Introduction

"My name is Chantal Lockey. I am from the UK. I am also a bereaved Mother to Marnie-Mae who died when she was just six weeks old to the horrors that is a cot death in 2004.

My work stems from my own loss. In many ways after the loss of our daughter we felt that we were left to "get on with it". This is why this book has been written - To act as an educator and training aid for professionals so that a high level of consistent care can be ensured internationally.

I have trained thousands of professionals over the last decade, all over the world. I am a Parent advocate, a government lobbyist and a PhD scholar.

CHANTAL LOCKEY

BA (Hons), MA, PhD Scholar

1. Infant Loss: An Overview and Understanding

"Like most mothers I was delighted when I found out I were expecting a baby. A new sense of purpose, hope, a fresh start, an exciting future ahead with our new found family status. The hopes and dreams start for your unborn baby at that very moment as does your boundless and unconditional love for them".

Very sadly for some, these dreams are shattered and they are left devastated when their much-loved baby dies.

The World Health Organisation estimates that over two million babies are stillborn internationally every single year and The Centers for Disease Control and Prevention state that in 2010 there were 2063 SIDS deaths in the USA and there are on average 300 cot deaths every year in the United Kingdom (The Lullaby Trust). There are also the issues of neo-natal deaths, which can be attributed to prematurity or medical issues.

The loss of a child is said to be the most devastating of losses that one can endure. It goes against the natural order of life and the forced separation between mother and child is not only devastating but also traumatic and one that really is never fully understood or accepted. A rollercoaster of emotions such as guilt, anger, shock and disbelief, denial, a feeling of disconnection, follow onto a deep depression and in some cases a feeling of anxiety and the associated panic attacks. Obviously during this period, the bereaved parents involved will clearly need a huge amount of support from not only family and friends, but also professional services and support networks.

Worryingly, this doesn't always seem to have been the case. Linda Sterrys study with The Scottish Cot Death Trust (2011) sadly shows evidence that support from professional services such as health care staff, the funeral director, police and the coroner's office was inconsistent and at times, of a very poor standard.

Pregnancy and Infant loss are sadly not uncommon. Therefore appropriate training for professionals in this area is vital.

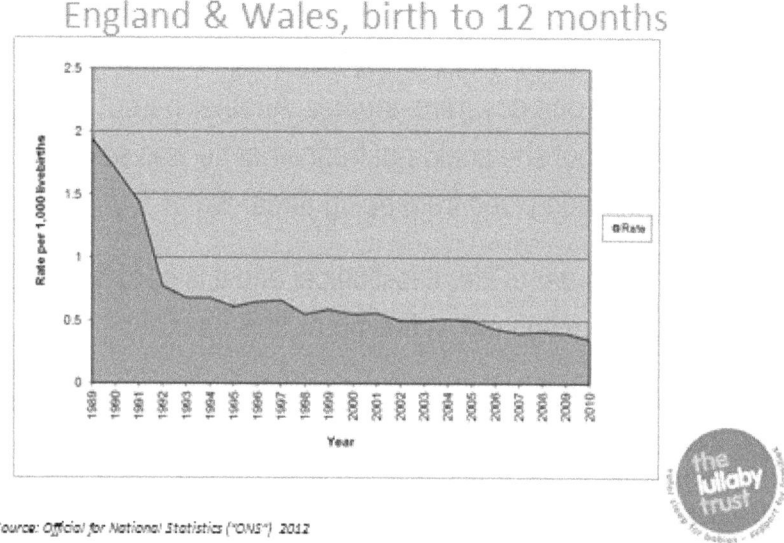

Rate of Sudden Infant Deaths per 1,000 live births:1989-2010
England & Wales, birth to 12 months

Source: Official for National Statistics ("ONS") 2012

Courtesy of The Lullaby Trust

2. The Initial Emotional and Physical Reactions to Pregnancy and Infant Loss:

An Understanding

Every parent's experience is individual but the death of a baby can bring a grief that is almost hard to describe. A grief that is so intense, so raw, so all-consuming and lasts much longer than other people may ever really realize.

It is a grief, "a pain" never experienced before.

Many parents have said that they have experienced grief and loss of relatives, particularly older people, but the death of a baby does not even compare to previous grief experienced or encountered,

The feeling of utter devastation and that life as you know it has been swept up from under you and that now, life has not logical meaning. After the loss of a baby the parents embark on what can only be described as an emotional roller coaster and finding a "new normal".

Emotional reactions

Most parents have said that they felt utter shock soon after losing their baby. A feeling that they were "in a bubble" or perhaps looking at himself or herself going through the motions but not really "being there". One mother described the days after her son died as a "complete blur". She could not recollect one day from another. Another parent said she could see a police officer talking to her but she could not hear what he was saying, more like a feeling that she could hear distorted noises from being under water.

A baby dying goes against the natural order of life. It is illogical and it is hard to take in, a feeling of disbelief and denial is very common with a feeling of "this cannot be happening".

The overwhelming feeling of guilt is also commonplace. Mothers in particular may feel guilty and blame themselves for their baby's death.

"I was her mum, I should have been able to keep her safe and protected. I let her down. I failed"

Anger is a common reaction to loss. The parents may be angry with themselves, with their partner, with their baby for making them feel so alone, with God, or with the health professionals who cared for their baby. They may also be angry or jealous with parents who have healthy babies. When your own life has fallen apart, it can be very difficult to accept that, for most people, life is going on as they planned.

"Why him? Why us?"

Physical reactions

Many bereaved parents have physical reactions to grief. These can feel very similar to intense fear and anxiety. They may have palpitations or chest pains. They may feel a heavy weight as if they cannot breathe.

They may feel sick and have diarrhoea, and feel that their stomach is tangled in knots all of the time.

They may have a lump in their throat constantly.

They may not feel like eating anything, or they may find that they can't stop eating.

They may feel exhausted but find it difficult to sleep. Their sleep may also be disturbed by very vivid dreams or nightmares. Some parents may wake up crying, or it may be that for a split second when they wake, they do not remember what has happened. When they do it is like finding out all over again.

Bereaved parents often say that their arms literally "ache" for the baby they were expecting to hold and cherish. Some mothers still feel their baby kicking inside them; others hear their baby crying.

It may feel comforting to just want to stay in bed and "hide away from the world". All these reactions are common and normal. Even though a baby has died, a mother's body will react in just the same way as it does when she has a live baby.

The Mother will have the usual vaginal blood loss that follows birth, and her breasts may start to produce milk. These physical reminders of the baby can be both painful and distressing.

"The biggest reminder of what she has lost".

Many mothers also get "after pains" as the womb contracts back to its normal size. Some have painful stitches or a caesarean scar and will need pain relief. In addition to their grief, many mothers get the normal "postnatal blues" a few days after the birth.

" I felt that I could vomit constantly. The gut wrenching pain in my stomach and in my heart were overwhelming and did not go away"

"My baby died when she was 3 days old. A day later my milk came in. It hit me hard that I was a mother now, ready to feed my baby and yet she was dead. It felt like life could not be more cruel"

.3. A Parents Perspective of Loss

A no holds barred, very personal Perspective of a mother losing her much-loved baby: A useful insight for Midwifery and Nursing Professionals

An electronic version of " Little Wings – A Mothers Story of Life after Loss"

Well done! I am impressed with you already. I never bother to read introductions. You could say that I am the hasty type. Well usually that is. On this occasion though, there was nothing hasty about me writing this recollection of our beautiful daughters Marnie Maes short six-week life with us. I struggled with the idea for quite a while I can tell you!. I didn't think I could handle it. By handle it, I mean I didn't think I could go through every single memory of Marnie in life and in death with a fine toothcomb. In many ways it would have been far easier for me to block it all out and never mention it again. It has been the most painful experience of my life and I am sure that nothing will touch that in the future. Did I really want to relive that over and over again?. A few things made me sit down and start writing however. One reason being I never ever wanted to forget. I never wanted to forget any of the funny little things she would do nor any one of her cute little facial expressions. As strange as it sounds, I didn't want to forget her in death either. I wanted to remember my visits to her in the chapel of rest and the day of her funeral. I was so scared that over time my memories of her would fade. I didn't want to forget. By writing Little Wings, every little detail will always be there and with me, as she will.

When Marnie died on 5 November 2004 at 6 week of age to SIDS or cot death, I truly felt that I would never get through this period of what can only be described as utter hell. I desperately wanted to feel that we were not alone in our pain. Of course we had amazing support from our family and friends but I really wanted to connect with other parents who had gone through the same situation. How had they coped? Was there any form of light at the end of a very long and darkened tunnel? Would time heal like all of the health professionals kept telling me was absolutely the case?. I assumed that there MUST be a book somewhere written by a parent who had lost a baby, I wanted to know that my constant rollercoaster of emotions were "normal"? And that I wasn't going completely mad in the over analyzing of Marnie's last moments until I felt like a mad woman. I felt further more lost when I realized that there was no such book. After writing about my own experiences, I can certainly see why. It is incredibly painful and difficult to relive everything over and over again. However, it was not all doom and gloom!. Writing about Marnie has helped me to come to terms with losing her, maybe in the tiniest way, but never the less. I have also written this book for you. Parents like us who suffer and continue to suffer. I would have done almost anything to come across an informal book like this when we lost Marnie. Every book that I picked up was filled with medical textbook terminology that you could barely read, never mind understand. There is nothing textbook about Marnie's book. What you see is what you get. There are no holds barred. It will make you smile, laugh and probably shed a tear or two. I expect you will feel like you have known me for years after reading my story!. I am so glad that for whatever the reason, you are taking the time to read Marnie's story. I hope that it helps you in some small way and I hope that it gives you, most of all, hope for your own futures.

About Us

Young, Happy go lucky, sociable people who live near the sea!. That just about summed Spencer and I up. We both worked hard and played even harder during our relationship of about seven months, particularly as Christmas 2003 was looming. It's just getting into the festive swing of things we would say in an attempt to convince ourselves!. Not that we needed an excuse really. By day I worked in a busy law firm and Spencer had all of the stresses and strains of running his own business. A glass of wine at the end of the day was much sought after!. Our first Christmas came and went in a haze of Christmas parties and work events. It came as no surprise when I was feeling a little worse for wear in January. All of the Christmas festivities had obviously taken their toll and I was convinced it was a classic case of burn out!. Something was niggling me though. I had put myself through the diet from hell and had exhausted myself on the cross trainer every night in a fight to get rid of that excess Christmas bulge and yes I wasn't losing a single pound. My period was late too. And would you believe it the thought of a glass of wine made me feel sick!. The alarm bells started ringing. Very loudly!. Nothing could have prepared me for when I saw two little blue lines on that home pregnancy test though. Shock! Amazement!, even a little horrified!. I can't tell you how many times Spencer and I read and re-read those instructions, just to make sure. Was the test working properly?. A mass purchase from Asda confirmed all (the woman at the pharmacy gave me a very strange bewildered look!) and that's when it really hit home. I was to become a mum!. My adventures as a carefree socialite for the time being, were over!!. Spencer and I hadn't planned the baby but we were so happy. We had just bought our new house with a nice garden and as a couple we were very happy together. This sealed the deal so to speak!. We felt so lucky!.

I had quite a normal pregnancy. I had the usual sickness, tiredness and carpel tunnel but all of my scans showed a healthy growing baby with no problems at all. Everything was normal apart from the fact that little one was breech so I was to be booked in for a caesarean section. We had found out at our 20 weeks scan that the baby was a little girl. We decided to name her Marnie Mae. I couldn't believe my luck. A girl!. Could life get any better?!. We got to work on the nursery – obviously everything was varying shades of pink!. We bought the pram, the sterilizer kit, the car seat and so many clothes, all neatly folded away in the nursery chest of drawers (all pink naturally!) and so many toys!. We were just so excited. I could not wait to meet Marnie. Here is a very good hint. Don't ever conceive in December. It means that you are at your largest and heaviest in August. The hottest month of the year!.

By this point, I was really ready to have the baby!. We were now ready for her Marnies arrival and I was finally given my date for my caesarean – 21 September 2004!. I was just so happy and excited, I thought I might burst!.

September 21st 2004 finally arrived!. It is no way an understatement to say I was terrified on that day. I too was unbelievably excited. Nine months of feeling pretty rough in all honesty, were soon to be at an end. I could not wait to meet her. I wondered if she would look like how I had imagined and pondered so, so many times. And here we were. I walked into theatre and wondered if my jelly like legs would hold me up. The delivery took much longer than I thought. There was a lot of commotion and I realized that Marnie had been born but there was no sound of her crying for a while. Just as I was about to panic, I heard her cry. I hadn't even seen her, and I burst into tears. Relief maybe. The doctors brought her over to me and WOW she was huge! a gorgeous little girl with great big eyes and a very loud cry!. They announced that she topped the scales at 8lb 12oz!. I was expecting a slight 7lb baby as I am only 5'3. I blamed Daddy myself.

Marnie Mae Pope was beautiful. A real little chubby cherub with beautiful blue eyes. I really was blown away. I couldn't believe that she was mine and oh my god! I was a mum!. You would have laughed if you saw me holding her in those first few days. I was so clumsy with her. I told you I wasn't a natural!. She just seemed so fragile. I didn't quite realize how long it would take to get her dressed. I wouldn't snap her little arms or legs off would I ?!. And honestly, how was I supposed to change her nappy, without getting weed on when she wriggled around so much?!. I used to dread it when my visitors would leave me alone at the hospital with Marnie. Not only because I knew I was not going to get any sleep (isn't sleep deprivation a form of torture in some countries?!) but I just felt that I couldn't cope on my own!. Those multitude of baby books didn't really give you the full picture! . My baby blues soon disappeared when Spencer took us both home and we introduced Marnie to her gorgeous milkshake pink nursery. I think she was rather impressed. We felt like a real family. As the days passed, Marnie and I got to know each other and the absolute terror that I felt when Marnie was born melted into a real sense of joy and a huge sense of pride. I had never felt so happy. I would never have believed it.

It became apparent that Marnie Mae was in no shape or form a textbook baby. She never stopped eating and never slept!. Instead, she liked to watch TV (we know all of the words to The Bear in the big blue house show). She liked to look at anything pretty like fairy lights and generally, she has to be involved in anything and everything. Nanny Jill called her "little Miss Nosy". She wasn't wrong there. People would comment on how unusually bright Marnie was and how advanced she seemed for a baby so small. She would hear my voice and turn her head to face me and she would watch the television with such concentration, it was scary!. Of course I beamed with pride. Not only was our daughter beautiful but she was very bright too. I felt truly honoured and yes I admit it, I felt rather smug too!.

Everybody told me that babies don't really do much until they are around three months old and that really, until that point, they haven't got a personality as such. Marnie seemed to smash that theory into pieces!. She made us laugh so much. Let me illustrate: Marnie had to be the hungriest baby in the world. Ever. She constantly shoved her little hands in her mouth and gummed them excitedly. I didn't have to guess what she wanted. Even when we kissed her she thought it was food and would try to eat at our faces!. She was a little animal (takes after Daddy obviously!). Marnie knew what she liked. She would sit in her bouncy chair watching cartoons, with her big blue eyes lit up, smiling and talking to herself. Marnie also knew what she didn't like!. Namely the dreaded crib!. One night we saw her little legs hanging out of the crib and then watched as her arms tried to hoist her up and out!. She was trying to escape into Mummy's bed no doubt!. I don't think she liked toy chickens much either. She used to punch her yellow chicken, watch it fall over and smile to herself. I don't quite know what the chick did to deserve that!.

Spencer always used to laugh at Marnie in her pink, frilly princess dresses I used to dress her in (it had to be done!). She wasn't the daintiest of little girls, she was a bit of a bruiser really, but she looked gorgeous in whatever she wore (and you knew it young lady). Marnie loved her cuddles and affection. If she wasn't permanently attached to somebody, we definitely knew about it. She never used to like it when I had to put her down. She used to cling on to my necklace in an attempt to stay latched on (good thinking - I told you she was clever). Not only did she love lots of cuddles, she loved being pampered. Well she is a girl!. She loved the baby massages that I gave her and having her magic cream rubbed into those gorgeous chubby cheeks of hers. She was a bit spoilt really. Marnie was so welcomed into our families. She was adored by everyone and was always centre of attention at our Sunday lunches. We felt like a proper family. We had to laugh when Marnie went to her first Halloween party, and when dressed as a little pumpkin with her spooky ghost slippers on her feet!. She was just adorable beyond words.

On Thursday 4 November 2004 we both had a lovely day together. We slept in and listened to my new Dido album until Marnie decided it was time to get up - she was bossy like that. She then had a bubble bath in her sink in her bedroom (I still wasn't that confident with her, slippery little sausage!) which she loved as she always did. Marnie was growing at such a fast pace that Daddy had given us some money to get some more clothes. We came back with numerous outfits, all pink naturally. I had felt very proud when out shopping. So many people stopped to compliment me on my lovely new baby. I was so proud. On the way home I saw that the shop windows had started being decorated for Christmas. I was so excited. What a fantastic Christmas we would have this year as a real family. We then went and spent the afternoon with my mum who was Marnie's biggest fan!. Needless to say Marnie was spoilt all day long.

We went home to see Daddy and I commented to him that I had never felt so happy and that I felt that as a family, we were so incredibly lucky. Life was now perfect. I was 24, we had a lovely new home for our lovely new daughter and the future just looked so bright for us three. I decided to get a head start that night as I was so exhausted. I kissed Marnie good night and admired her beautiful little face, still not quite believing that she was mine. That was to be the last time I saw my gorgeous little girl alive. Spencer told me that nothing was out of the ordinary that night. Marnie took 3oz of her late feed and then proceeded to wee all over him as he changed her nappy. She then settled down and very quickly, went to sleep around midnight.

I woke up at just before 3am with a start, expecting Moos to be stirring for her next feed. I looked at her and the first thing I noticed was that she has a small amount of blood coming from her nose. I looked at her more closely - it was dark - maybe my eyes were playing tricks on me - I realized her lips and around her eyes were blue. She wasn't breathing. I can only describe the events after finding Marnie like that, was absolute chaos. Utter panic and screams upon screams.

In that second I knew. I knew that Marnie was dead. I remember screaming her name over and over and attempting to bring her back. I remember blowing into her tiny mouth and rubbing her chest. I remember looking at her and just knowing that it was too late. But I carried on until Spencer's mum took over as I watched helplessly. I can't describe that utter fear I felt. It was a pain I had never felt before. The next thing I knew the paramedics were in my bedroom. As he rushed Marnie out of the house into the ambulance I saw her little limbs hanging loosely, my little sturdy girl was now so floppy. So lifeless. This can't be happening. This can't be happening. By now they were several police arriving outside my house. I went outside but the paramedic guys closed the door to the ambulance. I couldn't go in. So I stood there. Barefoot on that bitterly cold November night waiting. I looked up at the sky. I have never prayed so hard in my life. I stood there bargaining with God – please let her live. Take me but not her. I remember the moment when the paramedic came out of the ambulance. I remember his tear-stained face and I knew. He tried to tell me that Marnie had gone yet all I could hear was horrendous screams. I then realized that those screams were coming from me, hysterical and retching in the middle of the street.

I was literally picked up and taken into the house. I could not breathe. This was my worst nightmare. This can't be happening. I looked up. Why were there so many police in my house?. Did they think we had hurt Marnie? done something wrong? had we?. I saw the police officer crying. This can't be happening. The worst thing was when my Mum and Dad arrived. Spencer had rang them in panic when we found Marnie. I didn't want to have to tell my mum and dad. Seeing their grief and pain made me feel utterly responsible. Did they think it was my fault?. I couldn't do this. My mum asked "where is she?" and all I could say was "she is gone". My mum ran outside to the ambulance where she told me Marnie was laying under a little white blanket on the ambulance bed. Mum said she looked so tiny. I was asked if I wanted to see Marnie and I couldn't. I just couldn't.

The Coroners officer then arrived. He told us that they had to take Marnie. I felt powerless. I felt shocked. I wanted to scream - leave my baby alone, leave her with me. But nothing came out. Nothing. The guilt and upset I felt was unbearable. What if Marnie thought that I had left her? she needed her mum. We gave the Coroners officer Marnies favourite little cuddly toys, which he said he would keep with her. It sounds stupid, but that brought me some comfort. She likes those toys. The next kick in the teeth was being told that Marnie would have to have a post mortem. I try and block that thought from my mind because it is far too painful. I am the type of person that cried when Marnie had her heal prick test. I told you I was a wimp. It was unbelievably surreal when they took Marnie. I remembered my words to Spencer the night before "lucky", "happy". That was all gone. In the space of a few hours. Her pink pram was still in the hallway. Her bottles all ready for her feeds throughout the night were sitting untouched and the house was full of her clothes, toys and baby necessities. I picked up her pink baby blanket and sobbed. I could still smell her new baby purity and the not so fragrant odour of baby sick. I never thought I would like that smell. How things change. The days that followed Marnies death were one big blur. I couldn't tell you one day from the other. Spencer and I were still on a knife-edge which didn't help. We were awaiting to hear the post mortem results. We both agreed that we would not be able to deal with it, if in some way it had been our fault. I thought I would go mad. I analyzed Marnies last moments to pieces, over and over and over. Finally the Coroner did come back to us with an initial finding of Sudden Infant Death Syndrome. This didn't really help us. All that confirmed that was Marnie had died naturally. That we hadn't hurt her, but we needed to know more. It now meant though that Marnies funeral could go ahead. Funeral. God, it hadn't even crossed my mind. How very stupid of me. I am ashamed to say that I was in a fit state to plan the bulk of Marnies funeral. My parents did the bulk of it and I am so thankful for that. It was bad enough having to organize such basic things. I was asked to organize an outfit for Marnie to wear. The day before she died, we went on our girlie shopping trip and ironically I got her a lovely pink tracksuit with "Angel" written on the front. I remember buying that and thinking how pretty she would look in it. Now this would be the last outfit Marnie would ever wear. I was so angry. But I had to deal with it so I decided on her angel tracksuit, her I love my Daddy vest and her mouse slippers. She was to have her soft pink princess blanket too. As daft as it sounds, I wanted to her to be warm and cosy. Daft probably isn't the word, insane maybe is more appropriate?. I took some of her toys to the funeral home to be placed in her coffin. I also gave her my gold necklace that she so often used to swing off in an attempt to stay on my front, a silver cross to keep her safe and a photograph of Mummy, Daddy and Marnie and a letter asking her never to forget us. I remember going to the jewellers to buy Marnies silver cross, and the shop assistant stood there smiling asking if it was for a christening. We just nodded. I wish it was. I kept thinking. I wish it was. I was asked whether I wanted to go and see Marnie at the funeral home. I really was in a terrible turmoil. I had never seen somebody who had died before seeing Marnie that night and I admit it, I was so scared. I was scared that seeing Marnie days after death would be even worse than the images I held of finding her that night. But as her mum I felt that I needed to get a grip and do what was right for Marnie. So I went. I had the most wonderful funeral Director who held my hand as I walked into the chapel of rest. I don't think I ever held someone's hand so tight in my life. And there she was in a little Moses basket, in her pink outfit, with her little dummy in and all of her toys surrounding her. She didn't look terrible as I had thought, but she didn't look like Marnie either. She looked like a little porcelain doll. She didn't even look real to me. Her beautiful big eyes had sunken and her fabulously chubby cheeks had shrunk. I touched her little chest and in such a stark contrast it felt so hard, unlike her little soft chubby belly as been. I sat by her side and re-arranged her toys around her and tucked her in. The soft toys were freezing cold and the harsh harsh reality hit that Marnie didn't stay in that cosy little room all the time but that she had been in some type of fridge before my arrival. Of course I understand why this is necessary but the pain and sadness in that hitting home could have destroyed me in that moment. I just wanted to wrap her up nice and warm in her little blanket and to take her home. For her to wake up and this whole nightmare to be over. It wasn't ever going to be over though.

I went daily to see Marnie for the next three days. She was still my little moos and I was fully aware that I was on borrowed time. Very soon I would not be able to pop in to see her anymore. I sat beside her and spoke to her. I pleaded with her to wake up and I told her how much I loved her. I also told her that I was desperately sorry. I felt like I had let her down. I was her mum and I was supposed to make everything better. I had let her down. I had failed. On the third day the lady at the funeral home gently advised me that Marnie was "starting to go" and that it would be better if I didn't return again. It hadn't even crossed my mind that babies do not get embalmed. But then why would it?. This couldn't be happening. Not to me. Not to Marnie. On my last visit, I sat and stared at Marnie for hours. I didn't ever want to forget her. Would I?. Would I forget what she looked like?. It couldn't happen. I realized that it was probably time to go home when I would stare at her so much my mind started playing tricks on me. I could have sworn that I saw her sucking on her dummy, or her little chest rising in a split second. It sounds ridiculous but I had to check by placing my hand near her mouth to see if I could feel her breath. Logically, it was ridiculous. I was going mad.

The day of Marnie's funeral came around very quickly. I didn't want that day to come because this really would be the end. I didn't want to say goodbye. It had only just been hello. And now it was goodbye and this was wrong. Very wrong. I was also scared about how I would react when I saw her little coffin. I knew it was coming but to actually see it. I didn't know how I would cope. There was still a huge sense of disbelief. I knew it was happening. I knew she was gone but none of this was really registering. When the hearse arrived outside our house I immediately thought, well where is Marnie?. There were so many flowers and her coffin so was so so tiny, that I couldn't initially see her. When I did, the pain hit. I thought I would be violently sick. We arrived at the church and Spencer carried Marnie in, in his arms . Marnie had a very Christian funeral. It gave us some comfort. We sang all things bright and beautiful, because that's exactly what she was. We also played Clocks by Coldplay which just felt relevant "Lights go out and I cant be saved, tides that I tried to swim against, have brought me down upon my knees, oh I beg and beg and plead". I sat in that church with a huge photo of my gorgeous, smiling little Marnie up on the table, and on that very same table was my daughter in a tiny white coffin. This was not right. I still could not believe that this was happening. It couldn't be. I tried to concentrate on her lovely photo and not the though of Marnie, lifeless in that box in front of me. Block it out Chantal. Block it out. Burying Marnie was one of the hardest things I have ever had to do. I stood at the grave and I couldn't even cry. There was nothing left. I wondered if people thought it was strange that I wasn't standing there crying and wailing. Was it?. I felt numb. Seeing her tiny little coffin being lowered into the ground, all I could think was, I really hope it doesn't rain today. I wouldn't want her to get cold and wet. After the burial, I turned around and realized the extent of the size of Marnies funeral. There was a sea of black. Over 250 people attended Marnie's funeral, and she had over fifty floral tributes. That's one popular little girl.

I found it hard to leave the churchyard that day. It was a bitter November day and I just kept thinking that I hoped she was cosy in her slippers and that I hope she knew that I didn't want to leave her. We spent the rest of the day with our friends and family, drinking far too much. I remember looking out of the pub window that evening. It was dark and it had started to rain. I felt like my heart had been ripped out. I hoped she didn't feel scared or alone. Spencer and I went away to Lanzarote for a week after Marnie's funeral. Our families had thought it best. As we boarded the plane with excited holidaymakers, I wondered what on earth I was playing at. We have just lost our daughter and we were going on holiday?. I felt guilty. I felt guilty every time I smiled or had not thought about Marnie for the past thirty seconds. As luck would have it (not really) our hotel was jammed packed full of babies and toddlers. There were everywhere, with their proud, happy, smiling parents. Families. We weren't a family anymore. Was I still a mum?. I hated it. I was angry, I was bitter and twisted and I wondered how I would ever be happy again. I spent most of that week away sat by the pool crying. Spencer didn't want to talk about it. I think men and women differ so much in their approaches to grief. I wanted to talk all day about it. To get some sense of it but instead we just ended up arguing again and again because he couldn't deal with it. I am told that this is very typical with guys.

You know that sinking feeling when you arrive home after a week or twos holiday? well surprisingly we didn't have this on our return. Quite the opposite really. I felt that going away was useful but it was a case of you can run but you can't hide. I could have spent the week on the moon, and it wouldn't have helped me escape the pain. I was quite glad to get home and back to our familiar surroundings. I went into Marnie's nursery when we got home. That smell hit me as I walked in. Her smell. It was still there. The pain rose its ugly head a fraction higher. Everything was the same in there. I felt closer to Marnie in her nursery. Spencer however could not go in there for weeks. I found a pile of dirty washing. Her little baby grows covered in her sickly smells in the laundry bin . I couldn't face putting them through the washing machine. I wondered how long her smell would stay. I would spend a lot of time in Marnies room. Keeping her clothes tidy. Rearranging her toys. Talking to her as if she was still there. And then I would look at her empty cot and realized there was no baby that needed her toys or clothes rearranging anymore.

 All of her "new baby" cards were still hanging up in her bedroom. All the messages of congratulations. I would often look at them and wonder how this had happened. How on earth we had got to this stage. I didn't want to take those cards down. It was like I would be accepting it. They stayed up for a long time. I would sit in Marnies room and look through Marnies memory book that mum had organized for the funeral. There were so many lovely individual memories from various family and friends. Several messages of how cute Marnie looked on Halloween in her little pumpkin costume. That was just 5 days before she had died. The most painful thing about sitting her Marnies room was when I was looking at the video footage we had of her from birth. That was almost impossible. To see your little one chattering and wriggling about in such a perfect way, broke my heart. She looked so contented having cuddles with Mummy and I looked just so happy. I then started watching and re watching to see if there were any signs that something was wrong. Again and again. I couldn't find or see anything. But I continued to punish myself. I felt that I deserved the pain.

Spencer and I spoke about trying again for another baby very soon after losing Marnie. We found it so difficult to go from being a family back to being a couple. Life just seemed very shallow and empty and lonely. I felt guilty for thinking about another baby. I didn't want Marnie to think that she was being replaced or that my feelings for her had changed. I remembered my words to her at the funeral home "you will always be mummy's special girl". But I also knew that for my own sanity, we needed to try again. I found out I was pregnant in January 2005. Yes that soon. I wondered if we had done the right thing, I worried what people may think that I was pregnant so soon and I was terrified at the what ifs. What if this happens again?.   I will keep you posted....

4. When a Baby dies – What to expect as a Professional:

The physical signs to expect when a baby dies

As a professional working with infant loss, there is someone that you need to make sure has the upmost care. YOU.

" I was 19 and a student midwife the first time I attended a still birth. I could not believe what I was seeing and more to the point I could not believe that I had been given no training or advice on a stillbirth. It was heartbreaking and I had to hold on within a inch of my life not to lose the plot emotionally. I wish I had been told what to expect, not only emotionally but also physically so that I could have been more prepared and therefore more of a support to Mom"

When a baby dies, it is normal for the professional to be scared, anxious and concerned about how they themselves will react when facing a stillbirth.

What is important to realise is that you are a Midwife but you are also human. If you did not feel emotionally involved in some small way, you would not be normal.

When a baby is born still he or she may look simply like a sleeping baby. This is dependent on how long ago the baby has died in the womb.

With this is mind the baby may display the following physical signs:

The baby may appear bruised or may have reddened skin, which may or may not have started to peel

The baby's eyes may be closed or in some cases they may be slightly open

The baby's mouth may be slightly open

The baby may have blue tinged lips and their fingernails may be white or discoloured

As mentioned, it may be that a baby is delivered that really looks like he or she is just asleep and that there are absolutely no imperfections, however as a Midwife it is important that you are prepared.

Ultimately, as hard as it may be, your role is there to support the bereaved parents, and to keep them as calm as possible.

You may be at a point of shock yourself but it is important to retain a sense of normality in what is such an abnormal and devastating time. It may be that the parents are shocked by their baby's physical appearance and are scared of looking or touching their baby. The

Bereavement Midwife should focus on the baby's beauty, be able to focus on the baby and be able to touch the baby. If at all possible, being able to "coo" at the baby as if it he or she was alive is wonderfully reassuring for the parents and they themselves are then more inclined to be able to be more relaxed around their baby, spend time with their baby, bond, make memories and as a consequence will be able to grieve and heal.

It is important that you also gently prepare the parents for what their baby may look like, so that there is not a shock when their baby is born. You should explain as a professional that these signs are perfectly normal. Quite often when a parent has been explained to, the fear of the unknown diminishes somewhat.

" You are human – always seek the support of colleagues, family and friends"

5. A Baby that dies in Hospital

Some parents will never have the privilege of hearing their baby cry or to see them open their eyes. Sadly some women will be told that their baby has died whilst carrying them in their womb. The devastation that is stillbirth affects over two million families a year worldwide.

"I could not believe it. I felt like it was a dream. My baby was dead and then it hit home, I had to give birth to a DEAD baby, the terror set in at that moment "

It is paramount that hospital professionals are prepared for when a woman is admitted to be induced to have her baby that will sadly never cry, never open its eyes or never take a breath. The bereaved mother must NOT under any circumstances be admitted on to a ward where there are new mums with their healthy, living babies. A lot of UK maternity hospitals now have designated areas, which are kept away from delivery wards and provide a calming "suite" type environment where by Dad can stay and they can feel almost, that there are at a home from home. Simple touches like some pretty flowers in a vase, some bright cushions, and some pictures on the wall can make all of the difference in favour of a clinical environment. The father should be allowed to stay and support mum at all times.

- A specialist suite away from the delivery - A home from home area to comfort the bereaved parents

- A specialist Bereavement Midwife

- Dad to be allowed to stay with mum at all times

- The reassurance of that when their baby is delivered, that their baby will be treated the same as that of a live baby, and will be treated with the upmost of respect and care. The reassurance of that the parents will have informed choices at all times. The reassurance that the bereaved parents will be able to make choices with regards to their baby after birth.

Not only will the mother be devastated, in a state of shock and denial but she will also be terrified about giving birth. Women who are expecting their babies to be alive and well are themselves terrified of labour and the unknown but this fear will be multiplied somewhat with a mum who has been told that she will have to deliver her baby who has died. She will be terrified of what her baby will look like:

"I wasn't scared of the pain that I would experience with labour but I was so frightened about seeing my baby, After all she was dead. Would she look terrible?"

"I wanted to see my baby but I was just so scared. I felt in turmoil"

"My midwife took some photos of our baby girl when she was born. We were scared about seeing her. I looked at her photo and I fell in love with her there and then. At that point I wanted, no, needed to see her and hold her. I would have always regretted it if I had not met my daughter and we have some very special memories with her"

It may be that there is a specialist Bereavement Midwife that will be able to spend time with the parents and talk to them about their options. It may be that the parents will ask not to see their baby. This decision should of course be respected. However it is likely that the reasoning behind this is fear. The parents could be reassured that when their baby is delivered, that the baby will be treated just as if it was born alive and there are options to see their baby should they so choose.

Other parents will want to see their baby. They will want to hold them and touch them. They should be assured that they will have as much time as they need with their baby in the privacy of their own room. The parents should never feel rushed. The time that they will spend with their baby will be their **only** time. This must be respected.

Informed Choices

Their midwives should assist the bereaved parents so that they can make informed choices about what they would like to do with regards to their baby. It must be remembered at all times that is without a doubt, the bereaved parents should have choices, just as if they would if they baby was born alive.

The midwife may want to gently go through the options with the parents. There are various options available to the parents

- Would they like to see their baby?

- Would they like their baby to be taken away after birth to be washed and dressed and then returned to them?

- Would they prefer to see a photo of their baby rather than seeing their baby in person?

- Would they like to wash their baby? – this may or may not be possible dependent on how fragile the babies skin is after loss

- Is there a special outfit they would like their baby to be dressed in?

- Would they like their baby to be placed in a crib?

- Would they like any other family members to come and see their baby?

- Would they like to have their baby christened or blessed or would they like to visit the hospital chapel?

- Would they like a staff member to take some photographs of the baby?

- Would the parents like a staff member to take some family photos of the parents with the baby?

- Would the parents like the staff members to help in creating some memories for them? For example: a lock of baby's hair, some hand and foot prints. When a baby dies, these can be treasured keepsakes that parents will cherish forever.

The use of a cold cot is increasingly being used in the UK and Ireland and Australia with a view to these becoming available in the Unites States and Canada from 2014.

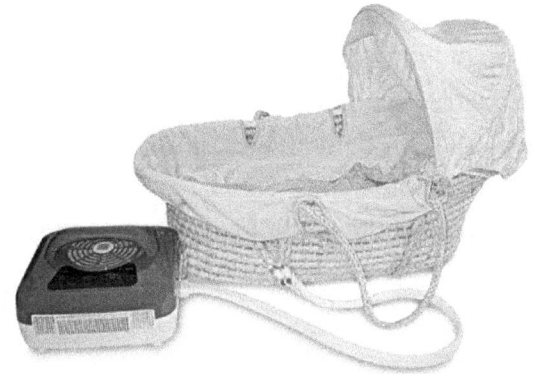

A COLD COT is shown above. It offers the opportunity for the baby whom has died to be placed into a baby basket to keep the sense of innocence, which will bring comfort to the bereaved parents. It also enables the family to spend longer periods of time with the baby as the cot keeps the baby's body cool and also will reduce the signs of decomposition which would have further more distressed the parents.

"To see Olivia lying in her little cot looking so peaceful was our last memory of her, it was a gentle one that we will always treasure"

THE LAST MEMORY of seeing their baby may be at the hospital or at the funeral home. It is the responsibility of the professionals to ensure that those memories are the best that they can be. It may be that the bereavement midwife may ask the bereaved parents what they would like their lasting memory to be.

" I wanted to bath and dress my baby, to hold him and to read him a bedtime story, the midwives kindly helped me to achieve this. I read Tommy a story and then I tucked him into his cot. He looked peaceful and cosy, we then walked away"

"It may sound strange but I wanted to change my daughter's nappy. It was something that I wanted to do for her and the midwife helped me to do this"

"I wanted to cuddle my son whilst he was still warm. I would not be able to touch my baby son if he was cold. It would be too much to cope with"

Photos

Many families request photos to be taken of their baby. Quite often these are the first, and only, family photographs they will have of their child.

Suggestions being:

- Baby in Mum and Dads arms
- Portraits of the whole family
- Close up of the baby's face
- Baby's whole naked body
- Close up of baby's hand, feet, fingers and toes
- Multi generational family shots
- Baby holding wedding rings
- Baby with teddy

There are some superb companies now who specialise in peri-natal loss photography and no cost to the families. Please contact our office for details of companies in your area (info@chantallockey.co.uk).

The parents may feel angry after the birth. Particularly if the baby looks "perfect" and they can see "nothing wrong" with their baby. They may want answers about how and why their baby has died. It may well be that the baby will be required to have a post mortem in order to give the bereaved parents those answers. All of these issues should be fully communicated with the parents at all times.

There must be nothing worse than giving birth to a baby and having to leave the hospital empty handed.

Some parents may wish to take their baby home with them. The cuddle cot is of great benefit should the family wish to take their baby home with them.

" I wanted to show Louis his bedroom. We also wanted our older sons to meet Louis in the comfort of our own home and not in a hospital. I took him home and held him as I sat in the rocking chair in his nursery and I sung to him as I would have if he had been alive. I will never forget that moment"

The bereaved parents will understandably be devastated and they will likely to be in a state of shock. The parents will need gentle guidance when leaving their baby at the hospital in the following areas:

- What happens to my baby now?

- Will my baby need a post mortem?

- Can you recommend a funeral director that has experience in looking after babies?

- What do I need to do about registering my baby's birth and death?

- What about work? Am I now not allowed to be on maternity leave?

- Is there something wrong with us? Do we have a genetic issue that will mean this could happen again? Nursing professionals will need to have a good knowledge of all of these areas so that they can gently direct the parents. It may be worthwhile for nursing professionals to have a list of contacts to hand which will include: funeral directors with a good reputation in dealing with infants, genetic counselling departments, counsellors who specialize with baby loss, the details of the local Registrar who will be willing to explain the sometimes complex procedures of obtaining the birth and the death certificate for the baby.

6. A Baby's Funeral Care

After receiving the post mortem results (if applicable) the bereaved parents next stage would be to organize a funeral home and consequently a memorial service. This may be done at home, at a funeral home or sometimes it may be that hospital professionals will assist with the arranging of a baby's funeral.

As illogical as it may sound some parents are consumed with grief and the feeling of being in a bubble and the feeling of total disconnection from the world, that it may not initial register that their baby will require a funeral.

" I could not believe that the fact that John would need a funeral did not cross my mind"

Midwives and Funeral Professionals have an enormous responsibility to gently guide the family through the planning of a baby's funeral because it may be the case that the bereaved parents are unable to do this alone. Many parents at this stage will still be in a state of shock, denial and of disconnection. Therefore, what may seem like simple choices or basic realizations to professionals, may not appear so to the bereaved parents.

"The lady at the funeral home asked me if there was an outfit I wanted to choose for my baby to wear. I felt like I should have thought of that. I had let my baby girl down again"

Many parents will be very fearful in seeing my baby at the funeral home or at the hospital after post mortem. Particularly in a situation when their baby had died suddenly and unexpectedly, perhaps in the middle of the night – for example a cot death. Professionals should be aware that the last image the bereaved parents have of their baby, who may have died to cot death for example, will not generally be one that they will want to remember.

 "I found my that my own daughter had died in the middle of the night. She had a blue tinged face and had a bloody froth coming from her mouth and also from her nose. To face your perfect, angelic looking baby being transformed in such a cruel manner is devastating. The fear then would be in this situation, several days after death, how much worse would my baby look?, I was terrified"

These quotes show the complete terror that bereaved parents may face when considering saying goodbye to their baby. There are also the issues of parents being fearful of what changes will be apparent to their baby after Post Mortem.

Based on this is may be that a bereaved parent will consider *not* saying goodbye to their baby. Of course this is the parents choice but it is often felt that this would be something that the parent would, in time come to regret and not assist them in their grieving by not being able to say a final goodbye.

Based on this and the professionals own judgement, it may be that the professional feels that they would like to reassure the bereaved parents and to even gently encourage the bereaved parents to perhaps see their baby.

One way of preparing the bereaved parents would be to take a photograph of their baby in the chapel of rest or at the hospital so that they can see that their baby on a photograph before seeing their baby in "real life".

This little bit of preparation for parents who may be averse to saying goodbye can simply put, make all the difference.

The funeral director or bereavement midwife should always assist the parents into the Chapel of Rest if applicable. To offer a holding hand to them should they need it and to keep the parents calm.

"My midwife was amazing, I was so terrified of seeing my baby. I was literally shaking. As we walked into the chapel of rest together she said:

Hello Poppet, there you are, aren't you beautiful

What a huge comfort to us her words were and as she spoke to our baby our fear subsided. Our baby was still that. Our little beautiful baby"

Any loss of life is traumatic and saddening for the family but extra care needs to be given to the bereaved parent of a baby. There is a sense of innocence, a sense that the baby did not get the opportunity to live and play as a child, a families dreams shattered.

The fact is that the infant has sadly passed away, but the funeral director and bereavement midwife can implement policies and procedures to ensure that the bereaved parents are comforted as much as realistically possible. This can be done in a variety of ways:

"We did not want to see our daughter in an open coffin - we did not want the last

image of our baby girl being in that box for which she would be confined to forever"

Professionals should offer alternatives in this respect. The sense of innocence needs to be preserved for the parents, to give them some form of comfort. The use of a Moses basket for the deceased baby is an example of this.

There has been a recent development in this area in the form of "Cold Cots" which we have already touched upon.

Thus allowing the baby to be laid into the crib which is kept cool. This is particularly helpful for when there is warm weather or the family would like to spend long periods of time with their baby, without the concern of increased decomposition thus distressing the parents dramatically.

The professional might think about further more comforting the parents by suggesting they bring in toys to surround their baby in the crib, or to ask if their baby had a favourite comfort blanket. The suggestion of a special piece of jewellery (perhaps twin pieces where by one piece is kept by the bereaved parent allowing a feeling of still being connected to their baby) or a St Christopher or other religious symbol. Professionals might encourage the parents to put family photographs or letters into the baby's coffin. It really can give the parents so much comfort:

" I didn't want my baby to ever forget us so we put lots of photographs in his coffin of his Mom, Dad and his big brother and our dog, it just felt that he was still a part of our family, that he would never forget us"

" We purchased our son a St Christopher for his final journey. I felt so scared for him and that he was alone. I put the St Christopher around his neck and I felt so much better. I wanted him to be safe"

" We just wanted our baby to be looked after, we saw her in the funeral parlour and she had a nappy on under her clothes and her pacifier in her mouth, holding her teddy, she just looked like she was asleep. She looked so peaceful"

The overwhelming feeling from parents is that they want their baby to be "looked after" and "to be safe". Just as in life. The above examples demonstrate how bereavement midwifes and funeral professionals alike can contribute to this.

The last image bereaved parents will have of their baby will usually be at the funeral parlour or at the hospital.

An everlasting image that will be on their mind for their rest of their lives. It is vital that the professional assists in making this a positive memory by using the examples above and by treating the baby as that, a well-loved baby that in death is being cared for and loved. This is reflected by the fact that the baby is surrounded by toys and is "tucked in" as it would have been in life. The harsh reality is that the baby has sadly died, but if any comfort can be sought and gained by the assistance of a caring midwife or funeral director, then it can make such a difference to the family.

The Bereavement midwife or funeral professional can suggest ways in which the babies funeral can be made to be special, to retain a sense of innocence and also to include older brothers or sisters so that the wider family can be involved in saying goodbye.

Candles - candles can be quite comforting and calming at a time of great distress.

Balloons - very often balloons are released either at the burial ground or as the family leave the crematorium. If small children are in attendance at the funeral service and appear to be in distress, then balloons can be a great way to distract them.

Glitter - instead of using sand for the interment of the casket, you can mix fairy dust or glitter in with a little sand and use that instead.

Doves - it is possible for families to release doves following a service.

Photos - families can be encouraged to take as many photographs of their baby and the service as possible. These can be on display and shared with everyone at the service.

Growing memories - these are seed impregnated cards that can be handed out to everyone at the funeral for them to plant in their own special place as a memory of baby

Bubbles - again these are a great way to get other children involved.

When the grave has been prepared for the burial, ask the family if they have a special blanket that could be placed in the bottom of the grave to cover the soil

Cover the blanket with rose petals.

Some funeral directors and hospitals choose to follow up with the family a month after their baby has died. Some provide some small gifts for any child siblings who have lost their brother or sister or perhaps even a card with a few kind words for the family. Quite often a month down the line after a baby has died, the visitors start to stop and it would be a welcome touch for the family to know that the funeral home and hospital has though of them and hasn't forgotten. Always use the baby's name in this respect rather than merely "he" or "she".

A suggestion for the Memory Box could include the following:
A small knitted blanked
A small teddy bear
The identity tag that was removed from the baby at the funeral home or hospital
A small nameplate engraved with baby's name if they were given one of 'baby of (parents names)'
Copy of the photographs from the service if applicable
A small bag with fairy dust if used at the service
A small bag of petals if used, a small candle

To sum up this chapter: The encouragement of placing toys, keepsakes and special letters and gestures in with the baby is very comforting for parents and other family members involved. The bereaved parents should be encouraged to visit their baby freely at the funeral home or to stay as long as possible in the hospital.

They should be encouraged to touch their baby if they so wish, to hold them, and to kiss them goodbye. The overwhelming point raised in this chapter is that the general consensus of bereaved families interviewed as part of this project, wanted professionals to treat their baby as if it was still alive, as it draws immense comfort to the parents. The professionals should use touches such as the nappy and the pacifier if the bereaved parents are in agreement to this. It is very distressing for the parents to see any sign of post mortem and it is the responsibility of the professional to ensure that are signs are hidden as much as is possible.

The use of a hat to cover any signs of post mortem entry marks, little gloves (to ensure parents do not see blue finger nails), a pacifier to cover blue lips are all examples of this in protecting the parents from further trauma.

A sense of innocence in a baby's funeral outlined in the examples given in this chapter offers comfort to the bereaved parents.

7. A Baby's Funeral Care – Making Memories

Creating Memories after a Baby has died:

After a loss of a baby, all that is left are memories. Sometimes a baby can die very soon after birth or even during delivery so it is so very important that further memories are made for the comfort of the family. This can be done in a variety of ways:

Hand and Footprints

Cutting a lock of the baby's hair as a keepsake

Photographs of the baby: Sometimes this can be considered a little taboo but it is a good idea to encourage the family to take photographs of their baby in death. Some parents may want family photographs with their baby, particularly those babies that have been still born because very sadly they will not have any family photos of their baby alive. Photos of the baby in death also assists the grieving process because it affirms to the parents of what has happened.

" I often look at the photos of my little girl in the hospital. I get some kind of comfort in seeing her looking so peaceful. Sometimes I need to look at those photos to make sense of a senseless situation, it may sound strange but I needed those photos".

Creating a Special Memory book: The Midwife could ask the parents if they would like a special memory book to be prepared. This could involve placing photographs of the baby in along with any scan photos and the baby's hospital band.

"After Sammy's funeral I took the time to look through the memorial book we had made. It was full of six weeks of wonderful memories of her, it was fabulous to have a keepsake like that. I was so grateful to our midwives for arranging this"

Creating a special memorial album : A Personal Perspective by Chantal Lockey

"This album was full of every single photograph I had of my daughter, including the scan photos during pregnancy and photos of carrying her. I also put in things like her NHS medical card, her wrist bands from the hospital, her little lock of hair, her order of service for her funeral and other special things. I think it is important for a bereaved parent to have these special things all together. It is very difficult to explain, but when my daughter died, it was a very surreal period. I had a baby, then in 6 weeks my baby was gone. I almost wanted some kind of evidence that she had even been here and that she was a little person, no matter how short her stay with us was"

Memory Boxes

"I have kept everything of my daughters. It is a personal choice but four years on I still have pretty pink boxes full of her neatly folded clothes and her little nappy's and dummy's. I probably go through these things once a year now, I will go through and tidy her little boxes, not really knowing why I am doing it, but it brings me comfort on bad days such as her Birthdays or on the anniversary of her death. I chose a few special outfits that reminded me of her with a smile, including her first pair of pink trainers and her Halloween costume which I put in glass fronted display boxes"

Take photos at the funeral and at the graveside

Again, this may sound a little taboo but taking photographs at the baby's funeral and of the coffin and floral tributes can help later on for the bereaved parents acceptance. It also paints a picture of the baby's life and death and the baby's journey.

Losing a baby makes no sense. It is illogical. By placing photographs in some kind of chronological order can help the bereaved parent come to terms with their loss.

We have included some visuals sourced from bereaved parents so that you may take inspiration in assisting your own bereaved parents:

Booklets for the Funeral

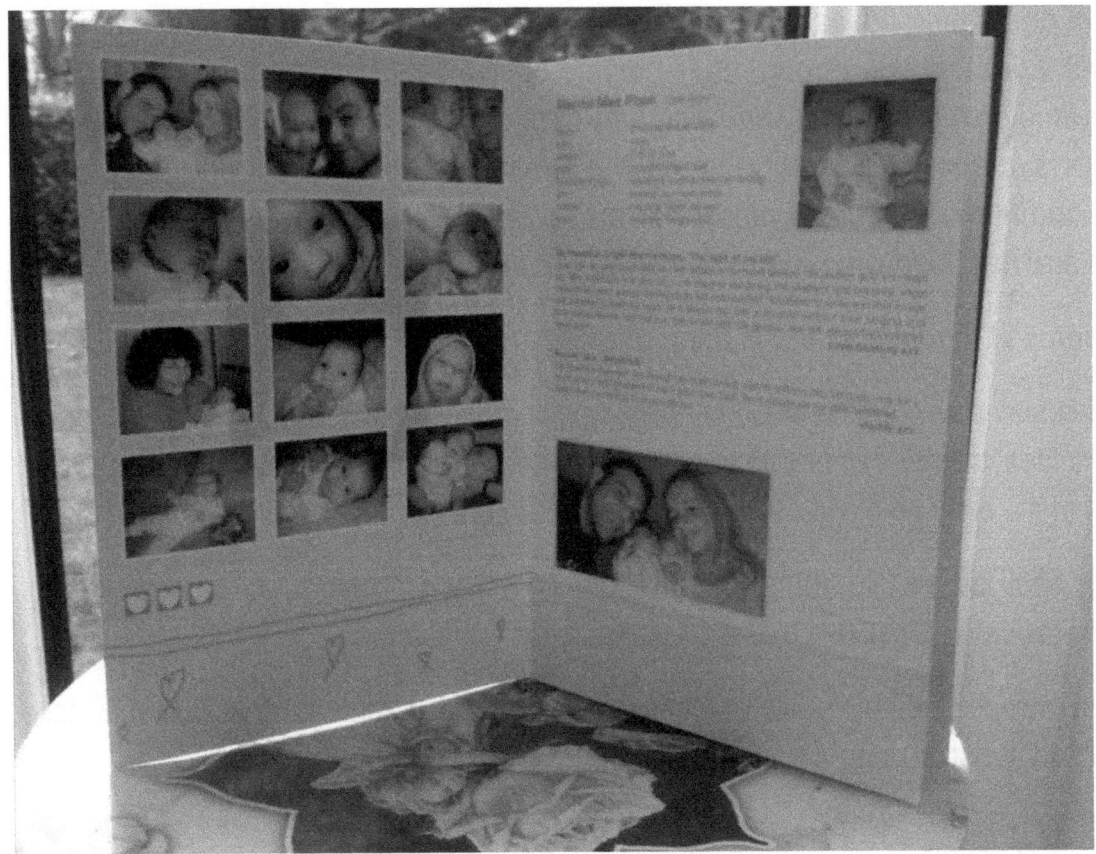

"A sense of innocence" Many parents will want to continue with this feeling of keeping the babies innocence, this can be achieved with floral arrangements in the form of a Teddy or a Angel.

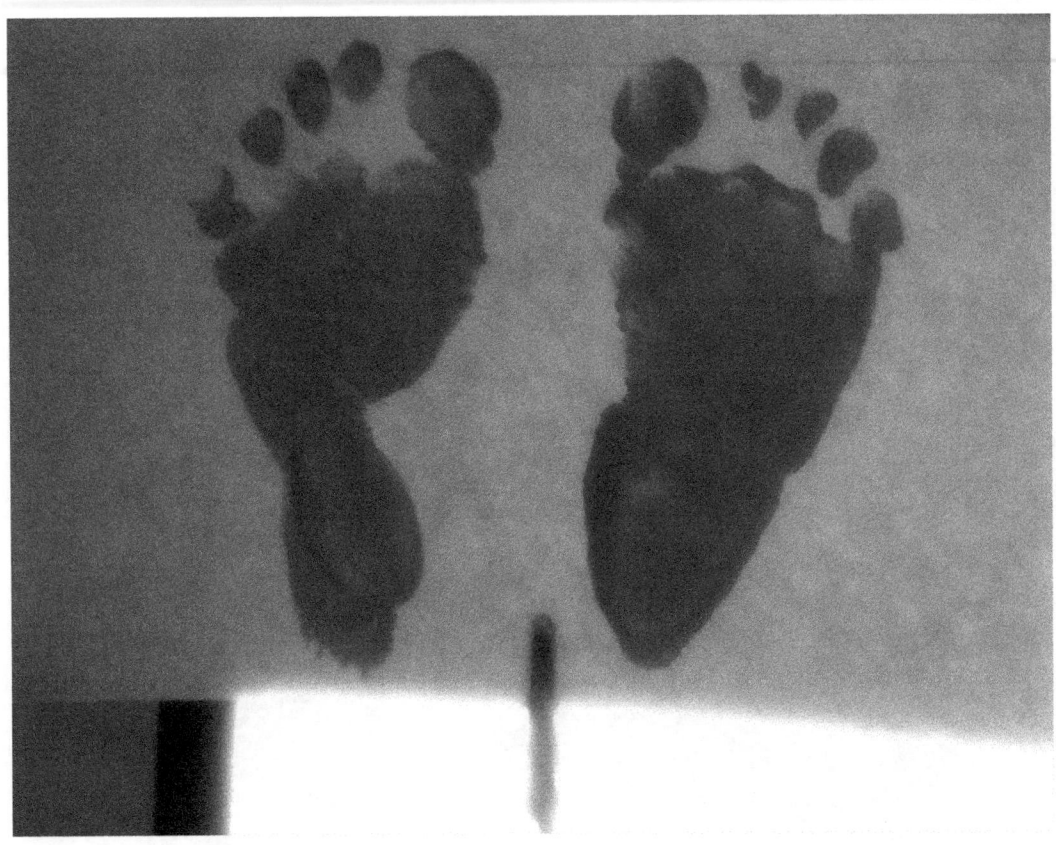

Hand and Footprints of the Baby

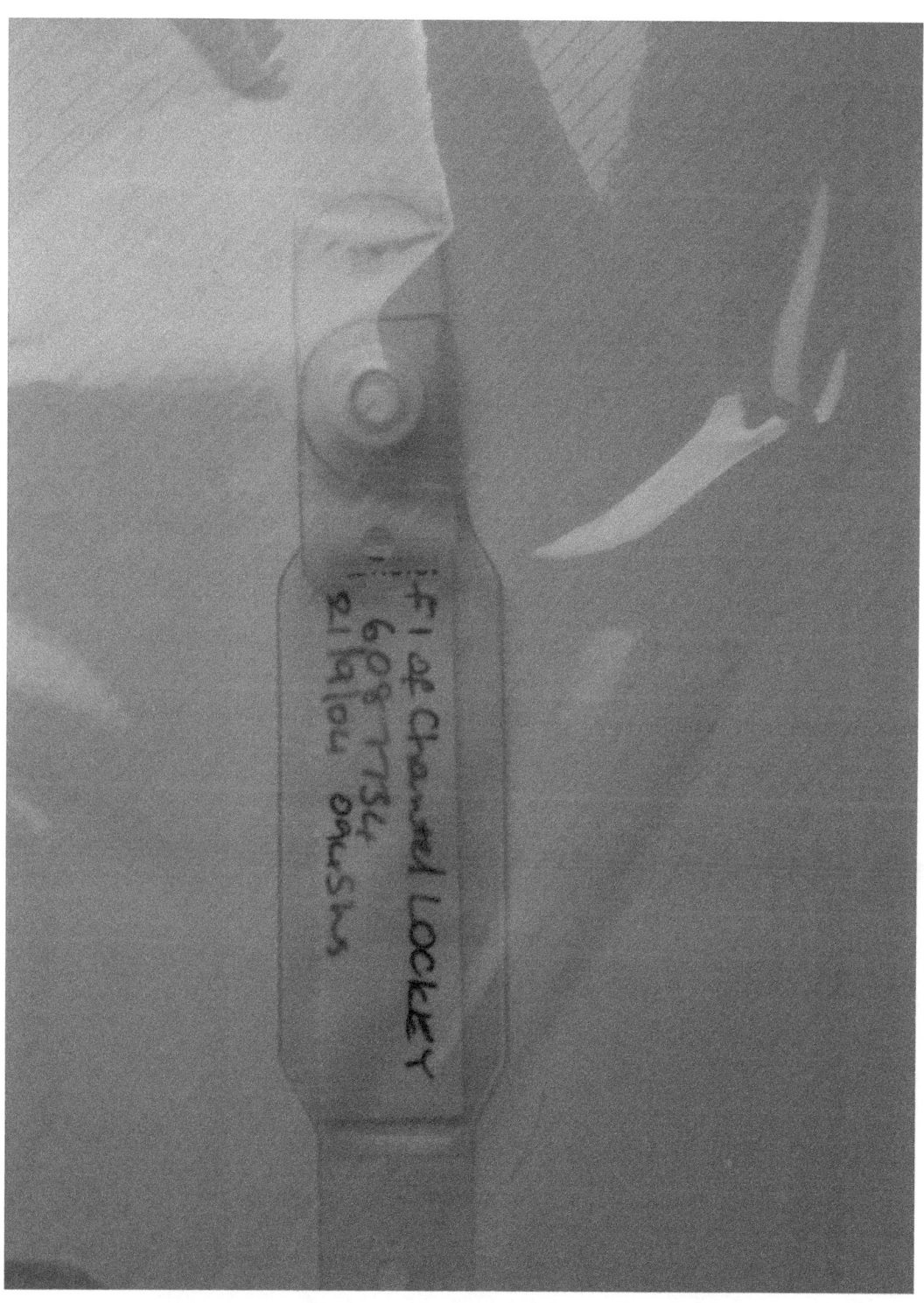

Keeping the Baby's hospital wristband and card as keepsakes for the parents

POPE
MARNIE MAE

On 5th November unexpectedly at home age 6 weeks darling precious daughter of Chantal and Spencer, and a much loved granddaughter. So sadly missed by all her family and friends.

Funeral service to be held at St John's Church, Moordown on Tuesday 16th November at 11.30 am followed by interment in the churchyard. All friends welcome.

Flowers may be sent to Alan Rice & Tapper Funeral Service, 987 Wimborne Road, Moordown, Bournemouth. Tel. 01202 549555

In loving
who die
tha
You w
world a
grand

Two lonel
Love Ber

Memory Boxes

Memory Boxes

Memory Boxes

8. Resources for a Baby's Funeral

Quite often when a parent has lost their baby, they will be in a huge state of shock and may be unable to make basic choices and decisions. It is the responsibility of the hospital and funeral professional to gently guide the bereaved parents with regards to choices and options for the baby's funeral. It may be that choices normally used for adults are just not appropriate when it comes to a baby or small child. We have compiled some resources appropriate for a baby's funeral:

Suggestions

He's got the whole world in his hands.

If I were a butterfly ,Id thank you lord for giving me wings...

Jesus bids us shine.

red and yellow and pink and green (rainbow song)

This little light of mine.

Somewhere over the rainbow.

Twinkle twinkle little star

Funeral Songs for Babies - Popular Music

"Amazing Grace" (Elvis Presley)

"In the Arms of an Angel" (Sarah McLachalan)

"Angels Among Us" (Alabama)

"As Long As I Can See the Light" (Creedence Clearwater Revival)

"Ave Maria", (Perry Como)

"Baby Mine" (Bette Midler)

"Because You Loved Me" (Celine Dion)

"Blessed" (Elton John)

"Borrowed Angels (Kristin Chenoweth)

"Bright Eyes" (Art Garfunkle)- click to see lyrics

"Butterfly" (Mariah Carey)

"Candle in the Wind (Elton John)

"Change The World" (Eric Clapton)

"Circle Of Life" (Elton John, from The Lion King)

"Close to You" (The Carpenters)

"Con Te Partiro/"Time to Say Goodbye " (Andrea Bocelli and Sarah Brightman)

"Don't Let The Sun Go Down On Me" (Elton John)

"Evergreen" (Barbra Streisand)

"Fly" (Celine Dion)

"Have I Told You Lately" (Rod Stewart or Van Morrison)

"Hallelujah" (Jeff Buckley)

"Hero" (Mariah Carey)

"Home" Daughtry

"I Am Your Child" (Barry Manilow)

"I Can See Clearly Now" (Johnny Nash)

"I'll Be Missing You" (P. Diddy, Faith Evans)

"I Will Always Love You" (Dolly Parton or Whitney Houston)

"I Will Remember You" (Sarah McLachalan)

"If" (Bread)

"If I Could Be Where You Are" (Enya)

"I'll Remember April" (Frank Sinatra)

"Imagine" (John Lennon)

"In My Life" (The Beatles)

"Keep me in Your Heart for Awhile" (Warren Zevon, he wrote it before he died of cancer)

"Knocking of Heaven's Door" (Bob Dylan)

"Lean on Me" (Bill Withers)

"Let There Be Peace on Earth" (Jill Jackson and Sy Miller)

"Life Is A Highway (Tom Cochrane)

"Longer" (Dan Fogelberg)

"Memories" (Elvis Presley)

"Memory" (Barbra Streisand)

"My Way" (Frank Sinatra)

"One Sweet Day" (Mariah Carey (featuring Boyz II Men)

"Only the Good Die Young (Billy Joel)

"Over The Rainbow" (Judy Garland, from Wizard Of Oz)

"Run to Paradise" (Choirboys)

"Seasons in the Sun" (Terry Jacks)

"She's Got A Way" (Billy Joel)

"Simply the Best" (Tina Turner)

"So Far Away" (Carole King)

"Softly as I Leave You" (Elvis Presley, Frank Sinatra, Andy Williams)

"Somewhere Over the Rainbow/What a Wonderful World (Isreal Kamamawiwo'ole)

"Stairway to Heaven" Led Zeppelin

"Stand by Me" (B.B. King)

"Tears in Heaven" (Eric Clapton)

"Tenderly Calling" (John Denver)

"The Rose" (Bette Midler)

"The Way We Were" (Barbra Streisand)

"To Where You Are" (Josh Groban)

"Unforgettable" (Nat King Cole/Natalie Cole)

"Up Where We Belong" (Joe Cocker, Jennifer Warnes)

"What A Wonderful World" (Louis Armstrong)

"Wind Beneath My Wings" (Bette Midler)

"Wish You Were Here" (Pink Floyd)

"Wishing You Were Here" (Chicago)

"You Are So Beautiful To Me" (Joe Cocker)

"You Are The Sunshine of My Life" (Stevie Wonder)

"You'll be in my Heart (Phil Collins)-

"You're My First, My Last, My Everything" (Barry White)

"You're the Inspiration" (Chicago)

"You've Got a Friend" (James Taylor)

Funerals for Babies - Poems

A Child Loaned

"I'll lend you for a little time

A child of Mine." He said.

"For you to love the while he lives

And mourn for when he's dead.

It may be six or seven year

Or twenty-two or three

But will you, till I call him back

Take care of him for Me?

He'll bring his charms to gladden you

And should his stay be brief,

You'll have his lovely memories

As solace for your grief.

I cannot promise he will stay

Since all from Earth return,

But there are lessons taught down there

I want the child to learn.

I've looked this wide world over

In my search for teacher's true,

And from the throngs that crowd life's lanes,

I have selected you;

Now will you give him all your love,

Nor think the labour vain

Nor hate Me when I come to call

And take him back again?

I fancied that I heard them say,

"Dear Lord, They will be done,

For all the joy Thy child shall bring,

For the risk of grief we'll run.

We'll shelter him with tenderness,

We'll love him while we may,

And for the happiness we've known,

Forever grateful stay.

But should the angels call for him

Much sooner than we planned,

We'll brave the bitter grief that comes

And try to understand."

Edgar A. Guest

Tears

If tears could build a stairway,

and memories a lane,

I'd walk right up to Heaven

and bring you home again.

No farewell words were spoken

no time to say goodbye

you were gone before I knew it,

and only God knows why.

My heart still aches in sadness

and secret tears still flow,

what it meant to lose you,

no one will ever know.

Author Unknown

My Little Angel

You've just walked on ahead of me

And I've got to understand

You must release the ones you love

And let go of their hand.

I try and cope the best I can

But I'm missing you so much

If I could only see you

And once more feel your touch.

Yes, you've just walked on ahead of me

Don't worry I'll be fine

But now and then I swear I feel

Your hand slip into mine.

There Is A Special Angel

There is a special Angel in Heaven

that is part of me.

It is not where I wanted him

but where God wanted him to be.

He was here but just a moment

like a night time shooting star.

And though he is in Heaven

he isn't very far.

He touched the heart of many

like only an Angel can do.

So I send this special message

to the Heaven up above.

Please take care of my Angel

and send him all my love.

Author Unknown

Heaven's Special Child

A meeting was held quite far from earth.

"It's time again for another birth,"

Said the Angels to the Lord above,

"This special child will need much love.

His progress may seem very slow,

And he'll require extra care

From the folks he meets way down there.

He may not run or laugh or play

His thoughts may seem quite far away,

In many ways he won't adapt,

And he'll be known as handicapped.

So let's be careful where he's sent

We want his life to be content.

Please, Lord, find the parents who

Will do a special job for you.

They will not realize right away

The leading role they're asked to play,

But with this child sent from above

Comes stronger faith and richer love.

And soon they'll know the privilege given

In caring for this gift from Heaven,

Their precious charge, so meek and mild

Is Heaven's very special child!"

– Author Unknown

Precious Son

God, I know you gave your precious Son

To give us life with You.

But we didn't want our son to leave,

Cause he was precious too.

We all are special in your eyes

And all to you return.

We know our son will not come back,

And for this our hearts still yearn.

Our time on earth is for learning,

And when our lessons are through,

Our Lord will choose the time we leave,

And we come back to you.

Our precious son is with you,

And there will be a day,

That we too will leave this earth,

And you will light our way.

His arms will be wide open,

And the wait will be worthwhile,

When we see again our precious son,

And the splendor of his smile.

Anon

I Only Wanted You

They say memories are golden, well, maybe that is true.

I never wanted memories, I only wanted you.

A million times I cried.

If love alone could have saved you, you never would have died.

In life I loved you dearly,in death I love you still.

In my heart you hold a place no one else could fill.

If tears could build a stairway and heartache make a lane.

I'd walk the path to Heaven and bring you back again.

Our family chain is broken, and nothing seems the same.

But as God calls us back one by one, the chain will link again.

Vicky Holder

Epitaph On A Child

Here, freed from pain, secure from misery, lies

A child, the darling of his parents' eyes:

A gentler Lamb ne'er sported on the plain,

A fairer flower will never bloom again;

Now let him sleep in peace his night of death.

The Day God Took You Home

In tears we saw you sinking,

And watched you pass away.

Our hearts were almost broken,

We wanted you to stay.

But when we saw you sleeping,

So peaceful, free from pain,

How could we wish you back with us,

To suffer that again. It broke our hearts to

lose you, But you did not go alone,

For part of us went with you,

The day God took you home.

Anon

God Took Him To His Loving Home

God saw him getting tired, a cure was not to be.

He wrapped him in his loving arms and whispered 'Come with me.'

He suffered much in silence, his spirit did not bend.

He faced his pain with courage, until the very end.

He tried so hard to stay with us but his fight was not in vain,

God took him to His loving home and freed him from the pain.

Anon

9. Relationships after Pregnancy and Infant Loss

Bereaved couples often feel cut off from each other and it is widely accepted that men and women grieve very differently. It is extremely hard to give support and understanding to someone else when a person is in such need of support themselves.

Men and women typically have different ways of expressing and dealing with feelings.

"I just wanted to talk and talk and talk about our son but my husband didn't want to at all. He would walk away and say he wanted to be alone. That hurt me because I felt that he was not there for me. I wondered if he even cared our son had just died"

"I could not even say my daughter's name. I had to cut off. Block it out. My wife thought I didn't care and we argued and argued for months. Of course I cared, I just could not keep on going over it over and over again"

For most mothers, the death of their baby is intensely physical as well as emotional. The baby that has been growing and moving inside the mother is suddenly gone. After the birth, her body still reacts as though she has a baby to care for. Many women are also more inclined to focus on their feelings and to want their partner to acknowledge these. They may need to cry and to be allowed to feel sad. They may need continuing reassurance that there was nothing that they could have done to prevent their baby dying.

Many fathers put their feelings on hold and get through by focusing on supporting the mother and planning for the future. Other people often assume that men will be strong and just keep going. Fathers are also generally expected to return to work very soon after the death of their baby and this too may lead some men to ignore their grief and to focus

"Everyone was asking how my wife was. Nobody asked how I was doing"

Family members may show far more concern for the mother than for her partner, who may feel left out and ignored. It is easy to see why bereaved couples may misunderstand each other and how this can lead to arguments.

These are all the more distressing at a time when many couples feel that they should be especially close and should be supporting each other. This can affect all aspects of a couple's relationship, including their sex life.

While sex may be a source of comfort for one partner, the other may not even be able to consider the idea, especially soon after the baby's death.

"I was horrified when my husband suggested love making. I was disgusted that he was thinking of his own needs after our baby had died. He said he just wanted to feel close"

It is important that the couple try to be patient with each other. The bereaved parents may speak to you about this area of their lives as they will see you as a confident, and a source of comfort. Many bereaved parents have found that by going to support groups together, to meet other people that are going through the same devastation, really helpful. It may be useful to find out the details of local support groups to you so that you can recommend these groups as well as any counselling organizations in your area.

An overview of the difference in ways that men and women may grieve:

MEN:

- Have a fix it nature – "How can I fix this?" or "What can I do?"

- Wanting to be the strong, dependable, keep-it-together husband.

- Feelings of "I have to do better – I am the husband."

- Will tend to compartmentalize grief.

- May throw himself into work to fill the need of wanting to control *something*.

- Work may become his safe haven because home feels (is) so out of control.

- Appear emotion-less, even though they are likely filled with emotions.

- Will not likely want to talk about what they are feeling.

- Men tend to want to *think* through their grief and rationalize the process.

WOMEN:

- After the initial shock, women tend to put their head down and deal with their grief right away and slowly work on getting better.

- Emotions spill over and she may not know why she is crying.

- May get to a point where she stops caring. It doesn't matter if the laundry, dinner, life, dishes, housework get done, or bills get paid. Little is important anymore because women may not know how to function in her new identity.

- Women want to *feel* through their grief.

- She wants to talk about her feelings and emotions.

- Will likely be the first to say something really stupid because she uses talking out loud to help sort her emotions.

- Afraid to laugh or be happy again.

10. Benefits that Bereaved Parents are entitled to after a Pregnancy and Infant Loss -UK Only

"I was on maternity leave when our son was born sleeping. It may sound strange but I was unsure if I had to go back to work the very next day. I was not a mother any more. My son was dead. Was I a mother? What happens now? I asked my midwife and she looked shocked at what I was asking. She did not know the answer to my question".

At what is a totally illogical and surreal time, midwives should be willing to expect questions about anything, as random as it may seem It would also be useful for midwifes to familiarise themselves with the below information:

What are bereaved parents entitled to?

This depends on many things, including the length of the pregnancy, whether their baby was stillborn or lived for a short time after the birth, whether they are employed, and their earnings before the birth.

http://www.moneyadviceservice.org.uk/_assets/downloads/pdfs/parents/bereavement_guide_english.pdf

The experience and the grief that parents feel when a baby dies after 14 or 16 weeks of pregnancy can be much the same as when a baby is stillborn. But for legal purposes, when a baby is born dead before 24 completed weeks of pregnancy, this is called a late miscarriage. Sadly, you are not entitled to maternity or paternity rights or benefits if you have had a late miscarriage. But you do still have some entitlements. Mothers are entitled to:

Sick Leave. A miscarriage is a pregnancy-related sickness. Your employer must not dismiss or treat you less favourably because you have a pregnancy-related sickness, even if you have only just started working there. The time you have off will not count towards your sickness record (though any sick pay you get will be counted) and is not time-limited. You need to get a Fit note (previously called a Sick note) from your GP.

Mothers may be entitled to:

Compassionate Leave and Time Off for Dependents. If you are not sick, your employer may give you Compassionate Leave or Time Off for Dependents(TOFD). You are legally entitled to TOFD in certain circumstances, but your entitlement to Compassionate Leave depends on your contract of employment and your employer's policy.

Sick Pay from your employer or income-related benefits from the state.

Fathers or partners may be entitled to: Sick Leave and Sick Pay, compassionate leave or Time Off For Dependents from your employer.

A mother's female partner has the same rights and entitlements as a father. If your baby was stillborn after 24 completed weeks of pregnancy OR if your baby was born alive at any stage of pregnancy and then died.

Mothers are entitled to:

52 weeks' maternity leave. You should normally have told your employer that you were pregnant before the 24th completed week of your pregnancy. If you gave birth before your maternity leave started, your leave starts the day after you gave birth.

Mothers may be entitled to Maternity Pay from your employer, Maternity Allowance, or income-related benefits from the state.

Fathers or partners may be entitled to:

One or two consecutive weeks' Paternity leave from your employer. You should normally have informed your employer that you planned to take paternity leave before the 24th completed week of the pregnancy.

Sick Leave and Sick Pay, compassionate leave or Time Off For Dependents from your employer. A mother's female partner has the same rights and entitlements as a father.

11. <u>Planning to return to Work</u>

When bereaved parents are ready to think about going back to work, they need to contact their employer, to discuss this.

Gradual " easing in" may be an option so that the bereaved parent can take steady steps back into employment.

Employers have a legal obligation to consider properly any request they may make for part-time hours, though they don't have to agree. Once they have agreed a date when they will go back to work, they may find it helpful to talk to their manager about how they are feeling and what might help them to settle back in.

They could also visit their workplace and have an informal coffee with their colleagues in small groups before they go back. This may be easier than repeating their story to many different people later. Unless they have experienced the death of a baby themselves, most people will have no idea of how they feel. They are unlikely to realize the full extent of how the death of their baby has had on them and on their family.

"I was really scared about going back to work. I felt really embarrassed and awkward for some reason. I didn't want to have to tell people my baby had died. I was dreading their reactions"

The early days back at work can be overwhelming. It can be daunting to leave the safety net of the home. The bereaved parent may also be worried about how they will manage their job

"I felt very anxious about going back to work. I was scared that I would just lose the plot and burst into tears and make a fool of myself"

The bereaved parent should be gentle with themselves. Parents should try not to put pressure on themselves to do more than they can. They should take time out if they need a break. They may find that the routine of work is helpful, and that it is a relief to have some structure to the days and weeks. However, their life and their priorities may also have changed a lot since their baby died. Things that once seemed essential may not seem so important now.

"I sat in my office on my first day back to work and I thought what is the point of this? Why am I bothering? What is the point of anything?".

Grief is tiring, they may be surprised at how exhausted they feel.

"I was exhausted by 11am. I felt heavy hearted and exhausted – in my mind and body"

Grief tends to come in waves. It is normal to have good days and bad days.

"I was fine for three days and then for no reason whatsoever, I burst into tears on the fourth day when making a cup of tea. I felt ashamed"

They may also find it helpful to find somewhere private to talk to a sympathetic colleague, phone a family member, If things are really getting on top of them, it may be sensible to go home for the rest of the day.

Many bereaved parents are nervous about how people at work will react to them. Some people may say insensitive things because they are shocked, or just because they don't know what to say. Others may be very supportive and willing to listen if they want to talk.

If people are insensitive or don't understand, they may simply not know how to react. There may also be someone who has been on maternity or paternity leave and returns to show off their new baby. Just as it is natural for them to have mixed feelings about other people's new babies, it is natural for them to want to share their excitement. All these situations can be really difficult.

Certain dates will be particularly difficult at work for bereaved parents.

These can include the anniversary of their baby's due date, and of his or her death. Many bereaved parents feel particularly sad on dates such as Christmas and on special days like Mother's Day and Father's Day.

Bereaved Parents may want to consider booking a day's leave on dates that they know are likely to be especially difficult for them. This can take the pressure off them at a time when they will feel the most emotional.

" I always take off Firework Day from work because that is the day that my son died. I always think I will be okay, but as the day gets closer, the memories come flooding back and I am an absolute mess. I like to hide away at home on this day every year. I don't want to see anyone"

12. Life after Loss: The Support required with subsequent children after loss

Support required in Subsequent Pregnancies

After a devastating loss some parents may decide that they want to try for subsequent children.

Any bereaved parent will agree that there is an overwhelming terror in the "will it happen to me again"?

It may be that bereaved parent has lost a baby to late miscarriage or stillbirth and there are unanswered questions about why that baby had died if the post mortem has come back inconclusive.

When looking at trying again for another baby. The feeling that one could not cope with going through such a terrible and devastating time once again. The bereaved parents require a huge amount of support during this time. The said parents may have feelings of complete guilt for contemplating another baby, but at the same token there is a huge feeling that another baby is the only obvious way to survive the grief and loneliness that the lost baby has left behind. The bereaved parent has feelings that any subsequent babies would not be to replace the lost baby but to help in healing their heartache and a feeling of incompleteness. Many bereaved parents have said (particularly when losing their first born baby) that it is near on impossible to go back to being a couple after having the joy of a baby in their life's and hence a family unit. There is a feeling of "empty arms", a feeling of how shallow life feels and a complete disconnection from life, which is often associated with a deep feeling of loneliness.

The professionals looking after a subsequent pregnancy after a loss should be aware that the parents might display a very irrational anxiety as to their baby's health and wellbeing. It is likely that the parents may "think the worst" for example if there is a lack of movement or if there are any twinges or pains.

"My pregnancy was totally different from my first child. I was anxious, terrified, convinced something bad was going to happen and I almost drove myself – and my husband mad with my constant worrying and over analysing. In truth I did not enjoy my pregnancy, I wanted it to be over as quickly as possible"

In subsequent pregnancies after loss there can be other concerns. For example the bereaved parents may worry if they will have the same love for subsequent children after loss. They may be afraid of bonding with the new baby, as they may be scared to – in case "it should happen again". All of these feelings are perfectly normal.

"I was so scared that I would not love my next baby. Rose was born sleeping and yet I loved her more than life itself. I didn't know if I was capable of that same love again. I was also scared to love again because I was terrified that I would get close and then the same thing happen to me all over again"

"I felt guilty about having another baby. I kept going to my baby's grave to tell my girl that I still loved her so much and I was sorry for having another baby, but that I just had to"

The Lullaby Trust in the United Kingdom provides the vital CONI scheme (Care of the Next Infant) which has proved invaluable to many families following a loss. The scheme provides bereaved parents with an Apnoea Breathing Monitor, paediatric first aid including that of resuscitation and a CONI "passport" which means if you have any concerns for your subsequent baby, then you can be fast tracked at your local Accident and Emergency Department.

"The breathing monitor was an essential element and part of our life's for my daughters first two years of life. It meant that a very anxious time was assisted by the fact that we knew our daughter was breathing, particularly during the night, and if there were any issues with her breathing, the alarm would sound and we would have the time to awake her and consequently "jolt her" into breathing again if necessary"

"The terror did not diminish as my second daughter grew. Any signs of illness resulted in many (probably unnecessary) trips to the hospital and the first few years, I silently wished away quickly. However the CONI scheme meant that I had the opportunity of starting to enjoy my second daughter, where if I did not have the breathing monitor or the related support, I do not feel that this would have been the case"

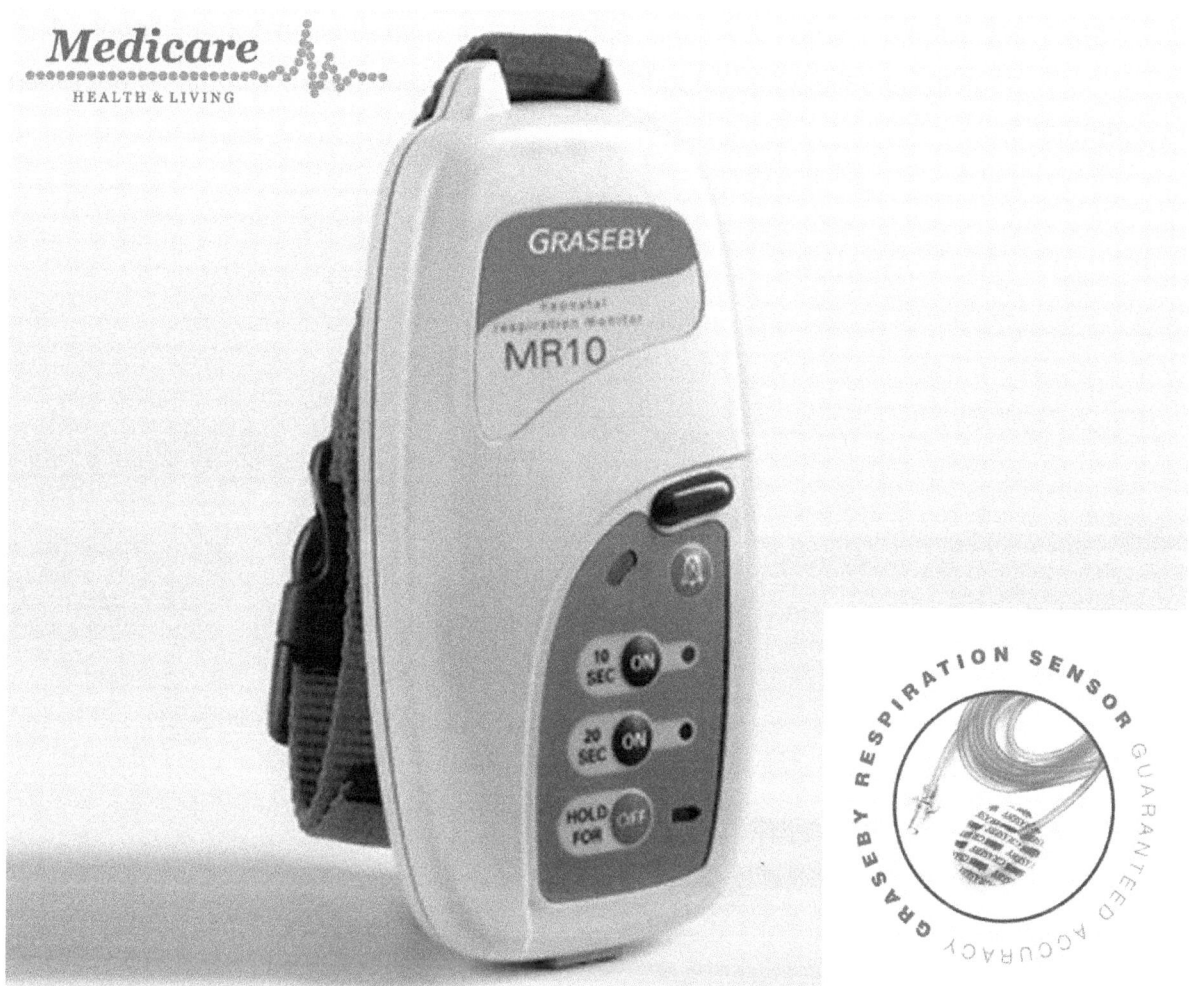

The Graseby MR10 Apnoea Monitor

The Health Visitor or any other Community Based Practitioners are essential in supporting bereaved parents with their subsequent pregnancies. It is an incredibly hard time from an emotional point of view. The approach to a new born baby is not anywhere similar to those who have not lost a baby previously. The bereaved parent lives a life of fear and terror that this subsequent child will die too. There is an enormous strain on the bereaved parent's relationship and it is likely that parents who have lost previously will adopt a very over protective approach to the subsequent baby. The parents need to be supported and reassured by their community based practitioner during this intense period in their life's and quite often will require more time and appointments with the said practitioner. This practitioner needs to be patient and supportive in what may seem a very irrational approach to parenthood.

13. Subsequent children after loss - A Personal Account

Electronic Version of " Rainbow through the rain"

The last time we spoke I had just found out that I was pregnant with Ruby. Do you remember the guilt I felt?. The hope I felt? and of course the utter fear. Would it happen again?. Ruby's pregnancy was a huge blur of continuous scans, Consultants appointments and regular emergency treks to the maternity Unit to "check" she still had a heartbeat. I think Poole Maternity got a bit fed up with me in the end!. I cant tell you how many times I was convinced Ruby was dead during my pregnancy. I had even accepted it before walking through the hospital doors on many occasions. I think it's is very fair to say that throughout the course of my pregnancy with Ruby, I held back. In a big way. I cared. Of course I cared but there was that little bit of self-preservation that I kept back. I had to. Because the same question kept cropping up time and time again in my mind - WOULD it happen again?. The twenty week scan was a bittersweet occasion. The Consultant told me that I was carrying another girl. As crazy as it sounds, I was so pleased it wasn't a boy. She would be just another Marnie wouldn't she?. She would make it all better, that I was sure of.

Of course we told everyone our "happy" news. People were over the moon when they realized I was pregnant again. It was "for the best" and it would ultimately mean a happy ever after, so why did I feel so utterly guilty?. Why didn't I feel particularly happy about it all?. I kept thinking that I had only buried Marnie months before, and here I was, waddling down the high street. I wondered what people must have thought. The guilt really was overwhelming. It consumed everything. I often would visit Marnie's grave to tell her that she would always be Mummy's special girl and that I wasn't trying to replace her or to forget her. The big question though was I trying to convince her or myself?.

During the latter stages of my pregnancy, Mum and I "braved" the nursery. It was hard. I suppose the realization kicked in when we had to sort out Marnie's things to "make way" for another baby. It wasn't a nice feeling. I was adamant that the new baby wouldn't wear anything of Marnie's. Marnie's things were so precious. I hadn't even washed a few of the last outfits Marnie had worn (I still have everything, neatly folded in pretty pink boxes). As I folded the new baby clothes and put them into what was Marnie's chest of drawers, the realization definitely hit. The guilt swallowed me up. In that second I wouldn't how I would cope with another baby. I really couldn't do this all again. What had I done?. I felt so bloody stupid and so irresponsible. However, it was all a bit too late in the day to be feeling like that. The months had flown by and before I knew it I was in front of my Consultant who was booking me in for an elective caesarean section on 5 September 2005. She was coming if I liked it or not.

My due dates with Marnie and Ruby couldn't have been any different. With Marnie's there was a buzz of excitement. The anticipation. The wondering of whom Marnie would look like. It was a good time. With Ruby I was feeling a mixture of dread - I was convinced that she would be born still born. There would be no heartbeat. My feeling were, let's just get this over with, and a state of numbness. I was in that bubble again. There was no excitement this time.

As I was wheeled into theatre, the first thing I noticed was the huge increase in doctors and nurses. Theatre was packed. My first thoughts were - See? They know the baby is going to be born dead too. Let's get this over....

As the epidural went in (and funnily enough this time around I didn't feel any pain, but then maybe I had stop feeling full stop) I lay back and started counting the cracks in the ceiling. For no reason at all. Then I started counting the doctors and nurses in the room. For no reason at all. And, in seconds, there was a baby's cry and then my doctor held up a very chubby, black haired baby. She was crying, she was breathing and Oh that was MY baby. I looked at her and I am ashamed to say I felt nothing. They handed her to me and I told them that "I would hold her later". She could have been anyone's baby they had just shown me. Anyone's. Spencer took Ruby off to get cleaned up and dressed. As I lay there getting sewn back up, I started counting the cracks in the ceiling again. They really should get this theatre re-painted. It looked ever such a mess.

After the doctors had finished with me, I was wheeled on to the ward where I saw Spencer feeding Ruby her first bottle. I looked at her closely. MY GOODNESS. She had jet black hair and reddish skin and she looked NOTHING like Marnie. Nothing. This isn't what I had expected. And then after all of those months it hit me. She wasn't Marnie. She never was going to be. She was Ruby and Marnie really wasn't coming back. What had I done?

I hadn't accepted Marnie's death and here I was with a brand new baby. What had I done?.

Over the next day or two numerous family and friends came to see me in hospital. They were all so happy for us and that our horror story had finally ended and we were now a happy little family. I smiled in all the right places, nodding in agreement, but all the time I stayed in that bubble and felt nothing. I felt like I had failed. Yet again.

Do you remember in the subsequent chapter when I told you about the CONI scheme? (Care of the next Infant? a scheme developed by FSID in the UK to help parents who have lost, with their new babies). Well thank goodness for them. Before Ruby was born they gave us an apnoea monitor. You attach the little probe on to the baby's stomach with a small piece of surgical tape and basically, if the baby stops breathing, the alarm sounds. From the day she was born Ruby was on the alarm. I would lay in my hospital bed listening to the click-click-click of the monitor which meant that she was still breathing. I would hold my breath if one of the "clicks" was a bit slow in coming around. That clicking could have driven me insane. But at the same token it was vital for my own sanity.

Having said that I don't think my sanity was that intact. I got up in the middle of the night during my hospital stay and I went to see if Ruby was okay in the nursery. The nurses had changed her baby grow and put her in a purple baby grow- that wasn't hers (but looked the spitting image of one that Marnie had worn). Maybe it was the lack of sleep or the drugs, but for a split second I thought it was Marnie in that cot. I did wonder if I was going mad.

Before long, it was time to leave the hospital and to go home. I really didn't want to leave. The hospital was my haven. My safety net with all of those Doctors around and drugs and monitors. If anything went wrong here I could just press the buzzer. What would I do if something went wrong at home?. I was terrified.

So, we took Ruby home. We took her into the same milkshake pink nursery that we had taken Marnie into on her arrival home, not even a year before. It didn't feel real. I felt like a fraud. We had a baby. We had lost a baby. And here I was standing in the same nursery with another baby girl in the space of a year. Ruby's first night at home was pretty traumatic. I felt like I would have a heart attack. I was so so terrified. Typically the CONI alarm went off through the night and after leaping out of bed for the third time, I wondered if this was a sign of things to come. Was it a false alarm or was she stopping breathing?. I also wondered how my caesarean section stitches hadn't burst open with all the leaping. Poor Rubes. Every time the alarm went off, I would shake her awake and she would awake with a fright, crying her eyes out. And then sat perched over her cot all night watching her. All night whilst shaking like a nervous wreck. I would sit there awake, night after night, wondering why on earth I had put myself through this again. I was so tired. I had the baby blues, I was so sore and yet the overwhelming fear that Ruby would die, beat all of that combined, hands down.

I was also obsessing about any potential signs of illness. I googled everything. And even though Ruby's breathing monitor was ticking away nicely, sometimes I would look into her cot and I would see the same blue tinged face that Marnie had on the night we found her, so again I would have to wake Rubes with a start until she cried loudly and started throwing her little arms and legs about. I would breathe a sigh of relief.

It sounds strange but despite doing everything for Ruby and watching her like a hawk, I could not at that point, have told you that I had bonded with her. I hadn't. It was all very mechanical. It was all about the fear of another baby dying. But I think at that point, that was as far as it went.

Until one day.

It was just an ordinary day really. She looked up at me whilst I was changing her nappy and she looked at me, and with a little windy smile. She broke me. I loved her like I couldn't believe. She was now 3 weeks old. And that was the start. Nothing has changed since that day. I am so grateful for that.

The love flowed and the bond had been made. I started to enjoy Ruby, but of course, those increased feelings of love, ultimately increase those of fear. In all honesty I suppose the first two years of Ruby's life, I was on a knife edge. I had done so much research into cot death and I had learnt that it can happen up to two years of age. Consequently, Ruby remained on her monitor until just after her second birthday. Those bloody false alarms came and went through those two years, and there is no denying it, that every one of those alarms could have given me a heart attack. As Ruby progressed and reached her little milestones, I would still wonder about Marnie. It felt so unfair that she had missed out on so much. You only realize how much when you see another child developing and growing into a little toddler. Its amazing how much they change and how much they can do. Her first tooth. Her first steps, her first words, her favourite things: food, TV programs, friends etc. I suppose silently, I wished away those two years. I wanted to get Ruby through that baby stage. Quickly. I can't say in all honesty that I believed that Ruby would stay however. I still had prepared myself a little bit in case it should happen.

I loved seeing all of Ruby's milestones, and celebrating all of her birthdays and Christmas times, but the whole time I still thought about Marnie and felt terrible that she had missed out on so much in life that was visible through Ruby growing and changing. I suppose that old word – guilt – cropped up a few times during those times too. Funny that. After two years I started to relax a little, Ruby came off her monitor – now this bit wasn't so easy. That beep beep beeping had been a regular fixture of my life for such a long time and it meant that I KNEW she was breathing. I can't tell you how often I checked Ruby in her cot each night when that monitor had come off!. I still had the same feeling of dread and fear as I walked into the darkness of her bedroom each night, half holding my breath, expecting the worst. People have said in the past, that how could I still feel like that, after all, by this stage Marnie was two years old, a toddler. Well let me tell you now, Rubes is eight this year and I still check her religiously at night. I can't see how that will ever go away. It's even worse when she is ill. I think the Paediatrics unit at Poole Hospital know us by first name. Or maybe I am more than likely known as "that crazy mother"!. But on the flip side of this, Ruby brings me so much joy in my life. I live for her. She is my happiness and I would do anything for her. Anything. I am so pleased that I have Ruby. Life would be a pretty dark and different place without her. I describe Ruby as my Best friend. It is made that a little girl of not even eight can be described as that, but she really is. She loves "chick nights" when we eat popcorn, watch movies and paint our toe nails. She loves going out for dinner at Aruba and talking to the Parrot! She loves the beach, her holidays and she loved visiting the "real" Father Christmas at Lapland last Christmas. She is just so precious,

So I think that is about the size of it. A story of utter hell that did have a happy ending (although I would have never ever have believed that). I still find it hard to believe that it will be nine years ago in November that Marnie died. Sometimes it feels like yesterday. A lady I know who had recently suffered a miscarriage asked me how I coped the other day. She was in such a dark place and was so low. I saw myself. She asked me if it gets easier in time, did I still get paranoid? Did it still hurt?. I suppose the answer to all those questions is yes. It does get easier. That raw pain that you never thought existed has faded away – but not entirely. It resurfaces its ugly head particularly at Christmas time or on Marnie's birthday. I am grateful that over time the pain has become bearable. And I think that's about as good as it will get, "bearable". The guilt? Well there is a small part of that that will always remain. I was Marnie's mum and I felt like I had failed her. But in 2010, 6 years after Marnie died, I finally sought Counselling. Its never too late so they say!. I am so honoured to have met the most remarkable Dr Hubbard, who in her ingenious fashion convinced me, told me that Marnie dying was simply not my fault. Now maybe this lady has a way with words or has magic powers or something, but in time, I accepted it. I finally got to the stage where I didn't think it was my fault, and do you know what, I walked out of her office smiling, and feeling like a huge weight had been lifted from me. A weight that had consumed me for nine years. A weight that was stopping me from living and a weight that meant I wasn't giving my all to Ruby, because I felt guilty. It was a great feeling. Not that it exactly started off like that. It was hellish going through every single detail of Marnie's death. I had blocked that night out from my mind over and over again. I would only have to briefly touch on the memory and I would immediately shove that memory back into the dark place it had been placed in. It was hard. And I almost felt that I was there that night once more. But like I said, afterwards, I felt so much better. Honestly, I would recommend Counselling to anyone who has gone through this horrendous loss. I feel that I can move on with my life and be a much better Mum to ruby. We have so much fun together and I didn't want to be consumed with guilt every time that happened. I was sick of living the bittersweet life.

So how are things now?. Things are going well. I can look at photos of Marnie now and smile and remember her little noises that she used to make and her little smile, without the gut wrenching feeling of pain. I think of Marnie and I hope she's okay. I hope she realizes that I haven't forgotten her and I hope she is happy – wherever she may be. There is no doubt in my mind that losing Marnie has changed my life forever. The person I was before Marnie died, isn't the same "me". I suppose there is a constant brick wall around me, that very few can break down. I can't say I relish the fact that I am like that but I think it is nature's way. I have a very strong bond with Ruby, as I mentioned, I would describe her as my best friend and there is no one in the world I would rather spend time with. Without going into too much detail, my relationship with the girls dad failed as do so many relationships after losing a much loved child, ultimately the differences in the way that we grieved, ultimately ended our relationship, sadly this is not uncommon after the death of a baby.

Ruby, of course knows all about her big sister. In fact, the day we bought Ruby home from the hospital we took her to Marnie's place. Ruby has been brought up with it. I still have photos of Marnie all around my house and we celebrate her birthday by sending her balloons and imagining her eating chocolate cake with her angel friends!. We decorate a mini Christmas tree for her at Christmas time and leave her eggs at Easter. I didn't want Ruby to be kept in the dark over Marnie's death and even, her existence, so I have always spoken about Marnie as a member of her family. Which she is . Ruby often asks why Marnie died and how unfair she feels that it is, because she would like somebody to play with. It breaks my heart, but I try to answer in a way that isn't too difficult for a seven year old to understand. I'm thirty three and I don't understand it so how could she?. People often ask me if I want more children and most are horrified when I say absolutely not. I don't think I could go through it all again. I think sometimes that if I hadn't got pregnant with Ruby so quickly after losing Marnie (about 8 weeks), I would have been too frightened to go for another. The fear is still there and now life is the best that it has been. Of course, I still check Ruby is breathing several times on a nightly basis. There is still that tiny bit of fear as I walk into her dark bedroom on a night and await to see her chest rise and fall and then that huge sigh of relief. I wonder when that fear might disappear, but I am realistic, and I don't think it will go away just yet. You really cant go through finding a child in the middle of the night, in the way I did, without it scarring you forever.

I hope that reading Marnie's story has helped you in some small way. Surround yourself with people that know and love you and know that in time, the pain will fade. I know you don't believe me -I said the very same thing.

Just trust me on this one...

14. Healing after loss: Family Inclusions and Marking Milestones

When a family lose a much-loved baby, that baby will still be considered very much a part of their family. Families may have photographs on display with their other living children, they may include their baby in Christmas and Easter celebrations and they may celebrate the baby's birthday every year. Families who have lost that have older children have found that by including their baby in day-to-day family life has assisted the healing process.

"At Christmas time we always take a small Christmas tree to Eden's grave, we sing her some Christmas carols, on her Birthday my sons kiss some balloons and send them up to heaven. Eden may not be here with us in a physical sense, but she is very much a part of our family. That will never change"

It may be that when a subsequent child after loss grows, that he or she is introduced to photographs of their "big" brother or sister. In this way it will never be a shock or a big issue, as they have always known about their brother or sister.

"On the day that Luke came home from hospital I took him to his sisters grave. It was a hugely emotional time, seeing Luke sat in his car seat on his sister's grave. It gave me some comfort though, it may seem totally illogical to some people, but my children were together. There is nothing more illogical that knowing one of your children is buried beneath your feet, I always say – do not judge me if you do not wear my shoes"

"We always have a messy chocolate cake party for Darcy' s Birthday every year. My other children love it and for us, it is a acceptance that yes she was here. She was a little life and for six amazing weeks, she brought absolute joy into our homes and hearts – that we will never ever forget. That is something to celebrate"

"Just because Toby is not here with me physically, I am and always be his Mom. I talk to him, I share my news with him, it may sound strange, but Toby is still very much a part of our family".

Including a baby that has died in day to day family activities can assist the bereaved family in the healing process.

Other bereaved families interviewed advised that they found the following activities a healing experience:

Healing through writing: Writing a journal or writing letters to their baby

A balloon release – Many found sending balloons to their baby in heaven with messages of love attached to them, very comforting

Healing through relaxation such as meditation, yoga or reiki classes to focus ones mind

Healing through craft: Making memory books of their baby or making small gifts to place on their baby's grave.

Healing through talking. Many of the bereaved families interviewed advised that talking to fellow parents who had lost a baby was one of the most helpful in the healing process:

" When I speak to Sam, she gets me. She understands every little emotion that I feel. She sometimes just nods as I talk as she feels the same. I have a super family and friends network but they do not understand me. How could they? They have never had to bury their own baby. Talking to Sam makes me feel that even if I feel that I am going mad with my constant up and down days, that what I am feeling is normal. It is normal for us"

15. In Conclusion

Losing a baby is the most devastating of deaths. It is quite often unexpected, it is illogical, going against the natural order of life and the bereaved parents are left feeling:

SHOCK, DENIAL, EMOTIONALLY DISTRESSED, ANGER, THE MOST GUT WRENCHING FEELING OF GUILT, DESPERATION, A SENSE OF "EMPTY ARMS", CONFUSION AND A FEELING THAT NOTHING MAKES SENSE IN THE WORLD.

Quite often when midwives first have contact with the bereaved parents the said parents may seem detached or "in a bubble". Many parents have described the days after losing their baby as a blur, a feeling that they are almost looking down at themselves going through the motions, but not feeling really THERE. That in fact this could be happening to someone else. I feel that this is nature's way to offer some kind of protection to the parents. What comes along with this, is the fact that the parents will not be a state of mind to consider even basic things that would seem obvious and apparent to others. Not only have the parents had to deal with finding that their much loved baby has died, they will quite often then have to contend with the fact that their baby has had to have a Post Mortem.

A parent's worst nightmare.

As previously mentioned the parents are in a complete state of shock.

"I felt that everything moved very quickly on the night that my daughter died. In the space of a few hours, I had gone to bed feeling that I was incredibly happy and lucky to have a beautiful daughter. In a few hours from this I had found her dead and then very quickly after this she was taken away by the Coroner for Post Mortem. She was gone and there was absolutely nothing I could have done to stop that. I was powerless and my worst possible nightmare was here. Right here"

It may be that the bereaved parents will therefore then ask questions and want answers from the their midwife with regards to Post Mortem. It is important that midwifery professionals should have an understanding of this area and to be able to speak freely yet gently to the bereaved parents.

SEEING THE BABY FOR THE FIRST TIME IN THE HOSPITAL OR FUNERAL HOME

When a parent finds their baby has died, it is without a doubt their worst nightmare.

" On finding my daughter had died in the early hours of the morning at home, she looked blue and she had a bloody froth coming from her mouth and nose. It is heartbreaking to find what was your perfect little baby, looking as they do after death. The terror is immense. That terror then follows through with me considering whether I would want to go and see my baby in the chapel of rest at the funeral directors. I felt obliged to go and see my daughter and to say goodbye but I was terrified. The immediate question was "would she look even worse several days after death"? and "would I be able to see evidence of the Post Mortem"? "

It is so vital and so important that the bereaved parent is encouraged to see their baby but also reassured that the baby looks "okay" and it would not be as frightening as finding the baby as they did.

"My funeral Director took photos of my daughter in the chapel of rest so that I could be prepared when I saw her for real. This helped so very much. I do believe that if these photos had not been taken and I had been prepared in this manner, that I am not sure if I would be able to "brave" seeing my daughter and obviously a final goodbye is essential in the healing process. I think that parents should be encouraged to take photos of their babies in death as it helps build a picture of the situation that has just happened. I still look at these photos even after almost ten years and I am so glad that I have them. For us personally we did NOT want to see our daughter in her coffin. I think it would have been too painful and the realization that that would be our final memory of her. Instead we had our daughter in a Moses basket at the funeral home, tucked up in her favourite pink blanket, surrounded by her toys, with her dummy in her mouth. We saw NO signs of the post mortem and she although looked very pale, she did not look as terrible as she did when I found her. The last memory I have of my daughter is a better one than the one I would have had of her had I not visited her at the chapel of rest"

This quote enhances why excellent professional care given to bereaved parents ultimately makes such a difference - in this instance, the bereaved parent had a final memory of their baby at peace, rather than the terror of her baby looking blue and "bleeding" from her mouth and nose.

MAKING MEMORIES AT THE HOSPITAL

Ultimately when a baby dies, memories are all that is left. There are memories that can be made by the Midwife professional in the hospital:

- Hand and foot prints

- A lock of baby's hair

- A copy of the funeral announcement to be given to the parents

- Photos of the baby – including family photographs

- Memory Books

- Memory Boxes

ORGANISING THE FUNERAL BY THE FUNERAL PROFESSIONAL OR BEREAVEMENT MIDWIFE

When meeting with the parents the following will need to be spoken about (as mentioned the parents are in a state of shock and quite often would not even think about such apparently obvious duties).

Choosing a Special Outfit (this included a Nappy and a Dummy for our daughter)

Choosing a Special Blanket to wrap the baby in

The child's favourite toys. Some parents may like to buy identical toys so that that they may keep one for themselves and somehow feel connected to their baby

Did the child require a St Christopher? Or another religious symbol or token? Parents can find this very comforting in keeping their baby "safe".

Preparing photos and a letter to be placed in the coffin

Preparing any jewellery or any special family items to be placed in the coffin

Burial or Cremation?

Religious or Humanist funeral?

Bearing the Coffin. Many parents decide to carry their own baby's coffin.

Flowers - "innocent" and "child centred" this can include floral tributes in the form of an Angel, a Teddy Bear or other arrangements with toys

Offering the parents advice on resources specifically for a baby's funeral (we have compiled a list which is included with this handout suggesting hymns, contemporary music and poems).

" We had a personalized funeral "booklet" produced for our daughters funeral. It included all of the photographs we had of her and also tributes from each member of our family. It may sound strange but we felt proud that we were able to show our daughter off in this booklet as many members attended the funeral had not yet met our daughter. Many people have said that they still have kept this memento nearly ten years on and for us, this means that our daughters memory is kept alive"

Considering whether the parents want the funeral to be videoed or for photographs to be taken. Again, although this may be slightly taboo in the UK, this is freely done in the USA and we feel that this is of benefit to the bereaved parents to look back on, even several years later.

Considering any special touches. These could include a **balloon release** after the funeral, a friend of mine released **butterflies** which was a lovely touch. **Rose petals** could be suggested for family members to sprinkle on to the coffin as it is lowered if the baby is being buried. Another suggestion is to give mourners a packet of **seeds**, particularly if there are children in attendance.

Encourage the parents to provide a **"Memory book"** to be placed at the funeral or wake so that mourners can write a few words of comfort or indeed their favourite memory of the baby. We found this comforting, amusing and a lovely collection of memories that perhaps we did not have ourselves.

Professionals should be aware that even after the funeral has taken place it is possible that the parents will want to return to see the staff at the funeral home or hospital. It is ultimately the last place that they have seen their baby before they have been buried. A degree of patience in this respect is required. I also think it necessary that professionals dealing with Infant Loss should have a knowledge of local support groups and counselling services for bereaved parents so that they can give the parents this information should they ask.

Finally understand your role in this respect. Understand the fact that YOU are taking care of a family's much-loved baby:

You are the person doing the very last in looking after for the said baby. A position of immense privilege and importance.

You never forget the care and kindness received by your midwife and funeral director in such a devastating time and those small things listed here make all the difference to a family going through the un – imaginable.

Further Reading: Suggestions

About What Was Lost: 20 Writers on Miscarriage, Healing and Hope. Jessica Berger Gross, editor,

After the Loss of Your Baby: for Teen Mothers. Connie Nykiel,

Beyond Prenatal Choice: Support and Information after Pregnancy Termination Due to a Fetal Abnormality. Centering Corporation,

A Child's View of Grief. Alan Wolfelt,

Death of an Infant Twin. Joy & Marvin Johnson,

Difficult Decisions: for Families whose Unborn Baby Has a Serious Problem. Centering,

Embracing Laura: the Grief and Healing Following the Death of an Infant Twin. Martha Wegner-Hay,

Empty Arms: Coping after Miscarriage, Stillbirth or Infant Death. Sherokee Ilse,

Empty Cradle, Broken Heart: Surviving the Death of Your Baby. Deborah Davis,

Ended Beginnings: Healing Childbearing Losses. Claudia Panuthos & Catherine Romeo,

For Bereaved Grandparents. Margaret Gerner,

A Gift of Time: Continuing Your Pregnancy When Your Baby's Life is Expected to Be Brief. Amy Kuebelbeck & Deborah Davis,

The Good Grief Club. Monica Novak,

The Grief of Grandparents. Centering,

Healing a Father's Grief. William Schatz,

Healing Together: for Couples Whose Baby Dies. Marcie Lister & Sandra Lovell,

Healing Your Grieving Heart after Stillbirth: 100 Practical Ideas for Parents and Families. Alan Wolfelt & Raelynn Maloney,

Life Touches Life: a Mother's Story of Stillbirth and Healing. Lorraine Ash,

Loving and Letting Go: for Parents Who Decided to Turn Away from Aggressive Medical Intervention for their Critically Ill Newborns. Deborah Davis,

Miscarriage: a Man's Book. Rick Wheat,

Miscarriage: a Shattered Dream. Sherokee Ilse & Linda Hammer Burns,

Miscarriage: Women Sharing from the Heart. Marie Allen & Shelly Marks,

Precious Lives, Painful Choices: a Prenatal Decision-Making Guide. Sherokee Ilse,

Remembering Our Angels: Personal Stories of Healing from a Pregnancy Loss. Hannah Stone,

SIDS & Infant Death Survival Guide: Information & Comfort for Grieving Family & Friends & Professionals Who Seek to Help Them. Joani Nelson Horchler & Robin Rice,

Silent Birth: When Your Baby Dies. Sharon Covington,

A Silent Sorrow, Pregnancy Loss: Guidance and Support for You and Your Family. I. Kohn & P. Moffitt,

Single Parent Grief. Sherokee Ilse,

Still to Be Born: a Guide for Bereaved Parents Who Are Making Decisions about Their Future. Schwebert & Kirk,

They Were Still Born: Personal Stories about Stillbirth. Edited by Janet Atlas,

This Little While: for Parents Experiencing the Death of a Very Small Infant. Joy & Dr. S.M. Johnson,

A Time to Decide, a Time to Heal: for Parents Making Difficult Decisions about Babies they Love. M. Minnick,

Unspeakable Losses: Understanding the Experience of Pregnancy Loss, Miscarriage &

Abortion. K. Kluger-Bell,

Unsupported Losses: Ectopic Pregnancy, Molar Pregnancy, and Blighted Ovum. Sherokee Ilse.

When a Baby Dies: the Experience of Late Miscarriage, Stillbirth & Neonatal Death. J. Kohner & R. Henley,

When a Grandchild Dies: What to Do, What to Say, How to Cope. Nadine Galinsky,

When Hello Means Goodbye: a Guide for Parents. Schweibert & Kirk,

When Your Child Dies: Tools for Mending Parents' Broken Hearts. Avril Nagel & Randie Clark

Resources for Professionals

Bereavement Care for Childbearing Women and Their Families. Caroline Hollins Martin & Eleanor Forrest,

A Caregiver's Handbook to Perinatal Loss. Gary Vogel,

Companioning at a Time of Perinatal Loss: a Guide for Nurses, Physicians, Social Workers, Chaplains and other Bedside Caregivers. Jane Heustis & Marcia Jenkins,

Death and Bereavement across Cultures. Colin Murray Parkes et al,

Giving Care, Taking Care. Sherokee Ilse,

Loss During Pregnancy or in the Newborn Period: Principles of Care with Clinical Cases and Analyses. James Woods & Jennifer Esposito (eds)

Midwives Coping with Loss and Grief: Stillbirth, Professional, and Personal Losses. Doreen Kenworthy & Mavis Kirkham

Motherhood Lost: a Feminist Account of Pregnancy Loss in America. Linda Layne

Perinatal Loss: a Handbook for Working with Women and Their Families. Sheila Broderick & Ruth Cochrane

When a Baby Dies: a Handbook for Healing and Helping. Rana Limbo & Sara Wheeler,

When a Child Dies: How Pediatric Physicians and Nurses Cope. Robert McKelvey

Resources for Helping Children

The Grieving Child: a Parent's Guide. Helen Fitzgerald,

Guiding Your Child through Grief. Mary Ann Emswiler & James Emswiler,

Healing a Child's Grieving Heart: 100 Practical Ideas for Families, Friends and Caregivers. Alan Wolfelt,

Parenting through Crisis: Helping Kids in Times of Loss, Grief, and Change. Barbara Coloroso,

Sibling Grief: After Miscarriage, Stillbirth or Infant Death. Sherokee Ilse et al

Books for Children

Am I Still a Sister? Alicia Sims

The Baby Project. Sarah Ellis

The Fall of Freddie the Leaf: a Story of Life for All Ages. Leo Buscaglia,

Lifetimes: the Beautiful Way to Explain Death to Children. Mellonie & Ingpen,

My Always Sister: Coloring Book. A Place to Remember

No New Baby: for Boys and Girls Whose Expected Sibling Dies. Marilyn Gryte

Sad Isn't Bad: a Good-Grief Guidebook for Kids Dealing With Loss. Michaelene Mundy

Someone Came Before You. Pat Schweibert

Something Happened: a Book for Children and Parents Who Have Experienced a Pregnancy Loss. Cathy Blanford,

When Something Terrible Happens: Children Can Learn to Cope with Grief. Marge

Heegaard

Where's Jess? Jody Goldstein,

Uk Support Organisations:

SANDS – Stillbirth and Neonatal Death Charity

Tel: 0202 7436 5881

Email: helpline@uk-sands.org

THE MISCARRIAGE ASSOCIATION

Tel: 01924 200799

Email: info@miscarriageassociation.org.uk

TOMMYS

Tel: 0207 398 3400

Email: mailbox@tommys.org

THE LULLABY TRUST (For babies lost to cot death)

020 7802 3200

Email: office@lullabytrust.org.uk

ACHING ARMS

Email: info@achingarms.co.uk

CHILD BEREAVEMENT CHARITY

Tel: 01494 568900

Email: support@childbereavement.uk.org

ANTENATAL RESULTS AND CHOICES (ARC)

Tel: 0207 631 0285

CHILD DEATH HELPINE

Tel: 0800 282986

CRUSE BEREAVEMENT COUNSELLING

Tel: 0844 477 9400

Email: helpline@cruse.org.uk

The Foundation for Infant Loss Training offers comprehensive training in infant loss and bereavement for professionals.

http//www.chantallockey.org

Email: info@chantallockey.co.uk

STOP MOTION
FILMMAKING

STOP MOTION
FILMMAKING

THE COMPLETE GUIDE TO FABRICATION
AND ANIMATION

CHRISTOPHER WALSH

BLOOMSBURY ACADEMIC
LONDON • NEW YORK • OXFORD • NEW DELHI • SYDNEY

BLOOMSBURY ACADEMIC
Bloomsbury Publishing Plc
50 Bedford Square, London, WC1B 3DP, UK
1385 Broadway, New York, NY 10018, USA
29 Earlsfort Terrace, Dublin 2, Ireland

BLOOMSBURY, BLOOMSBURY ACADEMIC and the Diana logo
are trademarks of Bloomsbury Publishing Plc

First published in Great Britain 2019
Reprinted 2020, 2021 (twice)

For legal purposes the Acknowledgements on p. viii
constitute an extension of this copyright page.

Cover design: Louise Dugdale
Cover image © Christopher Walsh

Bloomsbury Publishing Plc does not have any control over, or responsibility for,
any third-party websites referred to or in this book. All internet addresses given
in this book were correct at the time of going to press. The author and publisher
regret any inconvenience caused if addresses have changed or sites have ceased
to exist, but can accept no responsibility for any such changes.

A catalogue record for this book is available from the British Library.

A catalog record for this book is available from the Library of Congress.

ISBN: PB: 978-1-4742-6804-2
    ePDF: 978-1-4742-6805-9
    eBook: 978-1-3500-3162-3

Typeset by Integra Software Services Pvt. Ltd.
Printed and bound in India

To find out more about our authors and books visit www.bloomsbury.com
and sign up for our newsletters.

This book is dedicated to my parents, John and Mary Teresa Walsh.
The value that they placed upon education continues to inspire me.

This book is also dedicated to my wife Jennifer, and to my children
Nathaniel and Madeleine. Thank you for your love, and for your support.
I love you even more than puppets.

Contents

1   **Part one**

Puppet fabrication

109   **Part two**

The studio

165   **Part three**

Animation

261 Part four

Making a film

Acknowledgements

For their support and generous assistance, I'd like to thank Rohit Asokan, Rob Corbett, Evan DeRushie, Bruno Degazio, Maureen Furniss, Alexander Gorelick, Erik Goulet, Dale Hayward, Nic Hesler, Georgia Kennedy, Mark Mayerson, Corrie Francis Parks, Kevin Parry, Ken Priebe, Emiliano Paternostro, Mario Positano, Barry Purves, Neeraja Rajkumar, Justin Rasch, Ronni Rosenberg, Dhiman Sengupta, Anne Stewart, Anthony Straus, Angela Stukator, Noam Sussman, David White, Jason Teeuwissen, and Aldines Zapparoli.

Additionally, I'd like to offer a thank you to Carla Veldman for providing her insights into costuming for puppets, and to Kelsey Ryan for sharing her skills in the area of 3D printing. Brenda Baumgarten also deserves a very big thank you, for her generous sharing of knowledge in the area of puppet fabrication.

Finally, my most heart-felt thanks goes to James Caswell, Rosemary Travale, and Mike Weiss, for the wonderful illustrations and diagrams that they have contributed to this book.

' "There is no dead matter," he taught us, "lifelessness is only a disguise behind which hide unknown forms of life. The range of these forms is infinite and their shades and nuances limitless." '

-Bruno Schulz

'Fantasy is the very basis of my career, and movies allowed me to make reality of my dreams, breathing life into all the ideas that existed in my mind.'

-Ray Harryhausen

Introduction

There's nothing quite like stop motion animation. No other medium is as efficient at making the fantastic real. Conjure up some early memories you have of the medium. As you watched, you probably realized that something special had appeared on the screen, even if you didn't know how it was created. What was unfolding probably didn't seem quite real. But even so, it was tangible, like you could reach in and feel it. Hold it, even. Real, but not real. It was fantasy, come to life, and it was utterly, perfectly enchanting, in the truest sense of the word.

Enchanted. That's how I felt as a kid, when I stumbled upon one of the medium's most remarkable examples, and had my mind completely blown. It was late at night. Everyone else in the house was long asleep, and I was flipping through the channels, looking for anything interesting. I paused when I happened upon a very strange scene. It was live action, and it involved a young girl in a small room, surrounded by old and neglected objects. One of these objects was a dusty glass case. Inside, a rabbit, stuffed and mounted, was nailed into place. It was a pretty freaky rabbit, with bulging glass eyes and sawdust dripping from its seams. Suddenly, it came to life! With great effort, it freed itself from its constraints, and in a mad rush, it put on a red top hat and dainty white gloves, and smashed its way out of the case. After it pulled a pocket watch from its sawdust-filled guts, I was done. Channel changed. Nope. Does not compute. This made no sense. This could not be. The rabbit was a real rabbit, a real stuffed rabbit, that shouldn't be alive. But clearly, it was. Or was it?

Alone in front of the television, I was transfixed and a little freaked out. Had anyone else in the world seen this? Or was this some kind of bizarre transmission for my eyes only, a midnight screening from another, stranger, world? I flipped back, hoping I hadn't missed too much …

My own memories of being entranced by Švankmajer's *Alice* isn't that unique. Audiences have always been, and continue to be, in love with this strange form of artificial life called stop

Figure 0.1
Story of The Fox, Ladislas Starewitch, 1930.
A handcrafted wonder, brought to life by a master.

Figure 0.2
Alice, Jan Švankmajer, 1988.
Jan Švankmajer's version of Lewis Carroll's story provided just the right magical shock, at just the right time, to change my life forever.

motion. That love on the part of audiences is a wonderful thing, to be sure, but if you're reading this, you know that there's something more important that needs addressing. That question is: how was something so magical put on to a screen?

In some ways, the pursuit of an answer to that basic question is what's driven me onward in this medium, and ultimately, I think it's also what's inspired me to write this book. I wanted to share what I had come to know about stop motion, in the hope that others could then use that information to bring more magic into the world.

Book overview

The objective of this book is to provide you with the essential practical skills that you'll need to create a professional quality puppet animation film. With that objective in mind, the book is organized in a way that flows in a pretty logical fashion.

Part 1: Puppet fabrication

Puppet fabrication is a lot of fun (addictive, some would say), but it can also be pretty complex. That's why this section is extremely detailed, with each step of the process laid out and illustrated clearly. By the conclusion of this section, you'll have your very own professional-quality puppet that's ready for animation, and the skills to make more puppets.

Part 2: The studio

As you arrive at this section, you now have a puppet that's ready to go, but where are you going to animate this thing?! You'll need some kind of dedicated space, and that's what this section covers. It helps you to establish your own professional animation space, with lots of practical insights, and it does it with a keen eye on working within a budget.

Part 3: Animation

You've got a puppet, and a space to animate. Now it's time to jump in to what is in my opinion the most exciting part of the medium. Starting with introductory exercises and moving into more advanced work, this chapter aims to seriously raise your stop motion animation skills. Each exercise is carefully explained, and by the end of the section you'll be able to construct a detailed and professional stop motion shot, that can serve as a very solid portfolio piece.

Part 4: Making a film

The time has come to put it all together. This section breaks down all the key stages of making a short stop motion film, in detail. It's an examination of a pretty complex process, so along the way I use very clear examples from a variety of short films, and I provide you with lots of practical insights and suggestions.

As you can tell from the above description, this book isn't aimed at the complete novice. It's more suited for advanced artists who already understand the basics of the medium, and are looking to take their existing stop motion skills onward, towards very polished and professional levels.

Mixed throughout these four core sections you'll find additional information, in the form of highlighted boxes. These include:

- **Professor Roy boxes:** These boxes provide deeper insights into topics, without getting in the way of the main process stuff. As for who Roy is, keep reading.
- **Must-watch boxes:** There's an endless bounty of excellent stop motion out there for you to watch, but there are some that simply must be viewed, if you're serious about this medium. You'll be a different person after watching these highlighted films.
- **Artist highlight boxes:** There's an incredible range of excellent artists who have made their mark on the medium, and these boxes will introduce you to their work. Some of them are big names, while others are less widely known – but all of them will inspire you in your own work.
- **Interview boxes:** Asking a pro is a fantastic way to learn, and these interviews with major talents will offer you some great insights into the medium.
- **Pro tips boxes:** Short and to the point, these boxes provide you with even more professional insights, from some of the medium's leading artists.

Who the heck is Roy?

Roy was the very first puppet I ever animated,
way back when. He was created as a teaching
tool for me to use by stop motion maestro Alexander Gorelick (you'll find an interview with
Alex further on in the book). I worked for a long
time with Roy, and frame by tentative frame his
movements became smoother and more fluid.
As I worked, the character of Roy also began to
develop through my efforts. He revealed himself
to be good-natured, easy-going, and keen to
earn a laugh. For me, Roy represents the process
of learning about stop motion, and as such he
seemed like the natural 'mascot' for this book.
You'll find him throughout these pages, offering
you his own tips, tricks, and insights. He may
also be exploited for a few cheap jokes, but as
long as it's in the service of teaching stop motion,
Roy is cool with it, trust me.

Along with Roy, there are a number of other
original characters that you'll encounter within this
book. Most notably, there's Nia. She's the actual
puppet that you'll construct and animate. You'll find
out lots more about her in the following chapters.
All of these characters have been developed specifically for this book, and they're all eager to help you
proceed further along your stop motion journey.

Nia and her pals.
One big happy
stop motion
family!

Roy the puppet. Roy sounds a lot like 'Ray' – as in stop motion
legend, Ray Harryhausen. Coincidence?

How this book differs from others

Truth be told, there are lots of great books out
there on stop motion, and each offers solid insights
into many aspects of the medium. But there are
a few things about this one that makes it pretty
special.

It offers detailed training in advanced puppet fabrication

Making a simple stop motion puppet isn't too
tricky (and some methods for that are covered
in this book), but the process of making an
advanced stop motion puppet is complex. It's
huge fun, but it entails a lot of steps and stages,
and if any of those get skipped over by a book, it
can really leave the reader stranded. I've taken a
lot of care to ensure that doesn't happen.

It provides proven methods

I teach stop motion in the Animation Program at Sheridan College, a program that attracts some of the brightest and most talented young animation students from around the world. All of the content in this book has been 'test driven' by those students. Stop motion grads who were trained in these methods have gone on to work professionally in the online, television, and feature film stop motion industries.

It grows out of practical experience

Beyond teaching stop motion, I also mentor senior animation students as they create their graduation films in the medium. Over the years, I've worked closely in the stop motion studio that I designed at Sheridan, guiding lots of ambitious and talented young artists through all stages of making a puppet film. Combined with my experiences as an animator in the stop motion television industry, and from making my own short films that have played in festivals around the world, I've gained solid, real-world skills that I can share.

I'm confident that this book will help you in your effort to excel within the medium, but like

When read aloud, this book bestows dark puppet powers upon the reader. Proceed with caution.

any complex art form, it takes hundreds of hours to get really good at stop motion. There's no shortcut – I can't stress that enough. You learn by doing, and then by doing again and again, frame after frame, shot after shot. No book can provide that. You have to roll up your sleeves and get in there. This book encourages you to develop the confidence to do just that, but you must jump in, and get making stuff. Learn, by doing.

And seriously – why wouldn't you? The best thing about stop motion is that it's fun to do!

A (somewhat personal) philosophy

I call this a 'personal philosophy' because in a medium as rich and as complex as stop motion, the last thing I want to propose is the 'One True Stop Motion Way'. But I think that some kind of stop motion philosophy can help to guide you as you travel through the medium. When times get tough in the stop motion trenches, and you get discouraged or fed up (hey, it happens), being able to refer back to some foundational concepts can provide some much-needed support.

Tenet 1: The artisan

An artisan is a highly trained craftsperson, who manufactures specialized items by hand. Traditional examples of artisans include watchmakers, tailors, and blacksmiths. Whether it's strictly functional, decorative, or a mix of the two, the finished object is an expression of professional pride. The work represents the artisan. It's a calling card, if you will, of her skills. That's because everyone understands that to create a high-quality product, you need a lot of training. You don't arrive at 'deeply talented' in a month, or even in a year. An artisan embraces this fact, and doesn't run away from it, or give up when faced with a setback. She accepts that the journey she is on consists of many steps, not one giant leap. An artisan possesses a constant desire to become better in her work, to move towards the status of 'master', and to perhaps one day even create her – yep, you guessed it – 'masterpiece'.

Masterworks abound in the world of stop motion. Some completed films are masterworks. But there are also masterworks to be found within a film. Puppet designers and fabricators work tirelessly to create new wonders. Set and prop artists struggle day and night to create a world more fabulous than the one before. So many people, working so hard, to create the best handcrafted work that is humanly possible. That's stop motion.

Tenet 2: The performer

Civilization continues to depend upon performers to provide insights, observations, cautions, and commentary. Through their work, performers allow us to learn about ourselves. You wouldn't go out on date without first looking in the mirror, right?

Performers serve the same function, reflecting culture and society back to itself, so that it can gain deeper knowledge about itself (and to see if it has any spinach stuck in its teeth). Even when a performance is designed to provide so-called 'simple' entertainment, it's actually offering something deeply needed by the community, as it provides temporary relief from daily stresses.

Comedy performances often hold up the most unflinching mirror to society, in the forms of satire, spoof, parody, and farce.

Stop motion animators offer frame-by-frame performances that have the potential to be every bit as effective as any live Broadway production. Each and every day, stop motion animators strive to generate rich and affecting performances, for the benefit of the audience. These performances may cause laughter, or tears, or thoughtful consideration, or (in some wonderful cases) all the above.

It's important to note that just as in live-action cinema, or in theatre, performance is deeply tied to acting – and stop motion animation is no exception. It's impossible to overstate how important acting is to effective stop motion, and you'll find much more on the subject in this book.

Tenet 3: The magician

Stage magic isn't real magic. We all know that. It's illusion, misdirection, and sleight-of-hand. A good stage magician may even go so far as to point that out to the audience, at the start of the show! So why do audiences pay good money for something they know isn't real? I think part of the reason is that everyone, magician and audience alike, very much wish that stage magic was real. If someone could wave a wand and truly cause a rabbit to suddenly appear inside a hat (something that utterly defies all the rules of the natural world), it would mean that potentially anything could happen. If anything can happen, it ignites

Figure 0.3
Moral Orel, ShadowMachine Films.
Comedy performances often hold up the most unflinching mirror to society, in the forms of satire, spoof, parody, and farce.

Figure 0.4
Adelaide Herrmann, The Queen of Magic.
Herrmann was a great pioneer of female stage magic and illusion.

our imaginations. It introduces a sort of wonderful and mysterious ripple throughout all the 'normal routine' of everyday life. It provides hope that the mysterious still exists for humanity, regardless of science's incredible advancements. And it's an acknowledgement that life is a bit more fun when there's room for mysteries and miracles. Even if they're pretend.

Through stop motion, we take an object that is plastic, clay, metal, and foam, and we bring it to life on screen. This object doesn't just move like it's alive by following the laws of physics. Incredibly, the object actually conveys an active mind. It's thinking.

Even more remarkably, as the object is made to live and think, we begin to care for it. If it's heroic, we want it to succeed in its task. If it's a villain, we want it to fail. We laugh at it, or we feel sorry for it. In some cases, we even fear it. There's no heartbeat in the object, but on a very true emotional level, that animated object is alive.

Doesn't this qualify as magic? Like a stage trick, we all know the puppet isn't alive, but because our emotions are so engaged, we also know that on some level, it is. The puppet is both alive and not alive. There may be no potions, cauldrons, or puffs of smoke associated with stop motion's collision of 'real' with 'impossible', but there should be!

A TRIP TO THE MOON, GEORGES MÉLIÈS, 1902

Méliès was a stage performer, a magician, and a filmmaker, all rolled into one. This film, created well over a hundred years ago, is his most famous, and it continues to enchant audiences, in part because it invites viewers into a joyfully fantastical world in which almost anything can happen.

PHIL TIPPETT, SPECIAL EFFECTS ARTIST AND FILMMAKER

This is an interview I conducted with Phil Tippett for *Fangoria* magazine. Tippett is a Hollywood stop motion superstar. He's responsible for some of cinema's most memorable stop motion moments, with his Star Wars effects in the original trilogy in particular holding a very cherished place in the hearts and minds of literally millions of people the world over.

Here, I talk to him about his stop motion project *Mad God*. We go pretty deep into the medium, and things get more than a little (you guessed it) philosophical. It's been edited slightly, for this publication.

Q. What exactly is *Mad God*?

A. It's an expression of a sentiment that I've been developing over the years … very different from my theatrical film day job. I'm taking a much more protracted collage approach that allows me to operate outside conventional norms. My inspirations are Trnka, Starewitch, Joseph Cornell, Hieronymus Bosch, and Guy Madden.

Q. I know this project goes way back for you. Can you take us through its history a bit?

A. I began shooting MG on 35 mm film well over twenty years ago. The scope of the project was quite unwieldy and then the digital revolution hit and I was forced to reinvent my approach to my day job, and that took many years. At some point I was archiving the project and some of the guys at my studio noticed, and thought it was some ancient Czech thing from the 1930s. They were inspired by the *Star Wars* and *Robocop* pictures but their career paths fell in the digital age. They'd missed the era when you made stuff with your hands. They convinced me to restart *MG*, and volunteered to help. Suddenly I had a crew and cheap digital cameras and I took them up on the bet. Gradually the crew of volunteers grew and after a successful Kickstarter campaign I was able to begin to believe that this thing might actually be able to get produced.

Q. Your accomplishments in the visual effects industry are massive. You've built a renowned studio that continues to work on big-budget, high-profile Hollywood projects. So I have to ask: why make this intimate series of short puppet films, that aren't likely to see any profit?

A. I really have no choice in the matter. It is a creative obsession that I must pursue. If I do not do it no one else will.

Q. You've built up a renowned and respected cg visual effects and animation house. Why not make *Mad God* in cg? Why go 'back' to puppets – foam, rubber, wires, hot lights, aching backs, blistered fingers?

A. The digital realm requires that one work from the position of intension. *MG* cannot operate like that. I approach it more as a collage or painting that wells from the subconscious and as a consequence it requires an approach that allows itself to grow. When working with material objects they look at you and demand attention. They tell you things and maybe you wouldn't otherwise be so perceptive. It is about the process and listening to the things around you, hearing what they can tell you. That takes time. In the day job we work under the onus of production schedules. I wanted this to be like a much older way of working wherein the consequences of time were less relevant. That informs the process in a very, very different way. It takes longer to cook and therefore you get something unlike what is being made by production processes that are typically used in animation projects. Much of my day job involves shooting live action and I have altered my approach to animation much more along those lines.

Q. The story of *Mad God* is a mysterious one, with no easy answers. Events unfold in a cause-and-effect manner, but we can't necessarily understand how the rules work. We're outside of this world, and are only given a glimpse into it. In other words, this film is pretty darn experimental! How have audiences been reacting, considering your previous stop motion work (mostly notably on the original *Star Wars* films) has fit more easily into 'popular entertainment'?

A: There are two camps. One gets it and is very appreciative of an alternate voyage. Others expect a conventional approach and are flummoxed. It is to be expected. If some people are disturbed or confused, that's when you know you're doing it right.

Q. In addition to well-known and widely popular artists like Ray Harryhausen, you've also been influenced by certain European stop motion artists, like Ladislas Starewitch, and Jan Svankmajer. Svankmajer's work in particular is quite dark and disturbing, and intended for specific audiences that are open to truly strange and unique worlds. How does it feel to be using the medium of stop motion to journey to such dark regions of the imagination?

A: Those guys were huge influences. The consequence of shooting real objects in an unreal application creates a disorienting effect. One cannot deny the photographic reality of what is being seen, yet at the same time it may not compute in terms of everyday observation and expectation. I am very careful on *MG* to use conventional iconic everyday props and imagery as an anchor that allows me to take off. I've little interest in reality when it comes to the creative process. It's an argument I face frequently in my day job where everything needs to be faked to be 'real' … doesn't anyone realize that it's all pretend?

Q. *Mad God* has no shortage of goodies for horror fans. It's got monsters and gore and blood and guts, not to mention a general atmosphere of serious dystopian dread. And that's just Chapter 1! As you craft the project, are you drawing inspiration from horror movies that have left a mark on you, or from other forms of art … or from a darker place entirely? I know you're a follower of Carl Jung, who praised the benefits of confronting one's Shadow self …

A: Much of the approach to *MG* comes from the analysis of my own dreams. I don't mean by this that there is any symbolist or psychological philosophies that I am trying to get out. At some point I realized in the study of my own unconscious (dreams) that upon awakening, the narrative is generally very fractured and obtuse.

However, I came to find that if I didn't think, and wrote the experiences down as quickly as I could, that they self-assembled into a quasi cogent narrative. That idea guides me in my process. I don't move from a position of intention but from one that allows me to surprise myself as I was able to do as a child. That keeps me alive.

Q. Much of Chapter 1 of *Mad God* involves a literal descent for the main character. At one point, his vessel takes him through what could be described as a tomb that is filled with statues that represent human history and religion. Keen eyes will see the cult of Ray Harryhausen well represented! This sequence suggests a larger story (or perhaps a larger statement, at least) – can you talk about this sequence?

A: All of the stuff in that scene has an overloaded art historical approach. There's a great deal of stuff stuffed into *MG* that is not quite as blatant, but that was the set piece; the kitchen sink of meaningful objects that I've collected since childhood, And yes, I had no choice but to include the Cyclops from *The 7th Voyage*.

Q. The idea that alchemy and stop motion are somehow intertwined is a fascinating one. Both pursue goals that lie beyond the grasp of normal man. For alchemists, the goal is to arrive at pure metals, while for the animator it's the creation of life itself (albeit on-screen). Can you talk about this idea of stop motion animation residing within the realm of the 'dark arts'?

A. Once you put yourself in a darkened chamber closed off from the rest of the world, the act of animating becomes a calming, meditative one. Analogies to alchemy are romantic … there's that idea of operating outside the realm of the unknown, attempting to bring it into focus, that may have some oblique similarities.

Q. At times, *Mad God* subtly blends live action and stop motion. It makes the whole experience quite unsettling, because the audience's association with the on-screen character is always in flux. Is that a puppet? Is it a real person? Can you talk a bit about this blending, from a creative perspective? Are we seeing live action,

or some other form of magical animation trickery?

A: I ripped that off from Karel Zeman. He had no trouble trafficking between the two worlds. He's another huge influence.

Q. I understand your crew is made up entirely of volunteers. Some are employees from Tippett Studio, and others are eager art students. You have some very solid animators working (namely Chuck Duke and Tom Gibbons), but if we assume most of the crew aren't stop motion professionals, how do you see these artists with different backgrounds and skills growing as they work in this medium?

A. Some folks are craftsmen close to my age. Some are students. I have been very lucky in drawing in local talented and interested people who want to observe and participate in these ancient processes. Everyone brings something to the table and, I think, I hope it's as inclusive of an experience for them as it is for me.

Q. I'm assuming that with all these keen artists on hand, you've been placed into the role of 'mentor' for this project. If so, what kind of artistic philosophies do you use, as you guide these artists into the strange land of puppet animation?

A. My approach is somewhat antithetical to the manner in which much animation is done. I take a much more live action shooting approach. I do not use motion control because I need the performances to drive the action. I'm there on the set shooting and direct, in a sense, when Chuck or Gibby want to open up a performance I'll have the latitude to adjust the camera to suit their intuitions much like one would do with an actor on the set. My direction tends to be a general as I can make it. Many times the direction is 'DO NOT THINK'.

Q. What do you think it is about this process of stop motion animation that eternally attracts people?

A. I can only speak for myself – the magic comes from the same place it did for me seeing *7th Voyage* when I was seven years old. I couldn't understand it then, and I still don't.

Related approaches in stop motion

Although I'll primarily use the term 'stop motion' throughout this book, a more focused term for what we'll be looking at is 'puppet animation'. This is commonly what people think of when they visualize stop motion animation. But it's very important to realize that there are other forms of stop motion aside from puppet animation, that both stand on their own as forms of animation, and also (at times) are blended in with puppet animation.

How are these following styles of stop motion related to puppet animation? To begin with, they all share a common 'straight ahead' process. We'll deal with a 'straight ahead' approach in a lot of detail (especially in Part 3, which is dedicated to animation), but essentially it involves recording frame one, then two, then three, and so on, in order, through to the end of the shot.

Another manner in which they're related is that they are all quite physical. This means that physical objects are being animated in front of (or beneath) a physical camera, and the animator is also quite physically engaged during the process. You use your body, as well as your mind, when working in all these styles.

What makes these styles different, then, is primarily the materials being animated. Each material has its own look, and that can greatly influence the tone or 'feel' of a project. Beyond the actual look, each material also requires careful and specific attention when it comes to working with it. What might work when animating clay, for example, might not suit a project that's going to be done with sand.

Things get really exciting when these approaches begin to mix together, so the more that you know about all of these related forms, the greater the chance is that you'll create a truly distinctive and unique animated project. Read on, learn all that you can about each method, and then give them a try!

Replacement animation

It's essential to be comfortable with this method, since it's used so much in puppet animation, especially as a solution for mouth animation. Often while using a pre-planned chart, the animator selects her mouth shapes to suit the moment of dialogue, pops in the chosen mouth shape, poses the rest of the puppet accordingly, records the frame, and moves on. (This method is what we'll follow later in the book, when we get to animating dialogue in Part 3).

The replacement parts can be very sophisticated, as you'd find at a feature film studio, or they can be very modest – even pieces of paper with eyes or mouths drawn on them can act as replacement pieces. It's very much determined by the visual style (and budget) of the project. Even entire puppets can be replaced, which sometimes happens for projects that require very specific poses that are repeated a lot. No matter how it's being used, this method of animation typically requires careful planning in advance, especially when it comes to lip sync.

Clay

Clay animation is very well known, in part because it's such an accessible and understandable material. There's very few of us that didn't have great fun squishing this substance between our fingers, probably before we could even walk. Clay, which is sold under a variety of brand names, all of which are collectively known as 'modeling clay', is a wonderful material for achieving direct and immediate work. Art Clokey, creator of the world-famous clay character Gumby, said it perfectly: 'Clay is embedded in our subconscious. It has been there for at least 50,000 years'.*

Figure 0.5
Graveyard Jamboree With Mysterious Mose, Screen Novelties, 1999.
A fantastic example of how mixing animation styles can create a hugely entertaining experience. Puppet animation mixes with cut outs, which mixes with live-action puppets! Why not?!

*Quoted by Mike Antonucci (Knight Ridder), 'Gumby's creator formed a spirit in clay', The Milwaukee Journal Sentinel, 1 January 1998, p. 6E.

Figure 0.6
Morph, Aardman Animation.
Hugely charming and deeply entertaining, this show really proves the potential that clay has for stop motion artists.

Figure 0.7
(Re)Cycle, Lynn Dana Wilton, 2011.
This behind-the-scenes image nicely shows off the layered feel that cutouts can achieve.

When watching clay animation, it can sometimes be hard to figure out what you're looking at in terms of fabrication materials, and this can lead to frustration on the part of the hopeful animator. A puppet character may look like it's entirely formed from clay, when in reality it's actually made of foam latex or silicone, and has an armature offering internal support. Or the puppet may have clay on its surface, with an armature inside. Or, to add even more to the confusion, the puppet may have some parts made of clay, such as the face and mouth, while the rest of the body is formed from latex or silicone!

If you want to do puppet animation entirely in clay, keep things simple, and you'll be free to make lots of fantastic animation. Superb work can result. Just ask Aardman's Morph, who only continues to grow in popularity, more than forty years since first appearing!

With clay, you may also want to consider using an 'under the camera' method for animating, as opposed to pointing the camera in at the puppet, as you would with standard puppet animation. If the puppet is lying down, this prevents gravity from toppling it, and lots of great stuff can be made this way. Take a look at Aardman's *Rex The Runt* for an example.

Cutouts

This is a method of animation that is usually achieved 'under the camera', since it's a lot easier to get a cutout to behave when it's lying flat. Thin card is often used because it doesn't warp and is easy to work with. The pieces are held together by a variety of methods. Sometimes, some very thin wire is glued between the pieces to provide a joint that can then be animated, or you can use a small layer of wax to hold the joints together. This is my preferred method, because it allows the pieces to remain very flat on the animation surface. Avoid sticky tack, as it tends to have an elastic effect, resulting in pieces that move out of position after you've posed them. Beyond this, there are many other ingenious ways of fabricating cutouts, so do your research.

Because it often involves animated characters and elements that are made from flat pieces, this style is more closely linked to drawn animation than many of the others, and it's also closely associated in its look and process with digital, 'symbol-based' animation. But cutout animation is its own thing entirely. Amazingly fluid and sophisticated work can result from this method, and its innate graphic style can be a great way for a stop motion animator to explore the drawn world.

Silhouette puppets are a distinctive form of cutouts. They possess incredible visual power, and can entrance an audience in a very special way. The audience for this kind of animation is actively engaged, as the black shapes onscreen encourage the imagination. The suggestive quality of this form of animation, with its complete lack of interior detail, brings an automatic sense of mystery to the project. This style is an example of how a look can be so intense and particular that it's very likely to dominate the story or animation. If you're strong in design, and you want a stop motion style that will showcase your skills in this area, I can't imagine a better way to work.

Sand on glass

Like cutouts, this is another 'under the camera' method. As with clay, sand animation is very elemental in that it's truly 'of the earth'. But unlike clay, sand exists almost as a liquid. Its countless grains are very tricky to animate individually, so the dedicated sand animator typically embraces the idea of 'going with the flow'.

Sand animation evolves from one frame to the next, often leaving trails of itself as the characters and actions drift across the screen. There's nothing solid about sand animation (compared to other forms of animation), and that's part of its beauty.

Figure 0.8
A Tangled Tale, Corrie Francis Parks, 2013.
This lovely sand film blends the traditional technique with modern digital approaches, which results in a continuing evolution of the technique.

Ghostly and ephemeral by nature, this technique can be used to great effect to tell stories that shift in time and space. Each new frame of sand animation, by necessity, destroys the one that came before it. You start a scene with nothing more than sand in a bottle, and you end it the same way. Amazing!

Painted animation

This method involves the frame-by-frame creation of animation through painted or drawn images on a surface. It often occurs in an 'under the camera' method, but not always (some artists prefer to create animation that's painted on walls). Like the sand animator, the artist who works in this style has to embrace the fact that with every new frame, the old one is typically destroyed.

Another connection that this style shares with sand animation is its potential for fascinating and compelling transitions. Wide shots can be smeared and mixed, reforming as a tighter shot of the same location, or whole characters can be morphed into new poses or settings. And like sand, painted animation often leaves evidence of itself on the frame, as new drawings are formed over old ones. These visual trails can provide great energy to the animation, and provide it with a deep sense of atmosphere.

Object animation

Just as cutout and painted methods reside a bit closer to drawn animation, object animation lives closer to live action than standard puppet animation. In this style, everyday objects are brought to life through the frame-by-frame process. Sometimes the objects magically perform their standard function. An animated piano may play itself, for example. Other times, an object is given a character that seems suggested by its design – imagine a pair of scissors, animated to snap like a crocodile.

Sometimes, the object's everyday function is cast off, in favour of whatever role the animator has envisioned for the object. It may sound strange, but when I imagine an object playing at being something else, I always imagine the liberation that the object must experience. The boring old eggbeater, playing the part of the hummingbird, must feel pretty overjoyed at the chance to fly!

Allowing for life to reside within everything around us, and imagining this sort of playful chaos, was of great concern to the Surrealists in the 1930s, but it's also a central concern for children. A child will very easily act out an improvised story at the kitchen table, with the salt and pepper shakers in the starring roles. It's nothing out of the ordinary, for a mind that has yet to have rules imposed upon it. Wonderfully, animators who work in this style retain this way of thinking, even as adults.

Pixilation

Living even closer to live action than object animation, we find the style of pixilation. When objects come to life, we know that life is artificial, because objects aren't really alive (at least not in a biological sense). But when humans move about in a frame-by-frame way, the distinction between animation and live action pretty much dissolves. We understand, of course, that the humans onscreen are alive, and yet in pixilation, they live with a strange, unnatural life, and often perform truly superhuman feats (like flying). They are us, existing in our world, but at the same time they are beyond us, somehow, in a fantastical nearly-real realm.

Audiences typically know how this trick is achieved, but that's not the point. Being in on how it's done only seems to deepen the enjoyment of watching people flit and fly.

Inventive pixilation, done with a professional approach, consistently offers results that are fresh, entertaining, and deeply charming.

This kind of animation has nothing to do with pixels on computer screens. Check the difference in spelling!

NEIGHBOURS, NORMAN MCLAREN, 1952

One of the first (and certainly one of the most effective) pixilation films ever, this classic from the NFB (National Film Board of Canada) playfully proves how easy it is for people to forget their manners. The whimsical animation sets audiences up to be deeply shocked by the film's climax – McLaren was a master of manipulating the viewer. This and all of the NFB's remarkable animations are available online for free streaming.

Part one

Puppet fabrication

Part 1 of this book is entirely dedicated to puppet fabrication. As a quick glance at the Table of Contents will reveal, it's an extremely detailed section that provides you with very specific and practical instructions for the construction of a professional puppet from start to finish. Part of the reason for this level of detail is that it's a pretty complex process, but that's not the only reason this book examines puppets in such detail.

From the earliest examples of stop motion, through to the work that's being created today, a common thread that connects it all is a desire to record the trials and tribulations, the joys and the sorrows, of these miniature creatures. Many are small-scale representations of ourselves – perhaps exaggerated or distorted for dramatic or comedic effect, but human, nonetheless.

Their forms vary greatly, along with the actions they perform and the stories they tell. But whether they're made from humble pieces of wood and wire, or space-age rubber and stainless steel, stop motion puppets are almost always *expressions of the human experience*.

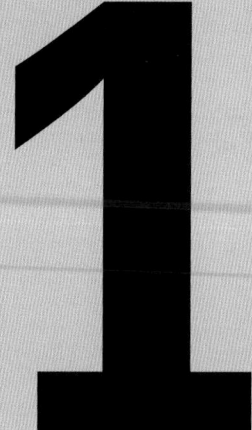

An introduction to stop motion puppets

In the end we're dependent on
the creatures we've created.

Mephistopheles (Faustus II, Goethe)

In this chapter, we'll begin the process of making puppets by
first attempting to understand puppets better, both in general
terms, and from a stop motion perspective specifically. Why
bother with these more abstract notions instead of just jumping right into making things? Just as you'd take the time to
get to know a living dancer, actor, or musician that you hope to
create a performance with, you owe it to the puppet that you
will *eventually* create to first understand its world a bit more
thoroughly. With this better understanding, you'll be in a better
place to create a better puppet, and in time, a better performance through that same puppet.

By the end of this chapter, you'll have a stronger understanding of the remarkable world of puppets, and a firmer
foundation upon which you'll be able to start fabricating your
own miniature performance partner. You'll also get to meet the
puppet that you're going to create, but I won't ruin the surprise. I'll let you read this chapter, first!

Figure 1.1
Midsummer Night's Dream, Jiří Trnka, 1959. A tender moment between puppets, in this beautiful production by the Czech master.

An introduction to puppets

Just by sitting on a shelf, a doll is doing what it's meant to do. That is, it's representing something *else* – a person, an animal, or a character of some sort. By contrast, a puppet may sit obediently on the same shelf alongside that doll, but it carries with it the expectation that it will be brought to life (or given life, depending on how you look at it). There's an *insistence* that surrounds a puppet. It's not fulfilled until it lives, even if that life is maintained, influenced, and ultimately controlled by, human hands. That's not to say that a doll can't have artificial life given to it. Who else attends the tea parties of little kids worldwide, if not 'living' teddy bears and dolls? But a doll doesn't *need* to be alive. A puppet does.

What can we say about this life that puppets acquire? Well for one thing, it's not true, biological life. It's pretended life. But rather than making things less interesting because it lacks a pulse, the opposite becomes true about the lives of puppets. This false life is capable of achieving remarkable things. Just look at Kermit the Frog! Yet it's all the result of the actions and words of a character that is only temporarily (and occasionally) alive.

Figure 1.2
Zimbo, Juan Jose Medina and Rita Basulto, 2015. The story of a marionette that longs to cut his strings. Cast in the role of the marionette? A stop motion puppet. A beautifully existential short film.

It's not that dissimilar to our own lives, really. We are born, we live, and then, inevitably, we pass away. When you consider things this way, it's easy to appreciate how existentially significant puppets are to an understanding of the human experience.

Complicating things further is the fact that the artificial life of a puppet is so deeply connected to the puppeteer or animator. When you make a puppet, and later perform through it, an amazingly complex relationship is formed. It can be a bit like a parent/child relationship – after all, the artist has given life to the puppet, as a parent does a child. It brings to mind poor Geppetto from *Pinocchio*, as he constantly frets and chases after his wooden child. The boy may be fake, but the emotions felt by the old carpenter are very real.

Yet this deep emotional attachment can also be broken very easily. All the puppeteer or animator has to do is place the puppet back on its shelf. Now it's just an object again – at least until it's time to perform once more. How can a relationship be so emotionally real, and at the same time, so imagined? How can it be so 'on', then so 'off'? You may have asked yourself this same question about a relationship you've had with a real person! Once again, we can learn a lot about ourselves through our work with puppets.

An overview of puppets

Of course, our medium doesn't claim ownership over puppets. They've been around for thousands of years in one form or another, and all of these types of puppets continue to be used today. Some

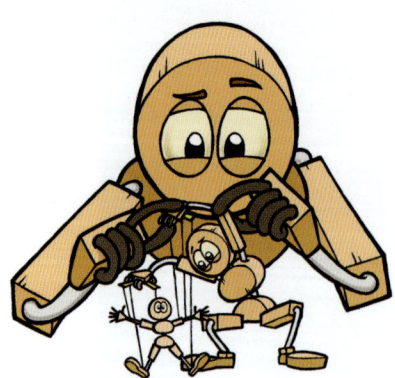

Here's Roy, animating Roy, as he puppeteers Roy. Don't think about it *too* much, or your brain will explode.

have been modified over the years by technological and artistic innovations, but most remain unchanged at a basic level. Regardless of style, they all provide artists with a way to make statements about humanity and the world in which we live.

Shadow puppets

The requirements for this form of puppetry are basic: a flat puppet, a strong light source, and a

Figure 1.3
Shadow puppetry.
Full of mystery and atmosphere, this ancient form of puppetry connects with audiences in a very primal fashion.

surface upon which to cast the puppet's shadow. The shadow puppet's origins may pre-date recorded human history, coming as it does from a time of fire and cave walls. Eventually, a screen would replace the wall, providing both a separation from the audience and a fantastic canvas for the puppeteer to tell the story. Movement of the puppet between the light source and the screen encourages changes in size and quality of the shadows, allowing for all kinds of creative transformations.

This style of puppet shares an aesthetic connection with the stop motion silhouette cutout in its reliance on the shape of a character's design rather than its detail.

Hand puppets

It doesn't get much more immediate than this form. Pull on a hand puppet, and you've got a living character, ready to perform. These puppets

Figure 1.4
Punch and Judy.
Punch and Judy, the original dysfunctional sit-com family, are still
going strong some 350 years since their creation.

have an additional advantage in that they allow
for surprisingly sophisticated performances. Hands
and wrists on their own are incredibly expressive,
so it's no surprise that a hand puppet would have
huge performance potential. A more complex hand
puppet may have mechanisms in the head to allow
for mouth movement, and possibly eye movement
as well.

> Prior to actual animation, try to 'hand puppet'
> your way through a stop motion scene. You
> can test posing, timing, and blocking this
> way, and it helps you to think through the
> entire shot, roughly and quickly.

Rod puppets

This form of puppet is essentially a hand puppet that has been modified to allow the puppeteer a greater amount of movement through
the addition of a rod that is attached to one (or
both) of the puppet's hands. This allows for a
greater range of expression and acting through
the puppet, and also more fully engages the
puppeteer, since more of her body is involved. A
rod puppet is relatively simple to fabricate and to
use, yet has great potential for complex performances, which explains why this puppet is such
a popular one. Take a look at the classic cast of
Jim Henson's Muppets for lots of examples of rod
puppets.

Body puppets

As the name suggests, this puppet requires more
of the puppeteer than the simpler hand and rod
puppets. In certain cases, *two* puppeteers are
required: one controls the head as well as one
of the arms of the puppet, while the other artist
controls the second arm. This allows the puppet
to feel very alive, and it also allows for some very
captivating acting, since the second arm is being
controlled independently of the other. In real life,
we're used to seeing a person's hands and arms
create poses that work together but here, strange
combinations of gestures and poses can result
since two minds are driving things. This can make
for a very interesting, and potentially very funny,
performance.

> **_LABYRINTH_, JIM HENSON, 1986**
>
> Executive produced by George Lucas and
> based on designs by legendary fantasy art-
> ist Brian Froud, this is a remarkable show-
> case for many forms of puppetry. In this
> film, Jim Henson further opened our minds
> to what can be achieved through puppetry.
> It's an incredible showcase of what the
> world's most talented artists can create,
> when their talents are truly allowed to shine.

Marionettes

For many people, this is the form that first comes
to mind when they think of puppets, in part
because marionettes have been used in film and
television quite a bit over the years. With marionettes, the puppeteer uses a control mechanism
that is attached to a variety of strings. The other
end of each string is then connected to a body
part on the puppet. By careful adjustments to
the controls, the puppet's body is brought to life.
Some marionettes also have a controlling rod,
which adds a certain amount of stability to the
puppet. A simple marionette will have only a
few controls, while a more complex puppet will
have a staggering assortment of controls and
strings, requiring very sophisticated work by the
puppeteer.

Figure 1.5
Royal de Luxe puppet company. Who ever said puppets had to be small? Certainly not the folks at Royal de Luxe. Their building-sized creations require cranes and heavy machinery to bring them to life.

An overview of stop motion puppets

A stop motion puppet literally stands alone, in a way that's very different from its puppet cousins. This is due in part to the armature that resides within it. Just like an animal's skeleton, the stop motion puppet's armature offers support for the overall puppet, allowing it to hold a pose on its own. But this is just a posed object, no different from a doll or statue. There's another component that's *critical* for life to occur, and that's the camera. As we all know, the camera records each new pose of the puppet so that it, along with all the other frames, can later be played back in quick sequence. When the viewer presses 'play', animation magic happens, and the puppet comes to life on the screen.

This combination of posing puppet, recording camera, and viewer playback means that very little suspension of disbelief is required when watching a stop motion puppet perform. Seeing is believing, and what the audience sees on screen *is* a living creature. No strings attached – literally! The audience doesn't have to pretend to not see the puppeteer behind, above, or underneath the puppet, because in this case the puppeteer truly doesn't exist! The stop motion puppet lives in an animated world, as opposed to a theatrical one.

This liberated quality makes the stop motion puppet very different from other forms of puppets that are more closely tethered to their human master. It also makes the stop motion puppet a solid contender for the 'most alive' puppet we can encounter.

All stop motion puppets can be posed, and they all need a camera, but are there other unifying aspects that further tie them together? That's a tough one, since a puppet grows out of human creativity. There's no limit to what kind of puppet an artist will dream up, fabricate, and bring to life. That being said, if we were to consider stop motion puppets, both past and present, we can find certain attributes that continue to be proven as 'pretty darn important' – common aspects that we should be considering, as we move towards fabricating our *own* puppets.

Figure 1.6 Homunculus. An ancient alchemist attempts to give physical form to the human spirit. This little creature was known as a homunculus, which is Latin for 'little man'. Sounds like just another day in the stop motion studio, if you ask me.

Overall visual appeal

This is very important, but it's also very tricky to pin down. That's because visual appeal in a puppet doesn't reside simply in its basic design as an object. Just because a puppet is a nicely designed 'thing', with an overall attractive look, that doesn't mean that it has true visual appeal *as a puppet*. A puppet's appeal is determined once it comes to life, so the question always has to be asked: does it look appealing, when it's living on-screen?

How do you ensure that your puppets will have strong visual appeal? There are lots of design guidelines (rules, even) that can help you, but even then, I'm a firm believer in trusting artists. If you're making a puppet for your own film, what *you* find appealing is what's right. And you'll learn more, as an artist, by trusting yourself and learning from the artistic choices that *you* make.

When the day arrives that you're designing something for a client, then the client's needs and wants will be vital, but I always tell students, 'It's your film, so trust your instincts'. By trusting yourself in this way, you're more likely to create a project that is distinctively you, and as a result, one that is *truly* special. And that's what the world wants, after all. Something special.

The armature

It can range from incredibly simple to mind-bogglingly complex, but the stop motion puppet's armature is an essential consideration, no matter what. The armature is important for a number of reasons (each of which is explored in more detail in the chapter dedicated to creating the inside of the puppet), but the primary reason is that without the armature, the puppet can't be effectively posed for animation.

When considering the armature for the finished puppet, it's vital to ask: does the armature's design and construction allow the puppet to do what it needs to do? If the answer is yes, then the armature for that puppet is an effective one. That doesn't mean it's a fancy one, or an expensive one, it just means that it's effective. A group project that I once mentored featured a tree sloth puppet. Its armature consisted of nothing more than a magnet in its stomach, that would hold the puppet on to a tree branch. That sloth wasn't going to be able to dance a ballet, but for the story at hand, it didn't need to. The final puppet laid firmly on its tree branch, and its mouth was animated, along with its eyes, and the final project looked great. Hence, it was an effective armature.

The face

We're trained in real life to expect information from this area, so it's no surprise that this region of the stop motion puppet is very important. But how does the specific puppet in question *use* its face? The answer may be that it doesn't – its expression may be completely fixed, forcing the puppet to express through other means, such as body language. A fixed face can also have the effect of causing the audience to 'lean in' to the performance, projecting emotions upon the fixed face that aren't actually being expressed through the animation. At the other extreme, the face may be incredibly expressive. To achieve this, it might make use of replacement faces, or have sophisticated adjustable mechanisms housed within its head. Many puppet faces reside somewhere in the middle of these extremes, with eyes and mouths that can be animated, but with an overall fixed face, that is made from a hard material.

Regardless of how expressive or not expressive it is, the face of the puppet needs to be carefully considered when evaluating its overall merit. As with the armature, if the puppet's face works for the intended project, it works. It's as simple as that. If the puppet needs to talk, or otherwise use its mouth, there's a *lot* that needs to be considered around how the puppet's mouth is designed and animated. You'll find more on puppet mouths, as you continue onward in this book.

Fabrication materials

The life that a puppet will have, and the performances that it will give, are at least in part determined by what that puppet is made from. A puppet may be made of little more than cheap foam, and be held together by hot glue and wishful thinking. Another puppet may be fashioned from the finest metal that money can buy, and have cast parts made from the very latest in lightweight, super-strong plastics. Still another puppet might be a raw chicken with armature wire stuffed inside. (Disgusting? Yep, but it was used to great effect on a very famous Peter Gabriel music video, back in the day. Go look it up!)

Regardless, the materials used for each puppet both influence and to some extent dictate, the life that the puppet will have once it's being animated. The cheap foam and wire puppet may not be able to achieve a very subtle performance, but it's light foam and flexible wires might make it extremely easy (and fun) to animate. The metal and plastic puppet may provide a remarkably smooth and subtle performance, but it can't compete with the raw chicken puppet when it comes to achieving blunt 'shock-value' animation.

And really, why would anyone want to compete with a raw chicken puppet? Disgusting.

Overall performance potential

To consider this aspect of a puppet, you need to forget about design and fabrication methods for a moment, and just consider things as an animator.

The 'eyes' have it. A puppet's face tells us much about the character of that puppet.

Figure 1.7
I Am Tom Moody, Ainslie Henderson, 2012. This short student film proves that the quality of a puppet's performance has little to do with the cost or complexity of a puppet, and everything to do with the animator's skill at conveying honest emotions.

You've already developed a good sense of the performance potential for a given puppet. Does its armature allow for the range of performance that is required? Does its face provide the amount and style of expression needed? Are the materials that it's constructed from going to be advantageous during performance? The answers to all these questions help you to determine the performance potential of a puppet. But as with overall visual appeal (which was considered earlier), things get pretty subjective at this point.

There is a mysterious relationship that exists when an animator connects with a certain puppet. For whatever reason (it really is a mystery, at least to me), sometimes an animator finds herself inspired and engaged by a particular puppet. It defies logic, it makes no sense in any way that can be charted or graphed, and as such is one of the most fun aspects of the medium. When this happens, regardless of anything else, a strong performance is already brewing, because a team has been formed – the team of animator and puppet. So rather than try to pull the mystery apart, let's just say that performance potential for a puppet is 70 per cent measurable, and 30 per cent 'the weird thing that sometimes happens between the puppet and the animator', and leave it at that. It's not a very scientific summary, but once in a while (especially in an art form as wonderfully weird as stop motion), I like to think that's ok.

What does a stop motion puppet do?

When you're trying to arrive at a deeper understand of a larger process – in our case, the larger process being 'stop motion' – examining the specific *function* of a component is pretty useful. When I pose the question 'What does a stop motion puppet do?' to students, they go through a range of reactions. Sometimes they're puzzled, because on the surface, the question seems completely self-evident. But as the discussion goes on, well – just keep reading.

The puppet serves as a focus for the audience's attention

When we watch a stop motion film, millions of years of evolution kick in, and our eyes are automatically drawn to movement within the frame. That movement is typically coming from the puppet, and once our eyes fall on it, we're deeply hooked. That's because we're compelled (through physical, cultural, and social conditioning) to identify with other humans, even when they're on a movie screen. In stop motion, of course, the puppet might not represent a human. It might be a monkey, or an alien, or a rock! But odds are pretty good that the character contains attributes that let us identify with it. It may have eyes that we can connect with, or it may be moving in a way that suggests a human consciousness is at work.

KING KONG, MERIAN C. COOPER, 1933
ANIMATION BY WILLIS O'BRIEN

This is the film that ignited Hollywood's love affair with puppet animation. He may have been nothing more than metal and rabbit fur, but good ol' Kong felt very real indeed for audiences all over the world. Even viewed today, it's impossible to not feel sympathy for the poor giant beast, as he wages his valiant battle atop the Empire State Building. Viewers were made to care about Kong, and this film serves as historic proof of stop motion's incredible ability to stir the emotions of audience members.

The puppet helps to moves things forward

I'm not necessarily referring to a puppet that pushes a box across the screen, although that certainly is a way of moving things forward! Instead, I mean that the puppet is typically the means by which *progress* is made within various key elements. These key elements include the basic situation (if it's a stand-alone scene) and the story (if it's a more complex project that's made up of various scenes). In a non-traditional or non-narrative film, it may be atmosphere that needs developing, or the overall tone. Even here, the puppet is usually essential, as it acts or reacts in response to the shifts that are occurring within the filmic world. Without the puppet's help in evolving these elements, we'd be in danger of having something that's flat and boring. Puppets make 'it' happen.

The puppet acts

The audience is connected to the puppet because the puppet is what the audience sees. As a result, any reaction that the on-screen performance manages to draw out of the audience needs to be credited to the puppet. As I mentioned earlier, in stop motion seeing is believing, and through the weird magic of animation, the animator simply doesn't exist in a stop motion performance. Yes, on a practical level the animator felt the emotion first, and skillfully transferred it frame by frame to

the puppet. But as far as the audience is concerned, it has just had its heart touched by the *puppet's* performance, not the animator's.

Stop motion audiences don't credit animators with performances, and I don't know a single stop motion animator who would have it any other way. An animator who desires this kind of direct approval from the audience performs on the other side of the camera, and goes by another name, which is 'actor', not 'animator'.

The puppet is a vessel for the animator's consciousness

Now *that's* a heavy statement. To understand it more fully, it helps to examine the actual process of animating a puppet. First, the animator rehearses the scene within his mind, moving through poses, blocking points, and emotional states, all in careful detail. He then repeats all of this as he transfers the performance outward, into the puppet.

It's during this transfer process that things can get pretty intense inside the stop motion studio. That's because the act of transference doesn't happen in a heartbeat. This is animation, after all. It happens slowly, frame by frame, over the course of hours, and the animator experiences every moment of this process as he physically interacts with the puppet. A finished clip may exist on the screen for only a few seconds, but the animator's mind may have resided within those seconds for an entire day of animation production. That strange, double-tiered, stretched-out experience of time, so particular to the process of stop motion, hasn't been experienced solely by the animator – the puppet's been there, too! To anyone looking in at the process, it's just someone moving an object, but for the animator and the puppet, they're on a journey together that exists outside (or at least 'to the side' of) the normal experience of time.

Scientists tell us that our experience of time is simply that – an experience. Time's true nature is far more complex. This is something that the stop motion animator comes to appreciate. On-screen time versus clock-on-the-studio-wall time are two very different things!

Introducing: Nia

In the next chapter, you'll meet your puppet companion for the next stage of your development as a stop motion artist. Her name is Nia, and she's been exclusively created for this book. What you see in Figure 1.8 is her final form, all ready for animation. But she didn't arrive on the scene like this. Instead, she was developed slowly and carefully. This development involved a variety of stages, which will be the focus of the following chapters.

Figure 1.8
Nia. Good things come in small packages. Introducing Nia, your companion along the stop motion journey.

ROBIN WALSH, PUPPET ARTIST

Robin Walsh has built, designed and performed everything from sock puppets for the Oscars to Hollywood movie monsters. She's a recipient of a Jim Henson Foundation Workshop Grant, and she has designed, directed, and performed two original puppet ballets (Stravinsky's *Firebird* and Prokofiev's *Romeo and Juliet*) with the Stanford University Orchestra. She has a BFA in Puppetry, and she's currently Head of Puppets at Screen Novelties. She's also performed some life-saving surgery on certain legendary puppets, as you'll soon discover.

It should be noted that although Robin and I share a last name, we aren't related (except by our love of puppets!)

Q. Why puppets?

A. I never really got a chance to choose puppets, they kind of had it in for me from the start. I grew up on Ray Harryhausen films, Universal monster movies, and of course the usual stop motion holiday fare. I didn't watch *Sesame Street*, so my idea of puppets was never limited to that. When I was four, I did see Disney's *Bedknobs and Broomsticks* on the big screen. I don't think I ever recovered from the wonder of watching a world where anything could come to life and dance, fight and save the day. From that point, I've never had a distinct line between what exists and what could be. My theory is if it doesn't exist and you want it to, then build it!

Q. Does 'Robin' go somewhere else, when she's performing through a puppet?

A. In 2003 I had the good fortune to become a master student under the amazing German puppeteer, Albrecht Roser. He had a unique way of combining scientific principles with artistic intent while building his puppets with the ultimate goal of getting to the point where 'technique serves performance'. When achieved, manipulation becomes a matter of intuition, rather than one of repetitious practice. In fact, one does not so much 'manipulate' the puppet, as work with the puppet as a partner in the performance. This practice led to what we called 'puppet zen'.

We learned that for a puppet to truly work on stage it must achieve that moment where the puppet comes to life in the mind of the audience, despite the knowledge that it is an inanimate object of wood and cloth. The triangle of puppeteer, puppet, and audience work together toward that moment of belief. When 'puppet zen' works, the puppeteer becomes as much a member of the audience as anyone. In that moment, the puppet moves of its own accord. The puppeteer no longer thinks on how to manipulate the puppet. The puppet informs the puppeteer and the performance becomes a matter of concentration and meditation rather than conscious choice. It can sound a bit crazy, yet one look at a puppet in Roser's hands and the possibilities shone through. As a student, that magic moment proved elusive – until one night when ... it worked. I was on stage holding the puppet, watching as it moved, seemingly without any effort on my part.

Q. **You conduct a range of puppetry workshops, which focus on very basic marionettes. Can you talk a bit about the value of a basic puppet?**

A. My favourite style of puppet, if I have one, is the scarf marionette. A very simple style of puppet, it consists of five wooden balls, a bit of fabric, and only four strings. It was actually created as an instructional puppet, to demystify the marionette and show students that a string puppet was not always a technical beast that took years to perform properly. But I soon learned that this puppet's simplicity was its greatest strength. Most scarf puppet heads are painted with a colour shift to provide a subtle focus to the head without adding a face. This inherent simplicity and nebulous nature allows the puppet to laugh, smile, frown and cry – letting the audience fill in the seemingly blank face with any emotion required for the given moment. The audience's power to imbue a puppet with emotion and subtext far exceeds even what the most realistic paint job or the greatest mechanism could provide. This extends from the 'puppet zen' approach to puppetry. You humble your own ego and arrogance and let the material or puppet become what it wants to become. The puppet character is evolved, rather than produced.

Q. **Have you ever met a puppet you didn't like?**

A. Oh, I've met several. Usually it's the one I'm working on at the moment, and it's not working out how I've planned. Of course, because I follow the puppet as a 'co-performer' rule, I must listen to it, even when I don't want to. But truthfully, the puppets I mostly don't like, or perhaps feel sorry for, are those who are being used as a 'hook' or device to spice up an otherwise less than perfect idea or show. But when you see puppetry performed with the care and respect it deserves, it can be truly astounding.

Q. **What are your thoughts on performance through a stop motion puppet, as compared to performance through other forms of puppets?**

A. Stop motion puppets are puppets, and therefore the animators are puppeteers. Both attempt to bring a puppet character to life. This is true for any style of puppetry, and each has its own unique idiosyncrasies. But stop motion is also a hybrid between traditional animation and puppetry. This gives stop motion the added ability to distort time, allowing for an entirely new realm of movement and character possibilities. In fact, after having worked in stop motion, I now use lessons learned from animation within my puppetry workshops, especially *The Animator's Survival Kit* and *The Illusion of Life*.

Q. **In terms of stop motion's role in popular culture, your restoration work on the Santa and Rudolph puppets from the Rankin-Bass television special is a big moment. Can you talk a bit about that experience?**

A. When the original puppets were discovered in 2004, after sitting in a metal tin in an attic for over thirty years, they naturally weren't in good shape. No longer could Rudolph's nose glow so bright – or at all. It had long ago been replaced by Play Doh and candle wax. His neck was broken, his antler and hooves chipped. Santa had fared even worse, with two broken legs, half of his moustache missing, no eyebrows and a crumbling beard. To clean and repair the duo properly meant dismantling them to some degree. Like everyone else, I was in awe of these puppets. It was as if I held my childhood in my hands – and then had to decapitate it. But managing to quiet the crying five-year-old inside of me, I put aside my memories and dove into the task at hand.

In view of the historical and cultural importance of the puppets, all work was geared towards conservation, leaving them as original as possible. As a professional puppet maker and puppeteer with a penchant for both stop motion and old puppet making techniques (I'd also been one of the key restorers for some Ray Harryhausen puppets) – I set to work. It was truly one of the greatest moments of my career and life. It was a rare opportunity to give back, to say 'thank you' for the many years and the happy memories these puppets had given me. And now, no matter where they are, simply knowing they still exist, makes the little five-year-old inside of me smile.

Character design

The path to a developed character is a mysterious one. Sometimes a character seems to arrive on the scene fully formed. Other characters evolve very slowly over time, with many artists adding aspects and traits in an organic fashion, until *something* seems to click, and a character feels 'right' (look up the history of Bugs Bunny, for an example of a very slowly evolving character).

This chapter first introduces you to some of the challenges that designing for stop motion puppets present, so that you can develop a character that will work when you get to fabrication. It also offers you some well-established stages of character development that can prove useful. You *may* be suddenly struck by divine inspiration for a character, and if so, congratulations! But typically, character development is a gradual process, not unlike sculpting, in which the final form often reveals itself through a gradual, exploratory process.

By the end of this chapter, you'll have a stronger understanding of a development process for character, and you'll be introduced to the star character of this section (and this book) – the one and only Nia.

Before designing: Essential considerations for stop motion

Just as you wouldn't design a bicycle with square wheels, there are some basic aspects of puppet design of which you should be aware, before getting started. Most of these considerations are made with animation in mind. Some design choices may *look* great, but if they don't allow for animation, they aren't suitable for your puppet.

You can't go wrong with 'humanoid'

Two feet on a puppet is just the right amount to keep it upright and mobile, while not creating excessive challenges down the road during fabrication and animation. Two hands are great for expressing emotion and performing actions, and one head and face is pretty useful as well. With your *next* puppet, you can make a four-legged creature, or a tentacle monster, or a three-headed Nia, or some wild combo of all of this … but first, start with a basic human.

Gravity is a serious downer

It's my book, and I get to make a few puns. As for gravity, this won't be the last time that I highlight its role in stop motion. In stop motion, we're *always* contending with this force as we struggle to pose things during animation. A general rule to remember is: the lighter you can make something in stop motion the better, since it will have less of a struggle with gravity, during animation. We can (and should) convey a *sense* of weight through our animation, but the puppet *itself* should be as light as possible.

Be mindful of proportions

You'll notice that in relation to her body, Nia's head is *fairly* realistically proportioned – it's a bit oversized, but not by too much. There can be a tendency when creating puppets to scale up their heads, sometimes by a lot. In part, this occurs because larger facial features allow expressions to read better on camera. Larger features are also easier for an animator to handle. I opted for a smaller head for Nia, because I wanted her performances to be about 'whole body expressions', and not just 'facial' expressions. Nia's hands are similarly proportioned – they're a *bit* oversized to allow for easier fabrication, clearer posing, easier animation, and better functionality when it comes to holding props – but they're *not* so huge that they push her into a more stylized design realm.

Keep the eyes simple

There are a lot of different ways you can approach designing and fabricating eyes for puppets, and each has its advantages and disadvantages. Basically, Nia's eyes consist of hard white eyeballs that have a black 'dot' on them that can be animated. It's simple, effective, and achieves great results.

Keep the mouth simple

As with eyes, there's many different ways that you can approach the challenge of mouth designs for puppets (several of which are explored later in this section). For Nia's mouth, we'll be going with simple replacement mouths that will be stuck to the otherwise smooth mouth area on her face. As with her eyes, this method is fairly easy to fabricate, works very well, and looks nice.

Who needs five fingers?

You'll notice that Nia has a total of four (not five) fingers. It's a long-held convention in drawn animation, to make animation a bit easier and faster, but it can be useful in stop motion as well. Fingers and hands, at the best of times, are quite tricky to fabricate, since they have to be both tiny *and* allow for precise animation. They also have to stand up to quite a bit of animation without breaking. A four-fingered hand looks very much like a five-fingered hand, and functions in the same way, but it's just a *bit* easier to create when we get to sculpting, moulding, and casting.

These feet are made for walking. And running

The feet and ankles of a puppet are placed under a lot of stress during animation, so the stronger and more reliable they are, the better. There are a lot of complex ways to design and fabricate feet, but we're going to keep it as straightforward as possible. We'll be using magnets in Nia's feet. Magnets have an effect on design, which is why Nia's feet aren't super tiny – they need to be big enough to house the magnets we'll be using. There are other methods for getting the puppet to remain in place, and we'll explore those in Chapter 3.

Design the costume to allow access to the armature

Remember that puppet parts wear down and break, and when they do, you need to access the armature to make repairs. A great looking costume that isn't designed with this in mind won't be so nice when it has to be torn apart to repair a broken arm or leg. Nia's costume isn't fancy, but it nicely expresses her basic character, and it will allow you to perform repairs.

Now that some constraints have been established (and explained), it's time to start the design process. The fun thing is that the following steps for development aren't specific to Nia. When you later develop more puppets that are based on your *own* designs, you'll be able to follow these same steps to success!

THE HAND, JIŘÍ TRNKA, 1965

Regarded as one of the most important stop motion films ever created, this short by the Czech master features a truly beautiful puppet. The design of the puppet (a scrappy little sculptor/clown) is perfect – at once subtle and expressive. The puppet not only *looks* wonderful – it's able to create lovely performances that range from 'charming', to 'sneaky', to 'heartbroken'. Beyond the puppet, the film's story is a powerful statement against tyranny and oppression, and is told with wit and charm. You owe it to yourself to watch everything Trnka made. It's all incredible.

Finding the character

There's been a lot of characters developed in the world of animation. Some of them are fairly generic, and achieve world-wide recognition. Others are wonderfully distinctive, engaging, and complex, but appeal to a smaller audience. Each animated character, famous or not, has gone through a certain amount of development process. This is a gradual evolution, that takes a character from a vague, general idea, towards something specific. The process for doing this isn't carved in stone, but what follows are some pretty standard stages of development that should prove useful. I've used Nia as the character example, but you can carry this process over to any animated character that you may find yourself developing.

Inspiration and reference

This early stage can be a lot of fun, since it's so full of potential. It's a chance to gather images and written descriptions of pre-existing characters and people that you feel somehow inform your character. You might select an image or description for something specific, (such as a hairstyle, or a facial design), but you might also include something that simply *suggests* an aspect of who you're developing. Once you've collected references, start refining. What you discard will be as informative as what you keep, since it informs what your character is *not*. Assemble all your images (digitally is easiest), take a step back, and consider what you have in front of you. Use this new knowledge to move you onward in your design efforts.

When I started to develop Nia, I only had a rough sense of her personality and her look. I knew I wanted to develop an adult female character. I wanted her to be fit, and to be capable of handling all sorts of animation situations, both subtle and broad. I also wanted her to be generally appealing in her features and physique. It's from those basic attributes that I began to gather my inspirations and references, and those led me to her character description and her physical design.

Character description

Developing a character description can really help you later in the design process, as well as during animation. A great example of this is the Disney character of Goofy. Art Babbitt was responsible for a lot of classic animation with this character, and he found that establishing a character description for Goofy was immensely helpful in developing and maintaining a consistent, entertaining character. The description helped to make Goofy feel *real*, and it helped other artists who would animate him to remain true to the character.

A character description has no set format or length, but you should aim for no more than a page in length, once you've fully refined it. You'll want to convey a sense of what makes your character distinctive. How does the character see her particular world? How does she see herself in relation *to* that world? How would she handle a specific situation (be it mundane, or outlandish)? What are her strengths? Her weaknesses? All of this will help you develop the physical look, and it will *also* help you when it comes time to animate.

I had some some fun with Nia's description below, as I image an over-the-top world for her that's full of adventure. But as you notice, it's all in the service of refining and clarifying Nia's *character*.

CHARACTER DESCRIPTION FOR NIA

Nia is in her early 20s, and thinks of herself as being 'of the world', since her family traces its roots to all corners of the globe.

Nia means 'purpose' in Swahili, and that very much describes her personality. When Nia knows what she wants, there's not much that can stop her. Her name also means 'bright' in Welsh, and once again, there's a lot of truth in a name, because Nia has a real spark to her. She's very quick-witted, and thinks fast on her feet.

Nia is the kind of person that you can drop into any situation and she'll adapt quicker than most. Like the time that she was mistaken for a secret agent, and found herself trapped on board a submarine filled with evil robots en route to Iceland. Nia came out on top (of the submarine, that is), while the robots met their watery fate somewhere in the north Atlantic. Anyone else might have panicked in her situation, but not Nia. That's because she lives in the moment, and is extremely aware of the *immediate* world around her.

She's quick-witted, that's for sure – unless she's been up too late the night before having fun with her friends. Epic online gaming sessions are one of her weaknesses. If she's had a late night, be prepared to meet the 'zombie' version of Nia, clad in pyjamas and bunny slippers, as she drags herself around the house. Just let her caffeinate herself properly, and all will be well.

You can certainly take a character's bio even further. You can explore her hobbies, her relationship with family, friends, and pets, her formative moments growing up … if it helps you to bring Nia to life more fully in your mind, then it's useful.

Design drawings for Nia

Drawing can play a large or small role in the development of a puppet. Are you confident when it comes to sketching your ideas and designs? If so, then you'll certainly want to do lots of playful sketches, as a way to find the character. Are your drawing skills not the strongest in the world? Then chances are you'll need to take more time to get good results.

Regardless of your drawing skills, it's important to remember that the actual, final look of the puppet is *not* something that exists on paper. The final puppet is a real, three-dimensional *thing*. If your fabrication skills aren't strong, all the fantastic drawings in the world won't result in a nice final puppet. Conversely, a very basic drawing can be just a starting point, and if you're a dedicated and talented sculptor and fabricator, a beautiful puppet can result from just a rough initial sketch.

One last thing on drawing skills: if you're weak at drawing, always look for ways to improve. Practice! These skills will help you with many stages of development in stop motion – character and set design, to be sure, but also for storyboarding and animation. Time spent on improving your drawing skills is *never* wasted.

You can make your Nia exactly as designed here, or you can give her your own distinctive twist. Just remember the design constraints discussed earlier. Don't get too extreme with your design choices, and you should be good.

Nia's character design was developed in collaboration with **Rosemary Travale**. Rosemary is an animation artist and stop motion filmmaker. She also works as a designer in the animation industry. Search for her award-winning work online!

Rough designs

The purpose of rough design work is to start moving towards what *is* and what is *not* the character. Rough means *rough* – let it be messy and raw. Go for loose, fast drawings. Don't spend too much time on each drawing, just keep exploring. I always tell students – there will be *so* much time later in the process to work tightly, but *now is not that time*.

Sketch a lot of ideas and shapes, and just keep drawing. Try to avoid editing yourself, and be open to surprises. Try new things. They're just lines on paper or on a screen – they shouldn't be precious!

Figure 2.1
Very rough designs.
Explore and have fun at this stage, and don't lose energy by trying to craft careful lines and precise renderings. You'll refine at a later stage.

Figure 2.2
Tighter roughs.
Still rough, but focusing on the head and face. The circled option shows that progress is being made. Through the process of designing rough, and then slowly refining, the final look of Nia is getting closer.

As you work in this rough fashion, certain features and shapes will start to stand out to you as effective or interesting. Let those elements inform each new drawing, and remember – work rough, and let it be fun. As you move through this stage, you'll want to gradually allow your drawings to 'firm up', as you slowly discover the character.

Action drawings

The purpose of action drawings is to see how your character will look as she moves through space, performing specific actions. It's a chance for you to imagine strong poses for your character, and then to see how those will look. As you work through some action drawings, you may find that the design of your character isn't suited for certain actions. That might mean you

need to do some redesigning, or that you need to be careful to not place your character into a situation that would require this impossible pose. Until you feel confident in the image, always draw light and loose, only darkening your lines as your confidence in the image increases. Be sure that you are maintaining proportions of body parts, and that you're connecting joints.

If establishing proper proportions and anatomy is a challenge, consider doing your drawing first as a stick figure (to ensure a strong structure), and then build upon that basic structure.

Figure 2.3
Action drawing.
This image shows how the drawing was constructed: rough, loose shapes to start, and then once you're happy with the underlying basic shapes, a more detailed line on top.

Story drawings

Story drawings can be a lot of fun, because they're a chance to place your character in situations and settings that can reveal aspects of her personality. You don't have to place your character in action/adventure settings, but it can be useful to remember that *conflict* is typically considered a strong basic ingredient in story. As you generate some story drawings, you'll be developing a stronger sense of just who your character is.

These drawings can also be great for judging just how at home (or at odds) your character seems within certain situations. A pirate character might not seem 'right' in a sci-fi space epic … but on the other hand, if you're planning to create a comedy, this sort of unexpected story situation might be a great thing!

Figure 2.4
Story drawing.
Showing off some clear character traits, Nia prepares to battle the undead. Nia's general design and character allows her to be dropped into a wide range of situations, which means that she can fit into all kinds of stories (realistic or fantastic).

Throughout all of these drawings (Rough, Action, and Story), you've been learning more about your character, testing her out and refining her look. Let this new knowledge sink in, as you begin to move towards the final stage of development.

THE NIGHTMARE BEFORE CHRISTMAS, HENRY SELICK, 1993

This classic stop motion feature has a cast of literally hundreds of puppets, each of which is superbly designed. For standard 'spooky' characters, the designs manage to be distinctive, while also working within genre expectations – a werewolf is a werewolf, after all.

These Halloween-style designs also manage to walk the line between creepy and fun. For the more original characters, like Jack and Sally, the designs are so strong that they've become a part of everyday popular culture, around the world.

Final design

Figure 2.5
Final design for Nia.
This image is
essential for
fabrication.
Notice that a few
construction lines
remain, and that's
fine. The version that
you've drawn should
have Nia standing
close to 23.5 cm (9
inches) tall, from end
to end.

When in doubt, you can simply scan or copy this image of Nia, scale it to the proper size, and print it out. Scale it so that Nia is 23.5 cm (9 inches) tall, and you are good to go.

An image of your character that's similar to Figure 2.5 is *essential* for moving into fabrication. You'll notice that Nia is posed in a very particular way – looking straight ahead, arms straight, hands flat, palms up. No colour, just line. This will allow you to effectively design and fabricate Nia's armature. This image is also vital because it will

serve as your *scale* drawing of Nia. Once it's a scale drawing, printed out, you can refer to it for all the sizing of Nia's parts. This image, at correct scale, can also be glued onto a board with a base, and used as a 'stand in' for Nia as you determine camera angles and set and prop sizes. Because it's so important, it's a good idea to save the image in a safe place, and make several copies so that you can always refer to it. Mark the image 'full scale', so that there's no doubt that it's sized correctly.

The maquette

A maquette is a full body sculpture of your character. It's not necessary for the process of fabrication that you're going to follow for Nia, because you're going to sculpt each body part on its own, so that you can create moulds from those parts. But if you like sculpting, you might want to create one anyway. It's a great way to explore a character, and if your sculpting skills are stronger than your drawing skills, you might actually want to do your design work through a maquette rather than drawing – just follow the general process used above, and think first in a loose, rough way, while also thinking about posing for action and conveying story. Develop the maquette carefully until you arrive at a final sculpture that you're happy with. Then, set the maquette aside, and get ready to do *more* sculpting, for the *actual* fabrication process that's laid out in Chapter 4.

Figure 2.6
Final design for Nia with colour.
Don't feel tied to these colours for *your* Nia. Pick your own! Consider combining colours digitally. It's a great way to see what combo works for you before committing.

BARRY PURVES

Purves' many award-winning (and Oscar-nominated) films are unified, in part, by a very distinctive approach to puppet design. His puppets are designed for limited facial animation, communicating instead through full-body animation that is often highly choreographed and poetic. His puppets always seem as though they were made to play their parts, which of course they were! Incidentally, many of his extremely nuanced puppets were created by Mackinnon and Saunders, and you'll find an interview with one of that company's senior members, just below!

Figures 2.7, 2.8, and 2.9
Nia variations.
Once you've successfully fabricated the basic Nia, just imagine the variations that you can develop!

IAN MACKINNON, OF MACKINNON AND SAUNDERS

Mackinnon and Saunders is one of the world's leading puppet making companies. They specialize in the design and construction of characters for television shows, feature films, and commercials. Some of their projects include Bob the Builder, Postman Pat, Tim Burton's *Corpse Bride* and Wes Anderson's *Fantastic Mr Fox*.

Here, co-founder Ian Mackinnon provides insights into the process of puppet design and fabrication.

Q. Mackinnon and Saunders creates some of the world's most remarkable stop motion puppets. Can you describe some core philosophies or guiding principles within the company that has allowed it to achieve such great results?

A. Try to keep the look of your work fresh. I don't think that Mackinnon and Saunders has a particular 'house style' – that may be because we work with a wide variety of designers, animators, and artists. Our overriding principle is to produce the best quality work, whatever the nature of the show. Whether we're collaborating with a well-established film director or a student, working on a major TV series or on a low budget indie project, we always try to find a way to do something new and exciting. Always do your absolute best to deliver the highest quality work.

As a puppet maker in a world of miniatures, you must have a keen eye for detail, and incredible patience (everything will take twice as long as you think). Perseverance is paramount – don't be disheartened if something doesn't initially work quite how you would like it to, failure is all part of research and development and informs future decisions.

Teamwork plays a big part in our workshop. We are lucky to work with artists and craftspeople who all bring something unique and special to the table. Recognize your strengths and weaknesses, and aim to work alongside other people in the team who can complement your own skills base.

There will be long hours of hard work and challenging problems to solve, plus seemingly impossible deadlines to meet so, most importantly, maintain a sense of humour throughout.

Q. Speaking very broadly, how would you define a 'good' character design, when thinking about fabrication for a stop mo puppet? How would you define a 'bad' design?

A. When thinking about the fabrication of a stop motion puppet, defining good or bad design is rather difficult as it's so subjective.

There are definite physical limitations to the materials used in puppet fabrication. That said, I would hate to limit the design at the outset and say that something is a 'bad' design just because it's going to be difficult to translate the design into a practical, expressive puppet. If a design looks great but is challenging from a technical point of view, then work with it – that's part of the fun of problem-solving and keeping the work fresh and interesting for yourselves and the audience.

Q. Transferring drawn designs through to a final stop motion puppet, whether for a client or for your own project, has all sorts of challenges. Can you talk about some of those?

A. The physical limitations to puppet fabrication include: weight issues, strength, durability, flexibility, softness, stretchiness. Whether it's metal, silicone, foam latex, fibreglass, or fabric, there are inherent properties that have to be taken into consideration.

The puppets need to be as light as possible. If a puppet is too heavy (or top heavy), it'll be hard to balance and will be unstable, making it more difficult to animate and possibly requiring support rigging. The weight mainly comes from the casting materials and the metal ball and socket armature. You should aim to keep the inner structure as delicate as possible with no excess weight; however, this has to be balanced off with a puppet being durable. A puppet might be on set every day for eighteen months during a feature or TV production, with little downtime for repairs, so the armature has to be engineered to be as robust as possible.

Q. It's always a challenge to retain a sense of life to a character, as it moves through so many stages of design and fabrication. Any advice or tips for keeping a character 'alive' through such a rigorous design and fabrication process?

A. Start with a quick maquette or sketch. Very often there is a real life and energy in these first character studies – a particular pose, expression, demeanour that can be lost as the puppet goes through many people's hands.

Keep referring back to these early studies throughout the process, check that a series of 'broken telephone' type refinements hasn't sterilized the original spirit and energy of the earlier designs.

Q. Any advice to the reader in general, as she moves through the process of puppet making? Any classic pitfalls to avoid? Any critical things to aim for?

A. Talk and work closely with the animator who is going to animate the puppet, they need to help guide the design and technical development of the puppet.

Work closely with the director and producer on the project, find out what the creative team want, what is their vision and expectation for the project? Do research, pull together reference materials and discuss them with the team as a basis for the design work that follows.

It's essential to work within time and money constraints. Work within the parameters available and adapt the design where necessary to make the best of a tight budget. Try to produce a prototype, or test parts of the model, prior to going into final construction/ duplication of characters.

Talk and work closely with the animator AGAIN once you've finished the puppet, get feedback – what's working and what problematic – learn your mistakes, and build on the successes.

Thoroughly document your all your work. Keep notes, drawing, scans, photographs, measurements, and jigs for future reference. Also keep copies of fabric, hair, paint colour samples. Often it's hard to remember where or what type of joint is located inside the many layers of foam or silicone and underneath a costume, but it may be necessary to get right inside to repair or tension an item sometimes whilst the model is still on set in the middle of a shot. Detailed plans of the workings hidden underneath help enormously to locate the specific area.

Always check the armature thoroughly before casting to make sure there are no dry solder joints (where the solder hasn't heated and flowed and gained full strength). This is much harder to fix once after the puppet has been cast and costumed.

Test the compatibility of the materials you would intend to use. Different materials shrink at different rates so, if you have a tight-fitting costume – for instance a sleeve that goes from a silicone hand to a foam arm – you have to make allowances to avoid 'stepping'. Also, some sculpting/modelling materials react to some mould making materials. Always do a patch test to make sure there are no bad reactions and also that you are using the correct release agents to stop the different materials from sticking together. Some materials are difficult to bond together – a glue that will happily stick foam latex to metal won't stick silicone to metal, and bear in mind that silicone is notoriously difficult to stick to anything.

Fabricating the inside

It's what's on the inside that *really* matters, right? This applies to people's personalities, but also to stop motion puppets. The puppet armature is the skeleton of your puppet, and as in real life, the design and construction of a skeleton largely determines what (and how well) that creature can perform its actions. This chapter provides you with all the information you'll need to design and construct a very sturdy and effective armature for Nia – an armature that will be highly reliable and responsive when the times comes to perform. It's also one that's likely to last a lifetime.

By the end of this chapter, you'll have all the practical skills required to make a complete aluminium block armature, and a deeper understanding of all the related materials and tools. You'll also have a better understand how to safely and effectively conduct yourself within a workshop environment, which will be essential for your armature work.

Overview of armatures

There's an almost endless range of ways to design an armature, and just as many materials that can be used to construct it. There's no one right way – there aren't even *ten* right ways! But there *are* some standard, time-tested approaches that stand out that you need to know about. In terms of fabrication challenges, from least complex to most, here's a brief summary of essential armature types.

Putty and wire

This approach results in a puppet that's literally all one piece. The various parts that need to move for animation can be posed, because they're made of wire, while the overall structure is fairly sturdy, since the 'bones' of the puppet are made of hardened putty (you'll find specific material information throughout this book). It uses simple materials and methods, so it's a great way to get a puppet done quickly and cheaply, and you can get great results. If you just want to start making puppets and animating them, or if you have a direct joke or a bit of specific acting that you want to accomplish, this method might be perfect. I've used this method for lots of puppets that just need to do a bit of animation, and it's very reliable.

The biggest drawback of this type of armature is that since all its bits are permanently connected, if something breaks during animation (an arm, a leg, a neck), you *cannot* easily replace that broken part. And over time, parts *will* break. Being able to replace a broken part is very important for most projects, so as fun as this type of puppet is, it's not well-suited to most serious projects, unless you know for certain that the amount of animation required is modest.

> This method of puppet making is so much fun, and is so useful, that you'll find a step-by-step process for this method, later in this chapter.

Brass tube

Brass tube armatures consist of tubes of metal that slide together in order to form a complete armature. Unlike the 'all in one' style, this type of armature allows for broken parts to be replaced, which is a great advantage. The materials and tools required for these armatures are affordable and fairly easy to come by, and depending on the methods used, a brass tube armature isn't too tricky to create, provided you have clear instructions. It also has the advantage of being super light, which is a great thing.

A downside to these armatures is that brass tubing is relatively soft, and so over time an armature fashioned in this way will invariably wear down. The brass pieces, although easy to slide together, can sometimes result in pieces that aren't entirely stable, which isn't great for animation, and since it can involve careful cutting of the brass and soldering small nuts on to the brass, this armature can require a fair bit of labour, all for an armature that isn't all that sturdy, relative to others. But it's a reliable option, especially if you're new to fabricating armatures.

Block

This style of armature gets its name from the basic shape of its main parts. These typically consist of a chest block, a hip block, and sometimes feet blocks, all of which are connected by lengths of armature wire. The blocks are typically made of aluminium (although can also be made from a very hard wood, such as oak or maple, or even from plastic), and as such are extremely strong and long lasting. Block armatures allow for very easy replacement of broken parts – pop out a broken part, pop in a new one, and you're back animating. Slick!

Block armatures require certain specialized materials and tools, and are significantly more complex in terms of fabrication methods when compared to brass tube armatures. Practice is needed to create a nice armature using this approach, so if you want fast and easy, this isn't the way to proceed. But if you want a reliable and professional armature, which allows for a great range of animation, is relatively affordable, is commonly used in the stop motion industry, and that presents an exciting challenge, then this is a very solid choice.

In fact, the block style of armature is *such* a good overall choice, that it's the armature style we'll be using for Nia!

> Since it requires training, practice, and dedication, if you can fabricate a nice aluminium block armature, you'll have effectively taken yourself to that 'next level' of stop motion skills. You'll be proud of yourself for what you've learned, and you'll be well on your way to being a stop motion professional!

Ball and socket

Sometimes referred to as B & S armatures, the design of these armatures is very similar to the human skeleton. Consider your own hip joint – there is a ball at the top of your femur bone, which fits into the socket of your hip. The ball rotates within that socket, allowing for a great range of movement, while also offering great stability. The B & S armature is typically used in projects that demand very high quality animation, such as feature films, television projects, and certain indie films. These armatures are super responsive, allowing for extremely subtle performances, and the good ones – that are professionally designed and fabricated from stainless steel – essentially *will not break*. What's not to love?

Well, to begin with, they are *very* challenging to make on your own, and as such can be a massive drain on your time and energy. Another challenge is that if you opt to purchase one (rather than try to make one), good ones are quite pricey. For a basic, well-made humanoid armature, it's not at all unusual to find a price tag in the range of $800 CAN, and prices rapidly go up from there.

You'll find cheaper ball and socket armature options online, but they are typically poorly made. A cheap armature might look great, only to reveal its weakness once you're animating, as it brings everything to a crashing halt. Do *very* careful research. Look for first-hand testimonials from impartial and experienced animators, before you commit to opening up your wallet for this kind of armature.

If you intend to pursue a professional career as an armature maker, or already have advanced skills in designing and working with metal, then attempting one of these armatures is a sensible ambition.

If not, I'd suggest that you leave the fabrication of this style to others, at least for now. Otherwise, you'll likely find yourself devoting all of your energies to the challenge of making the puppet's armature, rather than to the challenge of becoming a better animator, or to becoming a better filmmaker.

> **JASON AND THE ARGONAUTS, DON CHAFFEY, 1963 ANIMATION BY RAY HARRYHAUSEN**
>
> This classic fantasy film features a remarkable sword fight between live action soldiers and seven (yes, seven) blood-thirsty stop motion skeletons. These skeleton puppets are great to study in terms of armature designs, since they are essentially ball and socket armatures with minimal 'skeleton' details applied on top. There's lots to learn from these puppets – including how humanoid joints connect in a realistic puppet.

Introduction to Nia's armature

This is what you'll be working towards, over the balance of this chapter.

Nia's armature is a block style, and is made from aluminium. This armature will be super strong, will allow you to animate just about anything you can imagine, and will allow you to replace parts in

Figure 3.1
The completed Nia armature, back view.

the event that anything should break. It should also last you a lifetime. To create it, you'll need access to a selection of specific tools, along with specific materials, all of which are detailed below.

Cost, of course, is always a concern. The materials required for this stage are quite affordable, all things considered. The cost of tools will vary, depending on how many you already have access to, and how many you have to purchase or rent.

The main cost in making any armature is *time*. It's a careful and precise process, and shouldn't be rushed. From start to finish (depending on your skill level), it may take several days to complete this armature. But the payoff is an extremely reliable and durable armature that you'll be able to use for hundreds of hours of animation time. Personally, I've never worn out an armature block … even after spending many hours moving puppets!

The instructions for making Nia's armature, as with all the instructions in this book, are designed in a clear step by step fashion. Each main component of the armature has its own section, so that you can quickly find a specific stage of the overall process.

Commonly used materials

Armature making requires the use of a wide range of materials. There's some central ones that you'll find yourself using again and again, and since these are so important to the overall process, it helps if you know a bit more about them.

Aluminium armature wire

This kind of wire is very widely used in stop motion, and it's the main kind of wire you'll be using in fabricating Nia's moving parts. It's very easy to pose, yet is also quite strong, making it perfect for the tiny movements required in stop motion. It may *look* like regular steel wire, but it's not, so don't accept regular 'hardware store' wire – that kind of wire is too hard to work with, and too stiff. You'll find armature wire in art supply stores, and it can also be ordered online.

In Canada, we use two official languages (English and French), *and* we use two forms of measurement: U.S. and metric. Whenever possible, I've listed a size in *both* forms of measurement. If you're stuck for a measurement in *your* units, it's easy to find the conversion using an online calculator. On behalf of my entire country, I apologize for any confusion. At least we make good maple syrup.

There are two gauges you need for Nia: 1.6 mm (1/16 inch), and 3 mm (1/8 inch). You'll be using quite a bit more of the 1.6 mm (1/16 inch), so get more of that (several packages, or rolls, depending on how it's sold).

Adhesives

Any stop motion expert knows a thing or two about sticking things together. 'The right tool for the right

Roy wasn't too happy about posing for this image, but he managed to stick with it. You might as well accept this style of humour now, since it doesn't get any better as the book goes on.

job' is a popular saying among craft people, and you can extend that to adhesives – there's no one adhesive that is best for all jobs. Beyond the basic white glue, blue tack (or sticky tack), glue sticks, and hot glue, you need to know what to use when dealing with certain materials and situations.

Contact cement

Contact cement is extremely strong, and bonds quickly but not instantly, which can be a great thing if you need to carefully position a piece. For armature making, it's often used to glue foam to both itself, and to armatures. If needed, the bond this glue forms can be broken without causing damage, provided you're careful. Contact cement is *not* the same thing as rubber cement. Rubber cement doesn't bond as well, so don't get the two mixed up. The fumes from contact cement can quickly cause headaches, so always follow the product's guidelines.

Cyanoacrylate glue (CA glue)

CA glue goes by a variety of brand names, including the most famous – Krazy Glue. It provides an instant and *incredibly* strong bond that is highly unlikely to break. Since it can glue metal to metal, CA glue is essential for certain steps in the armature making process, as you want complete confidence that your pieces are secure before moving into animation.

Look for CA glue that is thicker, as opposed to runny. This is sometimes referred to as 'gap-filling glue', because it slowly flows into spaces as it bonds. With some puppet parts, gaps are unavoidable (such as when attaching brass stock to armature wire), so this thicker CA glue is very useful. If you can't find the thick stuff, the thin stuff works fine if you are careful in your application. CA glue loses its effectiveness rather quickly once the container is opened, so be sure to store it in an airtight container, with a pin or needle in the spout to ensure that the opening doesn't seal itself shut.

Handle this glue carefully, and respect its strength. If you *do* happen to glue your fingers together (it happens to everyone), don't panic. It won't burn or hurt. Acetone (or nail polish remover, which typically contains acetone) will dissolve the bond with no damage to your skin. Even warm, soapy water will eventually do the trick, if you're patient.

A specialty store (such as a hobby store) that sells CA glue will often sell 'debonder' as well. It's typically made with acetone, and breaks down the CA glue's hold. It can be useful to have on the shelf in case of CA mishaps.

Double-sided tape

A very thin strip of this specialty tape is especially useful on puppet costumes to keep things like coat flaps, belts, and jewelry in place during animation. If you have a 'grass' ground that consists of shaggy fabric, thicker strips of double-sided tape is great for holding the fabric it in place, while still being easily removable after that set is no longer in use.

Toupee tape

This tape is a gentle form of double-sided tape, and is handy for holding things like puppet hats or helmets in place. It's quite strong, but removes very easily, so it won't damage a delicate puppet paint job. And if you need to keep your own hairpiece steady in a strong wind, you'll be well-prepared.

Modeling putty

This is stuff is great, and is often used in puppet making, especially for forming 'bones' on leg and arm armatures. It's also useful for adhering certain puppet parts that resist other adhesives, and for patching or adding on to resin (plastic) parts. It often comes in two parts that you mix together, and in no time you have a super hard piece that didn't require baking. Some putty products have a very short working time, while others don't harden fully for an hour or longer, allowing for lots of sculpting time. Not all brands dry hard enough to be of use in stop motion, so do your research.

Brass stock

Brass stock is also known as brass tubing, and for most stop motion purposes (including Nia's armature) you'll be looking for the square and round tubes. They're used for a variety of purposes when it comes to puppet-making, and they come in a wide assortment of sizes. They can slide together to form tight bonds (always useful when working with armatures), and to make very strong end bits for puppet parts.

The specific sizes you'll need for Nia's armature are as follows: 4 mm (5/32 inch) round stock, 4 mm (5/32 inch) square stock, and 5 mm (3/16 inch) square stock. I'd recommend buying a decent supply, at least three or four pieces of each gauge. They aren't very expensive, and having extra on hand saves you the hassle of having to acquire more when you're in the middle of fabrication.

Aluminium

Aluminium is super light and incredibly strong, which is why it's the metal of choice for airplanes. Yet as hard as it is, aluminium can still be cut, shaped, and drilled, using simple tools. Think of aluminium as being like very, *very* hard wood, only shinier!

Aluminium is also *cheap*. For a few dollars, you can buy enough aluminium to make dozens of super strong, super reliable armatures. Aluminium has different ratings, based mostly on hardness. The aluminium you'll want for Nia doesn't have to be overly strong (you don't want it to be too hard to cut), so make sure you explain to the shop what you're using it for.

You'll want to find a piece of aluminium at least 10 cm (4 inch) × 20 cm (8 inch). In terms of thickness, I'd strongly recommend that you find a piece that's very close to 2 cm (3/4 inch). Since this is the approximate thickness of Nia's main blocks, it will save you a *lot* of cutting if the block is already the right thickness. A block that's the size that's described above won't cost much, and it will provide you with enough metal to make lots of armature pieces.

Overview of a workshop

An inexpensive (but bright) overhead light, positioned towards the front of you, is essential for the detailed work that you'll be undertaking.

Physical space is always a challenge in stop motion. You need it when animating, but you also need it for fabrication. If you have space that you'll be dedicating to animation, you may also be able to use that space to build the armatures. Since both animation *and* armature-making require a sturdy table, consider setting up your tools for armature making, and then when you're done, clearing it off for animation.

There's nothing special about the space that's required, but ideally it should be a place where noise and a bit of mess is ok. Mine is set up in a corner of my garage. If you can't arrange for your own workshop space, or aren't able to afford your own specialized tools, ask around. High schools, colleges, and community centers often have workshop facilities that can be borrowed or rented by students or individuals. Friends and family might have tools, or they might know someone who does. The nice thing is that you don't need access for months on end to these tools. If you plan effectively, two or three days should be enough workshop time to fashion Nia's armature.

All of the tools (and materials) required for this stage are detailed below. Most are quite commonly available. But if you're looking to borrow or rent

**Figure 3.2
The home workbench.**
An inexpensive (but bright) overhead light, positioned towards the front of you, is essential for the detailed work that you'll be undertaking.

some workshop space, there are few *essential* tools that you need to ensure will be available for you.

These essential tools are:

- a drill press
- a sturdy vice that is secured to a workbench
- a coping saw.

Working safe

If you don't have any experience with tools, don't let that put you off. I'm not a master carpenter or experienced at metal-working, but I practised and I learned.

You're intelligent and keen and you'll learn as you go. You *are* going to want to take your time and get familiar with the tools you'll be using. You want to be confident, so that you can be safe and so that you can do great work. None of the tools are particularly dangerous, but accidents *can* happen, so proceed slowly and carefully. Think things through in advance. It also helps to seek out someone who has at least some experience to give you some workshop training with these tools.

In addition to tool safety, all of the materials used during fabrication should be treated with respect. Always follow the product's guidelines, and use your common sense. Also, (no surprise here) – always wear safety glasses when sawing, cutting, sanding, or drilling.

Making the chest and hip blocks

Figures 3.3 and 3.4 are essential illustrations that you'll want to refer to regularly. The holes marked for rigs will be explained later in the chapter. A key measurement here is the drill depth for the body part holes, which is 1 cm (3/8 inch)

Take note of how the set screws tighten into the body part holes, effectively biting into the body part to keep it in place for animation. Each body part is tipped with round brass stock, so that the set screw doesn't destroy the relatively soft armature wire. All of the blocks (chest, hip, and feet) work in this fashion.

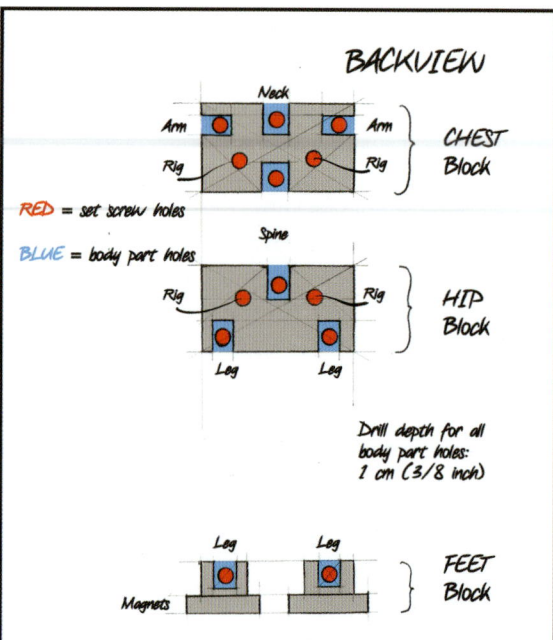

Figure 3.3
Armature Blocks.
Plan for chest, hip, and feet blocks, back view.

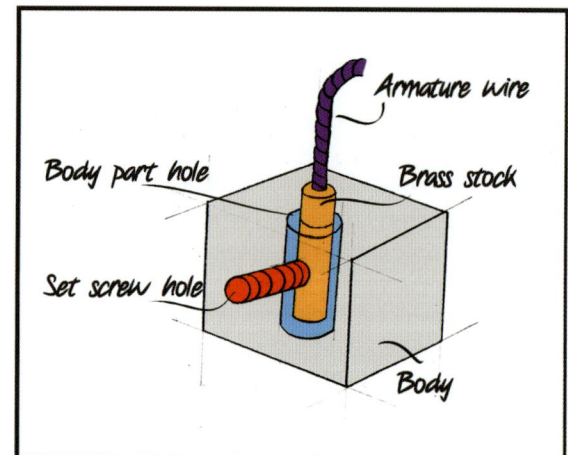

Figure 3.4
Armature Holes.
Set screw holes vs. body part holes.

As you study Figures 3.3. and 3.4, you'll see that Nia's arms, neck, spine, and legs are held in place by tiny screws (known as set screws) that come in at right-angles to the body parts. These are tightened on to the body part pieces to keep them in place. If a part breaks, you can loosen the screw, replace the broken piece, tighten the screw again, and you're back in action.

These two kinds of holes – body part holes and set screw holes – are *not* the same size (although they are very close). Each requires its own particular drill bit. All the specific bit sizes are indicated at the appropriate steps. As you create the armature, don't confuse the function of these holes. The different holes have been colour-coded in the illustrations to help keep things clear.

As you study the illustrations, you'll notice that there is only one specific measurement, and that is body part hole drilling depth – 1 cm (3/8 inch). Other careful measurements *will* be required, but in my experience, it's better to measure as you go, referring back to the scale drawing that *you've* created yourself. As you proceed, use your own eyes (and ruler) to judge things overall. This method allows you to make minor adjustments as you go along, based on what you see in front of you on your workbench. If a measurement needs to be made, or if something needs to be a specific measurement, it's clearly noted in the instructions.

Looking for suppliers for certain materials and tools? You'll find help at the end of material-heavy chapters.

MATERIALS

Aluminium, approximately 2 cm (3/4 inch) × 10 cm (4 inch) × 20 cm (8 inch). You'll have lots left for Nia's feet blocks, and for more armatures in general.

4.76 mm (6/32 inch) set screws, approx. 6.35 mm (1/4 inch) long × 20 (four for the chest block, three for the hip block, two for the feet blocks, and the rest because the screws are *very* tiny, and easily go missing!)

TOOLS

paper, pencil, eraser
light box (optional)
vice
drill press
3.97 mm (5/32 inch) drill bit
2.78 mm (7/64 inch) drill bit
coping saw
extra blades for coping saw
metal lubricant spray (e.g. WD-40)

metal file (medium coarse)
small precision metal ruler
4.76 mm (6/32 inch) allen key (also known as a hex key)
metal tapping tool
4.76 mm (6/32 inch) tapping bit
safety glasses
safety mask

STEP BY STEP

1. Lay a blank piece of paper over the final scale Nia design drawing, and trace Nia's outline. You can use a light box for this, or just tape Nia's design on to a bright window, and trace over it.
2. Using the outline drawing you've just made, create *another* tracing. This time, draw in the details of Nia's armature, using the finished armature drawing (Figure 3.6) as a guide. Don't draw the armature parts *too* close to the edges – remember that on top of the armature will be foam, silicone, and fabric.

Figure 3.5
Creating Nia's armature drawing.
You'll notice each of Nia's feet consist of a flat magnet with a block of aluminium on top. Specifics for the feet armatures are found later in this chapter.

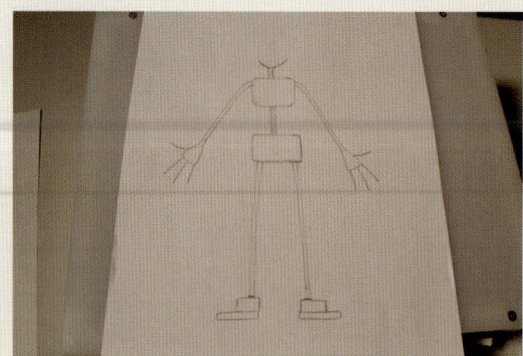

Figure 3.6
Nia's scale armature drawing.
Your scale drawing of Nia's armature should basically look like this.

3. Carefully measure the width and height of the chest block and the hip block on your armature drawing. Ideally, your aluminium is already the right thickness (approx. 2 cm or 3/4 inch), so that you don't need to measure for this dimension.

4. Use a pencil to transfer these measurements to the aluminium. Double check your measurements, before moving on.

Figure 3.7
Chest block, ready for cutting.
It helps to write the name of the part on the metal at this stage, for quick reference later.

5. Make sure that you're wearing safety goggles and work gloves for this stage. Secure the aluminium in the vice and spray a bit of lubricant on to your cut mark. Use the coping saw to carefully start your first cut by lightly scoring the aluminium, making a small groove. Start this cut slowly and carefully. Once the groove is established, you should be able to work away at a good

pace, stopping regularly to check that your cut is straight (and to rest your arms!) Regularly spray lubricant into the cut to make the going easier. Wipe away the aluminium shavings as needed, so you can see where you are cutting. Be patient, and stick with it. This stage takes time. Once the chest and hip pieces are cut, use a coarse file to take off any sharp edges, corners, or overly rough bits. If you have access to a metal grinder, you can use it to nicely smooth out the armature edges, and even give the blocks beveled edges.

Figure 3.8
Cutting the armature blocks.
Go slowly until you get a nice groove established in the metal. Watch that you don't drift off the cut line – check the straightness of your cut at regular intervals.

Practice makes perfect in all things, including armature-making. If your blocks aren't perfectly square and smooth, it doesn't mean that they won't function well once they're completely done. If you've *really* gone off, and your 'block' looks more like a 'lump', then you may want to cut a new block.

6. Using the armature drawing as your guide, measure and mark all the drilling points on to the blocks. Be sure to carefully refer to the armature illustrations (Figures 3.3 and 3.4) to guide you as you make your drill marks. It's very important at this point to remember that each body part hole (neck, arms, spine, legs) has an *associated* set screw hole, and that each set screw hole must come out *into* the body part hole.

Figure 3.9
Marking the drill points.
As with all stages of armature making, work slowly, and be
sure of your measurements before moving on.

7. Wear safety goggles and a basic safety mask
    for this step. If you have long hair, tie it back,
    and remove all jewelry. Review overall drill
    press safety items, then get ready to drill all of
    the *body part* holes. Do this for both the chest
    and hip blocks. Be sure to add some lubricant
    to the block's surface to ease the drilling.

    It's best to grip the block with pliers, since
    the block will get a bit hot as it's drilled. If you
    can't get a solid grip with pliers, you can hold
    the block with your fingers, just keep your
    fingers well back, and wear work gloves. To
    drill these holes, you need to use a 3.97 mm
    (5/32 inch) drill bit. Be sure to drill to the depth
    required for each hole (most drill presses have
    a device to prevent over-drilling). Remember,
    the depth of each body part hole should be 1
    cm (3/8 inch).

Figure 3.10
Chest block with body part holes drilled.
Notice the drill marks for set screw holes, which is the next
step.

> Once you've drilled one body part hole,
> create a 'depth gauge' by inserting a small
> nail into the hole, and marking the depth
> on the nail with some tape. As you drill
> each new body part hole, check the depth
> with your gauge, to make sure that they
> are all consistent. Each hole should be
> about 1 cm (3/8 inch) in depth.

8. Now drill all of the *set screw* holes. Do this for
    both the chest and hip blocks. To drill these
    holes, you need to use a 2.78 mm (7/64 inch)
    drill bit. Be very careful in how you position the
    armature before drilling each of these holes.
    You want each of these set screw holes to
    intersect with its associated body part hole, so
    that when you insert a set screw, it will effec-
    tively tighten on to the body part. Each set
    screw hole you are about to drill should end as
    you come out into the associated body part
    hole. Ideally, each set screw hole should come
    out centered into the body part hole. If there's
    ever any doubt about which holes are for *body
    parts*, and which are for *set screws*, refer back
    to Figures 3.3 and 3.4 before you drill!

Figure 3.11
Drilling the set screw holes.
Notice how the drill bit is nicely lined up to enter *into* the
corresponding body part hole.

Remember those rig holes (see Figure 3.3)?
Now is the time to drill them, using this
particular drill bit. These holes only need only
go in a few mm (1/8 inch), because they will
eventually house a rigging bolt. More on that
later.

Figure 3.12
Set screw hole intersecting with body part hole.
Ideally, each of the set screw holes you drill should come out nicely centered like this.

If the set screw holes don't come out perfectly centered into the body part hole, you should still be ok, since the set screws should still be able to bite on to the body part. If you're rather off, you'll know within a few more quick steps whether or not the error was fatal. If it was, try to re-drill new body part holes and set screw holes, using the same blocks. If there's no room on the block for more holes, it's back to the vice and coping saw. Just think of those toned biceps and triceps you'll soon have. Looking good, stop motion animator!

9. Wear safety goggles for this step. You're now going to create the screw threads for the set screw holes. This is a process known as 'tapping', and requires (as you may have guessed) a tapping tool, and a tapping bit to go with it.

Figure 3.13
Tapping the set screw holes.
Be sure to regularly 'back out' with the tapping tool. This will extract the metal filings from the hole.

Fit the tapping tool with a 4.76 mm (6/32 inch) bit. Squirt some metal lubricant into the first set screw hole, then carefully 'thread' the bit in, by turning the tool clock-wise into the hole. Apply steady pressure as you turn the tool. As you turn, you should feel a gentle grinding sensation as the bit cuts threads into the aluminium. After a few turns, 'back out' by turning the tool counter-clockwise, so as to remove the metal filings.

Blow out the hole, then continue to thread the hole until the tapping bit comes out into the associated body part hole, and can't go any further. Blow out the hole, reapply some lubricant, and repeat the process. This ensures that you have clean threads.

Repeat this process for all of the set screw holes, as well as for the rig holes.

10. Use the allen key to insert the set screws into all the body part holes. No need to put screws into the rig holes.

Figure 3.14
Inserting the set screws.
Tighten each one fully, to ensure that it has a clean path into the body part hole. Then back the screw out, to leave room for the brass stock that will be inserted.

It's time to test your results! Do this by inserting a length of 3.97 mm (5/32 inch) round brass stock into a body part hole. Tighten the associated set screw until it bites into the brass. Is the brass held tightly? Since this is the round stock that will be on the ends of all your body parts, if the screws hold the brass firmly, congrats. If the brass is loose, or not held in place at all, that's a problem. You'll need to track it down, and possibly re-drill. Test all of the body part holes in this way.

When the rig holes are needed (during animation that requires a rig wire, like runs and jumps), you can thread a 4.76 mm (6/32 inch) bolt into any one of these holes. You'll find more on rigged animation in later sections.

Figure 3.15
The finished chest and hip blocks
Awesome work, stop motion artist!

Making the feet armatures

Stop motion puppet feet can be very tricky to design and fabricate. Since they hold the puppet up, the feet (and ankles) need to be extremely durable. They also need to be very flexible for animation, and the challenge that comes from trying to combine these attributes (super strong, as well as flexible) has kept many puppet makers up late at night. How to ensure that the puppet will stand up, and remain stable? There are two main methods:

Tie downs

The tie down method involves inserting bolts up from under the set's surface into the feet of the puppet. The bolts thread into holes in the puppet's feet, keeping it stable. The great thing about this method is that since the hole in the foot can be very small, it allows for quite tiny puppet feet, which can be great for character designers. It also provides an extremely stable point of contact, provided that the foot is designed and fabricated well.

A downside to the tie down foot is that it can be tricky to make (very tiny parts that have to be super strong), and animation can become a bit more complex, since you need to account for the set holes. You can't just land a puppet foot anywhere during animation, it has to land *right* at the hole. This takes some getting used to when animating. If you are used to tie down puppets, or simply prefer that style, you can modify Nia's feet armatures to allow for tie downs, and Figure 3.19 clearly shows how that would look. If you go down this route, know that you'll also have to modify the moulding and casting process for her feet from what you see in this book.

Magnets

For this foot type, an extremely strong magnet (called a rare earth magnet) is secured in the foot. From under the set, another magnet connects with the foot, thereby keeping the puppet in place. An advantage of this type of foot is that it allows for relatively easy animation – you just need a ground surface that is thin enough to allow the magnets to connect. You also don't need to land a foot anywhere in particular, so that makes animation somewhat easier. It's also relatively easy to fabricate this kind of foot. A disadvantage is that in order to allow room for a big enough magnet, the foot tends to be on the big side, which can restrict the character design. And although magnets are very strong, they aren't as strong as metal bolts, so the puppet won't be quite as sturdy during animation.

It's important to realize that rare earth magnets are *not* your average fridge magnet. They are

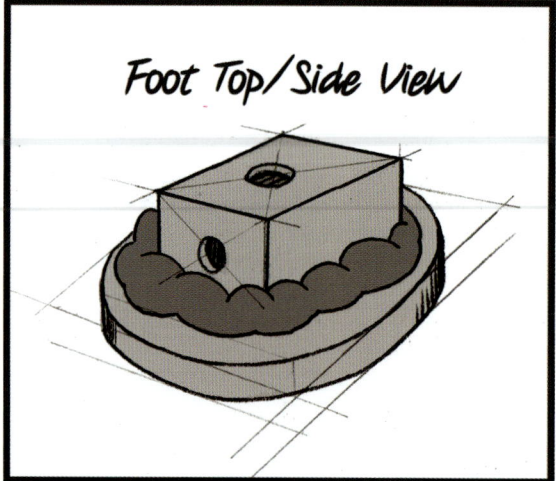

Figure 3.16
The foot block and magnet.
Modeling putty is used to connect the block and the magnet. The drill depth for the body part hole in the foot block is the same depth that used for the chest and hip blocks – 1cm (3/8 inch).

remarkably strong, so take care. Keep them away from electronics, hard drives, and bank cards. Take precautions so that they don't fly across your work bench towards each other – they break

easily, and cause nasty little blisters if your fingers get pinched!

Because a magnet foot is fairly easy to make, and because it allows for fairly easy animation, it's the foot style for Nia. You may notice that Nia doesn't have a toe portion that can be posed. Instead, her foot is one solid piece. All things considered, this is a modest compromise when it comes to animation. It means no toe animation, but Nia's magnet feet are *strong*, and durable and Nia will be extremely stable. This kind of foot will allow you to create great overall animation (if not fancy toe animation). Once you can confidently design and fabricate a foot like Nia's, you'll be able to try your hand at modifying that design if you want a foot that can be animated more fully.

Figure 3.16 is one that you'll want to refer to as you fabricate the foot armature pieces. You've already learned the essentials by making the previous blocks, and the feet are pretty simple in comparison, so this stage should go fairly quickly.

Incidentally, the feet armatures will eventually be encased in a *plastic shoe,* which you'll learn all about in a later chapter.

MATERIALS

Scale armature drawing of Nia (refer to Figure 3.6 to see how Nia's feet armatures are drawn).
Aluminium (use the same piece that you bought for the chest and hip blocks)
4.76 mm (6/32 inch) set screws, approx. 6.35 mm (1/4 inch) long × 2 (these are the same screws that were used for the chest and hips)
strong modeling putty
19.05 mm (3/4 inch) rare earth magnets × 2. Buy more than two if possible, as they are cheaper in larger volumes and you're sure to use them for other things. You may also want to buy at least two larger magnets at the same time. These larger magnets will be used to click on under Nia's feet during animation. Get 25.4 mm (1 inch) magnets for this.

TOOLS

paper, pencil, eraser	metal lubricant spray(e.g. WD-40)
vice	small precision metal ruler
drill press	4.76 mm (6/32 inch) allen key
3.97 mm (5/32 inch) drill bit	metal tapping tool
2.78 mm (7/64 inch) drill bit	4.76 mm (6/32 inch) tapping bit
coping saw	safety glasses
extra blades for coping saw	safety mask
vice grip	

STEP BY STEP

1. Use the scale armature drawing as a guide, and plan to cut two small square pieces of aluminium. These will be the ankle pieces. As you plan the pieces, make sure they are small enough to fit inside what will eventually be Nia's shoes. Before cutting, ensure that the aluminium pieces you're planning to cut will cover most of the 19.05 mm (3/4 inch) magnet's surface.
2. Mark the aluminium for cutting, as with the previous blocks.
3. Cut the blocks, using the same method that you used for the previous armature blocks. Make sure you have your safety goggles on.

Figure 3.17
Foot block on magnet.
Once the blocks are cut, double check that each will sit cleanly on the top of the magnet.

4. Mark the ankles for drilling, as with the previous blocks. As you create the marks, remember to line up the body part holes so that they will intersect with the set screw holes.
5. Drill the body part holes and set screw holes, as with previous blocks. Since the ankle pieces are so tiny, you'll want to use vice grips to hold the pieces steady while drilling. This stage can be tricky, because the ankle pieces are quite small. You may end up having to cut new ankle pieces and drill again. Fortunately, it's a quick task to cut more ankle blocks.
6. Ensure that both magnets are oriented in the same way, with the same polarity pointing

downward. Follow the instructions for mixing the putty, and secure the first ankle piece to its magnet. Keep the area around the set screw hole clear of putty. The putty bond between the block and the magnet should be very strong – if it's not, try another putty, or epoxy, or CA glue. This part of the puppet will receive further strength once it's cast in plastic (next chapter), but the stronger you can make it now, the better.
7. Repeat for the other foot.

Figure 3.18
The finished feet armatures.
Make sure that the bond between the magnet and the putty is extremely strong.

Figure 3.19
Tie down feet armatures.
Nia's feet armatures can be modified to use the tie down method, rather than the magnet method. To do this, you'd need to make the aluminium foot pieces a bit longer, then create a threaded hole in the toe area of the foot block for the tie down bolt. If you do this, be sure to also modify your process during moulding and casting.

Making the neck, spine, and legs

Along with the arms (whose fabrication is covered in the next chapter), these are the body parts that will be animated. As such, they are also the parts that will eventually wear out and need replacing. They are pretty quick to make, so consider fabricating several of each. Then, when they need replacing, you'll have extras ready. This will let you stay focused on animation, instead of switching gears back into 'fabrication mode'.

You'll start by creating some basic items that all the body parts will need.

MATERIALS

1.6 mm (1/16 inch) armature wire
4 mm (5/32 inch) round brass stock

TOOLS

pencil
rotary tool (or coping saw)
cutting disks for rotary tool
power hand drill (for twisting armature wire. If you
     don't have a drill, you can do it by hand)

wire snips
a nail
metal file (medium coarse)
safety glasses
safety mask

STEP BY STEP

1. Start by braiding a healthy length of 1.6 mm (1/16 inch) armature wire. Create about 20 cm (7 ¾ inch) in total. Do it by hand, or use a drill. From this braided length, you can snip off pieces, as needed.
2. With a pencil, mark cutting points on a length of round 4 mm (5/32 inch) brass stock. The length of each brass stock piece should be the same as the depth of the body part holes that you drilled, which is 1 cm (3/8 inch). These bits will be for the ends of the neck, spine, and legs. You'll need a total of nine pieces of brass stock for all the parts, but you might as well cut more – in case you lose some, and so you have them on hand to make more body parts. As you make your marks, be sure to allow for the thickness of your blade or cutting disk.
3. Wear safety glasses and a safety mask for this step. Cut the pieces using the rotary tool (see Tip Box), or a coping saw.

Figure 3.20
Cut pieces of brass stock.
These pieces are ready to be glued on to the ends of body parts. Also shown is a rotary tool, outfitted with a cutting disk.

4. With the metal file, smooth off any major rough spots on the ends of the brass pieces. Use a nail to further clean the inside of the pieces as well. With braided wire and cut brass pieces ready, you can now move on to the individual parts.

A rotary tool is a very useful addition to a stop motion tool kit. You can attach a number of different blades and bits for cutting, sanding, polishing, and etching all sorts of materials. Fitted with cutting disks, a rotary tool is great for cutting brass stock. Take time to learn how to use the tool effectively. Be sure to follow the safety instructions, and wear safety glasses and a safety mask – the tool creates a lot of dust as it works.

Making the neck

MATERIALS

final Nia design, printed to scale (Figure 2.5)
scale armature drawing of Nia
1.6 mm (1/16 inch) armature wire (already braided)
4 mm (5/32 inch) square stock, one length
1 small piece of round brass (already cut)

TOOLS

pencil
rotary tool (or coping saw)
cutting disks for rotary tool
CA glue
wire snips

metal file (medium coarse)
nail
safety glasses
safety mask

STEP BY STEP

1. Using 4 mm (5/32 inch) square stock, and the scale drawing of the final design, make a cut mark on the stock that measures approx. 1/2 of the height of the scale puppet head.

Figure 3.21
Measuring the stock.
This brass piece will eventually be embedded inside of the head.

2. Cut the square stock. Use the file and nail to smooth off the inside and outside of the brass.
3. Slide a piece of the cut round brass stock over an approx. 8 cm (3 inch) long piece of the braided armature wire. Use CA glue to secure the round brass to the wire. Let the glue fully dry (min. 10 minutes).
4. Fit the cut square stock over the free end of the armature wire. Push the stock on to the wire until it's well-embedded. Don't glue it yet. Use the scale drawing of Nia's final design (along with your scale armature drawing) to check for overall length. If the overall length is too long, remove the square stock, trim the wire, and fit the square stock on again. Check for length on scale drawing. Once you've got the right length, you can *now* glue the square stock on to the wire.
5. Fit the round end of the neck into the neck hole on the chest block, then tighten the set screw. The neck should be firmly in place.

Whenever possible, leave wires overly long until you're ready to glue. You can always keep trimming these wires until they are the perfect length, but if you cut them too short, you'll have no choice but to scrap the piece and start again.

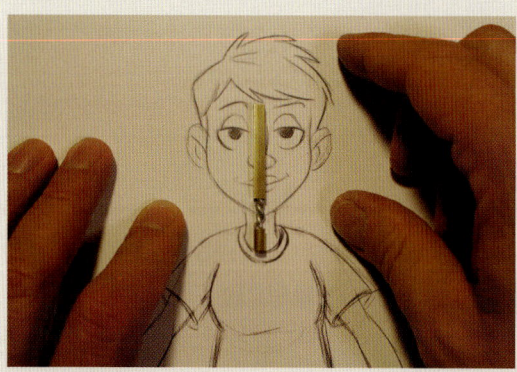

Figure 3.22
The finished neck.
The square end of this neck will slide snugly *into* the slightly larger gauge square stock that will be secured within the head (next chapter).

Making the spine

MATERIALS

scale armature drawing of Nia
1.6 mm (1/16 inch) armature wire (already braided)
2 small pieces of round brass (already cut)

TOOLS

CA glue
wire snips

STEP BY STEP

1. Use the scale armature drawing to determine a length of braided 1/16 inch wire for the spine. Allow for a bit more length than needed, and then snip the wire.
2. Slide a piece of round brass stock on to the end of the wire, and CA glue it into place. Let the glue dry.
3. Check the length of the spine once again, against the drawing.

4. Slide the remaining piece of round brass stock on to the other end of the wire. Check for overall length on the scale drawing. Trim the wire if necessary. Once the length is correct, CA glue this piece of brass on to the wire.

5. Fit one end of the spine into the spine hole on the chest block, and the other end into the spine hole on the hip block. Tighten the set screws. The spine should be firmly in place.

Figure 3.23
The finished spine and neck, secured within the blocks.
It's starting to look like a finished armature!

Making the legs

The legs are created in exactly the same way as the spine, except that you'll be using stronger wire. Nia's legs have to be strong, since they support the weight of everything above them.

MATERIALS

scale armature drawing of Nia
3 mm (1/8 inch) armature wire
4 small pieces of round brass (already cut)

TOOLS

CA glue
wire snips

STEP BY STEP

1. Using the scale armature drawing, size out a length of wire for the leg. Be generous in the length (you can trim to proper length later). Cut the wire.

2. As with the spine, slide a piece of round brass stock on to the end of the wire, and CA glue it into place. Let the glue dry.

3. Check the length of the leg once again, against the drawing.

4. Slide the remaining piece of round brass stock on to the other end of the wire. Check for overall length on the scale drawing. Trim the wire if necessary. Once the length is correct, CA glue this piece of brass on to the wire.

5. Repeat for the other leg.

6. Fit one end of the first leg into the leg hole on the hip block, and the other end into the leg hole on the foot. Tighten the set screws.

Repeat for the other leg. The legs should be firmly in place, and the armature should stand on its own (with a bit of posing).

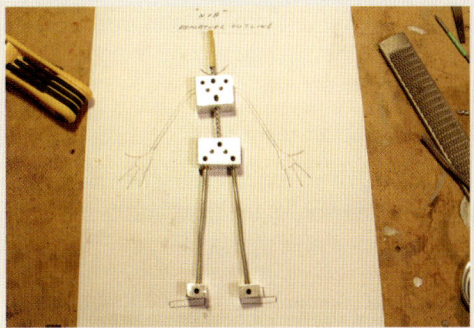

Figure 3.24
The completed armature, fully assembled.
Pat yourself on the back, because you've just completed a lovely aluminium block armature. Congratulations!

Depending on your skill level when you started this chapter, you've now learned a *lot* about precision mechanical design, armature making, and working with metal. Fantastic work!

STREET OF CROCODILES, THE BROTHERS QUAY, 1986

On many people's list of top animated films, this short offers a remarkable glimpse into a mysterious fantasy world of animated objects and half-formed puppets. Screws, metal joints, and cotton stuffing all peek out through gaps in clothing, and in one scene, the central character is actually disassembled by the other puppets, who then reassemble him using new parts.

SUPPLIER INFORMATION

Rather than listing specific stores and outlets (that vary from region to region, and that go in and out of business), what follows are some tips on tracking down the specialized materials and tools that are required in this chapter, regardless of where you live in the world. In many cases, if you start by looking up a particular product name, the company's website often leads you to local suppliers. I've only offered insights here into items that can be difficult to find. For more common tools and materials, look to your local hardware and art supply stores.

Stop motion social media spaces

Social media groups and websites that are dedicated to the medium are a great way to track down materials. Some groups have subfolders that list suppliers, and if you don't see what you need there, ask the group! I strongly recommend that you take advantage of social media to research any online vendors you may discover. Ask the group if they've had a good experience with particular stores.

Online stop motion resources

There's an array of companies that specialize in providing stop motion materials to artists. In some cases, you may be able to find most of what you need at a single source. Before you commit to an order, be mindful of shipping costs that the online store may add to your order. And be sure to ask the larger stop motion community if the store in question is reliable, and offers good materials.

Armature wire

You can usually find the basic required gauges of armature wire at art supply stores. If they don't have the specific wire that you need in stock, see if they can order it. It's also quite easy to get via reputable online stores.

Modeling putty, brass stock, specialty glues

Look for these materials at hobby stores that specialize in sculpting and miniatures. Model train shops are a good place to look, along with stores that specialize in RC (radio controlled) vehicles. Online stories carry these items, as well.

Liquid latex

This material is *not* to make Nia, but it can still be very useful to have on hand for making puppet skin (see below, in the instructions for making a putty and wire puppet). You can usually find it at art supply stores. The main bit of advice for this material – find the *thinnest* (most runny) liquid latex that you can find. It should flow like milk. If it's thin, then you can dip puppet hands into it, or paint thin layers on, and you'll get great results. If you get thick latex instead, it will go on 'goopy', with poor results.

Set screws

Look for online or physical stores that specialize in metal fasteners (yes, such places exist). If you are going to a store in person, ensure that they're open to the public, and be sure to bring along any relevant measurements. If you already have parts of the armature on hand, bring those too, so the staff can size things in person. This helps to avoid confusion when it comes to the small bits.

Tapping tool and tapping bit

These can be found at online and physical stores that specialize in metal-working tools. As with set screws, if you're going to a store, it's essential that you bring your measurements along (heck, bring this whole book!) so the staff can have a better sense of what you're building. It helps them in their efforts to help *you*.

Aluminium

You'll want to search for 'industrial material centers or suppliers' in your region. Call before heading out, and ask if they sell to the general public. They typically deal with large supplies of metal, but are often happy to sell you small pieces, for very cheap.

Make sure the thickness matches the dimensions listed in this chapter (you don't want to have to saw more aluminium than is necessary). Also, there are different kinds of aluminium, rated for strength, so tell the supplier what you're using it for, and they can suggest the right kind. You don't want super hard aluminium (it's too hard to cut and drill).

Rare earth magnets

Check with specialty hardware stores, and stores that cater to woodworking and cabinet-making. These craft people use the magnets for door and drawer latches. You will also find them sold through online hardware stores and online stop motion stores. Be sure you're getting 'rare earth magnets', since they are specially constructed to offer maximum magnetic strength. Some stores will offer 'coin shaped magnets' but they won't be strong enough for your needs.

Making a putty and wire puppet

This puppet-making process is less complex than the overall process for Nia. It gives you very nice looking results, and a puppet that's great for animation. The main drawback is that once a piece breaks, unless you can get a new piece into place, the puppet can't be used any more (making it inappropriate for longer or more complex projects).

The following techniques, specifically the process for making the head and arms, can also be combined with aluminium armature blocks. This would allow you to replace parts as they break, but wouldn't require complex moulding/casting.

MATERIALS

drawing paper
Super Sculpey (grey)
modeling putty (this will be used for the puppet's hard parts, but Super Sculpey can also be used)
bits of material (for costume)
19.05 mm (3/4 inch) rare earth magnets × 2
cotton balls
talcum powder
upholstery foam
1.6 mm (1/16 inch) armature wire
very fine floral wire (for fingers)
aluminium foil
liquid latex (the thinner the better)

TOOLS

pencil
eraser
masking tape
light box (optional)
sculpting tools
small jar or cup
utility knife
wire snips
contact cement
fabric glue
fabric scissors (regular scissors will also work)
spray primer (grey automotive primer works well)
acrylic paints
paint brushes

STEP BY STEP

1. Create a scale drawing of your character. Follow this with a scale armature drawing. Refer to the process laid out for Nia, earlier in this chapter, if you need clarification.

2. Use the scale armature drawing as a guide to create a spine made from braided armature wire. Make it overly long (you can trim it later).

3. Using the scale armature drawing as a guide, form a loosely shaped head from armature wire. Braid the end of the wire together to form what will become the neck (as with the spine, leave the neck overly long for now). Bulk up the wire with aluminium foil to keep it light, then add a thin layer of Super Sculpey. Sculpt the head, including the hair, nose, eyeballs, and ears. You should also sculpt on the mouth if it won't need to be animated, otherwise you will tack on replacement mouths during animation, or add digital mouths later.

> You can also make this head so that it's removable, so that if the body breaks, you can at least remove (and reuse) the head. To do this, sculpt your head around a short length of 5 mm (3/16 inch) square brass stock. On the neck of the puppet, use 4 mm (5/32 inch) square stock, and this way you can slide the head on and off the neck, as needed. Also, if you have a block armature, you can use this head with that armature. If you need further clarification, check out the process for making Nia's neck.

4. Bake the head. Then prime it and paint it, following the same methods you'll find for Nia's resin head.

Figure 3.25
The painted head.
This Super Sculpey head has a wire core, which is then bulked up with foil to keep it very light.

> If you're using putty for the following steps, it may come with safety warnings. If it does, be sure to follow them correctly. For example, you may need to use safety gloves, since contact with bare skin can cause irritation. Other safety concerns may also be present, so work safely.

5. Now to create the feet. Create a loop of armature wire around a magnet, and then braid the wire, so that it tightens around the magnet. As with the other wire parts, make the leg extra long, so that you can trim it to the correct length later. Determine which side of the magnet attracts another magnet – this will be the side of the magnet that will be the *bottom* of the puppet's foot, and will be the side that connects with the ground.

    Carefully apply putty to the *other* side of the magnet (the side that will be the top of the foot), which will secure the magnet within the wire loop. Bend the wire where the braiding starts, to form the ankle. Ensure the ankle of the puppet is well-secured with putty. Then build the foot up with more epoxy or Sculpey to make a shoe. Repeat with the other foot, making sure that the magnet is oriented in the same way as the first.

    Prime the shoes, and then paint them.

Figure 3.26
Magnets with putty.
Once the magnets are secured within the wire loop, they're ready to build up further with putty or Sculpey.

6. Now to make the hands and arms. Using the scale drawing as a guide, braid a length of overly-long armature wire that has a loop at the braided end. This loop will form the

palm. Use small bits of thin wire or floral wire to create the fingers, and secure them with putty. Pour a small amount of liquid latex into the cup. Mix acrylic paint to get the desired skin colour (match the skin on the face), and then stir a few drops of the paint into the liquid latex, tinting it. Wrap very thin layers of cotton (from the cotton balls) on to the hands and fingers to get a basic shape, and use an old paint brush to apply tinted latex to the cotton. The latex will act as highly flexible skin, and will bind the cotton on to the wire.

Continue until you have a good basic shape, and then dip the hands into the latex. By dipping the hands, you'll avoid brush marks, and achieve a very smooth skin-like surface. Apply two or three coats, or as many coats as are needed to get the hands to the desired size. Allow the latex to become tacky between coats. Once the latex is fully dry (leave it overnight to be sure), apply a layer of baby powder to the hands. This will take down the shine, and will also prevent the latex skin from sticking to itself.

If you now add round brass stock to the ends of these arms, you can use them in a block armature! Refer to the process for Nia's arms if you need clarification.

7. Lay all the parts on to the scale drawing, and begin to carefully trim all the wire ends to get the parts to scale. Don't over trim! Then carefully assemble the parts, using putty to secure them all together. Make sure the joint points are well secured with putty.

Figure 3.27
Assembled puppet armature.
Use just enough putty to do the job. You want the puppet to be as light as possible.

8. To bulk up the puppet, cut foam pieces, and then use contact cement to attach the foam on to the puppet. You can gently secure the foam with masking tape, while the glue dries. Once the glue is dry, trim the foam pieces to shape.

9. Make a simple pair of pants out of fabric by creating a front and back (trace around the puppet to get the shape). Leave room when cutting the fabric to fold in a seam. 'Sandwich' the puppet between the front and back, and carefully work around the seam, gluing it with fabric glue.

10. Make a simple shirt from one piece of fabric (see Figure 3.28). Wrap the piece around the puppet and glue the seams together with fabric glue. Get creative with how you apply these costume pieces, and you can hide the seams very nicely!

Figure 3.28
Pattern for one-piece shirt.
A piece of fabric cut into this shape can then be wrapped around the puppet and glued into place. As you can see, this is also a chance for the puppet to have a nice, relaxing nap.

11. For eyelids, pupils, and eyebrows, refer to how these are made for Nia. For mouths, you can apply clay or Sculpey shapes, use paper mouths, or add them digitally in post-production. That's it! You now have a highly animatable and very nice looking puppet, that's great for small bits of animation.

Figure 3.29
The finished puppet.
Fun and easy to make, this puppet is capable of very nice animation. Just remember that if a part breaks, this puppet will be pretty hard to fix.

MIKE EMIGLIO OF MFX & MANUFACTURING

Mike Emiglio is a designer, inventor, and fabricator for the special effects industry. Through his company MFX & Manufacturing, he also specializes in designing and fabricating ball and socket puppet armatures for stop motion. His clients have included Disney (*JoJo's Circus*) and Shadow Machine (*Titan Maximum*), and he created the armatures for the puppets in *Higglety Pigglety Pop!* (the companion piece to Spike Jonze's adaptation of *Where The Wild Things Are).*

Q. When someone is looking to buy a ball and socket armature, the question of cost quickly comes up. That's understandable, since a quality ball and socket armature can cost a lot. Just why is a quality armature such a pricey thing?

A. A top quality armature is one that is well designed and will stand up to the rigors of industrial stop motion productions. The process of creating a stop motion ball and socket is labour intensive starting from the design process from programming/set-ups for the machining process and onto the assembly and finishing process. A good quality armature should last a lifetime.

It should be machined with stainless steel that has high tolerances, as opposed to lesser quality ones that are made of mild steel or brass and some that may be either laser cut or water jet cut-out constructions. A high quality armature would have high temperature silver solder welded assemblies as opposed to low melt or fastener jointed assemblies.

Q. When researching armature makers, what should one look for?

A. You should look for a armature maker with proven stop motion experience, and the quality of craftsmanship that goes into all aspects of the armature. There are only a few specialists in the entire world that cater to high quality stop motion ball and socket armatures.

Q. Are there specific questions to ask an armature maker, before buying?

A. The questions to ask would include: what machine process do they use to create the joints – CNC or manual machining? CNC means 'Computer Numerical Control', and it's a more precise way of working than doing things by hand. You should also ask what type of material they are fabricating the armature from. The best is stainless steel, as opposed to mild steel or brass.

Q. I know that your customers are happy with the armatures that you make for them. Why is that?

A. My clients come to me because they know they are getting a high-quality armature, that is designed properly, with heavy duty components that will withstand the duration of production period and then some. I make armatures that are always made of the highest quality products, and 100 per cent machined construction backed with a 100 per cent guarantee. Plus, they look cosmetically beautiful!

Q. Any final advice for someone who is shopping around for a ball and socket armature?

A. Do your research and look out for the less expensive online armatures that are available, which are low quality, thin plated components, that use fastener connections, usually made of low quality metal alloy. They may be fine for demonstration or training purposes, but are not made for the intense and critical high cost nature of film and TV productions.

Fabricating the outside: Part 1

This is the first of two chapters that deal with fabricating Nia's exterior parts. In this chapter, the focus is on sculpting most of Nia's parts that will eventually be used in moulding. This chapter also provides an introduction to moulding and casting, and covers all of the fabrication steps for Nia's head and face parts. Her other parts will be moulded and cast in the following chapter.

Between this chapter and the next, there's a lot to learn. It's a complex process, but rest assured – it's all carefully laid out, step by step, with lots of images to help you along.

You'll also find a very detailed section on how to design, model, and print 3D mouth shapes for stop motion. 3D printing is increasingly a part of stop motion, so if you've already got some digital modelling skills, this section can provide you with some very exciting options.

By the end of this chapter, you'll have Nia's parts sculpted and ready for moulding, as well as her finished head and mouth pieces. You'll also be very well trained in moulding and casting, which are specialized skills that are essential for advanced puppet fabrication in stop motion, and that also have uses in a variety of related design and fabrication industries.

Introduction

As with armature making, the workspace requirement for this stage of fabrication is pretty simple. A large worktable and good lighting is essential, as is a window, for ventilation purposes. Since this stage takes longer than armature making, you'll need access to the workspace for a good stretch of time.

You'll be mixing and pouring liquids and things *will* get messy, so make sure that you put down lots of paper before starting. It can help to break the workspace into two sections: a 'clean' work area, for things like sculpting and general preparation work, and a 'dirty' work area, for things like moulding and casting.

This stage of fabrication requires less specialized tools than armature making, but it does require quite a bit of specialized *materials*. It's a good idea to go through all the material and tool listings in this chapter before you start, so that you can create a master list for when you're purchasing.

Supplier information for both this chapter and the next is included at the end of Chapter 5.

Sculpting: An introduction

Since the final puppet is a three-dimensional object, sculpting skills are very important for this stage of things. You'll want to be fairly confident in sculpting before heading into this section. If you aren't, take some time, and practice. You can practice in plasticine or any kind of cheap, available clay. There are some great how-to books that you can reference (with some listed at the end of this book), and with a focused effort, you'll find your skills increasing very quickly. Time spent working on this skill is a great investment, and will help to ensure that your final Nia results look as great as possible.

Sculpting tools

There are some beautiful (and expensive) sculpting tools out there, but you don't have to drop a lot of money to get great results. The basics are a great way to start, and they're all you need to make great puppets.

Plastic tools

A basic set of plastic tools is a great addition to your tool kit. Their smooth finish makes them a pleasure to work with. They're inexpensive, so they can be easily replaced if they wear out or go missing. They are also very easy to clean – just wipe them down when you're done, and they'll last for ages. Most kits come with a good selection of tools.

Smooth wire-end tools

A few basic wire-end tools are quite useful, especially for sculpting out spaces for eyes and ears. Grab a few that are rounded (various sizes), and a few that are slightly stretched, and you should be good.

Rake wire-end tools

These rougher wire-end tools can be very useful for refining a sculpture once its details are established. A fine one and a slightly rougher one should serve you well.

Bladed tools

These include scalpels and utility knives. They're extremely useful for removing large amounts of material, and for making dramatic cuts. They can also be used to refine a sculpture, even after it's been hardened. A few sizes will prove useful. Make sure that you also have replacement blades.

Always have a good supply of round wooden toothpicks on hand. Their fine points are great for detailed work (on hair, for example). And since they're short, they're very maneuverable in small spaces (like puppet ears). You can even clean your teeth with them!

Super Sculpey

All of the sculpting for Nia will be done using Super Sculpey. It's a polymer clay, which is easy to sculpt,

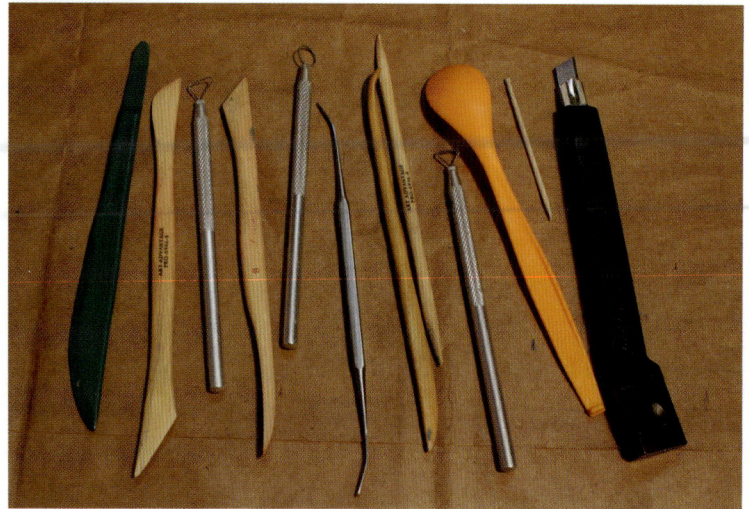

Figure 4.1
Basic sculpting tools.
They aren't fancy, but they get the job done. The tool on the far left is especially useful; it's the one I couldn't do without.

and which hardens when baked. Super Sculpey is particularly useful for our purposes, since it becomes *very* hard when baked (much harder than regular Sculpey). Because it's so hard, baked Super

Sculpey can be sanded to get a super smooth finish, which is great for puppet parts. It also stands up perfectly to the moulding process that you'll be using. You *could* sculpt in a clay that would remain soft (such as the clay made by Chavant), but a soft sculpt is prone to damage during moulding, and we want to reduce such risks as much as possible.

Sculpting the head

The following stages of fabrication were created in collaboration with **Brenda Baumgarten**. Over her career, Brenda has worked with many studios to create short films, television series and commercials. She was the Character Fabrication Supervisor for stop motion puppets used in the feature film *The Little Prince* (2015). Currently, Brenda is working in the puppet fabrication department at LAIKA. Visit her company's website at www.stopmotionsilicone.com

MATERIALS

final Nia design, printed to scale (Figure 2.5)
450 gram (1 pound) pack, Super Sculpey, (grey).
    This one package should be enough for all the
    body parts that you will be making.
3 mm (1/8 inch) armature wire
length of square brass stock (any gauge)

4 mm (5/32 inch) square stock, approx. 3 cm
    (1.18 inches) long
eyes × 2 – use the scale drawing of Nia to help
    you size the eyeball. You can use ball bearings,
    marbles, or beads. The colour doesn't matter,
    but they do need to be smooth.

TOOLS

small permanent marker
utility knife
wire snips
heat gun (or conventional oven)
sculpting tools
various fine sandpapers (220, 400, 600)

rotary tool
cutter bit for rotary tool
safety mask
safety glasses
work gloves

STEP BY STEP

1. Cut out a block of Super Sculpey that is the size of Nia's head. Use the scale drawing of Nia as your guide.
2. Lightly sketch the location of the facial features on to the block. Always use the Nia drawing

for reference. Push the eyeballs into the block. Be very careful in your placement. If they aren't well balanced, pull them out and try again.
3. Sculpt the head. Add and subtract material as needed, slowly refining as you go.

Work the head all over, being sure to turn it constantly as you check for overall balance. Reference the design drawing as you work.

Figure 4.2
Sculpting the head.
Rough in the basic shapes and features, before refining.

4. Once the head and face are well underway, add the hair. Locate the spot on the head where you want Nia's neck to be, and stick the length of brass stock into this spot. This forms a handle you can now use, so you don't damage the hair and ears.

5. Continue to refine. Hold the sculpture up to a mirror to check for symmetry and balance. Don't be afraid to get in there with a blade, and make some dramatic cuts (especially on the hair).

> Overly warm Sculpey droops and sags. If this starts to happen, carefully place the sculpture in the fridge for a few minutes, to harden it up again.

6. Once you're happy with the sculpture, it's time to bake the head. You can certainly do this in a conventional oven, but the following instructions assume that you have a heat gun, which allows for more controlled and detailed baking. Wearing a work glove, hold the head by the bottom of the brass stock handle, and use the heat gun to slowly bake the Sculpey. Turn the head regularly, so that the heat doesn't stay on any spot for too long – be careful you don't burn it! Keep at this for about 15 minutes. For our purposes, it's not critical that the sculpture is baked all the way through, since it's the *surface* that needs to be hardened for moulding. Allow the baked head to slowly (and fully) cool down. Avoid any sudden temperature changes, as this may crack the sculpture.

> Heat guns generate temperatures that can easily burn you, so treat them with respect. If you don't have a heat gun, you can use a conventional oven for baking all of Nia's Sculpey parts. The baking instructions are for baking thin pieces, so for Nia's parts (which are pretty thick), leave them in for approximately 30 minutes. After this time, they should be hard enough for our purposes.

7. Wear safety glasses for this stage. If needed, you can scrape the surface of the sculpture with the edge of a bladed tool, to further smooth it out (if this technique is new to you, test it out on a scrap piece of baked Sculpey till you get the hang of it). If there are any flaws remaining, you can still add small pieces of Sculpey to patch things. Once you've patched, use the heat gun again, this time baking just the patched area.

8. Wear safety glasses and safety mask for this stage. Perform a final finish, by carefully sanding the head. Start with the roughest paper (220), and work your way down to the smoothest (600). Work carefully (don't over sand), until you're happy with a final result.

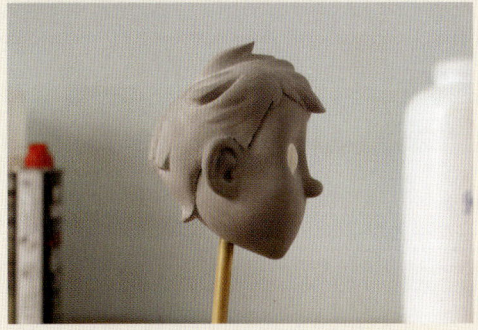

Figures 4.3 and 4.4
Final head sculpt, front and side view.
The final head sculpture should look nice from all angles.

9. Now, prepare the neck portion of the head for moulding. Roll out a Super Sculpey neck, using the scale drawing to determine thickness. Make the neck approx. 4 cm (1 ½ inches) long, and leave it unbaked. This may seem overly long, but this will make sense later once you're making a mould for the neck. Remove the brass stock handle from the head (it should just pop out), and position the Super Sculpey neck in the spot where you want Nia's neck to be. Trace around it with the marker, then set the neck aside for later in the process. Use the rotary tool to carefully cut out the hole in the head. Cut the hole to a depth of approx. 1.5 cm (1/2 inch). If you don't have a rotary tool, you can cut the hole using a utility knife. Work slowly, and don't cut out too much. Sand the edge of the cut to ensure a smooth finish.

10. Cut a piece of 3 mm (1/8 inch) armature wire, that's approx. 4 cm (1 ½ inches) in length. Push the wire into the hole, making sure it's nicely centered.

11. Slide the piece of 4 mm (5/32 inch) brass stock over this wire, and again ensure that it's nicely centered. You've now created a registration for the soon-to-be created mould.

Figure 4.5
Register for brass stock.
This register will ensure that casts of the head will have cleanly positioned brass stock embedded in them. If you're wondering what that means, don't worry. It will make sense soon enough.

WILL VINTON

If sculpting is your thing, the animated work of this legend will amaze you. For decades, Vinton's name was synonymous with clay animation. He formed a major studio around the medium (Will Vinton Studios), and his work was showcased in some of the biggest ad campaigns of the time. He created numerous television specials and series, with each frame of animation a sculpted work of art. Look for his feature *The Adventures of Mark Twain* – the detail and subtlety on display in this film is astounding.

Sculpting the neck

MATERIALS

Super Sculpey
3 mm (1/8 inch) armature wire

TOOLS

wire snips
heat gun (or conventional oven)
utility knife
various fine sandpapers (220, 400, 600)

STEP BY STEP

1. Take the Super Sculpey neck that you created earlier, and cut a length of 3 mm (1/8 inch) armature wire that is a bit longer than the neck. Slide the wire through the neck, and ensure that a bit of wire hangs out at each end.
2. Bake the neck, sand it to a smooth finish, and set it somewhere safe. We'll return to it during the moulding process.

Sculpting the hands and arms

As with the other body parts that you made in the previous chapter (the neck, spine, and legs), the hands and arms will *eventually* be animatable. But unlike the other parts, the hands and arms first need to be sculpted. We'll concern ourselves with fabricating the wire armatures for the hands and arms during the casting stage, which happens later.

MATERIALS

Super Sculpey
1.6 mm (1/16 inch) armature wire
10 small pins (for fingers)

TOOLS

final Nia design, printed to scale (Figure 2.5)
scale armature drawing of Nia
utility knife
wire snips
heat gun (or conventional oven)
sculpting tools
various fine sandpapers (220, 400, 600)
safety mask
safety glasses
work gloves

STEP BY STEP

1. Using the final Nia design image for reference, make a length of braided 1.6 mm (1/16 inch) armature wire, being sure to leave a loop for the palm area of the hand.

Figure 4.6
Wire arm for sculpting.
If you leave the end of the wire long enough, it can serve as a nice handle while you're sculpting.

2. Carefully apply Super Sculpey to get a basic shape for Nia's right arm. Stick in the small pins for the thumb and fingers. Check the scale armature drawing to ensure that the fingers and thumb are positioned correctly. Also check against the final Nia design drawing.
3. Apply Super Sculpey to the finger and thumb pins, and continue sculpting the hand and arm.

Constantly check your sculpture against the scale drawing, as well as the final Nia design image. Sculpt the full length of the arm, even though Nia's sleeves will cover the top portion. Better to have too much of the finished arm, as opposed to not enough; you don't want bare wire showing through under Nia's shirt sleeve.

4. When you're done sculpting, bake the arm and finish in exactly the same way as you did with the head.
5. Repeat for the left arm.

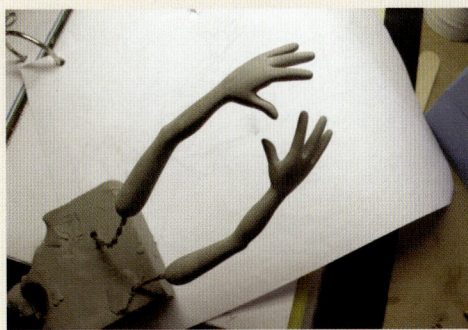

Figure 4.7
The finished arm sculpts.
Notice that they include a bend for the elbow. This will help during animation, as a visual reminder as to where the joint should be. You can include a bend like this, or sculpt your arms straight.

Sculpting the feet

We only need to sculpt one foot for Nia, since we're only creating one mould. This one mould can then be used to cast both of Nia's feet (left and right).

MATERIALS

Super Sculpey
4.76 mm (6/32 inch) bolt, approx. approx. 4 cm (1 ½ inches) long, × 1 (this is the same thread size as the set screws used in the armature)

4 mm (5/32 inch) round brass stock, approx. 2 cm long (3/4 inch) × 1

TOOLS

utility knife
heat gun (or conventional oven)
4.76 mm (6/32 inch) allen key (also known as a hex key)

multi-bit screwdriver (or one screwdriver, that matches the bolt)
various sculpting tools
various fine sandpapers (220, 400, 600)

STEP BY STEP

1. Remove the set screw from the foot block. Be sure to store it safely for later.
2. Insert the piece of round brass stock into the body part hole in the foot armature. Thread the bolt into the set screw hole and tighten it with the screwdriver, until it grips on to the brass stock.

Figure 4.8
Foot armature with brass stock and bolt.
This arrangement of brass stock and bolt will become vital when creating the shoe mould later.

3. Sculpt the shoe by applying Super Sculpey directly on to the foot block. Sculpt right up to the brass stock and screw. Make sure that the bottom of the shoe is completely flat, or else Nia will have trouble standing.

> The magnet in the foot block will attract your metal sculpting tools. You may want to use plastic or wood tools for this sculpt!

4. Bake the foot and finish it, using the same method as for the head and arms.

Figure 4.9
The finished foot sculpt.
The foot's ready for moulding. Make sure that you leave the brass and bolt embedded for now.

Moulding and casting: An introduction

It's time to move into the exciting stage of moulding and casting for your Nia puppet. It's the stage in which Nia really *becomes* Nia. You may have some experience with this stage of fabrication, or be completely new to it all. Regardless, it only makes sense to get a few things straight, before really diving in.

What is moulding? It's the process by which you create a shell around an object. In our case, the object will be various sculpted puppet parts. The inner surface of this shell will be an exact copy of the original part's surface and shape.

What is casting? Casting is the process by which you create a copy (or cast) of the original object. To create that copy, you need a mould in which to create it. You pour a casting material (just what that casting material is will vary) into the mould, let it cure (harden), then extract the cast from the mould. Need another cast? Simply repeat the casting process as often as required.

Why use these intensive processes? Why not just create one of everything, and save yourself a lot of labour? There're a couple of reasons. If there's one – and only one – of a puppet part, what do you do if something becomes damaged or breaks? Being able to create replacement parts that are exact replicas of the damaged part means that project can continue. Being able to create exact replica parts also allows for multiple puppets of the same character. This is essential for television and feature work, since the same character is often being animated in various scenes, by various animators, all at the same time.

Using this method of moulding and casting is also extremely useful if you need to make parts for 'replacement' style animation, such as mouth pieces.

Silicone rubber

This is the main material that you'll be using during this stage of fabrication. It's a flexible and tough rubber that comes in two parts that you mix together. Once it's mixed, it sets into its final form.

We'll be using only platinum silicones, for both moulding and casting. Platinum silicone is a kind of silicone that is easy to find at various suppliers, and can typically be mixed 50–50 by volume. This means that you'll be pouring the silicone into measuring cups, which is a pretty simple method (measuring other types of silicone can be more complex). This kind of silicone also resists heat well, which is useful for when the time comes for casting, since resin gives off heat as it cures. Platinum silicone is a bit more expensive than other kinds of silicone, but you'll be using such a relatively small amount of silicone for Nia's moulds that the difference in cost will be minimal.

Silicone is a fantastic material for creating moulds, since just about any material you pour into a silicone mould can be removed (or 'demoulded') once it's fully cured. That's because hardly anything sticks to silicone, and that's a great attribute in a moulding material. If you need parts that are flexible, silicone is also great for casting, and that's what we'll be using for Nia's neck and arms (it also takes paint tints very well, allowing for any kind of skin tone).

Nia's other parts – the hard parts (her head, her mouths, and her feet) will be cast in resin plastic (see below).

THE BOXTROLLS, LAIKA STUDIOS, 2014

The remarkable creative potential for silicone in stop motion is on full display in this feature film. With so many distinctly different characters, no other material but silicone could be tailored this way, while remaining flexible enough and strong enough for the stresses of animation.

There are a few important points to remember about the platinum silicone that you'll be using. (1) It doesn't like latex, so avoid wearing safety gloves made from this. Only use nitrile or vinyl gloves. (2) It can become easily contaminated. If that happens, it won't behave in the way you want it to. Contaminants can include things like household soaps, so be careful with containers and stir sticks.

Resin plastic

Like silicone, resin plastic, or 'resin' as it's often simply called, is an affordable, two-part liquid material that is mixed by volume, 50–50. Unlike silicone, resin cures into a super hard material. It turns into, well … plastic! Yet resin can still be drilled, tapped, sanded, and painted, so it's an overall great material for many of Nia's parts.

Smooth-On

The specialized materials used in this chapter are all made by Smooth-On, a major manufacturer of moulding and casting materials. As such, you'll see very specific Smooth-On product names in the Materials lists. Check the Smooth-On website for availability in your area. If their products aren't available where you are, don't worry. Other manufacturers make very similar products, and they can help you to find equivalent products that will perform in the same way.

Material costs

Silicones and resins are specialty materials, made for professional work, so you need to expect to spend a bit of money to acquire them. The good thing is that you're using a relatively small amount of materials, since Nia's not that big. As a rough estimate, you can expect to spend in the range of $200 CDN for the silicone and resin. It's a significant cost, but rest assured that the process you'll be following has been designed so as to minimize costs and maximize the use of materials.

> The methods you'll be using during moulding and casting for Nia are the same methods used in many other disciplines. These include jewelry-making, toy-making, and special effects work for motion pictures.

Working safe

All of the silicone and resin that you'll be using is quite safe, but it's still essential that you read and follow the MSDS (Material Safety Data Sheet) for these products. This sheet comes with the material, and you can also look it up online. The sheet details all health considerations involved with the product, and advises you on how to handle any accidents that you might encounter.

Silicone is quite safe to use. There's almost no smell, it cleans up easily, and if you get it on your skin, you can just wipe it off.

Resin is also very safe, but requires a bit more care. It gives off fumes, so have a fan going or a window or door open, to ensure fresh air. As it cures, it gets quite warm (even hot), so be mindful of this. If curing resin lands on a surface it can be nearly impossible to remove. For the same reason, don't get it on your skin. Always wear vinyl or nitrate gloves when mixing and pouring, and get in the habit of wearing safety glasses as well.

Moulding the head in silicone

Like most of the moulds you'll be making, Nia's head mould is a two-part mould. That means that (you guessed it) the final mould exists as *two* pieces, which fit together, prior to the casting stage.

The head will be moulded in Mold Star 30. This is a low-viscosity (runny) silicone, so bubbles will easily rise to the surface and harmlessly pop, which is a good thing for a mould, since bubbles in your mould means flaws in your cast. It's also very strong, and should last ages, so you can create lots of casts from it if needed. This is also the silicone you will be using for Nia's mouth shapes and feet. Plan your moulds carefully, don't build the mould walls too high (more on this below), and you may only have to buy one kit of this particular silicone.

> The more you learn about silicone and resin, the better you'll be at moulding and casting. Smooth-On products have very detailed product descriptions, and are written in a very accessible style, so check them out.

MATERIALS

Mold Star 30 Silicone, 473 mL (1 pint) kit (also used for Nia's mouth and feet moulds)

oil-based, sulfur free clay (This will be used for making mould walls. You can reuse it with each new mould you make, provided it's free of debris and contaminants)

silicone mould release

foam core or thin wood, for mould base

more foam core (for mould walls)

6 medium sized marbles

TOOLS

lighter fluid

small cheap paint brushes

glue gun

utility knife

large kitchen knife

pencil

ruler

cotton swabs

permanent marker

medium sized plastic mixing buckets with measurements (buy a good supply of these, you'll be doing a lot of mixing. Make sure they're smooth inside, to allow the silicone to be mixed fully)

strong wooden stir sticks (tongue depressors work well)

vinyl or nitrile gloves

safety glasses

safety mask

STEP BY STEP

1. You'll make part 1 of the mould first. Ensure that the registration brass stock is properly centered in the neck hole. Use the pencil to carefully work out a path for the mould line. This is where part 1 of the mould will meet part 2. It's critical that the line passes to the rear of the neck hole. Also, keep the line close to the back of the ear. Once you are confident in the mould line, trace over the pencil with the marker.

2. Lay the head on the large piece of foam core or thin wood, face up, in the center of the piece. Wedge a few chunks of clay under it to support it. Try to slightly tilt the head so that its chin is slightly up. This will help displace any air bubbles that might get trapped during moulding.

3. Sculpt in more clay around the head, carefully following the mould line that you drew on to the head. Ensure there's a nice amount of clay all around the head. Build the clay out so that it extends just a bit further than the registration brass stock. As you work, ensure that the clay meets the sculpture at a 90-degree angle all around. Once you've sculpted the clay all around, cut the edges of the clay squarely and cleanly on all sides. When you're nearly done,

Figures 4.10 and 4.11
The head with mould line, bottom and top views.
Keep the mould line close to the back of the ear. If there is any distortion in the mould, this is an easy area to clean up, and isn't seen by the camera as much as other areas.

use a small amount of lighter fluid on a brush to totally smooth out where the clay meets the sculpture. This will give you a very clean mould line.

4. Use the marbles to create 'keys' for the mould, by pressing them into the clay. Push them in not quite half way. These keyed areas will help to lock the mould together during casting, ensuring that the liquid resin stays in the mould.

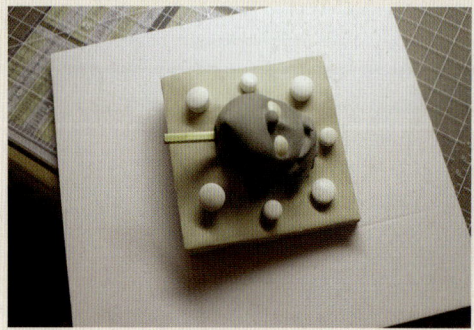

Figure 4.12
The head with clay and keys. Place the marbles close to the head, but be sure to leave a small gap. We used oblong plastic pieces for the keys, but your marbles will work great.

5. Measure for the mould walls. Measure from the bottom of the clay, up to the highest point on the sculpture, then add on at least 3 cm (1 inch). This ensures that your mould walls will be high enough. Don't make the walls too high, or you'll use up all your silicone!

Figure 4.13
Measuring for the mould walls.
It will be easier to measure and construct the mould walls if you've taken care to cut the sides of the clay base square and straight.

6. Cut the four walls out of foam core, and hot glue them into place around the clay base.

Make sure the walls are snug against the sides of the clay. Your silicone will run out through any gaps in your seal, so make sure that you glue the walls carefully. There should be just a small gap between the mould wall and the end of the registration brass stock. Use a bit of clay to fill in that gap.

7. It's time to calculate how much silicone you'll need for part 1 of the mould (don't worry, the math is simple). Measure the length, width, and height of what will be part 1 of the mould. Measure from the top of the clay up to the top of the mould wall. Make sure that your measurements are all in the same units (cm or inches). Multiply those measurements to determine the total volume of silicone you will need for the mould. Add a little bit to this volume (just to be safe.) *Half* of this final amount is how much Part A silicone you need, and it's also how much Part B you need (since the two parts get mixed 50–50).

Figure 4.14
Measuring for total volume of silicone for part 1 of the mould. Take note of how much total silicone you used for part 1 of the mould, because you'll use roughly the same amount for part 2.

8. There's no serious time pressure for these next steps, as the silicone takes several hours to set. Follow the product's info sheet carefully, as it will tell you exactly the best way to mix. Once Part A and B are fully mixed together, pour the mix into the mould, starting in one corner. Try to keep the pouring bucket raised as high over the mould as possible. This will create a long stream of silicone, which will allow any bubbles to pop before they enter the mould. Completely fill the mould with silicone.

Figure 4.15
Pouring the mixed silicone for part 1 of the mould.
Watch the mould for a while to make sure there are no leaks.
If there is a leak, use a bit of clay to plug the hole from the
outside.

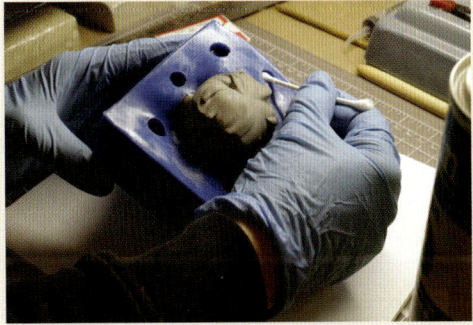

Figure 4.16
Coating part 1 with mould release.
Use a cotton swab to ensure that all of the surfaces of part 1
have been coated. Getting mould release on the sculpture is
fine. Don't forget to also coat the key holes.

Once the silicone is poured, gently tap the
mould base for a few moments, to help free
up any trapped air bubbles. Take note of the
time at which you poured the silicone. You can
refer to this when consulting the demould time
on the product's info sheet (it needs several
hours, at least). Once that time has passed,
it's safe to handle the mould.

> If you should run out in the middle of a
> pour, don't panic. Let it set, mix up some
> more silicone, and finish your pouring.
> You can do the same thing with resin.

9. Once the silicone is cured, pull the walls off, and
   flip the mould over. Carefully cut off any flaps of
   silicone (known as 'flashing'). Remove the clay.
   Clean out any little bits of debris that remain.
   Pull out the marble plugs. The holes created by
   the marbles that you now have in part 1 of the
   mould will get filled with silicone when you pour
   part 2, resulting in a silicone 'lock' that will help
   hold the mould halves together during casting.
   With this step completed, you now have part 1
   of your head mould.
10. To create part 2 of the mould, you'll be
    pouring silicone directly on to part 1. Although
    almost nothing sticks to silicone (making
    it great for mould making), *it sticks to itself
    extremely well*. For that reason, you need to
    create a chemical layer on part 1 first, so that
    the parts will separate. Spray all the surfaces
    of part 1 of the mould (that will come in
    contact with the poured silicone) with mould
    release. Follow the instructions for the mould
    release carefully.

11. Create foam core walls around part 1 of the
    mould. As with part 1's walls, make sure that
    these walls are at least 3 cm (1 inch) higher
    than the highest point on the sculpture. Make
    sure the walls are snug against part 1, and
    that the hot glue seal on the walls is tight.
12. Measure for the volume of silicone in the same
    way as with part 1. Before mixing, check the
    amount of silicone that you have left in your
    pint kit. It should be enough, but if it's not,
    you'll need another kit.
13. Mix the silicone. Pour it. Check for leaks. Let it
    cure. Break off the walls.
14. Carefully prise the two parts of the mould
    apart and remove the head sculpture. If there's
    any tiny bit of clay or debris in the mould, use
    a dull scraping tool to get it out. Be careful to
    not cut or damage the mould.
15. Pop out and discard the piece of armature
    wire from the neck area of the head. Ensure
    that the piece of registration brass stock is
    squarely seated in the mould, with a few mm
    (3/8 inch) sticking out into the mould area. The
    mould is now ready for casting.

Figure 4.17
The completed head mould.
Parts 1 and 2 of the head mould, ready for casting. Notice the
brass stock register that's seated in the mould.

Casting the head in resin

Time to make Nia's head! As you'll recall, keeping things lightweight is vital for a stop motion puppet, so to get the lightest head possible we're going to use a process called 'slush casting' (also known as 'rotocasting'). This involves pouring a small amount of liquid resin into the mould, and then rolling and rotating the mould as the plastic cures. This forces the plastic to the outside of the mould, resulting in a hollow head.

All of Nia's resin parts (her head, her mouth pieces, and her feet) will be made from Smooth Cast 300. This resin is quite strong, and its final cure colour is white, so it can be painted easily. As it cures, the resin will start to get very warm, turn very cloudy, and finally harden,

over the course of a few minutes. The actual cure time for the resin will depend on a variety of factors (consult the product's info sheet). No matter what, once you've mixed, you need to act fast, because once the resin begins to set, it happens *fast*, and at that point you're out of working time.

It's worth using a little bit of resin as a test, to get a sense for how it behaves and how fast it sets, before trying to cast a part 'for real'. You'll have plenty of resin in the kit that you bought for all of Nia's parts, so using a bit for a test is a good use of your resources.

MATERIALS

final Nia design, printed to scale (Figure 2.5)
Smooth Cast 300, 473 mL (1 pint) kit (this is
    enough for all of Nia's resin parts)

teflon tape
5 mm (3/16 inch) brass stock
talcum power

TOOLS

pencil
ruler
rotary tool (or coping saw)
cutting disks for rotary tool
small plastic measuring cups for mixing resin (get
    lots)

small wooden stir sticks
small package of uncooked rice (optional)
vinyl or nitrile gloves
safety glasses
safety mask

STEP BY STEP

1. Cut a piece of 5 mm (3/16 inch) brass stock that is just a bit shorter than the height of the head. Use the head mould itself to determine the length, measuring from the top of the silicone registration point in the neck, up to the top of the head. Next, ensure that the

small piece of registration stock is sticking out from the registration point. Slide the piece of longer stock over the smaller stock and under the silicone of the registration point. Once in place, the longer piece should sit in this space quite snugly.

Figure 4.18
Sliding the head stock over the registration stock.
The exposed end of the brass stock should sit very close to the top of the mould.

2. To prevent the resin from flowing into the brass stock, cap the end of the stock with a small piece of teflon tape. Since teflon resists heat, it won't melt during the resin's curing process. After taping, reposition the brass stock, if needed.

3. Apply baby powder to both sides of the mould. A light layer is all that you need. Make sure that it gets into all parts of the mould. The powder attracts the resin, which helps to ensure that the resin finds all parts of the mould.

4. Time to mix the resin. The volume of mixed resin that you need is enough to fill up approx. three-quarters of part 1 of the mould. Remember, you don't need both sides filled with resin because you are 'slushing' the resin to the outer edge, to get a hollow head. You can estimate this total volume roughly, since it's a very small amount of resin (use Figure 4.19 as a guide), or you can use the 'rice measurement' method (see the Professor Roy box).

Pour uncooked rice into the mould, until it reaches the approximate volume of what you intend for the resin. Then pour the rice out into a measuring cup (being sure that you get every last grain of rice out, you don't want any in your cast). That volume of rice is a good estimate of the *total* volume of resin that you'll need.

5. Once you know the total volume needed (it won't be much), use that to figure out how much of Part A and Part B of the resin you need. To do this, as with the silicone, just cut the total volume in half, and that's how much of each part you need. Before you mix, remember – once the parts are mixed, the chemical reaction is under way, and you don't have that long before the resin will start to set. Consult the product's info sheet first for specific instructions, and plan this stage carefully in advance, so that you don't waste precious time. And remember to have ventilation for this, as the resin's fumes aren't good for you.

6. Once Part A and Part B of the resin is fully mixed (the mix should go from a bit cloudy once the two parts are combined, to quite clear once you stir them fully), pour the mixture into part 1 of the mould. Snap part 2 into place, and start rolling the mould all around, turning it over and over, in all directions. Do it at a medium-fast speed. You want the resin to flow into every part of the mould's surface.

Figure 4.19
Assembling head mould for slush casting.
The blur in this image gives you a good sense of just how quickly you need to work at this stage of things! Note the relatively small volume of resin being used. Remember, you're making a *hollow* head, not a solid one.

7. As you roll the mould, check the remains of the resin in the mixing cup. Once the remains have set, you know that the resin

inside your mould has also set, and at that point you can stop slushing. Set the assembled mould 'hole down' on your worktable, and leave it undisturbed. Remember to consult the product's info sheet for final cure time information.

> It never hurts to let the resin cure longer than the info sheet states. Freshly cured resin is still very flexible, and it can distort as you demould it. If it's cool to the touch, it's safe to demould.

8. Once the resin is fully cured, use a pair of pliers to grab the small piece of registration brass stock from the hole, and slide it out. Retain it, in case you want to cast more heads. Now carefully crack open the mould parts, and remove the resin head. There you have it: Nia's head, cast in plastic, with a built-in brass stock that will slide over the neck armature. Nicely done!

9. Hold the head up to the light. If it seems too thin in any spot, or if any part simply didn't get formed in the cast, you'll need to recast, using a bit more resin this time. You may be able to pry the brass stock out of the old head to reuse it, but if not, you'll need to cut a new length. Fortunately, recasting doesn't use up a lot of product, and resin cures very quickly, so with just a few tries, you should be able to get near-perfect results. If any very tiny part of the head didn't form properly, or if there are small bubbles or flaws, don't worry. Fixing resin is pretty easy. It's detailed in the next section.

10. Finally, slide the head on to the neck armature that you made in Chapter 2. Checking against your scale drawings of Nia, her head should rest at a height that looks natural, bearing in mind that her neck is still just bare wire. If the head is sitting too high or too low, you will need to adjust the neck armature. If the head is too high, one way to do this is by cutting down the neck's brass stock a tiny bit. If adjusting doesn't work, you'll need to create a new neck armature, using the length of the head's brass stock as a guide.

Figures 4.20 and 4.21
The cast head – front and bottom views.
Notice how the brass stock is nicely seated in the bottom of the head. The slightly smaller stock on the neck will slide into this, creating a nice fit.

Patching and sanding the head

Although Nia's head probably came out of the mould looking pretty great, it might have a few flaws that need touching up. For all of this stage, work very carefully and slowly. Don't be aggressive in how you approach this stage – these are the finishing touches before you paint, so if you damage the head, you might have to recast.

You can use these exact same techniques on Nia's other resin pieces (mouth pieces and feet).

MATERIALS

modeling putty (make sure the brand is strong, and safe to paint. Apoxie Sculpt is a good brand)

TOOLS

various fine sandpapers (220, 400, 600)
utility knife
rag or paper towels
safety glasses
safety mask

STEP BY STEP

1. If there are any tiny holes in the resin, you can easily patch them with a very small amount of modeling putty. Press a very tiny amount of the mixed putty into the holes, and smear the excess putty off. Ideally, there should be no putty left on the surface, only in the filled holes. You'll sand any excess putty down, but the less you have to sand, the better. If there are any larger holes or gaps in the cast, you can use the putty to actually sculpt in the missing piece. This only works for very small flaws (if there's a large flaw, better to completely recast the head).
2. Once the putty is dry, sand any excess down. Be very careful you don't over-sand. The resin sands down very fast, and if you aren't careful, you'll do serious damage before you know it. Even if there is no putty to remove, you can use sandpaper (or the utility knife) to remove any tiny flaws on the head. Once all your patching and sanding is done, make sure that the head is wiped down to remove any dust before moving on.

You can also use modeling putty at this point to add on specific facial details that weren't in the original sculpt. For example, if you were making a 'Devil Nia', you could sculpt putty horns on to her forehead, let them dry, and paint them as you would a non-modified resin head. Endless creative variations!

Painting the head

As awesome as resin is for making puppet parts, it's not the easiest material in the world to paint. In part, this is because the resin's surface is so smooth that paint has nothing to grip on to, so if you just slapped a coat of acrylic paint on Nia's head right now, it would scrape or peel off as soon as you started animating her.

That's why the priming stage of painting is so essential. The primer paint is specially designed to grip to the resin surface. After the resin is primed, regular acrylic paint will adhere quite nicely. Do your research carefully for plastic primer paint (not all brands work well), and do a test on a scrap piece of resin to ensure that it adheres very well, before using it on actual puppet parts.

Rather than painting Nia's head at this point, you may prefer to wait until after you've cast her arms in silicone. By waiting till then, it gives you more freedom when mixing the colour of her skin in silicone (see 'Casting the hands and arms in silicone'), since you won't have to mix silicone colours to match a pre-existing painted head. Make sure you're only using matte (flat) finish paints for Nia's head. If you use glossy paint, the studio lights will create an unflattering shine on her during animation.

The exception is her eyes and her lips, which you can seal with a paint-on glossy finish if you like.

You can use these same painting techniques on Nia's other resin pieces (mouth pieces and feet).

MATERIALS

final colour design for Nia

can of plastic primer spray paint, white or black (look for Citadel brand). White is easier to paint over, but black stands out better on the resin, so you'll know where you've applied it. It's up to you.

assorted acrylic paints, non-glossy

matte (flat) finish (spray or paint on)

glossy acrylic finish, paint on (optional)

TOOLS

4 mm (5/32 inch) brass stock (use this as a handle, to hold the head while you paint. If you don't have a length of brass that you can use for this, fashion some kind of handle that you can slide into the neck hole)

assorted paint brushes, various sizes and styles (if you're handy with an airbrush, you can use that instead)

hair dryer (optional)

water container

mixing surface (plastic container lids work great)

rags or paper towels

vinyl or nitrile gloves

safety mask

STEP BY STEP

1. Wear gloves for this stage, and a safety mask. Slide the head on to the brass stock handle, and then spray the head with primer. Do this somewhere that is well-ventilated, and out of the wind. Consider spraying into a large cardboard box, so that the excess spray is contained. Follow the instructions on the paint can carefully, and avoid extreme temperatures (hot or cold), to ensure best results. Let the primer dry fully. The dried primer should resist scratching quite well (do a scratch test on a scrap piece of resin).

> Priming is a vitally important stage of painting. If you use too much, it will run and streak. Use extremely light passes of spray, turning the head as you work. Use only enough to just cover the resin's surface. If you've never done this before, practice on scrap pieces of resin first.

2. Mix your skin paint, keeping it fairly thin. If you've already cast Nia's arms in silicone, match the paint to that skin colour. Once you have the paint mixed, do a test on a hidden part of her head, or on a scrap primed piece. Use the hair dryer if you want to speed the drying process. Do another scratch test to ensure the layers of paint are adhering. Reference the dried colour with your final colour design, and move the paint test into different kinds of light (bright light, dim light) to see how it looks. Adjust the paint colour if needed.

3. Paint the skin area of the head, using several thin coats. If you go into the hair area don't worry, as you'll soon be covering it with dark paint anyway. Be careful around her eyeballs – you'll paint these in a later step.

4. Mix the colour for Nia's hair, and follow the same process that you used for her skin. Rather than making her hair full black,

consider using very dark blue or dark brown, since pure black for puppet hair tends to hide the sculpted details. Also, consider painting in some details of hair, just to break up the dark colour a bit. Finish her hair with a creative bit of tinting if you like, just to keep things stylish and fun!

5. If you want, add a very small amount of pink colour to her cheeks and nose, to add some life. Blend it in nicely with her surrounding skin.

6. Mix some thin white paint, and paint Nia's eyeballs. Use *very* thin coats, since you don't want any brush strokes here. After the paint is dry you can add a thin layer of glossy sealant if you want shiny eyes.

7. Make sure you're completely happy with your paint job, and then spray matte (flat) finish on to the head. If you used gloss on the eyes, cover the eyes with a layer of clay before spraying. Use a very thin coat of finish. This seals the paint in, and helps prevent paint

damage during animation. After spraying, remove the clay on Nia's eyes very carefully, so that you don't damage the paint job on the eyes. There she is, Nia's completely finished head!

Figure 4.22
Final painted head.
Keep a small container of Nia's skin paint handy, in case any touch-ups are needed during animation.

Sculpting the master mouth

Since the mouth area on Nia's head is one solid surface, the mouth shapes that you'll create will be stand-alone sculpted shapes that adhere very easily with a bit of wax or sticky tack. They'll swap out smoothly during animation, and will provide very nice results for lip sync animation and general facial animation.

Imagine an animal puppet with a muzzle, beak, or jaws. How would those mouth shapes be sculpted, moulded, cast, and animated? Imagine replacement eye areas, or even whole faces. With the moulding and casting methods you're learning, you'll be able to try out all kinds of variations, as your experience increases!

MATERIALS

Smooth Cast 300 (just a small amount)
modeling putty

TOOLS

Nia's head mould
paper, pencil, eraser
utility knife
heat gun (optional)
sculpting tools

various fine sandpapers (220, 400, 600)
safety mask
safety glasses
vinyl or nitrile gloves

STEP BY STEP

1. Determine the specific mouth shapes that you want for Nia. Search for animation mouth shapes in books and online – they're all over the place. Whatever style and shapes you go with, make sure they can be sculpted, and that they are effective for animation (for both lip sync and acting). When in doubt, use Figure 4.26 as a guide for your designs and shapes.
2. Sketch the mouth shapes on paper, and keep them handy for reference while sculpting.
3. Using Nia's head mould (and your resin casting know-how), cast just the face and mouth portion of Nia's head. This small portion of Nia's face is needed because we want the contour of her face to match the contour of the mouth shapes. This way, the mouth shapes will sit nicely on Nia's face.
4. Using modeling putty, sculpt the 'most open' mouth shape on to Nia's face. This mouth shape should include teeth, but don't over-sculpt them (see Figure 4.26 for reference). This will be the 'master mouth' shape. Once you've finished sculpting, allow the putty to harden fully.

Figure 4.23
Sculpting the master mouth shape.
Sculpting at such a small scale presents its own challenges. As small as Nia is overall, these mouths will be even smaller! Take your time, and be patient.

There are other ways to create mouths that don't involve moulding and casting. On set you can use clay mouths or paper cutout mouths. Or you could animate entire scenes with no mouth on Nia, then create mouth shapes in Photoshop and apply them digitally in post-production.

Moulding the master mouth shape in silicone

From this sculpted master mouth, we'll create a mould of the mouth shape and the resin Nia face. We'll then use this mould to cast all the other mouth shapes (each of which will be a modification of the cast from the master mouth mould). By always starting with a cast from the master mouth mould, we'll have a generally consistent mouth that will allow for smoother mouth shape transitions during animation.

MATERIALS

Mold Star 30 Silicone, 473 mL (1 Pint Kit) (also used for Nia's head and feet moulds)
sulfur free clay
silicone mould release
foam core or thin wood, for mould base
more foam core (for mould walls)
2 medium-sized marbles

TOOLS

[see the Tools section for 'Moulding the head in silicone'] lighter fluid
small cheap paint brushes
glue gun
utility knife
large kitchen knife
pencil
ruler

cotton swabs
medium sized plastic mixing buckets with measurements
strong wooden stir sticks
vinyl or nitrile gloves
Safety glasses
Safety mask

STEP BY STEP

1. Create a two-part mould of the master mouth and resin face, using the same methods that you used for Nia's head mould (there's no

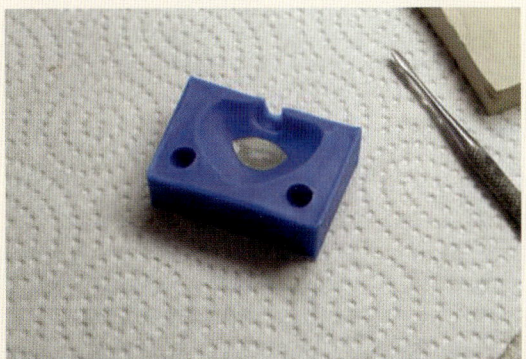

Figure 4.24
Part 1 of the master mouth mould.
Notice how the master mouth shape is nicely seated in the mould, and has a smooth surface. This is important, because it ensures that all the mouth shapes will conform neatly to the surface of Nia's face.

need to mark a mould line with marker for this mould). For part 1, build the clay up to just below the face. Use the two marbles to create keys.

2. After part 1 of the mould has set, break off the walls, turn the mould over, and carefully remove just the resin face piece. The Super Sculpey mouth should still be in the mould. Leave it there (or place it back into the mould, if it's still attached to the resin face). Make sure that the mouth piece is nicely seated in the mould, and that the surface of the mouth piece is smooth and consistent (you may need to patch it with a bit of clay).

3. Create part 2 of the mould, using the same process that you followed for part 2 of Nia's head mould. Remember to use mould release, or your two mould parts will stick together, and you'll have to re-do most of these steps! Not fun.

Casting the mouth shapes in resin

MATERIALS

designs of the required Nia mouth shapes
Smooth Cast 300 (you will use a very small amount)
modeling putty

TOOLS

small plastic measuring cups for mixing resin
small wooden stir sticks
vinyl or nitrile gloves
various fine sandpapers (220, 400, 600)

utility knife (fitted with a very small blade)
safety glasses
safety mask

STEP BY STEP

1. Mix a very small amount of resin and pour into the 'lip' side of the mouth mould. Overfill the mould very slightly with the resin, and then apply the other part of the mould. Once the resin has set, pop the moulds apart. You now have a master mouth shape cast.

Figure 4.25
Cast of master mouth shape.
Most of the mouth shapes that you'll create for Nia will start out as this cast master mouth shape. Notice the resin flashing that needs removing.

2. Create the first required mouth shape. Depending on the shape you need, you may need to cut off or sand down whole parts of the master mouth cast, and then build back up with putty. Use your mouth shape drawings as a guide. Try to leave the upper lip intact as much as possible, so that it remains consistent from mouth to mouth. Of course, if you have to modify the upper lip to get the desired mouth shape, so be it (an 'oo'-shaped mouth being an example). Once the putty has fully set, use the utility knife and sandpaper to finish off the mouth shape fully.

3. Repeat the above process for each mouth shape that you need. That is: create a cast of the master mouth shape, then modify that cast to create the required shape.

4. If you have access to animation equipment, shooting a quick test with the mouth shapes at this point can be very useful. Use a very short bit of dialogue (a word or two is enough), and animate the shapes to that dialogue. You can place the shapes on to the resin face piece that you used earlier, adhering them with a bit of sticky tack. If your shapes don't animate smoothly, or if you discover that you need an extra shape (or two), now is the time to deal with that. If you need further insights into animating with dialogue, you can refer to the chapter dedicated to the topic.

Painting the mouth shapes

Paint the mouth shapes following the same process that you followed for Nia's head. Avoid painting individual teeth, as the vertical lines are hard to keep consistent from mouth to mouth, and the variations will be distracting during animation. Check out how the teeth are painted in Figure 4.26, as reference.

If you want glossy lips for Nia, you can add a glossy finish to them. Otherwise, finish the mouths with a matte finish as a way to seal the paint and to protect against damage during animation.

Create labels to go along with the mouth shapes ('ah', 'oo', etc.), and store the mouth shapes safely in a way that allows you to see the specific shapes quickly and pick them up easily. Once you're animating, you won't want to be slowed down by trying to find the right tiny little Nia mouth shape!

Figure 4.26
Basic mouth shape kit.
This basic set will serve you nicely for lip sync and acting. If you want to create even more shape variations, go for it. Having options during animation is a great thing. Notice how the pieces are raised up in the box – this makes it easier to lift them out during animation.

Pupils, eyelids, and eyebrows

Along with the mouth, these features are the main means by which Nia communicates during animation, at least from the neck up. In some ways, the pupils, eyelids, and eyebrows are even more important than the mouth for performance, since they're all located around the area of the eye. As powerful as these features are to the animated performance, they are all quite simple to fabricate.

Pupils

Wait to make these until you are tinting the silicone for Nia's arm. Mix a small amount of black silicone, and then dip the end of a paint brush into the silicone and carefully dab the silicone on to a piece of plastic that has been coated with petroleum jelly. Make lots of pupils in one size – they're so tiny that they easily go missing during animation, so you'll want lots of extras. You can also make more pupils of varying sizes (they're fast, cheap, and easy to make). It can be fun to play with pupil sizes during animation, to get different effects. Once the silicone has cured, you can peel the pupils off and use them on Nia's eyeballs. Coat her eyeballs with a tiny bit of petroleum jelly as well, and then use a toothpick to move the pupils during animation. Another method for creating pupils is to mix some black clay with soft wax (see below). If you use this method, make sure the finished pupils are very thin, otherwise they can look a bit silly. As you animate, be careful that the clay doesn't cause ugly smears all over the eyeballs. If they do, carefully clean the eyes with a cotton swab and a touch of soapy water. Swab very gently, so that you don't scratch the paint finish.

Eyelids and eyebrows

The easiest (and in some ways best) way to create eyelids and eyebrows for Nia is to mix coloured clay with soft wax. Use more wax than clay. The wax/clay mix stays firm during animation, and won't smear on to Nia's head as much as pure clay would. Even with wax mixed in, you'll still need to keep the face area tidy as you animate – clean the area in the same way that you'd clean Nia's eyeballs. Alternately, with the skills you now have, you could cast various stages of silicone eyelids for Nia. You could also create silicone (or resin) eyebrows. Personally, I like being able to custom sculpt these features frame by frame so I can get very specific expressions, which is why I stick with the clay approach.

> **TUBBY THE TUBA, GEORGE PAL, 1947**
>
> In this short, Pal – the undisputed king of replacement animation – creates a very effective talking tuba character, all through replacement head pieces. The time invested in sculpting, moulding, and casting was offset by the relative speed in which the animation could be created.

3D printing a mouth kit

Decreasing costs for printers means that this method of puppet making is becoming increasingly viable for artists. It has particular value in the area of replacement mouth pieces. These pieces are obviously smaller than entire faces and heads, which keeps printing costs down. Also, replacement mouths need to register very cleanly on the puppet, and are often variations on a main shape. Since a printer can create the same basic shape, again and again, the printer is a great tool for creating effective replacement mouths.

What follows are detailed, step by step instructions for making printed mouth pieces, from someone who has followed the very same process. Consider this method for making Nia's mouths, or for some future puppet! A bit of caution, though – they require a fairly advanced amount of computer modeling skills, so bear that in mind before you fully jump in.

During my final year in the Animation program at Sheridan College, I created my graduation film project in stop motion. My film included some lip sync elements for the main character, and instead of sculpting all of the necessary mouth replacements by hand, I decided to try 3D printing them.

This is a tutorial for a mouth kit with a fairly simple design that will be painted by hand after printing. I used a combination of Maya and Zbrush to create the kit – this workflow was the most logical path for me to personally take, as I had some basic knowledge of animating and 3D modeling in Maya before starting the project. It's possible to make face replacements with Maya, Zbrush, Blender, or any combination of 3D programs that can export to a printable format. Use whatever you're comfortable with to get an end result that suits your project!

> This section on 3D printing a mouth kit was developed in collaboration with **Kelsey Ryan**. Kelsey is a Canadian stop motion artist, who works as an animator and fabricator. Search for her outstanding work online. In her own words, here's the process that Kelsey used for her printed mouths.

> Depending on what version of Maya and ZBrush you're using, the details of what follows may be slightly different for you, since software is always getting updated. Help Menus and online resources are always standing by to help!

STEP BY STEP

1. Plan your facial expressions. Use your project's designs and storyboards as a guide, and create a list of all of the different 'extreme' mouth shapes that your puppet will need. This includes all of the major facial expressions it needs to make (happy, sad, scared, yawning, etc.), as well as all of the phonetic shapes needed for lip sync. Draw out what all of these mouths look like from the front and side views to use as a guide for the 3D models later on.

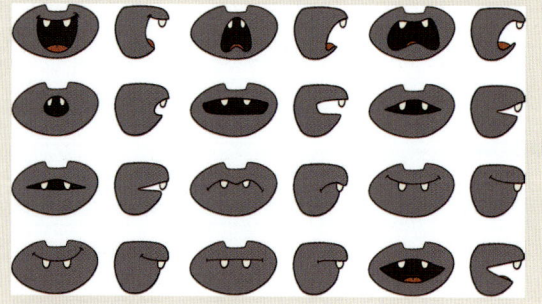

Figure 4.27
Mouth shape drawings.
Drawings of each required mouth shape from front and side views to use as reference for the 3D models.

There will likely be a visible seam where your replacement parts connect to the rest of your puppet's head, and it's up to you to decide whether to keep that seam visible as a stylistic choice, or remove it in post-production after animating. In this puppet's case, the different textures in the design mask that seam on its own – the snout is a different colour and texture from the rest of the head, which makes that seam look natural.

At this point you should also consider how the puppet's mouths will attach to the head, and where any required registration points will be on your model. Generally, any mouth replacements will attach via a magnet embedded in the puppet's face. As for registration, it will depend on the design of your puppet – for this puppet, a shallow indentation on the top of each piece fits right underneath the nose, ensuring that each mouth will attach in the same spot every time. Registration points could also be placed behind the mouth, where each piece connects to the magnet.

Figure 4.28
Replacement seam and registration points.
The green line indicates the seam where the edge of the mouth pieces meet the rest of the head. A shallow indentation on top of each mouth piece will ensure that the pieces align under the puppet's nose in the same place (pink line).

It's important to know the scale you are working with when designing your mouth kit. At this point you may find it helpful to sculpt a to-scale version of your puppet's head, so that you can accurately measure the dimensions of the area you'll be printing. This sculpture can be a useful guide for creating your 3D mouth model, and the dimensions of the sculpture will be useful later on when you're preparing files to be printed.

2. Model a basic 3D mouth. This is a neutral mouth from which you will derive all of the expressions you planned out earlier. Generally, an open and expressionless mouth is good for this – it will be fairly easy to alter this shape into more specific open and closed mouths later.

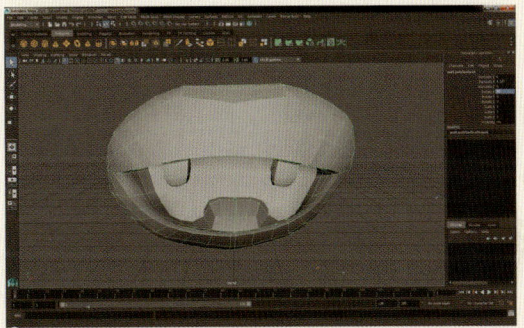

Figure 4.29
Maya screenshot of mouth template, front view.
Finished model of the neutral, open mouth.

Since you will be animating with this mouth in 3D before printing it, you should build this 3D model the same way you would build a mouth on a character intended for 3D animation – with two important differences. When working on a solely 3D project, different elements (such as teeth or a tongue) can be built as completely separate elements from the main mouth and simply grouped together for animation. For this method of 3D printing, this structure will likely not work. The printer needs to be able to read your model as one solid, hollow object. Because of this you should build any elements you want included in the print, like teeth or tongues, into your main mouth shape from the beginning. The simplest method of doing this will be to extrude these shapes from your main model, rather than building them as separate assets and merging them later. The reason for not merging things together is that many printers require all of the polygons in your model to be quads – meaning they each only have four sides and vertices. If you try merging different pieces together, you may not be able to easily make a clean connection between them, and could end up with unpredictable, non-quad polygons in your mesh. If you keep these things in mind while modeling this first piece, it will make the rest of the process much easier later on.

3. Set up registration points and scale. It's important to build your registration points into this first instance of your model, so that they will be exactly duplicated on each further shape you create. Add indentations or extrusions to inconspicuous areas of your model that will fit together with the rest of the puppet's head. Also be sure to create an area on the back of the mouth where you can attach something magnetic – so that the mouths will stay attached to the head. To do this, select an appropriate area of the back of the mouth, and use the extrude tool to create an indentation large enough to accommodate a small magnet, wire, or other metal material. It should only need to be a couple of mm deep.

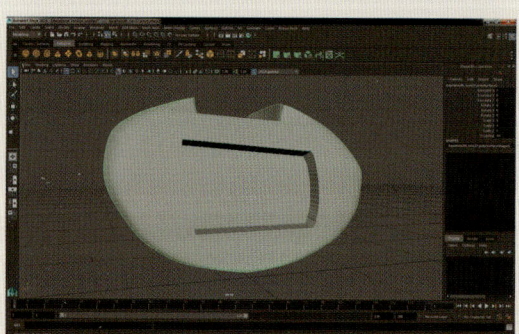

Figure 4.30
Maya screenshot of mouth template, back view.
Back view of the neutral mouth, showing the registration point on top, and indentation on the back.

In Maya you can set your project's scale to match the real-life units of measure of your puppet. By default Maya should be measuring in cm, but this can be checked or changed in the Settings/Preferences menu, under 'Working Units'. To make working to scale easier, each square of the grid in Maya can be set to equal one unit in your chosen unit of measurement – this can be checked in your Grid Preferences.

You can check the scale of your model by going into Create>Measure Tools, and using the Distance Tool. Make sure that you're looking at your model from a flat view, like the front or side (not the perspective view). Use the distance tool to click on the beginning and end of a distance on your model to check the scale, and make the appropriate adjustments so that it fits the scale of your puppet.

At this point it's also a good idea to do a test print of your model, so that you can check that the sizing and registration looks right on your puppet (or on the sculpture you made earlier). Registration points and the general design of the mouth should be locked down at this stage, while you're only working with one mouth shape – it would be difficult to fix these things identically on more than one model later on!

4. Set up Tools and Subtools for sculpting expressions in ZBrush. Once you're happy with your mouth template, you can export it from Maya as an .obj file and start creating your mouth shapes in Zbrush. The option to create an .obj might not be available by default when you go to export it – if you don't see it, open the Plug-in Manager in the Settings/Preferences menu, scroll down to 'objExport', and make sure that the 'Loaded' box is checked.

After exporting, open up Zbrush and click the 'Import' button in the Tool box on the right. Load in your .obj file. (If your model has any polygons that aren't quads, you'll see a popup to let you know at this point – if this is the case, you should fix your geometry before going any further.) Click on your model's thumbnail in the Tool box, then click and drag in the workspace area to set it up for editing.

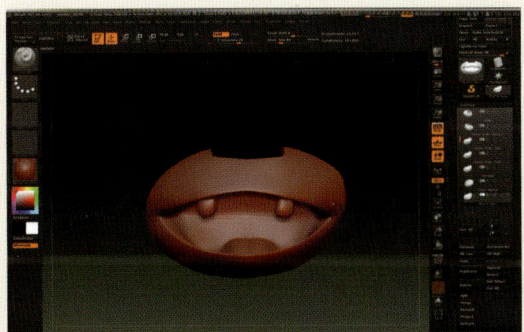

Figure 4.31
Zbrush screenshot of mouth template.
Neutral mouth template in Zbrush, with additional polygons
that create a smoother surface.

Zbrush organizes 3D objects as 'tools'
and 'subtools'. For this project your mouth
template will be your main tool, and all of
the new expressions you're sculpting will be
subtools. To add subtools, click 'Append'
in the Subtool menu, and select your mouth
template. Do this for every expression
you're making, and rename your subtools
to match each expression. Make sure there
is a subtool for your template mouth as well
– this way you can toggle visibility between
the template and each expression to ensure
that your sculpt is in line with the template.
Your subtools will be created in the same
area of the workspace as your main mouth
shape – this is good, as you will be able to
see differences between your models clearly
when toggling between them.

5. Sculpt your expressions. Once your subtools
are set up and labeled, you're ready to start
sculpting. Be sure to mask off any areas that
you don't want changing size or position on
any of your models – such as registration
points, outer edges, or details like teeth. Editing models in Zbrush is a lot more like working
with real clay – anything can move if you push
it, so make sure to mask anything you don't
want moved around.

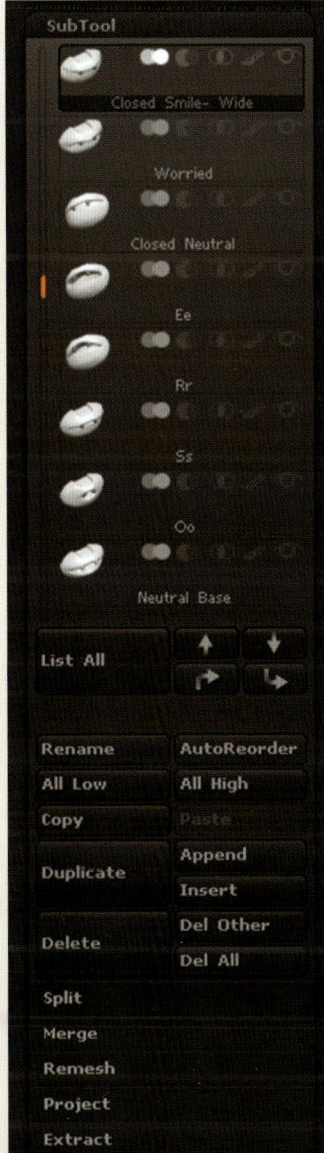

Figure 4.32
Zbrush screenshot of subtool menu.
Subtool menu, listing the new expressions.

To sculpt (and print) smooth, detailed
expressions, your model will likely need a
denser number of polygons than the initial

Maya model had. Remember that every polygon on your model represents a single flat plane – in order to give the prints a smooth, rounded appearance, large polygons will need to be broken down into smaller pieces. Open the Geometry menu, and click 'Higher Res'. You will see this adding more polygons to the geometry in the workspace, as well as increasing one subdivision level in the geometry menu. Subdivide your model a few times, so that you have a smoother surface to work with.

Zbrush has many different editing tools available to edit your models with, and by experimenting with them you can discover some interesting effects. However, a few of the basic brushes should be able to do pretty much everything you need for this project. The main three I found myself using are Move Topological, Smooth, and Inflate. Move Topological lets you select an area of the model's surface and push it around in space – similar to sculpting with clay. If your mesh is looking too bumpy, the Smooth tool can even out the polygons in an area. And if your model starts to look too caved-in or crumpled from moving and smoothing, the Inflate tool will push your edges back out again. Use these tools to sculpt each of your expressions, making sure to flip back and forth between your models and the template to ensure that they are all lining up correctly.

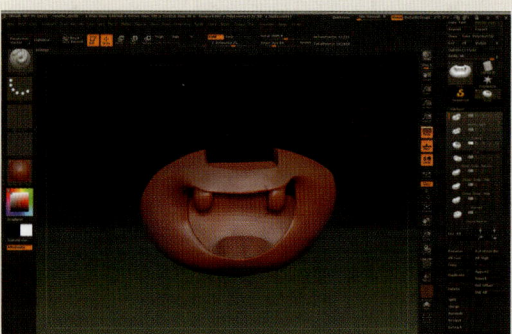

Figure 4.33
Zbrush screenshot of a sculpted subtool.
Finished model of the open, smiling mouth.

6. Export Subtools. Once all of the facial expressions have been sculpted, they can be exported from Zbrush and brought back into Maya. Make sure to export the higher-resolution, subdivided versions of each mouth (including the original template), and to export them all at the same subdivision level – they will all need to have the same polygon count to animate with them in Maya. Export each expression subtool from Zbrush as a new, separate .obj file.

7. Clean up the expressions in Maya. When you bring the higher-resolution sculpted expressions back into Maya, there's a possibility that some of your geometry won't look quite right at first. In Zbrush you were able to freely push polygons around, which could make some of the geometry look crumpled when it's brought back into Maya. Before animating, you will need to straighten out all the geometry, and make sure that there are no overlapping polygons or vertices in any of the 3D models. The main places to look for messy overlaps are the places where the geometry has the densest number of polygons – these tend to be around the edges of facial features, or in the corners of the mouth. On this model, the problem areas were around the bases of the teeth, the center crease of the tongue, and the corners of the mouth on more extreme expressions, like the smile. To straighten out this crumpling, zoom into a problem area and move the vertices of the polygons one by one, untangling them as you go. Although this may seem like a tedious job, these overlaps can cause errors in the printing process – the printer needs to read each mouth piece as a solid, hollow object, with clearly readable inner and outer faces.

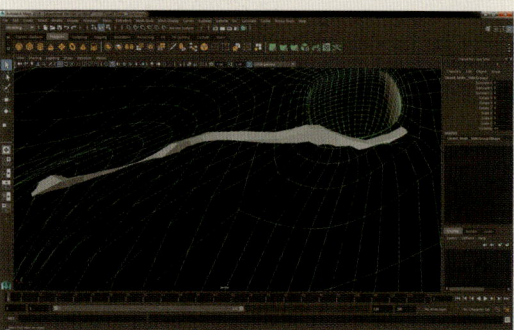

Figure 4.34
Maya screenshot with example of bad geometry.
This image and Figure 4.35 are taken from inside the roof of the mouth – the sunken area in the top right corner is a tooth. The geometry in light grey was pushed through the roof of the mouth while sculpting, and belongs on the outside of the model.

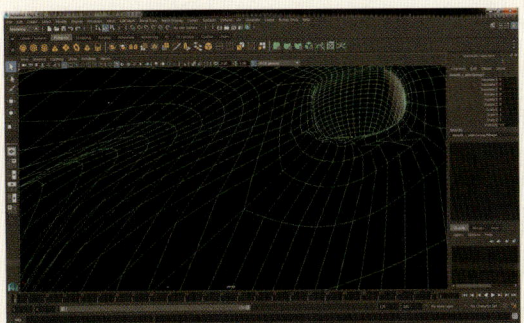

Figure 4.35
Maya screenshot with example of fixed geometry.
This is the way the model looks after the outward-facing geometry has been pushed back to the outside of the model. There are now no overlapping polygons or vertices.

After straightening out the geometry, it's important to check that each object's normals are facing the right way. In Maya, normals can tell you which way your polygons are facing – all of the normals on your object should be facing outward. To check this, go to Display>Polygons, and click on Face Normals. There should be a small line pointing outward from every polygon in your model. If any normals are pointing inwards, reverse the normals on those polygons so they match the rest of your model – if this has happened anywhere on your model, it will likely be in one of the 'crumpled' spots that needed to be cleaned up earlier, so pay close attention to the geometry in those areas. You should be able to unify all of the normals on an object using Normals>Conform, but if this doesn't work, polygons can be individually selected and reversed as well. This is another necessary step to ensure that the printing process goes smoothly later on.

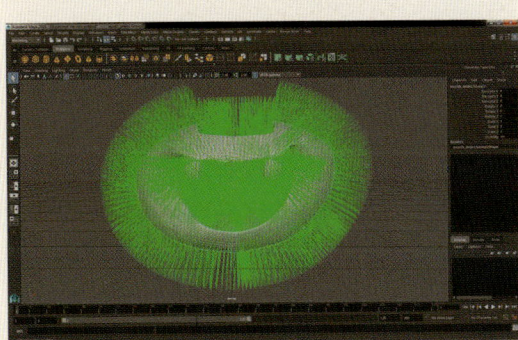

Figure 4.36
Maya screenshot of expression with normals.
Each green line pointing out from the model is attached to a polygon.

8. Set up blend shapes. Once all of the expression models have been cleaned up, you're ready to set them up for animating! To get started, open a new Maya project and import all of the cleaned up, high-resolution.obj files for your mouth template and expressions. Arrange them so that they're easy to see and work with – placing the base template in the center of the workspace and lining up the expressions above or beside it works well. Then you can begin connecting the expressions to your template mouth as blend shapes. In Animation mode select one of the expressions first, then shift-select the mouth template. Go to Create Deformer>Blend Shape, click on the option box, and name the blend shape. Repeat this process until all of your models have been connected to the template.

Figure 4.37
Maya screenshot of workspace, connecting blend shapes.
The expressions are lined up above the base mouth template.

9. Animate the mouths. Import the audio track that you would like to animate to into your Maya file. This way you can scrub through the audio as you animate – though you may find an x-sheet helpful to have as well. Go to Window>Animation Editors> Blend Shape – this will open up a new menu. You will see the blend shapes you set up previously, with slider bars to control how much they deform your base template model. Animate your lip sync by moving the blend shape sliders in time to your audio track. Remember to set a keyframe on each blend shape every time it is moved. You might prefer setting your keyframes to Stepped mode as well – which means that instead of Maya automatically

inbetweening your keyframes, your blend shapes will only move when a keyframe is set. To do this, open the Preferences window and go to Animation>Tangents, and set the default in to 'Clamped' and the default out to 'Stepped'.

Figure 4.38
Maya screenshot of animating with blend shapes demonstrating ability to combine them.
This is a mid-point between the Neutral Closed mouth and the O mouth, creating a smooth inbetween position.

10. Export 3D files for printing. Once you are happy with your animation, it can be exported for printing. You will most likely want to export your mouths as.stl files, but be sure to check the settings of the printer you'll be using to make sure. To export a single mouth shape, go to the frame of animation you'd like to export, and select the mouth object. Go to File>Export, and select the file type STL_DCE. This will create an.stl object of this single animated frame.

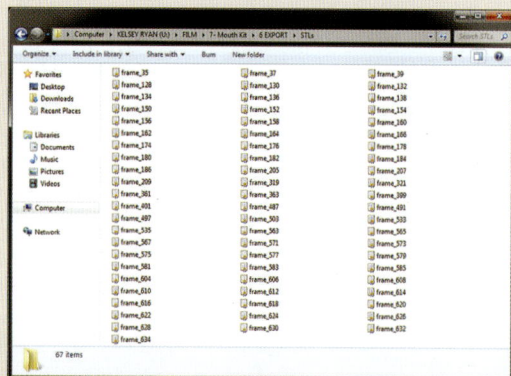

Figure 4.39
Exported files with frame numbers.
The file names here correspond to each mouth's frame number in Maya.

Be sure to name your exported files in a way that they will be easily identifiable, especially if your mouth kit has a large number of pieces. Use a file naming convention that makes sense to you – naming each file after its corresponding frame number in Maya works well, and makes it easier to sort through your printed pieces later. You may want to write this frame number on the back of your final printouts too, for easy reference while animating.

11. Send your files to the printer. 3D printers can print your project in a variety of ways, using a wide range of materials. For this project you will likely want to print using a standard PLA plastic filament, one of the more common materials used. Depending on the shape of your pieces, the printer might need to create a support structure to hold up any overhanging parts of the mouth. The way this support is printed depends on the type of printer being used. Some printers will print these supports using the same plastic as the rest of the project – the supports can be cut or snapped off after printing is finished. Other printers will use a different type of plastic to fill in the space around the overhangs, which can be dissolved in a chemical bath after printing, leaving a clean print behind.

Before starting to print your mouth kit, be sure to confirm that the scale of your files is correct with your printer – even if your Maya files appeared to be the correct scale for your puppet, this may need to be inputted into the printer again at this stage.

12. Attach magnetic materials to the prints. Depending on the strength of the magnet embedded in your puppet's head, it may not be necessary to use magnets in each mouth replacement. Using a small rare earth magnet in the puppet's head is recommended for this reason – your 3D prints will be very lightweight, and as long as there is something small and metallic glued inside the indentation on the back of each piece (such as a few small pieces of wire) the mouths will stay in place on the rare earth magnet. Using magnets on both the puppet's face and the mouth kit may not be a good idea – depending on the strength of the magnets, the head and mouth may snap together when the magnets attract, potentially

moving your puppet during animation! This shouldn't be as much of an issue if you are using weaker magnets, though. For most cases, one rare earth magnet on the face and wire backings on the prints will work well.

Figure 4.40 **Magnet on puppet face, wire backing on mouth pieces.** Small pieces of wire have been glued inside the indentation on the back of each replacement mouth.

13. Smooth the prints. Depending on the resolution of the printer you're using, and the material that you are printing your parts out of, there may be small ridges along the surface of your prints. Each of these ridges are a layer of whatever material you're printing with – the higher the resolution of the printer, the smaller and less noticeable these ridges will be. The degree to which these can be smoothed out will depend on the material you're printing with – if you're using a standard PLA plastic filament, they can be smoothed out with acetone. To get a smooth, consistent surface finish, quickly dip each piece in a small cup of acetone. Don't hold it with your fingers – use something magnetic to pick the piece up, such as a dowel or pencil with a magnet attached to the end, and hold that while dipping the print in the acetone. About one or two seconds should be all the time needed, as any more time could end up warping the details of your print – the acetone is basically melting the surface layer of the plastic. Leave each piece to air dry.

14. Paint the finished pieces. Once each piece has been smoothed out, it's finally time to paint the mouth kit. It is useful to mix all of the paint you'll

need beforehand, and keep each colour in a sealable container – this way you won't have to worry about running out of paint later on and trying to mix exact matches for your colours. Depending on the number of pieces in your kit and the complexity of your prints, it could be a good idea to keep the colour palette relatively small – the more colours involved, the harder it will be to consistently replicate the paint job on potentially dozens of different mouth shapes. By using one flat colour for each part of the mouth (outside surface, inside the mouth, teeth, tongue, etc.), your paint job will be easy to replicate over and over. Start with painting the inside of the model – since the pieces are so small, this will be the toughest area to paint – and work your way towards the outside.

Figure 4.41
Final printouts, painted.
I made a lot of mouth shapes! You could also create a more basic kit, to save on time and cost.

Figure 4.42
Final mouth on puppet.
A frame from the film, with a finished mouth on the puppet.

DANIEL BAKER, SPECIAL EFFECTS ARTIST, 3D PRINTING ARTIST

Daniel Baker has design and fabrication experience in everything from stop motion puppets to large museum displays. He also co-developed the Special Effects Program at Sheridan College, a program that teaches practical effects fabrication techniques for television and film, theme parks, and museum display projects.

Q. 3D printing opens the door to all kinds of creative possibilities for stop motion artists, most notably in the area of replacement faces and mouths. But what people sometimes don't realize is that the 3D printed parts in feature films are the result of entire departments working tirelessly to create a beautiful product. For an indie stop motion artist, working mostly on her own, she needs to think practically – what can one person achieve? What essential advice would you offer to someone wanting to use 3D printing for facial parts for a short stop motion film?

A. There's a lot that can be done with 3D printers. The key is to understand the printer you are using. You should know what that printer can and cannot do. Once you are ready to print a digital file you should consider the following things:

- Orientating the file
  The quality of work created by printers will vary depending on how you orient the digital file on it. It might print fine vertically, but not as clean horizontally. If you don't position the file effectively, you'll be spending time cleaning up the print, which can be time consuming if you have multiple mouth replacements.
- Speed of print
  If the printer is slow, producing prints might effect the schedule of your production as well as limit the number of prints you can produce.
- Detail of digital file
  If the digital file is highly detailed, it might not transfer to the final 3D print depending the level of detail the printer can produce. For example if your model has very fine lines and textures in the face they might not be transferred to the print, and will have to be added in.

The real limitation is what the artist can achieve with the time and budget that's available.

Q. Prices for printers and printer media continue to drop, while quality rises. What makes for a good 3D printer, when it comes to stop motion?

A. When looking to invest in purchasing a 3D printer consider the following things:
- Print quality
  Printers vary in the quality of prints that you can achieve. Most printers work laying down successive layers of material until the entire object is created. This can leave fine striation lines in the print that need to be cleaned up. Printers that can produce higher quality print are easier to clean up once they are printed.
- Material used
  There is a variety of material that printers use to produce a printed object.
      Not all printers can print all materials. When investing in a printer you might want to consider the cost to purchase additional material. The printer might produce very fine quality prints but the material used to print might be expensive and it could be very costly to print multiple parts. These different materials include PLA, ABS, Resin … do your research, so you know what you are getting into, and what is the best choice for your needs.
- Print size
  Each printer has its own maximum print size that it will allow you to print. In the case of stop motion you might not need to invest in a printer that has a big printer bed if you are printing replacement mouths. But the printer could also be used to make armature, set pieces or props, so depending on the scale, it might be better to have a larger print bed.

Q. Beyond printing for facial parts, can you discuss some other uses for printing in 3D when it comes to stop motion?

A. As I touched on above, there's a wide range of applications for 3D printers in stop motion. Replacement mouths are just one way of utilizing them. Printers can be used for creating set pieces, props or even armatures.

If your film requires different scale props or puppets, printers are great to accurately reproduce objects. You can achieve a long shot of the entire set by shrinking down the models and printing them in smaller scale. This will allow you to create interesting scale and perspective on a smaller animation stage.

Armatures can be designed digitally and then printed for test animation before you invest in expensive machined armatures. I have made replacement arms with wire and epoxy. Over time and use the epoxy can start to break, and the fingers become loose, and you have to replace the arm. You can replace the epoxy with printed parts and secure the wire to them. This will give you longer use then the epoxy method

Q. I know you're a highly trained sculptor, and accomplished with moulding and casting as well. How do feel about this movement towards 3D printing? Will it replace physical items entirely one day?

A. I am very pro 3D printing. I believe it is a great way to enhance the art of stop motion. I don't feel that it will ever replace fabricating a physical puppet, prop, or set. They are good to get the first sculpt or design for the project. But you will still have to finish the piece. You can print a drinking glass for the puppet to hold. But you will still have to clean up the print, mould it and then cast it in a material that will simulate the look of glass. In the case of replacement mouths or heads, you will still need to clean up the pieces and paint them, bringing the overall look together. They can help achieve designs that might not have been possible before for indie filmmakers.

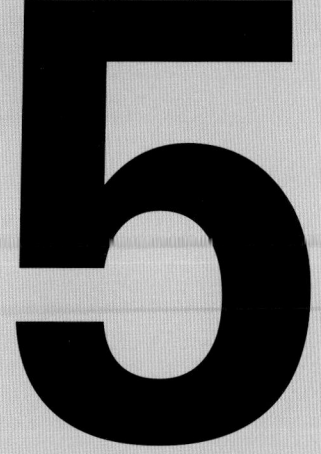

Fabricating the outside: Part 2

In this chapter, you'll build upon the skills that you've developed in the previous chapter as you continue to create Nia's exterior. The focus here is on moulding, casting, and finishing her hands and feet.

By the end of this chapter, you'll have taken your moulding and casting skills that much further. And more importantly, you'll have a finished Nia puppet, that's all ready for her costume!

Moulding the hands and arms in silicone

To create the arm moulds, we'll be following essentially the same process that we used for moulding Nia's head. However, the silicone we'll be using is different. We'll be using Smooth Sil 945. This is a firmer and stronger silicone than the one we used for the head. It needs to be stronger because as you'll see, we'll be putting more pressure on this mould when casting the arms, in an effort to get the thinnest seam possible on the final arms.

MATERIALS

Nia's arm sculpts, with armature wire ends
    snipped to approx. 3cm (1 inch)
Smooth Sil 945, 473 mL (1 pint) kit
sulfur free clay
silicone mould release
foam core or thin wood for mould base
more foam core (for mould walls)
approx. 10 medium sized marbles
4mm (5/32 inch) round brass stock, cut to the
    length of the armature wire at the ends of Nia's
    sculpted arms

TOOLS

lighter fluid
small cheap paint brushes
glue gun
utility knife
large kitchen knife
pencil
ruler
cotton swabs permanent marker
medium-sized plastic mixing buckets with
    measurements
strong wooden stir sticks
vinyl or nitrile gloves
safety glasses
safety mask

STEP BY STEP

1. Nia's arm mould is a two-part mould. As with the head, mark a mould line along the entire surface of the arms (first in pencil, then in marker).
2. Slide the round brass stock over the armature wire on the ends of the arms. Arrange the arms on the mould base and build up a clay foundation, carefully following the line that you drew on the arms. Make sure that the arms don't touch, and that there's a nice amount of clearance all around. Place the marbles in the clay to create keys.

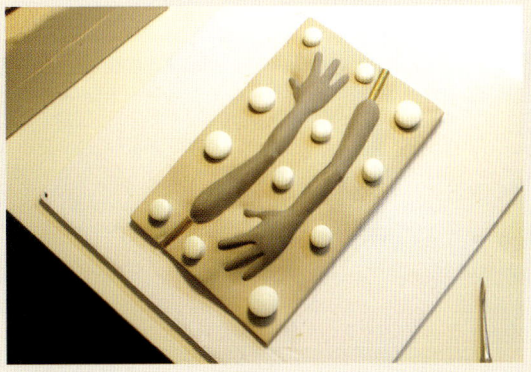

Figure 5.1
The arms with clay and keys.
Sculpting around the fingers is tricky work. Remember to keep the clay at a 90-degree angle wherever it meets the arm sculpture.

3. Create part 1 of the arm mould, following the same methods used to create part 1 of the head mould. Be sure to follow the kit's instructions carefully as you prepare and pour the silicone.

4. After part 1 of the mould has set, remove the walls and create part 2 of the mould, following the same methods used to create part 2 of the head mould. Remember to use mould release!

5. After part 2 of the mould has cured, remove the walls, and separate the mould parts. Carefully remove the arm sculpts, and there you go – completed arm moulds!

Figure 5.2
The finished arm moulds.
Be sure to remove any debris from the moulds. Use a dull scraping tool to avoid damaging the mould.

Making the hand and arm armatures

There's no way around it, hands and arms are tricky to make for stop motion puppets. They need to look great, but they also need to be flexible for posing. They have to be strong enough to hold props, but they also have to be *small*. In each of those tiny silicone fingers are wires that were perfectly positioned within the mould – and getting that right takes practice. Be prepared to pour several sets of arms before you're truly happy. Fortunately, wire is cheap, the amount of silicone needed is modest, and you'll learn fast. Once you're getting beautiful results, be sure cast even *more* arms, because you'll want extras during animation.

MATERIALS

floral wire, approx. 26 gauge (This wire has cloth on it, and is for the fingers. If you can't find wire that is specifically 26 gauge, refer to the images in this section for sizing)
1.6mm (1/16 inch) armature wire
Two-part liquid epoxy adhesive (a good brand is Quick Cure 5. Another brand that is commonly available is made by Lepage. You'll often find this item sold in a kit that has two syringes, side by side.)
woven cloth tape

TOOLS

needle nose pliers
stir sticks

scissors
vinyl or nitrile gloves

STEP BY STEP

1. Using the hand mould as the guide, braid a length of 1.6 mm (1/16 inch) wire, looped where the palm of the hand is. Leave a few mm (1/8 inch) of clearance between the palm wire and the edge of the mould.

Figure 5.3
Armature wire with loop for palms.
The overall length of the braided arm wire isn't important (yet), but it should at least extend past the end of the mould's edge.

2. Using a strand of floral wire, make several tight loops of floral wire around the 1/16th inch armature wire, starting at the base of the wrist. Once the loops reach the first finger (or thumb, if that's where you are starting) tightly crimp the floral wire where the mould ends, then bend it back to the palm area. Loop the floral wire through the armature wire once more to anchor it. Carry on looping your way along the 1/16th inch armature wire until you reach the

Figure 5.4
Forming the fingers.
Keep the floral wire as neat as possible as you work.

next finger in the mould. Form this finger in the same way that you formed the first.

3. Carry on along the hand, working your way around. As you work, keep the wire very neat and compact. The tidier the hand armature is, the nicer the final arm and hand will be, and the better it will animate.

4. Once all the fingers are created and anchored, grab the end of each with the pliers and carefully twist the finger wires to braid the fingers. After you've braided the last finger, continue making tidy loops with the floral wire along the armature wire until you've return to where you started. Snip the floral wire and ensure that both ends of the floral wire are neatly tucked into the palm area.

As you twist each finger, try to ensure that the fingertip's pad, which is the wide, fleshy part of the fingertip, is oriented in the mould in the same way that a human finger pad would be. This will allow for better animation, and will prevent the wire from tearing through the cast silicone.

5. Lay two small squares of cloth tape down, sticky-side up, and lay the hands on them. You're about to pour some glue on to the hands, and the tape will prevent the glue from running through, on to the table. This textured tape will also give the silicone something to grab on to during casting.

6. Get your gloves on. Mix a small amount of the two-part liquid adhesive epoxy. Use a stir stick and follow the product's instructions. Apply a thin, flat layer of the glue on to the palm of each hand. You want to make sure you've covered the entire palm area. This will effectively 'lock' all the wires in place. Be careful to not put glue on to the actual wrist or fingers. Let the glue dry fully, then trim the excess cloth tape from both hands.

7. Use the utility knife to cut a long thin strip of cloth tape. Wrap the thin strip neatly around the length of the arm, starting at the palm (don't put tape on the fingers). The textured tape will give the silicone something to grab on to during the casting process.

Figure 5.5
The finished arms.
Make several pairs of these armatures, so that you can cast several sets of arms.

BALANCE, CHRISTOPH AND WOLFGANG LAUENSTEIN, 1989

This short film about a group of fisherman poised on a floating platform won the Oscar for Best Animated Short. It's wonderful in all ways, but when watching it again, pay particular attention to the hands of the puppets. They're oversized, which allows them to effectively hold all the props required by the story. They also work from a design perspective, since the film is rather surreal and otherworldly.

Casting the hands and arms in silicone

Up to this point, the only material that we've poured into our silicone moulds has been resin. But in this case, since the hands and arms have to be flexible, resin isn't going to be suitable – we'd end up with solid arms and hands! Instead, we'll be casting in coloured silicone that has an armature embedded within it.

The arms will be cast in (yet another) silicone, called Dragon Skin 10 FAST. It's flexible, tough, and can be tinted. The kind we're using cures quickly (approx. one hour), which is also very useful if you need to cast some hands in a hurry. This silicone doesn't come pre-coloured to match Nia's skin. Instead, the silicone is clear, and needs to be tinted to match the desired colour, using specially formulated tints. Testing will be essential, to get the right skin colour.

MATERIALS

473 mL (1 pint) kit of Dragon Skin 10 FAST
SILC PIG silicone tints sample pack (As with all
    the other specialized materials, these tints are
    made by Smooth-On. This sample pack is
    pretty cheap, and provides all the tints you'd
    need for any realistic skin colour, as well as
    fantasy skin colours.)
silicone mould release

TOOLS

two small resealable plastic containers
small mixing cups
wooden toothpicks
stir sticks
CA glue
vinyl or nitrile gloves
talcum powder
several heavy bricks or books (to weigh down the
    mould)

STEP BY STEP

1. First you need to tint the silicone. Clearly label the resealable containers 'Part A' and 'Part B'. Following the product instructions, pour out approx. 125 ml (1/2 cup) of Part A into its labeled container. Do the same for Part B. As long as the silicone parts haven't been mixed together, they won't cure, so there's no time pressure while mixing the colour. Once the parts are mixed together, you have a set amount of time to work. You'll find that working time on the product data sheet. Don't worry, it won't set nearly as fast as the resin.

2. As you prepare to start mixing colour into the silicone, there are two key things to consider: the *opacity* of the silicone, and the *colour* of the silicone. Mix in a few drops of 'White' tint into Part A and Part B, and mix thoroughly (as you tint, be sure to add the same amount of tint to *both* parts). This is creating a base of opacity – if you don't have opacity, the finger wires will show through the silicone! You can gauge the opacity by looking at the stir stick after you've mixed. Can you see the stick clearly? Just a bit? Not at all? Best to aim for some opacity now (in other words, you want to be able to 'sort of' see the stir stick), because the later tints are going to continue to increase the opacity.

3. Add in a few drops of 'Flesh' colour into Part A and Part B and mix. It's called 'Flesh', although it's certainly not *everyone's* flesh colour – but that's what they call it.

Figure 5.6
Tinting the silicone.
Remember that as you add tint to one part of the silicone, you should add the same amount to the other part as well.

4. Then add 'Brown' into Part A and B and mix, adding a bit more until the desired colour is reached. Only add a few drops at a time …

5. Then a little bit of 'Yellow' to Part A and B, and mix. Work slowly and carefully, as you try to establish Nia's skin colour.

> Dedicate a stir stick to each tint, and to each container of silicone. You don't want to 'cross contaminate' tints with other tints, or with the silicone.

6. Once you've achieved a look you like, mix a very small amount of Part A with Part B. Allow the test patch to dry fully, then brush it with some talcum powder to take the shine off, and check the patch in various lighting situations. If you've already painted Nia's head, compare the test patch to that. If you're happy, you're ready to go. If not, keep tinting, slowly.

7. Now that your silicone is tinted, cover the containers for Part A and B, and set them aside for now. Spray both sides of the arm mould with mould release. Make sure that you fully coat all parts of the mould – all around the inside of the arm cavities, and all surfaces.

8. You're now going to create a *skin coat* of silicone. This coat will create a silicone 'shell', so that the armatures will stay in place. Use a stir stick to drizzle some of Part A into a small mixing cup – you don't need too much. Then drizzle the same volume of Part B into the cup, and mix fully. You now have a small batch of mixed silicone. Drizzle the mixed silicone into one part of the mould. Remember, you don't want to fill the mould – you just want a very thin layer, to act as a shell. Repeat on the other part of the mould. Use a toothpick to pop any small bubbles that form in the silicone. Let this silicone cure.

9. Now you're going to secure the armatures into the mould. Arrange the armatures carefully in one side of the mould. Use whichever side of the mould you think the armature will rest in the most comfortably. It's critical that no part of the armature touches any part of the mould. Once

Figure 5.7
Creating the skin coat.
By creating this skin layer, your armature will sit nicely in the center of the cast, right where it should be (as opposed to the edges, where it can be seen, and where it can easily tear through).

the armatures are posed, carefully *remove* the armatures, and set them to the side.

10. Mix another small amount of Part A and B. Drizzle a small layer of silicone into the mould, and then place the armatures back into the mould. The armatures should now be nestled in this new silicone layer. Once this layer dries, the armatures will be secured.

11. Lay the two mould parts side by side. Make sure you have them aligned so that you can quickly fold them together after you've poured the silicone in – they'll be filled with silicone, and you don't want it to run out before you get the mould pieces together. You're going to fill each part of the mould with silicone, so mix enough of Part A and B for this. Drizzle the mixed silicone into both sides of the mould. Make sure you've filled each side completely. If they're a bit overfilled that's ok.

12. Quickly flip the moulds together, making sure that they lock together. Lay the locked moulds flat and weigh them down with the bricks or books. Ensure the weight is evenly spread over the moulds. The more weight, the tighter the mould parts will lock, and the less flashing you will have to deal with. Some silicone may squirt out the sides, which is to be expected. Use your mix cup to tell you when the silicone is fully cured. When it's cured, pop open the moulds, and remove the cast arms.

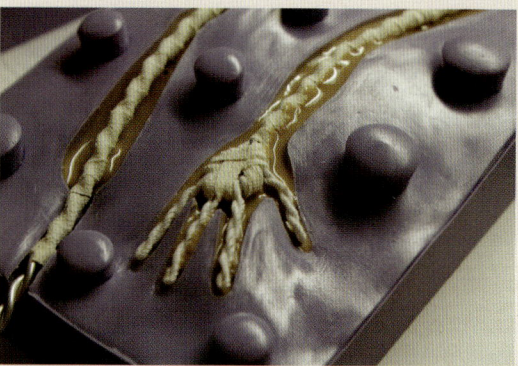

Figure 5.8
Securing the armatures within the mould.
This layer of silicone acts as a sort of glue, further ensuring that the armatures stay right where you want them during the casting stage.

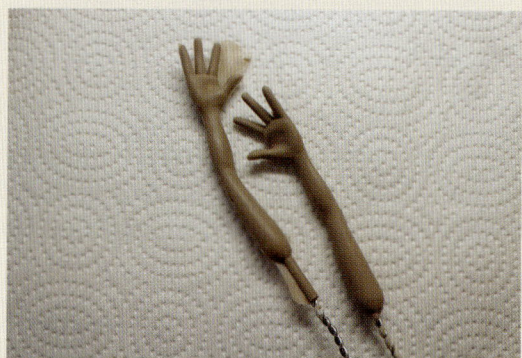

Figure 5.9
Cast arms ready for finishing.
There will be some 'flashing' (extra casting material) at the mould lines, much of which you can carefully pull off. Further tidying will happen in the next step.

Finishing the hands and arms

Even the best cast arms and hands will have a very thin seam that runs around them from where the two parts of the mould met. We want to remove that seam, so that Nia's arms are nice and smooth, all around. This is a process known as 'seaming', and is the last stage in fabricating the arms.

MATERIALS

small amount of Nia skin silicone, already mixed
lighter fluid
colourless makeup powder (This is not the same
  as talcum powder, since talcum powder has a
  slight sheen to it. You *can* use talcum powder,
  but this stuff works better.)
clay (any kind)
4 mm (5/32 inch) round brass stock, short length

TOOLS

wire snips
rotary tool (or coping saw)
cutting disks for rotary tool
small mixing cups
wooden stir sticks
cuticles scissors (or very tiny scissors)
small cheap paintbrushes
cotton swabs
vinyl or nitrile gloves

STEP BY STEP

1. Start by setting up a length of clay, where you'll stick the arms to cure once you've finished seaming.
2. Clean the first arm with a cotton swab dipped in lighter fluid. Carefully trim any flashing from the arms and fingers. You want the surface of the arm to be smooth, with perhaps a few indents (from cutting the flashing). You *don't* want any flashing left sticking *out* from the arm. Once you've finished trimming, clean the arm again with lighter fluid, using a cotton swab.
3. Pour out a small amount of Nia skin silicone, and mix in a small amount of lighter fluid. The lighter fluid acts to thin the silicone, so you can apply a very thin patch layer to the seam. Using a paint brush, work your way around the seam, carefully applying a thin layer of silicone to cover the seam. Only patch a bit of the seam for now – the silicone will cure quickly, so once it starts to get tacky, move on to the next step.
4. Dip a brush in the makeup powder. Hold the brush up to the seamed area, and blow on the brush. This will lightly dust the drying silicone with powder and ensures that the new layer of silicone will have the same matte finish as the original layer. Stick the arm into the clay to let it fully dry (wire end first, silly!)
5. Once the silicone is fully dry, use a cotton swab with lighter fluid to clean off any part of the seam that hasn't been patched. Thin a small amount of skin silicone as before (with lighter fluid). Repeat the above steps, patching a small amount at a time, and adding powder, until the entire seam has been covered. When you're done, gently brush off any excess makeup powder.
6. Cut the wire ends to length. Be careful to not trim too much! Cut two pieces of 1 cm (3/8 inch) round brass stock. Slide the brass over the armature wire ends, but don't glue them yet. Insert the arms into the appropriate body part holes in the chest block. If they don't match up with the scale drawing, trim the end wires a bit, and check again. Once they are right length, use CA glue to attach the brass stock to the arms. The arms are now ready to insert into the chest block, and are ready for animation.

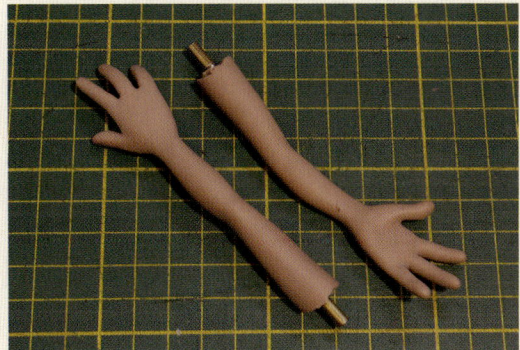

Figure 5.10
The finished arms.
You did it! Give yourself a hand! Puppet fabrication puns are wonderful, aren't they?

Moulding the neck in silicone

Nia's neck is very simple – it's nothing more than a silicone tube that slides over the neck wire. Before you can make this neck tube though, you need to create a two-part mould for it, using the Super Sculpey neck sculpture that you created, way back when you sculpted Nia's head.

MATERIAL

neck sculpture (created when sculpting Nia's head)
Smooth Sil 945 (the same silicone that was used for the arm mould)
3mm (1/8 inch) armature wire
4 medium sized marbles

TOOLS

lighter fluid	cotton swabs
small cheap paint brushes	permanent marker
glue gun	small mixing buckets
utility knife	wooden stir sticks
large kitchen knife	vinyl or nitrile gloves
pencil	safety glasses
ruler	safety mask

STEP BY STEP

1. Ensure that the neck sculpture still has its pieces of armature wire extending from both ends before you proceed. By this point in the fabrication process, you've created more than your fair share of two-part moulds, so moulding this little neck shouldn't present you with too much of a challenge! Refer to earlier sections (moulding the arms, specifically) for guidance. Remember to create keys in the mould, and remember to use mould release. You can reference Figure 5.11 to see what the neck mould should look like.

Casting the neck in silicone

MATERIALS

The mixed 'Nia skin' silicone that was used for the arms
3 mm (1/8 inch) armature wire, cut to the same length as the wire space that is in the mould
silicone mould release

TOOLS

small mixing cups
wooden toothpicks
stir sticks
vinyl or nitrile gloves
talcum powder
several heavy bricks (to weigh down the mould)

STEP BY STEP

1. You're going to cast the neck using essentially the same process that you followed for casting Nia's arms. Skin coat both sides of the neck mould, following the same process used for the arms.
2. Once the skin coat has set, place the piece of 3 mm (1/8 inch) wire into the mould.
3. Overfill both sides of the mould with Nia skin silicone, close them up, and place weight on the assembled mould. Allow the silicone to set.
4. Separate the mould pieces, and slide the wire out of the neck. You now have a neck tube that can be slid *over* the neck armature piece.
5. Tidy up the neck using the exact same process that you followed for the arms and hands.

6. Trim the neck tube to the correct length. To determine the length, make sure Nia's head is sitting at the correct height on the neck armature, and cut a length of neck tube that is just slightly *longer*. Remove the head from the neck armature, and slide this tube over the neck armature piece, put the head back on, and check for length. Trim the silicone neck tube further, if needed.

Nia's fabrication is nearly completed. If you started this process with little or no experience in moulding and casting, stop for a moment and consider all that you've learned over these past chapters. It's a remarkable accomplishment! Now push on, you're nearly there.

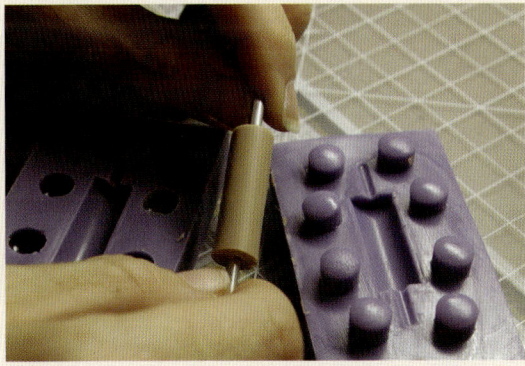

Figure 5.11
The finished neck tube.
Once the wire has slid out, this silicone tube is a very simple, but very effective, solution for covering Nia's neck armature.

Moulding the feet in silicone

This is going to be a one-part mould, as opposed to the two-part moulds we've made for the head, arms, and neck. That means you'll only pour silicone once to create this mould. Once the silicone for this mould has set, the foot sculpture should just pop out, as should the later resin casts. You only need to create one mould (even though Nia has two feet), since both her feet are the same.

MATERIALS

Nia's feet sculptures, with brass stock and bolt inserted
Mold Star 30 Silicone, 473mL (1 Pint) Kit (also used for Nia's head and mouth moulds)
oil-based, sulfur free clay
foam core or thin wood (for mould base)
more foam core (for mould walls)

TOOLS

pencil
screwdriver
hot glue gun
CA glue

utility knife
ruler
vinyl or nitrile gloves

STEP BY STEP

1. Set Nia's foot on the foam core or wood base. Use a drop or two of CA glue to secure the foot to the foam core. Make sure that there are no gaps between the foot and the foam core. If there are, use a bit of clay to fill in the gap.
2. Since this is a one-part mould, there's no need to build up a layer of clay. Go right to creating mould walls around the foot. You will need to custom-cut a piece of foam core to allow the bolt to stick out through the mould. Use clay to fill up any gap in the foam core around the bolt.
3. Mix and pour the silicone. Allow the mould to set. Break off the walls and pull the foot (and mould) away from the base.
4. Unscrew the bolt from the foot (it should come out easily) and pull the bolt out of the mould. Retain the bolt for casting.
5. Remove the foot sculpture from the mould. Remove the brass stock from the sculpture and retain it for casting. It might be stuck, but

should come out with a good tug. Clean out any debris from the mould. The mould is now ready for casting.

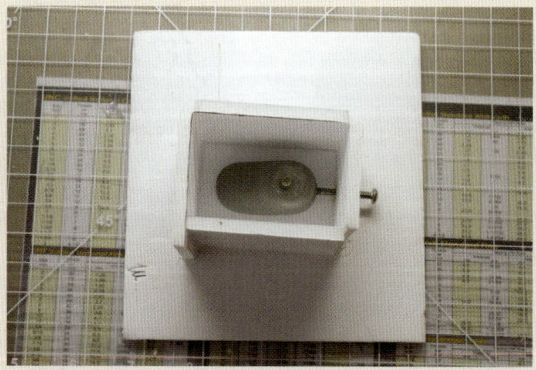

Figure 5.12
Foot sculpture with mould walls.
Notice that the bolt goes through the foam core wall into the foot. Remember to seal any gap around the bolt with clay.

Casting the feet in resin

You need the actual foot armature for casting, *not* the sculpture, so break the Super Sculpey off from the foot armature. You should be able crack it out fairly easily.

MATERIALS

foot mould
Smooth Cast 300
round brass stock that was used in sculpting the foot bolt that was used in making the foot mould
petroleum jelly

TOOLS

small plastic measuring cups for mixing resin
screwdriver
4.76 mm (6/32 inch) set screw
4.76 mm (6/32 inch) allen key (also known as a hex key)

small wooden stir sticks
vinyl or nitrile gloves
talcum powder
safety glasses
safety mask

STEP BY STEP

1. You'll essentially be using the same process that you followed for casting Nia's head. Powder the mould with talcum, then apply a very thin coat of jelly to the brass stock and replace it into the foot armature. The jelly will allow the brass to be easily removed from the cast.
2. Turn the foot armature upside down and place it into the mould, making sure that the brass stock is seated in its hole in the mould.
3. Coat the bolt with jelly and push it through its hole in the mould. Thread the bolt into the armature block.

Figure 5.13
The foot armature ready for casting.
The foot armature should be nicely supported by the brass stock, and be further secured by the bolt.

4. Mix and pour the resin into the mould. Allow the resin to set. Unthread the bolt, pop the foot out of the mould, and remove the brass stock from the foot.

5. Carefully thread the original set screw back into the threaded hole. The resin should have threads in the set screw hole (thanks to the bolt), which will allow the set screw to thread into the foot, and eventually into the block. If the resin isn't allowing the screw to go in, you can always drill out the resin a bit, to allow

access to the armature block. You can then use some coloured clay to fill in this space, once you've painted the foot.

6. Trim any resin flashing and carefully patch and sand any flaws, following the same process that you used for Nia's head and mouth shapes. Sand the bottom of the shoe until the magnet is almost visible, and make sure the bottom of the foot is perfectly flat. Any irregularities will cause trouble during animation.

7. Repeat this process, for Nia's other foot.

Painting the feet

Using your colour image of Nia's final design, paint Nia's feet following the same process that you used for her head and mouth shapes: prime, paint, and seal.

Magnet wands

To get Nia to stand in place during animation, you'll use more rare earth magnets, which will connect to Nia's feet from beneath the animation deck. These 'under the deck' magnets are sometimes referred to as 'magnet wands' – a short length of wood (round or square) with a magnet attached at one end. The piece of wood makes the magnet easier for your hands to find, during animation. You'll need two of these for Nia, but I recommend making a few more, since they are also handy for other stop motion tasks.

Of course, if you've designed Nia's feet to use tie downs, you don't need magnet wands!

MATERIALS

25.4mm (1 inch) rare earth magnets × 2
magnet cups to match magnets (optional, but magnet cups greatly increase the strength of a magnet, so get them if you can)
short length of dowel (round wood), or any small scrap wood, to approximately match the size of the magnets
small wood screws, with flat heads (not rounded)

TOOLS

pencil
coping saw (or any kind of wood-cutting saw)
vice
screwdriver

Figure 5.14
Nia's finished resin feet.
Since the resin is quite strong and is cast all around the aluminum foot armature, Nia has very sturdy feet that should hold up very well during animation.

Figure 5.15
Magnet wand.
Take note of the magnet 'cup' that surrounds the actual magnet. These cups greatly increase the strength of the rare earth magnet. The coloured tape makes the wands easier to spot in a darkened studio.

STEP BY STEP

1. Secure the dowel in the vice. Cut a short length. This is your 'wand'.
2. Place the magnet cup on the wand, and attach it with a wood screw.
3. Orient the magnet so that it will attract, and not repel, Nia's foot. This is *extremely* important, because once you drop the magnet into the cup, you can't get it out to fix your mistake, and you won't be able to unscrew the cup from the dowel. And the last thing you want is a magnet wand that undermines the very reason you made it! Once you know for sure that the magnet is oriented correctly, drop it into the cup.

If you can't find magnet cups, you can just hot glue a magnet directly on to a small piece of wood. Even without the cup, it should still be strong enough to do the job. Again, just make sure that you have the magnets for the wand oriented correctly before you glue.

If you have access to a metal grinder, grind down a deep notch in the cup before dropping in the magnet. That way if you ever need to reuse the magnet (or need it to have a different orientation), you can get a screwdriver under the magnet, and pop it out.

Adding volume to the puppet's armature

All that remains for fabricating your Nia puppet is to add some foam to give her some shape. You'll use a soft foam that allows for easy posing of the armature, but is firm enough to maintain a good sense of volume as you animate. It's a pretty simple process – you're basically going to make an 'armature sandwich', with the foam as the bread!

Nia may be all done, but she's probably a bit chilly, since she doesn't have any clothes yet! Fortunately, that happens to be the focus of the very next chapter.

MATERIALS

final Nia design, printed to scale (Figure 2.5)
upholstery foam (Look for foam that's medium density. Foam that is too dense will inhibit posing during animation.)

TOOLS

contact cement
scissors
utility knife
permanent marker
ruler

STEP BY STEP

1. Set Nia's feet, arms, and head somewhere safe (you don't want to scratch them or damage them). Assemble the armature so that the neck, spine, and legs are attached.
2. Lay the armature on a table, then measure and cut two pieces of foam: one will be for Nia's front, and the other will be for her back. The length of the foam should run from the top of the chest block down to the bottom of the legs. The width should be just a bit wider than the blocks.
3. Trim out hollow spots in each piece of foam for the chest and armature blocks so that the armature sits snugly within the foam.
4. Apply a thin layer of contact cement to each side of the foam. Let the contact cement sit for

a few minutes so that it becomes tacky. Ensure that the armature is placed correctly within the foam, and then press the foam sides together. Apply gentle pressure – if you squeeze the foam too tightly, the glue will seep through the foam entirely, and the foam will become very compressed and gummy. Allow the foam to fully dry.

5. Using the final Nia design as a guide, carefully trim the foam to give Nia her shape. Attach her feet, arms, and head at times, to check that her overall shape is working. If you trim too much, you can glue some foam back on and continue trimming. Once you're done, cut careful slits in the back of the foam to allow later access to set screws. Attach her feet and head, and you now have a 100 per cent completed Nia puppet!

Figure 5.16
The completed Nia puppet.
Lightweight and durable, Nia is easy to pose and easy to fix.

SUPPLIER INFORMATION

This section offers advice on *how* to locate certain materials, as opposed to listing specific vendors. That's because specific vendors come and go, and the world is a big place – so providing a relevant list for where *you* specifically live isn't very feasible.

As with armature making materials and supplies, remember to consult stop motion social media spaces for regional help.

Moulding and casting products

Start by searching for sculpting supply stores and special effects shops. Stores that carry silicone and resin will likely carry most of the other specialized items, like plastic measuring cups and oil-based clay (art stores also carry this kind of clay).

Vinyl and nitrile gloves

These can be found at most drug stores and hardware stores. Remember to avoid latex gloves, as silicone doesn't react well with latex.

Primer paint for resin

Hardware store brands might work, but the best kind is specially formulated for model kits and role-playing figures, so try hobby stores and comic book stores.

Eye beads, floral wire

Try craft stores or art supply stores.

Various tapes

Look in sports supply stores or hardware stores. Also look in craft stores.

Two-part liquid epoxy adhesive

As fancy as this product's name is, it's quite common, and is sold at hardware stores.

Colourless makeup powder

Look for this at high-end makeup stores and at theatrical supply stores. If you can't find it, you *can* use regular talcum powder, but it tends to give silicone a slightly shiny look (which doesn't look as good in front of the camera).

Upholstery foam

You can buy large chunks of this at fabric stores. If you can't find it there, find any thrift store cushion that is firm, and pull out the foam. In a pinch you can even use dollar store kitchen sponges!

The costume

Covering up puppet bits is the very basic thing that the costume does. In a very real way, the costume *completes* the character. Imagine a doctor, an opera singer, and a construction worker. To a large extent, it's the specific costumes of these characters that help to immediately differentiate each of them. An effectively costumed puppet will help your audience to understand your character better, and will inspire the animator to create richer performances.

This chapter offers you some important considerations that you should keep in mind as you design puppet costumes. It then shows you step by step instructions for fabricating Nia's specific costume. As with previous fabrication chapters, this one also lays out all the materials and tools that you'll need.

By the end of this chapter you'll have a better understanding of costuming for stop motion puppets, and you'll have the practical training necessary to fabricate Nia's costume. You'll then be able to expand upon these skills as you take on more costuming challenges, further along your stop motion path.

Figure 6.1
Opera singer costume, *Prima Donna*, Seema Virdi, 2013.
This comedic Sheridan College film features a beautifully
costumed puppet whose character is very nicely clarified by
her costume.

Overview of costumes for stop motion

Designing and creating a costume for a puppet is very much like designing and creating a costume for a living person. A pattern using the person's specific measurements is first made. That pattern is then traced on to the chosen fabric, which is then cut and assembled into the final costume. Creating a costume for Nia will proceed in exactly the same way.

If you don't have any experience with sewing, this stage of production might be rather challenging. Machine sewing is a delicate art, to say the least. You need to know how to use the machine, and you also need to be familiar with a variety of stitching methods, and have experience using them. You *can* use the following instructions to help you hand-sew Nia's costume. It will take longer by hand, but you can still get very good results.

If you're really stuck when it comes to sewing, the good news is that there are lots of folks out there with great sewing skills, who would likely love the challenge and fun of making Nia's relatively simple costume. Hand this nice person a plate of homemade cookies (the internationally recognized currency for 'favour-asking'), along with this book and your finished Nia puppet, and all will be well.

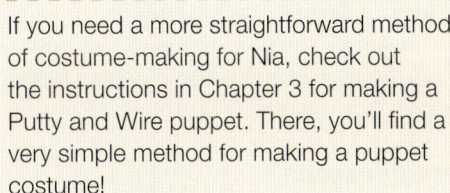

If you need a more straightforward method of costume-making for Nia, check out the instructions in Chapter 3 for making a Putty and Wire puppet. There, you'll find a very simple method for making a puppet costume!

Essential considerations

As fun as costume design and fabrication can be, it's useful to keep a few things in mind before you dive in.

Armature access

Always keep in mind that puppet parts often need adjusting or replacing. To deal with this, there needs to be decent access to the armature to allow for these 'operations'. Take it from me, there are few things more painful than having to rip a lovely costume apart, just to patch an arm or leg. The more you can plan access into your costume, the better. Even then, you may need to rip a few stitches to get access, but that isn't the end of the world, since it's usually a quick patch up. But the less damage required to the costume, the better.

Ease of movement

If a puppet can't be posed, it can't be animated! This can be a real challenge with costuming puppets when you need to create a form-fitting costume that shows off the puppet's shape. Create a costume that's too tight, and the puppet literally can't be posed. Alternately, creating a loose and baggy costume might make animation easier, but it can actually *hide* the posing of the puppet, as the puppet gets lost inside all that fabric! Finding a middle ground is often the best way forward.

Ornaments and accessories

Adornments and extra bits are often what truly sell a costume. Imagine a witch character, with a cobweb-inspired shawl, a bone necklace, and a belt made of strange charms and creepy little details. She might look wonderful, but animating her could be a huge challenge if all those bits aren't properly secured! As you dream up your designs, be sure to give attention to just how any loose bits can be secured when it comes time for animation.

Camera concerns

Not all patterns and designs look good on camera. Fabrics with thin stripes and certain weaves can often 'buzz' and shimmer in a very distracting way once in front of a camera. When possible, always test fabric selections in front of a camera, before committing. Even better, see how the material looks when animated, to be extra certain that your choice is a good one. A quick animation test on a fabric choice can save a *lot* of trouble down the road.

The research stage

In Nia's case, we informally included costume design into her character design stage. In part, this was so we knew very early on just how much of the Nia puppet would require silicone skin, versus how much of her would be covered by fabric. No sense worrying about fabricating skin if we're never going to see it! Also, Nia's character allowed for a simple costume – she's an 'everyday' sort of character, who is suited to a simple T-shirt and a pair of pants.

But in other cases, detailed costume design work comes about via its own research, and that can be a huge amount of fun, as well as a chance for great creative expression. As with character design, consider making a collage image of all of your inspirations, and from that collage start sketching out your own ideas on to your character's actual design. As you craft your costume, make sure that you remember the considerations for stop motion, as outlined above.

**Figure 6.2
Nia T-shirt
variations.**
A T-shirt design, painted or attached directly on to Nia's shirt, is a great (and simple) way to express character. There are endless options, but here's a few to get you started. Each conveys a very different sense of character!

Figure 6.3
Rigoletto, Barry Purves, 1995.
Here we see wonderfully ornate costumes that offer rich visual pleasure for the viewer. This film is a puppet costumer's dream come true!

Choosing fabrics

It can be a lot of fun searching for just the right fabric for your puppet. You can head to actual fabric stores, but since you don't need a lot of material for a puppet, thrift stores can also be a great (and affordable) resource. You can make some very unexpected and fun discoveries in these stores. As you search, keep in mind the weight and scale of the fabrics. You want something that matches the scale of the puppet and its world, but that also won't impede the movements of the puppet. In short, you want fabrics that are believable, and that are also not too thick or bulky.

You also want fabrics that won't *fray* a lot while you work with them, and that are generally easy to work within during sewing, and during animation. The fabrics for both Nia's shirt and pants are cotton; the shirt is a thin cotton stretch,

and the pants are a denim-looking fabric, which is also a thin cotton. Her pants fabric has the *look* of denim, but not the *thickness* of it. Real denim would be far too thick to work with at this scale, and would look very awkward on Nia!

Figure 6.4
Fabric for Nia's costume.
Match the colours you see here, or have fun picking own your own custom combinations. Notice Nia's unpainted head and rough seams in her arms. See below for details.

The following instructions for Nia's costume-making assume a certain amount of sewing knowledge, but any unfamiliar terms or concepts can be quickly clarified through an online search.

Making Nia's costume

For Nia's costume, rather than completing each item fully before moving on to the next, you'll instead be working on *both* her shirt and her pants, at the same time, as you move through to completion. The specific stages that you'll follow are: pattern-making, cutting the fabric, and finally pinning and sewing.

Compared to the previous chapters on fabrication, gathering materials and supplies for costume-making won't require materials from a wide range of suppliers. Just about everything that you need you'll be able to find at a fabric store,

and anything that they don't carry you should be able to find at an art supply or craft store.

The process of costuming can be surprisingly rough on the puppet, since it gets flipped over and turned around a lot on the worktable. There are also sharp pins and snipping scissors flying around, which can cause scratches to paint and silicone. Consider casting a temporary head and arms for the costuming stage (or re-using early attempts that aren't perfect), and keep your proper 'camera ready' head and arms safely stored during this stage.

As for Nia's feet, you'll probably want her to stand at times as you work on her costume, so you'll likely need to use her final feet during costuming. Just be careful with them, and be prepared to touch them up if scratches happen.

The following stages of fabrication were created in collaboration with animation artist **Carla Veldman**. Carla's puppet costume work has appeared in a range of stop motion projects, and her animated work has appeared in both commercial and independent film pieces. Her own films have played in animation festivals, internationally. Look for her films, online.

MATERIALS

final Nia design, printed to scale (Figure 2.5)
final colour design for Nia
thin paper or tissue paper

TOOLS

sewing machine
serger (optional)
pencil, pen, eraser, markers
quilter's iron (a specialized 'mini iron', for small, precision work)
liquid seam sealant (Fray Check is a good brand, but other brands are fine)
pin cushion and pins

thread (to match shirt and pants fabric)
fabric snips
stitch ripper
seam gauge (a specialized tool measuring seam allowance)
fabric scissors
fabric glue
double-sided tape

STEP BY STEP

1. Trace the pants on to a piece of thin paper or tissue paper. As you trace, give yourself some extra room for the seam allowance – this is the space taken up by the edge of the fabric, and by the seam itself.

2. As you trace the pants, you only need to draw one side of a pant-half. You should then cut the pattern on a fold (see Figure 6.5). This ensures that your final pattern (and later, your cut fabric pieces) will be equal on both sides. This is very beneficial when it comes to matching pieces up for sewing together, so it's highly recommended! You can use the same technique on the shirt as well.

Figure 6.6
Wrapping the pattern around the puppet.
If there's not enough seam allowance, Nia's costume will be too small or too snug, so take your time getting the pattern right.

Figure 6.5
Cutting pattern on a fold.
Using this method for cutting ensures a symmetrical pattern, which makes sewing much easier.

Figure 6.7
The finished pant pattern.
You'll eventually trace out two of these shapes on to your fabric in order to make the pants.

To ensure that the pants pattern piece is the right size, wrap the pattern around one half of the puppet (see Figure 6.6). Do the edges of the pattern meet the center of the puppet, both in the front and back? If they do, will there be enough extra room for seam allowance? It's best to err on the side of more seam allowance; if there's too much, you can always trim it down after you've sewn it. Line the pattern up on the puppet, and ensure that there's enough room around the waist, as well as in the crotch area.

If the pattern piece that you cut turns out to be too small, simply redraw it a bit bigger, then cut it out and test it. Repeat until you're happy. Once you have this one final pant pattern piece, that's all you'll need.

3. Trace the main part of the shirt pattern in the same way that you traced the pants – don't trace the sleeves yet. Don't cut the neck hole too big, since it will get bigger when you eventually use some of the fabric to create a seam. Once you've drawn half of the pattern, fold this

Figure 6.8
Shirt pattern pinned to puppet.
Notice the dotted line showing seam allowance.

pattern in half and cut it, just as you did with the pants. Pin the pattern to the puppet. Does the pattern piece reach both sides and have some extra room for seam allowance? If not, trace a new one with more allowance.

4. Draw the pattern for the shirt's sleeve. You'll notice that the shape of the sleeve that gets sewn to the shoulder has an inverted curve to it, when compared to the sleeve hole (see Figure 6.9). This will allow the sleeve to curve down into the underarm, once sewn. If you make a sleeve that ignores the opposing curve, it will come out puckered and rumpled, and you will have to do a lot of adjusting to make it fit properly.

Figure 6.9
Drawing shirt sleeve pattern.
Be sure to include the opposing curve pattern.

Once you have the shirt sleeve pattern drawn, cut it on a fold as you did with the main shirt pattern and the pants pattern. That's it! Your patterns are done, and it's time to move on to cutting.

Figure 6.10
Final patterns: Pants, shirt, and sleeve.
You'll use each of these patterns twice when cutting out fabric.

5. Lay the fabric out on the table, making sure that it's 'right side up', and that the grain of fabric is properly positioned (for more on fabric grain, see the Professor Roy Box below). Pin each pattern piece, and trace it on to the fabric. Then, remove the pattern, flip the pattern over, pin the pattern again, and trace it again. Do all of this while the fabric is lying right side up, and you'll ensure that when you sew your pieces together, the rough side will be inside, and the 'right' side will be on the outside.

Fabric grain affects how the material behaves. The grain is often a visible thing, and you can confirm it by pulling on the material and taking note of how it behaves and stretches. For both Nia's shirt and pants, you want the material to stretch horizontally, so that the clothes will stretch around Nia's body.

6. Carefully cut the fabric. After the main pieces are cut, measure around the neck of the puppet and

Figures 6.11 and 6.12
All costume pieces ready for pinning and sewing.
Now is a good time to double-check that all of your pieces match your patterns.

cut out a rectangle of fabric for the shirt collar. Leave enough seam allowance for both the seam joining the piece at the back of the neck, as well as for the collar, that needs to be stitched to the neck hole, folded over, and stitched down.

7. It's time for pinning and sewing. If your fabric is prone to fraying, zig-zag it first. Alternately, you can serge it on a serger if you have one. A serger is a type of sewing machine that is used for sealing the edges of fabric to prevent fraying. If you don't have a serger, you can put liquid seam sealant on it, though be safe, test the liquid on a scrap of your fabric first. Clear nail polish can do the trick too, if you're in a pinch.

> A zig-zag stitch is a stitch that you can select on your sewing machine that runs the needle in a back-and-forth motion. When you use it to sew along the edge of a fabric that tends to fray, it holds the weave of the fabric in place and prevents the individual threads from splitting off.

8. Match up your pants pieces, and place them right side together. The 'right side' of the material is the side that will eventually be on the outside of the pants. By assembling them and sewing them right side together, you'll later be able to turn the pants inside out, which will reveal the right side. Pin the matched pieces along the 'U' curve at the top. On the one side, pin them just a little way up from the bottom of the 'U'. (If you're not sure where the 'U' curve is, you can see it clearly in Figure 6.14. It's more of a 'half U' curve, actually).

Figure 6.13
Pinned pants fabric.
Make sure the fabric is pinned right side together.

Put a few stitches below the pin to make the crotch seam, but leave the upper part open, to be hand-stitched later when you are stitching the finished pants onto the puppet. Using a straight stitch, sew the one 'U' side, back-tacking where you begin the stitching and also where you end the stitching.

> 'Back-tacking' means go back over your stitch a few times, to ensure that it's extra strong. This will help to prevent the garment's pieces from pulling apart.

Figure 6.14
Stitching the pants.
The 'U' curve of the pants, neatly stitched.

> **DEBORAH COOK**
>
> A remarkable talent in the puppet-costuming world, Deborah Cook is known for her work on *Corpse Bride, Fantastic Mr. Fox, ParaNorman*, and *The Boxtrolls*. Creating a lovely miniature costume is tricky enough, but fashioning it in such a way as to allow for ultra-precise animation is another. Her gorgeous puppet costumes are works of art, and marvels of design and engineering.

9. Take note of the piece that you kept open, then open the pants, and fold them so that the crotch seams you just sewed are lined up and touching each other. Pin along the insides of the pant legs and stitch those together, giving enough seam allowance in the crotch area. You will need to have enough room to put a few snips in the fabric, because it tends to

clump up a little due to the excess fabric from the seam allowance.

Figure 6.15
The stitched pants.
Only a few final steps remain before the pants are complete.

10. Try the pants on the puppet. If the legs are too roomy, take them in a little. If they're too snug and you have room to let them out a bit, go for it. If there's not enough room to do so, it's back to adjusting the pattern and re-cutting.

11. Once you're happy, you can hem the pants. Hemming is a finishing method that used on openings in garments. It ensures that the opening won't fray, and that it looks nice and neat. To do this, turn the pants right side out, fold over the raw edges to make the pants and their waistline the length that you want, and use the quilter's iron to press them, to keep them folded in place. You can either machine-stitch them if there's enough room, otherwise hand-stitch them with a needle and thread. Hand stitch the pants up the back using a

Figure 6.16
Pressing pants with a quilter's iron.
Press the hemmed edges when you're finished to give the pants a bit more of a worn-in look as opposed to a 'freshly sewn' feel.

ladder stitch to hide the stitching, and there you have it – Nia's finished pants!

12. Now it's time to pin and sew Nia's shirt. With right sides together, pin the top edges of the shirt, and sew them. Once sewn, pull the pieces open and lay the shirt out flat. Then pin the shoulders of the shirt to the shirt-sleeves. Once pinned, sew the sleeves in place.

TITUS, JULIE TAYMOR, 2005 COSTUMES BY MILENA CANONERO

This film isn't stop motion, although director Taymor certainly has a strong background in puppets – she staged the very successful Broadway version of Disney's *The Lion King*, which made wonderful use of puppetry. In this bloody and brilliant adaptation of the Shakespeare play, costumer Canonero creates costumes that are wild blends of styles and periods. The costumes are unexpected and daring, and serve as a great example of how powerful costumes can add real energy and depth to a production.

Figure 6.17
Shirt and sleeve pieces sewn together.
For the following steps, you'll also need the rectangular collar piece that you cut out earlier (not shown here).

13. Next, pin the shirt collar in place around the neck hole. Start by taking the rectangular collar piece and, with its right side and the shirt facing each other, wrap it around the opening of the neck hole along one of the

collar's long edges. Make sure that the edge of the collar and the edge of the shirt meet up – this is your seam allowance for attaching the collar to the shirt. The seam that you make to join the short edges of the collar's rectangle together (to make the rectangular piece into a circular collar) can either line up with the shirt's already-existing shoulder seam, or else be positioned centrally on the back of the shirt.

Pin the long edge of the collar to the shirt first (remember, right sides together), making sure to leave some space around the short edges so that you have enough seam allowance there to join the collar to itself afterwards.

Try the shirt on the puppet to determine how much seam allowance you'll need for that seam. Once you've determined the seam allowance, stitch down the long edge of the collar around the neck hole. It's often better to hand-stitch this, since it's so small. Once that's finished, pin and stitch together the short ends of the collar (right sides together) so that you've joined it into a circle.

Figure 6.19
Finishing the collar.
Once the collar is sewn, carefully trim off any extra bulky seam allowance that's left over.

Figure 6.20
The shirt with sleeves partly done.
Take your time fitting the shirt. You want Nia to look as nice as possible during animation.

Figure 6.18
The attached shirt collar.
Hand stitching the collar is a good idea, since the piece is so small.

14. Following that, from the outside of the shirt, fold the collar over, and tuck the raw edge into the inside of the shirt. Adjust for the final height you want the collar to be, then pin and hand-stitch it into place, using the invisible hem stitch to hide the stitches in the crease/seam of the collar (see Figure 6.19).

15. Fold the shirt, right sides together, and pin down one side of the sleeve and shirt. Sew

them together, and try the shirt on the puppet – is it fitting well? If it's not, adjust accordingly: take it in, let it out if possible, or redo part of the sleeve.

16. Once you're happy, carefully make a few snips in the fabric in the seam allowance right by the armpit of the shirt, in order to free up the fabric a little. Don't snip too far in, or you'll have a hole in the shirt! You can now sew the other side of the shirt (either with the machine, or hand-stitch, using a ladder stitch).

17. Try the shirt on the puppet. Make any adjustments that are needed. Determine the hem lengths for the sleeves and pin them. If you don't want the stitching to show on the hems, use an invisible hem stitch.

18. Hem the bottom of the shirt as well, fit it on the puppet, and you're done!

Figure 6.21
The completed Nia puppet and costume.
Nia is ready for animation!

After all that hard work, your Nia puppet is finally done. From a rough initial idea, through to a completed puppet, you now have all of your hard work right there in front of you. You'll notice that in Figure 6.21, Nia is featured with her animatable facial features. It makes for a nice photo, but you should leave these *off* your puppet for now, until it's time for animation. This will minimize the chance that clay or wax will mark her face, prior to her going in front of the camera.

This concludes the section on Puppet Fabrication. You've now got a very professional stop motion puppet, which is full of animation potential. Nia is just waiting to come to life! But before that can happen, you'll need to establish a bit of physical space that will allow that life to happen. Fortunately, you'll find everything that you need to know about that in the very next chapter.

Part two

The studio

Part two of this book is dedicated to helping you get
everything ready prior to animation. That 'everything'
begins with establishing an effective space in which you
can create your animation. With that accomplished, this part
moves into chapters that train you in camera and lighting
for stop motion. An animated puppet will only *really* look its
best when it's lit and photographed effectively. And since
your objective is to become a well-rounded stop motion
artist, who eventually has what it takes to make an accomplished short film, all of these skills will prove essential.

Physical space

The focus of this particular chapter is the creation of a modest but effective home studio space. The insights you'll discover here are based on how I've set up my own home studio, in which I've shot many stop motion projects, both for myself and for clients. Its design is based on commercial stop motion studios that I've worked at over my career, which I then modified to better suit a home space. I assure you that what you'll find here has been developed with a budget in mind. Costs can add up quickly, and I've done my best to offer economical solutions, as well as tips on cutting further costs, whenever I can.

This chapter also shows you in detail how to construct an animation deck, which is the specialized stage that Nia is animated upon. It's an essential item for any stop motion studio, but it isn't exactly something that you can buy at the corner store!

By the end of this chapter, you'll have a much better understanding of the specifics required to create a modest but effective home studio within which you can start to seriously apply yourself to your stop motion training.

Figure 7.1
Komaneko:
The Curious Cat
It doesn't take
a lot of fancy
equipment to
set up a home
studio, just ask
Komaneko! A
stop motion cat
makes a stop
motion movie,
in this charming
Japanese series.

(Almost) any room will do

Just what is a 'studio'? At its core, a studio is a space dedicated to making something. If you're a commercial animation studio, that space might take up a huge amount of real estate. But if you're working on your own, *any* space that you can dedicate to your work can be your studio.

Figure 7.2
The Amautalik, Inhabit Media, 2014.
A small studio space requires you to be creative. On this particular project that I shot for a client, I used a puppet, along with modest set pieces, on a green screen background. An expansive Arctic vista was then added in post-production.

Over the years, I've mentored many stop motion student films. Some of those have been created on campus in a fairly spacious studio room, while others have been created, quite literally, at home. The student has pushed his bed to one side of the room, set up some animation equipment, and made a stop motion film!

The strong films that result from this 'bedroom studio' approach prove that it's not how *much* space you have, or how fancy it is, it's how you *use* that space. If you have talent and passion, a small studio space isn't going to prevent you from making great work. And just think about the convenience – after a hard day of animating puppets, you'll be able to just take a few steps to the side and fall into your bed for a good night's sleep. Nothing beats a short commute between work and home!

I practice this same approach – of making the most of a small space – with my own home studio. I've managed to dedicate a single (and very cozy) room to my studio efforts. I work within the constraints of that space, and I don't let the lack of real estate hold me back from dreaming up (and making) my stop motion films.

That being said, you can't exactly set up a stop motion studio *anywhere*. There *are* a few specific attributes that you need to look for, as you set things up.

Dedicated space

Your animation studio space may not be huge, but if it's dedicated to your project, you're well on your way. As with all forms of animation, stop motion takes a lot of *time*. But unlike a computer animated project, or a project that's drawn on paper or tablet, you can't pack up the stop motion work and do it on a laptop somewhere else. You need to know that your studio space (and your sets and puppets) can remain undisturbed for the length of your animation. Couldn't you animate for a bit, take things down so the space can be used for something else, then set things back up again? Yes – but it's not ideal, and should be avoided, if at all possible. You owe it to yourself, and to your stop motion aspirations, to have a space in which you can work. Even it's just for the length of your project's animation.

A solid, level floor

This is important, because a bouncy or uneven floor means that even modest shifts or wobbles will work their way up into your stop motion project. Depending on your studio floor, you may find that you need to keep yourself in a certain spot when recording each frame, so that you don't cause the set to shift! It's just 'one of those things' in the life of a stop motion artist, but the more you can do to address this when setting yourself up, the better. The more level and sturdy your floor, the happier you will be long term.

Reliable, convenient electricity

Ideally, there should be several wall outlets in your studio space. The more outlets, the easier it is to plug in your equipment and lights, and the less tripping hazards you'll have, because you won't have power cords snaking their way around your feet. If there are no outlets in your space, can you safely and easily run power and power bars from somewhere else, to your space? As for the actual electrical usage, you won't be putting a huge strain on any of the outlets, and the wiring in most homes and buildings is quite adequate for what you'll need.

Control over lighting

There's no reason why you couldn't set up a studio space in a corner of a larger room. But if the rest of the room needs to be used for other things besides stop motion, how will you ensure that the lighting in your studio space can be controlled? You don't want your lighting to change in the middle of a shot, because someone turned on the overhead lights to do laundry! Professional studios solve this by hanging heavy black curtains around each studio space, so that it becomes a self-contained 'world', but that's not the most practical or affordable solution at home. Better to find another solution, such as avoiding the use of overhead lights entirely, and using smaller desk lights for areas of the room that need lighting. Since a desk light doesn't cast light very far, this lets you maintain lighting control in your shooting area. Of course, the *best* solution is to have a room that is used only for animating, if such a thing can be arranged. You'll also need to address unwanted light coming in from exterior windows. Unless you plan to do all your animating at night, a couple of black garbage bags or some cardboard taped to the window works well. Neighbours may suspect that you're a vampire, but that's their problem.

If you *are* a vampire, you probably have your windows covered already, so you can skip this above step.

A large, sturdy table

This table can serve a couple of functions in your studio. It's a worktable for making puppets and sets, but once those stages are completed, it can then be used as the surface upon which you will place the animation deck. Avoid using a table with folding legs, since they tend to be not sturdy enough for animation. You should also look for a table that has a lot of clearance under its surface – you can use this space to store items in bins, and it also provides you with more room for your feet and legs, while you're animating. A very simple solution for a sturdy table can be found at a store like IKEA. You can buy a very robust table top, along with the four metal legs that screw into it. Very simple, very sturdy, and extremely affordable.

Making the animation deck

The animation deck is the stage upon which you create your animated performances. It sits *on top* of the sturdy table, allowing you to stand in front of the set-up, and animate comfortably.

Start by measuring the surface of the table you'll be animating upon. Reduce these dimensions by a bit, and that is the width and depth of the animation deck that you will be building. By making the deck a bit smaller than your table, the deck will rest securely on the sturdier table.

The completed deck will have legs that you will custom cut to suit your own height. Everyone likes to work at a different height, but personally I like to have my elbows at about a 90-degree angle while animating – so I make my deck legs accordingly. Just don't make the deck too low, or too high – you're going to be spending a lot of time working at it, and you want to avoid muscle strain as much as possible.

Before you buy your materials (especially the lumber for the frame and the legs), do your measurements for the frame, and determine the height of your deck legs – this will tell you how much lumber you'll need to buy.

Working safe

As with all fabrication stages, you need to be mindful of safety concerns when you're constructing the deck. You'll be cutting wood, so be sure that you're wearing safety glasses, and that you're being safe around the saw blade. Work in a space that's big enough for the lumber and tools. Depending on where you're working, you may also want to put down a tarp or a blanket to prevent damaging the floor.

MATERIALS

masonite (also known as hardboard) for deck surface (these boards often come pre-cut to a size that might work for you. If the pre-cut size isn't right, buy a bigger size, and ask the store to cut it for you, or cut it yourself)
lumber for deck frame and deck legs, approx. 2.54 × 7.62 cm (1 × 3 inches) × whatever length you've calculated
small box of medium length wood screws (long enough to secure the legs to the deck)
finishing nails
4 small 'L' shaped metal brackets (optional, to secure the deck legs to the table)
small wood screws (for 'L' brackets)

TOOLS

pencil
ruler
hand saw (or power saw)
hammer
power drill
drill bits

screw driver bits for drill (you could just use a regular screw driver, but using the drill will be a lot faster and easier)
medium grade sandpaper
safety glasses

STEP BY STEP

1. The masonite that you'll use for the deck's surface may already be an appropriate size for your deck. If it's not, you'll need to cut it to size. Once the masonite is the correct size lay it down on the ground.

2. Measure each side of the masonite. Transfer those measurements to the wood and cut the pieces for the frame. Sand the ends of the wood down a bit, to prevent splinters.

3. Assemble the frame on top of the masonite, ensuring that all of the pieces fit cleanly around the outside edge. Drill pilot holes through the frame pieces, in the spots where you intend to insert screws.

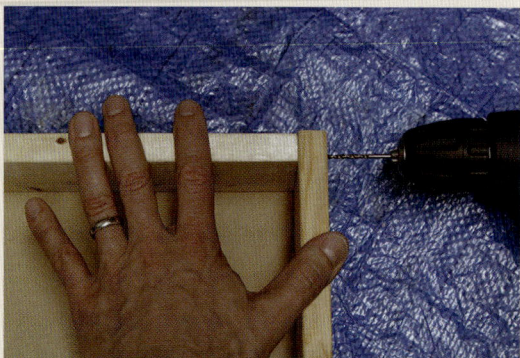

Figure 7.3
Drilling pilot holes.
Pilot holes are small holes that you drill *before* inserting the screws. These holes help to prevent the relatively soft wood from cracking when you insert the screws later.

4. Insert the screws into the pilot holes. Don't over tighten, or you'll crack the wood. When you're done, you should have a sturdy frame.
5. Slide the masonite out from under the frame, and place it on *top* of the frame. Ensure that its edges are flush with the frame. Attach it to the frame with small nails. Once the masonite is attached to the frame, flip it over once more. You should now have a shallow 'box'.
6. Determine the height that you want your deck to be, and use that height to calculate how long to make the deck legs. Each leg consists of two lengths of wood, each cut to the length you just calculated. Ensure that the ends of each piece are level, or you'll have a wobbly deck. Assemble two of the leg pieces into an 'L' shape (see Figure 7.4). Drill two pilot holes, and insert screws to complete the leg. Repeat for the other legs. You should now have four 'L' shaped legs. Ensure that they are the same height, so that your deck won't wobble.
7. Secure the first leg squarely into a corner of the deck. It should sit snugly. Drill two or three pilot holes from the outside of the deck, being sure to drill through into the leg. Then insert screws to secure the leg to the deck. Repeat on the other side of the leg. Repeat on all the legs.

Figure 7.4
Attaching the deck legs.
Make sure that the leg is pulled in tight to the corner of the deck before you insert the screws.

8. Flip the deck over. Ensure that the deck doesn't wobble. If it does, further trim or sand down the legs as needed.

Figure 7.5
The finished animation deck.
This deck can also be used for tie-down puppets, since the masonite is easy to drill through.

Set the deck on to your table. To keep the deck from shifting during animation, you can use a metal 'L' bracket to secure the deck legs to the table. If the surface of the deck sags, wedge a piece of wood underneath the surface to stabilize it. Reposition this wedge as needed *before* each shot, to ensure that it's out of the way of your puppet's magnets or tie downs. You don't want your puppet's movement on the deck blocked by a misplaced wedge!

You can paint this deck as needed, or add a textured surface, to create whatever look you want for your project. To save on wear and tear, you could tape or glue a very thin skin of plastic over the deck, then paint or texture that surface, instead of the deck itself.

This deck is fairly lightweight and portable, so you can easily remove it from the table if you need the table's surface for making puppets or sets. Then just set it back up when it's time to animate. This can be a great solution when working in a small studio space.

BOTTLE, KIRSTEN LEPORE, 2011

This bittersweet story of a long-distance relationship has been a huge hit with audiences worldwide. The film's stark contrast to a 'studio' stop motion film, since *Bottle* was created entirely outdoors. Lepore's characters carry out their touching and funny tale, oblivious to the wildly shifting landscapes. It's as though they only care about each other, and uncontrollable aspects of setting and lighting only serve to emphasize the power of their relationship. This film wouldn't be half as impactful if it had been created in a fully regulated studio space.

The computer

For just about any stop motion project these days, you're going to need a computer. You'll use it for capturing your frames during animation, and also for doing a lot of other tasks, from editing storyboard panels together into a motion picture file, to editing the final animation, to working with your sound and music, to doing visual effects.

As for memory and hard drive requirements, today's computers typically have more than enough of both to handle the animation stage of your production. As for other motion picture work (editing, sound, visual effects), the more memory and hard drive space you have, the better. If you're considering a laptop versus a desktop, I'm of the opinion that for a home studio, a laptop computer is a slick way to go, because it's small, portable, and powerful. But a desktop style computer is completely fine (and often more affordable) – you'll just need to design your shooting space around its size. If you have the space and the funds, you may consider adding a very good monitor into the mix, because so much of stop motion depends on how the image looks. But again, most modern computer monitors are excellent, and are completely sufficient for most projects.

There are many exciting stop motion apps available for tablets and phones. These options are immediate and fun, but are typically limited in their functionality. They also don't allow for a professional workflow, so for more advanced projects, the app option should probably be avoided.

Should you use a Mac or a PC? It's the question that has plagued artists since the days of the caveman (when all they had to animate were rocks). I am a Mac guy myself, but whatever works for you. Remember it's not the computer that makes the great stop motion project – it's *you*.

One bit of computer hardware I would strongly recommend that you invest in is an external hard drive. Get into the habit of regularly backing up your project to this drive. During the animation stage of a project, I back up externally at the end of every day. If you can't afford your own external drive, then back up to someone else's computer, or to some form of cloud storage, daily. Animation is just too labour-intensive to run the risk of losing all of that hard work.

but has a wide array of very advanced features as well, all for a relatively low cost.

Because Dragonframe is so essential to stop motion, this book assumes that you have a certain amount of proficiency in it. As such, you won't find a lot of basic instructions in this book, so if you're new to this software, take the time to get proficient with it. You'll find more about Dragonframe on the company's website, which has lots of constantly updated tutorials.

Overview of Adobe applications

Adobe creates a wide range of software that is used in the motion picture world. These applications are currently available via online subscription through Adobe's Cloud service. You subscribe, then download the software to your machine, and receive updates accordingly. There are four applications by Adobe that are of central importance for stop motion work.

Photoshop

This is one of Adobe's first (and most popular) applications. It's used to modify still images, and can be used in stop motion to edit individual frames of animation.

Photoshop is an excellent choice for 'cleaning up' frames that need colour correction or rig removal. Also, you can use Photoshop to create images for backgrounds for green-screened animation. These are just a few uses of Photoshop for stop motion; there are lots more you'll discover over time.

Premiere

Premiere is used for editing motion picture projects (including animation). You import your footage and sounds, arrange and manipulate them in a timeline until you're happy, then export the final project. As simple as that sounds, Premiere is an extremely powerful piece of software that lets you try out all kinds of creative choices with the click of a button. As you craft your stop motion project's final blend of picture and sound, you'll spend a *lot* of time inside this application.

After Effects

If you're dreaming up an effects-heavy stop motion project, After Effects will help you realize your vision. Whereas Photoshop is mostly used on individual images or frames, After Effects is typically

Roy's hard drive has just died, and he has no back up. He's lost months of work. Roy is *not* a happy puppet.

Software essentials

You'll need software for the animation stage, but also for all the other motion picture and sound work that's required to make a stop motion film. There are *lots* of options out there. Some options are quite cheap and in some cases, free, which is great – but because they are very inexpensive, they may not allow you to do all that you'll want to do on your project. The applications listed here are not super cheap, but they *are* extremely powerful, and are used widely by professionals around the world. That makes them a solid investment that you're likely to get a lot of use from as you carry on in life. These applications have also proven themselves to be extremely useful in the world of stop motion, which is why they'll be focused upon quite closely in later sections of this book.

Overview of Dragonframe

There's a wide range of frame-capturing software out there, but only one has distinguished itself in recent years as the software of choice for the medium. Dragonframe serves the needs of everyone, from feature film projects to grade school students. Dragonframe's greatest strength is that it was designed in part by an artist, rather than strictly by a computer programmer from outside the medium. As a result, it does exactly what a stop motion animator wants it to, in a sensible way. It can function as very basic frame-grabbing software for simple projects, used on motion picture footage. In other words, After Effects lets you manipulate entire shots, rather than just frames. It can be used to create wildly extravagant composites, but it can also be used to do very subtle things. It's great for handling rig removal, colour correction, and green screen work. You can also use it for adding post-production effects like fog, smoke, water, fire, explosions, and just about anything else you can imagine.

Audition

While the other Adobe applications deal primarily with images, Audition is designed to assist with sound. It allows you to professionally set up, monitor, record, and (if needed) manipulate whatever sounds your project requires, whether it's effects, music, dialogue, or narration. Audition then allows you to save that sound in file formats that can be easily shared with other applications, such as Dragonframe and Premiere.

THE STREET, CAROLINE LEAF, 1976

This much-praised NFB adaptation of a Mordecai Richler story shows what can happen when an artist is able to sink into a studio experience. To tell the story of a Jewish family in Montreal that's struggling to deal with an ailing grandmother, Leaf painted each frame on glass. The entire film carries with it a sense of intense concentration and dedication to a very specific atmosphere and tone. The film has a deeply intimate, almost claustrophobic feel to it, which comes in part from the nature of the story, and in part because you feel like you are right there with Leaf in her darkened studio, as she painstakingly crafts each and every frame.

Additional studio items

Every stop motion project and studio space has its own particular requirements, and over time, you'll slowly acquire more tools and items to help you along. But there are certain items that make the process of stop motion much easier, and these are found in just about every studio space.

Computer cart

Since you stand while animating, your computer needs to be at a height that's comfortable, or else you will very quickly strain your back, neck, and arms. If you're using a laptop, you can use a small but sturdy cart. I set a metal box on top of my cart and then put my laptop on that, as a way to get my computer up to a comfortable height. Ideally your cart should have wheels, so that you can easily move it around the studio space, as you set up the camera for each new shot.

Grip items

Grip equipment does exactly that – it grips (or secures) items into their place, safely and effectively. Grip equipment is often used to fasten elements in front of lights in order to achieve a final look. It's also used to secure set pieces, or to hold certain visual elements within a scene. For example, a tree branch that can be seen dangling behind a set's window may be held in place by a piece of grip equipment.

What follows is a brief list of some of the most common (and useful) pieces of studio grip equipment that you might want to invest in. Bear in mind that professional grip equipment can be quite expensive. Before spending, think through the task at hand and see if there is a more affordable way to achieve it, before spending big money. Hardware stores offer lots of different clamps, fasteners, and assorted hardware bits that can do the trick – and are a lot less expensive.

As you continue to set up your studio space, remember that in time you'll use up floor space well beyond your animation table and deck. Your computer cart, tripod, grip equipment, and light stands all need a good amount of space, so be sure to allow for that in your planning. And don't forget to allow space for the most important piece of the stop motion studio – you!

Light stands

These are important. Photography stores carry a wide selection of basic stands that are typically used for holding studio lights and flash equipment, but they're also great for grip purposes as well. Their height is adjustable, and you can attach a range of items to them fairly easily. These stands are also pretty cheap and quite sturdy. Since you'll also be able to use them to hold lights, a couple or three of these are essential studio items.

> Stands can easily tip over if they're holding up a heavy weight. Be sure to safely secure your stands!

DIY stand adaptors

A lot of basic hardware store clamps that are useful for stop motion can't grip the smooth peg end of a light stand very effectively. This little home-made adaptor solves that problem by offering something for a clamp to grab. It is also very useful for inexpensive clamp-on lights (see Chapter 8 on Lighting).

Figure 7.6
Stand adaptor.
Take a small wooden block and drill a hole in one end that is just big enough to allow the block to slide on to the stand's peg, and deep enough so that the block rests securely. Then drill another smaller hole in from the side, to allow a bolt to tighten on to the stand's peg, as pictured. That's it!

Clamps

Clamps come in all kinds of sizes and styles, and over time you'll come across just the right ones to serve your specific studio needs. You can find specialized ones (like the one pictured below) at photography stores, and at suppliers of film and television equipment. You can find cheaper, more general ones at hardware stores.

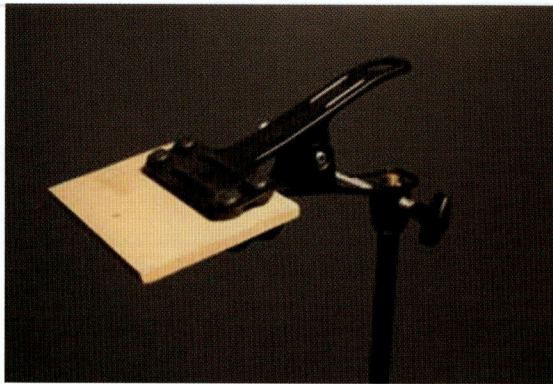

Figure 7.7
Clamp.
Clamps can be attached to light stands and used for all kinds of purposes. Secure a thin piece of wood in place (as pictured here), and you can then attach clamp-on lights to the wood. You can also hot glue some strong wire to the wood as a way to suspend items for lighting effects. Use the same method for suspending set items, like tree branches.

Grip stands

Grip stands (also known as C-stands) use an ingenious system of adjustable joints and arms, which allow for very precise and secure positioning of items on set. They are also extremely useful when it comes time to rig a puppet for jumping or flying.

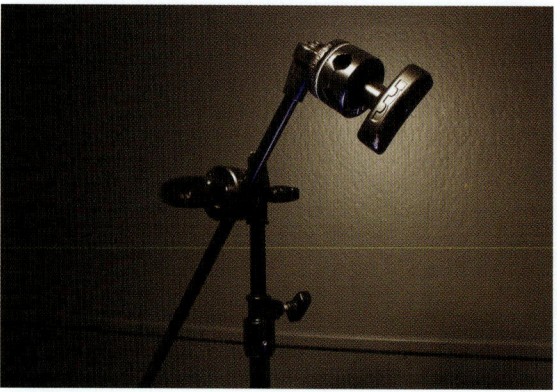

Figure 7.8
Grip stand.
These extremely useful stands come in various sizes, and can be used to hold all sorts of things, large and small.

They're also pricey, and take up a lot of floor space, so before buying, try to envision simpler and cheaper ways of achieving what you need to do. But if you can afford it, and if you have the floor space, nothing beats a grip stand. Look for them at the same specialty stores that stock the other grip items listed above.

Grip stands also come as simple arms that can be attached to an animation deck. These arms are a bit cheaper and take up less floor space, which makes them a good alternative for a small home studio.

Finishing touches

You'll always be adding to your studio's list of equipment, but to wrap up the essentials, there are a few more important items that you'll want to secure for your studio space:

- a small selection of basic hand tools (pliers, screwdriver, utility knife, etc.)
- a small floor mat (to prevent sore feet, legs, and back)
- one or two power bars
- a few extension cords

Tools of the trade: The stop motion animator's on-set toolkit

Take a look inside the kit of a stop motion animator and you'll find an eclectic assortment of mostly everyday items that nonetheless serve very specific purposes. A stop motion animator is constantly contending with the effects of gravity, so you'll notice that a lot of the items listed below are used for securing and stabilizing puppets and set items. And of course, since the stop motion animator operates within a miniature world, a lot of these items are geared towards precision work. Having these materials and tools within arm's reach will make your daily animation life a lot easier.

Figure 7.9
Helping hands.
This is a very useful and affordable tool that has two adjustable clamping arms that can hold small items on set. It's also great for holding props during construction and painting. Look for this tool at hobby stores.

JIM DANFORTH

Although not as well known as Ray Harryhausen, Danforth was responsible for some of the finest special effects stop motion during the medium's Hollywood heyday. Danforth's special effects work wasn't confined to stop motion – his work as a matte artist and special effects miniature artist brought countless fantasy, horror, and sci-fi worlds to life. An examination of his incredible work continues to provide inspiration to today's animation and effects artists.

Figure 7.10
Home studio set up.
An effective home studio doesn't have to take up a lot of space, or cost a fortune – it's the quality of the work that's created in it that space that *really* matters.

medium-sized tool box

small plastic containers (look for ones with internal dividers – they are useful for storing puppet facial bits)

power drill (for tie down puppets)

drill bits

small scissors

blue tack

snot tape (this transparent and rubbery adhesive works like blue tack, only stronger. Gross name, useful material)

green-screen tape (you can use this to wrap puppet rigs, which makes them easier to digitally remove in post-production. There's nothing particularly special about this tape, and even green masking tape can work)

florist's wire

straight pins

hot glue gun

china marker

needle and thread

dental wax (you can find this soft wax at the drug store. It can be mixed with coloured clay to make eyelids and eyebrows for puppets, and for securing small things on set)

wooden toothpicks

wooden skewers

tweezers

needle-nose pliers

cotton swabs

assorted bits of armature wire (different gauges)

hand wipes (especially if working with clay)

Lighting

The process of lighting for stop motion can be a journey of discovery, as you carefully position your lights in an effort to make your scene perfect. As you work, you may find yourself feeling a bit like a sculptor, as your lights seem to 'carve out' areas of light and dark on your set. You'll be amazed as you watch your sets, puppets, and costumes quite literally shine with brilliance as their textures and colours come to life. It's a process that is endlessly exciting and fascinating.

This chapter explores the fundamentals of lighting for stop motion, much of which grows out of live action filmmaking. It also shows you all sorts of ways that light can be used in stop motion, and it covers basic set-ups as well as more complex situations. You'll also find specific advice on what kind of lights you might want to include in your own studio kit.

You may want to jump between this chapter and Chapter 9 on Camera. That's because if you don't know how to set your camera effectively through the animation software, no amount of lighting skills will be able to get you a solid-looking stop motion image. By the end of this chapter you'll have a strong practical understanding of how to use light effectively, so that you can communicate exactly what you want to through your stop motion scenario.

Figure 8.1
The Little Prince, Mark Osborne, 2015.
The right light fixture, positioned in just the right manner, can bring wonderful life to your scene. Here, the perfect lighting makes for a tender moment, filled with a peaceful sense of security and calm.

Lighting styles

As you start to think about lighting for stop motion, one of the challenges you'll quickly be confronted with is how to *describe* the look that you're going for. But describing that look can be tricky. How do you pick the right words to conjure up something that's so purely visual? As a place to start, many artists find it helpful to begin by picking from two main styles – high key and low key. This is a general way to at least begin the process of lighting – and from there, you'll be able to get more specific.

High key

Don't be confused by this term – it's not in reference to a light's *physical* location. Rather, it's in reference to the *amount* of the light. 'High key' lighting means there's a high amount of light coming from the key light. (What's a key light? See below.)

Typically, with a high amount of key light comes a lot of visual energy – things are bright, and vivid, and lively. Consequently, this style of lighting is often used for comedies and for generally 'up tempo' stories. It's also a style often used in projects aimed at kids, because it typically feels fun and exciting.

Low key

'Low key' lighting means there's a low amount of light coming from the key light. In contrast to high key lighting, you typically see this style of lighting used for scenes that are restrained in terms of energy and mood, or when the environment insists upon it (imagine a candle-lit dinner).

It's important to note that there's no hard divide between 'high key' and 'low key' styles. A sequence in a film might be entirely high key, entirely low key, or some combination of both. There's also no hard rule about the type of story that works best for a lighting style. A sad story about a lonely man on a park bench might use high key lighting, simply because it makes sense for the time of day!

At the very least, though, being able to describe the scene that you are lighting as 'high key' or 'low key' lets you start to think about

Figure 8.2
Timmy Time, Aardman Studios.
Bright and filled with light (as well as laughs and charm), this series is a great example of high key lighting.

Figure 8.3
Snip, Terril Calder, 2015. A moving short film about reconciliation, this film makes great use of low key lighting to bring the audience into a world of dark forces that are eventually overcome through bravery and love.

the general look, and it also lets you communicate what you are aiming for to others. This is extremely helpful, if you are working with other artists on a project.

The first step towards learning practical lighting skills is grabbing a light – any light – and start moving it around a subject. Lighting is an active, hands-on process. You don't even need to be looking through a camera or at a monitor, at least not yet. Use your *eyes*, and learn from the changes that you see as you move the light around.

Basics of lighting

Once you have a sense of the overall lighting style that you want to create, you can get more specific. But how do you do that practically? If you have a scene laid out in front of you, and a bunch of lights standing by, how do actually use those lights to create the style that you want?

Since most scenes for stop motion involve at least one figure and a background, we typically assign a specific purpose to each light we're using, as well as a name that refers to exactly *what* it's lighting within the scene.

Key light

If something is 'key', it's essential, and that's a good way to think about this light. The key light is the brightest source of light in the scene, and is usually the first (and sometimes only) light that you will set up. In the real world, the sun is the brightest source, so for most exterior scenes, it's likely that you'll be replicating the position and quality of the sun itself. If it's a night scene that's set outdoors, you'll often be replicating the moon's position and quality. As you'd expect, there are exceptions to this rule. For example, if your scene is at night and your character is seated beside a campfire, then the brightest source of light will be the fire, making the fire itself your key light.

Typically, for interior scenes, your key light is often replicating a ceiling light or another lighting fixture located somewhere in the room itself. We might see the actual light fixture in the shot (for example, if a character is seated by a reading lamp), but often the key light for interiors doesn't appear on-screen at all. Rather, the light fixture is suggested through the lighting to exist 'somewhere near the ceiling' of the scene.

The amount of light – from your key light, or any other light – can be adjusted in a couple of different ways. First, you can physically move the light closer to or further away from your set. The closer the light, the brighter the scene – the further away, the less light you'll get. Another way you can vary the amount of light is through the addition of diffusion paper. This specially designed translucent paper is placed in front of the light and effectively 'cuts' the amount of light that hits your subject. If you diffuse the light, make sure to only use paper specifically designed for this use. Regular paper or tissue can catch fire if placed too close to a hot light!

Of course, in addition to the amount of light, you can also change the *direction* of your light as well, by moving the light up, down, left, or right relative to the subject.

> If your scene doesn't require a very specific key light position, placing your key light above and to the front of the character is usually a safe bet, whether your setting is an exterior or interior.

Fill light

Let's imagine your key light is in place. If you *only* used a key light for your scene, you might have a very dramatic image, with some intense areas of brightness, and also deep shadow areas as well. This might be the exact look that you're going for, but typically, this stark and intense look is 'smoothed out' to some extent by the addition of another light, known as the fill.

This light is typically placed on the opposite side of the set from the key light, and its name explains its role. The fill light 'fills in' the dark shadow areas created by the key light, so as to allow at least some details in those shadow areas to read more clearly. Since its job is usually to gently level out the overall light, the fill light is often from a source that offers 'indirect' light (see section below).

As with the key light, the amount of fill light can be adjusted to fill in the shadows, more or less, depending on the desired look. Do you want to show off the puppet fully, revealing all the lovely detail that you put into it? Then use a lot of fill light. Do you want something more dramatic, something that reveals how sculptural and angular the puppet is? If so, use *less* fill light.

This balance (or ratio) of key light to fill light is a fundamental one, and getting it just right takes time and patience. There's no 'correct' ratio, so play with the 'key light to fill light' relationship, and see what kinds of moods and looks you can achieve, and what works for the context of your scene.

Back light

As your key light and fill light join forces out in front, there's often another light that's hard at

Figure 8.4
Key light only.
Where's the key light located? When you observe the areas of brightness, as well as the shadows, you find that the key light must be coming from high up, to the front of Nia, and on the left side of the frame.

Figure 8.5
Fill light only.
Compare this 'fill light only' image with the key light image. Like the key light, the fill light is located high up, and to the front of Nia. But in this case, the fill light is located on the *right* of the frame, and is obviously far less bright than the key light.

work behind the scenes – or more accurately, behind the puppet. This is the back light, and as you might expect it is typically positioned to the rear of the scene, casting its light on to the scene and *towards* the camera. This light is typically a form of direct light, and its purpose is a subtle but important one: the back light helps to separate (or 'pop out') the subject from the background. It can be positioned on the same side as the key light or the opposite side (you'll decide as you go through the lighting process which you prefer), and typically it's positioned at about the same angle as the key light. Essentially, if your back light is positioned effectively, it creates a subtle but flattering highlight area on your subject, and this edge is what causes the subject to 'pop' out

from the background. Because of this edging effect, the back light is also sometimes referred to as the 'rim light'.

Don't confuse this light with the background light (see below). That being said, if you're clever, you might be able to set up your back light to do its main job as described above, *and* have it also serve a second function – that of background light.

Background light

With the key, fill, and back lights established, there's a final component to consider – the background light (not to be confused with the back light). The background light provides illumination to the actual background itself. If your background is full of texture and detail, the background light might be a direct light that you aim across the set from the side or top, thereby bringing out the beautiful details. But if your background is rather plain, flat, or overall nondescript, the background light might make use of lighting cookies or barn doors (see below) to add visual interest. Remember though, that the main area of interest is typically in the middle ground and foreground of the scene. The background is exactly that – background. It shouldn't distract from the important areas within your scene. And remember that your background is often out of focus or very softly focused – further reason to not spend *all* day on this area (as fun as it might be!)

> ### *THE LITTLE PRINCE*, MARK OSBORNE, 2015
>
> The stop motion sequences of this feature are breathtaking, and achieve an original look in part through the use of paper for certain puppet and costume elements. As light passes through the paper, it suggests a remarkable delicacy and sensitivity, which is very much in keeping with the tender source material, the classic book by Antoine de Saint-Exupéry.

Figure 8.6
Back light only.
Notice how the rimming effect of the back light helps to define Nia in space, separating her from the background area. It's also super dramatic! Look for this heavily backlit look in thrillers and suspense films.

Figure 8.7
Background light only.
In this example, the flat background is given some added interest, as it is 'broken up' into patches of light and dark. This is being achieved with the help of a cookie (see the section on Shadows).

As with lighting style, there's no hard rule to what each of the above lights are doing. A key light, depending on how it's positioned, might also cast light on the background, making it a 'key light/background light'. Alternately, a background light might also serve the purpose of backlighting the puppet, making it a 'back light/background light'. You can conceivably light your entire scene with a single light source (if it gives you the look that you want).

Three-point lighting

You'll find this concept referred to a lot in the world of lighting. It describes a lighting set-up that is often used for still photography, as well as for filmmaking. The 'three points' refer to the three physical lights involved. Typically, these three lights are key, fill, and backlight. Once you get those three lights established for your scene, guess what? You've got a three-point lighting scenario!

Since it's a standard approach, and one that offers a basically appealing and 'safe' look, it's good to understand three-point lighting. But not every scene needs it, or benefits from it. Don't be afraid to get dramatic with your lighting, and to break some rules to get an exciting look. Be daring, shoot tests, and refine your look accordingly.

Figure 8.8
Key, fill, back, and background light.
All the lights are at work in this final image: First, Nia is nicely illuminated in a basic way – we can *see* her plainly. She also has a sense of volume, which is provided by shadows that are not distracting. She's also nicely separated from the background, which itself has a bit of visual interest added, through the use of dappled shadows.

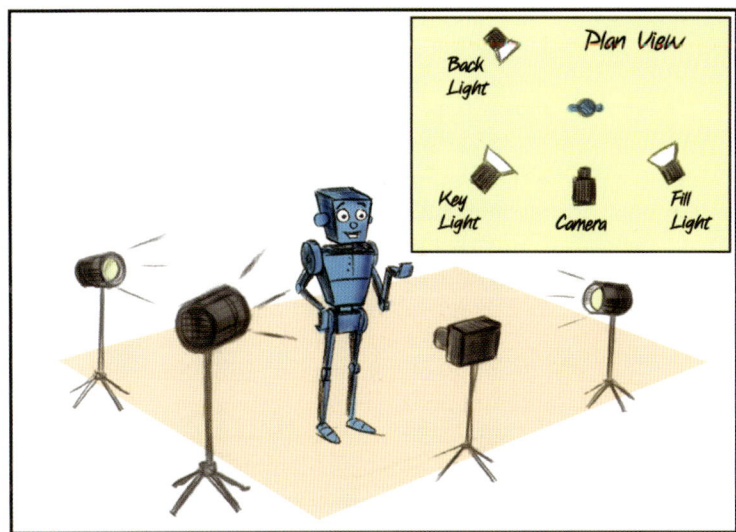

Figure 8.9
Three point lighting.
Key, fill, and back light, all working together to give you a professional looking image.

Aiming the light

The main lights discussed above are standard when it comes to lighting a scene effectively. But they're really just the beginning of what you can do with light in terms of creating a look and establishing a mood. Depending on how you 'throw' light around your scene, you can achieve an endless range of different looks.

Direct

Direct light is light that travels from a source directly to the subject. The light isn't bounced off other surfaces, nor is it greatly diffused. This light typically stems from a single, intense source. Think of a flashlight, a candle, or the most intense direct source imaginable – our sun. Now, picture the effect that the light from the sun has on a landscape on a sunny day. More specifically, picture the *shadow* areas that it creates. On its own, a direct light causes deep, dark shadows on the subject.

Not surprisingly, the key light is typically (but not always) a direct light. It may be somewhat diffused or softened, but it typically maintains its 'direct', or 'sun-like' quality.

Direct light has a lot of uses when lighting for stop motion. It's very good at conveying 'time of day'. Position it high to suggest noon, place it low to suggest sunrise or sunset. It can be used to bring out details and textures in your sets and puppets, and it can offer exciting and dynamic drama and mystery.

To set up a direct light, you need a light with an intense light source (which most lights have – it's called a bulb), and you need to point it directly at your subject. Voila! You now have direct light. But more specifically, there are various *types* of direct light, each of which is tied to the location of the light, relative to the subject. Each offers a very dramatic, and very different, look.

You could add one of the following direct lights to an established three point set up, or

You can 'diffuse' (or soften) a direct light by securing diffusion paper in front of it, often by using wooden clothes pegs. This specially designed paper comes in various thicknesses, and it can help take the hard edge off the light that's created by a direct light. You can purchase it at supply stores for photography and motion picture production.

you could use one of these direct lights to serve as a key, fill, back, or background light. It's up to you – whatever looks right for the situation.

Types of direct light

Frontal

Essentially this light is placed just behind the camera, and shines directly on to the subject. Placing a light here offers an intense light that serves to simply (and somewhat roughly) illuminate your character. It can also flatten out the character, and make him appear isolated and 'pinned down' by the lighting. If you need to create a 'deer in the headlights' feel, this is the way to go.

Top

If you're looking to isolate your character in space while maintaining a somewhat realistic quality, consider top lighting. This results in a lot of structural highlighting and long, dramatic shadows that are cast downward towards the ground. As with frontal light, it can create a 'pinned down' feel, and also an 'interrogation' feel. Since its direction is essentially realistic (overhead, like the sun), this lighting position is generally perceived by the viewer as stylized, but not *overly* so. Do a search for 'Marlene Dietrich' to see how this style of direct light can achieve amazing looks!

Side

Side lighting, as with front and top lighting, causes long dramatic shadows, adding additional visual interest to any scene. It's also a great way to suggest 'time of day'. Side shadows are prevalent when the sun is rising or setting, so try this light position (along with yellow and orange gels) when you need to ensure that your audience knows what time it is.

Add a blue gel to your light to convey a winter feel (when the sun is *always* low in the sky). You'll find more about lighting gels later in this chapter.

Under

This is classic horror movie lighting. Why is this form of direct light used so often in this genre? Because light coming from this direction is the absolute *opposite* of what we understand as the normal direction of light – from above, as the sun shines down. Lighting your scene from below instantly tells your audience that your stop motion world is an inverted world. Even the most friendly looking puppet will look evil if you hit it with light from below!

Back

Positioning a direct light behind your character so that the light shines *into* the camera is a useful way to create a striking silhouette for your character. It can also create a great sense of mystery, since a character lit in this fashion has little illumination on the camera-side. The stark silhouette raises the question, 'Who *is* this character?!' It can build great tension and excitement for your film, and can create a very striking effect.

On set lights

Sometimes you'll have a direct light actually appear on camera – an example would be a living room scene where there is an actual floor lamp in the shot. This type of direct light is often simply for show, with the *actual* illumination for the scene coming from an off-screen source.

As dynamic, exciting, and useful as direct light is, it *isn't* a great option if you're trying to convey things like 'soft', 'gentle', 'silky', 'snowy', or 'overcast'. Further, if used on its own, it can create tricky pools of intense darkness and light, which might look good in a still frame, but could cause headaches when it comes to blocking and staging puppet movement (this is looked at in more detail, later in this chapter).

Fortunately, there's another kind of light that you can use as an alternative to direct light which will let you achieve a whole other range of looks.

Indirect

Indirect light is light that *eventually* reaches its subject, but not before bouncing off something else. Imagine dropping a thousand plastic balls into a room. The balls would bounce about madly, hitting every surface available, from all directions. That's what happens with indirect light – it bounces around a lot. As a result, this type of light has no strong sense of direction. It seems to just 'exist'. A great example of this can be found on an overcast, snowy day. The light from the sun travels through the clouds (where it bounces around), and then proceeds to bounce off all the snow, with the end result being a subject that has a sense of weightless limbo, since almost all shadows have been effectively eliminated by the bouncing light.

For stop motion artists, this kind of light can be extremely useful, because it can act as a 'base' layer of illumination for a scene. Bounce a bunch of light around the space (off ceilings, walls, bounce boards) and instantly your scene is lit. What's more, you have no problematic shadows to deal with, as you sometimes do with direct light. You can move your set pieces and puppets around in this space, knowing that no matter what happens, your blocking and staging won't run into lighting or shadow problems. Indirect lighting can let you get shooting quickly, and that can be a good thing, especially if your film is more about story than lighting, or if you need to work on a very tight time budget.

Since indirect light generally brings light to a subject without conveying a specific direction, the fill light is often (but not always) an indirect light, because it gently fills in the deep shadows that are often created by the key light. To set up an indirect light, you need to *bounce* your light off

something before it hits the subject. This means aiming your light at a wall, at the ceiling, or at a bounce board (made of simple white foam board) that is angled appropriately near the light itself.

As useful as indirect light can be, it *doesn't* convey strong drama, and it doesn't highlight the angles and shapes of your world as powerfully as direct light. If you need your lighting to be dramatic, direct light works better. But if lighting isn't the focus of your film, indirect light may be just the thing. You can also *combine* direct light with indirect light within a shot, to achieve an even wider range of looks.

Lighting for colour

With digital technology that lets you see on screen exactly what you'll be recording, lighting for stop motion is truly a case of 'what you see is what you get', assuming that your monitor is effectively calibrated. Point your camera at your scene (after you know how to set it effectively – see Chapter 9 on Camera), get a live image on your monitor, and start lighting.

You'll quickly notice that different colours react differently when hit by studio lights. A very dark colour may appear to 'swallow' all of the light, and as a result will not show any detail on camera. A lighter colour may 'blow out' when lit, causing all the details of your subject to wash away. Direct light might make your colours pop

Figure 8.10
Spider's Anatomy, Vojtech Kiss, 2014.
This film uses intense and wildly stylized colours as it explores a character's struggle within a surreal and ominous world.

in a wonderful way, or wash them out completely. Indirect light might bring out a lovely vibrancy to your colours, or it might pull the whole image down, into something that lacks visual energy. The best advice is to take your time. Vary the angle of the light and the intensity, its directness versus its indirectness, play with all the variables that you can, for as long as you can, until you're happy.

Your puppet is typically the most important thing, and its costume and skin tone need to read on-screen in the way you that makes you happy. Darker skin needs more light on it to bring out its details, while lighter skin sometimes reflects so much light that you'll need to knock down the amount of light you're using. Take your time, learn as you go, and don't start shooting until you're satisfied. Or until your shooting schedule insists that you've got to start animating, whichever comes first!

Colour temperature

This is an important term in lighting, but can lead to confusion. It doesn't refer to how physically warm something is, but rather how to how warm something *looks*. Some light looks 'warmer' (more orange), while other light looks 'cooler' (more blue). Depending on a variety of factors, a given light bulb can look warmer or cooler, and the resulting light created by that bulb can greatly affect the look of your scene. Incandescent bulbs (the ones with wire filaments that get hot) tend to have a warm orange colour, while LED lights tend towards the blue. You can correct a bulb's colour using gels (see below), but as bulb technology continues to improve, LED bulbs (that are cool running and energy-efficient) are more readily available in both warmer and cooler looking options.

> White balance is the term used for determining 'true white' within the specific context of a scene. All digital cameras have an 'Auto White Balance' option, which is typically fine to use. Just be aware that you can play with this to get drastically different looks. Give it a test sometime, and see what stylized looks you can achieve.

Lighting with gels and filters

You can dramatically change the colour of the light in your scene by placing a special lighting gel (in sheet form) over your bulb. Gels typically come in large sheets and can be cut to size, and held in place with wooden clothes pegs or tape (if the bulb is cool, like an LED bulb).

You can get gels in subtle colours, which can be used to gently 'warm up' or 'cool off' the colour of light given off by a bulb. For example, you could warm up a bluish LED light with an orange filter. You can also buy wild colours, and suddenly you have a scene that's psychedelic and over-the-top. Gels are a lot of fun to play with, especially if you are telling a genre story, or a story that is highly theatrical or stylized. They can be purchased at lighting supply stores, and since stop motion lights are typically pretty small, a single piece of gel of any given colour should be enough.

Lighting for black and white

There's nothing quite like a beautiful black and white image. It offers a mood and atmosphere all of its own. One factor about working in black and white that you'll come to appreciate is that you don't have to worry about the colour of the light coming from the bulb. If you're seeing the image in black and white, and you like the look it creates on your set, then you're good to go. There's

Figure 8.11
The Lighthouse, Simon Scheiber, 2016.
This film uses beautifully nuanced black and white imagery to tell the story of a lonely lighthouse keeper who finds himself in uncharted territories.

no need to 'correct' a bulb's colour, and that frees you up to use just about any kind of fixture and bulb that you can get your hands on.

Remember that you aren't just creating an image in 'black' and 'white' – you're actually working with huge range of greys. Some of those greys will be very dark, some very light, and everything in between. The way that you vary the *brightness* of your image is how you'll achieve all these greys. *Contrast* is also hugely important when working in black and white – you can create a 'low contrast' image (that has a general level of basically similar greys), or a 'high contrast' image (that has areas of wildly varying greys).

When animating for a project that will be black and white, I prefer to set my camera so that I'm actually recording frames in black and white rather than in colour, even though I could remove the colour in post-production. I do this because I want to see the grey scale image as I light my set, so that I can adjust contrast and brightness effectively, on set. I often go so far as to create my sets and puppets in greys! That way, I'm *always* seeing and thinking in terms of contrast and brightness. As you continue to work in this way, you'll be amazed by just how many gradations (from true black to true white) you'll discover, as you craft your project.

Adjustments to the look of your footage can be done in post-production, for both colour and black and white projects, but the more you can handle in front of the camera, on-set, the better. It's easy for post-production manipulation to feel 'added on', while manipulations that are done at the time of animation often have a richer, more authentic feel.

STORY OF THE FOX, LADISLAS STARE-WITCH, 1930

This remarkable achievement, made largely by Starewitch himself, is a wonderful stop motion study piece for its effective, economical lighting. Working on a modest budget, using his own skills and creativity, Starewitch manages to create both realistic lighting situations, as well as more expressionistic ones, all in black and white. The whole film is wonderful to look at, but the exterior 'moon-lit winter night scenes' are especially convincing, atmospheric, and clever.

Shadows

Effective manipulation of shadows is an essential part of lighting for stop motion. They can be used to convey setting; cast some strong vertical shadows on a set wall, and you instantly have a prison cell. They can be used to communicate time of day, with long shadows suggesting sunrise, sunset, or winter. They can also be used to establish the mood and atmosphere of your project. If a scene is cloaked in shadows with whole areas of the image obscured by darkness, you're well on your way to creating an effective piece of drama. Shadows are very powerful, but they can also be tricky to manage. Read on, and as you start to craft some shadows on set, remember the value of experimentation. Move your lights, cast some shadows, and have fun learning.

Shadows on characters

If the lighting on a puppet's face is *too* even (meaning no shadow areas at all), it can make your puppet look very flat. And since you spent all that time making it dimensional, this is something you probably want to avoid! Fortunately, a very small amount of shadow is sometimes all that it takes to bring dimensionality to your puppet. As you play with the shadows on your puppet, pay special attention to the head and face, since this area is typically where your audience will be looking.

As you light, look at the *quality* of the shadow. It may be hard, or it may be soft. A hard shadow results when the light 'falls off' into darkness quite quickly, and it's often the result of direct lighting. With a soft shadow, the light falls off more gradually, with a slow transition from bright to dark. A hard shadow might be just the look you want, but you can still create a slow drop off by filling in the shadow area with other light sources. After all, that's what your fill light is for!

Which kind of shadow looks better on your puppet – hard or soft? It depends entirely on context. A scene featuring a rugged-looking puppet may call for hard shadows. A scene featuring a character with a smooth appearance might play best with soft shadows. These are the decisions that you'll need to make through the process of lighting.

As you play with shadows on your character, remember that key light typically falls from 'up high' (like the sun). With that in mind, be sure to watch out for the dreaded 'shadow moustache'! This is the result of a hard shadow being cast downward, by the puppet's nose. It can be quite distracting for an audience (and sort of hilarious, once you notice it). You can avoid this by being mindful when you're positioning the direct lights, and by filling in shadows areas effectively.

> For medium and close up shots, use mini bounce boards to fill in shadows under your puppet's face. To make one, just take a piece of white foam core or paper, and tape it down securely on your set. Voila! It will bounce light up, and nicely fill in any dark areas. It's a very fast and very effective lighting tool. It's not really possible in wider shots, though, since you'd see the bounce board in the shot!

Shadows on backgrounds

A background that is one solid expanse, regardless of colour, can really flatten out a scene, robbing it of life. Varying the brightness on that background by using shadows (either dramatic or subtle) can nicely 'break up' that big flat area. You can also make a background more interesting with shadows by bringing out its texture, if it has one. Position a fixture so that its light is falling very much across the set, and watch the textures pop out! Background shadows are usually created in a way that sees them fall on the background

only, and not the puppet. This way, your puppet is free to perform without worrying about distracting shadows (see below, in Advanced Lighting).

As with any work you do with backgrounds, remember that you typically don't want your audience's attention completely focused 'back there', so be cautious with how dramatic or intensely you light this area. Remember that your wonderful puppet is the star, not the background!

How to create effective shadows

In this chapter's introduction, I mentioned the idea of 'sculpting' with light. Some of the tools used to create effective lighting carry that analogy further, since these tools allow you to break up, shape, and cut the light within your scene. Ideally, these lighting tools are held in position with the help of grip stands, but grip stands are pricey – so be creative.

Flags

In lighting terms, a flag is anything that 'flags' or 'cuts' the light before it hits your scene. A flag performs the same function as a barn door or a piece of black wrap on a light fixture (black wrap is explained below). The difference is that since a flag is physically further away from the light source, it can be micro-positioned to get a very specific cut (see the important rule below for creating hard and soft shadows). Professional flags are available, but you can make your own very simply with a piece of sturdy cardboard or foam core.

Black wrap

Black wrap is a very sturdy form of foil wrap that's used by lighting professionals. It's highly flexible, heat resistant, and reusable. You can use it to make DIY barn doors on just about any household lighting fixture. Wrap some around the light, and form it until you're casting light in the way you like. You can also use black wrap for animation. Just glue a piece of it to fabric or paper, and you now have something that looks like cloth or paper, but can be posed frame by frame, thanks to the stiff black wrap. It's great stuff! Look for it at supply stores for photography and motion picture equipment.

Cookies

Not the chocolate chip variety, unfortunately. In lighting, a cookie is short for 'cucoloris'. A cucoloris is basically a flag with shapes cut into it, so that you can cast specific shadows on to your set. As with flags, you can make your own cookie – just get some board, design the shapes you want, and then cut them out. You can create a 'prison bars' cookie, a 'bare branches' cookie, a 'window frame' cookie – there are all sorts of options. Some online research will show you all kinds of styles (or invent your own that's just right for your scene).

The world of lighting is filled with basic rules and principles, and you'll come across them all as you continue to learn. Here's one for creating shadows that can really help you in your efforts. The rule is:

The *further away* that the shadow-casting object is from the light source, the more distinct (or 'hard') its shadow will be. Conversely, the *closer* the shadow-casting object is to the light source, the more diffused (or 'soft') the shadow will be.

By moving your cookie or flag closer to or further away from your light, you'll be able to create a wide range of shadow types. Just remember that direct light is better for creating shadows, as opposed to indirect light.

Figure 8.13
Creating hard shadows.
To create a distinct shadow, position the shadow-casting object (in this case, the cookie) *further* away from the light source.

Figure 8.14
Creating soft shadows.
To create a soft shadow, position the shadow-casting object *closer* to the light source.

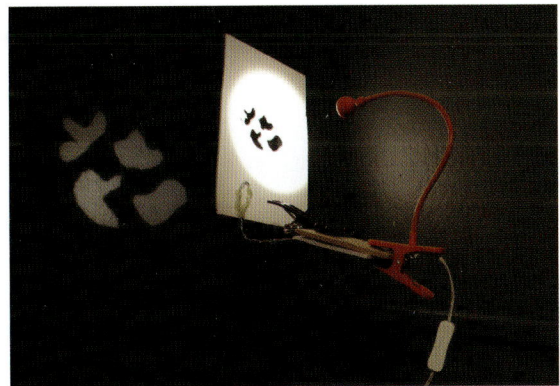

Figure 8.12
Lighting cookie.
The abstract 'blob' pattern in this cookie breaks up an otherwise uniform light. Because it doesn't imply a specific setting, but instead just breaks up the light, I get a lot of use from this particular pattern.

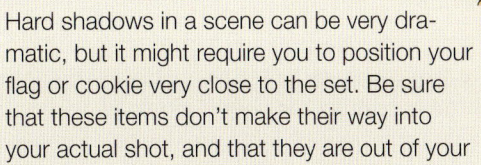

Hard shadows in a scene can be very dramatic, but it might require you to position your flag or cookie very close to the set. Be sure that these items don't make their way into your actual shot, and that they are out of your way when it comes time to animate!

Working safe

All lights require electricity, and many of them give off heat. These two things (heat and electricity) represent the main safety issues when lighting a stop motion project.

You should have a pair of work gloves to protect you from hot bulbs. Fortunately, LED lights are much cooler to the touch than older incandescent bulbs – but they still give off heat. Be mindful. If you're using black wrap on a hot light, the wrap will also be very hot (it's easy to forget this!) Be careful to not encase the light fixture completely with the wrap. If the heat generated by the bulb can't escape, you risk damaging the bulb and the fixture. You also increase the risk of fire.

Only use gels that are specifically designed for lighting, since they resist heat. Never use regular coloured paper or plastic sheets, as these can easily catch on fire. As for safety with electricity, the nice thing about lighting for stop motion is that for most home studio projects, you aren't using massive amounts of electricity, since the lights are small. But of course, you need to be cautious.

Don't overload wall outlets, and whenever possible, plug lights (and any equipment) into a quality power bar that has a surge protection switch. If you overload these power bars they'll switch off instantly, preventing a blown fuse or tripped circuit breaker. If your lights trip the power bar, you know you are running too many things off that bar. Of course, lighting cords and cables create tripping hazards, so be sure to tape them down neatly, once you've set up a shot.

Light fixtures

As with every stage of setting up your studio, what you purchase in terms of light fixtures will depend very much on your budget. As you'd expect, professional lights are designed to allow pros to do their job well, and the pricing for these lights reflect that. These lights will give you great results, but will also empty your bank account very quickly. Alternately (or in combination with pro lights), household lighting fixtures can provide great results and cost a fraction of what a pro light will set you back. These are fixtures that you can purchase at just about any hardware store, and with a bit of creativity, you can use these to achieve excellent production value. Personally, I take huge satisfaction when I achieve a beautiful lighting set up in my studio, knowing that I pulled it off with inexpensive lights.

Professional studio lights

These come in a wide range of sizes and designs. At one end of the scale you'll find dainty little fixtures that use 100 w bulbs, and at other the end you'll get monster fixtures that can handle 650 w bulbs. These big fixtures will provide quantities of light that simulate a nuclear blast (a stop motion-scaled one, that is). Pro lights fixtures are often divided into 'lensed' and 'non-lensed' categories. For both kinds of lights, be aware that their bulbs burn *very* hot. The bigger the fixture, the hotter the bulb, so a large 650 w light bulb requires serious respect, in terms of potential safety hazards.

Lensed lights

These fixtures have a specially designed lens (originally invented for lighthouses) that condenses and amplifies the light. They can be further adjusted so that the spread of light that they give off is very narrow, or very wide. They also have 'barn doors' (hinged metal flaps that can be positioned to shape the light) and slots to position other modifying screens and gels. As you'd imagine, these fixtures are incredibly versatile and useful, with their cost being their main drawback. You're looking at spending hundreds of dollars on each of these lights, even for the most modest fixture. Bulbs for these lights are quite costly, and can be tricky to find. That being said, if you can afford these fixtures, they *are* fantastic.

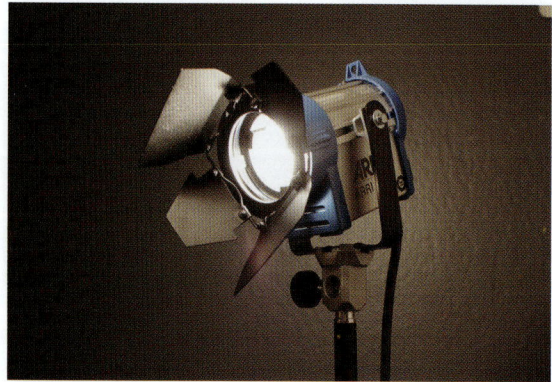

Figure 8.15
Lensed light.
Note the handy 'barn doors' that can be adjusted, allowing you to further shape your light.

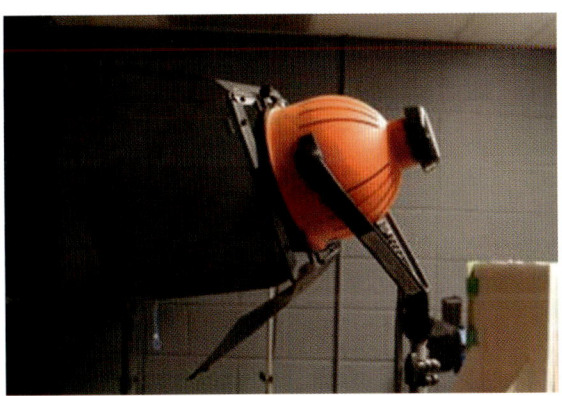

Figure 8.16
Non-lensed light.
This studio light is great for providing a basic blast of light to a scene. The kind pictured here is a popular style, and is often referred to as a 'redhead', due to the colour of the fixture. I know, it's not red. It's orange. I don't make up light fixture nicknames, I just use them.

Non-lensed lights

Without a lens to focus the light, these fixtures create a more general illumination. Depending on the fixture, you can get very bright bulbs that offer a huge amount of illumination. Imagine a big, unruly flood of direct light, and that's what you'll get from these fixtures. You can use them as direct lights (if you can deal with their hard shadows), but you can also bounce their light off bounce boards (or even ceilings and walls), and quickly create a very satisfying indirect look. They typically come equipped with barn doors, and they aren't as expensive as lensed fixtures (although they are still pricey). As with lensed lights, their bulbs are tricky to track down, and are expensive.

Light banks

Rather than a single source of light, these fixtures provide an array (or bank) of lights. This, combined with the designs of the bulbs, provides an intense but soft light. Light banks are fantastic for creating a fast lighting set-up. Plug the fixture in, point it at your set, and things look good. Certain manufacturers now offer LED banks (as opposed to fluorescent), and that means high-energy efficiency and lights that are cool to the touch. As with the other pro lights, light banks are very pricey. Check online for DIY methods of making LED light banks. If you're up for the challenge, you can make your own!

Household lighting fixtures

These easy to find fixtures are highly affordable, and for the most part, use very common bulbs. For these fixtures, it helps to get familiar with various bulb options, since different style bulbs create different styles (and colours) of light. 'Old school' incandescent light bulbs give off a lovely warm-coloured light, but are hugely inefficient energy-wasters, and are getting harder to find each day, as they get phased out of use. They also generate a lot of heat, which can make a small studio uncomfortable. LED bulbs are very widely available, are very efficient, and don't create heat. Look for warm-coloured LED bulbs, because otherwise these bulbs have a rather cold, blue-leaning light that you may need to correct. Overall, though, LED bulbs are a great way to go.

Some popular household fixtures are listed below, but this is really just a start. If you come across a fixture that's affordable and will give you a look you want, go for it. Remember, it's not how expensive the light fixture is, it's how effectively you use it to create your desired look. I've got an LED penlight that only cost me a few dollars, and I use it all the time to get very appealing mini-highlights in my shots.

Basic work lights

These are extremely useful fixtures. I have four of them, in different sizes, and I use them all the time, for all sorts of reasons. They're my 'go to' lighting fixture for a lot of the projects that I create. You can find them at any hardware store. They're very affordable, and they use cheap household bulbs (incandescent or LED). The clamp-style versions are especially handy, since they're lightweight, easy to attach to lights stands, easy to adjust, and the light that they give off can be 'sculpted' quite nicely by the use of black wrap.

Flexible utility lights

These are often sold as simple little reading lights, and they're super cheap at IKEA-style stores. You'll often find that these fixtures come with built-in bulbs, so try to find one with a bulb that offers you the light you want. They often provide a very intense 'spot'-style light, which can be good or bad, depending on your needs. The best thing about these fixtures is how flexible they are in their positioning. This allows you to achieve quite precise angles for the light. I often use a light like this to create an accent in a scene or for dramatic highlights.

Miniature lights

A stroll through the flashlight section in your hardware store will turn up all kinds of fun options that you can use for creative stop motion lighting. You'll find pen lights, puck lights, clamp on reading lights … these are all (typically) LED fixtures that are light weight, and great for detailed lighting. I'll often secure one of these into place with tape, in order to get very specific lighting highlights. Since LED bulbs use very little energy, miniature lights can run for a long time on their battery – just make sure that the battery is fresh before animating a shot. You don't want your light to slowly fade out over the course of animating the shot!

Light stands

You could invest in building a lighting grid over your studio space to hang overhead lights, but unless you're setting up a serious professional shop, or are very accomplished at home renovations, a grid isn't very practical. Instead, studio lights, and most of your household fixtures, require a stand. These were mentioned in the previous chapter, but they bear further consideration here, since they can be used for grip items as well as for lights.

Basic lighting for stop motion

Lighting is a craft that serious artists devote their entire careers to, but that doesn't mean that you *have* to spend ages setting up lighting for a scene. Your story may not call for it. Maybe you're more interested in showcasing the animation in the scene, or the dialogue, in which case you may just want things to be illuminated in a very simple fashion. Or maybe you want the lighting to look decent, but are on a very strict deadline, and need to get things going as quickly as possible. In all these cases, there are some standard approaches that can get your very pleasing results, quickly.

To get a basically pleasing image for your scene, follow this one simple instruction: bounce light everywhere. With indirect light (and lots of it), you'll have few distracting shadows, and your scene will have a generally pleasant look. There you have it! You can achieve this basic look by pointing strong lights at bounce boards, or bouncing light off the walls or ceiling. If your scene is lit in this style, you'll be able to set up each new shot quite quickly (all things considered), with very little adjusting of lights required. More than a few television series have used this method for lighting, precisely because it allows the production to meet the always-insane production deadlines. A 'bounced light' approach can make your production schedule very happy indeed!

Advanced lighting for stop motion

You can think of 'advanced lighting' as any lighting set-up that requires you to carefully break the image into areas of bright and dark. Once you start crafting like this, you're working towards something beautiful and sophisticated, but that brings with it greater challenges. These challenges take *time* to address, so be prepared. Of course, the trade-off for the time invested is a beautiful scene! The following are a few aspects of lighting to be aware of, if you want to *really* use light to its greatest potential.

Directing the eye through lighting

The human eye is attracted by any number of factors, and live action filmmakers as well as animators have learned how to take advantage of that. Movement will attract the eye, as will areas of general visual interest: colourful areas, areas with strong shapes, and areas that are bright. And brightness is where lighting comes in. By using light to make certain regions of the frame brighter, you can make your audience pay attention to that specific location. A general rule to keep in mind is that the area (or areas) in

Figure 8.17
Basic stop motion lighting kit.
Quality lighting comes from practice and skill, not from expensive fixtures. The black chunks (top left) are pieces of black wrap, the ultra-useful lighting foil. The pen-like device is an LED penlight (very useful for creating tiny 'hits' of light).

Figure 8.18
I'm Scared, Pete Levin, 2016. Photo credit: Colin Crump. As the characters in this short film explore their strange world, layers of dappled light provide atmosphere, mood, and visual interest to the scene.

which your characters will perform is usually the brightest, while backgrounds tend to be at least a bit darker in comparison, so that attention isn't taken away from the characters. You can also use this to tell your audience where something is *about* to happen. Imagine a stop motion scene that is set in a theatre. The theatre's stage is empty, but there is a spotlight on the center of a darkened stage. As an audience member, exactly *where* do you expect an entering puppet to stop? Within the pool of light, of course. This use of light builds a sense of expectation and tension within the audience, and as simple as this example is, it illustrates how light can be used to direct *and* engage the audience. Learn to use light like this, and you'll learn to control your audience's attention in a very professional fashion. Once you have the hang of this, you can even use light to *misdirect* your audience. What if the puppet in the example above actually takes its place *away* from the spotlight? Perhaps the puppet enters, clears its throat, the audience looks across the screen to where it stands in shadows … and

As you light your scenes, get in the habit of looking at the actual high-resolution frames themselves, as opposed to the frames as displayed by Dragonframe. To do this, simply go into the folder that holds your high resolution frames for the shot, and examine them using your computer's default image viewing software.

you've now taken your audience by surprise. And in part, you did it through the use of light!

Lighting for emotion

We may not always notice it as we move through our daily lives, but light deeply affects us at an emotional level. Here's an example: you're at a fall fair, on a crisp autumn afternoon. There's the smell of the food, the sounds of the carnival rides, and the crystal sharp sunlight, surrounded by the deep blue sky. This moment has a particular mood to it, a tone. Now picture a twilight moment by the edge of a quiet river on a warm summer night. All is quiet, except for the sound of crickets, as a full moon rises slowly behind the trees. Again, the moment carries with it a particular atmosphere, a feeling. Lived moments like these are truly special – magical, even. And they carry within them the range of human emotions, from the darkest and scariest, to the most hopeful and joyous. Over time, these moments become precious memories that make us who we are as individuals. Now ask yourself – how much of that magic in these memories comes from the *light itself*?

To really excel at lighting for stop motion, you certainly need to study lots of movies (stop motion and live action). You need to study lots of photographs, and you certainly need to practice your lighting in the stop motion studio. But you also need to truly open your eyes and look around you, *in the real world*, and *feel* the emotions of light.

If you can develop your understanding of how light in the real world effects our emotions, and if you can let that emotional understanding lead you in your efforts on-set, you'll then be in a better position to create truly powerful lighting for your stop motion worlds. Your scenes will feel real *emotionally*, even if your sets and puppets are highly stylized, and even if your setting is completely fantastical. If you can do this – if you can light not only for realism but for emotion – you'll be moving well past the basics, and towards a true mastering of the craft.

Blocking considerations for lighting

If the riverbank scene described above was translated into stop motion, the lighting for it would be advanced, because the pools of light and dark on-set that would be created by the moonlight through the trees would present serious blocking challenges when it comes to animation.

Essentially, blocking refers to the puppet's specific movement through the frame over the length of the shot. For example, a shot may begin with the puppet in the background on frame right, and end with the puppet in the foreground on frame left. Does the complex lighting that you've set up work with the blocking of the shot? If your puppet's final position in the frame is an area of deep shadow, it might be very distracting for the audience to suddenly lose sight of the character in

VITTORIO STORARO

Few cinematographers have built a career so confidently upon the idea of lighting for emotion. Storaro is responsible for some of the most remarkable lighting scenarios we have in cinema. These scenarios don't astound because of their realism (any novice cinematographer can replicate reality), but because they affect the audience deeply, in their hearts.

this way. No one wants to spend hours animating a puppet into a final spot, where the light only serves to confuse or frustrate the audience!

The pop-through for lighting

To prevent problems with the puppet falling into unwanted shadows, you can create a quick test animation that will reveal any issues with lighting. This test animation is known as a

Figure 8.19
Old Man, Alicia Eisen, 2016. Light isn't just something that makes physical things visible. It can also make *emotions* visible.

'pop-through'. This is essentially a rough (and relatively quick) version of the finished shot.

To create a lighting pop-through, ensure that the camera angle is how you want it, and that all your lights are in place (see below, A lighting process for stop motion).

Pose your puppet as it will be for the start of the shot, and place it in its appropriate spot on the set. Capture a frame, and then move the puppet to the next major point along its path within the shot, reposing it if necessary (usually only if its posing is dramatically different). Capture another frame. Repeat this process for each major position for the puppet within the shot. Once you're done, flip through the frames from start to finish. Does the lighting work with all of the puppet's positions and poses within the shot? If not, tweak your lighting and/or your blocking, accordingly. This test doesn't have to be the same duration as your actual shot will be – remember, you're just testing for how the lighting works with the movement of the puppet through the frame. You can also use a pop-through test to ensure that your focus is correct within a shot, and to help you plan your blocking and staging.

When a pop-through is created to match the duration of the actual shot, it can also help you to plan out timing and posing concerns, making it a great help for animation. Accordingly, you'll find more information on creating animation pop-throughs, in Part 3.

Remember, 'bounced light' is the friend of every stop motion animator who simply wants a pleasantly lit scene that allows the story and the animation to be showcased. If your attempts at advanced lighting are driving you crazy, consider simplifying your approach. You might be able to find a middle way that lets you get *some* amount of drama out of your lighting (perhaps in the background, away from your animation), while at the same time letting you get things lit relatively quickly, so that animation can begin.

> The following lighting process will help you now, but it will prove even more valuable during the filmmaking process, which we look at in Part 4. Be sure to refer back to this, once you're making a film!

A LIGHTING PROCESS FOR STOP MOTION

Playing while setting up your lights is vital – but so is getting your project done! The following process is one that's generally followed in television and feature stop motion productions (and for most live action productions as well, incidentally) and it's one that I've streamlined for indie stop motion projects.

1. Forget about lighting for a moment. Think about any movement of the puppet through the frame for the shot that you're setting up.
2. *Roughly* frame up your shot with the camera, as per your boards. Keep the camera angle a bit wide for now (you can always tighten the angle later in this process).
3. Now, ask yourself these essential questions:

   - Have you left room for all puppet movement that will occur in the shot?
   - Does your camera angle look nice at each major moment within the shot?
   - Does your depth-of-field work effectively for the shot? (see Chapter 9 on Camera)
   - Does the framing you've created 'hook up' with the shot before, and the shot after? (See Chapter 16 on Production).

4. At this point, refine the framing if you need to. Take your time. Move carefully and mindfully. A strong frame-up is essential. Don't rush this.
5. Once your frame-up is perfect, or as close to perfect as you can get, you now have a 'locked frame'. That means that you don't move your camera, or its lens angle, any more.
6. Now, with the 'canvas' set, you can begin the process of lighting for this specific frame. As you light, ask yourself these questions:

   - Does the lighting allow the essential visual elements to 'read' on camera effectively? Is any region too bright? Is any region too dark?
   - Is the lighting for this shot consistent with the lighting for other shots within the scene that you've already completed?

- If this is the first shot for this scene, does the lighting work effectively to convey the emotion and overall mood/tone of the scene?
- Does the lighting cause any problems for blocking and staging of the puppet movement? Consider creating a lighting pop-through to test for this.
- Does your lighting bring the viewer's eye directly to the main area of interest within the scene?
- Have you left room for *you?* It's very easy to forget that you need room to animate!

7. As you light, keep checking how things look through the camera. Only worry about how it looks within your frame, because *that* is what matters now – the area within your locked frame. You'll tweak your lighting (a bit, or a lot) for every new shot, anyway.

8. As you work, you may find that you need to change your camera position or lens angle a bit. Fair enough, but only a *bit!* Don't undo all of your progress by wildly rethinking things – the time for that has come and gone.

9. Carry on lighting, but with each adjustment (of lights and camera) you should be *reducing* how much you are adjusting.

10. Finally, lock the lighting. With lighting locked, and your frame locked, you'll be able to move on to the animation stage. Repeat the above steps for each shot in your project.

Light flicker

Anyone who has done even a bit of stop motion has probably encountered light flicker. It's the fluctuation of light that only becomes evident when you play back the animated frames. If a few frames have flicker, it might be completely unnoticeable to the audience, so consider letting it slide. But if flicker becomes excessive, it can be a seriously distracting problem. It's all the more frustrating, because sometimes it's quite hard to determine *why* the flickering is happening. To eliminate (or to at least greatly reduce) light flicker, it's important to isolate the cause of the problem.

First, make sure that you're reviewing the high-resolution frames that Dragonframe records, as opposed to the low-resolution playback frames. The playback frames in Dragonframe sometimes exhibit flicker for a variety of reasons, but often that flicker *isn't* occurring in the high-resolution frames. In addition, make sure that your camera is set to record at 100 ISO (you'll find out more about ISO, and how it's controlled by Dragonframe, in Chapter 9). Digital cameras have the ability to boost the brightness of an image, but since it's an electronic process that has to be applied to each frame, the brightness of each image may not be precisely the same over an array of frames. For a series of still images, that's rarely a serious problem, but for animation, it's an issue. Light fluctuations over an entire shot can occur, as each frame is slightly less (or more) bright in relation to the others that are racing by on-screen. Shooting at 100 ISO means your camera is boosting your image's brightness as little as possible, thus, less visible fluctuation over the course of your frames. This means that you'll need more light on-set, but that's a small price to pay in order to reduce flicker. Again, if you're asking yourself 'What the heck is ISO?', it's explained more fully in Chapter 9.

Once you've ensured that you're shooting at 100 ISO, if you still have light flicker, you can continue to search for the cause. It might very well be human! Since the animator is standing so close to the scene during animation, if you're wearing anything *but* dark clothing, you may be reflecting light on to the scene. Take your stop motion fashion cues from goths, metal heads, and ninjas, and always dress in dark clothes when animating.

Stop motion message boards and online groups have endless threads (and arguments) around the topic of light flicker. These resources offer a lot of suggestions, but of course, not all advice is good advice. Don't go throwing out your lights and camera parts, just because someone online recommends that as the only solution!

Roy is ready for stealthy martial arts combat.
Also, stop motion.

this turned on (you'll find it within Dragonframe's preferences).

If you determine that the flicker isn't coming from unwanted light on-set, you may find that the actual flow of electricity to your lights is causing fluctuations. Big appliances that draw large amounts of electricity such as washers, dryers, and furnaces can cause your studio lights to shift in brightness ever so slightly. Do what you can to 'shoot around' these problems – maybe that load of dirty laundry can wait till you've finished your current shot.

Some animators have also had luck shooting with a slower shutter speed, as they believe the longer exposure 'evens out' any lighting imbalances (see Chapter 9 for more on shutter speeds). Still others feel that using a lens that has a manual control for aperture helps reduce flicker, since digital aperture lenses create slight brightness discrepancies from frame to frame (again, see Chapter 9 to learn more about aperture).

As you can see from all these possible reasons for flicker (and all the possible solutions), it's a never-ending headache for stop motion artists. Once you've done your best to reduce it to the utmost, unless it's completely destroying your animation, move on. If it's very modest, your audience will be so busy enjoying all the beautiful components in your project (like story, animation, sets, props, and sound), odds are they won't even notice a little bit of flicker.

Beyond your own reflection, look for other physical causes that might be affecting the lighting. Your computer monitor might be casting unwanted light on your scene, and causing flicker. Dragonframe has a fantastic feature, called 'Black Out', which causes the monitor to go to black when capturing a frame, in order to prevent monitor flicker. Make sure that you have

Digital tools like After Effects can be of great assistance when it comes to fixing problems, including light flicker. You'll find more on this in Chapter 17.

Further tips for lighting

Lights on, lights off

As you add lights to a scene, it can be tricky to determine just what each light is actually doing to your scene. You can address this by isolating your lights as you set them up. Once you have a light roughly in place, simply switch it on and off, and observe the differences in your scene. Then adjust the position of the light accordingly. Figures 8.4–8.7 illustrate this process of isolating lights.

Use your nose

Well, use your *puppet's* nose, actually. For many shots, your audience's attention is likely to be on the character's face, so as you set up lights, look at how shadows are falling around the nose of the puppet. The nose, of course, sticks out from the face, so it's a good location to study for the effects of your lighting efforts, since it's capable of casting a strong shadow.

As you study the lighting in this region, consider some essentials: do you see distracting double shadows around the nose? If so, try to 'kill' them, by getting it down to one shadow, ideally the one created by the key light. Is the shadow extremely dark? You might be creating the dreaded 'shadow mustache', so consider brightening up that shadow by adding some fill light from underneath (perhaps by using a mini bounce board).

A high light means a low shadow

Lights that are positioned up high will create shadows that fall lower in your shot. This can help to do away with unflattering shadows on puppet faces. Conversely, lights that are positioned lower will have shadows that are cast higher in your scene, and that can cause annoying shadows on puppets and on sets. Of course, if these are precisely the kind of shadows that you need for your scene, then go for it!

Get hands on

With a light fixture in position, you can create rough shadows by simply holding your hand up in front of the light. By varying the angle of you hand, and its distance from the fixture, you can quickly rough in shadows on your set. Then, when it comes time to set up a flag or a cookie, you'll already know the basic angle and position that you should use for your lights and shadow-creating tools.

DREW FORTIER, LIGHTING DEPARTMENT, *THE BOXTROLLS*, *FRANKENWEENIE*

Drew Fortier is a lighting and camera specialist. He's worked on several stop motion feature films, including *Frankenweenie* and *The Boxtrolls*, as well as many stop motion television series and independent films.

Q. A feature film is a huge production. It's not just one person running around, doing all the lighting! Can you roughly outline the structure of a lighting department for a stop motion feature, and what each position is responsible for?

A. Most stop motion films have multiple sets (called units) shooting at once. When you're at the peak of production that means a film could be shooting on 30 plus units at once. That's way too much for one director of photography to be working on all at once. So there are multiple camera teams that are shooting at the same time. Scenes from the film are divided up, and assigned to these different teams. On *Frankenweenie*, director of photographer Pete Sorg had four other teams shooting at the same time as his. Each team runs as it own little complete film crew.

Usually each team will be made up of 3–4 people. There is a Light Cameraman (LC) who acts as the director of photography for the team. They are responsible for overseeing all aspects related to the visual image: framing, composition, lighting, and camera movement. The LC has the ability to bring elements of his own style to the sequences they are working on, but ultimately he's there to help bring to life the look that is established by the DOP. The LC will be in breakdown meetings alongside the DOP, and work hand-in-hand with the visual effects department to oversee or offer notes about any post work that may need to be done to the shots, or grading that needs to be added in post.

There is a gaffer, whose job is to actually execute the lighting design of the LC. This involves setting up everything from C-stands, to placing lights, to balancing power loads, to programming the DMX for animated lighting effects, to rigging green screens. They work with the LC on set to bring to life their ideas and overcome any technical aspects that might be involved with lighting a scene. There usually is a far bit of custom lighting equipment to build as well – things like wiring small practical lamps on set, or creating small rigs to hold things like bounce cards and mirrors in the smallest of spaces, while still allowing access for the animator to shoot.

There is a camera assistant, whose job it is to make sure the camera equipment is ready to shoot. Things like keeping the sensor clean, keeping track of the lenses and keeping them in good working order are a top priority. Since time is always of the essence in a stop motion production, the camera assistant tries to stay a little bit ahead of everyone else and tries to foresee any technical problems that might slow down the shoot.

They will also work closely with the animator to make sure they have everything they need to shoot. Things like having a comfortable shooting environment, and providing them with access to any reference the animator might need. The camera assistant is also responsible for maintaining focus on a shot and often for programming the camera move if the shot calls for it. This also requires working with the animator to get the correct timings for the puppet's movement, as well as maintaining focus for the shot.

Often, a move or focus will have to be tweaked during a shot, as the animation can change at the last minute. If it's a very complicated shot, a dedicated motion control programmer will be on the crew, to alleviate some of the work load from the camera assistant.

Q. Can you talk a bit about considerations that need to be made when lighting in relation to the animators?

A. When lighting a shot, you can't just put a light anywhere you want. You have to constantly be thinking in the back of your head, 'How will the animator will be able to move this puppet?' Things like leaving them access to the puppet, which sounds like a simple thing, can become a huge battle. Lighting for a stop motion set is very much the same as lighting a live action film. Only lights and cameras are about 500 times bigger for a puppet then they are for a human. Which means you can run out of space on set very easily, especially on interior sets.

So when lighting you have to get creative. Using bigger sources of light further away from the set can help. Or things like plating a wall (which means you take a static frame of the scene without the puppet, take the wall out, and add the missing wall back in post after the animation is complete). Also you can get creative with using smaller lights as well. With a DSLR on a stop motion shoot, you have the added benefit of controlling your shutter speed. This allows you to use smaller and dimmer light sources, but have a long exposure to make that dimmer light seem brighter. This lets you wire up say a small 3 v bulb in a practical puppet-sized lamp on set, and actually have it able to light up the set.

Even with these tactics, for a lot of shots, it still comes down to a bit of a struggle to leave room for the animator. And sometimes the only way to allow the animator to shoot is to sacrifice something on your end of things. Change a camera angle so the camera rig is in a different position. Or dare I say it, make the lighting a little less the perfect, 'cause at the end of the day if the animation is bad, it doesn't matter how good the lighting is!

Q. *Frankenweenie* is a black and white film, as opposed to a colour film. What challenges did that present? What pleasures?

A. Shooting in black and white was a fairly big adjustment from shooting in colour. Especially when the majority of your film takes place at night and all the characters have dark hair, and you put them against black back rounds, or a dark night sky. They would just disappear and blend in to the scene. I found I had to really work so much more subtle light into a scene. A particular scene I worked on in *Frankenweenie*, with Edgar sneaking into the school to electrify his pet rat, had a lot of dark corners in the room. I didn't want to have this magical rim lighting following him around to separate him from the background. That can very quickly look fake, and distract your eye from what's happening in the scene. So I started to just put subtle hits of soft light on the walls just behind the characters to give them some separation. I used soft racking lights to bring out the detail in the room. As a result, I ended up using more lights then I regularly would, but the end result is very slick and subtle. None of it was motivated from a source, but it doesn't draw the eye, just allows you to see the action of the character freely and uninterrupted.

There was a great simplicity to shooting in black and white. To not have to worry about colours matching between shots, or scenes, or worrying about gels burning out on lamps, was refreshing. I found I was just able to focus on simply the white light, and how it would react to everything. I find myself craving to be able to work in black and white again. It was a lot of fun!

Q. These days, lighting effects in stop motion are often a blend of physical, 'on-set' tricks and digital effects created in post-production. Can you discuss some of the on-set effects that were created in *Frankenweenie*?

A. The best thing about stop motion is that you can do all sorts of in-camera lighting tricks. One of the most rewarding is being able to animate lights within a shot. I was fortunate enough to work on a lot of the end sequence on *Frankenweenie* where the windmill is burning. The fire was all CG, but we added layers and layers of animated light to the set to help sell the look of the CG fire. The fire at the start of the scene begins at the base of the windmill, and slowly spreads upwards to the top. We had to create an effect that would make it look like the flames were growing up the windmill and licking the top of it. So we devised this system that involved 4 inch wide and 1 foot long rollers. They were hollowed out, and had these hand-carved blotchy circles carved out of them in all sorts of various shapes and sizes. We could shine a light through them, and the light would be broken up by these curvy shapes. We mounted the rollers onto a small stepper motor, and that allowed us to rotate the cylinders at tiny intervals.

Dragonframe has the ability to communicate with the motion control rig, to advance the stepper motor every time an animator takes a frame. Then we wired up four small 100 w halogen bulbs to shine through the roller. So as the light passed through the cylinder, you got this organic looking shape, that was wonderfully animated. It was constantly changing, much like the light from a real flame. I based this whole rig at the bottom of the windmill and focused the light to spread up the entirety of the windmill. As the light travelled up the building it would change shape and get wider, etc., making it look very organic. To top it all off, each of the bulbs was wired up to a DMX lighting board and on its own channel. In Dragonframe you have the ability to control the intensity of lights, and can even program key frames throughout a timeline. So I had each light essentially animating to its own lighting pattern, flickering up and down at different intensities from each other. All of this combined really made it feel like the whole windmill was lit by real fire. I had to use about eight of these rollers at once when the whole windmill was on fire!

A lot of the other effects in the film involved electrocution. The actual bolts of lighting were created in post, but again we used practical lighting to help augment how the light would react on set. Another great thing in stop motion is that you can shoot multiple passes for each frame taken. So we would have our 'beauty lighting' pass, which would be the nicely lit pass, without any lighting effects, and then we would have our effects pass, which would be any effects, like the lightning. For those lightning passes, we would sometimes have a small rice light (which is a small light bulb, the size of a grain of rice) that would be put in the frame for the effects pass. It was placed there by the animator, and would create the light from the lightning as it hit. In post they would simply use the light created by this bulb, and not use the bulb itself.

Camera

With all of the intense labour that goes into a stop motion project, it can be easy to forget the camera, as it quietly clicks away. Yet without it, the entire medium of stop motion wouldn't exist. The frames that your camera dutifully records *are* the project. Without the camera, you'd have no recorded frames to play back. No recorded frames, no stop motion!

But much more than simply being a device that records your work, the lens and the camera are absolutely essential creative tools for our medium. What (and how) your lens and camera sees is what (and how) your audience will see. That means the lens and camera are in a very real way a direct 'tap' into the vision you have in your head for your stop motion world. And that tap goes right to your audience. Just as important, the emotions that are evoked by the way you use the lens and camera will be the emotions felt by your audience.

This chapter introduces you to the essential aspects of the lens and camera, so that you'll be able to capture remarkable looking images. You'll probably want to move between this chapter and Chapter 8 on Lighting, in order to maximize your training. By the end of this chapter, you'll be well on your way to using the lens and camera to transfer that remarkable stop motion world in your head on the screen, for audiences to enjoy.

Figure 9.1
Nia poses for the
camera.
The DSLR (digital
single-lens
reflex) camera
is essential for
high-quality stop
motion projects.

Essential camera considerations for stop motion

What's stopping you from grabbing any old digital camera, connecting it to your computer, and getting down to the business of creating stop motion? It's not like the stop motion police are going to arrest you. But using just any digital camera, despite being convenient and cost-saving, isn't going to help you in your desire to make a great looking stop motion project.

First of all, you'll want to avoid the so-called 'point-and-shoot' style of camera. In order to keep things quick and easy for the user, this kind of camera greatly restricts the amount of control that you can have over your image. And you want to be able to control your image as fully as possible.

Webcams can be great. They're cheap, they typically connect easily with Dragonframe, and they can offer a pretty nice looking image, all things considered. These cameras can be great for introductory projects, and for creating animation for a portfolio, when it's the quality of the animation that matters, as opposed to the quality of the image itself. But webcams simply can't provide the very high image resolution we typically expect in professional looking projects, and as with the point-and-shoot camera option, the humble webcam can't offer much in the way of true professional image control.

There are also lots of stop motion apps out there that work with mobile phones and tablets. It's all very slick – a camera and software, all in one handheld device! But again, while these options may be fine for introductory projects, they lack the true image control needed for most serious projects.

That's why for more advanced stop motion projects, and for any project in which you want true control of your frame, a DSLR camera is the way to go.

DSLR cameras

DSLR stands for 'digital single-lens reflex camera'. Without diving into the technology too deeply, a single-lens reflex camera uses a mirror behind the lens to send the light from the image to the viewfinder. When taking the actual picture, this mirror flips out of the way, allowing the light to pass through the lens into the camera's body, where a sensor records the image.

This design has a range of advantages in the world of still photography, but for stop motion purposes, the main thing to realize is that this style of camera has a very large image sensor, relative to other lower-end cameras. This large sensor allows for fantastic resolution within the recorded image, and provides an overall image quality that will look stellar on even the largest movie theatre screens, not to mention the screens of handheld devices.

Besides the fantastic image quality provided by DSLR cameras, the manner in which they interact with lenses make them ideal for serious stop motion projects. DSLR cameras are designed to work with very high quality lenses. These lenses transmit and focus light in a very precise fashion, ensuring that the image that's recorded on the sensor has incredible integrity. The precision lenses for DSLR cameras are also designed to allow the photographer (or animator, in our case) the ability to vary the amount of light that is transmitted. As you'll learn in this chapter, being able to precisely control the amount of light that's traveling through the lens is essential for achieving masterful results.

Like most high-performance tools, DSLR cameras don't come cheap. But it's hard to argue against this particular cost, when you see the quality of image they provide. And with prices constantly dropping, what literally cost tens of thousands of dollars just a few years ago can now be purchased at any electronics or camera store, for a few hundred dollars. The DSLR camera is likely going to be the most expensive single item that you'll be acquiring for your stop motion project. If you buy a new camera (which almost always comes with a lens), they typically begin around $500 CAN, but can cost much more than that.

Obviously, you'll want to do a good amount of research before committing to any purchase. Does the camera that you're considering work with Dragonframe? A wide range of DSLR cameras do, but be sure to check Dragonframe's website for a list of compatible cameras. Also, check online reviews of the specific model that you're considering. Have other stop motion artists used the camera? Are they happy with the results?

> When it comes to price, you can sometimes save literally hundreds of dollars if you're ok with buying last year's model.

The great thing about investing in a DSLR is that most (if not all) also record high definition video as well as still images. Having an HD video camera as well as a stop motion camera is a very nice perk, in case you want to develop your live-action filmmaking skills as well. You'll just need to purchase a memory card that's big enough for all the data.

For years now, I've used a Canon DSLR (one of their Rebel models) for all the stop motion that I've created. This is also the model of cameras we use in our senior studios at Sheridan College. Stop motion films created with these Canon cameras have played at festivals all over the world. A good number of television productions have also been created using this model. It's a solid choice, because Canon makes a great product that's reliable and affordable (the Rebels are priced quite reasonably, all things considered). The lens that it comes with is variable (it can zoom in and out), and it offers a very high quality image. I use the one lens that came with the camera for everything that I shoot. My camera is a few years old now, but it's a real workhorse – it continues to function perfectly, and it gets me exactly the image that I want.

That being said, there's a wide selection of manufacturers to choose from – Canon is just one of them. Just be sure to do your research before you commit. And even once you do purchase, shoot some tests as soon as you get it. Most reputable vendors have generous exchange and return policies, if you aren't happy with the model that you've chosen.

The camera lens in detail

The study of light (and its transmission through materials) is its own area of scientific specialization. Of course, you don't need to become a physicist to use a camera effectively, but you do need to understand the principles that govern a camera's lens if you want to be a pro.

Lens focus

Dragonframe can control nearly every aspect of your image, except for lens focus. You need to do that manually on your camera lens, by adjusting the focus ring.

Being able to manually control the focus means you can actually animate your focus within your shot, frame by frame. In the live-action world, this shifting of focus is often referred to as a 'rack focus', and it can be a very effective way to take your audience's attention from something in the foreground to something in the background, or vice versa. Animating the focus takes some practice, but it doesn't take long to get good at it. It's easier to see the results of animated focal changes when you have a shallower depth of field (see below), so set your lens accordingly, and do some tests. You'll be impressed by the dramatic effect it might be able to provide your project.

The aperture

The lens aperture is the opening within the lens that allows light to pass through, so that it can hit the sensor that's located within the camera's body. The aperture (on a DSLR) is variable – you can make it bigger or smaller. When dealing with the lens aperture, you'll often hear the term 'f-stop' used. F-stops are standardized numbers that refer to the size of the aperture opening. The specific f-stop numbers differ from lens to lens, but they typically range from approximately 1.4 up to or beyond 20.

Here's where it gets a little bit confusing – the *bigger* the f-stop number, the *smaller* the aperture opening. It's a strange way to number things (every student of photography would agree), but for our purposes as stop motion artists, understanding exactly how these f-stop numbers are determined isn't vital. What *is* vital is that you understand that a change in the f-stop (meaning, a change in the aperture size) results in a change to how much of your image is in focus. This, in turn, has earned its own very important term: depth of field.

Depth of field

Depth of field (which is often used interchangeably with the term 'depth of focus') refers to how much of your image is in focus, when the lens is focused at a certain distance. For example, if your lens is focused on your puppet, and that puppet is 30 cm (12 inches) away, the image isn't *only* focused at precisely 30 cm. It's also focused at a point a bit closer to the camera, as well as a bit further away. You can think of this as a zone, or region, of focus. This zone is what's known as depth of field, and it's typically within this zone that you'll want to keep your puppet, while animating. Your puppet may go in and out of this zone, for a variety of reasons, but typically, this 'sweet spot' is where most stop motion performances takes place.

What effect does the aperture have on the image's depth of field? When the aperture is big (a low f stop number), your image will have a 'shallow' depth of field, with less of the image in focus. Inversely, when the aperture is small (a high f stop number), your image will have 'deep' depth of field, and more will be in focus.

> The bigger the aperture, the shallower the depth of field. The smaller the aperture, the deeper the depth of field.

Effective control over the amount of focus in your image is extremely important. It's a subtle but powerful way to direct the attention of your audience to the areas that you feel are most important. In keeping with this, the use of focus in Figure 9.2 seems to suggest that 'only Nia is important in this shot', while Figure 9.3, through its deep focus, suggests to the viewer that 'everything' in the frame is important.

Once you're effectively controlling depth of field through the use of the aperture, you can create a shot that makes use of shallow depth of field or deep depth of field, depending on the needs of the shot. Each approach has its own advantages, as well its own challenges. Understanding them more fully will help you make the right choices when it comes to developing your own distinctive look for your project.

Figure 9.2
Larger aperture's effect on depth of field.
With the focus set on Nia, and a large aperture (I used an aperture of 5.6), foreground and background elements are 'soft'. This is shallow depth of field.

Figure 9.3
Smaller aperture's effect on depth of field.
For this image, I left the focus untouched from Figure 9.2, but this time, I used a small aperture (an aperture of 32). As a result, the foreground and background, as well as Nia, are all in sharp focus. This is deep depth of field, or 'deep focus'.

Shallow depth of field

As discussed above, shallow depth of field is a great method for directing the audience's attention. But its usefulness doesn't end there. Take another look at Figure 9.2, specifically in the areas that are not in focus. The fuzzy foreground and background have a dreamy quality to them. The overall look of the image is sort of romantic and lyrical. It's an artful look, and one that has a certain softness and mystery to it. In short, shallow focus can bring a lot of feeling and emotion to your scene.

Working in stop motion with a shallow depth of field can also provide you with a way to highlight the fact that you're working in miniature. Since depth of field tends to be at its most shallow when the lens is focused 'close up', a miniature stop motion landscape close to the lens often appears profoundly out of focus, compared to the same landscape when it's full-scale. This is a strong visual clue regarding scale, and typically signals 'miniature' to our eyes.

The challenge of working with shallow depth of field in stop motion is that it can be very tricky when it comes to animation. A very shallow depth of field provides an extremely narrow region of 'in focus' space for your animation. It's easy to forget about focus, especially when lost in creating an animated performance, because the image on screen may be sharp enough for your animation purposes, but not for viewing by your

audience. Many animators have had their hearts broken (and their production schedules blown) when they realized, after hours of animation, that their puppet was *slightly* out of focus for much of the shot, due to shallow depth of field.

As with advanced lighting, a pop-through test is needed here – this time, to ensure that the depth of field is sufficient for your animation. Record a number of frames with your puppet in place, moving it very slightly closer (and further away) from its initial mark. Review the high-resolution frames, and if the puppet goes out of focus in any significant way, you'll need to rethink things. Make your aperture smaller, or 'widen' your camera angle (more on that later in this chapter), or modify the placement of your puppet within the frame. You should also make use of the Focus Check feature in Dragonframe (which you'll find in the software's Cinematography Workspace).

Deep depth of field

Deep depth of field is often referred to as 'deep focus', and with good reason. If you look at Figure 9.3, you'll see that it shows not only the middle ground clearly, but also the foreground and background. Unlike shallow depth of field that has a limited range in which the performance has to occur, deep focus can provide you with far greater performance freedom, since your puppet will be able to range closer and further away from the camera while still staying in focus. As such, if your story is more about performance and story as opposed to mood, deep focus is a great way to go. Deep focus can also be useful if your puppet is going to roam around a lot within the shot. Set your lens with a small aperture, do a quick focus test to make sure you're good, and away you go. In the same way that using indirect (bounced) light lets you move on from the lighting process, using deep depth of focus lets you 'set it and forget it', so that you can get on with things.

And just as shallow depth of field can emphasize the miniature nature of your stop motion world, a deep focus approach can help to create the illusion that your stop motion world is full-scale.

One possible disadvantage of shooting with deep focus is that it can rob a scene of some of its artfulness, since there's less atmospheric 'fuzziness'. If you take a look at Figure 9.3, you'll see that the painted clouds in the background are very sharply focused. Do we really need to see the clouds in such focus? They'd probably look more effective (and convincing) if they weren't so sharp, but that's the hazard of deep focus. This can cause further problems, beyond just mood, since often you actually want a foreground and background to be at least somewhat soft, so that the puppet stands out nicely as the center of attention.

Deep focus's requirement of a smaller aperture also means that you'll need more light, or a slower shutter speed (more on this below).

Shooting with an f-stop of around 8 is pretty safe for many stop motion situations. This will provide you with a good amount of depth of field, so that you have room in which to safely animate, while still providing you with some flattering softer focus on foreground and background elements. Just remember that your own tests, and your own artistic intent, will determine what f-stop is *truly* right for any particular shot.

CITIZEN KANE, ORSON WELLES, 1941. CINEMATOGRAPHY BY GREGG TOLAND

It's impossible to examine the artistic potential of depth of field in filmmaking and not highlight Toland's work in this classic Hollywood film. By staging pivotal sequences in extremely deep focus, Toland allowed Welles to compose extremely complex shots, with remarkable action taking place in the foreground, middle ground, and background, all at once. These sequences have become legendary, and it all comes down to the transmission of light through the tiniest of apertures!

The relationship between aperture, shutter speed, and ISO

If the aperture was the only variable we had at our disposal in photography, our photographed images would be pretty limited. Most images using shallow depth of field would be blasted with far too much light, while images created with a small aperture might have deep focus, but would be too dark to show off any details. Fortunately, there are other variables that we can use to get just the look we want for our stop motion project.

Shutter speed

Imagine a darkened room. The door opens, letting in light from the outside, then closes again. Just how much light is allowed into the room is determined by how long the door is left open. The camera's shutter works the same way. It's a door in the camera body that allows light to enter (via the lens) so that it can hit the sensor. How long this door is opened for (or how briefly) is what's known as shutter speed.

This ability to vary the shutter speed when using a DSLR becomes essential as you vary the aperture in the lens. That's because by varying the shutter speed, you can 'correct' for how much (or how little) light the aperture is allowing into the camera. Consider the earlier images that illustrate shallow and deep depth of field – Figures 9.2 and 9.3. One image used a large aperture (letting in lots of light), while the other used a small aperture (letting in little light), yet both images are equally bright. I achieved this equal level of brightness in both images by varying the shutter speed. Figure 9.2 (with its big aperture) had a shutter speed of just ¼ of a second, while Figure 9.3 (with a small aperture) required a whopping 8 seconds of exposure, in order to get the same brightness.

The larger the lens's aperture, the faster the camera's shutter speed must be, in order to achieve an image that has a correct level of brightness. Alternately, the smaller the lens's aperture, the slower the camera's shutter speed must be, to achieve the same level of correct brightness.

It's important to note that when you're shooting things that move around on their own (also known as 'the real world'), a variable shutter speed has significant effect on the image (see Motion blur below). But in the stationary world of stop motion, the variable shutter speed's main use is to control the overall brightness in the image, in relation to how the aperture is set.

Motion blur

When a moving object is photographed, it tends to 'smear' the image somewhat, depending on the shutter speed and the speed of the object. This smear, also known as 'motion blur', is missing from stop motion, since the puppet is always at rest when recorded. This is something that's typically sensed by the audience, rather than actually noticed, and it's a part of what makes stop motion feel 'real, but not quite real'. Many artists embrace this as a hallmark of the medium, but there are times when the illusion is desired. There are ways to create blur in stop motion – namely by using a long shutter speed and actually moving the puppet (often along a track or wire), during the exposure. These days you can achieve blur using digital tools in post-production, if you feel it's necessary for your project. You'll find more on this in Chapter 17 that's dedicated to post-production.

THE MASCOT, LADISLAS STAREWITCH, 1933

A subtle hallmark of Starewitch's animation is his highly effective use of frame blurs to add a dimension of liveliness to his work. You'll find them sprinkled throughout his films, but there are some especially effective examples in this short film. It's startling even today, to see his stylized puppets 'zip' so realistically through space.

If you've never set up a project in Dragonframe before, now would be a good time to get familiar with the basics of the software. In no time at all, you'll have a project set up, and a decent grasp on the basic controls, at which point the following information will be a lot more useful.

ISO

The relationship between aperture and shutter speed is an important one, but there's a third (and final) variable that we can use, in order to determine the quality of our stop motion image, and that's something known as ISO.

ISO is an acronym for 'International Standards Organization'. What do those words have to do with taking nice pictures? Not much, so for our purposes, it's easiest to simply think of ISO as essentially meaning 'sensitivity to light'. The higher the ISO number, the more sensitive the camera's sensor is to light. The more sensitive the sensor is to light, the brighter the image will be, depending on how the aperture and shutter speed are set.

On most DSLR cameras, this sensitivity ranges from around ISO 100 (which is not very sensitive) to ISO 6400 and beyond (which is sensitive enough to create a bright image with almost no visible light at all, if the aperture and shutter speed are set effectively). This variable sensitivity to light, when combined with the variable shutter speed and variable aperture, ultimately allows you to create an endless array of looks within your image.

When shooting in the 'real world', a variable ISO can be a great thing for a variety of reasons. For example, if your subject is moving very fast (like a race car), you can shoot with a high ISO, which allows you to also have a very fast shutter speed. This fast shutter speed ensures that your image of the fast car will be nice and crisp, without any blur. Very handy!

But when working in stop motion (where nothing is actually moving within the frame), using a high ISO isn't the way to go. The specific reasons why are laid out in the previous chapter, in the section entitled 'Light flicker'. In that section, it's recommended that you simply lock your ISO at 100 (Dragonframe has a lock icon to allow this) as an easy way to reduce flicker.

That being said, it's still important to know that ISO *can* be varied, and that it's the final (of three) variables that you can use to modify the basic look of your image when it comes to the lens and camera.

As with everything in stop motion, it's through your own practical application of all this 'aperture/shutter speed/ISO' information that you'll truly start to understand (and make use of) the interconnectedness between these three variables. Fortunately, Dragonframe's design takes into account the importance of how aperture, shutter speed, and ISO work together, as you'll see when we look at Dragonframe's Cinematography Workspace.

Depending on what version of Dragonframe you're using, the details of what follows may be slightly different for you, since software is always getting updated. Help Menus and online resources are always standing by to help!

The cinematography workspace in Dragonframe

For most projects, Dragonframe has two main interface windows: the Animation Workspace, and the Cinematography Workspace. The Animation Workspace is used during animation (so we'll look at that later), while the Cinematography Workspace is used as you light your scene and set up your camera. As you'd expect, it's this workspace window that's more important for our efforts right now.

Dragonframe is designed to 'talk' to your DSLR in a variety of ways, and it's in the realm of camera communication and camera control that Dragonframe *really* shines. As you work within the Cinematography Workspace, Dragonframe allows you to tweak a huge array of camera settings, without actually touching the camera at all. As you explore its features, be sure to use the software's tutorials and help options (both within the software and online) to reveal everything that you can do.

All of the controls within this window are useful, but there are a few that are truly essential for you to know about.

Controls for shutter speed, aperture, and ISO

Now that you know all about the importance of shutter speed, lens aperture, and ISO (as well as their interconnected nature), you'll appreciate the fact that Dragonframe has located the controls for all three right on top of each other. You'll find them in the Camera Settings window.

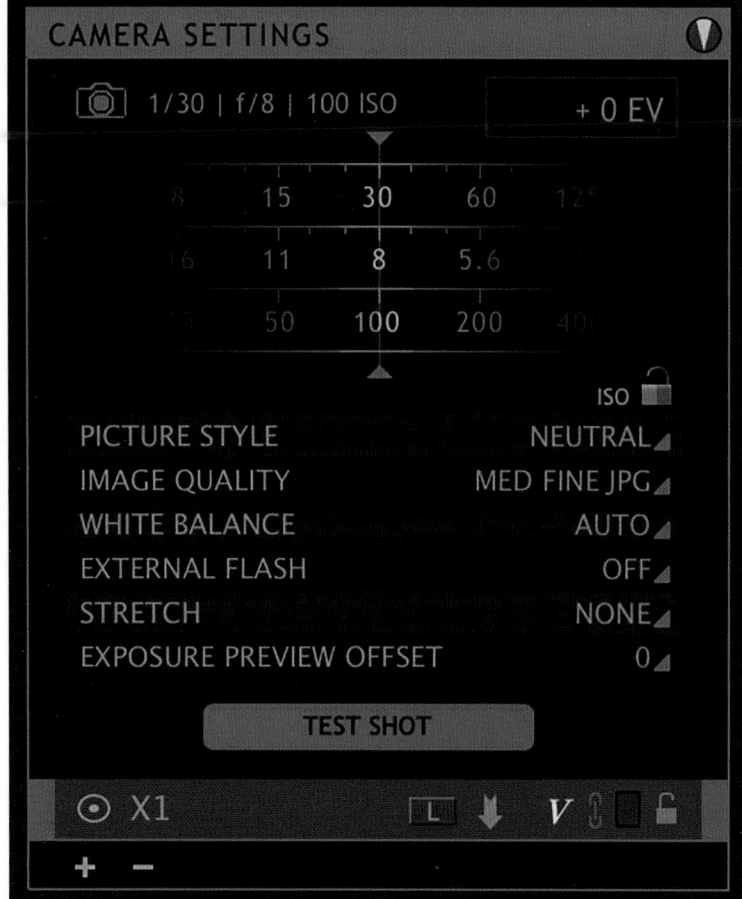

CAMERA SETTINGS

⌖ 1/30 | f/8 | 100 ISO   + 0 EV

	15	**30**	60	125
8				
16	11	**8**	5.6	
	50	**100**	200	400

ISO 🔒

PICTURE STYLE   NEUTRAL
IMAGE QUALITY   MED FINE JPG
WHITE BALANCE   AUTO
EXTERNAL FLASH   OFF
STRETCH   NONE
EXPOSURE PREVIEW OFFSET   0

TEST SHOT

⊙ X1   L ↓ V 📷 🔒

+ −

Figure 9.4
The camera settings window in Dragonframe. Dragonframe does a great job of ensuring that the essential camera and lens variables are easily accessible.

With your camera connected to Dragonframe and the Cinematography Workspace open, you can manipulate each control ring and instantly see the effect that has on the brightness of your image.

By using these control rings and the earlier part of this chapter as a guide, you can record a range of test images as a way of more fully understanding concepts like depth of field. To do that, arrange some objects close together, one behind the other in front of your camera, and throw a decent amount of light on the objects. Lock the ISO at 100, and set the aperture 'wide open' (towards the lower numbers). Adjust your shutter speed until you get a decently bright image, and record a frame. Now adjust the aperture to be very small, and compensate with the shutter speed until your image is about as bright as the previous one (if you hover over the border between the control

rings in Dragonframe, you can actually adjust both rings together, which helps to maintain consistent brightness). You'll now need a very slow shutter, depending on how much light you're using. Record a frame. Compare the two frames for depth of field, and you're on your way to securing a strong practical understanding of these essential principles. Refer to Figures 9.2 and 9.3 for guidance.

Besides shutter speed, aperture, and ISO, you'll notice additional controls in the Camera Settings window. Be sure to take the time to understand each of them, but the most important controls are:

Picture style

This control allows you to choose a basic 'look' for your image. The 'Neutral' setting will give you an unbiased and accurate recording of the colours in front of the camera. Another useful setting is 'Monochrome' – use this setting if you're creating a black and white project. Dragonframe will not only display your frames as black and white during animation, but will capture them in this format as well.

Image quality

This control allows you to set the overall image quality (and size) of your recorded frames. As mentioned previously, DSLR image sensors are incredible things: even at the lowest resolution setting, the captured image still exceeds current high definition standards. I typically set image quality in the middle (Medium Fine Jpeg). This setting provides me with excellent resolution that allows me to enlarge and reframe if needed in post-production, yet the frames are still easy to manage, since they aren't massive. This file format looks great in front of audiences, from the biggest screens to the smallest.

Outside of the Camera Settings window, the Cinematography Workspace has many other lighting and camera tools. Some of the most frequently used ones are highlighted below.

Live View

Dragonframe puts the DSLR into a sleep mode after it's been inactive for a while, in order to prevent the camera from overheating. The Live

View button wakes up the camera, so that you can continuo lighting or framing up your shot. If the camera is being shut down and you find this is preventing you from getting work done, you can extend the time in the software's Preferences window.

Aspect Ratio Mask

Most DSLR cameras record a high-resolution image that has an almost square shape to it. For motion pictures, however, the standard shape of the frame tends to be more rectangular: think of a 'widescreen' look. By using the Aspect Ratio Mask (16:9 is pretty standard), you can impose a mask over the square image you're actually recording, and see how it will look in your final film. As for how to create this widescreen look in your final footage, that's discussed in more detail in Chapter 17 dedicated to post-production. I typically use a pre-set Mask ratio (you can decide which Mask you want), and leave it on at all times during production.

Focus check

As discussed earlier in this chapter, adjusting focus is about the only variable Dragonframe can't control on your DSLR, but it can help you to check it. As you set up your shot, you can use this control to effectively 'zoom in' on your image to make sure the focus is perfect on the region of the image that's most critical. This is a great feature and is one that I use for every shot before I begin animation. Focus control is so critical that I also shoot a test frame before animating, and go out of Dragonframe to view the high-resolution image itself, just to be sure.

I can't stress this enough: the very best way to learn about lenses, cameras, and Dragonframe is to jump in and shoot lots of test footage. 'Purposeful play' is truly the best way to learn. Assuming that you aren't swinging a sledgehammer around your studio, you're not going to break anything (in the camera, or in Dragonframe), and you'll be amazed at how quickly you start to get the hang of it all. If you *are* swinging a sledgehammer around, that's a very strange approach to the medium, but if it works for you – so be it!

Figure 9.5
Spider's Anatomy, Vojtech Kiss, 2014.
A great example of how lens and camera variables can be used to help communicate both story and emotion. Also – stop motion water! How do you do that? Part 4 will reveal all.

Camera placement and angles

Where should you place your camera as you frame up a shot? As you ask yourself this question, it's vital to remember that in stop motion there are actually two cameras at work. There is the 'storyboard camera', (which expresses itself at the storyboard stage through the panel drawings), and there is the 'physical camera' that you use on-set. Since it's a drawing on a piece of paper or a screen, the storyboard camera can do all kinds of wild things. Almost *no* rules govern what it can show – even the rules of perspective need not apply, if you want to be really wild.

But unless you're a studio that can afford computerized camera-control systems, the physical camera is bound by all sorts of constraints: tripod height, lens angle, lens focus, the animator's access to the stage ... the list goes on. All of which is to say that the more your storyboard shots match what the physical camera can achieve, the better. This doesn't mean that your camera positions have to be dull, it just means that your creativity needs to operate within certain boundaries. Even the world's greatest painters still have to stop when they get to the edge of the canvas!

Determining the best angle for each shot at the storyboard stage as well as on-set is a big part of a director's job.

filmmaking how-to guide (not to mention in every movie), and odds are you're instinctively familiar with them already. That's because regardless of where (or when) we were born, we've all grown up surrounded by motion pictures that use these same basic angles.

The angles include: high (bird's view), low (worm's view), long (also called 'wide – angle'), medium, and close-up. They some-times get blended together to create hybrids (an example being the 'medium close-up' shot), but essentially, these basic angles constitute the core 'visual grammar' of motion picture storytelling.

But just as a writer has to select the perfect word when crafting a story, a storyteller who deals with visual sequences (such as a comic or storyboard artist, as well as a filmmaker) has to choose just the right angle for every shot. Many angles can work for a given shot, at least in terms of conveying the basics of story, but is it the very *best* angle for that moment? Effectively discerning which angle is ideal and which is not is an acquired skill that comes through practice and through the study of the medium.

Consider the following example. Your character has just had his heart broken. What's the best camera angle for this situation? It's an emotional moment, so perhaps you should use a medium or even a close-up angle, so that your audience can clearly see your character's emotional state. Shot in this way, even a puppet with a fixed expression will seem to 'emote' to the audience, if only because the audience feels so physically close to it! Alternately, perhaps you want your audience to feel emotionally distanced from your character. If that's the case, then maybe you should place the camera far away. This physically distant camera will cause your character to seem isolated in the frame, which can work to deepen the sadness of the moment. And if you place the camera at a high angle, looking down – the sense of isolation intensifies even further, and you officially have a tear-jerker on your hands. That's the power of angles!

Basic camera angles

These are basic positions that the storyboard and on-set camera can occupy, and there are basic directions in which it can look. You'll find examples of these basic camera angles in every

WHAT'S THE BEST WAY TO TELL THE STORY?

Version A

Version B

Figure 9.6
Simple vs. complex camera angles.

You can convey the same story sequence in more than one way. Consider Figure 9.6. In that image, Version A uses very basic camera angles. These basic angles allow the story to unfold in a simple way, and are easy to recreate with the physical camera, on-set. The angles aren't that dynamic, but they work, and they let your project move forward effectively, since you can set these angles up pretty quickly.

Version B uses more complex angles that add a lot of visual interest, but they'll be tricky to achieve in the studio. And does all that visual energy coming from the strong angles *distract* from the story and animation? Since it looks like the scene has quite a bit of dialogue, perhaps the added visual energy that these angles offer is badly needed to keep the scene from becoming a boring collection of 'talking puppet' shots. Because it's complex, Version B will take longer to create than A, but B sure has cool angles! Version A isn't as fun, but you'll meet your deadlines, and your story and animation will be nicely showcased. Which version is the right way to tell the story? It's up to you, as director.

As you select your angles, it helps if you can determine what the 'normal' camera height is for your story. Try to think of the camera as another character within your scene. What height should it be at relative to the other characters? You'll vary this height from shot to shot, of course, but knowing this 'normal' camera height can help you maintain a basic visual flow from shot to shot within your scene. You'll learn *lots* more about visual flow in Chapter 16 dedicated to Production in Part 4.

Another way to maintain smooth visual flow through your camera angles is to avoid using angles that are almost, but not quite, the same. Practically speaking, if you find that you have a sequence of shots in your boards that continually returns to *basically* the same angle, consider shooting these shots from just one.

This simplifying of angles will also help your shooting schedule. Every time you move the camera, you need to invest time in that move as you clear space for the tripod, get your new frame established, and light it. But if you can shoot a string of shots from the same position, one after the other, it helps you get the most from your day. Then in post-production, of course, you'll edit them into the correct order.

Only move the camera to a new angle (at the storyboard stage, and on-set) when it's really necessary. Changes to camera angles and positions should be *motivated* by something. If they happen for no reason, they will quickly become confusing and distracting.

Watch out for random low angle (worm's view) shots in stop motion. The visual drama that a shot like this can offer may not be worth the production time it can eat up. You'll need extra fabrication time to create a ceiling or sky background, and you'll also need extra time to position (and light) this awkward set piece in front of the camera. You may also need extra animation time, if the ceiling or sky prevents easy access to the puppet.

Lens angles

In addition to the basic camera angles that we have as our visual building blocks, we also have another way of thinking about camera angles. These are 'lens angles', and these become especially important when we're working with the on-set camera. More specifically, when we're working with its lens.

The lens that comes with most DSLR cameras is a variable focus or 'zoom' lens. It's called a zoom because by adjusting the lens, you can zoom in on your subject without physically moving closer to it. With a zoom lens, you can shoot an image that has a 'wide-angle' field of view (when it's zoomed out), or an image that has an enlarged and 'narrow angle' field of view (when it's zoomed in, which is also known as 'telephoto').

As you'll see below, this variable angle feature on a zoom lens makes it extremely useful for stop motion. But an image created with a wide-angle on a zoom lens has some very different properties compared to one created with a narrow angle. These differences will seriously affect your image.

Wide-angle

When a lens is zoomed out to its wide-angle position, its depth of field is increased, which is quite useful for keeping the action within your scene in focus. But a wide angle presents some serious challenges for stop motion. For example, if you're setting up for a close up shot, a wide-angle lens setting will require you to move your camera in very close to the puppet to get the frame you want. Since your camera is now so close to the puppet, this makes accessing the puppet for animation quite tricky, and increases the risk that you'll bump

the tripod or camera. A very wide lens also means that you're seeing a lot more of the background. As a result, you may find yourself having to fabricate (and light) more of your set walls, in order to satisfy the wide-angle lens. Considering how labour-intensive stop motion is in general, this can be a serious factor when it comes to production costs and time.

Narrow angle

When a lens is zoomed in to achieve a narrow angle, its depth of field becomes shallower. As you've learned earlier in this chapter, narrow depth of field can make animation tricky, since it reduces the area of focus needed for animation. Typically, at least for stop motion, the narrow lens doesn't diminish depth of field *too* much, and if you compensate with a smaller aperture, your focus will still be deep enough. The greatest advantage of shooting with a lens zoomed in is that it allows for that critical physical space between the camera and the set. This space gives you room to work, and it minimizes the chances that you'll bump the tripod or camera. This allows you the peace of mind that you'll need in order to create effective animation.

If you like the roomy access to the puppet that zooming in the lens offers you, but you don't like the shallow depth of field this gives you, you can try shooting the shot with a slightly wider lens angle, which will increase the depth of field. You can then digitally *enlarge* the shot to the desired framing in post-production. You can find more on this in Chapter 17.

HENRY SELICK

With a number of renowned stop motion features to his name, Selick is, of course, an extremely experienced and talented stop motion filmmaker. Among his many stop motion talents is his ability to make extremely effective choices about where to put the camera for each shot. Study his films, shot by shot, to see how these decisions expertly convey both the story and the emotion of the moment.

Effective framing and blocking

Framing and blocking refers to the establishment of the actual frame in which your animation will occur. Whether you're setting up a simple wide shot that will allow you to create some portfolio animation, or a more complex one that has to work in relation to shots that come before or after it within a sequence, an effectively framed and blocked shot is key. Below, you'll find some essential advice that should help.

Framing

Just what is framing for stop motion? It helps to think of a picture frame, as it surrounds the image and contains it. The frame that you create with your camera for stop motion does the same thing: it establishes the actual stage within which your performance will take place. If you zoom the lens in, you have a 'smaller stage' in which to act the puppet. If you zoom the lens out, the stage is much larger.

But as you set about framing up your shot, what factors need to be considered? At the most basic level, the framing for your shot should allow the animation to play out in plain view. Further, it should allow any other critical elements (aside from animation) within the shot to show (or 'read') clearly. Arranging your frame so that the action occurs towards the center of the frame is always the safest way to achieve this. Frames that are 'edge-heavy' (in which the action occurs towards the very edges of the frame) can be very dramatic, but they can also be tricky during animation as you struggle to keep the puppet within the frame. These shots can also be hard to work with in editing.

Additionally, an effective frame should do its best to flatter the subject of the shot. Assuming that subject is your puppet, does the puppet look as good as possible within the frame? Puppets, like people, look better from certain angles, and the more you can frame with that in mind, the better. Is the frame visually balanced overall, not just in terms of the puppet's location, but in terms of all visual elements, including sets, props,

and lighting? This attention to composition needs to be considered for the entirety of the shot. Your framing may look nice for the start of the shot, but will it be effective halfway through, and at the end? Remember that you aren't framing for a still photograph, but rather for a performance that will happen over time, within your frame.

> Be mindful of your Aspect Ratio Mask in Dragonframe. Get in the habit of using this mask to show you the specific frame size that you'll be working with in post-production, rather than the 'full' DSLR frame.

You may find yourself setting up for a shot that will stand alone, such as a piece of character animation that's destined for your demo reel, or a bit of physical comedy that plays best in a single shot. If that's the case, your framing concerns are limited to that single shot. But many times, you'll be framing up for a shot that will exist among many others. This kind of shot must satisfy the above requirements for good framing, but it will also need to be framed so that it can 'hook up' with the shot that came before it, as well as the shot that comes after it. When the time to edit arrives, you want shots that connect nicely, not in a jarring fashion. It's tricky stuff, to be sure, so you'll find *lots* more on shot hook ups in Chapter 16 dedicated to production.

Figure 9.7
Bone Mother, See Creature Studio, 2018 Sometimes the perfect camera position for the shot means that the animator has to do some serious contortions. Here, Sylvie Trouvé watches the monitor as she positions the puppets. Just another day in the life of a stop motion animator!

Figure 9.8
Effective framing.
A good frame needs to allow for all of the action that will occur over the course of the shot. In this example, Nia is going to eventually straighten her arm – so the framing needs to allow for that action.

Figure 9.9
Starting pose for a shot.
In this example, the camera is set up effectively for Nia's first blocking point within the shot. But will it be effective later in the shot, as Nia moves towards the right?

Figure 9.10
Final pose within the same shot.
As Nia arrives at her final blocking point within the same shot, we can see that the framing for this entire shot is effective, since it allowed for *all* the action to occur, from start to finish.

Effective blocking

Blocking is the process by which you ensure that the puppets will be in the right place at the right time, over the course of the shot. Blocking has its roots in live theatre, and in that context, the director breaks down each scene of the play to determine just where the actors should be positioned. In theatre, the physical space for this positioning of actors is the stage itself. But in stop motion, the stage is the frame that's created by the camera's view.

What makes for effective blocking? If the puppet's movements within the frame over the course of the shot have been taken into account so that we can simply see things clearly, then you're well on your way. This movement within the frame may be up and down within the frame (known as 'x and y axis' movement), it might be towards or away from the camera (movement of this nature is said to be occurring along the 'z axis'), or a combination of various directions. As with good framing, a well-blocked shot looks visually pleasing and balanced throughout the shot – at the beginning, at the middle, and at the end.

Ultimately, a well-blocked shot does more than simply allow for all action to be shown clearly. It actually suggests (or even reveals) something bigger. Imagine a shot in which an insecure character gains confidence. This change in state will of course be expressed through animation (and possibly dialogue), but blocking can also play a part in 'selling' this idea of growing confidence. If the shot is blocked so that the puppet begins the shot far away from camera, but gradually moves closer, this increase in size will help to emphasize the acting and dialogue. In other words, growth in size on screen equals growing in confidence. Compare this blocking choice to a shot that sees the puppet moving *away* from the camera – or from frame left to right. Would those other choices be more, or less, effective for the shot in question?

We looked at using a pop-through for lighting in the previous chapter, but you can also use a pop-through to help with framing and blocking challenges. To do this, first establish a rough frame for your shot that you think will work for the entire shot: its beginning, its middle, and its end. Pose your puppet as it will be for the start of the shot, and place it appropriately within the frame. Capture a frame, and repeat this for all the main points of the shot, through to the final pose and puppet placement. When you review the frames, you should be able to tell whether the frame you've established is effective or not. If it's not, you can modify the framing, before actual animation.

> Pop-throughs are also very useful for animation, and you'll find out more on how to use them for animation later in the book.

As you can imagine, the process of blocking for your shot is closely tied to the process of framing, since your shot is only effectively framed once you've taken into consideration the shot's blocking requirements. Often, a shot gets reframed somewhat as the process of blocking is worked out. The frame shifts a bit to accommodate the blocking, and the blocking gets modified somewhat in consideration of the framing.

Additional camera requirements

Obviously, the DSLR camera is your main camera purchase but there's some related equipment that you're also going to need for stop motion.

> One camera item that you don't need for stop motion is a camera memory card. That's because you'll be recording frames directly on to your computer via Dragonframe, as opposed to storing them on a card. Of course, if you want to shoot still frames or video on to the camera itself, you *will* need a card.

Tripod

When selecting a tripod for stop motion, the sturdier the better. That's because during animation,

if you're going to bump into anything, odds are it will be the tripod, since its legs take up quite a bit of room within the studio, right near where you'll be standing. If your tripod is solid, a slight bump might not shift your camera at all.

Of course, the sturdier the tripod, the heavier it is, which can make it tough to position as you set up each shot. It can also mean that it's more expensive. The tripod I use in my studio is sturdy enough, yet is still quite lightweight. Considering it will likely be the only tripod I ever buy, it was relatively affordable (under $80 CAN) and it works great.

You might want to consider a tripod that's designed for video cameras rather than still photography cameras. Since video cameras need to pan and tilt in a very smooth way, this kind of tripod can make 'on the tripod' camera moves in stop motion easier.

External power adaptor for DSLR

It's highly impractical, if not impossible to use a battery in the DSLR when shooting stop motion. During a day of animation, Dragonframe is communicating with your DSLR constantly, and even the strongest battery will soon be drained by all of that hard work. Now imagine that midway through animating a shot the battery dies. How do you get the camera off the tripod so that you can recharge or change the battery, without messing up your shot?!

Instead, you'll need to get an external power adaptor. This adaptor typically plugs in to the camera as a battery would, and has an electrical cable running out of it, so you can plug it into the wall. They generally aren't that expensive, and they're essential, so before you purchase a DSLR, make sure one of these adaptors is also available for the model of camera that you've selected.

USB cable (DSLR to computer)

Most DSLR cameras come with a cable that allows them to be connected to your computer, typically via USB. This cable is the method by which your camera sends all of its information to Dragonframe, including the frames that you'll be capturing. If your camera didn't come with a USB cable, you'll obviously need to pick one up at a camera or electronics vendor. When it comes to cable length, things get a bit tricky. A longer cable means more freedom to move around in your studio, but a longer cable can cause connection issues. I'd advise that you get one that's on the longer side, and try it out. If it has issues, return it and get a slightly shorter one.

Camera moves

As you'd imagine, when it comes to animating camera moves, the more that you understand the principles of animation, the better your camera moves will be. That's because you'll be literally animating the camera, frame by frame.

Even a modest camera move can bring a lot of visual excitement to a stop motion shot. But moving the camera during your shot is tricky, in part because you typically also have puppets moving around within the frame. It's a lot to manage, to say the least. But it's certainly possible, so you'll definitely want to explore them.

My advice on camera moves is to practice them on their own for a while and then, once you understand their potential and their limitations, you'll be in a better position to decide how and when to work them into your projects.

'On the tripod' camera moves

Although they take practice, camera moves don't have to be complex things. For example, you can zoom in or out, frame by frame, to create new camera angles within shots. This can offer a huge amount of visual excitement to action or comedy scenes, and has required little more than a gradual adjustment of the lens. Be mindful that as you zoom in or out, your focus is also likely to need to be adjusted, frame by frame.

A modest tilt (when the camera pivots up or down) or a pan (when the camera pivots to the left or right) can be achieved in much the same way that you'd animate a zoom, or your focus – a frame at a time. Before animating, adjust the tension on your tripod head accordingly, and give it a go. These simple moves can be great for modest reframing within shots. An example would be a shot featuring two characters, when one character leaves frame. Without too much trouble, you could animate a slight camera pan to simply re-balance the frame,

on to the remaining character. These 'on the tripod' moves can provide you with great results, and typically don't take too long to learn. Some quick tests will start to show you how it's done.

> When creating a camera move, it can be hard to track the movement as you flip your frames, because there is simply so much visual information to take in. Try focusing your attention on the *edges* of the frame as you flip. It's here that issues related to smoothness of the move will reveal themselves. If the term 'flipping frames' isn't clear, go check out the Animation section of this book.

Tracking shots on a tripod (when the entire camera is actually moving along a path) is hard work, but certainly possible. The results are usually a bit rough, since you're actually bending or crouching down, and sliding the whole tripod! But give it test, and see what you think of the results, and of the back strain. You can also fashion a simple DIY track, from a length of wood into which you insert two 'train tracks' of thin plastic. Attach the camera onto a piece of wood that has grooves cut to match the tracks, and you can now smoothly track your camera! There are lots of other DIY methods, so do your online research, and see what you can come up with.

The salon stand

These big stands go by various names, 'salon' being one of them. Some of them are on lockable wheels, so that the stand can be moved around during set up, then locked off for stability during animation. Others have camera arms that come in from the side, or from above, allowing the camera to take up its position within the shot, which can allow the animator a good amount of easy access to the puppets.

Rigs like this are great devices for camera moves, since they typically allow for incremental movements along a variety of axes, so there's no end to the slick camera moves that you can pull off. The challenge, as you'd expect, is their size and their cost. They're simply too big and too expensive to be practical for the home studio artist; but if you find yourself in a professional studio that's equipped with one, you're in for a treat.

Motion control devices

You're formally in the 'big leagues' if you're animating with a motion control system. Essentially, this is a computer-controlled device that allows for extremely precise and complex camera moves to be created. The system can be pre-programmed by a camera professional, and since they are programmed in, moves can be modified or perfectly repeated, as required. This frees up the animator to concern herself with achieving a great performance, rather than worrying about moving the camera. It can be a bigger beast than a salon stand, and not surprisingly is even more expensive.

As Part 2 wraps up, take a moment to consider how far you've come. You know how to set up your own stop motion studio space. Beyond that, you have the practical skills to use light effectively, so that your stop motion world looks its best, and conveys the mood and atmosphere that you intend. To top it all off, you now understand the principles of cameras and lenses, and how to use these tools to showcase your miniature world in the perfect way.

Lights, camera … so what about the action? That's Nia's department, of course –your faithful acting partner has been waiting patiently, as you've been getting everything into place. Now, her time has arrived. Move along to Part 3 stop motion artist – it's time to get animating!

JAMIE CALIRI, FILM ARTIST, CO-CREATOR OF DRAGONFRAME

Jamie Caliri is a director and cinematographer who makes hand-made films. His credits include director on a wide range of commercials and music videos for major clients. He is also the co-creator of Dragonframe, the world's leading stop motion software.

Q. You and your brother Dyami seem like the ideal team to create Dragonframe – he's a programmer and an engineer, you're a filmmaker and stop motion artist. Can you provide some insights into the process, the back and forth, between you and your brother, that occurs during the development of Dragonframe?

A. When we're working on development, we Skype every day. I'll send him plans, diagrams, details on new buttons, all kinds of details. 'When this is turned on, it has to do this, but it shouldn't do that', all kinds of specifics. From that, he'll come back with all sorts of questions about functionality, and we go back and forth. I always think of it like a tennis match. If I reach for outside insights, it's primarily into the world of animators, to get their opinion on what works, what doesn't, what new functions would be great, that sort of thing. Then we put it all in, and test it. Sometimes new ideas don't work out, but that's why you do tests. I've got a nice studio space here, with lots of equipment, so I can put the software through its paces, practically, right on site.

Q. Few things occur by accident when designing software. Can you talk a bit about some guiding philosophies that you held as essential, as Dragonframe went through its development?

A. We've really focused on working with animators, to give them the tools that they need. Since I relate to animators on a practical level, and since I have such a clear path to my brother, there's been no disconnect between the user and the developer. Sometimes a developer can make something that works great for his needs, but it falls down for the user. We've managed to avoid that. I also really wanted to keep things that are vital, and that are used a lot, right up in front for the animator to access. Things like frame rate. An animator should be able to see, right up in front, that rate he's shooting at. What aspect ratio are you working with? Again, that needs to be *right* there. A lot of that comes from my work as a cinematographer, and working with all this gear. Things need to be clear, and right there in front of you, so you can do your job.

Q. **In your role as a film artist working in live action and animation, clients turn to you to bring something distinctive to a project, as a way to ensure that the project stands out. What advice do you have for a young film artist who is in the process of establishing her own artistic voice?**

A. Remember to respect your audience's time. Watching a film is an experience, so step back to see your shots and moments as if you are seeing them for the first time.

Q. **Any advice on staying true to a directorial vision, when faced with the intense challenges that production presents – things like meeting deadlines, appeasing clients, overcoming various production challenges, and so on?**

A. Just keep making all of your shots as good as possible. Great work will give people confidence in you. If you start to give up on your vision, you will lose your momentum and the respect of those around you. Most important, don't be afraid of losing the job. Be willing to walk away if you can't make it great.

Q. **Today, with more motion picture content washing over us then at any other point in human history, it can all get a bit numbing. What captivates you, what grabs you, as an audience member?**

A. It's the classic things, the things that endure. I like simple stories and classic filmmaking with interesting characters.

Part three

Animation

This section assumes that you have a certain amount of familiarity with the basics of animation, and the basics of animating with a puppet. If you're completely new to it all, you may find that some of the concepts and terms within these chapters are a bit confusing. Not to worry. There are all kinds of excellent and affordable resources out there, both in book form and online, that will help you get up to speed in short order. And always remember that even if you *are* new to it all, every frame of animation that you create (even if it's not beautiful) means that you're learning more, and getting better.

10

Before animating

This chapter presents you with some fundamental ways to consider animating in stop motion. Now let's be clear – you *could* just start moving Nia about on your deck, while clicking frames in a frenzy. If you did this, nobody would blame you. You've invested a remarkable amount of hard work thus far, and you want to get Nia moving. But if you can extend your remarkable patience just a *bit* further, by the end of this chapter you'll possess some very useful 'big picture' concepts surrounding the process of creating stop motion. These concepts will not only help you to improve your work, but they'll make it all just a little bit easier on your body and mind.

**Figure 10.1
Bringing Nia to
life.**
Flowing forward
is the only way, in
stop motion.

Some essential considerations

Some of these tips should be useful to you immediately, while others might only prove valuable
once you've been working for a while. But *all*
of these have proven their value through the
honest-to-goodness daily grind of creating stop
motion animation. Use them in good health!

Animator 'flow': Moving within your workspace

Once you've settled into a shot, there's a kind
of physical flow (or rhythm, if you prefer) to the
work. This is the constant back and forth, as
you move your body (and your concentration)
between the puppet and the computer monitor.
If you've ever rocked a baby to sleep, or fallen
asleep in a hammock, you know the calming
effect that this kind of repetitive movement
can have. In the case of creating stop motion,
the rhythm doesn't put you to sleep. Rather, it
provides you with an effectively calm state of

mind in which to perform. Don't wait for this work
rhythm to find you. Instead, actively seek it out.
It's in this zone that good work happens.

Fitness

As the proud owner of an entirely unremarkably
physique, take it from me – you don't need stacks
of muscles to create stop motion. That being said,
the muscles that you *do* have need to be in good
shape. You'll be using those muscles all day long,
day after day, and if they aren't at least decently
fit, the quality of the work with suffer, and so will
your body. Stop motion shouldn't hurt the next day!

Core muscle strength is especially important.
These are the muscles of your torso, abdomen,
and back, and they provide you with the stability that you need to create the precise posing of
the puppet. Your shoulders, arms, and neck also
get a big workout during a day of stop motion,
and strong leg muscles will help you to take

the pressure and weight off your lower back as you work. Flexibility is also important, so don't neglect that aspect of things, as well.

> If muscle strength or mobility in general is a serious issue for you, there are lots of ways that a studio space can be modified to allow you to work. For example, a desk and animation deck can be modified to allow you to sit while you animate if standing isn't realistic or possible.

The mind's eye

By this, I mean visualize, visualize, visualize. Don't just jump into a shot and start animating. Consider it. Think it through, in your imagination. You're an artistic person – your power of imagination and your ability to *see* those imagined things in your mind is the envy of the non-artistic world!

Start by visualizing the key points within a very simple shot. Then, as you animate, imagine specifically where your puppet is *going* to be later in the shot, and what pose it will be in. In time, as you practice this skill, you'll be able to visualize complex three-dimensional movements that lie ahead of you within the shot. You'll also be able to use the visualization powers to rehearse aspects of your performance. This will allow you to effectively test out whether something is dramatic, or funny, in a manner that is very frame-specific.

As you see the shot unfolding frame-by-frame in your mind, you'll *also* start to see the challenges and pitfalls that each frame may present,

> Drawing skills in the world of stop motion are never wasted, and they can be quite useful as a visualization tool. During the planning stage, try sketching out specific poses that you want to convey in the animation. The very act of drawing the poses will help solidify them in your imagination.

and this will help you to be prepared prior to animating. This can include blocking and staging challenges, and challenges that will come from animating with props and set pieces.

Of course, gravity, fussy puppet parts, and looming deadlines will do everything they can to mess with all this careful visualization. And of course, you'll want to modify what you've visualized, in response to the actual positioning of the puppet, and in response to your own instincts as a performer. But by doing this advanced mental work, you're effectively creating a path for yourself, within your mind, that's dedicated to the specific shot that you're about to create. You can then use this path to help you make more confident choices during the process of creating the actual animation. When you're done with that specific mental path, you can simply erase it and lay down a *new* one, for the next shot.

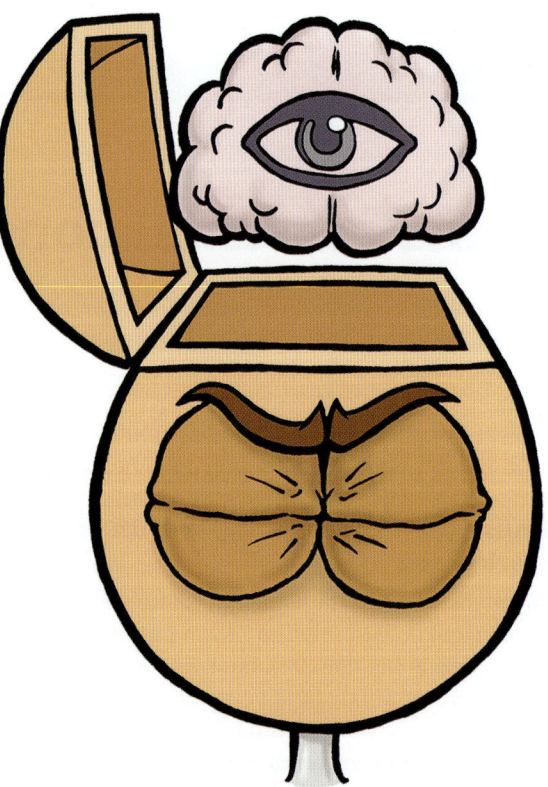

As you develop your mental abilities, you'll eventually be able to 'pre-animate' the shot, all within your mind. Trippy stuff!

PAS DE DEUX, NORMAN MCLAREN, 1968

This NFB film takes live action footage of ballet dancers and essentially deconstructs their movement, further and further, until human bodies become almost pure, abstract movement. I can't think of another film that so effectively reveals the process all animators go through, as they visualize their work. You'll come out of this one slightly hypnotized, and seeing the world of movement in increments you didn't even know existed.

Straight ahead animation

If you consider the list of animation principles (see below), you'll note that straight ahead animation is there. But it's one principle that has *extra* importance in the world of stop motion, because it highlights a vital aspect of how we actually *create* our work, and how we need to *think,* in order to do what we do.

There are endless connections between stop motion and live action motion picture. Both are based in physical reality, since they both use real lights, sets, and actors (or puppets). But it goes deeper than that. Consider a live action performance, that's recorded by a live action camera. The action occurs, and the camera records it, starting with frame 1, then 2, on so on, *in order*. It doesn't record frame 1, then 8, then 40, then back to 2. Stop motion happens the exact same way, only a *whole* lot slower. This process shared by both mediums is what's known as 'straight ahead': an orderly and linear recording of images, one after the other. And you need to *think* like that, as a stop motion animator.

Perhaps stop motion is simply live action, that's figured out how to use the principles of animation to create the illusion of life?

This method of creating animation in a straight ahead fashion can strike terror into the hearts of animators who are coming into stop motion from drawn or computer animation. 'What do you mean, no breaking down the shot, no establishing your key poses and then "filling them in" through inbetweening?! Where's the safety net?! I can't perform like this!'

It's tough stuff, to be sure. But it's what the stop motion animator just accepts as the way it's done. And as your experience grows, this way of working and thinking will cause you to become an animator who is very strong and very confident. It's the reason we see stop motion animators able to move into drawn and computer animation as needed, assuming that the necessary drawing and software skills are present, of course. A strong animator is a strong animator, regardless of medium.

Embracing the idea (and method) of straight ahead is all well and good, but I'm always quick to remind students that stop motion isn't *blindly* straight ahead. You don't just start moving a puppet and capturing frames, hoping for the best. Early masters of the medium *had* to work this way, recording frames without seeing inter-frame relationships. But to do this, they devised certain technical tricks, along with mind-blowing levels of deep concentration. Their powers of visualization were truly astounding, because they *had* to be in order to create their performances. Today, with frame-referencing software as part of our method, animating blindly is like eating soup with a fork. It might work, but you'll wind up with a heck of a mess.

The importance of flipping frames

There's a reason why we have frame-referencing software: it's so we can construct careful animation that is as beautiful as humanly possible. Movement is essential for the creation of this beautiful animation. It doesn't just happen in the final product when we watch it played back. It's an essential part of the actual *process.*

Consequently, animation cannot be created *within* a single frame, since a frame is a still image.

Movement occurs *across* frames, or *between* frames if you prefer, as those frames replace one another, in front of our eyes. And to get things moving, we *have* to flip those images.

ABF: Always be flipping!

I came up with the acronym in class as a way to emphasize and embed something that's incredibly important for creating effective stop motion. And so we have ABF. ALWAYS. BE. FLIPPING. Students quote it back to me after they've finished my course, so I guess they agree. Either that, or they just want to get me back for annoying them for weeks on end. Whatever the reason, if ABF sticks, I'm glad. In my opinion, if you're not busy posing the puppet, you should be flipping frames.

But just because ABF is vital, that *doesn't* mean that you should just randomly pound away on the arrow keys!

This entire book uses 24 fps as a base. It also assumes that you'll be animating on 2s. To achieve this, you *could* set your frame rate in Dragonframe to 24 fps, and capture two frames at a time, but this makes flipping frames quite tedious. With this in mind, set Dragonframe to 12 fps, and capture *one* frame at a time. The resulting animation will play correctly. Then, if you need to double frames (or half playback speed) in post-production to maintain the correct playback speed, you can.

Certain frames, certain rhythm

I'm a firm believer that finding a personal rhythm while flipping through a specific set of frames both simplifies the animation process, and leads to strong animation. Here's how to go about doing just that. If you're new to Dragonframe, you'll obviously want to take some time to get familiar with the basics of the software, before trying this out.

1. Grab any object that can be easily animated along the surface of your deck, and set up a file in Dragonframe. Ensure that you are in the Animation Workspace. Ensure that your frame rate is set for 12 fps.
2. Shoot a handful of held frames. The number of frames doesn't matter.

Held frames are frames in which no animation occurs. You're just recording the stationary object, repeatedly. These held frames are also referred to as 'holds'.

3. Ensure that you're on live view, with its red border. Also ensure that you're 'sitting' on the next frame that will be recorded. For example, if you have already recorded ten held frames, ensure that you're sitting on frame 11.
4. Move the object slightly, which you'll observe in live view – but don't record the frame yet.
5. Follow this step precisely: flip *back* one frame, then back another frame, and finally back one more. Now go *forward* a frame, forward another frame, and finally forward once more, into red (live view), which shows you your newly posed object (see Figure 11.2).
6. Repeat this specific flipping pattern several times, as you study your animation and its relationship to the live view image. Create a rhythm with your flipping. Roll back, then forward. Roll back, then forward, always going into live view, until you're satisfied with how things are moving. How do you know for sure that things are moving properly? That comes from experience and skill, and is a separate concern right at the moment! Record the frame.
7. Repeat this process, starting at Step 2, gradually animating the object along its path. You're now 'building' your shot, one frame at a time, straight ahead.

You may find that you're more comfortable viewing *more* recorded frames than the amount I've laid out here. That's great, I'd only suggest that you don't flip *too* many frames; it quickly becomes

Recorded   Recorded   Recorded   LIVE

> Your official stop motion mantra: 'Back, back, back. Forward, forward, live'. Find the rolling rhythm in these words, and start building your animation performance, a frame at a time, via this rhythm.

tedious, and overly tiring. Just make sure that you *do* find a rhythm for rolling your frames, and make sure that you're looking at what you're planning to record *in comparison* to what you've already created.

Once I've recorded several frames in this way, I play the animation at full speed. I playback either from the very beginning of the shot, or by using the short play option (if I'm well into a longer shot). Playing back regularly is necessary in order to judge for timing, performance, arcs, and overall quality.

And remember: ABF! Annoying, I know.

'The Principles of Animation' in stop motion

The 'Principles of Animation', as they have come to be known, are time-tested guiding concepts for our medium. They were originally intended to help animators who were working with pencil on paper in their job, but they're just as essential for stop motion (with a few modifications, that you'll see noted below).

Here they are, then, as they are typically understood and accepted:

Squash and Stretch *
Anticipation
Staging
Straight Ahead and Pose To Pose **
Follow Through and Overlapping Action
Slow Out (Acceleration) and Slow In
   (Deceleration)
Arc
Secondary Action
Timing Exaggeration
Solid Drawing***
Appeal

*In the case of a solid puppet like Nia, this principle doesn't easily apply, since Nia cannot be easily deformed in the same way that a drawn character can be. That being said, clay puppets can be perfect for exploring Squash and Stretch.

**As discussed earlier in this chapter, Straight Ahead *is* stop motion! As for 'Pose To Pose', we can most certainly create stop motion that is strongly posed, and that moves from one strong pose to the next, over time (creating the effect of 'Pose To Pose'), but we *achieve* it in a straight ahead method.

***Solid Drawing is not generally applicable in stop motion, since everything in front of the camera is a real, three-dimensional object.

Figure 10.2
Core reference frames for animating. This is where animation happens! Your final shot may be hundreds of frames long, but it's the recorded frames that are *closest* to live view that are the most crucial to the 'building' of your shot.

> Some experienced animators swear absolute allegiance to these principles. Others take issue, claiming that some aren't essential, and are subjective or conditional in their importance. As you develop *your* animation skills, you'll no doubt develop your own views on this list.

The *principles* are exactly that – the absolute basic concepts needed to create animation. At this point, if you need to learn about them, there are endless sources out there in the form of books and online resources. But to *write* (and read) about the principles in any serious detail is futile, because they apply to *animation*. As I mentioned earlier, animation *is* movement; it isn't to be found in a still image, and it isn't to be found in the written word. You need to be actually animating, and flipping your images, and playing things back, in order to *really* learn about these principles. So that's where we'll contend with the principles of animation in more detail – during the many animation exercises that you'll find in later chapters within this part.

Before going onward, do you deeply *understand* each of these principles, and their importance? Some are concerned with helping you to show off your animation more effectively to your audience (such as Staging and Appeal), and are best considered a bit later in your training. Others, such as Anticipation, Slow Out (Acceleration) and Slow In (Deceleration), apply directly to the objective of creating convincing animation, and as such are *very important,* right from the very first frames of animation that you create.

These principles, the ones that are specifically tied to *how* things move, are the principles that are very closely tied to the laws of physics. And if there's one science that every stop motion animator needs to be friendly with, it's physics.

This book uses the term 'Acceleration' instead of Slow Out, and 'Deceleration' instead of Slow In. These terms (Acceleration and Deceleration) are easier for everyone to understand, when discussing the specifics of movement.

Mechanical physics

When animators aren't animating, they tend to be observing the world around them. They observe how people and animals act and react in certain situations, so that they can later incorporate this into their character performances. But they are also observing things at a more basic level. This is the level of how things move, *devoid* of character. These are the basics laws of *mechanical physics* that are being observed, and it's these laws that are of utmost importance for every animator who is starting out. As you think about physics in animation, it can help to ask yourself questions, and then imagine the answers as they'd be expressed through animation. Who knows, one day you may find yourself animating these very scenarios (or ones just like them)!

Here's some example 'mechanical physics questions', to get you started:

- How does a race car accelerate slowly?
- How does the same car accelerate rapidly?
- How does an apartment building fall over?

Figure 10.3 Movement In Life.
The world never stops moving! But that movement isn't random, it's governed by the laws of physics, and it's the animator's job to understand those laws, and replicate them through animation.

- How does a motorcycle that's making a tight turn *not* fall over?!
- How does an elephant skip rope (lots of potential character animation there, obviously – but lots of mechanical physics, too!)
- What happens when a small rubber ball rolls off a high table, on to a tile floor?
- What happens when a bowling ball does the same thing?
- What happens when a person tries to push a large weight along a flat, slippery surface?
- What happens when an asteroid moves through space?
- What happens when the same asteroid collides with a larger one that's moving much faster, from the opposite direction?

You'll notice that a primary concern for most of the above questions is *energy*. How energy is generated in various situations, and how it's transferred – from points within a body or object, as well as from one body or object to another. *Gravity* is also a major consideration, and more specifically, its effect on objects that are at rest, and that are moving. Fortunately, you don't have to earn a degree in physics to become a great animator (although I'm sure it would only help). You're already a pro at mechanical physics – at least at the level of knowing when it looks 'right', and when it looks 'wrong'. After all, you've been observing it your entire life. From the first time you dropped a stuffed toy as a child, you've been learning about gravity, and you learned a lot more the first time you fell and scraped your knee. Playing at marbles taught you all sorts of things about energy transfer. All of this mechanical physics knowledge, before you were even five years old! Now, as an animator, you just need to develop your ability to *convey* what you've been observing, through animation. And that happens through practice.

If you're not familiar with them already, do a search for 'Newton's Laws of Motion'. There're only three of them, yet they govern the entire world of mechanics (and by extension, the world of animation).

Being able to convincingly simulate the laws of mechanical physics is obviously important when trying to create action-oriented animation. But it's just as important for character performances. If your character doesn't move convincingly, you run the risk of creating a terrible distraction for your audience. The viewer will be too busy noticing that the movement is 'wrong' at the level of mechanics to notice any other aspects of performance. Like static on the radio, sloppy physics in your animated performance only gets in the way of clear communication. Think of time invested in honing your abilities to create convincing physics (even through simple animation exercises) as time spent ensuring that your more complex character performances will ring through loud and clear for the viewer, when that time comes.

A question of style: Limited animation vs. full animation

In an earlier chapter, we considered the concept of 'style' in reference to lighting. If something has style (be it a lighting design, or a piece of animation), it's distinctive in some way. In animation, this distinctiveness often results from how the animator handles the basic principles (see above). This use of the principles results in what we call 'limited' animation, and 'full' animation.

Limited animation

This style of animation gets its name from the restricted, or 'limited', way in which it makes use of the principles of animation. In limited animation, you won't see a lot of anticipation, acceleration, deceleration, or any of the other principles connected to mechanical physics – at least not in comparison to 'full' animation (see below). The net result of this approach tends to be, quite simply, less animation. As a result, extremely strong posing becomes very important in limited animation, since it can communicate a great deal to the audience, regardless of how much animation is involved. For the same reason, timing can also be put to great use in limited animation, since just like a strong pose, it can communicate meaning to the audience regardless of how much (or how little) animation is present.

Figure 10.4
A Krampus Christmas, Screen Novelties, 2013.
A strong pose can say so much about a character. Watch anything created by Screen Novelties, and you'll see great examples of excellent animation posing, as well as energetic animation that's *fun* to watch!

When watching limited animation, the audience is asked to imagine more movement within the on-screen world, in the same way that looking at a rough sketch causes you to imagine more detail 'into' the drawing. Limited animation asks the audience to do more work, and that's not always a bad thing, since a working audience is an *engaged* audience (you'll find more on this idea of an engaged audience in Part 4).

Limited animation can be used in all sorts of contexts, and for all kinds of reasons. It can be a great style to use when creating intense, high-energy animation, or for certain kinds of comedy, since the lack of nuance to the movement can both heighten and sharpen the overall tone of the piece. It can also be the style of choice for projects that are running on a very tight dead-line, since less animation in a shot often means that more shots can be completed in a day. This time-saving (and by extension, money-saving) aspect of limited animation isn't seen by every-one as a good thing, though. For some artists (and audiences), the notion of limiting the work in this way is just another way of saying 'make the work lower quality, just to save some money'. This can be a hard pill to swallow for a hard-working and talented animator whose goal is to create the finest work that she possibly can. Working

in a limited style, then, can sometimes feel like 'dumbed down' animation, when you long for something more nuanced.

> To learn more about the history of limited animation, look up the American anima-tion company UPA, and the television studio that further evolved the approach, Hanna-Barbara.

I learned a *lot* about limited animation the moment I began working professionally as a stop motion animator. I was working on a television series that, due to major deadline challenges, required a staggering amount of footage from the animators each day. To meet these challenges, I had to focus my efforts on creating extremely economical animation, which could instantly communicate the *essentials* of the shot. As I planned the shots, I had to distill each of them down to their core poses, and when it came to animating them, I had to do away with any 'frills' that would consume too much time. As I contin-ued to refine my skills in this way, I came to real-ize that limited animation is, in a way, a bit like an animation megaphone. It *shouts* its message

GERALD MCBOING-BOING, ROBERT CANNON, 1950

This charming short film tells the story of a special little boy who uses sound effects to communicate with the world, rather than words. It's considered by many to be one of the first, and best, examples of purposely limited animation. Working at the legendary UPA Studios, the artists on this film were attempting to push the medium in daring ways. This film remains a fantastic exam-ple of how excellent designing, planning, staging, and posing can be used to create an effective film, despite there being almost *no* animation.

to the audience very loudly, and very clearly, and knowing how to shout clearly is very useful when your job is to communicate. It can also be blunt and hard on the eyes, but again, we take the good with the bad.

As useful as limited animation is, there's no denying that there are times that simply getting the point across clearly isn't enough. There are times that a different style is required – one that allows for more nuanced communication.

Full animation

Full animation contains a *lot* of what limited animation does not: lots of anticipation, acceleration, deceleration, follow through, and so on. That's because full animation takes the principles of animation that are linked to mechanics *very* seriously. If a simple animated action (a ball rolling across a table, for example) can be completed in just ten frames using limited animation, the same action done 'fully' might take twenty frames, as the animator expresses more increments of movement. As with limited animation, very strong posing is essential with full animation, but these strong poses are typically more blended *into* the overall animation – they don't stand out in quite the same way as they do in limited animation.

There's many ways to further describe the actual look of full animation. You'll hear it referred to as 'robust', 'lush', or 'rich'. It's also described as looking 'smooth'. This notion of smooth is a complex one, and you'll find more about it in the next chapter.

Because full animation more fully replicates movement as it occurs in the real world, it's generally considered to look more 'real' than limited. It's also typically the style that animators long to master, since it can be very effective at expressing sophisticated aspects of *character.*

Imagine a shoulder shrug, conveyed through limited animation. The shoulders go up, and are held in that pose for a moment. Then they go back down. End of action. Now imagine the same action fully animated. The shoulders go up, but with a slight hesitation at the start: they creep up, tentatively. Once they are up, they hold, before going up again, and again, ever so slightly … before suddenly *dropping,* completely, settling fully with a sense of exhaustion and exasperation.

In this example, the same basic action has occurred (a shoulder shrug), but it was conveyed

in very different ways, in terms of complexity of performance, and in terms of expression of character. Precisely because it's so nuanced, full animation takes serious amounts of time to create (when compared to more limited animation), which is a huge consideration when planning a project. And if you're paying others for their time to create animation in this style, a project done in this way can get very pricey indeed.

There's a reason why animated feature films cost millions of dollars to create – in part, it's due to the sheer cost of labour that it takes to create the full animation that most audiences have come to expect from these projects. Even if you're making a very modest animated film (on your own, or with a small crew) the choice to make use of full animation is one that needs to be seriously considered in advance. The choice to go 'full' can add incredibly amounts of time to a project – but of course, the final work can be stunning.

> If you're still working hard simply to get the principles *themselves* under control, let alone being stylish with them, don't worry. Carry on in your training, knowing that this idea of style is one that you'll soon be coming back to as you become more accomplished.

Full animation is the style that I insist that my students aim for, for the very reason that it *is* challenging, and because it asks a lot of the animator. To animate in this style, one has to have discipline, commitment, and a depth of professional courage (see more on this below, in 'Earning the pose'). These are good traits to have as *any* kind of professional, and they really get developed through creating stop motion in this style. I always tell my students that I want to help them build 'animation muscle', and working in a full style does this. It's heavy lifting! An additional benefit to learning in this style, right from the beginning, is that if an animator has been trained to create full stop motion, then that same animator, with practice, can 'pull back' on the fullness in order to create more limited animation, as the need or the desire arises.

In the feature film world, a stop motion animator creates a few seconds of finished, full animation, *per week*! If you're aiming for this kind of 'feature film' style, be prepared to invest hours into creating just a few frames of full animation, even if the same bit of animation could be created in a fraction of the time, using a more limited style.

Figure 10.5
Fantastic Mr. Fox, Wes Anderson, 2009.
How would you describe the animation style, or mixture of styles, that are used in this feature?

Mixing styles

You don't have to maintain a clear divide between full and limited. You can create a distinctive style by creating a *mixture* of the two, by varying how much of the principles (or how little) you express. For example, you might decide to use very little anticipation in your animation, but go pretty 'full' with the other mechanical principles. This could provide sudden bursts of visual energy to your animation. Alternately, you could choose to use an *excess* of anticipation and *less* of the other mechanical principles. The resulting animation will reveal the intentions of your character's movement long before it actually happens, which can be hugely entertaining in certain situations. Typically, however you are mixing full and limited animation should be maintained throughout the project, in order to create a cohesive overall style – but not always. Sometimes an animation's style is partly defined by the very fact that it's a seemingly endless mixture of varying amounts of principles. Take the time to experiment with mixing more of 'this' with less of 'that', and see what different 'animation recipes' you can cook up.

Is full animation 'better' than limited? Is a certain mixture of limited and full better than other mixtures? No one style of animation is the best. Whatever style or mixture works best to connect with the audience is right for that project. Most people would agree that certain styles work better than others in certain contexts and on certain projects, but what looks good in terms of animation style is ultimately incredibly subjective. It often comes down to a question of taste – on the part of the artist, the client, and the audience. And as we all know, taste is a very individual thing.

Figure 10.6
Robot Chicken, Stoopid Buddy Stoodios.
This show is a great example of highly stylized animation, that's wild, unpredictable, and funny to watch. To see just how effective the animation is at maintaining audience interest, try watching it with the sound off. It's just as engaging, which can't be said about all television animation which so often relies heavily on its dialogue for entertainment value.

SYLVIE TROUVÉ

The stop motion work created by Sylvie Trouvé through her company See Creature is proof that there are no hard rules when it comes to animation styles. With her partner Dale Hayward, Sylvie works in whatever style (using whatever technique) is best for the particular project. It's this creative and personal approach to animation that attracts clients to her company.

Animating on 1s and 2s (and 4s, and 8s) …

There's another basic variable that can affect the movement of our animation. As with limited and full animation, this variable also operates on a very basic level. In fact, it happens right at the moment that we record our images.

Animating on 1s (Singles)

For a moment, let's assume a frame rate of 24 fps. When we animate on 1s, every one of those 24 frames has been recorded individually. Consequently, each of those 24 frames has required a repositioning of the puppet (of course, if the puppet is in a held position, there's no repositioning required, but you get the idea).

Animation created on 1s shares certain attributes with full animation. First, it can look more 'real', in that it mimics the manner in which live action film records movement on every single frame. Because there's animation on every frame when shooting on 1s, this method is the preferred way to animate camera moves (camera moves created on 2s tend to strobe or jitter).

Because animation on 1s provides so much detail of movement, it's often the method used by feature films, whose goal is to 'wow' an audience with extremely detailed work. This leads to the other attribute that animating on 1s shares with full animation: it takes a lot of time to create! It literally takes twice as long, when compared to shooting on 2s (see below).

Animating on 2s (Doubles)

Again, assuming a 24 fps situation, when we animate on 2s, we record not one but two frames for each distinct moment, resulting in a total of 12 movements per second, since 12 × 2 equals 24. Amazingly, the resulting animation (assuming it's done well, of course), still looks great. The benefit of this is obvious, and very attractive – by shooting this way, you can literally cut in *half* the actual amount of animation that you need to create, compared to working on 1s, without compromising the quality to any serious extent. That's why it's used in so much television work and on indie films. It's how I animate my own projects, it's how I created all of the television and client work that I'm involved with, and it's how I teach my stop motion class.

In his book *The Animator's Survival Kit*, Richard Williams admits to being addicted to animating on 1s, in part because of the simple fact that more animation on the screen means more for the eye to enjoy. But he's also the first to admit that mostly, animating on 2s looks perfectly fine, provided that the animation is well done.

4s, 6s, and 8s: The animation pop-through

It stands to reason that if you can animate on 1s and 2s, then you can animate on 4s, 6s, 8s, and so on. Let's again assume that a project is created at 24 fps, in order to simplify the following math. At 24 fps, a shot created on 4s would have 6 distinct movements per second. A shot that was animated on 6s would have a mere 4 distinct movements, and one animated on 8s would have just 3 distinct movements. The resulting footage wouldn't be useable as final animation, but it *can* be of use to the overall animation process.

This rough test shot that is the same *duration* as your actual shot is called an animation pop-through, and it's extremely useful for pre-planning. Yes, the footage will look blunt, since the puppet will jump to its next pose and its next blocking point, but since it's the correct duration, it should give you an overall sense of how the shot will play out, once its animated, from beginning to end.

As with a blocking or lighting pop-through, the animation pop-through shouldn't take ages to create. Don't let it drain all of your energy and time. Plan it, shoot it, play it back, learn from it, and let that knowledge sink in. Then, armed with this new wisdom, set up to shoot your *actual* shot. You won't directly use any of the pop-through footage in your final animation, but that's not why you created it. It's to serve as a frame-accurate 'study' for the final animation, in that it can show what the basic structure of the shot might look like, before you commit.

Creating a pop-through for every single shot might not be necessary, or realistic. If you're confident in what you need to do, just go for it. But when in doubt, shoot a pop-through.

As an animation teacher, I've evaluated a *lot* of college-level stop motion over the years. What I find fascinating is that within that animation, certain recurring issues around posing the puppet show up in the work, especially when the student is just starting out. Once I draw attention to these issues through critiques, students can see them

quite clearly, and can work at avoiding them in the future. These two recurring posing issues are explored below.

Earning a resting pose

As its name suggests, a 'resting pose' is a pose that a puppet can occupy during a shot, sometimes for just a few frames, or for much longer (see the next chapter for more on poses). When the puppet is positioned in just the right resting pose, it can convey a complex state of mind

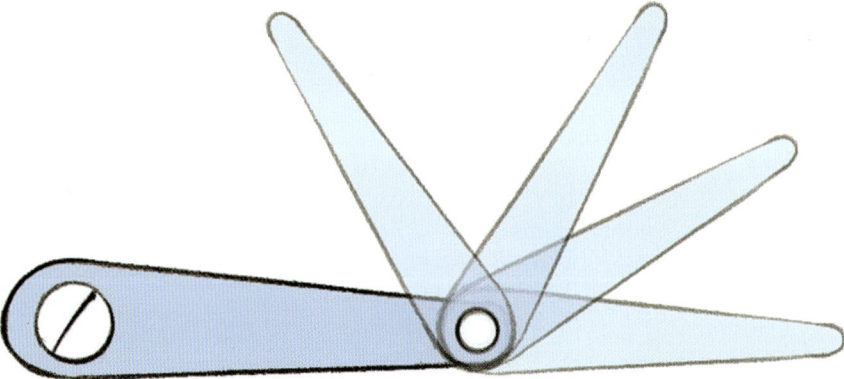

Figure 10.7 Limited deceleration versus full deceleration. Illustration A shows limited deceleration, which is easy to achieve but results in animation that often feels abrupt. Illustration B shows deceleration that is fuller. The effort and patience that you invest in those increasingly tricky final movements of deceleration will be worth it in the quality of the final animation.

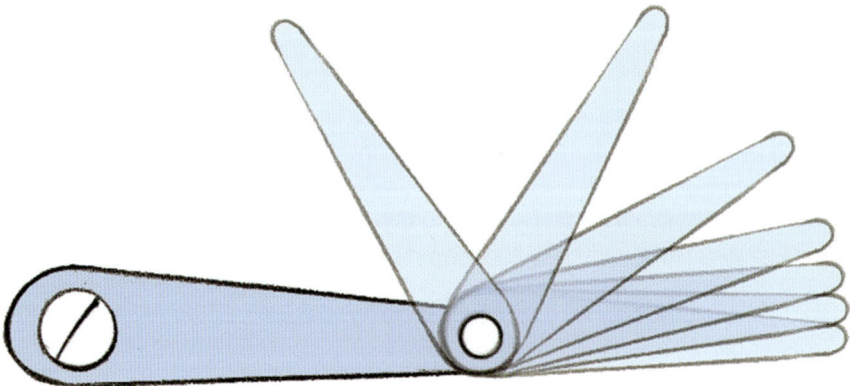

instantly, making it a sure-fire way to effectively communicate with the audience. But this doesn't mean that you can instantly force a puppet into that pose, during animation. If you think of a resting pose as a destination, you *arrive* at that destination in part through the creation of careful and precise *deceleration.*

Creating full deceleration in stop motion animation can be both nerve-wracking and frustrating. If something is decelerating, each incremental movement must be smaller than the previous one. As each movement becomes smaller, the risk of 'blowing it' increases. It can begin to feel a bit like you're performing open-heart surgery, or disarming a bomb! All it takes is one increment that is either not decreasing in terms of spacing, or one that is actually *increasing* in its spacing, to ruin things. If this happens, you now have to delete at least one frame, possibly several, move the puppet back to an earlier pose, and go for it all again. Is it any wonder that many new animators shudder at this challenge, and resort to very limited animation at this point? They'll often rush a part, or entire puppet, into a pose after just a few modest frames of slowing down.

This choice to suddenly create 'limited' animation amongst what is an otherwise fully animated shot may allow the animator to move on in her day, but upon playback the shortcut will show up very clearly. If you find yourself just wanting to 'get it over with' when decelerating into a pose, try to catch yourself, and don't give up. Just a *few* more frames of animation can make a huge difference. Every time you watch that fuller animation, you'll be glad you invested a bit of extra time and effort.

Letting a resting pose read

Another common posing problem which students often encounter is tied into the concept of timing in stop motion (you'll find more on timing in the following chapters). In my experience, learning effective timing in general is one of the hardest things for stop motion students to get

comfortable with, and more specifically, how to time poses.

Often, students create animation that's a showcase of good resting poses, all of which flow too quickly into each other. Upon playback, we get 'pose, pose, pose', with no time to let the viewer understand each pose, or to properly feel the significance of the pose in terms of performance. I suspect this grows out of an honest desire on the part of the animator to 'give' lots of performance, but sometimes *not* moving the puppet (or at least, not moving it too much) is exactly what *has* to happen, so that the audience can understand what's going on.

How long is long enough, in terms of letting the pose communicate effectively to the audience? There's no set rule, and there's no way around it, it takes *lots* of practice to develop this skill. It also takes lots of playback! If the puppet has achieved a pose, and everything is held, try capturing a bunch more 'held' frames … then play it back. Is this hold too long? Not long enough? Capture or delete frames accordingly, and carry onward. This really is one of the hardest things to get good at in terms of performances in stop motion, so if you find yourself struggling, know that you aren't alone! Stick with it, and hopefully the exercises in the following chapters will help.

Issues around timing and poses *can* be addressed in post-production. It's often just a matter of cutting out held frames to shorten a hold, or copying and pasting them in to extend it (provided the entire frame is held). But I encourage students to strive for quality performances 'on-set', in front of the camera, rather than rushing through the animation, and making notes on how to fix it later. The better your performance upon playback in your studio, the more the performance will be a *true* expression of your own acting skills through the puppet, and the prouder you will be that you managed to pull it off with no 'fixing' required in post.

Remember ABF, and remember to regularly play back your animation, at full speed. These are the only ways to ensure that your animation is working effectively.

The critique

It's only natural that as soon as you start to create your animation, you'll crave feedback. A loved one might gush about the quality of your animation, but unless Grandma is a stop motion animator, her opinion is probably just a *little* bit biased. A peer may happily offer insights, but is that person developed enough in the medium to give you the quality of feedback that you deserve?

The obvious answer is to show your work to an animation teacher. After all, an animation teacher is not only trained in the medium but is practiced at helping others get better. But what if you're developing your stop motion animation skills *outside* of a formal school setting? It's essential that whoever you show your work to is further along the stop motion animation path than you are (and the further along that path, the better).

One option is to explore the world of stop motion animators who are already doing good work. This can include commercial animators, indie artists who are making their own projects, and even senior students (provided that the quality of their work is very high). If you're shy or unsure, remember that these artists weren't always where they are now. They developed their skills over time, just as you are doing, and they know exactly the challenges that you're facing. Reach out with a brief message that introduces yourself and your work, and politely present your request.

Another avenue that you can explore in order to receive feedback is social media groups and forums that are dedicated to stop motion. In these online communities, you are certain to get fast feedback. They are typically very supportive and inclusive, but it pays to be a bit cautious when you're first starting out. General comments of support (which you are sure to receive) are nice, but they don't help you to improve through *specific* critique, and that's what you need.

Making good use of solid criticism is an acquired skill. It can hurt to hear that your work is flawed, especially when you've worked so hard on it, and hurt feelings can sometimes get in the way of learning. But if your overall objective is to become a strong animator (and we both know that's precisely what you want), then the only way to achieve it is by trying, getting legitimate feedback, and then trying again.

11

Introductory exercises

OK, let's animate. The introductory exercises that you'll find in this chapter will help you to build strong skills in animating basic human movements. It will also help you to develop greater overall confidence, and establish good workflow. In time, as you get stronger, you'll be able to evolve and improvise upon these exercises, even as you move on to more complex things.

By the end of this chapter, you'll have some solid clips of 'realistic human movement' to show off, but just as importantly, you'll also have a clearer sense of just who Nia is *to you.* Go with it, and let her personality mature in the same way that your skills as an animator are going to grow – frame by frame. Then, when it's time to move on to more performance-based animation, you'll have a stronger connection with Nia, which is essential.

As you make your way through the exercises, remember that there's no shortcut to becoming a talented stop motion animator. It's only through lots of practice that you'll be become skilled. In other words, firing off *one* attempt of each of these exercises won't be much help. You'll want to create a first attempt, then a second. Then a third. And so on.

Figure 11.1
Simple beginnings.
Getting to know Nia, frame by frame.

Giving life

You needed a *work* space in which to first fabricate Nia, and then of course you had to create a *studio* space in which to create the animation. Now, as you begin to animate, you need to develop a certain kind of *mental* space that is conducive to creating an effective performance.

Emotional empathy

Simply put, emotional empathy is the ability to feel what someone else is feeling, within a specific situation. With this in mind, it's easy to see why strong empathetic abilities are extremely useful when it comes to creating quality stop motion. If you can clearly imagine the emotions of a character within the scene, and if those emotions can be alive for you as you animate, frame by frame, the better the puppet performance is likely to become.

Do you need to actually *be* in a homicidal rage when animating a violent scene? I hope not (and so does everyone around you). Do you need to *literally* cry endless tears while animating a scene of heartbreak? If so, things would get very damp on set. But even if you aren't showing it in any visible way, you should be able to 'go there', on a certain level. A well-trained animator feels it all, frame by frame, even as she stays cool and collected, in order to make the animation. She has to in order to make the madness, or the heartache, or the comedy *real* for the audience.

If being emotionally empathetic isn't easy for you, you may need to determine the emotions from the outside. Take careful observations from your vantage point, and then convey what you've observed, through the puppet. Do what you have to do, but always remember that your *audience* craves animation in which your characters act and react honestly. In the same way that an audience can instantly recognize bad physics, it can discern between an animated performance that rings true in terms of emotion, and one that feels false.

Animism

Animism is the belief that some form of life (or some form of 'spirit') exists within all objects. It's at once a very primal and a very complex concept. It extends into the weird world of quantum physics, while also reaching back to the dawn of humanity, and religion, and our search for meaning within a vast universe. But since this is a textbook dedicated to stop motion and not to comparative religion or abstract physics, I'm going to drastically simplify 'animism' into something that can be useful when creating animation with puppets. It's all here in the following statement: puppets are alive. Those physical objects, that we craft from metal and wire and plastic, *are alive*.

Do I *really* believe this to be true? The more important question is: does thinking like this help to create better stop motion? I think

Figure 11.2
Old Man, Alicia Eisen, 2016.
From the shadows, the animator provides life to the puppet.

is alive, you're far more inclined to treat it as if it *is*. And that's good for performance.

Giving life to objects is a basic human action. Most of us sadly move away from it as we age. Think back to your own childhood when you played with your favourite doll, action figure, or stuffed animal. There was no question, back then, that the toy was *alive*. If you could do it when you were little, you can do it now!

so. This way of thinking can lead to a deeper respect for objects, and out of that respect can grow an increased sense of connection *with* that object. In this way of thinking, one wouldn't say 'I'm a living, thinking human, so I'm obviously more important than that lifeless object that I'm about to animate'. Rather it's more a case of saying 'That puppet and I both have life within us, and as a result, we are *both* important'. Thinking this way means that you approach the puppet in a way that doesn't automatically place you and your own ego in a position of dominance. Rather than a 'puppet master', it places the animator into more of a 'puppet partner' position.

Depending on how you see the world around you, and the medium of stop motion, these notions of empathy and animism may strike you as bit too pseudo-mystical for your purposes. But isn't this tension between the rational and irrational – the idea that Nia is *not* alive, yet *is* alive – part of what draws us to this medium? Maybe this is where the magic of the medium (or at least some of it) resides. And if you can embrace this poetic approach in a playful way, or in a serious way, or both, you'll very likely see positive results in your animated performances. After all – how can it hurt?

In my own classroom, I sometimes simply inform students at the start of class, in a very matter-of-fact manner, that the puppets are already alive. That's it. And in my experience, if you pick up something that you've just been *told*

Some best practices

You've set up some lights, you've got Nia ready to go, and your camera is framed and focused. Do some stretches, take some deep breaths, and check out some more tips that will help you to create solid work.

Keeping it smooooth

When looking at full animation in the previous chapter, we considered the term 'smooth'. But the concept of smooth in animation is more complex than it might first appear. It's true, full animation is, typically, quite smooth. But *limited* animation can also be very smooth in its own fashion, provided that it's free of 'pops'. What are pops? Different animators may call them by different names, but pops are essentially glitches within the animation. They're disruptions or 'hiccups' in the flow of things, that distract the eye and diminish the effect of the animation. Pops are the bane of animators everywhere, because they sneak into the animation without the animator noticing it. All of a sudden, during playback (and sometimes not until after *many* playbacks) – there it is. Pop spotted. You didn't see it before, but now you do. And then, depending on how severe it is, the pop needs to be corrected (more on that below).

They're nasty little troublemakers, and they come in two forms: pops in arcs, and pops in spacing.

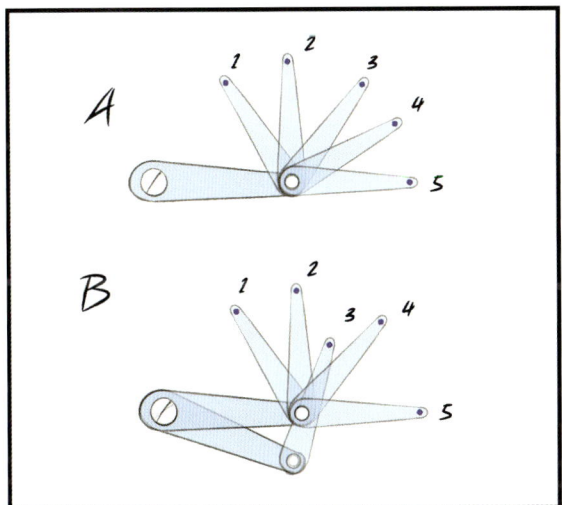

Figure 11.3
Pops in arcs.
Illustration A shows a smooth arc, that will playback nicely.
Illustration B shows a 'pop' in the arc, occurring at movement 3. After
this pop, the movement continues along its original (and smooth)
path, but the damage has been done. On playback, the animation
will have a bump in it that distracts the eye. This is the 'pop'.

Pops in arcs

As you'll know from your study of the principles of
animation, movement in the real world typically
follows an arc. The arc may be gentle, with hardly
any variation, or it might be extremely sharp and
dramatic. Regardless, it most often follows a predictable path that can be charted, and that's consistent with the overall movement. But since the
arcs in stop motion are created straight ahead, it's
quite easy for an arc to break from this predictable
path for a frame or two, only to return to the correct
path a few frames later. That 'blip' in the expected
path, that break from realistic movement, is a pop.

> The movement of a butterfly is an exception
> to this idea of 'smooth arcs', since butterflies
> fly in a very erratic path in order to confuse
> predators. When you animate a butterfly, you
> need to think 'overall direction' of movement,
> rather than 'clear, smooth arcs'.

Pops in spacing

Spacing pops are similar to arc pops, in that they
are violations of the real world of physics. When
something is speeding up or slowing down, it

may do so slowly, or quickly, but it does it in a
fairly predictable fashion. An accelerating object
(when convincingly depicted in animation) moves
a bit in one frame, then a bit *more* (in relation to
the previous frame), and so on. What does *not*
happen in the real world is a movement of acceleration, followed *immediately* by a movement of
consistent (or diminished) spacing, followed by
acceleration again. Increases and diminishments
in spacing certainly *do* happen, and sometimes
very dramatically, but they occur over a number
of frames, not instantly. Again, as with pops in
arcs, the straight ahead nature of stop motion
makes it very easy for these issues in spacing to
occur. And before you know it – pop!

Pops are *especially* troublesome for stop
motion animators to fix, because of the labour
that's required to remove them. If you only
discover a nasty pop in frame 10 after you've
completed thirty frames of animation, the only
way you can get rid of that pop is to – you know it
– delete your frames back from 30, fix the pop at
frame 10, and re-animate from there.

Lots of flipping of frames will help you to
catch pops before you record them. Scan the entire
frame before you record, as you hunt for pops in
all the moving parts. Then, make sure that you
regularly play back, and keep your eyes peeled.
Deleting one or two frames in order to get rid of a
pop hurts a lot less than deleting ten or twenty.

Figure 11.4
Pops in spacing.
Illustration A
shows smooth
deceleration in
which the spacing
between each
point continues
to gradually
diminish, until the
movement ceases.
This will playback
nicely. Illustration
B shows a 'pop'
in the spacing,
occurring after
movement 4,
when the spacing
suddenly (and
without reason)
increases, before
once again
decreasing. When
played back, this
animation will
have a pop, which
will distract the
eye.

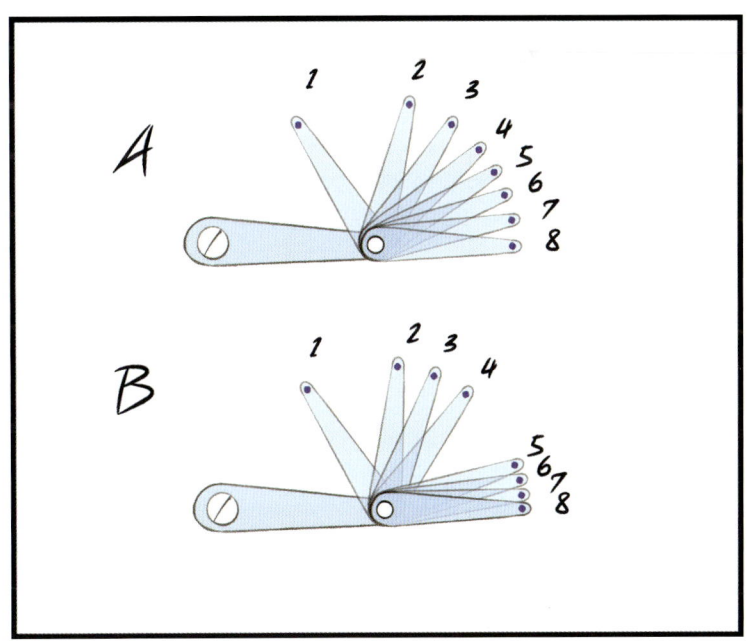

Roy has a strict 'No pops allowed' policy. He claims that they carry diseases. Whatever you say, Roy.

Strong and effective posing

The previous chapter emphasized the importance of good posing, and also looked at some of the challenges that new animators face when trying to achieve them. In fact, poses are *so* important in stop motion, that you really *should* know a few more things about them, don't you think?

Resting poses

A 'resting pose' is a relatively static pose that the puppet can remain in for a time. Some part of the puppet might keep moving (an impatiently tapping finger for instance, or some secondary action on a coat or dress that settles), but the puppet is essentially at rest. These resting poses are a critical part of the grammar of animation, because they can communicate a lot to the audience, and they can do so instantly. Through a clear resting pose, the audience gets the message about the character's state of mind, and that's an essential part of acting, and of animation.

Effective resting poses are also, quite simply, nice to look at! And on a very simple (but important) level, this *satisfies* your audience. Just as effective lighting and camera work is aesthetically pleasing, so is an effective pose. It just looks good, plain and simple.

Since it tells the audience something *and* is nice to look at, an effective resting pose occupies the audience, at least for a time, and that can be a huge advantage to an animator, since it means that the animator doesn't have to be actively animating the puppet *constantly*. To do so can be exhausting, and can ultimately result in animation that looks too 'busy'.

> **RUDOLPH THE RED-NOSED REINDEER, ANIMATION BY TAD MOCHINAGA, 1964**
>
> This is perhaps the best-known stop motion Christmas special. The Japanese-born, Chinese-trained Mochinaga and the rest of his Japanese animation crew knew the value of strong posing when it came to puppet animation. When faced with any number of challenges that *you* might face, an effective pose can be the clearest and most effective way to get the basics of the shot across to the audience. When holiday season rolls around, tune in to this classic, and learn how the master did it.

> A puppet that's held for *too* long can become boring to look at, and can very easily be robbed of its animated life. That being said, you'd be surprised by how long a puppet can continue to look 'alive', if it's very carefully posed!

The value of a resting pose doesn't end here. An audience can only really look at one thing at a time, so a puppet that is no longer moving allows the audience's attention to be shifted elsewhere, to something that *is* moving. Controlling where the audience is looking within the frame is an extremely important part of an animator's job, and resting poses are essential to this. If we didn't use resting poses, the entire frame would be a buzz of non-stop animation, making a scene pretty hard to follow! And just in case you're wondering, you'll find exercises to help you develop this kind of 'audience control' in later chapters.

As important as resting poses are, they *are* tricky to achieve, and not just because decelerating into them is challenging (see the previous chapter). There's also the challenge of arriving at a resting pose that looks good. You can work hard to get the puppet into a pose so that it can rest, but if an arm is jutting out oddly, or the head has an odd tilt, your audience is going to be staring at this awkward pose for quite some time. Yuck. Practice is the only way to get better at arriving at truly good poses.

Figure 11.5
Resting pose.
The image on the left shows Nia carefully posed so as to convey weight. She has a relaxed look, and can exist in this pose for some time, all the while remaining 'alive' to the viewer. The image on the right is stiff and rigid, and communicates 'lifeless puppet', as opposed to 'living character'.

Action poses

Just like the resting pose, 'action' poses are also very important for clear communication. An action pose is one that 'sells' a specific action (or portion of an action). Action poses are important because actions are often *fast*. And for an action to appear as fast on screen, it can't have a lot of frames of animation. This means that whatever frames *are* being used to convey the action have to be very clear.

Studying the 'key', or essential poses for actions, prior to animating, can be very helpful in this case. Typically, you'll find most key poses for actions broken down into three main poses: set up, action, and follow through (more on this later in this chapter). An online search for just about any action will provide you with these key poses, which can serve as great reference for you. If the action allows it, *always* perform the specific movements of the action with your own body as you plan the animation. Once you can feel it in your own body, it's much easier to find that essential pose with the puppet. It will also help

you find the individual poses that will make up the actual animation.

Good resting and action poses *are* essential, no doubt about it. But please don't think that the quality of all the other 'inbetween' poses that you will create aren't *also* vital! If you don't take time to create good posing in *every single frame*, the overall animation will suffer.

> Since strong resting and action poses are so *very* important, once you can consistently achieve them in your stop motion, it's time to congratulate yourself. You're now *clearly* communicating with your audience!

Quality, not quantity

I always remind students that beautiful stop motion animation takes time. That's just the way it is, and there's no way around it. You can't bake a delicious cake in five minutes just by turning up the oven to 1,000 degrees! All that you'll get is a charred mess (and maybe a visit from the fire department).

But of course, there has to be *some* kind of balance. In a classroom situation, you can't hand in three frames at the end of a session and expect an A+. If you're making your own film, an animation schedule that creeps out further and further along the calendar can be a very scary thing. And of course, in the commercial world, the same holds true; a production manager who expects a certain amount of footage from you each day may not be too pleased if you have nothing to show for a day's work.

Do unto puppets

Imagine a giant hand suddenly reaching down and picking you up. You had better hope that the giant at the other end of that hand is a *gentle* one!

Figure 11.6
Set up, action, and follow through.
Take your time and do your research, to determine the very best poses that will convey your action clearly and precisely.

Treat Nia (and every puppet) as *you'd* want to be treated. Move the puppet's parts in small increments – even the biggest of movements during animation are relatively small, so there's never any reason to suddenly and violently yank on Nia's parts. Again, think about how *you'd* feel! The fact that you worked so hard to make Nia should help – you know better than anyone the work that went into her. But even if you're handling a puppet that you didn't make, treat it well (see Animism, above).

That being said, sometimes you have to be tough! It's your job to create the animation, and poses *have* to be achieved, and they aren't always easy on the puppet. Extreme poses can look fantastic, but they can also require wild stretching or compacting of the puppet. At times, you'll find it necessary to all but crush poor Nia, and parts sometimes break as a result. It's an occupational hazard for every stop motion puppet, and remember – Nia was designed to allow for replacement of broken bits. Sometimes, you just have to say to yourself (and to the puppet) 'It's all in the name of performance', and go for it. Nia will forgive you if you break her arm, or her leg, I assure you. Especially when it's in the pursuit of great animation.

Action analysis

Action analysis is a central part of animation training, but the term 'analysis' can be a bit misleading. It feels a bit *formal*, doesn't it? A bit removed. It suggests that you stand *outside* of something, take it apart (in the way that a mechanic would an engine), study the parts, and learn what you can. When it comes to animation, this might mean watching movement as it occurs 'live' before our very eyes, or watching it on video reference so that we can study it frame by frame. This is all extremely helpful, to be sure. But a *richer* type of analysis occurs by getting *inside* the action by performing the action yourself (if it's possible), and ultimately, by *animating* it!

As you prepare to animate actions, you'll need to think them through carefully. *That's* analysis. Then you'll need to act out the movements repeatedly, before and *during* animation (assuming it's an action you can perform). *That's* analysis, too. As you do all this, you'll be learning and understanding more about movement with every frame that you record. Then, as you play back your animation, you'll study it carefully. You'll ask yourself, 'Does this action look right?' If so, why? If not, why not? *All* of this is action analysis.

In other words, animation *is* action analysis, and action analysis *is* animation.

You'll notice that some of the exercises that follow are officially labeled 'Action Analysis'. These are milestone exercises that are opportunities for you to express what you know, thus far. When you get to them, imagine you're on stage, and the spotlight has come on. It's time to show what you can do. If they turn out well, you'll have a great addition to your demo reel!

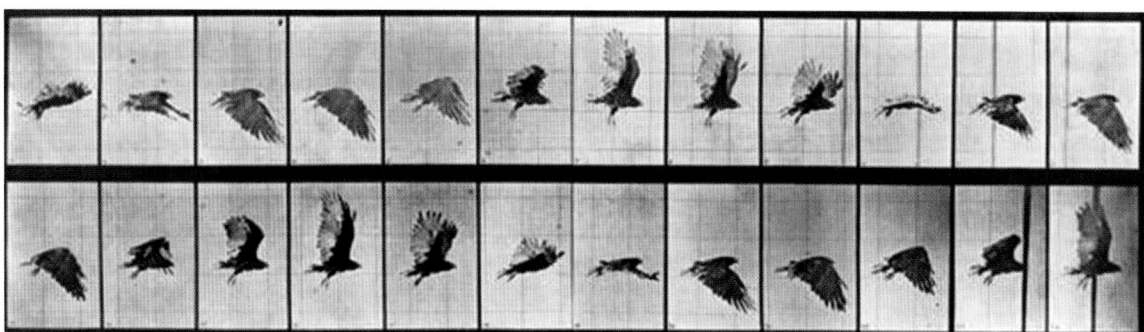

Figure 11.7
Action analysis.
Eadweard Muybridge's sequential photographs of animal and human movements are still referred to today by animators. But video and photographic reference should be just the beginning, when it comes to action analysis.

MOVEMENT EXERCISES

Pretend that you're learning to juggle. You don't rush into it by throwing ten objects into the air all at once. You start with one. You toss it up, and catch it. Then you move on to two objects, and so on. In other words, you build on your skills, progressively. These exercises are presented in a similar way. First you'll get one of Nia's parts moving effectively, and then another, and then another. In time, you'll get *all* of Nia moving effectively through space and time.

Another juggling analogy. When you have those ten objects in the air, you can't just suddenly decide that you're going to *not* juggle one of them. If you do, that object falls to the ground, followed by all the others. It's the same way with Nia. Once you have a lot of parts moving, you have to *keep* them moving, at least until you can effectively decelerate them in a convincing fashion. If you forget to animate a part that you've started moving, even for a single frame, you'll have a nasty pop in your animation, and no one wants that.

You'll notice that these exercises aren't presented in a 'Step by Step' format. Instead, they're described in enough detail to get you going, and then it's over to *you*. I firmly believe that there's no better way to learn how to animate well then by *doing* it.

When you resurface, check back with the book, for more insights into the exercise.

You'll notice that following exercises focus entirely on 'body' animation, while Nia's facial features remain fixed, throughout. Facial animation is looked at in detail in the following chapter.

Arm extension

If you're very new to animating in stop motion, this exercise will provide you with productive challenges. If you're more experienced, it's a great warm up exercise that has a surprisingly rich range of variations (see below in 'Going further with this exercise'.)

Direction

- Get Nia framed up. Make sure that she's posed in a relaxed manner, as you see in Figure 11.8. The final pose that you will animate the arm into is shown in Figure 11.9.
- As you prepare, make sure that the magnet wands are securely connected to Nia's feet from beneath the deck's surface. The magnets allow you to easily reposition Nia in front of the

Figure 11.8   **Figure 11.9**

camera. If you've gone with a tie-down foot option for Nia, now is obviously the time to drill the holes and get her bolted into place.

- As you frame up, ensure that the frame will look balanced at the beginning, middle, and end of the action. Leave room for the action to happen!
- Try to keep the action relaxed and casual; after all, she's just straightening her arm. It's a very normal, everyday thing to do. Act it out yourself.
- Try to keep the spacing and timing simple for now. You can get more complex later.
- Remember to consider all of the principles of animation. You'll want to start with a bit of anticipation for the actual movement, before moving into the movement itself.
- Don't go overboard with the follow through, and remember to fully decelerate into the final pose.
- For now, don't bother animating Nia's fingers. Animation using her *wrist* is certainly reasonable, but think of her fingers as a solid mass. You can get into 'finger animation' later.
- If this is your first or second take, don't stress. Do careful work of course, but don't take all day to create this. Maybe 20 minutes max? Get a take done, learn from it, let your confidence grow, and go again. If you've created several takes already, and you're feeling good, now might be the time to really dig in, and try to make the animation as full and as nuanced as possible.

When you've finished animating an action, get in the habit of shooting some held frames of Nia in that final pose. These held frames are easier on the eyes when looping the animation during review. If you want, you can then accelerate Nia *out* of this pose, creating a series of actions separated by held frames (a good way to hone your skills at letting poses 'read').

Things to consider as you animate

- ABF! You need to flip your frames, so that you can see (and feel) the flow of animation between your recorded frames and your current (aka live view) position.
- Typically, there is a hierarchy of moving parts within a movement, with the 'boss' part being the part that *drives* the action. It's this primary part that you should always pose first, as you work your way down (or up, or along) the jointed part. In the case of this exercise, you'll want to pose the most upper part of the arm first, and then work your way down from there. There are lots of examples of 'hierarchy in animation' that you can look up: a dog's tail, a piece of seaweed, a page turning, a pendulum (to name just a few)!
- As you animate, are you visualizing the final pose that Nia's arm will occupy?
- As you flip, your main focus must be on the specific parts that you're animating, but also look at Nia *overall*. Don't let the puppet start to shift and jitter, because you've been too focused on just the arm.

Troubleshooting

- If the entire arm is a bit too much for you to handle, *reduce* the number of parts that you're animating. Get Nia in her first pose, but leave her shoulder and upper arm rigid, and perform the extension using only the elbow joint and wrist joint.
- Does Nia's arm seem too 'rubbery' in your animation? As you'll recall, there's no bones in there, just wire, so you need to be mindful of that as you pose her arm. You'll need to maintain a consistent location for both her elbow joint and her wrist joint, throughout these exercises.
- Does the animation feel overly tentative? Maybe you're trying to be too careful, too perfect, too 'full'. Go again, and just let the action happen. Who cares? You're learning! Relax.
- Animating follow through on this exercise can be a tricky thing. If you follow through too much at the wrist, and then

come back up, you'll be inclined to want to move the hand downward yet *again* in an effort to settle it further. Before you know it, Nia is waving! Go again, and lay off on the follow through this time.

Going further with this exercise

- Try the same thing with Nia's other arm.
- Create versions that are more complex: a fast extension; a *very* fast extension (that slows down abruptly at the end); a slow extension, a *very* slow extension, and so on.
- Extend *both* arms, but mix up the timing: start animating one of the arms several frames before the other, but try to have them arrive at their final pose on the same frame.
- Try variations on the simple extension: rather than just straightening her arm, lower Nia's arm to her side; start with her arm straight up in the air, then lower it completely to her side.
- After settling Nia's arm (or arms) into a final pose, shoot some held frames. Then, continue animating back to the first pose. How long should you hold for? Play it back, and see what feels right. Remember, figuring out how long poses need on-screen for them to read effectively is *hard*. This is good practice!
- Add a bit of head movement into the action: a simple tilt in any direction is a good challenge. Don't overdo it.
- Add a bit of finger animation: try to get Nia to 'point' at the end of the extension, or try a bit of elegant posing with the fingers as you arrive at the end of the extension.

If you decide to create multiple attempts within one file (rather than creating a new Take or Scene for each attempt), shoot a handful of frames after each effort, so that you'll have a visual divide between attempts. This will make it easier to distinguish between attempts later. You might even shoot a few frames of a title card between takes, that simply says 'Attempt 1', 'Attempt 2', and so on.

Torso rotation

This exercise is a bit more complicated than the previous one, in part because of the simple fact that you're animating more parts now. This exercise is also challenging because it involves movement in three dimensions (whereas the arm extension just dealt with two dimensions: 'up' and 'down'). This animation in depth, often referred to as 'z-axis' movement, gets pretty intense, but it's good to get into this sort of three-dimensional movement sooner, rather than later.

Direction

- The direction for this exercise is much the same as for the Arm Extension. Try to let the movement feel relaxed and natural. Start with a pose similar to what you see in Figure 11.10. A midway pose should look like what you see in Figure 11.11, and a final pose is shown in Figure 11.12. As always, be mindful of framing considerations.

Figure 11.10   Figure 11.11   Figure 11.12

- The action begins with Nia's torso. It drives the action, so pose it first, flip to ensure that you're are happy with its position, and *then* move on to posing her upper arm, then lower arm, and so on.
- As her torso decelerates into its final pose, the arm carries onward, heading towards *its* final pose. Ideally, this 'chain' continues, as her upper arm then decelerates into its pose, followed by the lower arm, and finally the hand.
- What about Nia's head in all of this? If you try to keep her face perfectly still, you'll struggle a lot, and you'll still likely end up with annoying jitter. Rather than fight this losing battle, work in a modest bit of head animation. Once the head is *purposefully* moving, it's much easier to control.

Things to consider as you animate

- Watch the screen, not the puppet. When you're flipping frames, where is the movement happening? 'Nia on the deck' should look generally balanced, but 'Nia through the camera' is what is essential to your animation.
- Remember the idea of 'hierarchy', as discussed in the Arm Extension exercise. If Nia's torso is the 'boss' in this exercise, what effect does that have on the other parts, and on the order in which you pose them, before recording?
- As you flip frames, try to isolate each moving part and consider it on its own. Does the part follow all the principles of animation? Is it moving in the way that you want it to? Is it 'doing' what it's supposed to be doing? If not, adjust it. Once you've addressed all the parts, you're ready to record. As you become more experienced, you'll be able to look at the whole puppet, overall, as one big moving 'thing', but for now, this isolating method keeps things more manageable.

Troubleshooting

- Accept the fact that this exercise is a tricky one. If a first take looks rough, who cares? You're learning. Set up, and go for it again. The next take will look better. And the next one? Better still.
- If there's too much going on in this exercise to handle right now, simply forget Nia's head. Seriously. Just ignore it, or even take it off her neck! Now you can focus on *just* her torso and arms until you're more confident.
- As with the arm extension, if your early attempts feel overly cautious, or tense, maybe you're trying *too* hard. As you go for it again, keep reminding yourself of what the action is: the chest rotates, and the arm follows along. Get that across to the audience, and you're good. Once you are communicating this, you can do more attempts that will look more full.

Going further with this exercise

- This exercise can allow you to become very graceful in your animation. Even if you were born with two left feet (like me), that doesn't mean that you can't express great beauty of movement *through* Nia. Let her take the lead, while you record the frames!
- Rotate Nia in the opposite direction, using her other arm.
- Go for a different sense of timing: faster; slower; more 'graceful'; more 'blunt', and so on.
- Bring Nia's head into the action in a more complex fashion. Try turning her head in the *opposite* direction to the torso. This can result in some really dynamic and exciting animation and poses.
- What about Nia's *other* arm that *isn't* coming across her chest? Try to do something interesting with it. What new pose can *it* arrive at by then end of the exercise?
- Explore the idea of 'drag' in animation. That's when a part trails *behind* the lead part, only to eventually catch up, and carry onward along the path. It can add a great deal of realism and visual interest to your animation.

Try to resist the urge to move on to more complex exercises until you're able to create solid animation at your current level. If you dash ahead too soon, the resulting animation will only showcase your impatience, rather than your talent.

WILLIS O'BRIEN

A true pioneer in stop motion, O'Brien was responsible for bringing to life one of cinema's most enduring stop motion characters – King Kong. When the film premiered in 1933, the world had never seen anything like it before, and much of this was thanks to O'Brien's talent and dedication. But he started out by making simple puppets, and then learning how to animate them, one frame at a time. Keep that in mind as you continue to hone your *own* skills. There's no telling where your dedication and talent might take you.

Knee bends

Nia is *really* going to get a workout with this one, and so are you! Remember the juggling analogy from earlier? With this particular exercise, you'll be getting a *lot* of Nia's parts moving – everything from the ankles up, in fact – and once each part is moving, you'll need to ensure that it's being animated effectively.

The single biggest challenge within this exercise is Nia's *legs*. With just a slight adjustment of her legs, everything further up (hips, torso, arms, head) will shift dramatically. It will take some getting used to, but once you're animating this exercise effectively, you're really moving onward in your skills.

Direction

- Your starting pose should look like Figure 11.13 and Nia's final pose should look similar to Figure 11.14. You'll obviously need a wider frame for this exercise, so adjust your camera accordingly. You might be able to simply 'zoom' the lens out, but you may need to adjust the tripod as well.
- Nia's ankles are the 'boss' parts on this exercise, so always pose them first. After her ankles, work your way up the rest of the puppet's central parts, then outward into her extremities (in this case, Nia's arms). Remember ABF.
- Settle in on this exercise. It takes time to do it well.

Things to consider as you animate

- You'll quickly discover that Nia's leg wires are surprisingly stiff, since they're made from a thicker gauge of wire than her arms. As such, they require real force to move them.
- You'll notice this especially at the points where they connect to the hips and feet.
- As Nia lowers, try to adjust *both* of her legs together, rather than one at a time.

Figure 11.13   Figure 11.14

Try to hook your fingers around her lower legs and pull, while pushing with your thumbs on her upper legs. This will cause her entire body to lower more evenly.

- As you work, you may realize that something on Nia needs adjusting, or has come loose. This exercise is tricky for Nia, since it's the first time that all of her parts have been put to work. You may need to take a break to tighten a set screw here or there. Once Nia is tuned up properly, these sorts of mid-shot adjustments should be a rare thing.

If a puppet needs adjusting during a shot, try to fix it while leaving it in place on the deck. If you can't, you'll have to take the puppet off, but even then, try to keep it posed, so that it's easier to get back into the shot. With some practice, you'll be able to pop Nia out of a shot and back in again, without it showing in the slightest. This is a lot easier when she's in the middle of a big move, since the generous spacing makes it much easier to sneak her back into place.

Troubleshooting

- As you pose Nia's legs, you'll find that her feet want to shift on the deck. This is always a challenge with puppets that use magnets in their feet. It takes practice to get used to it. Get in the habit of checking the feet as you flip frames, to ensure that they are staying in place.
- If you animate the action so that Nia accomplishes the knee bend a bit faster, it obviously means that you'll have fewer frames to pose. The resulting action may not look lush and 'full', but if you take care to fully decelerate Nia into her final pose, it can still look very nice.
- If all those moving parts are causing you grief, just pose Nia's arms out at her sides, and forget about them. Focus on the legs. You can even perform 'surgery' on Nia, and remove her torso so that she's just

hips, legs, and feet! She'll understand. Once you're move confident with this exercise, you can put her back together.

Going further with this exercise

- Make the knee bend a 'very slow' knee bend. This will be tricky and time-consuming, but it will make you a stronger animator. If you can nail this, that's great progress!
- Work in a variation for Nia's upper body and head. What other combinations of gestures and poses can you come up with that are graceful, or funny, or forceful? How do these variations express aspects of *character*?
- Ready for a *real* challenge? Reverse this action. In other words, start with Nia 'down', and then animate her into her 'standing' pose. Why is this variation so challenging? It's those leg wires again. It's easier to pull forward (to make Nia lower), than it is to push them in (to make her stand). Try it. You'll see what I mean. No one said this was easy.

Unfolding

This exercise shares a lot with the previous one, in that you'll be animating Nia's entire body. But it also lets you work in some of the rotational challenges that you dealt with in the 'Torso Rotation' exercise. Here, you'll be rotating *both* Nia's hips and chest block, as she slowly 'unfolds' herself over the course of the exercise.

If you've already tried your hand at getting Nia to stand up (a variation that was presented in the previous exercise), then you know the challenge that awaits you. This exercise is also a chance for you to be very *expressive* with Nia. She starts out small, but ends up big – and any time that a character gets to change states so dramatically, there's often great opportunity in terms of performance.

Don't just stand Nia up – let it be fun, energetic, and expressive. After all the hard work that you've put into fabricating her, Nia is finally alive! Let that joy show itself in the animation!

Figure 11.15   **Figure 11.16**   **Figure 11.17**

Don't lose your head during this one. Well, don't lose *Nia's* head, actually. If you pose Nia with her head down (which might happen in this exercise), her head can slide off her neck, and the fall could damage her paint job. To help keep her head on, apply a small amount of tack to the neck brass stock. When you slide the head back on, the tack should provide just enough grip to prevent heads from rolling.

Direction

- Nia starts as show in Figure 11.15. Over the course of her action, she'll eventually achieve a pose similar to Figure 11.16, and by the end, she'll be 'unfurled', as in Figure 11.17
- As reference, do a search for time-lapse footage of a growing fern (you'll find lots of good examples online). It's that same sense of 'unfurling growth' that you'll be going for in this exercise. To achieve this effect, you'll need to decelerate Nia's parts in sequence. As she rises up, her legs and hips straighten and find their final poses. From there, you'll want to get her spine straightened and her chest posed. Then, you'll continue onward to her head, arms, and finally her hands.
- As you get closer to the final frames, make sure that nothing else is moving on Nia except for the final bit of animation on her hands (and fingers, if you're up for the challenge). If you can do this effectively, you'll have controlled the attention of your audience *right* down to the final frames of careful animation, which is a sure sign of a talented animator.

Things to consider as you animate

- Take the 'Direction' for this exercise to heart. Let the action be big, and full of life.
- Compare the positioning of Nia's hands in Figure 11.16 to their positions in Figure 11.17. As Nia's hands move up towards their final poses, you'll need to roll them over, and that's a tricky bit of animation. Be sure to test the movement yourself, with your *own* hands, to get it right.
- Remember all that stuff about honing your visualization skills, as a way to improve your stop motion? Keep seeing where Nia is *going* to be, as you animate.

Are you relying on the onion skin tool a lot? If you want to build stronger animation muscles, switch it off. Animation is movement, and onion skin denies that movement, by making you think about just one static frame. Use ABF instead!

Troubleshooting

- As with any wider-angle shot, keep an eye on Nia's feet. It's easy to forget them when you're intensely focusing on the other parts, and by the end of the action they're sliding and jittering all over the deck!
- If you're struggling with this exercise, follow the same advice that was offered in the previous one: get the main action over with, quickly. If you accelerate Nia fairly aggressively out of her starting

pose, you can get her standing up over just a few frames. Then, take time and care to decelerate her into her final pose, and you'll be surprised by how good it can look, once the exercise is complete.

- If you find that this exercise is really beyond you, consider heading back to some of the earlier exercises and renewing your confidence. Then, come back to this exercise. It will be waiting right here for you!

Going further with this exercise

- You've gone 'small to big', so why not try 'big to small', by reversing the entire exercise.
- Try animating Nia from any extreme 'full body' pose into another one through careful, full animation.
- Shots won't always have the puppet looking at the camera! To prepare for this, attempt this exercise again, only this time with Nia's *back* to the camera. You can obviously create the same challenge by staging *any* of these exercises in the same way.

Now that you've been working with Nia for a while, are there aspects of her personality that seem to be revealing themselves? Be open to this process of character development that occurs *through* animation, and let Nia continue to develop!

A TOWN CALLED PANIC, STÉPHANE AUBIER, VINCENT PATAR, 2009

This extremely fun (and funny) stop motion feature from Belgium is a master class in timing for animation. Being little more than tiny posed figures, the puppets are intentionally very limited in how they can move, but that has nothing to do with how effectively those movements are *timed*. As you work with Nia, your focus is on timing for realistic human animation, but this film will greatly expand your *overall* understanding of the concept.

Animating impacts

When I'm animating, few things give me greater pleasure than creating a really effective impact. Impacts are, well … impactful! They tend to have a lot of visual energy, and at this basic level of 'eye candy', an energetic impact is fun to animate, and fun to watch. Impacts are also a cornerstone of physical comedy, and of action stories.

Beyond that, they're a basic part of realistic animation! Of course, not all impacts have to be filled with energy. You can have a very *gentle* impact, but it needs to look right, no matter what. If we return to mechanical physics for a moment, when an object in motion suddenly encounters another object, you have an impact. And that has to be animated effectively.

Impacts are *very* much about timing. If you time an impact (and its follow through) correctly, you should be able to *feel* the impact when you play it back, even before you add sound effects. On the other hand, if you miss the mark with your timing, the impact can feel 'soft' or 'flat'. Get it timed right, and it's right. Get it timed wrong, and it's wrong. Impacts are very black and white in this way, so use them to improve your animation timing, whenever you can.

Before you spend a day smashing things into Nia, there are lots of *other* ways to practice impacts that are quick to set up, and that won't needlessly damage your awesome puppet. Here are a few ideas to get you started, but you'll come up with your own in no time. For all of them, think through the actions carefully beforehand, and be sure to play them back as you animate. Be sure to animate not only the impact, but also the *consequences* of the impact.

- Animate two balls of clay that roll towards each other, and then collide. There's endless variations within this that will let you explore all kinds of animation challenges: create a 'head on' collision; create a collision where one ball hits the other from the side; make one ball much bigger than the other and see how that plays out; animate one ball rolling with much more energy then the other, and so on.
- Animate toy cars around, until the inevitable 'crash' happens. If you animate them as if one is a timid driver, and the other is aggressive, how does that all play out upon impact? Crash them again, in different ways.

- Of course, you *can* use Nia to practice impacts. Maybe she gets hit by a snowball? Make a snowball from white clay, suspend it from a very thin wire (which you won't really see, since it will only be in a few frames), and then 'fly' it into the shot, from off-screen, towards the unsuspecting Nia. Whack!

Animating with props

Up to this point, you've been bringing Nia to life in ways that have focused entirely *on* Nia, and nothing *but* Nia. But as with any active character, Nia will eventually want to interact more directly with the world around her. One way that she'll do that is by grabbing *hold* of something – namely, a prop.

You'll find more specific insights into fabricating props in the chapter dedicated to Production (in Part 4 of the book), but now is a chance for you to try your hand at making something simple, since you're going to need this prop very soon. It's the bat prop that Nia will use for the Puppet Smash exercise.

Before fabricating this simple prop, why not jump ahead to the Props section of Chapter 16 on Production in Part 4? What's explored in that part of the book will be of use to you now.

Since it's pretty straightforward, we won't bother with a detailed 'Step by Step' process. Figures 11.18 and 11.19 should provide you with enough information. The most important things to remember are as follows: the bat must match Nia in scale, it must be light, it must fit nicely in Nia's hand, and it must be sturdy.

If you *really* don't feel like taking the time right now to make a bat, you could just use a pencil or other similar object.

Figure 11.18
Crafting a bat prop.
I went with a very basic design for this prop, but feel free to design *your* bat however you want. I made the bat from pine, which is light and strong, but you could use balsa wood, Super Sculpy, or pink foam, which is a common material for making props and sets. Pink foam is discussed in more detail in Chapter 16.

Figure 11.19
Finishing a bat prop.
Once you've made that bat, a quick coat of stain or paint can provide you with a nice final finish.

Figure 11.20
Simple prop rig.
If a prop needs to be suspended during animation, consider using a simple prop rig like this one. It's just a rare earth magnet with some armature wire glued on to it. Some sticky tack (or glue) can hold the prop to the wire. If possible, hide the rig behind something on set, so that you don't have to remove it in post-production.

When animating with a prop, it's important to realize that even though a prop may be secured in a puppet's hand, the prop isn't simply a part of the puppet. Depending on the nature of the prop, it may need to be animated a little, or a lot. For example, if a character is holding a flagpole, the flag on the end may need to be animated in *every* frame (if you want to suggest a wind or breeze). Another prop (like a cell phone) may need only a modest amount of animation, since it doesn't 'do' much. Regardless, a prop adds complexity to every shot, if only because it needs to be attended to by the animator, frame by frame.

Conveying weight in stop motion

When it comes to conveying weight when animating props, here's my general advice: always remember that animating objects so that they appear to be heavy has *consequences* – both within the animated world, and in the world of your production.

We'll use the example of Nia trying to lift a cannon ball. Within the animated world, Nia will first need to bend down very low, as she begins to struggle to get her fingers under the ball. Then she'll struggle to get her hands under the ball, and then the *serious* strain begins as she attempts to stand back up, *and* to keep her fingers from slipping apart.

This is very hard work for Nia, and the *consequence* is that she's going to be exhausted if she manages to actually lift it. If she can't handle it, and accidently drops the ball, we have further consequences – the floor cracks, or far worse – Nia breaks her foot! These are some of the consequences of a heavy object *within the animated world*.

In the real world of the production, animating the action described above has real world consequences. It will take a long time to create this scene, *because everything that was described must be animated*. And as Nia begins to actually lift the ball, she has to do it *extremely slowly*, in order for it to be convincing. This slow movement will consist of heaps of animation, and all of it will be tricky, since the increments will be so small.

None of this is to scare you away from animating heavy things. Instead it's to make you aware of the challenges involved in conveying weight, so that you can plan accordingly when sizing up a shot (or when imagining your own story). The Puppet Smash Action Analysis will provide you with a great chance to explore the challenges of providing weight to props.

Of course, it's not only props that require animated weight. Characters also need to seem as though they have real mass. Let's consider the average person, of average mass – someone like Nia. As this person moves through life, her body may be struggling against gravity's effect on her mass, *but it doesn't typically show that struggle*. If you try to keep this in mind, you won't lose yourself in trying to *constantly* convey weight, when your efforts might be better applied elsewhere. Consider reserving your efforts in this area for moments when it can really convey something to your audience. For example, if Nia is very tired, or very depressed, that would be a time to animate her 'weighed down' – legs bent slightly, shoulders slumped. Or, if Nia slips and falls, it's time to show the effect her weight has, through a well-planned and well-animated impact.

If your character is massive, or is carrying a huge weight as part of its costume (think of a knight in full armour), then you've got your work cut out for you. If your production schedule allows you time to convey all that weight with every frame, then all is well. But if not, try to find a compromise in how you animate the character's mass. Consider animating it in a way that *suggests* how heavy the character is, but can be animated easily enough to meet your production's demands. Try to use strong posing that sells the idea of 'heavy' – perhaps the knight constantly has slightly bent knees, as a result of all that heavy gear!

Providing a sense of weight to a character during a walk or a run is a special situation that merits a bit further consideration, so you'll find more on this topic in the following chapter.

Action analysis: The puppet smash

Don't panic. Despite this exercise's colourful name, no puppets will be harmed. Instead, it's Nia (and you) that gets to smash something, using

Figure 11.21   Figure 11.22   Figure 11.23

her awesome new bat! This action analysis allows you to personalize things, and it lets you apply a lot of what's you've learned so far from this chapter. Nia's entire body can be animated in this, and all of the mechanical principles of animation can be put to good use. You'll get a chance to express strong poses (resting and action), strong timing, and strong 'impact' animation. You'll also get to show off your skills animating props. It's a complex exercise, so plan it out carefully, and dedicate a good amount of time to doing it. And be sure to have a 'smashing' good time!

There's no sense dwelling on how bad that joke was. You have a stop motion exercise to set up, so you'd better get going.

> It's not necessary, but you may *want* to use an x-sheet to help you plan out this exercise. There's a section dedicated to the x-sheet in the next chapter.

Direction

- Take your time setting all this up. There are a lot of visual elements involved, so don't start animating until everything looks nice and balanced.
- It takes time to get the bat secured in Nia's hands. Be patient.
- Sculpt a small piece of clay into 'something' for Nia to smash. Now is the time to decide – will you be animating this object so that it appears to be hard? Soft? Will it break into shards? Or simply squish around the bat? Whatever you decide for the *nature* of the object will greatly influence the animation, once Nia smashes it. I went with a simple tube shape, which will show off compression nicely.

- The action begins with Nia posed as shown in Figure 11.21. Make sure that she's positioned slightly *behind* the clay object. This will allow the action to read clearly on camera. This is a chance for you to work on your staging and blocking, as well as your animation.
- The peak of the anticipation for the action is shown in Figure 11.22, which you'll want to personalize as you animate, obviously. And then the final approximate pose is shown in Figure 11.23
- The bat should stay on screen through the whole shot, so frame up accordingly. Remember that effective framing for your shot is an essential part of stop motion.
- It helps to think of this one exercise as having basically *three* important portions: anticipation for the action, the action itself, and the follow through on the action.

Things to consider as you animate

- Planning is essential on this one. It might help to sketch some of the essential poses in advance, and be sure to act it out, before and during animation. Get the action straight within your own bones and muscles to help you translate things into Nia.

- See the extreme poses in your mind's eye well in advance of arriving at them in the animation.
- Don't forget to effectively manage the bat when you're posing Nia. It's a major visual element in the shot, so if it's popping around in the animation, it will be very distracting.

Troubleshooting

- If the bat really won't stay secured in Nia's hands, perhaps it's simply too heavy? If so, whip up something fast that is *ultra* light, and go again. Remember that it can be essentially weightless in reality, while you *imply* that it's heavier, through how you animated it.
- If raising and lowering Nia's legs is too challenging, you can simplify the leg animation and instead focus more on her upper body. Just make sure her legs are well posed, and then limit the animation to her upper body. It will still look like a 'smash'. Once you're getting good results in this way, add leg animation back into the mix. Alternately, just animate Nia's legs *downward* as she smashes (rather than 'upward' during the anticipation).
- If you greatly simplify the extreme poses, you can simplify the entire exercise. Visualize Nia performing a much more modest action, in which she simply raises the bat a bit, then drops it on to the clay. Simple. Get that looking good, then make the action bigger (and more extreme) in later attempts.

Going further with this exercise

- Stage Nia facing in the *other* direction, and go again.
- Rather than an overhead swing, try swinging the bat out to a side.
- Change the weight of the bat by animating the action as though the bat is incredibly heavy (or perhaps Nia is super weak?)
- Change the clay object, so that the impact allows for variations in animation. If your first effort saw the object 'splat' like a melon, this time animate the object as though it was made of concrete.
- Express *character* through the action: try a confident Nia, a tentative Nia, a bored Nia, a scared Nia. This expression of character can be tied to the object that is being smashed, to help with the acting. For example, if Nia's scared, perhaps it's because she has to hit a beehive!
- Work a 'step' into this. Perhaps as Nia comes down with the bat, she takes a step *forward*, and plants her foot again, in order to *really* add some force to the smash. Raising Nia's foot off the deck is covered in detail in the next chapter, but if you're up for it now, why not try it? You're sure to learn a lot, no matter the results. Just be sure to plan it out carefully.
- Use your animation skills and your creativity to *surprise* the audience. What if Nia has a *huge* wind up, but at the last moment slows her swing down dramatically, so that she merely *taps* the object?

SEAMUS WALSH, SCREEN NOVELTIES

Together with Mark Caballero and Christopher Finnegan, Seamus Walsh runs Screen Novelties, a LA-based animation studio that specializes in stop motion for television and commercials. They've brought everyone from Fred Flintstone to SpongeBob SquarePants to the gang from *Adventure Time* to stop motion life.

As with Robin Walsh (who was interviewed earlier), I'm not related to Seamus. What's with all the stop motion Walshes? I have no idea.

Q. Think back to a very early experience creating stop motion. What was that project, and what was the experience of trying to perform through a stop motion puppet like for you then?

A. I made my first animation when I was nine, I begged my parents to buy me a roll of super 8 film for our movie camera. 50 feet of film gave you a little over two minutes for a quick story. Luckily the camera we had had a 'single frame' option on it! We made a mini space epic, with me and my friend and my sisters 'flying' in a spaceship and running around on various planets. It was mostly live action, but I did a few animation shots to spice it up.

I animated some toys I had, a robotic spider and scorpion fighting I think.

My dad was such a good sport. We didn't have a tripod, and he realized that for animation that was going to pose a problem. So he sat himself in a chair and balanced the camera on his knee while I animated the creatures on the ground. He managed to keep it pretty still actually!

I was too young to think about 'performance' then – I don't really think I thought about that until high school when my friends and I had a public access show that I would do animated linking skits for. I guess I was too lazy at that time to make real puppets, I mostly used found objects or clay blobs. I remember making a thing about an amoeba family rolling into a room and watching television. I think that was the first time I recognized getting some 'character' into the animation. The learning process was so slow back then. You had to fill up the roll of film, which took weeks, and then send it off for developing which took another week. The wait was excruciating and not very conducive to learning quickly. But it was still fun.

Q. As you continued to practice animating, how did you know that you were getting better?

A. It wasn't till college that I started to get some decent results. I remember just making a bare armature walk back and forth on a tabletop, then doing hops and jumps. I was trying to get realistic weight into it. I had no frame grabbers and had to wait several days to get the film back until I could see if it worked.

I remember getting stuff back from the lab and being happy that I was finally feeling like I was getting it. I did a hopping run that had some convincing weight and had follow through in the arms and hands – yay! Then a single frame grabber became available for me to use, and I thought 'Wow, now I'm really going to be able to make the animation great!' I animated a bunch of walks and jumps again. When I got the film back, I was bummed. I had lost the dynamic action I had gotten before. I realized it was because I was so in awe of the fact that I could reference the previous frame, I had lost sight of the big picture. Everything was even and smooth, but the 'life' wasn't there. That was a great lesson to learn right away, and I've never forgotten it. The frame reference is there to help you take risks and push your performance to new heights, not to make it smooth.

Q. Imagine a fairly straight forward shot. Not crazy long, no crazy rigs. It's mostly a performance piece. As an experienced animator, can you talk a bit about the 'planning out' process that you'd use? I know some animators who like to really carefully chart things out in advance, and I know others who like to jump in, thinking it through more in the moment.

A. I think I'm somewhere in the middle. I always think about the entire scene and how this particular shot contributes to the overall timing of a sequence. I like to carefully look at the shot previous and the shot after, even if they're still just storyboards, because all of that really affects the timing and the approach. Then I act it out myself several times until I feel like I've internalized the performance. Then I jot down a few marks on my exposure sheet, usually circles with an 'X' to note the points where the character is going to hit their main poses or vowel sounds for the scene. If I've internalized the performance, the acting will flow out. To sum up, I like to plan major points I want to hit, but I try to leave some things to be improvised as the shot unfolds.

But honestly, often on paying jobs, there is a lot of pressure to get the quota of seconds done, and you're lucky if you get 5–10 minutes to think about a shot before you launch.

Q. **There's one particular formative experience you've had that I'd like to ask you about. You and Mark Caballero worked with Ray Harryhausen in the early 2000s, to help him complete his film** The Tortoise and the Hare. **Not many stop motion animators working today actually worked alongside the master like this. Looking back on that experience, how did it affect you and your work, as you've carried onward?**

A. Well of course it's still surreal to think that we actually did that. To get to meet and even befriend someone who was such an inspiration as I grew up is just insanely lucky. It was cool to watch his creative process, it was very matter-of-fact in that old school way, which was great because it was so unpretentious. His imagination and enthusiasm were still going strong at his age, which was so inspiring. Ray's work is truly art. You're watching the creative explosion of an amazingly unique artist. I know that working with him showed me the value of keeping your vision controlled and singular. It made me wary of any situation where stop motion might be turned into a 'factory' process. Ray did almost everything himself and that's why you feel such a creative spark in his work.

Q. **The work that comes out of Screen Novelties shows off a real love for stylized looks that feel fresh and fun, while also feeling nostalgic and warm. Can you talk a bit about your inspirations and influences, either from within stop motion, or from other forms of art?**

A. Thank you for those kind words! We have almost too many inspirations. We admire work that is loose and experimental but still with a very deliberate design style. Rankin/Bass, Garri Bardin, and Bretislav Pojar come off the top of my head as huge influences. But there are so many more, from Henson, Okamoto, and Lotte Reiniger. It basically boils down to unpretentious, bold artistic statements, whether esoteric or commercial. Everything from Paul Klee and Calder and Fischinger to Ward Kimball and Rod Scribner and Frank Zappa. I could talk about this all day but I don't want to bore you with lists!

Q. **Screen Novelties has brought some very beloved cartoon characters to life, including The Flintstones. You've even brought Sponge-Bob SquarePants to life, in his very own Christmas special! Can you talk a bit about the process of translating such well known drawn characters into stop motion, specifically from the perspective of animating them?**

A. We do really enjoy translating well known characters from 2D animation into the dimensional realm. It's a very specific challenge. You have to find the essence of the character without getting too literal about the translation. We always get the model sheets of the character, but if you 'trace' or measure things out, it just won't work. You have to push it in the right places. That's where you have to have the taste and design sensitivity to get at what makes it feel like the character. We usually dub it the 'puppetization process'.

From an animation standpoint, you have to trust your poses and stick with them. A lot of 2D characters hit a strong pose and then milk it for as long as possible. That's not usually a bad thing, it actually shows the graphic strength of the pose. Stop motion tends to not follow that pattern so much, but I think it can look really cool if done right. I guess people feel like the character will seem dead if it's not moving all the time, but if your timing and poses are full of energy then it can totally work.

Q. Back to advice for incoming animators! Imagine a really strong animation demo reel from a young stop motion animator. What do you see in that demo reel?

A. Snappy timing, economical action, and strong poses. Inventiveness in the poses, not just using the stock things that work. Always compare your work to the best stuff you've ever seen and strive to get there. It'll push you to take your work to the next level. Learn from the greats in 2D animation how to get great poses and apply that to your dimensional work.

Q. Any further advice for an upcoming stop motion animator who is keen to break in (to stop motion, not your house).

A. Make your own films. And try to do almost everything yourself. Make films and put them in festivals and/or online. With luck, someone will recognize your talent and offer to pay you to make stuff. The simple films that Mark and I made when we were starting out got into festivals, and a recruiter from MTV was at one of the screenings and offered us jobs based on that. From there, you need to have a focus on what you want to do with the medium. Where you want to take it, that is unique to you.

Don't look at stop motion as an 'industry' to get into. It's an art form. It's an art form that is really just too crazy to try to put monetary value on, the numbers just don't add up. You have to do it because you're passionate about it. Having a backup skill to make money is probably a good idea.

Q. Final question. Plaid or paisley?

A. Plaid.

12

Advanced exercises

Now that you've got a strong foundation in creating realistic human movement in stop motion, this chapter will guide you through the challenge of using that movement to express emotion. It's not just actions you're going to communicate now, but feelings. In other words, it's time to get acting!

That alone is an exciting challenge, but this chapter also examines other advanced concepts and techniques, including walks, runs, and rigging. And since Nia is going to be so busy with all of this frame-by-frame action, there's also a section on puppet repairs (think of it as a day at the puppet spa for the hard-working Nia).

If you dedicate yourself, by the end of this chapter you'll have some strong acting pieces to show off. And in a certain way, Nia will be truly 'free'. She'll be able to act, run, walk, and jump across your animation deck, confined only by the edge of the deck, and your own imagination. It won't be easy (these exercises are called 'advanced' for a reason), but if you're willing to put in the hard work and the disciplined practice, then the reward will be fantastic.

Figure 12.1
Facial
Expressions.
Clear and effective
communication
through Nia's
facial elements is
essential.

Facial animation for Nia

Nia's facial elements are expressive, but they don't allow for extremely subtle or nuanced expressions. This had its advantages when we were dealing with fabrication. It kept things relatively straightforward. But when it comes to acting, it *does* present a challenge – how do you use Nia's fairly basic facial pieces to effectively convey a wide range of emotions?

The answer lies in finding very clear expressions that convey precisely what you intend. Once you get the hang of animating her features, you'll actually find that there's quite a range of emotions you can convey. Combine just the right mouth shape, tipped at just the right angle, with just the right angle of an eyebrow, and you've suddenly got a very subtle expression. When this is used in combination with all of the animation in the rest of Nia's body (not to mention the acting within the dialogue that you might be using), you'll find there's not much holding Nia back, in terms of acting.

Once you've had some practice animating Nia's facial elements, consider taking the time to arrange all of her features into a basic 'resting'

facial expression, and record it as a reference image. Do the same for some other basic expressions: tired, confused, surprised, angry, and so on. You'll still have the freedom to come up with variations on these expressions as you animate, but they may prove useful at a future date, at least for reference.

> For a reminder of the methods used for creating Nia's facial features, refer back to the section 'Pupils, eyelids, and eyebrows' in the Fabrication section. Those methods have an impact on the animation techniques you'll need to use.

Pupils

Of all of her facial features, you'll need to pay special attention when animating Nia's pupils. If you animate them effectively, you can provide a great deal of life to Nia, since a character's eyes

Figure 12.2 Animating Nia's pupils.
Make sure that you have extra pupils on hand, in case Nia's pop off mid-shot!

tend to reveal so much about what a character is thinking and feeling.

At a very basic level, you'll need to ensure that Nia's pupils are always working in unison. Keep them from crossing, or going off in different directions (unless you are intentionally going for a bit of comedic weirdness, of course). It's surprisingly easy to lose track of this when you're handling all the challenges of a shot!

> Very slight and occasional movements of Nia's pupils, that don't shift her attention significantly, can be a very effective and simple way to convey 'thinking'. Try moving them in a very tiny square pattern, or triangle, with several frames spaced between each movement. Eye movement like this is almost like a progress bar on a computer – they tell the audience that 'processing' is occurring within Nia's mind.

Always remember that your audience is constantly looking to Nia's eyes in order to understand the moment. *Where* is Nia looking? *Why* is she looking there? As she is looking there, what is she thinking? When does she shift her attention to something else, and why? And what does all of this tell us about Nia, and her state of mind?

Imagine a shot in which Nia is cautiously moving away from a potentially dangerous situation. How would you animate her pupils, as this shot progresses from beginning to end, frame by frame? Would her eyes ever leave the threat? If so, when? And why?

Eyelids

If Nia's pupils are the main area of interest within her face, then her eyelids are a close second. The positioning of her pupils may show us that Nia is looking at that alien space ship that has just landed, but it's her eyelids that help express how she is feeling about it (which is probably pretty amazed, I should think).

Of course, beyond expressing emotion, eyelids simply add a sense of realistic life to Nia. She needs to blink, to keep her eyes moist! With this in mind, throwing in an occasional blink is a quick and easy way to keep Nia 'alive' when posed. Don't overdo it, though – too many blinks will become distracting. I typically animate normal blinks by putting a fully closed lid on the eyeball, for one frame. That's it. It's enough for the audience to register it, but it doesn't distract from the main animation. Slow blinks obviously need more stages of lids, so play around and see what works for you. If I'm turning a puppet's head from one main pose to another, I'll often animate a blink as the head turns, and I'll also begin the pupil animation towards the new position, at the same time.

If you're doing a lot of eyelid animation, things can get messy pretty easily, since eyelid clay can start to build up quickly on the eyeball. It's important to be mindful of this, so you don't end up with a shot full of mucky eyeballs. And be sure to keep Nia's pupils positioned correctly when working with blinks! An applied lid can cause the pupil to shift, so make sure that you check this before recording the next frame.

> A cotton swab can be used to remove clay or wax from Nia's face. Moisten the swab very slightly with water, if needed. You can also use a wooden toothpick to get at stubborn bits, just be very careful not to scratch the paint job. If you do, you'll need to touch things up (see 'Fixing the puppet').

Figure 12.3
Various eyelids for Nia.
Having an assortment of pre-sculpted clay lids can speed things up during animation, since they can be quickly put on and removed as needed. You'll need to give them a final sculpt, once they're in place.

Eyebrows

Eyebrows can offer additional punctuation to what Nia's eyes and eyelids are expressing. For example, a surprised expression (wide eyes) is emphasized by posing Nia with 'upward' eyebrows. But eyebrows can also offer surprising *twists* to expressions, if they are played in contrast to what's expected. Imagine Nia's eyes wide in surprise, but with 'angry' (downward tilting) eyebrows. The resulting expression would be 'alarmed confusion', which is quite a complex expression. Position one brow in an 'angry' position and the other in a 'surprised' position, and Nia's expression shifts towards 'bemused confusion'.

The ability of Nia's eyebrows to enhance expressions is increased by the fact that her brows have visual contrast – they are dark, on top of her lighter skin. Because of this, the audience notices their positioning and movement readily. Be aware of this, not only for their acting potential, but also because you need to keep them under control! You don't want Nia's eyebrows shifting from their realistic positioning, like two creeping caterpillars. Always refer back to your reference images of what a 'resting' Nia face looks like, if in doubt.

If you find this style of eyebrows messy, you could sculpt a range of eyebrow expressions for Nia, either from Super Sculpey or modeling putty – just use a bit of dental wax to keep them in place during animation. You won't be able to animate them in the same way as soft clay brows, but they'll be tidier.

Figure 12.4
Container for facial animation.
Over time, you'll wind up with lots of eyebrows and eyelids, of
various stages and shapes. You'll also have mixtures of coloured
clay for when you need to create more lids and eyebrows. Keeping
that all together in one container will make your life much easier.

Mouth

With no formal registration spot on her face, you'll
need to determine the precise location for Nia's
mouth to reside, and then maintain that. If you
have a reference image of your 'resting' Nia face,
it can help to keep things consistent. A tip I often
use to maintain registration when animating
mouths like Nia's (beyond flipping frames) is to
ensure that the upper lip and upper teeth remain
generally in the same place, and allow the bottom lip and teeth to move as needed.

This non-registered type of mouth has some
advantages. Since you can freely move it around,
you can do some unique and subtle things. For
example, if you need to animate Nia chewing,
you can achieve this with just one mouth shape
(a neutral, closed mouth). The mouth shape
moves up, then down on a slight arc, then back
up, and so on. You can also use this method to
settle Nia's entire mouth area at the end of a
piece of dialogue, simply by decelerating the
final mouth shape over a few frames. You'll create a very nice effect, which gracefully finishes
off the mouth movement. You can do the same
thing at the start of dialogue, as well. As you'd
expect, there's more on animating with Nia's
mouth shapes in the next chapter, 'Animating
dialogue'.

As you're discovering, even though Nia's
head is a solid form, and even though her individual features are somewhat limited in how
much they can be animated, the combination

of all the elements can provide you with a great
range of expressions. Try to remember that
your audience isn't looking for utter realism
but instead is looking for a form of shorthand
(more on this below, in the intro to the Acting
Exercises). And when in doubt, study some
Clint Eastwood clips! He's a master of 'less is
more' in his facial expressions, and through his
restraint, Eastwood causes the audience to lean
in, towards his performance.

The 'Kuleshov Effect' is very useful for puppet animators to understand. Show the movie
audience a shot of a bowl of soup, followed by a
shot of an actor with a neutral expression, and
the audience will believe that he is conveying
'hunger'. Replace the bowl of soup with a fierce
lion, and the audience will now believe that he is
conveying 'fear'. In other words, film audiences
eagerly read into character expressions, so use
this to your advantage – when working with puppets, and while editing your projects.

Restrained is all fine and good, but what if
you want to go wild and crazy in your facial
animation? Feel free to go for it – it may just
mean that you need to create some custom-
ized cartoony facial elements for Nia to get
the 'Tex Avery' style working for you.

Using Nia's hands for expression

You'll find that Nia's hands are extremely useful as a way to emphasize, accent, or complete an overall 'full body' pose. Beyond that, they are also extremely useful as acting tools on their own. A single hand is capable of all sorts of things. It can point, in order to direct our attention gently or abruptly (depending on how it's animated). It can provide an accent to a point that's being made by dialogue (think of the classic 'Aha! I've got it!' hand pose). It can convey impatience, through a simple tapping finger, just as easily as it can convey tender

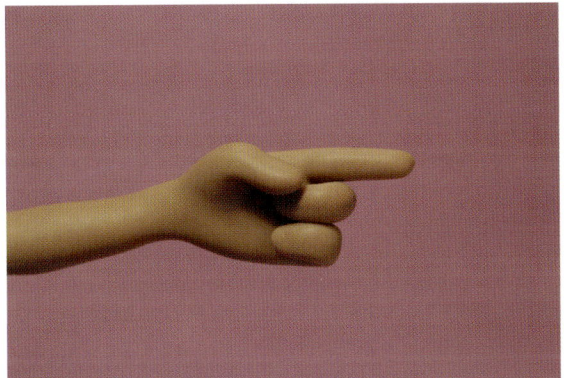

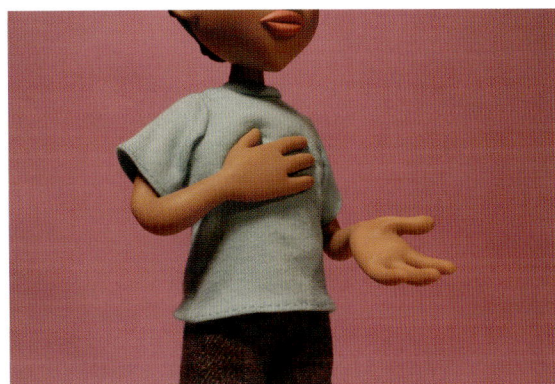

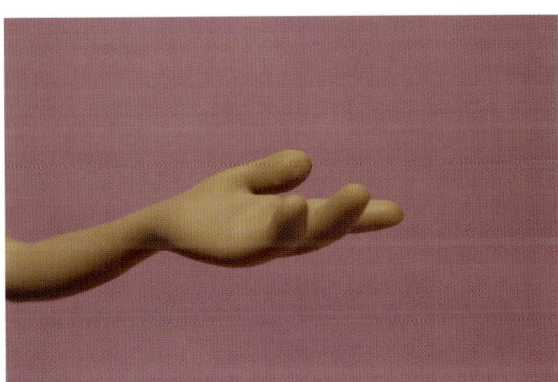

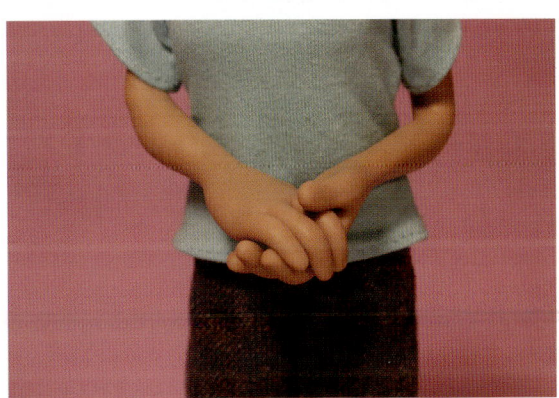

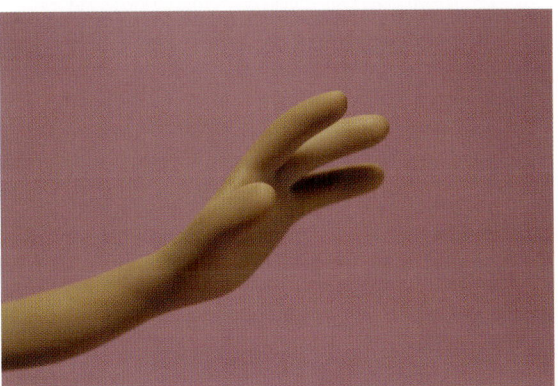

Figure 12.5
Nia's hands can be very direct in their posing and acting, as well as very subtle.
They certainly weren't easy to make, but it was worth it, when you now consider how much acting power they possess.

Figure 12.6
They say that the eyes are a window into the soul.
But in animation the hands can be just as revealing.

affection – imagine a mother's hand, gently reaching downward, to assist her child.

As you'd expect a *pair* of hands is even more expressive. They can work together to powerfully clarify a character's state of mind, or add some excitement to a piece of dialogue. They can mirror each other in their posing, they can complement each other with slight variations on a common pose, or they can dramatically differ from each other, offering a wide range of performance possibilities.

> You owe it to yourself to invest a good amount of time specifically animating Nia's wrists and hands. Animate them through a range of poses. Use them to express clear emotions, and clear gestures. Your aim is to determine what they can and cannot express, and to find the angles and poses that look the most flattering and convincing.

Using the x-sheet

The term x-sheet is short for 'exposure sheet', and dates back to when animation was shot on physical film that was exposed to light, frame by frame. The x-sheet is also sometimes referred to as a dope sheet, and it's basically a tracking list of all the frames within a specific shot, to which you can add your own notes. You can create your own x-sheet template (like the one pictured here), or find one online. Dragonframe also offers an x-sheet window that you can activate while animating.

At its basic level, the x-sheet helps you to keep on track during a shot. No matter how strong your visualization skills are, and no matter how much you've rehearsed, without some kind of chart, you might lose track of things (especially on longer shots). You may find yourself skipping over major blocking points, or losing yourself in a bit of inspired acting, and soon your shot is of no use to the larger project, even if it has some great animation in it. When you have an x-sheet to go along with a shot, it's a constant reminder

> The danger with x-sheets is that they can easily feel too restrictive and confining. With practice, you'll find a way to create animation that satisfies the x-sheet's requirements, but which also retains a sense of freshness and life.

that you need to stick to what you originally envisioned.

Every animator has a distinctive way of working with the x-sheet. If there's no dialogue in the shot, I first confirm the specific length of the shot in frames, and then fill in the 'Frame' column on the x-sheet (see Figure 12.7). Then I visualize the specifics of the shot, from beginning to end, and act it all out carefully in my mind within that specific frame count. Once I can see the shot in my mind, I translate that to the x-sheet, mostly by writing in very modest notes, but also with simple sketches that will remind me of certain essential poses. Then, as I animate, I compare my progress with the x-sheet, to ensure that I'm generally on track. For shots that are quite simple, I'll rarely look at the x-sheet. Instead, I just 'go for it', and check the x-sheet occasionally. For more complex shots, I'll refer to it more closely. But regardless of the shot details, I use the x-sheet to *guide* the animation, not to dictate it.

> The specific length of a shot will often be determined by the animatic reel (more on that in Part 4), but if you need to determine the length of a shot strictly from your imagination, you can use a stopwatch. You won't be completely tied to this running time while animating, but it provides you with enough of a range to fill in frames on an x-sheet.

If the shot I am animating does have dialogue, then I tend to use the x-sheet in a more formal fashion. That process is covered in greater detail in the following chapter, which focuses on animating dialogue.

If the x-sheet is such a useful tool for planning shots, why are you only hearing about it

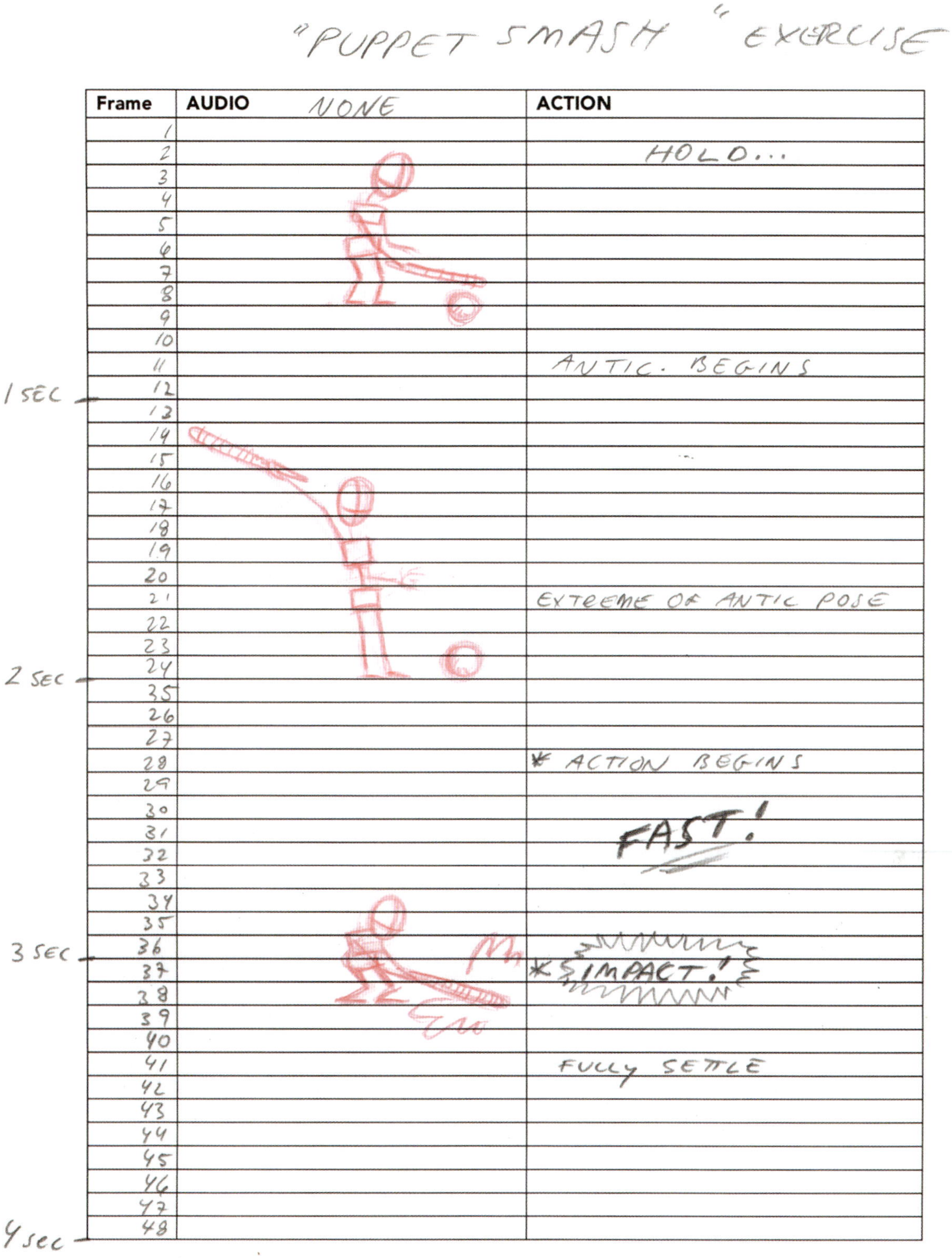

"PUPPET SMASH" EXERCISE

Frame	AUDIO	NONE	ACTION
1			
2			HOLD...
3			
4			
5			
6			
7			
8			
9			
10			
11			ANTIC. BEGINS
12			
13			
14			
15			
16			
17			
18			
19			
20			
21			EXTREME OF ANTIC POSE
22			
23			
24			
35			
26			
27			
28			✱ ACTION BEGINS
29			
30			
31			FAST!
32			
33			
34			
35			
36			
37			✱ IMPACT!
38			
39			
40			
41			FULLY SETTLE
42			
43			
44			
45			
46			
47			
48			

1 SEC — (at frame 11/12)
2 SEC — (at frame 24)
3 SEC — (at frame 36)
4 SEC — (at frame 48)

Figure 12.7
A completed x-sheet.
An example of an x-sheet, marked up for the Puppet Smash exercise. You can easily make your own template, based on the column headings you see here. You should be able to get 48 frames on the template page, which is four seconds of screen time (when shooting at 12fps).

now, when you're already well into animating Nia? In part, it's because we haven't looked at animating with dialogue yet (which is when an x-sheet is extremely useful). But there's another more fundamental reason. Strong character animation in stop motion comes from studying motion and performance, and then translating that through the puppet, straight ahead. It *doesn't* come from charts. Once you have developed strength as a stop motion animator by focusing on actual animation, there'll be lots of time – and reasons – to work with x-sheets more closely.

To sum up, there's really no right or wrong way to use an x-sheet in stop motion. If there's a note that will help you to create good work, write it in! Ultimately, the x-sheet is a tool to help you in your effort to create great shots. If you can consistently do that with nothing written down except a few quick notes on a napkin, that's great. But the x- sheet is standing by, ready to help.

ACTING EXERCISES

There are as many approaches to acting in stop motion as there are stop motion animators, but here's how I personally see things. It's an approach that has very much informed my own animation over the years, and it also helped to shape the following exercises.

Take a look at Nia. She's a wonderful thing. But part of her appeal is that she's *not* utterly realistic. This is not a flaw in Nia. It is, in fact, a strength. She is a distillation of a human being. She represents a human. She's a symbol that says 'human'.

Your audience knows this. And rather than being disappointed, your audience is happy about this fact. If your audience wanted utter realism, it wouldn't be watching a puppet film. Your audience wants to fill in some blanks and to connect some dots – so *use* that, to your advantage. This will make your life easier as an animator since you won't be losing yourself in an endless, and ultimately futile, quest for 'realism' through Nia, and it will be giving your audience what it truly wants – a 'puppet version' of the human condition.

This doesn't mean that your acting should be blunt, predictable, or clichéd. And it certainly doesn't mean that it should be dishonest, or lazy. Your job, as animator (and as actor) is to honestly feel the emotions, and then to translate that through the puppet in a way that retains the honesty. Just as Nia is a distillation of the human form, you need to distill the human experience through Nia. Even if your animation isn't technically marvelous, even if there are some rough edges to things, if you can get honest human emotion through to your audience, through Nia, then you're doing your job well.

If we put 'emotional honesty in animation' aside for just a moment, what if you're more interested in cartoon-style acting, intense physical comedy, or pure action animation? In all of these cases, it's often more about entertaining your audience, rather than carefully conveying emotion. If that's your ambition, just crank up the cartoony intensity in the following exercises. There's also lots of ways that you can create zany variations on the exercises, which should suit your wilder style. And remember, you can always throw in a good 'slip on a banana peel' moment, whenever it suits you.

For most of the exercises, you'll be animating Nia as she interacts with an imagined off-screen character. Unlike the previous exercises, these acting challenges don't have an obvious 'beginning, middle, end' structure, but you'll still need to *find* that sense of structure within the emotion. This is what's often referred to as the 'emotional arc'.

You can think of this as the development of the emotion within the clip, from beginning to end. It's complex work, but each exercise provides suggestions that should help.

You may get frustrated at times, and find that the emotional state is not coming through, or that it feels 'one note' (a flat expression of a basic emotion, often the result of a weak emotional arc). But that's part of learning. Stay open to what you're trying to communicate, and keep working on finding the right ways to get Nia to express the emotions through her posing. And never forget that your audience is at the other end of all this, waiting (and wanting) to feel it, too.

Friendly

Since this is our first acting exercise, this seems like a reasonable emotional state to begin with, doesn't it? After all, who doesn't like a nice warm welcome? In this exercise, everything is right in Nia's world. There's nothing but blue skies and sunshine, and Nia hasn't a care in the world. It's a wonderful day, indeed.

Figure 12.8
Nia greets her friend.

Figure 12.9
Nia listens approvingly.

Figure 12.10
Nia loves what the friend has proposed.

Direction

- Frame up a shot of Nia that basically replicates what you see in Figure 12.8. You want to give her enough room within the frame to act freely, while remaining on screen. As with the exercises in the previous chapter, try to keep the lighting effective, and generally flattering, but simple. The emphasis here is on acting, not lighting.
- You can stage Nia as though this character is off screen to the left, or to the right – whatever works for you.
- Before you animate, determine for yourself specifically where the off-screen character is. Lock Nia's eyes on that spot, and ensure that they stay there – don't let them wander aimlessly.
- A possible emotional arc for this exercise could be:
- Nia offers a happy greeting to her arriving friend.
- Nia listens attentively to what her friend proposes.
- Nia thinks it's a great idea, and is completely on board!
- Since all of this is occurring without actual dialogue, feel free to imagine what the off-screen character is saying to Nia. Focus on Nia's actions and reactions, and on ensuring that they are conveying the central emotional state, which in this case is 'friendly'.

Remember, an 'emotional arc' is the progression of the emotion over the course of the shot. Feel free to develop your own emotional arc for each of these acting exercises, as long as they conform to the central emotion!

Performance suggestions

- How do 'friendly' people act?! It's surprising how easy it is to dive into a shot without actually thinking about (and observing) the way that humans express themselves! So do your research.
- When preparing, it can help to think of other words that can be associated with the central emotion. In this case, think about words like 'approachable' and 'open'. How would you convey these through Nia's stance? How would you convey it through her hands and her facial features? All of this can be very useful when imagining strong poses that you'll eventually use to 'sell' the emotional state. You can use the images at the start of this exercise to help you develop some strong posing ideas.
- You need to feel 'friendly' as you create this exercise! That doesn't mean that you need to start literally hugging everyone within arm's reach (although don't let me stop you), but it *does* mean that you need to make the emotion real inside you, even as you carefully and methodically move through the shot. It's what animators do. Feel it, and convey it.

Things to consider as you animate

- Apply the skills that you developed from the previous chapter's exercises. To create a convincing piece of acting, Nia's movements need to follow the laws of physics, as well as the principles of animation.
- High quality performance animation takes time. Rome wasn't built in a day, and a nice clip of Nia performing isn't going to be created in ten minutes of dashing out frames.
- If something's not working, don't be afraid to delete some frames, reposition Nia, and re-animate. Or start over entirely. They're just frames, stored on a computer. And you're learning.
- Don't hesitate to sketch out strong poses that you want to go for, if that helps you to plan out Nia's emotional state and how it will be expressed. Simple stick figures are really all that you need – it's just a rough guide to assist you in the shot.

Frustrated

In this exercise, we're encountering a side of Nia that we've never seen before. Our typically good-natured and easy-going companion is clearly fed up. She's heard enough nonsense, and she's not putting up with it anymore. What's gotten her so worked up? It's up to you, as you think through the situation, and the performance!

Direction

- As with the previous exercise, this one relies upon the imagined off-screen character, who will be a focus for Nia's frustration. It's often said that acting is really about 'reacting', or responding, to another character's actions or words. This exercise can be a good place to explore this idea.

- A possible emotional arc for this exercise could be:
- Nia doesn't like what she's hearing.
- Nia throws it right back.
- Nia's temper boils over!

Figure 12.11
Nia is not amused.

Figure 12.12
Nia gives her adversary a piece of her mind.

Figure 12.13
Ka-boom! Nia loses her temper completely.

Don't feel that you need to animate Nia's facial features endlessly. A strong arrangement of eyelids, brows, and mouth that conveys 'frustrated' may be all that you need, for the whole exercise. It's a big, outward emotion, that should come through Nia's entire body, rather than just her face.

to her face. Then, with the audience now looking specifically where you want it to be looking – animate the eye roll. It's a valuable trick of the trade: get the audience to look where you want it to, then do the thing that you want it to see.

Performance suggestions

- As with any emotion that you're trying to convey, think about what bits of animated action 'sell' the emotion. Try a tapping finger towards the start of the piece – it's simple and clear, and it implies a building pressure that is likely to soon blow up. In other words, it suggests that the emotion is going to progress. Then let it!

- If Nia is feeling on edge, really consider the word 'edge'. And think of the word 'sharp'. How can you animate Nia so that she appears sharp? Lean her forward, give her edges, point her fingers, and so on. Think 'prickly', like a cactus. Taking that further, think about a knife. It has hard edges. It cuts. Bring this into your actual animation, in terms of how Nia moves.

- Compromise isn't a part of this bit of acting. So think 'obstruction' in the way that you pose Nia. She completely disagrees with her off screen opponent, so nothing is going to get past her. She's like a wall.

- Try an 'eye roll' at the end of the clip, to really bring home the idea that Nia is fed up. Can you animate it effectively so that it actually reads as an eye roll? And just as importantly – can you animate it so that your audience actually notices it? It's a subtle bit of animation, and can get lost if Nia's whole body is moving. To make it work, try to settle all of Nia into a pose. Once she is settled, animate a modest bit of facial animation (perhaps her mouth shifts slightly). This will bring the audience's attention

Things to consider as you animate

- It's vital to get to know what Nia can and cannot do. You'll find that the 'crossed arms' pose in Figure 12.11 is a challenging one to achieve effectively, due to the thickness of Nia's arms. Always take your time to find a version of a pose that works as well as it can, or rethink your posing entirely based on what the puppet is able to achieve.

- Go towards the emotion. This can be applied when you're planning the shot, and most certainly while you are animating. This will bring you further into the emotion, which can help you to create a more effective performance. It can also help you in your efforts to create an emotional arc. To go closer to an emotion means you are traveling along that emotion. And this is just the kind of movement you want, to create a dynamic performance.

- What about the personality that Nia seemed to be developing over the course of the exercises in the previous chapter? She was 'becoming Nia' in a way that had a lot of freedom to it. Now that she is acting in these exercises, is there still a 'real Nia' under all this? If so, does that personality show through in *these* exercises? Are all of these complex layers of performance actually a manifestation of *you*, the living and breathing animator? Welcome to the kind of thinking that keeps stop motion animators awake at night!

Reviewing professional clips of stop motion is a great way to learn more about acting through puppet animation. It really lets you dig into precisely how an effective performance is created. What's essential is that you can step through the animation frame by frame, so make sure that the video player you're using can do this. QuickTime and VLC are both reliable players, in this way.

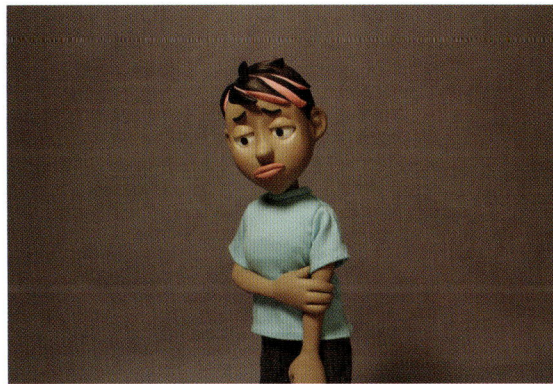

Figure 12.14
Nia pulls inward, trying to protect herself from the bad feelings.

Gloomy

Poor Nia. Things were so sunny just a few exercises ago. Now, storm clouds are overhead, and Nia's feeling low. Everyone feels pain. It's a part of being alive, as hard as that can be to accept.

Direction

- This exercise doesn't require an imaginary off-screen character. That's because when we feel down, we often retreat into ourselves, in order to heal (or sometimes to make ourselves worse, sadly). As a result, this is a very 'inward' acting exercise, as opposed to the 'outward' style of the previous ones. The challenge, then, will be to convey an inward struggle in such a way that clearly communicates to the audience, and doesn't just read as a 'puppet that isn't doing anything'. As always, strong and clear posing will be essential.
- You're going to need to take Nia *down* in this exercise, there's no way around it. It won't be much fun – not in a conventional sense anyway. But it does present a fantastic acting opportunity. A possible emotional arc for this exercise could be:
- Nia's had a rotten day. Everything went wrong.
- Nia wonders, 'Is there any path out of this mess? Why me?'
- Nia hits the bottom. She's done. That's it. Time to climb into bed and pull the covers up.

Figure 12.15
Stress and worry are wearing her down.

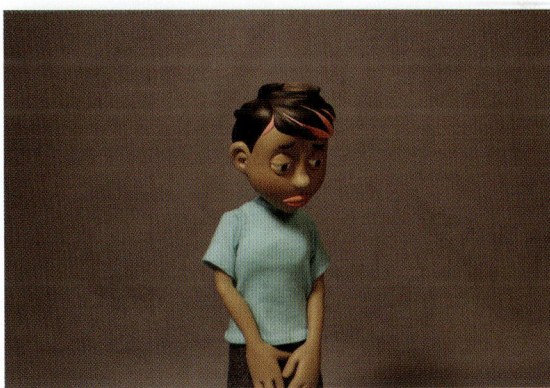

Figure 12.16
That's it.
Completely defeated, and in serious need of a hug.

It's tough work, animating a sad moment. You have to feel it, just like the character. Roy made this drawing to cheer you up, once you're done animating.

Performance suggestions

- It's true that the entire body's posing tells us a lot about how someone is feeling, but in this particular exercise, consider paying special attention to Nia's face. When someone is sad, we're inclined to focus on the person's face. We scan it as a way to find clues as to what's wrong. The eye area, in particular, will prove important.
- Let yourself feel it. Scenes that involve difficult emotions can be tough, but also strangely therapeutic. You go through it, just as Nia does, but then you come out of it at the end, unscathed. Nia will too.
- In comparison to the previous exercises, which carried within them a certain amount of outward energy, this one calls for slowness in Nia's movements. It calls for lack of energy, because Nia has none. She's spent it all. She's wiped out. She's done.
- Consider the word 'sinking' as you plan, and as you animate. Poor Nia's

only going in one direction in this one, and that descent is a very strong form of emotional arc.
- See what happens to the performance when you push it. Don't just make Nia a 'little bit sad'. Amplify the depth of her emotions. In the same way that you might make an animated action a bit exaggerated to make it come through more clearly, do the same with Nia's emotional state.

If you decide that Nia needs to shed a few tears in this exercise, you can use glycerin. It's a fluid-like gel, that looks just like water, but can be animated frame by frame with a toothpick or other similar tool. It's nice for stop motion, since it won't damage a puppet's paint job. You can also use it to animate water trickling down a window, or as slime on a monster's jaws! Now that's versatile. It's available at most drug stores.

Things to consider as you animate

- Allow yourself to be surprised by what you might find within the main emotion. Perhaps there's a touch of anger in Nia's sense of gloom? Regret? Shame? A dominant emotion can contain other facets, and if you can express all of that, you're creating some very complex performances.
- As you animate these darker regions of the human condition, what can you learn about the way that you handle these kinds of emotions? What do acting exercises like these teach you about yourself? And how can you bring that wisdom into further animation work?

Amazement

Figure 12.17
Ho hum.
Just another boring day in the stop motion studio.

Figure 12.18
Something new
What is that?!

Figure 12.19
Utterly remarkable!
Nia can barely believe her eyes!

From the looks of things, Nia seems to be feeling a bit better, at least compared to the last exercise! She's not so sad, at least. A bit bored perhaps? But that's all about to change.

This final acting exercise involves 'changing states'. That's when a character's dominant emotion transitions into a new one. These moments are great fun for the audience to watch, because they are literally seeing, before their very eyes, a character *progress emotionally*. It's like time lapse of a flower, opening its petals. Instant development! Which leads to instant audience satisfaction.

These moments also tend to cue the audience that the story is taking a new turn. Things are developing, and development keeps your audience engaged and connected to your project.

Direction

- This exercise once again makes use of an imagined off-screen character or situation. Have fun with what you imagine is going on off screen. Since you aren't actually showing it, you can surprise Nia with just about anything that you can dream up! It can be subtle, or wild (as you'll see below).
- A possible emotional arc for this exercise could be:
- Nia is minding her own business.
- Nia witnesses a UFO landing.
- Nia is dumbfounded, as the other-worldly visitors exit the spacecraft.
- Getting the emotional transition to work just right, in terms of its timing, is tricky on this one. It takes lots of playback, lots of flipping, and quite likely some deleting and re-animating until you get it just right. It's worth the effort though, since a clip of this nature, that's well-animated, will look great as part of your portfolio.
- This exercise will also benefit from very strong posing to convey 'amazement'. Make sure you have your poses clearly visualized, and possibly sketched out, before you begin animating.

Performance suggestions

- Transition between emotional states tends to read more clearly when there is a significant emotional distance to travel. If you perform Nia so that she's 'extremely bored' at the start, it will give her a long way to go in terms of acting, as she becomes 'extremely amazed'. Since it will happen fast, it will have a lot of energy to it, and will be exciting to watch.
- How does someone express 'boredom'? The body is relaxed, since there's nothing for it to do. Perhaps Nia scratches her head absent-mindedly … looks around a bit, casually.
- Her eyelids might be a bit droopy, while her eyebrows are probably low as well. Again, *relaxation* is the idea here.
- How does someone express 'amazement'? The body is alert and ready for action. Muscles get ready to act. The hands are ready to defend, or attack. The body leans inward, in order to bring the head closer to the situation, so that the senses can take in more information. Nia's eyes are vital now – the lids pull back to give maximum vision, as she tries to take it all in. The brows go up, and the mouth opens, as the jaw goes slack. Those must be pretty amazing looking aliens!

Things to consider as you animate

- This may be a chance for you to let things get pretty 'cartoony'. Research cartoon 'takes' which are basically variations on ways that a character can express sudden amazement. Then, experiment. Creating a modest sense of amazement is fairly easy – creating something intense and wild takes more planning, as well as more animation. They're also a lot of fun to create!

- How is the process of creating an acting exercise like this one, that's generally pretty fun and light, different from creating the previous exercise, that was pretty heavy and dark? Is one easier for *you* to create? Is one more satisfying for you as an animator, and actor? Everyone has different sensibilities, and being mindful of what you are learning about yourself as you work can help you to develop your own distinctive vision, and learn what kinds of scenes and stories appeal to you, personally.

Going further with acting exercises

- Come up with your own emotional states to explore. 'Friendly', 'Frustrated', and 'Gloomy' are just the beginning. What about all the other emotions that make up the human experience? You've just begun!
- Create more 'changing states' exercises, similar to the 'Amazement' exercise. Nia can transition between emotions that are very close to each other (imagine 'Flirty' transforming to 'Shy'), or between emotions that are extremely far apart (imagine 'Confused' giving way to 'Outraged'). As you prepare to create these transitions, be sure to carefully think through what is specifically causing these transitions. Being clear on this will provide you with greater confidence, as you perform through Nia.
- Try blending the concepts within the Puppet Smash exercise in the previous chapter with the acting exercises found in this one. The more that you can effectively mix complex physical actions with strong emotional performances, the more compelling your work will become.

If you aren't familiar with the idea of 'cycled' walks, take some time to research them. They aren't used that often in stop motion compared to drawn and computer animation, but when they are, they can save a lot of animation work. Just know that that they require careful planning and testing, to ensure their effectiveness.

Walks and runs

The time has come for Nia to throw off the tyranny of magnets (or tie-downs), and walk on her own two feet. Freedom at last! Nia is no doubt pretty excited about this opportunity, but hopefully she's not the only one. That's because a well-animated puppet walk is excellent proof that you're a dedicated and competent animator. It's proof that you can animate an entire puppet (not just an arm, or a range of parts) in a convincingly realistic manner. Not everyone can do that, so it's a real benchmark for your animation skills.

On top of that, once you are competent at animating walks, you'll be able to work them in to any of your action or performance animation, with fantastic results. Sometimes even a half step is all it takes to provide a huge amount of additional interest to a shot. Imagine the Puppet Smash Action Analysis from the previous chapter, only this time Nia takes a big, confident step into the downward swing. Or an 'Amazed' Nia, taking a cautious step forward towards something remarkable.

As exciting as animating walks can be, there's a reason why we've held off on attempting them until now. They require a solid amount of foundational animation skill if they're going to look professional. If you think back for a moment to the introductory exercises, we began with just one part (Nia's arm), being moved effectively through the frame. Now, as we tackle the walk, every single part of Nia will be moving.

As tricky as walks are to animate, there *is* a process that you can follow that makes them a bit easier to accomplish. A 'step by step' for walking, if you will. That process is laid out below, as well as some tips to help you as you learn. The good news is that since a walk is such a rhythmic (and therefore repeated) action, once you get the basic process straight, you can repeat that process with each new step.

The strongest piece of advice at this point (beyond the basic process) is this: just keep walking the puppet. I'm always amazed when I introduce students to the puppet walk. The first step that they animate is wobbly, and awkward … but the very next step is more confident and realistic. The next step is even more so, and so on. It's like watching some form of evolution, played out over a few frames! So keep going. Keep walking Nia. You'll see your progress almost instantly. Get feedback on that progress, take that feedback to heart, and then carry onward. It's endurance work, to be sure, but you'll be a much stronger stop motion animator if you stick with it, and it's *essential* for your overall success in the medium.

Basic walk

A basic puppet walk is really important to master. Once you can effectively create one, you can innovate on it, and create all sorts of walk variations. The walk laid out in the images below (and in the process underneath) is very basic. It contains no aspects of character – it's strictly mechanical. Get the mechanics of your walk sorted out first, and you'll then be able to add personality to that mechanically correct walk, in future attempts. What's depicted is also very limited in its style. If you create it using only the essential frames shown, it will play back very fast! But it's good

Figure 12.20
The basic poses
for a basic walk,
starting from a
resting position.

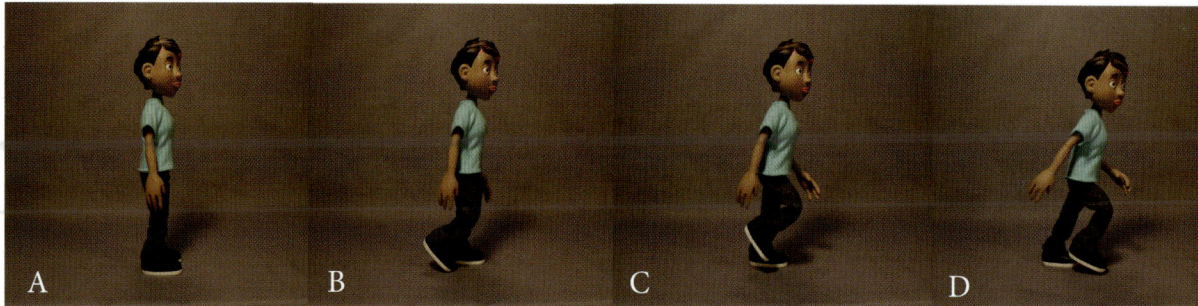

A   B   C   D

for a start, and once you have the hang of the process, you can create other attempts that will be much slower, and more nuanced, in a more 'full' style.

The following process assumes that you went with the magnet foot design for Nia, as laid out in Part 4. If you modified Nia to have a tie-down foot, you'll find that much of the following process can still be applied. You'll just need to plan out (and drill) your tie down holes, in advance.

As you prepare to animate, remember ABF, remember to play back your entire clip regularly, and remember that walking a puppet is a serious challenge, so be sure to pat yourself on the back a bit, for all that hard work!

Process

Since Nia only has one magnet in each foot, and since only one foot is ever fully in contact with the ground at any time, you only really need one magnet wand for a walk. But having an extra wand on hand can sometimes offer a bit more gripping power, if it's needed.

1. Position Nia in a neutral pose, similar to Figure 12.20A. Frame your shot wide enough so that Nia has a bit of room to walk forward a few steps. She's going to step forward with her right foot (the foot closest to the camera), so position the magnet wand under her left foot.
2. Capture a few held frames, just to make playback and looping a bit easier on the eyes.
3. With one hand, grip Nia's left foot very firmly, so that it won't shift on the deck. As you do this, bend the ankle on that leg forward, ever so slightly. When you flip frames, you'll notice that this single bit of tiny movement has had a big effect on Nia's position in the frame. Don't capture the frame yet.

During a walk, the puppet's ankle (on the foot that has the magnet wand attached) is almost always the 'boss' part, in terms of hierarchy. Adjust Nia here first, and then work your way up the rest of the puppet, working from the core parts outward to the extremities.

4. While ensuring that Nia's left foot stays securely in place, carefully bring her right leg forward (Figure 12.20B) You'll sometimes hear a walk referred to as a 'controlled fall' – a fall that is prevented by the front foot 'catching' the body. Remember that as you animate, and it will help you to keep your priorities straight. If Nia doesn't get her front foot out in front, she's going to fall on her face. Literally!

Since it's often supporting all of the puppet's weight during a walk, Nia's ankles are under a lot of strain. This pressure can lead to loosening of the set screws, or wearing away of the wire. Always check on these parts before attempting a walk, and be sure to keep them in good shape!

5. Now for Nia's arms. We'll keep their movement very simple and mechanical, and we'll only worry about a basic movement that originates mostly at the shoulders and elbows. In later attempts, you'll want to also use her wrists and even fingers to express character, but not now.

When adjusting her arms, it helps to regularly remind yourself of the term 'opposites

forward'. So if Nia's right leg is coming forward, then you need to bring her opposite (left) arm forward, too – opposites forward. If the left arm is coming forward, then the right arm has to be going back. It's surprising how easy it is to get lost in this, so just remember – 'opposites forward'.

Beyond Nia's arms and legs, there's really no need (on this basic walk) to pose the hips, spine, chest, or head. All of that is for later attempts.

6. Flip frames. Tweak parts accordingly. You may need to adjust the hips, spine, chest or head a fraction, but most of your adjustments will be to the legs and arms. Keep flipping, and adjusting. Be mindful of all the principles of animation. When you're happy, record that frame.

7. Onward, using the same process, as you create a frame that looks similar to Figure 12.20C, followed by a frame that looks similar to Figure 12.20D. Remember to get that front leg coming forward, and that front foot coming out with its heel sticking forward, in order to catch Nia's fall. Don't step Nia out too far – this will shift her mass out very far over the magnet, and she's likely to topple over! A short step works better.

8. As you create a frame that looks like Figure 12.20E, you can breathe a bit easier, because Nia's front foot has now stopped her fall. You should be able to actually feel the stability that this new pose provides her. Make sure that her heel is planted cleanly, at a crisp angle. This creates a strong pose that will contrast nicely with the next pose, when her front foot is fully planted. As for her arms, they should now be at their 'extremes', forward and back. Flip and adjust repeatedly until you're happy – then record.

9. Now that you're a bit rested, it's time for the trickiest point in the walk. This takes time, so be patient. To create a frame that looks like Figure 12.20F, you're going to need to swap the magnet from Nia's rear foot to her front foot. To do this, hold Nia in place by gripping her right foot and leg with your right hand. With the other hand, remove the magnet wand from the rear foot. Gently tip Nia forward, so that her front foot is now flat, and apply the magnet to that foot. Nia is now secured – but is leaning forward in a very crazy way!

Now for the hard work – starting at her ankle, you'll need to repose Nia. It's not as hard as it sounds, provided that you flip your frames a lot as you adjust, and be patient. And in fact, much of Nia will 'magically' repose, simply by adjusting that ankle. The absolute priority at this point is to ensure that Nia's front foot has not shifted. When compared to the previous frame, the front foot should simply be 'slapping' down on to the deck, in a satisfying fashion. It shouldn't be 'skating', either forward or back. If it has shifted, getting it back to the right spot is your priority. If it's not positioned correctly, no amount of posing is going to get Nia in place. And you will weep sad, bitter stop motion tears, I assure you.

10. Once you've captured the previous frame, and assuming that your blood pressure has stabilized, create a frame that looks like Figure 12.20G. With this frame, Nia's next step has begun, and you'll proceed onward, using the method already laid out, and the remaining images (Figures 12.20H and 12.20I) to guide you. Nia is officially off and walking!

If you're looking for a new fabrication challenge, consider devising and fabricating a hinged foot, which has a toe section that can be animated. If you do, remember that beyond the redesign and fabrication, you'll also need to cast Nia's foot in silicone, rather than resin, so that it's flexible.

Runs

If you can walk Nia, you can run Nia, since an animated run grows out of what you learned and applied during the walk. But in order to create an effective run, you need to keep a few important things in mind.

Clear and effective action posing is essential. That's because, as with any fast action, there simply aren't many frames in which to convey the run effectively. Take special care to suggest weight convincingly through these poses. To do that, once the forward foot is planted, that planted leg has to *really* bend down. It does this in part to absorb the energy from landing, but also so that it can then use that energy to launch forward and up. Show this pose clearly, and you're on your way to creating an effective run.

A convincing run also makes use of fairly aggressive movement through the frame. In other words, there's usually quite a bit of spacing between poses. If you don't cover a lot of ground between the strong action poses you're creating, the poses can start to 'stack up' on themselves, and the whole thing can very easily start to look otherworldly, in an odd, slow-motion sort of way.

In some ways, a run is sensed by the audience, rather than clearly seen. To get that 'sense of a run' across, you'll need to keep it very basic and obvious: clear posing, and cover lots of ground.

An additional challenge when learning and practicing an animated run is that they tend to look their best when the puppet is completely off the ground, at least for a frame or two. To achieve this, some form of rig is required, and that introduces certain complexities. You'll find out more about rigging Nia later in this chapter.

Figure 12.21
A simple foot rig.
This is a clever way to 'fake' Nia into the air when doing a run, without needing a formal rig. Just find a small piece of sturdy metal that is attractive to magnets, and bend it sharply to the angle shown. The flat piece can now be held by a magnet from under the deck. If you paint the rig to blend in with your ground, no one will even know it's there!

Action Analysis: A slow, relaxed walk

Now that you've had some time to practice the basics of the walk, it's time to push yourself to create a really nice portfolio piece, in the form of a slow and relaxed walk.

A slow walk is hard, since it involves a *lot* of animation. And relaxed is also hard, since it requires a looseness to the animation that can't really be faked. If you're tentative or unsure of yourself and your skills, a walk is likely to come out a bit stiff, or uptight – the exact opposite of relaxed.

Because this kind of animation exercise quickly reveals an animator's basic skills, it's quite often a required task during animation tests for projects. When that time comes, the more confident you are in your puppet-walking skills, the better your animation test will be.

> What this sort of effort *doesn't* show off is your acting and performance skills. Once you've nailed this exercise, create more walks that are also very high quality, but aim to express your acting and performance animation.

Direction

- The basic direction for this Action Analysis is utterly simple. From a relaxed resting position, Nia takes two natural, slow steps, and then comes to rest. That's it.
- The challenge lies in the quality of the animation. It needs to be slow, relaxed, and full. Let Nia have a bit of looseness to her limbs. She's just taking a few steps, no big deal (at least, that's how it should look, upon playback).
- In terms of what qualifies as 'slow', we won't impose a specific frame count. But upon playback, each step should take approximately one second to occur (so that's approximately 12 frames, per step). There's no need to precisely follow this, but it can help you as you plan things out. The slower, the better.

- Let this exercise take a few hours, if needed. You'll be glad that you invested the time, when you see how nice the animation looks.

Things to consider as you animate

- The camera can be a bit misleading. It's easy to lose yourself in posing and flipping frames, without realizing that the puppet is leaning away from the camera, and is about to tip over! To prevent this, keep an eye on the puppet as it proceeds across the deck, from all angles, not just through the camera's eye.
- Once you've animated a portion of the walk, you can literally count how many frames of animation that action required, and repeat it for the other leg. You can repeat both the number of frames, and the posing.
- Walks can be prone to having lots of little pops in them. As you flip, keep reminding yourself that a walk requires everything to move in the same direction across the screen. Even when an arm is swinging back, it's only swinging back in relation to other parts – it's actually still moving forward, as part of the entire body's movement. A nice walk should have smooth arcs, on all parts, all the way through.
- Now that your skills are more advanced, try to think of Nia as one organic, living, moving 'thing', rather than individual parts that need adjusting. Visualize the next pose in its entirety, pose the puppet accordingly, flip frames, and then correct the posing by adjusting any part that requires it. Think of it as 'macro' work, followed by a few 'micro' adjustments where needed. Once you've become practiced in this more advanced method, it can save you animation time, and can result in more fluid and expressive animation.

Troubleshooting

- When you stop Nia, remember that there is a *lot* of energy moving her forward by this time, and that energy needs to be dispersed. In other words, don't bring her to an abrupt halt. Decelerate Nia carefully, into her final pose, with various parts coming to rest at different times, in order to create a more complex and layers bit of animation.
- If you're struggling, is it because you're bending Nia's knee after impact? If you are, don't. At least not for this particular walk. Upon impact, a bent knee can add a lot of fun weight and bounce to the animation, but it also adds an incredible amount of complexity for animation, which is why it's not included in the process above. Of course, if you've been doing walks for a while, feel free to add the knee bend. If it's done well, it can look stellar.
- If the upper body is simply too much to handle, just take Nia apart! Loosen the set screw in her hip block that secures her spine, and voila – literally half as much puppet to worry about! Reassemble Nia when you're ready to bring her upper half back into the mix.
- Don't lean Nia too far forward as she walks. The more she is leaning forward, the harder she will be to control. The same goes for the length of her steps – the wider the step, the harder she will be to control.
- Always remember that you can sketch out the poses for the walk, before animation. As you sketch things out, it gives you some quiet time to really contemplate and visualize each part of the walk. Use the sketches for reference, as you animate.
- Just keeping walking Nia! It will seem like you're walking a million miles, because it will be hard work, but with every single step that you animate you'll get better. If you dedicate an entire day to walking Nia, you'll be amazed at your progress.

Going further with this exercise

- Once you get the hang of a basic walk, you can innovate endlessly. A few suggestions are depicted below to get you thinking, but why not try a 'tired' walk? Or a 'dizzy' walk? What does an 'elegant' walk look like compared to a 'cautious' walk? There's a huge amount of character that can be expressed through the way that someone walks, so set aside a good amount of animation time, and explore this area as much as you can. With dedication, you'll have even more solid portfolio work to show off, and you'll be an even stronger animator.

A bit of searching will provide you with lots of detailed breakdowns of various walks, and their main poses. Use them to guide you in your further efforts.

Figure 12.22
Proud walk.
The lower body for this walk would be much the same as a basic walk, but the upper body and head are handled differently.

Figure 12.23
Sneaky walk.
You'll need to take Nia down low and decelerate carefully into that 'low' pose, possibly even holding there for a beat, as she glances around. Then accelerate up and forward, only decelerating again once the new 'low' pose is reached on the next step.

Some animators find that using video reference is quite useful, especially when planning out complex human movements, such as walks. You can find footage that matches, or create your own. As you consider video referencing, remember that animation is an artistic representation of reality, distilled through the animator – it's not actual reality. Whenever possible, try to use video reference to clarify complex actions, and to inspire yourself, but then turn your attention back to creating a fresh performance through the puppet – one that expresses your own imagination, and your own body's understanding of movement, emotion, and physics.

Rigging the puppet

Do you know how hard it was to resist calling this section 'Getting Riggy With It'? Very hard. Anyway, if you want to make Nia jump, run, fly, or otherwise break free of gravity within a shot, you're going to need to rig her so that she can achieve that. But rigs aren't just used for 'off the ground' situations. You'll also make use of them for shots where Nia can't use her feet to get a secure grip. For example, she may need to be seated on a high chair, which leaves her feet dangling. By running a rig wire out of Nia's back from her rig point, you could secure that wire to a screw in the chair, and there you go – Nia is secured, and ready to be animated.

If you recall from way back in Part 1, you created rigging holes in the back of Nia's chest and hip blocks. To make a rig for these holes, you'll

Figure 12.24
Nia on a rig.
When a puppet simply must leave the ground, a rig is the solution.

Larger productions have staff within the puppet department that are specifically tasked with designing and fabricating very advanced puppet rigs, for just about any situation that an animator could face. Indie projects, on the other hand, need to be a bit more DIY!

need to gather some readily available materials and tools. The following images and their captions explain how to create a simple rig, using those materials. Since Nia has holes in both her chest and hips, you can use whichever rig point works best for any individual shot that you're are setting up.

To make a simple rig, you'll need:

a generous length of 3 mm (1/8 inch) armature wire
a 4.76 mm (6/32 inch) bolt, that's long enough to stick out a short distance from the armature block (I'd recommend taking an armature block to the hardware store and sizing it there)
a 4.76 mm (6/32 inch) wingnut
two small washers that fit snugly on the bolt
screwdriver (that matches the bolt's head)
wire snips
pliers

Figure 12.25
Basic hardware for a simple rig.
Assemble the hardware as shown, then screw the bolt into a rig hole on Nia's armature block. If the wingnut won't stay tight, you can replace it with a 'locking' nut (available at any hardware store).

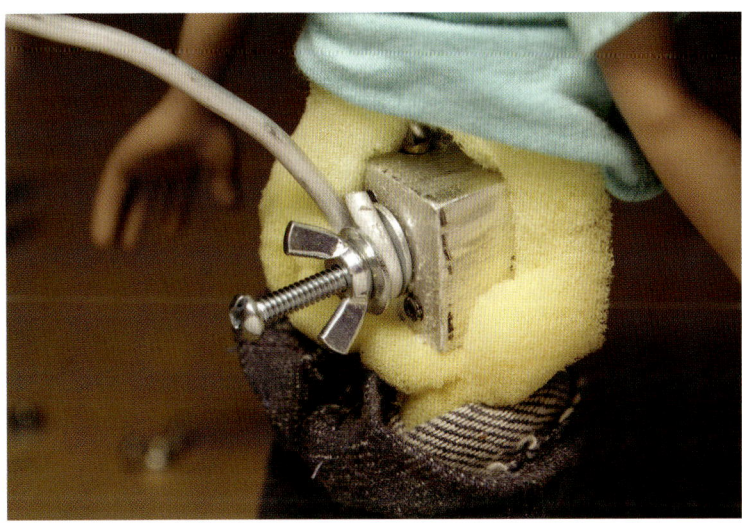

Figure 12.26
Rig in detail.
Make a tight loop in the end of the armature wire, secure it around the bolt *between* the washers, then tighten the wingnut. Secure the other end of the wire to a stand, and you have a rig. If the 3 mm (1/8 inch) wire is too stiff, use a thinner wire. You may need to rip a few stitches in Nia's pants to make things work, but that's easy to patch once you're done the rig shot.

As you practice animating with a rig, there's some important considerations to keep in mind:

- A good rig doesn't need to be fancy or expensive! It just needs to do its job effectively.
- A rig needs to support the puppet very well. The less drifting, swinging, or rebound in the rig, the better. Any of this kind of unpredictable or uncontrollable movement will drive you mad, as you try to battle both the rig and the other challenges of your shot.
- A rig needs to be stable all the way along its length. This includes where it connects to the puppet, the length of the rig itself, and its final anchor point. Any weak spots along the way are potential points of unwanted movement.

It takes patience to deal with rigs while animating. I always like to put significant effort into creating an effective rig prior to animating, and just as much time ensuring that it's strongly attached to the puppet, as opposed to slapping a wire on to the puppet and dashing into the shot.

Where there's a rig showing, there's a need to *remove* that rig! With this in mind, there are some best practices you should be aware of before creating shots that will require rig removal – and that's covered in Part 4, in Chapter 16 that focuses on Production.

Figure 12.27
Feathers, Group Film, 2016.
In this Sheridan College film, we see two examples of rigs. The flying puppet is rigged from above, and the box (that the flying puppet has knocked over) is rigged from below. In post-production, both rigs will need to be digitally removed.

> Whenever possible, hide a rig behind a puppet or set piece. If you can stage your shot so that the rig is completely invisible, there'll be no need to remove that rig during post-production.

RAY HARRYHAUSEN

There's no way a single box can possibly do justice to this legend – yet no other stop motion artist more richly deserves to be highlighted. Harryhausen's work spanned nearly six decades, during which time he created some of the most memorable and remarkable works of stop motion fantasy that cinema has to offer. His work combined remarkable technical skills with fantastic character animation abilities, and all of this work was created well before frame-grabbing and frame-referencing software was available. His importance extends well beyond the world of stop motion, as fantasy filmmakers the world over look to him as a primary influence, to this day.

Fixing the puppet

The most common repairs that you'll need to perform on Nia will involve replacing moving parts, due to broken wires. These breaks typically occur at the joint points in the wires, since that is where most stress occurs. If a wire is on the verge of breaking, you'll often be given notice by the wire, in advance of it actually breaking. The part will feel 'off' in the way that it responds to movement. This advance notice can allow you to think ahead, and sometimes still finish the shot, before starting in on your repairs.

When replacing a part, you may find that the brass end piece has become wedged in its hole. If that's the case, you can use sticky tack to draw it out. If that doesn't work, you can remove the associated set screw, and use a small nail to work the stubborn brass out.

Other times, force on the joints may cause the bond between the brass stock and wire to loosen. A drop or two of fresh glue will cure the problem – just be sure that you remove the part fully from the armature before gluing. You don't want to glue a part into the armature! If that does happen, you can use acetone to break down the glue.

> CA glue (the kind used to bond brass stock to wire) loses its effectiveness fairly quickly, once opened. Be sure to use the freshest glue possible, to ensure strong bonds.

If a small tear or break develops in the silicone of Nia's arm, it can be patched with a bit of patience, using the same method you followed when seaming Nia's arms. Refer to the section called 'Finishing the hands and arms' in Chapter 5 for a reminder on this process.

When a wire inside Nia's arm or finger breaks, performing 'surgery' isn't very practical. There's no efficient way to fix the wires, and to access them you'd have to do quite a bit of damage to the silicone. In this case, the easiest solution is to simply swap out the broken arm and replace it with a new one. You can always hold on to the damaged arm, because there may other situations where it could still be used. Part 1 of the book advised that you cast extra arms when you were in fabrication mode. If you didn't, or if you've used them up, it may be time to set up for a bit more moulding and casting. If you do set up, make as many arms as possible. Once cast, the silicone in Nia's arms stays viable for ages, so even if you don't use the replacement arms any time soon, they'll still be in good shape for whenever you *do* need them.

> If you need to perform a repair on Nia mid-shot, try to do it at a point in the shot when spacing is on your side – ideally in the middle of a large move. This wide spacing will make things a bit easier to get Nia posed back into place, after the repair.

Another common 'illness' for a puppet is minor paint scratches. You likely have touch up paint still standing by for Nia's shoes and head, but if you don't, you'll need to mix some up. Take your time mixing this so that its matches perfectly. Test the paint colour on hidden parts, because if the colour doesn't match, you'll only be making the damaged area more noticeable.

When doing a touch up, carefully clean the area first. Then, using a small piece of sponge and a *very* tiny bit of paint, carefully dab on the repair colour. Spread the layer of paint out (through gentle dabbing), and it should blend in nicely with the rest of the paint job. When it's dry, seal it in the same way that you sealed the part, during fabrication.

PAYTON CURTIS, FEATURE FILM ANIMATOR (PART 1)

Payton Curtis began his career working at a variety of Canadian stop motion studios, where he animated on commercials, music videos, and television projects (both series and specials). He then made the transition into feature films, where he worked on *Fantastic Mr. Fox, Coraline*, and *ParaNorman*. Most recently, Payton has established his own company, Mechanical Farm, which is located in Belwood, Ontario.

Payton and I had a nice long chat, so you'll find Part 2 of this interview at the end of Chapter 14.

Q. First, a fairly straightforward technical question. On features, do you shoot primarily on 1s or 2s? Or do you mix it up?

A. Primarily 1s, depending on the film. They had a wonderful idea on *Coraline*, which was that the 'real world' would be on 2s and the 'other world' would be on 1s, giving the two separate worlds a distinct look. The real world being a little choppy and the other being 'perfect' and smooth. Unfortunately, this idea was abandoned. Not really sure why. If you look closely, you'd see that many shots on the film are mixed 1s and 2s. They were used mainly for efficiency as scheduling was tight. On the other end of things, we shot *Fantastic Mr. Fox* entirely on 2s to give it a more 'rustic' or 'classical' feel. Only shots with a panning camera were done on 1s, to avoid the awful strobing that occurs if shot on 2s. On a big screen, a camera pan on 2s can be enough to give you a stroke.

Q. Another technical question – can you describe the general work flow for you, as an animator on a feature? To be more specific, can you take us through the process you would follow for ONE shot on a film, from beginning to end, in terms of your involvement.

A. Much is involved. You would first have a meeting in editorial with the director, lead camera, and editor. Going through the storyboard to find key gestures, character movement, facial expressions, dialogue, anything that may be needed for the current shot as well as the previous and following. Then it's off to the 'facial animation' department. These are the people charged with animating the character's dialogue and expression. I always had complete faith in their judgement – they are experts, after all. I always thought my strength lay in action, not dialogue, so it was a great relief to have a department dedicated to this.

You then talk with your camera team to figure out what is needed for execution. When shooting in 3-D, you have to make sure that your effect is going to work; without testing the 3-D camera, the entire shot could be blurry. The slightest error in distance the camera travels between the two exposures needed for 3-D can spell disaster. Worse thing is you only animate using one of the two 3-D exposures. So you don't notice the error until you've finished the actual shot. After action is established, you then move on to the puppet department to discuss exactly which puppets are required.

This then leads to a visit with the wardrobe department to make sure continuity is correct. Because you shoot out of sequence, your puppet may have just fell into a mud puddle, or ripped a hole in her jeans, just previous to the shot you're about to create, and wardrobe will ensure the costume is in its correct state. The slightest error in costume could mean starting all over again from scratch!

Then to the rigging department. If a puppet needs an aid moving through space, jumping, running or handling props, a member of the rigging team will come up with clever levers, winders, or pulleys to help your puppet defy gravity. These people are fantastic! Some of the most ingenious devices I've ever seen are conjured by these people and of course, in the final cut, all of their work is invisible! Then you go back on set with everything you've gathered and shoot a block.

A block (also known as a 'pop through') is the shot filmed on 5s or 10s (5 or 10 fps). It's a basic test to prove lighting, rigging, and animation are in sync. Also, the post effects wizards can spot any potential disasters or discuss a specific effect that may have been requested by the director.

After this, back into edit a second time to discuss the block and make any alterations before going back out to shoot a rehearsal if needed. This is a much more involved effort where you shoot on 2s or 3s, including facial expression and any other details that will be present in the final product. I personally prefer to just go for the shot.

Sometimes when you just 'wing it', you surprise everyone, and yourself, with a wonderful and spontaneous performance. I find that often when something is rehearsed over and over again, something is lost. The 'forest for the trees' conundrum. Henry Selick understood this perfectly. He always reminded animators fussing over their work to look at the bigger picture. 'Does it tell the story?' he'd often ask. If the story is weak or lacking, beautiful animation will make no difference, it'll just be 'lipstick on a pig'. Of course, if your spontaneous effort doesn't get a pass, it's back to edit to iron out the problems and go back for the third and final pass.

Q. You've mentioned that on *Coraline*, your approximate quota of animation that you had to deliver was five seconds per week. How did that break down, during a work week?

A. Those five seconds per week are only finished frames that end up in the film, no rehearsals or pop-throughs. Depending on the week, sometimes this was quite simple to achieve. Say for instance you have a single character who remains stationary, then five seconds is more than reasonable. In fact, it wasn't uncommon to double or even triple your quota in a week. On the other hand, a shot that is extremely difficult, for instance the floor disintegrating, and *Coraline* falling into the web, took weeks to plan. I worked with camera and rigging for ages, to prepare. So when we actually approached that shot, testing and correction took well over two weeks. Everything possible was done in camera, which can slow an animator down significantly. Then, quota can be a little tough to meet!

Q. In your experience, is the animation style of a film established as part of pre-production tests and run-throughs, with various

departments and crew consulting? Or is it something that firms up only once the actual shots are being turned in during production?

A. The style is supposed to be established by lead (or key) animators early on in production. But since the film takes a year to two to complete, many fresh new ideas or styles surface, and if possible are worked into the film. The best animated films in my opinion are seamless. You should not be able to tell who did what shot, a definite style should be set in stone very early on (Disney's Studio were masters of this). I think it's distracting from the story if style or character performance varies, especially in the main character.

Q. On the topic of animation styles for features, can you tell us a bit about how the styles are determined in terms of what directors convey to you? Is it all through example footage of previous projects, or through discussions? Through acting things out live, or letting animators go crazy for a while and then see what style is emerging, to then focus it from that?

A. It's a bit of everything you mentioned, really. It could be reference from old films, clippings from a magazine that show a certain pose, perhaps more and more animation tests … mainly though, once a hard line for a character is established, you play. By this I mean play it out, act it out, with the director, to see what works. Personally, I like to fumble through my work without live action reference. I've tried using live action reference, but I found myself spending too much time trying to mimic the reference footage rather than letting the puppet lead me.

Q. With so much going on around you, how do you stay focused, so that you can give the performance that you need to give?

A. I can really only stay focused while actually animating the shot. Until then, everybody is tapping you on the shoulder. When you are finally 'launched', everyone who helped bring it along, camera, rigging, sets, post, etc. leaves you to it. If I really wanted extra privacy on a tricky shot I would stay after hours when the building was empty. Very quiet and peaceful and absolutely no distractions, except for other animators. If anybody else is kicking around, it's nice to take a coffee break and discuss progress or problems. As everybody knows, a fresh set of eyes or perspective can be the quickest cure for a stale situation.

13

Animating dialogue

In this chapter, our focus will temporarily shift away from 'full body' animation towards a more specialized form of stop motion – animation dialogue. Yep, the time has come to (literally) give Nia a voice! In some ways, animating dialogue in stop motion is a bit easier than full body animation, since it places an emphasis on one part of the puppet specifically. Yet, as you'll soon see, it requires its own specialized form of concentration and dedication.

It's important to acknowledge that not all stop motion projects require dialogue. But mastering this method of animation is essential if you want to be considered a professional. Most television and feature film projects tend to be very dialogue heavy, and if you can't show your proficiency with animating dialogue, you'll be limiting your chances for success. Fortunately, animating dialogue is both fun and addictive (in a healthy way). In the same way that simply bringing a puppet to life is satisfying, seeing a puppet actually talk is a pretty magical moment. And of course, dialogue can add a huge amount of storytelling potential to a project, as well as performance opportunities.

By the end of this chapter, you'll have a solid practical understanding of how to approach animating dialogue in stop motion. And, with some practice, you'll have some very nice portfolio clips that will nicely show off your skills in this area.

These dialogue animation skills, when combined with all of the animation skills that you've amassed from previous chapters, mean that you'll be now be very well equipped to handle a wide range of animation challenges, as you move further into the medium of stop motion.

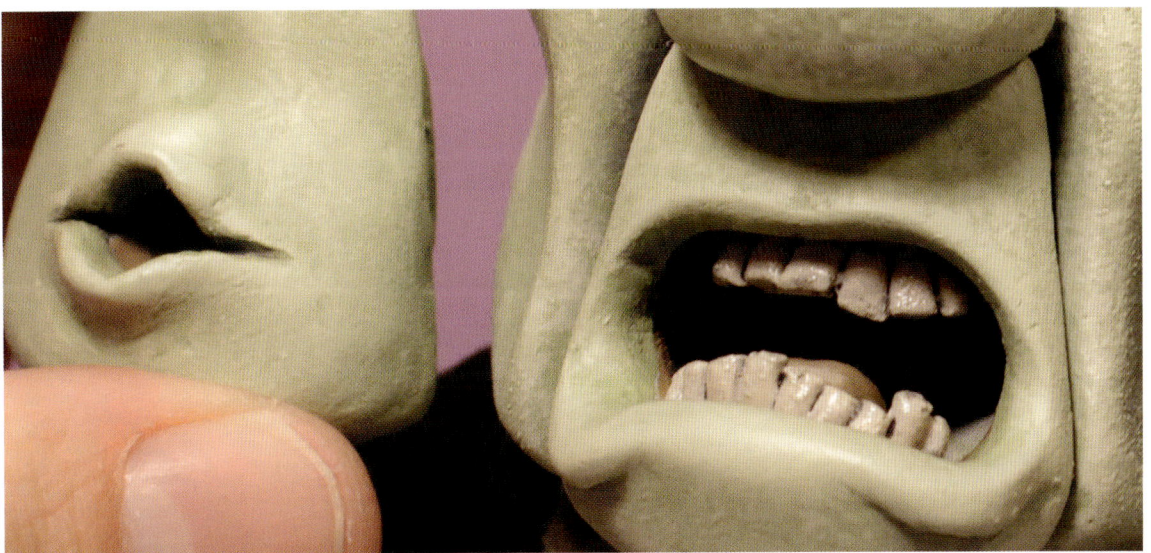

Figure 13.1
Replacement Mouths, Mad Lab Productions. Just one of the many ways to approach animating dialogue in stop motion.

Mouth animation vs. whole body

Figure 13.2
Basic posing with lip sync.
Here's Nia saying the line 'What have I done?' The voice acting might be great, and the lip sync animation might be accurate, but the flat posing doesn't convey much to the audience.

Figure 13.3
Strong posing with lip sync.
Nia delivers the same line of dialogue as in Figure 13.2, but it's now accompanied by stronger posing, which carries a lot more performance weight.

Sometimes, mouth animation for dialogue in stop motion can start to feel as though it's a separate and distinct 'thing' from body animation. That's partly due to the process that's typically used for dialogue animation; it's often pre-planned and structured, whereas body animation is able to follow a slightly more organic path. Also, creating mouth animation can seriously absorb your attention as you strive to get perfect synchronization. Then, with that sorted (at least for your current frame), you move your attention back to the rest of the puppet, to achieve the right pose. Again, this can result in a feeling like mouth animation is distinct from the rest of the puppet.

The key, of course, is to be absorbed by all of the animation as you are creating it. Lip sync is vital, but it can't come at the expense of overall animation quality. As you develop your skills at animating lip sync, try to always remember that the mouth needs to look good (which often means that it simply syncs up with the dialogue), *but so does the entire puppet*. A perfectly synced piece of dialogue animation isn't much fun to watch if the rest of the puppet has been neglected.

Being mindful of context can really help. As the animator, *you* may be very focused on choosing the mouth shapes that sync up the best, but what about your *audience*? Does it share the same specific interest? If the main focus of the shot is full body animation as Nia performs a very strong action, and if it's framed from a distance, your audience is going to be focused more on the big movements, as opposed to the relatively minor variations in mouth shapes. Alternately, if you're animating a close up shot of a puppet, and the emphasis is clearly on the mouth, then guess what? That mouth animation *has* to look great if only because the mouth will be so big in the frame! Context is king, but finding the balance between how much effort and energy to invest, and where to invest it, within a dialogue shot is vital.

The great thing about working with dialogue is that it often gives you obvious and natural acting moments that you can focus upon in your animation. Always look for points within the dialogue that are made more interesting by the voice actor. Perhaps the actor emphasized a certain word or phrase, or created an interesting pause or inflection at a certain moment. These spots are often natural locations where you can create some strong posing.

Dialogue can also greatly simplify the planning of a shot. If Nia is shouting 'It's over there!' the dialogue makes it pretty clear that you're going to animate Nia pointing in a specific direction, and doing that at a particular time, which will be when she hits the word 'there'.

Animating directly to the accent points or to the specifics of the dialogue is often

Figure 13.4
Mouth kits, *Life's A Zoo*, Cuppa Coffee Studios.
These replacement mouth shapes are in various stages of being painted. The more puppets you have, and the more complex their designs are, the more challenges you'll have when it comes to lip sync animation.

Figure 13.5
Life's A Zoo, Cuppa Coffee Studios.
The mouths in Figure 13.4 are now complete, and connected to the finished puppets. As you can see, when your cast consists of these many different creatures, your work is cut out for you when it comes to designing, fabricating, and animating lip sync!

necessary, but it can sometimes result in clichés, and in somewhat lazy performances – so be mindful. Try to explore contrasting or unexpected actions and poses, and see what they can add to the scene. It can be a really delightful moment, when you realize that that the voice actor delivered a line in a certain way, but now the puppet can perform it in a contrasting or surprising way.

As you practice this, you'll find that you're creating exciting and unexpected work, which develops out of the dialogue, rather than simply following along with it. Lip Sync Exercise 2: Acting and Lip Sync, will help you develop these skills.

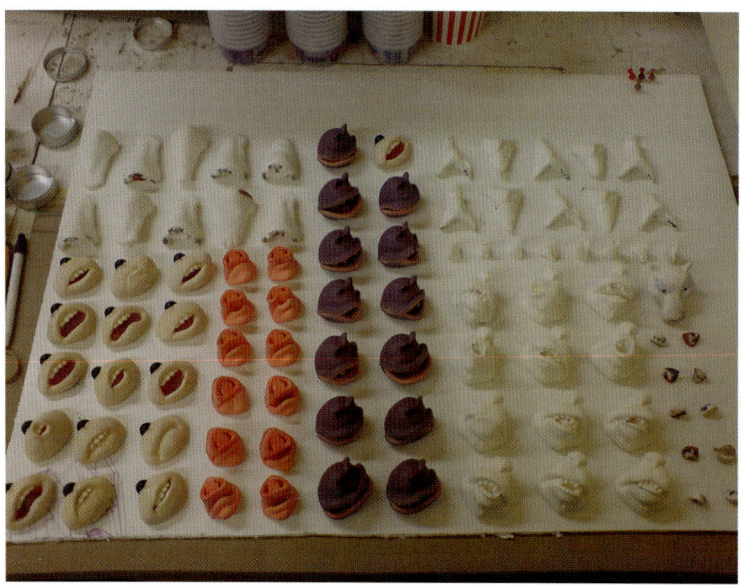

Basic workflow overview

Every animator will have a particular way of working with dialogue that's the result of personal tastes as well as personal experience. What follows is how I approach every shot that I create, if it involves dialogue. Feel free to modify this workflow for yourself – but it at least gives you a place to start!

This workflow is designed specifically with portfolio development in mind, in which the quality of the recorded dialogue isn't absolutely vital. If you're recording final audio for a film, you may want to approach things slightly differently, since you need very high quality recording (you'll find more on recording quality below).

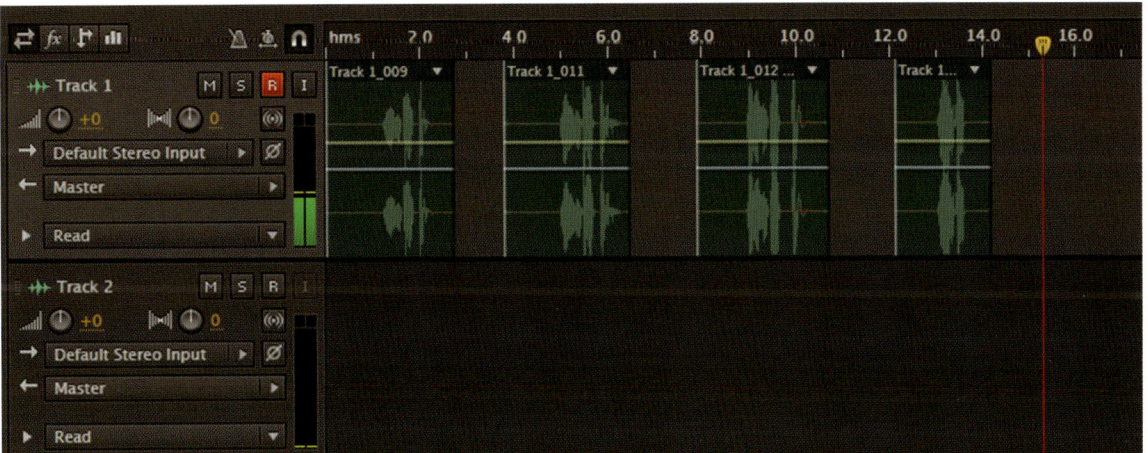

Figure 13.6
Multi-track
recording in
Audition.
In this multi-track
setup, Track 1
is being used
for 'practice'
recordings of a
line of dialogue,
while Track 2
will be used
for 'actual'
recordings, once
the voice talent is
warmed up.

1. Record dialogue in Audition (or similar software).
2. Import dialogue into Dragonframe.
3. Use Dragonframe to break down your audio on to an x-sheet.
4. Make note of required mouth shapes on the x-sheet, beside the corresponding moments of dialogue.
5. Rehearse the shot's actions and acting, while playing back the audio.
6. Make further notes on the x-sheet, as needed.
7. Animate!

PENNY CARTOONS, PEE-WEE'S PLAYHOUSE, 1986–1990

This is a series of charming animated shorts that were created by Aardman for this iconic live-action television show. Each cartoon features a clay girl with coins for eyes, named Penny (get it?), who tells the viewer about aspects of her life. Since she talks a lot directly to the camera, these clips involve a lot of lip sync animation. As you watch, notice how the main mouth shapes are emphasized through the animation. Then be sure to cancel anything you have planned for the next days, because once you watch a bit of *Pee-Wee's Playhouse*, you'll be hooked, and need to watch the entire series!

Recording dialogue in Adobe Audition

Audition is a very reliable, professional, and affordable audio recording software, that can handle all of your stop motion needs. To be clear, if you have a different audio recording software package available to you, you don't have to use Audition – use whatever works! It is vital that the software creates audio files that can be read by Dragonframe, so do your research.

The process in Audition for dialogue recording is pretty basic: you set up a file, you press 'Record', you perform your dialogue (or have your actor perform it), and there you have it. Of course, to ensure that you are recording effectively, it's a little bit more detailed than that, so Audition has a very useful Help Menu. There's also lots of support online if you run into trouble, or need to clarify thing further.

Depending on what version of Audition you're using, the basic steps needed to set yourself up may differ somewhat from what follows, since software is always getting updated. Help Menus and online resources are always standing by to help!

STEP BY STEP

1. If you're using an external microphone, make sure that it's properly connected to your computer.

2. Launch Audition, go to the File menu, and create a New Multitrack Session. This multiple track option allows you to organize your recording somewhat, so that you don't have dozens of takes in one massively long file. For example, you can put practice recordings on Track 1, and when you're ready, you can switch to Track 2 for proper recordings. Structure your session however you want, but rest assured that regardless of which track you record on, all of your recordings will be accessible later in the process.

3. If you're using an external microphone, you may need to tell Audition to recognize it. Do this by going to Audition Preferences, then to Audio Hardware, and look in Default Input. Select your external mic from there.

4. On Track 1, click the small square button marked 'R'. This button readies the track for recording. You should see the Monitor Input come to life, which indicates that your microphone is ready to go (see Figure 13.7).

5. When you're ready to record, just click the red button that's located towards the bottom of the main window. You're recording!

6. When you're done, click the record button once again to stop recording. If you navigate to the folder in which you've saved the file, you'll see each recording listed as.wav file. It's this file that you'll take into Dragonframe as you move onward.

Ideally, your recorded dialogue should be neatly 'trimmed', with no unwanted space or unwanted audio on either side of the dialogue. This can be done in Dragonfame, but it's more professional to trim it in Adobe Premiere (or other editing software). If you're not sure how to do this, refer to Chapter 15 in Part 4 that's dedicated to pre-production.

As you record, there are some basic best practices that can help you get better results:

- Record in a location that is as quiet as possible. Turn off fans, air conditioning, and anything else that might cause background noise.
- If you're using an external microphone, make sure that you're quite close to it when recording. Do some tests, to ensure that your recording is coming through properly. Use the Input Monitor to help with this. Your volume when recording should never go into the 'red' on the meter.
- To ensure that the volume of your recording is decent, don't listen to it played back through headphones. Instead, use the computer's speakers, with their volume set appropriately.
- Get in character! You may not be a professional voice artist, but you might be pleasantly surprised by what you can achieve. Other people are only going to hear your final (good) takes, so don't be shy. Remember that you'll need to animate to this dialogue and it's more interesting if there is some range within the recording. Don't just say the lines – perform them. Think the lines through, and discover ways to make them interesting and dynamic.
- Always record a variety of takes, so that you'll have more to choose from later on.

Audition has a range of effects that you can apply to voices. Want to sound like a robot? Or a squeaky mouse? Play around in the software, and search for online tutorials, to find out more about the fun that you can have playing around with voice effects. It opens up a whole new world of performance opportunities.

Figure 13.7
USB Microphone.
Very high quality microphones such as this one made by Blue are relatively affordable (under $100 CAN), plug directly into your computer via USB, and can provide great results.

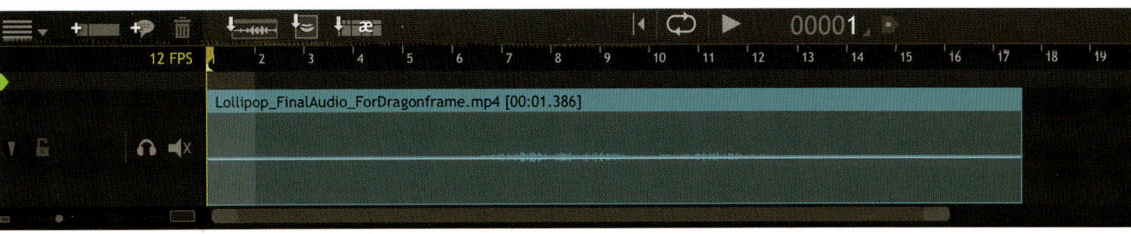

Figure 13.8
The audio
workspace in
Dragonframe.
Here's the
recorded audio
for the first Lip
Sync exercise
(see below) once
it's imported into
Dragonframe.
Notice how the
sound is now
associated with
specific frames
of animation.
You need
frame-accurate
representation, to
break down your
dialogue.

Microphones

Most laptop computers come equipped with built-in microphones that can provide a basic recording that will let you grab some dialogue very quickly so that you can get animating. However, the results will likely sound pretty hollow and with a lot of distracting background hiss.

If you want to be more professional, you'll need to secure a higher quality microphone (and by 'secure' I mean buy, beg, or borrow). Fortunately, these are good days to be in the market for an affordable, high quality microphone. As a result of digital audio's continued growth, there are now fantastic microphones out there that serve the needs of professional podcasters, musicians and voice artists. These mics are extremely easy to use, are quite affordable, and provide great results. If you can afford to buy your own, it can be a great addition to your studio. You'll be able to record audio (dialogue and sounds) whenever you need to, and if you set things up carefully, you can get very professional results that can be good enough for serious projects.

If you're going to use one of these mics to record for a film, you'll find lots of online tutorials that can help you to maximize the quality of home recording, so do your research.

Breaking dialogue down in Dragonframe

So far we've only considered Dragonframe's ability to help you set up your camera, and to help you animate. But the software is also designed to handle dialogue. In just a few simple steps, you'll be preparing (or 'breaking down') the dialogue that you just recorded in Audition so that you can begin mouth animation.

As you follow this process, you'll notice that it's tailored to working with a physical x-sheet, but if you prefer to work digitally, you can modify the process accordingly. X-sheets were looked at in detail in the previous chapter, so refer back, if you need a refresher.

STEP BY STEP

1. Open a file in Dragonframe. In the Animation Workspace, make sure that you are working at 12 FPS.
2. From the Window menu, select 'Show Audio'. You'll now see the Audio Workspace icon as an option in the top right corner, alongside Animation and Cinematography. Switch to the Audio Workspace.
3. Import the dialogue that you recorded in Audition. To do this, click the 'Import Audio' button. If you aren't sure what button this is, hover over the buttons to get a pop-up label. Once imported, you'll see your dialogue displayed as a timeline (see Figure 13.8.) This timeline shows you specifically how long your dialogue is in frames.
4. Fill in your x-sheet with the same number of frames.
5. Take a minute to play around with how Dragonframe lets you interact with the dialogue. Do this by 'scrubbing' (sliding back forth) along the timeline, either by using the arrow left and right keys or by grabbing the slider. Scrub slowly to hear your dialogue in slow motion, and scrub faster to hear it closer to full speed.
6. You now need to 'break down' the audio on to the x-sheet. You'll use this breakdown guide to help you select Nia's mouth shapes, and you'll also use it as a general guide, during animation. Starting at the beginning of the dialogue, scrub along until you hear the first part of the first word, then make

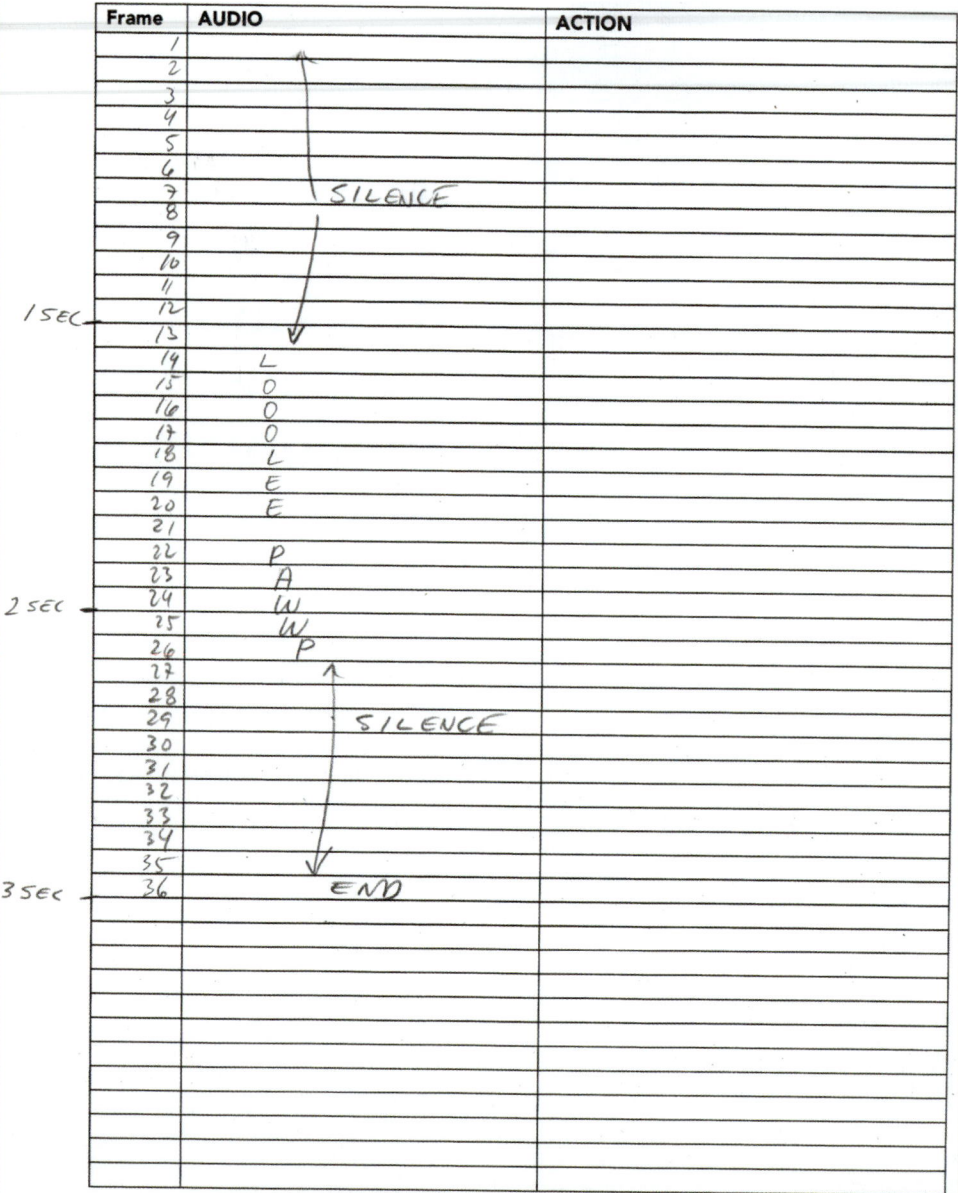

Figure 13.9
Dialogue breakdown.
Here you see the breakdown for the first Lip Sync exercise (see below). This illustrates just what a breakdown looks like, but remember that the specific frame at which each sound occurs in your recording will depend on *your* specific recording!

note of that sound at the same frame, on the x-sheet. Figure 13.9 gives you an idea of what your x-sheet should look like, as you break things down.

7. Carry on like this throughout the entire dialogue. Some animators like to be extremely detailed in their breakdown, while others prefer a more relaxed approach, knowing that they will 'firm it up' during animation.

8. Once you've broken some dialogue down, play it back several times at full speed and compare it with what you're seeing on your x-sheet notes. Scrub it some more as well, to confirm that you've transcribed things accurately.

Selecting mouth shapes

With your dialogue broken down, you now need to select which of Nia's mouth shapes will work best for each moment of dialogue. When we were designing and fabricating Nia's mouths, you would have worked through the various mouth shapes needed for your kit (either the basic one depicted in Figure 4.26 or something more detailed). Refer to that kit now, as you work through the broken-down dialogue on your x-sheet. Move from start to finish, and as you move through the dialogue, make a note of the mouth shape that will be used to convey that particular sound.

> If you change a mouth shape a frame or two *before* you actually hear the sound, it tends to look more accurate. Play around with this off-setting through your own tests, to get a sense for what looks best.

This process of effectively selecting mouth shapes takes practice. Assign too many shape changes, and you'll have a constantly buzzing distraction. Assign too few, and you'll still have a distraction, but now it's because your animation is wooden and stiff. Assign the wrong shapes, and once again, your audience is distracted, as it tries to figure out what's wrong with the lip sync. Keep

> There's an alternative method of mouth animation that you can explore with Nia, which involves applying digital 2d mouth shapes. Create these shapes by either drawing them physically and scanning or photographing them, or by drawing them digitally. Crop the mouths in Photoshop and save them as.png files, then bring them into Premiere and apply them to Nia's blank mouth area, frame by frame, in accordance to the dialogue.
> Just be aware that although this method can speed up on-set animation time, it adds significantly to post-production.

Roy doesn't normally have a mouth, but in the interest of cheap comedy, we thought you should see what he'd look like if he did.

it modest but accurate, try not to overthink it, and you'll be allowing your audience to pay attention to the more important things within the shot, which is typically the body and facial acting.

Fortunately, as with so much in stop motion, the proof is right there on screen for you to quickly learn from. If it looks and sounds good during playback, you're doing it right. If it doesn't, you'll know, and you'll be able to fix it before carrying on.

NICK PARK

One of the most recognized stop motion artists out there, Nick Park's remarkable work has been essential to the ongoing success of Aardman Animation. His characters Wallace and Gromit are among the most-loved stop motion characters we have, serving as a constant reminder of how deeply charming the medium of stop motion can be. His work is wonderful for all kinds of reasons, but when it comes to animating dialogue, Park has the ability to make mouths actually fun (and funny) to watch. Study all of his projects, and think about the careful planning and attention to detail required to get such perfect performances.

Viewing audio while animating

Dragonframe's dialogue animation tools aren't limited exclusively to the breakdown stage; the software also offers great help during animation as well. With dialogue loaded, you'll be able to hear the dialogue as you flip, during animation, and you'll be able to flip ahead to hear what sound is coming up. Your x-sheet will provide you with the same information, but it's really good to be able to hear this while animating.

You can also *see* your audio, as you're animating, which is also a great help.

In the Animation Workspace, you'll find a button near the bottom right of the main window that will display the loaded audio at the bottom of your animation window. This is extremely useful for keeping mouths on sync, since you can effectively see 'into the future' of your shot's audio.

Make use of this option, while also referencing your x-sheet, and you'll be creating very nice lip sync animation in no time. Of course, that's assuming you put in some dedicated practice. Fortunately, the following exercises are designed to help you do just that!

> Depending on your comfort level and the complexity of the dialogue and the shot, you might not need to perform all of the prep work that was described in this section. Instead, you could simply import your audio into Dragonframe, display it your Animation Workspace, and select Nia's mouth shapes as they are needed, while you animate. It very much depends on how detailed you want (or need) to be with your dialogue planning. Whatever works for you, and the project!

Lip sync exercise 1: Lollipop!

Just as we began our animation exercises with the relatively simple arm extension, we'll start our lip sync exercises in a way that introduces the basics. With just a single word, you'll learn a lot about the practical process of animating for lip sync in stop motion.

Obviously, you'll need to find a voice actor for Nia (for this exercise, as well as the next). This could be yourself, or you may need to enlist the help of a generous voice actor, which in this case can be a friend, roommate, or family member.

Why the word 'lollipop'? Mostly because it consists of several syllables, and because it requires a nice range of mouth shapes for it to read effectively on screen – all of which means that it's a good challenge.

Direction

- For this exercise, you'll want to frame Nia in a close up shot, so that her face is of central interest.
- Since this is an intro exercise, it should just be about lip sync. Don't worry about facial animation or body animation just yet (that will come next). Beyond nailing the lip sync, this exercise is also a chance for you to work through the various stages that were laid out earlier: you'll need to record the dialogue, break it down on an x-sheet, assign mouth shapes, and then animate it.
- A note on recording the dialogue: don't worry if the delivery of the line isn't that dramatic, at least not for this exercise. But do make sure that it's very clearly pronounced, with each specific part of the word emphasized. For exercises like this one, it's often a good idea to actually over-emphasize the sounds and shapes when recording, so that it's a bit easier when animating to connect sounds to mouth shapes. In other words, if you were writing the word as you'd want to record it, it might look like this: 'Loool-eee-Pop'.
- It won't sound completely realistic, but it will be good for this exercise.

Things to consider as you animate

- Remember, the proof is on the screen, during playback. If the mouth shapes work, and if they sync up, then you're good. If they don't, delete frames, adjust your notes, and go again. Fortunately, it's a very short piece of dialogue, so creating numerous attempts shouldn't cause you too much grief!
- ABF is as vital during animation for dialogue as it is for action and acting!
- In the previous chapter, I mentioned that a mouth shape can finish off a bit of dialogue, by animating the final shape (usually a resting mouth shape) for a few frames, as it finds its final location on Nia's face. Now's the time to see how it looks! Try it at the start of the dialogue, as well.

Troubleshooting

- Does the mouth animation seem overly busy? Maybe you're simply trying too hard, and forcing more shape changes than the eye cares to see.
- During playback, the mouth shapes should match up very well, in terms of sync. If they don't, you might be changing shapes too soon, or too late, or you might have made some poor choices when selecting your shapes in advance. Take your time, and keep trying. It's just one word, so you'll get it, with practice.
- It's easy to 'zoom in' so much with your attention while animating mouth shapes that you become overly critical and uptight. Take a well-earned break, and watch your attempt later, this time looking at Nia's face overall, and not focusing too much on the mouth. The main thing is that the mouth animation matches up nicely, and that it's not distracting.

Going further with this exercise

- Create another attempt, and see if you can get it to read with less mouth shape changes. Often, you don't actually need as many mouth shapes as you thought you did, when planning things out. You can think of it as 'full' animation when you are using a lot of mouth shapes, and 'limited' if you are just getting the basic idea of the movements across. Knowing how to achieve both is important.
- Go for it again, but put away the x-sheet. Just try it with the dialogue loaded into Dragonframe (and viewable in the Animation Workspace), and your mouth kit standing by. Make full use of ABF, and be sure to playback regularly. You might be surprised at how easy animating dialogue can be (at least with a simple line, such as the one used in this exercise).
- Record a new line of dialogue, this time a longer one, and go through it all again! You might even want to record a short sentence that you can animate, now that you're getting the hang of it.

Working with dialogue gets easier with practice. Your ears will get used to hearing words slowed down, natural moments in the dialogue that can work with poses will become evident more quickly, and you'll get more precise at picking mouth shapes that work for each sound. Keep practicing!

Prima Donna Replacement Faces

Seema Virdi

seemavirdi@gmail.com
seemavirdiportfolio.blogspot.com

Figure 13.10
Mouth kits, *Prima Donna*, Seema Virdi, 2013. The perfect mouth kit for a cartoony and comedic film about an opera singer! Since the character only sings, there was no need for 'talking' mouth shapes. Why make dozens of mouth shapes that won't even be used in the film?!

Lip sync exercise 2: Acting and lip sync

Now that you have the basic process of getting Nia's mouth shapes to sync up to dialogue, it's time to move your skills further along by leaps and bounds. Now, on top of ensuring that you're maintaining lip sync, you'll need to get solid acting into the mix, through both Nia's facial features and her full body.

This one asks a lot of you, and if you can make it happen, it will be time to celebrate. That's because this challenge is essentially a culmination of the skills developed in this section. So do some stretches, make sure Nia's all tuned up, and get ready for some serious animation!

Direction

- The most sensible framing for Nia on this exercise is one that shows her entirely, so that she has room to perform. Don't worry, the details of her mouth animation will still show up, even if she's framed from a distance.
- The first thing you'll need to do is select the line of dialogue that you want to use. You can use one of the suggestions listed below, or come up with your own. If you're going to create your own, just make sure there's some emotional state being expressed within the dialogue, so that you'll have more to work with in terms of performance, during animation.
- Here are some suggestions for lines of dialogue, but feel free to write and record your own. You'll notice that many of the emotions they convey are similar to the emotions that you animated in the previous chapter.
  - 'Hey! It's so nice to see you, it's been forever!'
  - 'No, that's not what I meant at all! You're totally putting words in my mouth!'
  - 'Ugh. Pizza, milkshakes, and roller coasters do *not* mix well'.
  - 'Why me? Seriously. I'm asking you. Why me'?

- 'Am I insane, or is that an alien spaceship?'
- Remember, your voice actor doesn't have to be a professional to provide you with something dynamic and interesting. And if the final result isn't going to win any acting awards, don't worry – it will be absolutely fine for this particular context.

As an alternative to recording your own lines, you can find a few lines of dialogue from a favourite movie. Choose something that will offer you a range of poses and expressions to explore, and that's not too complicated or lengthy (at least for now).

- Record your dialogue, and break it down on an x-sheet in the same way that you did in the previous exercise. Then, as you review the dialogue, work out your acting. In the same way that you planned out performance points along an emotional arc in the previous chapter's exercises, plan out strong moments now, only this time with the dialogue as your guide. Ensure that you have some clear poses in mind that work with the audio (either directly, or by creating some kind of interesting contrasts).
- The planning out stage for this exercise will take some time, since there's quite a bit to think through. Time invested up front in planning can actually save time once you get animating, since you'll have greater confidence and be able to roll onward without second guessing yourself. Be sure to put all of your well-developed visualization skills to work on this one, as you think it all through.
- Once you are confident that your 'full body' animation is going to work for the scene, do the same for any facial animation. With that accomplished, you can move on to planning out your mouth shapes. Make notes on your x-sheet as needed, check it all through once more, and then it's time to animate.

Things to consider as you animate

- Working in a procedural way on this exercise can be helpful. I typically like to pose the puppet's body first, and ensure that's positioned effectively, in accordance with the dialogue (and the x-sheet, if I have any posing notes). Then I'll adjust any facial features that require animation, again flipping to make sure all is well. Next I'll think about mouth shapes, and I'll consult my x-sheet once more for applicable notes. After tending to the mouth animation, I'll flip again, this time focusing my attention on that area, and listen for how it syncs up. I flip some more, this time looking at the whole frame, and once I'm happy, I record.

- Do you find animating with dialogue a lot easier in terms of acting, compared to acting in the previous chapter that had no dialogue? If so, maybe it's because you now have clear points of interest to focus your acting and posing upon. Or maybe you find it harder? It can be quite tricky to try to hit all those dialogue points, as opposed to just 'flowing' through an emotion, as you did previously.

- With Nia's mouth smaller in the frame than it was in the previous exercise, you'll likely find that there's less attention paid to the mouth, when you play the clip back. And since her whole body is acting now, this further reduces how much we notice her mouth. That's something to bear in mind, when animating dialogue in the future.

- Always consider what your audience is truly paying attention to – and then focus your energies there.

- As you plan, and as you animate, try to create contrasting or unexpected poses, actions, and reactions, which offer new complexities or 'shading' to the dialogue. You don't want to stray too far away from the true intention and purpose of the dialogue, but finding unexpected and exciting ways through it can be one of most exciting parts of animating these kinds of shots.

Troubleshooting

- Does the finished clip play back with a bit too much frantic energy? Perhaps you used too many poses in your desire to make the shot as exciting as possible. Remember that with the addition of dialogue to your animation, the audience isn't just watching now, it's listening, too. That's a *lot* of information to take in, so sometimes limiting the visual energy within the animation can help the entire shot come through more clearly.

- Maybe your finished shot has too much emphasis on the mouth animation, and not enough on the body? This might result in your shot feeling a bit 'talky', and result in it looking a bit, well … boring. Live and learn. Next time, make a point of getting some more visual interest going in Nia's body animation. Finding a balance between too much going on, and not enough, will come with practice and experience.

- When you play the shot back after completion, is the entire screen black? If so, you probably left the lens cap on the camera for the entire shot. Set Nia down carefully, and go have a nap, because you're obviously deeply sleep-deprived.

Going further with this exercise

- Now that you are effectively creating animation that involves acting and dialogue, you can go where you want with things. Record different dialogue that conveys a very different sense of emotion, and animate that.

- If your acting style in the clip is fairly natural, create another attempt, only this time with the specific intention of making the acting 'bigger'. The dialogue will remain the same, obviously, but amplify your poses and gestures – let it be 'cartoony'. You may find that this take is more effective than the more 'natural' one. Or you may find that it's silly, and too obvious. Either way, you'll be solidifying your own personal acting style as a result of pushing yourself in this sort of way.

Figure 13.11
Halloween Project, Mad Lab Productions.
Here's a puppet that was created through my production company, that makes use of replacement mouths. Note how the creases on either side of the nose act as a perfect place to hide the seams for the replacement pieces.

As you carry on working with dialogue in animation, remember the importance of context. If the details of the mouth animation are vital to the shot, then focus your effort and talent in that area. If the main area of focus is not on the mouth animation (which is often the case), your main challenge with the mouth is to keep the animation free of distraction, so that the audience can focus on what's important.

The creative challenge of figuring out how to make a stop motion puppet talk effectively is a fantastic one. There are clay mouths, hinged mouths, cg mouths, paper mouths, or replacement mouths that are similar to Nia's in terms of animation methods, but that are far more complex in terms of design and fabrication (see Figure 13.11). If you find yourself really excited by dialogue animation, and by what different kinds of mouth designs can offer, you might want to revisit Part 1 of the book. Now that you're clearer on the animation process for dialogue, you're better equipped to think about more advanced mouth animation solutions, that might work with different kinds of puppet heads.

But don't go back to Part 1 yet! In the next chapter, you're about to have the opportunity to show off just about everything that you've learned thus far. Your puppet making skills, your lighting and camera skills, and of course, your animation skills are about to be put on full display. It's a chance to show yourself off as a veritable stop motion mountain of talent. You don't want to miss out on that, do you?

- Animating in stop motion is like a live performance and regardless of how much you plan, it can and will take on a life of its own. The more prepared you are before you shoot that first frame, the more you can alleviate the stress of trial and error once you're into a shot. This will leave you more time to focus on executing your best performance.
- Get in touch with professionals. Spend time learning about various studios and individual artists that are producing stop motion animation and become familiar with the style and content. This is a small world and many people in the stop motion community travel all over to work on different projects together, so understanding who you're working with, their skills and styles can be invaluable for a future point of reference. Find studios or projects that you admire and that inspire you, and contact the animation supervisor or recruiting department to introduce yourself. Have a prepared website that includes a demo reel or student film and résumé posted online for them to view easily. In some instances, you may be able to set up a studio visit or a test.
- There are many cases where a student film has opened up an opportunity for a job, sometimes it's in animation but sometimes there is another skill that gets you in the door. Even if there isn't currently a job or internship prospect available at that time, meeting people and seeing the space or caliber in which they work can be an inspiration and a good starting point.
- Develop your acting skills. Coming from a theatre and performance background, I learned that when breaking down a scene with actors, everything ultimately comes from intention or objective. We learned to ask ourselves about the relationships, what is happening in the scene, why does each character do what they do, and how do they get what they want. There is generally more opportunity for complex acting on a feature, although sometimes there are genuine acting moments on a series where this can be applied. As a character animator, this is your background work – sometimes you get this from the director, but like an actor, you must come to the table with your own set of tools.
- Practice, and be curious. Always add to your knowledge and visual memory bank. Get your hands on to puppets to practice and improve your skills as often as possible. Spend time observing daily life and be curious about how to animate everything from emotional subtleties to quick fleeting actions. There's a natural curiosity for animators to spend time clicking through an interesting shot frame by frame to figure out how it was done. If I'm curious about a movement, I find myself pausing live action or animated films and clicking through frame-by-frame, taking mental notes on tricks and ideas to try.
- Follow direction. Every project is different in terms of budget and style, but the one thing that must be consistent is your ability to execute what you are being asked to do. Ultimately, your job is to animate what the director wants. There are still many opportunities to add your input as the animator. In some cases, you may be asked for your creative input or given the reins to bring ideas about the shot to the table, but the main focus should be on achieving and capturing the director's vision, not your own.
- The best way to find freedom in your work is to develop trust with the director. Once the foundation of this relationship exists, you will have the confidence and platform to push your work to new levels.

14

Putting it all together:
The showcase shot

As this chapter begins, you're at a pivotal point in your training. You've acquired a serious amount of practical skills in a wide range of stop motion areas, and the time has come to put all that together. As you might imagine, the 'putting together' is going to happen in front of the camera, for your audience to enjoy. More specifically, it's going to take the form of *one* beautifully planned and executed shot.

But this chapter isn't *just* a summary of your many stop motion skills; it also presents you with a final important challenge. You've proven that you can create performance animation involving *one* puppet, but can you achieve the same results with two?

Proving this is essential, because animated interactions between characters is a big part of many projects, whether it's an indie effort or a major commercial production. As for who these two characters are, Nia is one of them (of course), while the other is someone you're about to meet for the first time.

By the end of this chapter, you'll have a solid showcase clip that will clearly convey to your audience the depth and breadth of your stop motion skills. And as a result of the steps required to create this showcase clip, you'll also have a deeper practical understanding of the process that professionals use when they tackle the same kinds of shots in their daily lives.

Finally, and perhaps most importantly, as this chapter (and section) comes to a close, you'll have proved to yourself that you're ready to move on to the final part of this book. There, you'll face your biggest, and most exciting, stop motion challenge to date: developing and creating your very *own* stop motion film.

Figure 14.1
Nia Makes A Friend!
It's time for a new challenge: animating more than one character.

Overview of the showcase shot

Just what is this showcase shot that you're going to be dedicating yourself to for the next little while? You'll notice that unlike earlier exercises in this section, there're no specific photo images to guide you along, or to show you essential beginning, middle, and end posing. That's because you're ready to take it over for yourself. You're going to set yourself up, entirely on your own, using all the skills that you've developed thus far.

Of course, you need *some* description. So here's the shot, broken down into specific statements. Each statement is a main point in the shot, as it progresses from start to finish. You can think them of each statement as a story moment, or 'beat', that has to be conveyed clearly to the audience if the shot is to work.

1. Lumpy is very sad.
2. Nia enters, not noticing Lumpy.
3   Nia suddenly notices Lumpy.
4. Nia offers a friendly greeting.
5. Lumpy is so happy to finally have a friend!
6   Two new pals, together forever.

To further help you along, you'll see the shot roughed out in a storyboard sequence below (Figure 14.3), along with some insights into how to go about creating a rough board for yourself.

There are a lot of considerations to work through as you envision this shot, but let's start with the most important one – just who the heck is Lumpy?!

Fabricating Lumpy

Meet Lumpy, Nia's acting partner for this exercise. Lumpy is literally nothing more than a roughly sculpted chunk of clay, with two hard eyeballs stuck in! Lumpy's not very fancy, but Lumpy's full of charm – and totally sufficient for our purposes.

With regard to eyeballs, you can make them very quickly by creating two Super Sculpey balls. Before you bake them, carefully poke small holes into them. Once they're baked, paint them white with black pupils around the holes, and you can then insert a toothpick or pin, in order to animate them. Beyond eyeballs, Lumpy's features are extremely simple – just clay eyelids and a mouth. That's it.

As you dedicate a bit of time to making cute little Lumpy, keep the details of the shot in mind. Lumpy needs to be small enough so as to seem cute, but big enough so that animation is fairly easy. For how Lumpy compares to Nia in terms of size, refer to your own quick boards, and to the rough board image below (Figure 14.3).

**Figure 14.2
Lumpy.**
Lumpy is *mostly* eyes, so be sure to use them to communicate effectively with the audience.

Feel free to design your own version of Lumpy. Just make sure that your version can achieve everything that's required in the exercise, and that it's simple and appealing in its basic design.

Animating with more than one puppet

Throughout this section, I've stressed the importance of effective timing in stop motion, and the challenges that come along with that. As you prepare for the task of animating *two* puppets, this topic of effective timing takes on even greater complexities. As your characters proceed within the shot, a continuous *exchange* will be happening between them. As the shot unfolds, the action of one character will force a reaction from the other. This reaction will in turn cause further actions and reactions to develop, and so it goes. All of this back and forth is tracked by the audience as the shot proceeds, as the audience slowly builds its understanding of the shot.

What does all this have to do with effective timing in animation? Effective timing is the way that you, as the animator, will ensure that your audience is watching *where* it should be, *when* it should be, and for the length of time that it should be, so that these vital exchanges are witnessed and understood. Time the exchanges effectively, and all of the complex relationship (and story) information that you're trying to convey will be communicated clearly. Time the exchanges poorly, and instead of having the exciting back and forth of a tennis match, your shot will look more like a train wreck, with all its essential bits of communication piled one on top of the other into a jumbled heap.

I'll highlight one moment in the shot that you're going to create, in order to illustrate how important timing is in this context. We'll look at the point in the shot when Lumpy is about to react to Nia's friendly greeting. We know

how Lumpy's going to react, but exactly *when* does that occur? On what frame, precisely? The answer doesn't reside on your x-sheet (unless you create wildly detailed x-sheets). Instead, the answer will be found on screen, as you flip your frames and playback your animation. And ultimately the answer will be found within your own timing instincts.

How do you nail down something that's so vital? Well, it's not the first time you've heard me say this: it's going to take some serious *practice*. With every attempt that you create, you'll be getting better.

> When animating with two puppets, always be asking yourself, 'Are my animation choices ensuring that the audience is watching the puppet that I want it to be watching, for this particular point in the shot?'

KUBO AND THE TWO-STRINGS, LAIKA STUDIOS, 2016

As with any stop motion feature, there's almost no end to the spectacular things on display here. But when considering the challenges of animating more than one puppet, be sure to the study the truly remarkable fight scene between Monkey and Sister. It was animated by Justin Rasch, and it just may be the best fight scene ever created in stop motion, since King Kong fought the T-Rex.

Prep work

There's no prep process that's written in stone for a shot like this, but I find the following steps work quite well. If you follow them, they'll help to keep things flowing forward efficiently, and they'll also help you to be as prepared as possible for when it comes time to animate. You should also be able to carry this basic process onward to your own film, or to any project that requires efficiency (which is every project, when it comes right down to it!) In time, you may find that you'll want to tweak this process, so that it better suits your own personal needs.

As you tackle each of the following steps, try to keep the 'prize' in mind, which is the finished shot. Take your time on each step, of course, but don't lose yourself in it for countless hours. Each step is just that: a step. It's not the destination. Keep pushing forward, towards animation.

As you set up, be sure to consult your boards, and also the specifics of the exercise in the 'Description' section below, to make sure that you're accounting for everything.

> You'll notice that many of these steps were looked at in detail previously in the book. But now it's time to apply them in this 'showcase' context. As you follow these steps now, be sure to refer back to their detailed sections, as needed.

Step 1: Quick boards

The example boards in Figure 14.3 were created pretty quickly, and that's a good thing. They're just for the purpose of conveying the essentials of the shot. These include:

- Essential framing for the shot
- Main blocking points, to show where the characters need to be, and when they need to be there
- Direction arrows, to indicate major character movements
- Clear eyelines, that show where characters are looking, and when
- Major actions, such as Nia's wave
- Major changes within a character, such as when Lumpy reacts to Nia's friendly wave

You'll notice that the posing and facial expressions in these boards aren't extremely detailed. As the animator, those are specifics that you can sort out on your own as you think the shot through, and as you animate.

Figure 14.3
Quick boards for the showcase shot.
Since this shot has fairly complex action and acting, a quick storyboard will serve as a great reference, both during prep and during animation.

Creating a rough board for a shot like this will help you as you plan for shooting it, but it's also good practice for what lies ahead of you when it comes to developing your own film. Effective storyboards will be required fairly early on in that process, and they'll have a huge effect on just about every part of your production.

For this shot, if your drawing skills aren't the strongest, simply use Figure 14.3 as a guide for this exercise. But do know that for future efforts, clear and simple boards are an essential part of any serious stop motion project, big or small. Fortunately, 'clear and simple' *doesn't* require great drawing skills – just strong visualization skills and some basic drawing ability, so not to worry. You'll find more on storyboards in Part 4.

Don't worry too much about having set pieces in this shot. A very simple background and ground that can be nicely lit will do just fine. Of course, if you want to add in some simple set items, feel free! Just be sure to keep those items out of the way of your animation, and keep them plain so that they aren't distracting.

Step 2: Framing

No doubt your framing skills have improved considerably from all of your animation practice, but this exercise has a few additional challenges to keep in mind. The content of the frame changes quite a bit over the course of the shot, since you have two characters moving about. It opens with lonely Lumpy, but your frame can't just concern itself with this moment in the shot. If you frame too tightly on Lumpy, it might look flattering at the start, but there'll be no room for Nia to enter, nor room for her to carry out her performance!

Further, once Nia hits her mark beside Lumpy, will the frame still look generally balanced as the two get to know each other? What about once Lumpy moves in closer to Nia? Effective framing needs to consider all the main moments within the shot, from beginning to end. Sometimes, an effective frame isn't so much perfect for every moment, but it's the very best that it can be, in consideration of the whole shot.

Reference your storyboards as you tackle your framing, and seriously consider creating a quick pop-through, which will help you to very quickly resolve any framing issues (as well as a variety of other concerns, as you'll see). If you need a refresher on creating a pop-through for framing and blocking, you'll find it in Chapter 9 dedicated to Camera.

Step 3: Blocking

Precisely where are your characters going to be within your frame at every major point within the shot? Will these positions work with all of the actions and performances that are required within the shot? This shot is fairly straightforward to 'block out', since Lumpy mostly stays in one place, and Nia enters along a straight line, stops beside Lumpy, and remains there. But you still want to ensure that these paths and positions are effective, before animating. For example, as Nia walks into the shot, you don't want her to stop *too* close to Lumpy, or else Lumpy won't have room to happily slide over to cuddle with her, towards the end of the shot.

You don't necessarily need to have it worked out *precisely* in advance (as with live actors, these blocking points will shift a bit, once the puppets start performing), but the clearer that you are on it before animating, the better.

As with framing, consult your boards regularly, and use a pop-through to quickly test out who goes where, and when!

> The draw tool in Dragonframe can come in very handy for shots like this. For example, you can draw a blocking point on your screen to indicate where Nia should stop once she has entered the frame, so that she's in just the right place with regard to Lumpy.

Step 4: Lighting

As you start to think about lighting, refer back to Chapter 8's section called 'A lighting process for stop motion'. As you follow along with that process, you'll notice that framing and blocking concerns need to be well sorted out before lighting can begin. Keep that in mind, as you work on creating this lovely shot that's going to show off your skills so fully.

When it comes to the details of the lighting for this shot, make your lighting dramatic or subtle. Make it high key, low key, or any combination that works for you. Cut the light and throw wild shadows, or keep it cool and smooth. However you approach it, make it *beautiful*. Remember, this shot is your showcase piece that's intended to convey as many skills as possible – and lighting is *definitely* one of them.

Just remember that you also need to *animate* within your beautifully lit frame, but I cautioned you enough about that in the chapter on lighting, right? How can you make sure that your characters can be animated within your wonderful lighting? Yep. You guessed it. Yet another reason to create a pop-through, this time for lighting.

Step 5: Act it out

As you act, and visualize, you'll probably find that you'll work back and forth between this step and the next (Step 6: X-Sheet). You can do this by first acting out a shot entirely, so that you know how long it will be in terms of frames. Once you transfer that to the x-sheet, you can work back and forth, breaking each acting moment down in terms of the details of performance, so that you can transfer it to the x-sheet in as much or as little detail as you need.

Acting out, and then animating, a shot between two characters is a particular challenge that's pretty specific to the world of animation. That's because live action actors typically inhabit one character at a time on stage or screen, whereas animators can be many characters, all at once, within the same shot! It's a big challenge, but it's one that really is one of the most enjoyable aspects of creating character animation. It's especially exciting when you have characters with very different emotions and states of mind, such as in this exercise. Lumpy and Nia are in very different places emotionally (at least until they become friends at the end), but both characters need to come across as emotionally honest and compelling in order for the audience to feel connected.

Figure 14.4
Dogonauts: Enemy Line, Justin and Shel Rasch, 2013. Action scenes between puppets can present great challenges, as well as great rewards. The physical back and forth between the characters drive the scene, whether it's a dance, or a fight – like this one.

It's the back and forth between characters that's often the most fun to perform, and to watch!

shot performed for the very first time, as it plays out in your imagination. What follows, of course, is the very serious business of ensuring that what just worked for you, and that made your cry, or laugh, or cringe, makes its way on the screen for others to enjoy in the same way.

Step 6: X-Sheet

Depending on your personal preference as well as your skill level, create an x-sheet that's detailed enough to help *you*. It might be very detailed or it might just have a few essential notes. Once you've completed an attempt of this exercise, you may find that things would have gone better with *more* detailed notes on your x-sheet. Or, you may discover that you're completely fine with very little written down.

Step 7: Finals

Fortunately, this doesn't refer to final *exams*. It's a term that stop motion has picked up from the world of live action film and television production, and it's in reference to the 'final' adjustments that are made before it's time to shoot (or in our case, animate).

Camera

Check your tripod to ensure that it's fully locked down. Consult your framing and blocking pop-throughs one last time to make sure that you haven't missed anything. Double check your camera settings one last time, through Dragonframe.

Lighting

Compare your live view in Dragonframe to your lighting pop-through to make sure that nothing in your lighting has shifted. Ensure that you've got room to work, and that no lighting equipment is going to be seriously in your way during animation. If it can't be avoided, at least ensure that you are clear on where the hazard is, so that you can avoid it. If you're using any mini-bounce boards, ensure that they are taped down, or otherwise secured.

Puppets

What happens to live action actors, just before the camera department calls 'Action'? They get a final bit of make-up applied, they get their costumes adjusted one last time, and they ensure they are on their correct mark for the start of the shot. That's precisely what happens for puppets, too!

It's now that those visualization skills that you've been honing are really going to be put to use. You'll be visualizing not only how and when the puppets move through the shot, but how they relate to each other and how they develop emotionally as the shot progresses.

The process of acting out a shot like this can be really exhilarating. In one way, you're the *performer*, testing out various poses and expressions for both characters (within your mind, or by using your own body). Yet in another way, you are also a very privileged *audience*, since you are seeing the

Figure 14.5
Slate frame.
A slate frame, captured at the start and/or end of a shot, allows you to ensure essential information travels along into post-production. A small dry erase board works great.

Pay special attention to the faces of puppets when doing finals. That's the area where the audience is often looking, and it's also the spot on the puppet that far more likely to accumulate distracting bits of things like clay and wax.

Slate

A slate is yet another bit of live action that has made its way into the stop motion process. It's a card that's recorded for one frame, that contains essential information relating to the shot that's about to occur. At its most basic level, a slate should at least contain the specific shot number, so that you know what you're looking at when it comes time to edit. Beyond this basic info, a slate will sometimes also contain the animator's name, any notes for post-production (such as notes regarding rig removal), and a colour or greyscale card that will help with balancing the look of the film later in production.

It's good to get into the habit of shooting a slate, since you'll need to do it on each shot of your own film when the time comes, and on professional projects as well.

Exercise: The showcase shot

You'll find that most of the details for this shot are laid out in the images and in the written description, both of which are at the start of this chapter. The quick boards will also guide you along, as will your acting preparation and x-sheet.

Direction

- As blunt as this may seem, your main direction for this exercise is 'create a great shot'. You've spent a lot of time and effort to get yourself to a point where you can size up a shot like this, and then tackle it. Apply all of the animation skills that you've developed thus far, and make it gorgeous.
- Beyond that, here's *one* further bit of direction, which pertains to the challenge of animating not one but two characters: *make sure that the audience is looking at the most important character for that particular moment.* If you can achieve that in your first attempt, you've done well. If you can achieve that, *and* if you've created a compelling performance, while keeping everything looking beautiful, then you've *nailed* it.
- It's hard to place a time frame on how long this shot is going to take you. It will depend on your skill level, and on how deep you go into the shot. To be safe, you should set aside half a day. That way you won't feel rushed, and you'll be able to give it your all.

Things to consider as you animate

- Because there's nothing other than gravity securing this puppet to the deck, it might take a bit of practice to get the hang of animating Lumpy. A bit of pressure will help secure the puppet to the deck, but if you do need to pick Lumpy up for a bit of sculpting work, or if you knock the puppet over by accident, you should be able to get the weird little creature back into place with a bit of frame flipping.
- As you'll recall from your acting exercises, if an animated character travels a great emotional distance during a shot, it's more dynamic and exciting for the audience to watch. With that in mind, if you start the shot with poor Lumpy *extremely* sad (rather than just *slightly* sad), you'll have an exciting distance to travel as Lumpy eventually arrives at extremely *happy*.

- As your audience's attention shifts from character A to character B, how do you handle animation for character A, now that the audience isn't watching it? Well, if you're confident that the audience isn't looking at character A, why animate it? Just make sure that you've effectively decelerated it into a strong resting pose, because if it stops abruptly, or hits an unflattering resting pose, it will only distract the audience.
- ABF! You didn't really think I'd stop nagging you about this, did you?
- A reminder on the importance of good timing: each character needs to have it within that character's own animation, but also *between* the two characters, as they act and react.
- When posing the characters' eyes, be sure to maintain strong eye contact between them. Make sure that Nia is looking *directly* at Lumpy, and vice versa. It's essential for creating a convincing performance, since eye contact connects characters to each other, and deepens their exchanges.

Troubleshooting

- The duration of this shot is quite long, and that invariably increases the chance that 'something' is going to happen. The 'something' could be anything from a bit of light flicker to a bumped tripod leg, to who knows what else. That's stop motion for you! Do your best to be vigilant, and to prevent or correct any mishaps, but don't lose your cool if something *does* go wrong. Learn from it, but unless it's a total disaster, keep going with the shot. It's a painful but necessary part of your training. Facing these sorts of challenges with confidence and a cool head is what it means to be a professional.
- If walking Nia in at the start of the shot is too tricky, figure out another way to stage the exercise that makes it a bit easier, but still shows off your skills. Perhaps the clip begins with Nia already well into the frame, so she doesn't have to walk as much, or (even easier) the shot begins with her already standing beside Lumpy. She looks down, suddenly notices him, and the shot goes on from there.
- Concentration and focus are vital, but if you're trying too hard the animation is going to feel forced and tense. If a first attempt doesn't provide you with solid results, consider simplifying the entire shot in terms of the animation style. Instead of going for completely full animation, limit things a bit, so that you aren't agonizing over each frame. It's just *one* take, after all. Let it be fun. It's surprising how the act of giving yourself permission to enjoy the work can translate into animation that's more relaxed and enjoyable to watch. Then, go for full animation in later attempts.

Going further with this exercise

- If you keep the same basic structure of this exercise, but change the *personality* of Lumpy, you have a whole new shot in terms of performance potential. Imagine a 'grumpy' Lumpy, or a 'dangerous' Lumpy!
- Change Nia's personality, and see how it plays out. Instead of 'friendly' Nia, imagine a 'disgusted' Nia, or a 'frightened' Nia. What kind of emotional arc would she follow?
- Come up with an entirely new situation involving these two. Follow the same process of development, and try to keep it relatively simple in terms of action and performance, and have fun. You've got all the skills now, run with them! Better yet, make Nia run!
- As you change the situation, change the lighting and framing as well. Perhaps you use your skills to convey a 'horror' atmosphere, and Lumpy gets redesigned into a blood-sucking monster. Perhaps you convey a wintery atmosphere, and poor Lumpy is shivering, and in need of warmth?

- Create an attempt where you live dangerously. Skip the boards, get a shot set up quickly, do away with the pop through, and forget the x-sheet. Use your visualization skills to imagine the shot fully, and then go for it. It might work out great, or it might be a flop. No matter what, you'll *learn* lots – about where your skills are at, and about what you *personally* need going into a shot in order to feel comfortable.
- Add a simple camera move to the shot. A simple pan, for example, can help to balance out a frame. A camera move can also add some visual interest to the overall shot.
- Additionally, you can add a zoom in or out to the camera move to add even more visual excitement (and animation challenges).
- Bring in some dialogue, for one or both of the characters – this will add a whole new level of exciting challenges!
- Bring in more set items to add visual interest to the shot, and to provide further atmosphere. Once you do, then guess what? You're (almost) making a short film!

ANTHONY SCOTT

Anthony Scott is something of a legend amongst stop motion animators, and a quick glance at his CV will tell you why. The list of characters that he's brought to life is incredible: Gumby, The Pillsbury Doughboy, Jack Skellington, James (of the Giant Peach), The Corpse Bride, Coraline, ParaNorman, The Little Prince, and more besides. If you've been astounded by a high-profile stop motion performance, there's a good chance that Anthony Scott was at the heart of it. His demo reel is online, go check it out. You'll be amazed, and inspired.

The online portfolio

After much practice and feedback, the time will eventually arrive when you want to transition somewhat from *creating* the animation to *showcasing* it. The same goes for your other skills, like puppet fabrication and lighting. A short stop motion film is a great showcase in and of itself, because it acts as an all-in-one portfolio piece. But what if don't *have* a short film yet, but still want to get your work noticed?

Within an online portfolio, you can personally manage what and how the world sees your stop motion talents. And best of all, you can easily update that work as you develop your skills, so that you're always presenting yourself in the best professional light.

There's no need to reinvent the wheel in terms of how you put yours together. There's a wide range of hosting options and templates that will let you show your work off professionally. Do your research, and check out examples of how (and where) other stop motion artists have set themselves up. This kind of research is also a great way to widen your list of contacts within the medium.

> For inspiration and guidance on what your online portfolio might look like, search for ones created by recent grads of major animation programs. These artists are typically *very* serious about showing themselves off professionally and effectively, and are using the latest and greatest hosting sites and templates.

Most portfolio sites and templates allow you to collect your work into major sections. For example, based on the skills you've developed thus far with the help of this book, you might set up sections for 'Puppets', 'Lighting', and 'Animation'. In time, as you create more work, you might create additional sections like 'Sets and Props', as well as 'Films'. This sectioned format is a very sensible way to organize things, because an industry visitor to your portfolio might be looking for a very specific skill, and you want to make

Figure 14.6
Portfolio website,
Evan DeRushie.
A great example
of an effective
online portfolio
page, that
showcases the
artist's contact
info, latest work,
demo reel, and
some concise bio
information.

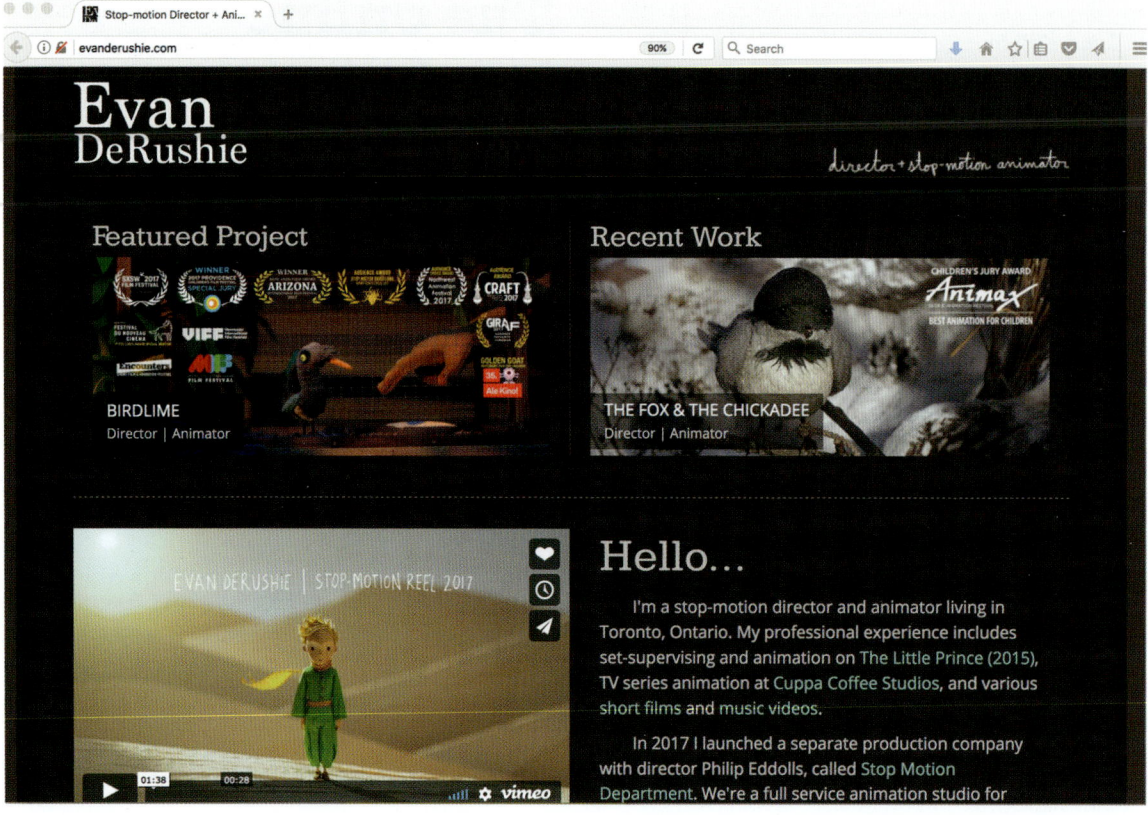

that search as easy as possible. Or, a visitor might want to 'graze' a bit, and get a sense of your overall talent. Again, this sectioned method of portfolio makes that very easy.

Over my years of working with graduating animation students, I've seen a lot of online portfolios get put together, and I've seen the results once those portfolios have gone out into the world. With that in mind, I've pulled some of my insights together, into a handy dandy Online Portfolio Dos and Don'ts list.

Do

- *Show your final online portfolio to trusted eyes, before sharing the link more publicly.* In the same way that you need serious critique for your animation work, you need serious insights into whether your portfolio is working or not. What should you keep? What should you remove? What should you emphasize? Is there anything else that stands out that could make it better? You need an honest and professional opinion. Take that

opinion to heart, make the changes, and *then* share.

- *Place your current contact information in a very easy to find place on the main page.* If your contact information changes, update it on the portfolio immediately. People are busy, and if they can't find out how to reach you in order to talk with you about your work, they'll move on.

- *Ensure that your still images can be enlarged fully.* This way, a visitor can really take in all of your beautifully detailed work. A series of postage-stamp sized images that can't be enlarged isn't going to do the visitor (or you) much good.

- *Include a range of animation work so that a visitor can see your overall skills.* Ideally, your animation section would include: very strong basic and advanced exercises, some lip sync work, and some very strong walks that express a variety of character traits. If you also have additional acting pieces that are impressive, that's great to include as well.

- *If your animation work is very short, loop it.* Nobody minds seeing a very nice piece of animation played back several times. Looping the clip also saves the visitor from having to click 'play' again, and the easier you can make it for a visitor to appreciate your work, the better.
- *Use Vimeo, YouTube, or another major video sites to host your animation clips, rather than the portfolio page itself.* You can count on these major sites to play your video effectively, time after time, whereas a portfolio site isn't likely to be as reliable. And you want your beautiful animation to play properly!
- *Keep the navigation methods on your portfolio very simple.* Remember, you want a visitor to remember how lovely your work is, not what a pain your portfolio page was to use.
- *Keep the overall design very clean and simple.* Let your work speak for you, don't hide it behind an overly fancy template or interface. People are visiting your portfolio to see your strong work, nothing else.
- *Allow your distinctive personality to shine through.* If you have a wicked sense of humour, let it show in the portfolio. If you love cute and cuddly more than anything in the world, again let it show. Just remember the above point, about keeping it clean and simple, and be sure to let your stop motion work be the *main* thing.

Don't

- *Expect the world to come to you.* You need to go out to the world by sharing your work. Your portfolio might be of exceptionally high quality, but if you don't get it out there, no one is going to see it.
- *Include weak work.* It only serves to bring your whole portfolio down, and it tarnishes your other work that might be very strong. If you don't *have* a lot of strong work yet, include what you do have that's impressive, and schedule in time to create more. Or, consider keeping your portfolio link private, until you have better work to show.
- *Set yourself up for defeat.* Don't create sections of your portfolio that will require updates that you won't be able to honour. Blog and journal sections are fun for a while, but unless you're right on top of them, they

can start to look bad on you, once they haven't been updated for months!

- *Allow your portfolio to fall behind your skill level.* Life gets very busy, and if you're creating some great new work, you might not feel like taking the time to post it to your portfolio. But it's important. Put up the new (and better) stuff, and if the older stuff isn't as good, or is redundant now, take it down. Your portfolio might be the only way that the world can learn how great you're becoming at stop motion – so keep it current.
- *Get discouraged.* Your hard work may not get noticed right away. The stop motion world is a small place, but that small place is filled with a lot of talent, and all of it is vying to get seen. If the world seems to be ignoring your work, the best way to deal with it isn't to turn your back on it all. It's to keep making more work! You have talent and skills, and as you create more work, you'll improve. When you later share that improvement, the world *will* take notice. The world loves beautiful stop motion, but it also loves hard work and dedication. You'll be showing off both if you don't let concerns over 'likes', 'shares' and 'views' get you down. Instead, go back to the studio, and get busy making more lovely stop motion.

As this section concludes, your work in the area of animation is far from done. In some ways, you're really just getting started. As I've stressed throughout, the exercises presented here should certainly set you upon a solid path, but it's over to *you* to carry things further. With what you've learned here, you can (and must) take your animation training onward, if you want to truly excel.

Go beyond the exercises presented in this section, and as you do, never forget that what you are creating isn't just between you and your puppet. The *audience* is what you are really doing this for, as you strive to communicate something that's inside of your heart and head. You want that audience – be it one person, or a hundred, or a thousand – to see, hear, and feel precisely what you are intending. You aren't going for a simulation, or a rough version, or a 'sketch' of what's inside of you. You're going for a perfect transfer, on to the screen. Let that desire to create crystal-clear messages lead you, and let the puppet be the means by which you can achieve that desire. Speak to your audience, through the puppet.

PAYTON CURTIS, FEATURE FILM ANIMATOR (PART 2)

This is Part 2 of my chat with feature film animator, Payton Curtis. If you're looking for Part 1 of our interview, you'll find that back in Chapter 12!

Q. The relationship between a stop motion animator and his or her animation director is typically a very important one. Can you describe what in your opinion makes for a great feature film stop motion animator director?

A. That one is simple: going to bat for you. You've got enough on your plate to deal with from day to day, what with prepping and shooting. So a good animation director will help to ensure that you're getting everything sorted out when it comes to sets, puppets, wardrobe, you name it. A good animation director will float between all departments making certain that everything that's getting put together for you is being made 'animator friendly'.

Q. What are some of the biggest challenges in being a feature film stop motion animator?

A. The biggest challenge is keeping your chops up! Unlike most television series (which are quite forgiving), feature work, generally speaking, demands the utmost attention to detail and quality of performance. In a 50–60 hour working week, spanning two years, you're required to stay sharp and give it your best from shot to shot. That's a very difficult thing to do. If you have an off day, everybody notices it and it'll be there on display for the world to see!

Q. Biggest rewards?

A. Meeting a childhood hero like Bill Murray (a true gentleman) on *Fantastic Mr. Fox* and hanging out with him was pretty cool. Working with Henry Selick was a treat, I was a huge fan of *Slow Bob In The Lower Dimensions* in high school.

But the absolute best is working with the best artists in the business! Painters, sculptors, camera people, animators, designers, effects wizards, wardrobe, riggers, set builders … These people are the reason you give it your best day to day. That immense wealth of talent keeps you on your toes! You don't want to disappoint all these brilliant people by shooting a poor performance. You want to make them proud of their efforts by doing the best you can.

Q. Looking back at your successes thus far as an animator, was there a moment that has proven to be pivotal, or key, in terms of your development? Even a childhood thing, perhaps, that 'makes sense' in some way today?

A. Not to be grim, but losing my mum as a boy was tough. I grew up fast and learned, arguably the greatest lesson a kid can learn – take nothing for granted. Work hard, stay true to yourself, and expect in return only what you put into your efforts.

Q. Other pivotal, professional moments that stand out that you'd like to share?

A. A few, but the standout moments professionally were working alongside people that had an impact on me and whom I admired through the developing years. Henry Selick of course, also people like Trey Thomas, a fellow animator on the film.

Trey and I split an 'Other Mother' sequence on *Coraline,* once I had proven myself to be relatively competent. Trey is a great supporter of other animators' work and has no ego, a very rare thing in film. Seeing my work along with his was a kick. He was the 'Godfather' of animation on *Coraline*. Trying to mimic the masters and make seamless cuts from one animator's work to another was a great challenge. And of course, for professional and personal reasons, meeting Julianna Cox. An amazing animator who worked on *Coraline*. We were pals throughout the two years on the film – and now we're married. That's pretty pivotal, I'd say!

Q. If someone reading wants to be where you are professionally down the road, but is just starting out in formally learning about stop motion, what insights could you share to help him or her in that effort?

A. Practice. Whether it's music, sports, academics, or animation, you must focus and improve your skills constantly. And don't wait for others to motivate you. I'm self-taught, I was so impressed with the work of Phil Tippet, that I started studying the craft on my own. By the time I stumbled into my first audition in Toronto, I was better prepared than most who were trained. Now more than ever before, anyone can take up stop motion in their own homes with as little as a computer and a cheap digital camera. So get cracking! We are all students of this beautiful medium, for life.

Part four

Making a film

Welcome to Part 4, where you'll meet the ultimate challenge of applying everything you've learned so far to making your very own short stop motion film. In the previous part, you concerned yourself with creating great looking *shots*. Now, the challenge becomes stringing those great shots together into longer scenes and sequences that will then eventually form a final film. This 'stringing together' will present you with all kinds of new challenges. You're about to learn a lot more about yourself as an artist, about stop motion, and about filmmaking.

Artists get better by finishing a project, and then stepping back from it in order to appraise it, and then making the next thing. Depending on how much work is involved in your stop motion film, it may be quite some time before you complete it, which means it might be quite a while before you'll be able to step back from the final film. With that in mind, if you are very new to stop motion filmmaking, *go easy on yourself,* by starting with a very modest film.

Then, as you develop it, don't worry if what you're making doesn't look, sound, or feel like something coming out of an established feature film studio! In fact, be glad that it doesn't. Let the giant productions do their own thing. Instead, give the viewer *your* imagined world, as expressed through stop motion. It will be special, in a million little ways, because it's honestly *you,* and no one else. And it will be awesome.

15

Pre-production

Since this chapter is dedicated to pre-production, we'll examine the 'getting stuff ready' stage of the process. As you move through this chapter, you'll notice that there's a particular focus on story. That's because the story in your film is like the foundation in a house – if it's strong, you can build beautiful, soaring things, that truly last. If it's weak, no matter how much effort and talent goes into later stages, it may look nice, but it's only a matter of time before things come crashing down.

Of course, a good story is just the starting point. From there, this chapter will lead you through the process of translating your story into the world of motion pictures, as you create a rough version of your actual film in the form of an animatic. What exactly is an animatic? Well, you'll have to read the rest of the chapter to find out!

By the end of this chapter, you'll have a clear understanding of the story development process for a stop motion film. You'll also have a clear practical understanding of how to create the essential elements of story for your film, which you will then take onward, into actual production.

Figure 15.1
Rough
storyboards,
The Champ,
Rosemary
Travale, 2014.
Even quickly-
created story
sketches must
have excellent
clarity, as shown
here.

Story

Figure 15.2
Epic of Gilgamesh.
This one has it all: romance, adventure, and intrigue. It's also
considered the oldest written story, dating back to around 2100 BCE.

Stop motion is a fairly young medium, but telling
stories goes *way* back. And as long as we've
been telling stories, we've also been making

insights and observations into how those stories
work. What are the components of story, and how
do those components go together? Then, once
they're fitted together, how do they interact with
each in order to become this amazing thing we
call a 'good' story?

Basic components of story

I firmly believe that for any film, nothing is more
important than story, so I really hope that you
take the time to make yours as strong as possible. Remember, the world already has enough
mediocre, ho-hum stories. What it needs is great
stories – stories that fascinate, and inspire, and
entertain … and that deeply connect with the
audience, because they feel honest, and true.

Through developing stories for my own
films, and through helping to develop stories
for filmmakers that I've mentored, I've come to
hold certain aspects of solid story as being pretty

essential. Some of these concepts are truly 'classic', in that they were first identified thousands of years ago, while others are more modern. But all of them are things you should be aware of, and consider, as you develop your own strong story.

Story structure

This concept is first in the list, because it's foundational. Pretty much anything that occurs over time (a sports event, a plane ride, you name it) has a basic shape to it, and that shape is determined at least somewhat by *time*. In other words, there's a beginning, a middle, and an end to the thing, over time.

Consider music. A piece of music begins, it carries onward, and then it concludes. Yet think about how many styles of music exist, and how many songs there are in the world! Over the course of a few minutes, the music may develop in different ways – in its melody, or in its rhythm, or in its overall complexity. But it *will* develop, somehow. And then, without fail, it will conclude. Stories are no different from music in this way. They have a beginning, a middle, and an end, yet

Strong story structure is like a skeleton. It provides something solid, that the rest of the story can grow upon.

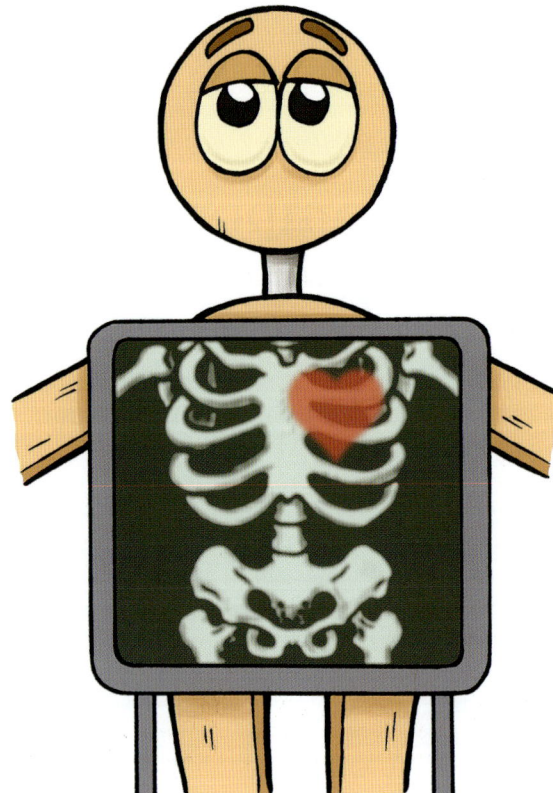

Figure 15.3
Rise of the Living Corpse, Chris Walsh, 2010.
Even the shortest of animated stories needs structure. Here, the zombie bursts from its grave, attempts to climb out, then suddenly gets crushed by its own tombstone. Beginning, middle, and end (not to mention, comedy gold).

upon that basic structure, storytellers can construct tales that are wonderfully varied.

If a story recognizes these three main parts, it's said to adhere to a 'three-act structure', with each main part (or 'act') operating in quite specific ways, in order to create a story that satisfies the audience. A lot of people swear by this approach to story development, and it can certainly provide you with a finely crafted tale. If you're fascinated by story, you really should learn more about it.

On the other hand, some people find this formal approach to be quite restrictive, and believe that it leads to a story whose shape is too easy to predict. I think that both sides of that argument have merit, but no matter how structured (or not structured) you want your story to be, there's no way around the fact that your film will start, it will progress, and it will end. Does your story develop and move forward, with this in mind? Make sure that something happens (even if that 'something' is very quiet, and small).

Character

You may be developing a story that focuses entirely on mood or atmosphere, in which case the question of character may not apply. But for a great many stories, the central character that moves the story onward, also known as the protagonist, isn't just central to the story. Rather, that protagonist *is* the story. Think of Charles Dickens's *A Christmas Carol*, in which mean old Scrooge progresses through a series of supernatural experiences on Christmas Eve, and eventually (spoiler alert) learns to love Christmas, himself, and the world around him. In this example, the story's development is tied to the actions and words of the protagonist, but also to the development of the actual *character* of Scrooge.

Does *your* story have a clear central character, who will effectively and actively move things onward? Does it have a character that ideally can change (or be changed) in some way, over the course of your story? Think back to Chapter 2 on Character Design, and the character bio that was provided for Nia. That bio was an attempt to bring the character of Nia to life, even before she became a puppet. Does your character feel alive in this way, as you develop your story?

> **HEDGEHOG IN THE FOG, YURI NORSTEIN, 1975**
>
> The enduring power of this perfect little gem of a cutout film has a lot to do with the effectiveness of the central character. The little hedgehog is very brave in certain ways, yet is also easily frightened by the mysterious world that he finds himself in. He's playful, funny, and charming, yet reveals deeper complexities of character, as the film progresses. He's also very *active,* and very determined, which are always great character traits, because they tend to move the story forward.

Objective

In the real world, being 'goal-oriented' is an attribute that's usually encouraged. Achieve what you set out to achieve. Go for it. Get it. So why should the characters in our stories be any different? At the very least, a character who is trying to achieve, to obtain, or to accomplish something (which is known as the character's 'objective') is being *active*. And active is good, when you have an audience that wants to see things progress. An active character doesn't have to be an action hero. Even a lazy character has an objective: to continue napping on the couch!

Your *protagonist* should have an objective, but so should all of your characters. And as the storyteller, you should be mindful of all of those objectives as your story progresses. Does your

character achieve its objective, or not? If it is achieved, perhaps it's in a way that surprises the character (and by extension, the audience). Think of your audience. Does it want your character to ultimately be satisfied? Or frustrated? And can you play with this somehow, while still being respectful of the importance of the objective to the story? We'll continue to consider the audience, later in this chapter.

Motivation

'What's my motivation?' is the classic question that's asked by actors as they grapple with a role. It's a basic question, because a character's motivation is the fuel that drives the character towards its objective. A character may struggle to get an apple out of a tree (with the objective being 'get the apple'), but the motivation that drives that struggle is vital. In this case, if the character isn't motivated (maybe he just ate a big meal and isn't hungry), he won't be inclined to work very hard to get that apple. But if he's starving, or (better yet) if his *family* is starving, you now have a deep, essential motivation. And that's good for a story, because it makes it easier for your story to progress and develop. Further, if you can make your audience aware of the depth of the motivation, you have a great chance to align your audience with your character's struggle, or at the very least to have your audience better understand your character's actions and words.

Drama and conflict

Drama doesn't necessarily mean 'heavy and serious', although that's often what we think of when we hear the term. In a storytelling sense, drama refers to the back and forth, the struggle, that occurs within a story. How do you get a struggle? You need to go back to the idea of a character and its objective. If a character too easily achieves its objective in the story, that's it. End of story. No drama. But if there's a challenge or 'obstacle' (which is the term most often used in storytelling) placed between the character and its objective, guess what? There's your drama. Or more correctly, there's your *conflict*.

Conflict in a story can be big, like a war between nations, or it can be far more modest – think of a character trying to get out of bed in the morning. Conflict can involve another character, or it can be an internal struggle. Conflict can be humorous or serious; it's up to you as the

**Figure 15.4
Basics of story.**
Here we have
a character, its
objective, and an
obstacle to that
objective. Where
it all goes from
here, and whether
it's compelling or
not, is up to the
storyteller.

more complex story, without getting in the way of the main, or literal, story. An example would be the wolf in the story of Little Red Riding Hood. Is the wolf just a wolf? It can be just a wolf. In some ways, that's sufficient for a child who is experiencing the story for the first time. But can the wolf also be something else? Something more? If so, then you're dealing in subtext and metaphor.

Trying hard to fill your story with subtext and metaphor is dangerous business. What should be hidden is now visible for all to see, and before you know it, you've got an audience that's feeling bored, and insulted, because you've hit it over the head with something that's now too obvious. But if you can sense subtext and metaphor bubbling within your story as you create it, sometimes that's enough, at least for the time being. No need to look it directly in the eye, at least not yet. Later, once your literal story is well-developed, you can go through your story again, and consider how (or if) you should hone these more abstract things.

Won't the audience assign its own sub-meaning to your story, regardless of whether you are actively making use of subtext and metaphor during the development stage? Yep. That's because the audience is thinking, and is constantly attempting to find bigger meaning in stories. But if you're careful, you can purposely provide a richer experience to your audience.

> Your story doesn't have to be complicated. It doesn't have to be 'important', or attempt to do something a story has never done before. Who needs that kind of pressure when crafting a story?! It can be very straightforward and simple, but if it succeeds in keeping your audience's attention, then you've already set yourself apart from a lot of other stories!

storyteller. But it's all for the purpose of engaging your audience, and maintaining its interest in your story. Make it dramatic, through conflict, and your audience is much more likely to remain engaged, because it wants to see how it all gets resolved.

Subtext and metaphor

Subtext is the meaning that resides *beneath* the literal meaning of a story. In a similarly 'invisible but visible' fashion, stories often serve as metaphors for larger things in our lives. Because they are pretty abstract, and because they require a bit of work to perceive and appreciate, subtext and metaphor can provide an audience with a

Challenge your story

Push on your story. Walk around it, and give it a shake. Does it stand up? If it does, you'll be able to build upon it, and that's what you want. Go through your story, moment by moment. Does each portion of your story serve a purpose? It doesn't have to be a big, showy, explicit purpose. It might be very subtle. But purpose needs to be there, and you need to be able to identify it. Is the moment revealing some story point? Is it deepening the audience's understanding of your character? Is it increasing tension, or suspense? Is it slowing things down, as you give the audience a chance to reflect or recover? *If it turns out that a moment in your story doesn't serve a purpose, cut it out.* Or at the very least revise it, until it does serve a clear purpose.

Story tempo

Yet another connection between film and music? Yes, and there's more that we'll look at as the process of filmmaking continues! Tempo is the beat, or rhythm, of something that is occurring over time. With that in mind, have you considered the tempo of your story? Many stories start out slowly, as they establish a world and situation, then speed up and become more intense, as they move towards their conclusion. That's pretty classic, and it certainly works. But there are other tempos you can consider. Your story can instantly start off wildly intense and frantic, and stay that way all the way through. Can your audience handle it? Maybe. Maybe not. But it's worth considering, as you develop things. Or, your story can move very slowly, all the way through, from start to finish. This might allow you to establish and maintain a very meditative, contemplative mood. But will it succeed with your audience? Maybe. Maybe not. There's no hard rule to tempo, but you absolutely need to be aware of its importance, and use it purposefully as you develop your story.

Related to tempo, and carrying on with the connection between music and film, you should be able to 'conduct' your story, as you play it out in your mind. Think about a piece of classical music. Its energy can ebb and flow. It can shift from state to state, and from mood to mood. Moments of wild intensity are only powerful because they stand in contrast to the quieter moments that surround them. Variations provide interest.

As you play your story out in your head, does it have variation? Does it have 'high' moments that contrast with 'low' moments? If the answer is no, are you keeping it 'flat' on purpose? Is there a reason? If so, fine. But an accidently flat story risks losing its audience, simply because it lacks this form of texture.

> Be patient with your story, as you develop it. You may find that it presents you with challenges that you can't solve right away. Go away from it for a bit, then come back. Sleep on it. But don't give up. Respect your story by allowing it the time it needs to reveal itself.

Endings

How many films (features, and shorts) have you watched that have strong stories throughout, but somehow fall flat in their ending? It happens frequently enough, and to stories crafted by very talented artists, that it proves one thing: endings are tricky.

How do you satisfy your audience, without being obvious? How do you provide your characters with what they deserve, but in surprising ways? How do you wrap things up, but not too neatly? Do you leave some elements within the story unresolved? If so, what things?

A story whose ending doesn't reveal itself to you easily during development isn't a 'bad' story. It may just mean that you have a chance to surprise your audience with an ending that it couldn't have imagined, but that feels perfectly right when the final credits roll.

How do *you* end *your* story effectively? You can start by making sure that your character objectives have been dealt with. But there's no easy answer, beyond that. At the very least, you can increase your chances of having a strong ending if you at least take some *time* to craft it. You might find that you need to head back to earlier parts of your story to revise, so that an ending works properly. You might think up a great twist that can be revealed in the ending, but does it really work? Think on it. Sleep on it. Show it around.

Think of your story's ending as your final opportunity to make a good impression on your audience. You wouldn't end a great job interview by dumping a glass of water on the interviewer's head, so value the final moments of your story in the same way. Give the ending to your story the attention that it deserves as you develop the overall thing, so that your audience is left loving your story all the way through, not just up to a certain point.

The audience

Gather up ten people, and we'll call them our audience. Now ask each member of that audience what it wants from a story, and you'll get ten very different answers. That's because while an audience in some ways works as one overall 'hive mind' in the way that it sometimes reacts and responds, that audience is ultimately made up of individual humans, each of which has a lifetime of experiences and expectations that they bring into the mix. Yet despite the individual nature of an audience, you'd be hard pressed to find anyone in the world who doesn't want to feel *engaged* by a story they're being told.

How the story achieves this engagement can be very simple and direct, or very complex and sophisticated. But if it's not happening, if the story isn't in some way engaging, then what do you have? You have ten people (or twenty, or thousands), who are disconnected from the story. And that means that you've lost your audience. For a film-maker (and for any kind of storyteller), that's fatal.

How can you avoid this? For a start, try ask yourself the following questions.

Who is my audience?

You can't know precisely who is going to be watching your film, but thinking about this is extremely useful as you develop your story. Perhaps your story is aimed specifically at kids. If so, what age level? And is there anything in your story for adults to appreciate as well?

Perhaps your 'target audience' is sci-fi fans. If so, what does a sci-fi fan expect? And more importantly, is your story doing something different (even in a small way) within the genre? If your story offers a spin, an inversion, or a new take on genre expectations, your story will stand out to your target audience.

Perhaps the audience you envision for your film is one that wants structure and convention to be thrown out, and wants to see an attempt at something utterly new, and strange, in terms of how a story is told, and what happens within a story. Yet even in this case, you are *still* thinking about the intended audience that you hope to connect with through your story.

And of course, as so many filmmakers long to do, if you want to tell a story that is for 'everyone', have you really taken the time to craft a story that accomplishes that? It's not an impossible task (after all, we all know about hunger, and love, and loss, and fear), but 'everyone' is still a specific audience, when you stop and think about it.

Does my story have unexpected moments?

Remember that you want an engaged audience that is actively paying attention to your story. With this in mind, why not take your story 'over there' at a juncture, when simply 'going here' was to be expected? Have a character react to a situation in a manner that surprises you, yet still seems honest.

If you can surprise *yourself* as you develop the story, that surprise will later be felt by the audience, when it experiences the story for the first time.

And if you then find that a new direction is too extreme, or doesn't work overall, so what? Revise, and carry onward. At this early stage, you haven't invested weeks of work on puppets, sets, and animation, so now is an excellent time to play around in this way. It's all part of developing something fresh, and engaging. Then, once you're happy with it, you'll lock it in.

Is my story 'time well-spent'?

It's strange to think of wasted time, when we're discussing short-format films. But it's amazing how a badly put together story can feel like an eternity for an audience, once it's on the screen. Don't waste your audience's time.

Figure 15.5
Gerald's Last Day, Justin and Shel Rasch, 2009. How could an audience *not* love this little guy? This film does a fantastic job of connecting with the audience on a very honest emotional level.

Figure 15.6
Pineapple Calamari, Kasia Nalewajka, 2016.
This film is wonderfully strange, and extremely funny, in a highly unique way. And it most definitely does *not* waste the audience's time!

This isn't to suggest that your story needs to be a showcase of pratfalls, explosions, or car chases (although all that stuff is fun, if it's done well). All it *really* means is that you remain mindful of your audience in this way as you develop your story. Be aware that your viewer has agreed to pause in her otherwise busy life, in order to consider what you have to say. Repay that, by providing an engaging story, that's worth that time it takes to watch it.

Essential considerations for stop motion

The following isn't an attempt to rain on your stop motion parade. I'm very much in favour of projects that push things further – for the medium of stop motion, and further for individual artists, who want to grow and mature. I'm constantly amazed not only by what upcoming stop motion artists attempt, but by what they achieve. It's endlessly inspiring. But if you consider the following as you develop your project, it might help you to push things more effectively, in the ways that you really want, and it might help you to arrive at results that are more deeply satisfying, for both you and the audience.

You have to make all this stuff.

It's a sobering moment in every stop motion project's development. The artist pauses, looks around the studio space, and mutters 'I can't believe how long this all takes'. This isn't to scare you off, it's just the truth. And in fact, the labour and intensity of the medium is probably part of what hooked you on stop motion in the first place!

But as you get caught up in the excitement of developing a story and planning out a film, it's easy to avoid thinking about the actual work that will be involved. This isn't to put you off a story that will require hard work in order to get it to the screen. You just don't want to find yourself up to your neck in seemingly endless challenges, when what you really wanted to create was a finished film. *You have to make everything that will appear in front of the camera.* Keep this in mind as you develop your story, so that things don't get too ambitious.

Assuming that you are basically a crew of one (or a few), here's a very general rule of thumb, that can help you to keep your project under control as you develop the story: Create a story that requires only a few puppets, and only a few sets. What's a few? If your puppets are very simple, it might mean three or four. If they're very complex, it might mean two, or even one. The same goes for sets.

Finish your film

On the topic of finished films, I'm a big fan, with 'finished' being the key word. I'm less a fan of films that have a few shots done, before being abandoned. That's not a film, that's an attempt. Attempts are essential, but it's not the same thing.

I can chart my own development as a filmmaker by the finished films that I've made, more than by the ideas that I've sketched out and put in a drawer, or by the puppet designs that I've developed, then moved on from. I see the same progress with student filmmakers that I mentor. When they finish a film, they can stand back from it, and learn. It may contain moments that you wish you could do over. In fact, it almost certainly will, since the animation you create towards the end of production will be more accomplished then the first shots you created, if only because you're a better animator by then! But that's just the way it goes.

Remember, your audience wants your film, and it won't be nearly as critical of your work as you are. So hand it over! Learn from the finished film, and from the world's reaction to it. That's how you become good at filmmaker – by making *more* films, not by making just one attempt at the perfect film.

Identify your priorities

Most people start out to make a film that is strong in all ways. But it can be helpful to spend some time thinking about what it is that you really want to showcase in your film. You know enough about the medium now to address this with some confidence. Do you want to show off your puppet design and fabrication skills? Then craft a story that will allow you to do that. Perhaps the main thing for you is animation. If so, what kind of animation? Comedic? Heartfelt? Physical? Once you think it through, let your developing story show that off. If instead of a particular element, you want to show off your overall stop motion filmmaking skills, that's great. In that case, devise a film that doesn't require you to lose yourself in one particular area, and will instead allow you to focus on making the whole thing strong, but in a manageable way.

Savour the process, while moving onward

There is so much to do when making a stop motion film, that if you don't let yourself enjoy the stages, you might get so impatient and frustrated along the way that you turn your back on the whole thing. 'Mindfulness' is a term that can certainly come in handy. The more present you are in the moment, the greater the chance is that you'll find personal pleasure (and satisfaction) in that moment. Thinking like this can get you through a lot of late nights!

That being said, more than a few stop motion filmmakers have loved the stages of making stuff for a film so much, that they've lost sight of the main objective that got them going in the first place: achieving a finished film!

As we start to look at the specific stages of development for your film's story, you'll notice that things start out general and rough, and move towards something more specific and locked down. Firming up your story for production is a bit like crafting a sculpture: you'll want to work rough at first, then move into the detailed work as time goes on.

Social media can be a great way to inform the world about your film, but at these early stages, it's worth asking yourself just how much you want to share during development. Share a little, or a lot, or none at all? Pick an approach that works for you, making sure that you spend a majority of your time making your film, and not posting cool process pictures on social media!

Story pitch

The story pitch involves a storyteller (you) conveying the basics of your tale to someone else (the audience). Does the story make sense to that audience? Is it clear from start to finish? Does it engage? If so, then the audience has 'caught' what you've pitched, and that's a good indicator that your story is strong enough to move onward in its development.

But just who are you pitching to? Well, it could be a powerful producer who will give you a bag of money to make this film (wouldn't that be nice?), but at a basic (and perhaps more realistic) level, you can pitch to anyone who wants to hear it. That can be a classmate, or a friend. It could be a stranger on a bus. It doesn't have to be an animation expert, just someone who is attentive, interested, and willing to hear you out.

You might also consider pitching to a small group of people. If you do, pay attention to your audience's reaction, and let them talk afterwards, as a group. Does your story raise questions for them? One person might 'get' a subtle part of the story, while another might be confused. Who is right? Let them talk it through, and try to stay quiet. Be patient, and let them talk. With everything *they* say, *you'll* be learning more about how to make your story more effective. And as you eventually take part in the conversation, you'll find yourself understanding your story better and better, as you continue to externalize aspects of the story with the group. Sometimes an aspect of story seems clear in our own heads, but it needs clarifying for others.

After you've pitched your story, revise things as you see fit. Then, pitch it again. Present your

Damien, a little boy aged 9, is sleeping in his bed. His mother stands over him. His walls are covered in wrestling posters featuring 'Brent McCoy'. The same thing is on his sheets and pajamas, and there are wrestling toys scattered on the bed and floor. This kid clearly loves wrestling, and counts himself as one of Brent's biggest fans.

His mother places a large wrapped box on to the bed and says "Happy Birthday, sweetie!". Damien wakes up and excitely starts tearing into his present. When he opens the lid to the box, his eyes go wide. He reaches in and pulls out A CHAMPIONSHIP WRESTLING BELT, that he holds above his head.

He quickly jumps out from under the covers and jumps off the end of his bed. He starts flexing and doing some classic strong guy poses while yelling "Mom! Mom! Look!! I'm the HEAVY WEIGHT CHAMP!"

Suddenly, the door to the room busts open and Brent McCoy is standing in the doorway. He yells " No. I'M THE CHAMP!" and starts running into the room. He tackles the boy to the ground with an elbow drop, while Mom looks on, horrified.

Damien and Brent fight, busting up the room in the process. Brent quickly rolls Damien up into a pin. A referee suddenly slides into frame and gives a three count. Brent stands up victorious and is handed the child sized belt by the ref, which he tried to put around his waist. It's way too small and after a few attempts, he relents and puts it around his wrist like a bracelet instead.

Brent puts his arm around the ref and the two of them exit the shot, slamming the door as they leave. Damien, still on the floor, bruised and bloody, regains consciousness and groans. He blinks for a second or two until the realization of what just happened sinks in.

Suddenly filled with vigor he jumps up and down and runs around the room happily yelling "BRENT McCOY WAS HERE! BRENT WAS IN MY ROOM! THIS IS THE BEST BIRTHDAY EVER! THANKS MOM!!!!" He wraps his arms around his mother who looks shocked. Then she smiles, returning her son's hug. The End!

Figure 15.7
Story pitch, *The Champ*, Rosemary Travale, 2014. This film from Sheridan College has a clear, effective pitch. It covers all the key moments of the entire story, from start to finish, without getting weighed down by details. Look for this same film later in this chapter, to see how it moves through the story development stages.

revised story to that same person or group, but also to someone new. Having a fresh audience can be very useful, because that new person has no preconceived notions or opinions that will carry over. That's very valuable!

In the same way that you dealt with feed-back during animation critiques, don't take story pitch feedback personally. It's not about you, it's about your story, and its effectiveness. But also remember – it's your film. You are the one who is investing so much of yourself, so *you* are the boss. Of course, if elements of your story pitch continue to confuse or fall flat with your audience, you should at least consider that pretty carefully.

Script

The script stage allows you to expand on your story after the pitch stage, and to begin the process of working out the details. A film script follows a very standardized format, the specifics of which you can easily find online or in a script-writing guide book. This formatting isn't just to challenge your

word processing skills. It actually allows someone to 'read' your film, in a fairly detailed fashion, while still allowing a lot of room for development.

A good script has just enough information to convey the basics, but not so much detail that it kills the reader's imagination. That's essential in the mainstream animation industry, where you need to convey a specific version of the story to other members of the crew (usually the storyboard-ing team, and later design crew), as they begin to visually and sequentially interpret the story.

In the world of the indie stop motion film-maker, what value does the script hold, if she isn't passing the story along to a crew? It still allows her to further externalize and formalize the story, and it makes it more concrete in the world out-side of her head.

It also begins the process of breaking the story down into specific moments (or scenes), and can provide her with a way to flesh out the story quickly, since words can be revised more easily than images. Can you proceed to the next stage without a formal script? Absolutely. But any step that helps you to sharpen and focus a story is one that you should seriously consider.

INT. Damien's bedroom. Mid Morning.

DAMIEN, age 11, is sitting on his bed, a large present box with a big bow is next to him. His room is covered in wrestling posters and toys and other wrestling paraphernalia, most of which is dedicated to BRENT McCOY. MOM is standing next to the bed. She is early 40's and dressed casually.

MOM
Happy Birthday, Damien!

Damien opens up the present, ripping off the bow. He reaches into the box.

DAMIEN
Oh WOW!

Damien pulls out of the box and raises above his head a championship wrestling belt.

DAMIEN
(excitedly) YEAHHHH!

Damien jumps off the edge of the bed onto the carpet in the middle of the room. He starts flexing and doing classic strong guy poses while mom looks on, amused, in the background.

DAMIEN
Mom! Mom! Look! I'm the CHAMP!
GRRRRRRR!

Sound of door slamming is heard off screen. Mom and Damien look towards the door in shock, Standing in the open door frame is BRENT McCOY, looking angry. Brent is late 30's, a very large wrestler, in his wrestling uniform.

BRENT
(angrily)No. **I'M** THE CHAMP
RRRRRRR!!!

Brent runs across the room and lunges at Damien. Mom looks horrified.

DAMIEN
UAGHHH!!!! (as Brent tackles him)

Figure 15.8
Script excerpt, *The Champ*, Rosemary Travale, 2014.
Compare this to the story pitch. How does the script differ from the original pitch?

Concept art and designs

Assuming that your story is now clear enough to proceed, you can now start developing other aspects of your film that grow out of your story – namely, concept art, and designs for both your characters and your sets and props.

Some animation artists argue that the written script should be developed after story sketches and rough boards have been created (see below). This way, the *visual* storytelling within the film is being privileged, rather than the *literary* version. Others like to see the visuals and the written version develop hand-in-hand. It depends on the specifics of your story, the context in which you are working, and on what works best for you, as a filmmaker.

Figure 15.9
Concept art, *Stubborn,* Eustace Ng, 2017.
The warmth and charm of this Sheridan College film comes through clearly in this development art, which establishes a clear stylistic path for the project.

Concept art

Concept art is development art that is created for the purpose of further clarifying the look, vibe, or feel of your stop motion world. The specifics of this art can be anything really, provided that it helps to move your imagined world and story closer to something 'real'. Often, concept art is environmental in nature, and brings in colours, shapes, and textures that suggest the details of the world. It can help you to see visualize your story more clearly, which is why concept art development and story development often go hand in hand.

If your drawing skills aren't that strong, and you find yourself struggling to create original concept art for your world, you can instead pull together a collection of pre-existing art by other artists that suggest the world that you want to create. This can be a very good source of inspiration, and since it's strictly for your own creative

reference, all is well. Just be sure that you move beyond this, in order to make something that's distinctively you.

Character designs

Figure 15.10
Early design work, *Stubborn,* Eustace Ng, 2017.
These early explorations of different looks and styles will inform later design choices as the characters move closer to fabrication.

At this point in a project's development, the process sometimes goes two ways at once. If you jump too vigorously into design before your story is visually clarified, you might find yourself with designs that don't have a home in the film. On the other hand, if you *don't* get your designs underway, you may find storyboarding to be a struggle, since you don't really know what to include when you draw your scenes and characters! Each artist should find her own way through this particular process challenge, but no matter when you specially want to get into it the designs are, obviously, essential.

Unless your story idea features Nia exclusively, you'll need to design and fabricate whatever characters that are required by your story. And since there's an earlier chapter dedicated entirely to character design for stop motion, I'll let you refer back to that, as needed. Instead, let's consider some designs and puppets created by artists for their own films. Notice how all of these artists explore character design possibilities, before settling into a final look. Also notice how each character presents its own set of distinctive fabrication challenges, which of course is part of what makes puppet-making so exciting!

> As you think through character and set designs, you'll likely be faced with questions that can only be answered by storyboards. Depending on the specifics of your film, you *may* want to get your rough boards done first, or at least get them well underway, prior to spending too much time on designs. You'll see why, as you carry on through the process.

Figure 15.11
Character design, *The Champ*, Rosemary Travale, 2014.
Exploring a character's design from various angles is essential.
Here we see the many sides of Brent the wrestler. All that bare
skin will present some fabrication challenges, but it's pretty
essential for a wrestler puppet!

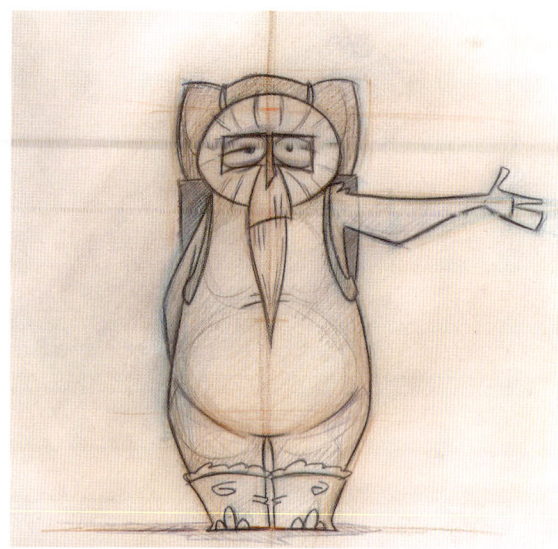

Figure 15.13
Final character design, scale drawing, *The Arctic Circle*,
Kevin Parry, 2010.
In this Sheridan College film, notice how the character is posed
here, to allow for the next stage, which is armature design.

Figure 15.12
Finished puppet, *The Champ*, Rosemary Travale, 2014.
The fun and cartoony style of the drawn character translates very
well into the actual puppet. This puppet also features a simple
and effective solution for lip sync, which involves stylish flat
mouth shapes that tack on to the otherwise smooth mouth area.

Figure 15.14
Final puppet, *The Arctic Circle*, Kevin Parry, 2010.
This image shows very good puppet posing, in order to convey
not only character, but also shape. In the bottom left of the image
you can see a mini bounce board for lighting (see Chapter 8 on
Lighting for more on this).

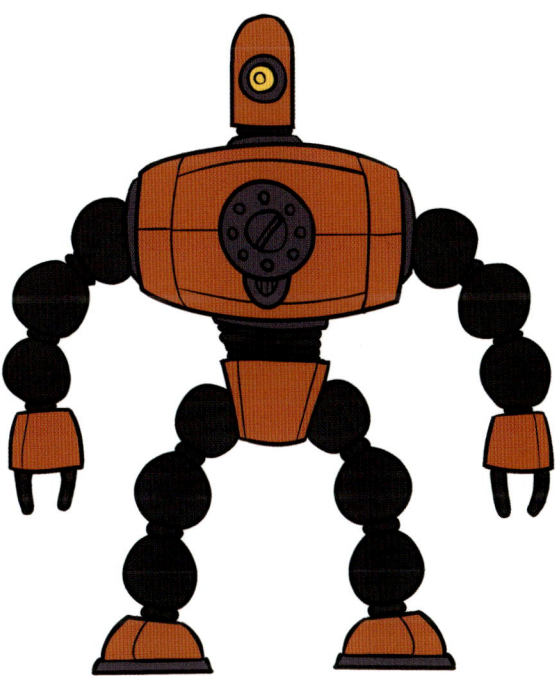

Figure 15.15
Final character design, *That One With The Robot*, Erik Blohm-Gagné, 2015.
With the character design for this Sheridan College film finalized, fabrication challenges can now start to be addressed.

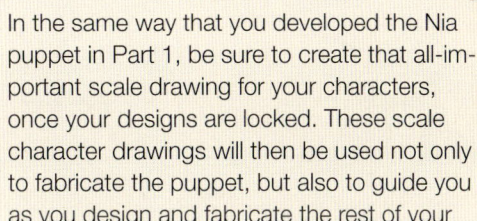

In the same way that you developed the Nia puppet in Part 1, be sure to create that all-important scale drawing for your characters, once your designs are locked. These scale character drawings will then be used not only to fabricate the puppet, but also to guide you as you design and fabricate the rest of your world, including your sets and props.

Set and prop designs

With your story developed sufficiently for you to consider such things, you'll want to start thinking through the specifics of just where your story is going to take place. If your story takes place in one specific location, you'll be able to spend more time making that one set look amazing. Alternately, if your story involves a range of locations, then you'll have your work cut out for you when it comes to set design and fabrication.

Do you envision a very distinctive visual style for your sets and props? If the film you are picturing is heavy in this way, then even a desk lamp or house plant might need to be styled to suit that distinctive look. Sci-fi films are often very heavy on production design because futuristic space ships and alien worlds often need to look completely different than regular old Earth 'stuff'. This can be a very exciting challenge, if you're up for it.

Figure 15.16
Final puppet, *That One With The Robot*, Erik Blohm-Gagné, 2015.
This puppet has a great sense of personality and charm. He may destroy your city, but you still have to love him. The accomplished paint job does a great job of adding a real sense of weight and age to the puppet.

Figure 15.17
Set designs, *That One With The Robot*, Erik Blohm-Gagné, 2015.
A story featuring a giant robot requires a giant city set (even if it's all small scale). And that requires careful designing and planning. Be sure to check in the following chapter, to see how these same designs were translated into three-dimensional pieces.

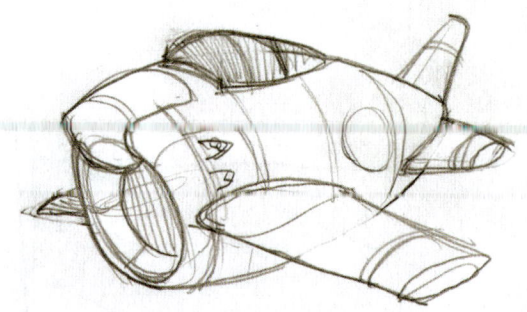

Figure 15.18
Airplane design, *That One With The Robot*,
Erik Blohm-Gagné, 2015.
A very fun design, that is both realistic *and* stylized. Check in the
next chapter to see this design's final three-dimensional form.

Figure 15.19
Set designs, *The Champ*, Rosemary Travale, 2014.
As always, work through your ideas in a quick, loose fashion. You'll
tighten things up later. Check the next chapter, to see how all of
these set and prop designs moved from drawings to actual objects.

On the other hand, a more 'everyday' location
(an average bedroom set, for example) will typically be quicker to design, because you can simply look to the real world to guide you. In these
cases, some artists like to go for strict realism,
even hyper-realism, while others like to slightly
tweak things, in order to create a modest sense
of style, while still keeping things fairly easily to
design.

Beyond the everyday, the world of your film
might be stylized, yet very minimal. In the same
way that theatre sets often suggest locations, the
set for your film might consist of nothing more
than a few items, distinctively lit. This approach
can allow you to focus on things like story, character, and animation, rather than sets.

Regardless of how you envision your sets,
there's a few essential considerations to keep in
mind as you 'set' about designing things. Look,
I haven't used a pun in ages, so just let me have
that one, OK?

- **Don't overbuild.** Why would you design
  (and later fabricate) an entire castle, if you're
  only going to see the castle gate in your
  film?! How do you know if you're only going
  to see the castle gate? That's where rough
  boards come in, so don't design too much
  until your boards are well underway (which is
  the next step in development).
- **Test things out.** Think fast and cheap. You
  can quickly get a very rough version of a set
  piece in front of the camera, by fashioning
  very basic cardboard versions. Just make
  sure that you're always working to the scale
  of the puppets. Get these mock-ups in front
  of the camera, and frame up according to
  what your rough boards are telling you, all
  for the purpose of determining if your designs
  and overall plan for your sets are working.
- **Allow access for animation.** This one
  is hugely important, yet it can be very easy
  to overlook. What good is a beautiful set if
  you've built it so deep that you can't reach
  the puppets during animation? Consider
  restricting set details to the background,
  away from where animation will take place.
  In keeping with this, be careful designing
  sets that have a lot of foreground items, since
  these are very difficult to animate around
  without bumping. If you want foreground
  items, consider shooting elements on green
  screen, and compositing them in later.

The scale character drawings you made to
help with armature design are also extremely
useful when designing sets and props. Use
them to ensure that the size of everything
you're making works, in relation to the size of
the puppets.

- **Allow access for lighting.** Attic sets, and
  sets requiring ceilings, are notorious for being
  hard to animate within, and also for being
  tricky to light. If possible, plan your sets so

that they are clear from above, and you'll have a much better time lighting.

- **Allow for puppet movement.** Remember that your puppets have to move throughout your set. Are doorways wide enough? Is the space between furniture sufficient? How will the puppet stand on your set? Puppets with magnet feet typically need fairly flat ground, so can you 'fake' texture and variations with paint effects? Tie down feet present their own issues, since you'll need to think about how you'll drill through a set, and get foot bolts up to the puppet.

- **Think through the function of set pieces.** If a set piece such as a bed or chair is going to directly interact with a puppet, then that item will take time to design and fabricate. First, it needs to be sturdy, in order to support the puppet. You may also need to figure out how your puppet is going to remain secure during animation. For example, a small puppet, sitting on a high chair, may have its feet dangling in mid-air. If that's the case, feet magnets will be of no use! You may need to use rig points in the armature, and bring a wire out to the chair. Set items that don't need to support puppets simply need to look right for your world. As such, they likely won't take as long to design and fabricate, depending on their complexity.

- **Cost things out.** This applies to literal costs, but also to cost of your own labour. That heavily designed rocket ship interior, filled with amazing gizmos and fantastic machines, could become quite costly in terms of building materials. It also might cost a lot in terms of labour. Think carefully about what you can afford, and always cost things out before committing. And think about what you want to showcase through your film. If the answer is production design and fabrication of sets and props, that's great. But if it's not, then it might be time to rethink that rocket ship a little bit!

> Don't lose sight of scale, and of the realities of your puppet. If your story calls for the character to take a book down from a shelf, you don't want that shelf to be so high on the wall that the puppet can't reach it. You also don't want the book to be so big that the puppet can't even hold it!

Prop design is closely associated with sets. Back in Part 3, when we were getting ready for the Puppet Smash animation, we briefly looked at prop design and fabrication, in order to create the bat prop. Working through prop designs for your film proceeds in much the same way. Think through everything that the character has to do with the prop. Keep the prop light, and ensure that it's as easy as possible for the puppet to work with. You'll find more on fabrication for props (and sets) in the following chapter.

And remember, you can always hold off on taking designs for characters, sets, and props through to completion until *after* your story is visually firmed up. You don't want to spend too much time designing something that isn't going to be shown in the actual film (even though it might still result in some nice work that will good in a design portfolio!)

Story sketches and rough boards

Growing out of your story pitch, it's time to get specific. It's at this stage that your story starts to really take on its true shape. As you begin to sequentially tell your story, you'll be choosing the specific angles and camera set-ups. You'll be deciding the edits and transitions that move your story forward effectively, and you'll be creating the overall flow of your film, from beginning to end. As you might expect, a stage that's as important as this can take a long time to work through, depending on how complex your story is. Be sure to refer back to Chapter 9 dedicated to Camera, since so much of storyboarding is tied to what you do with the camera, and where you place it, to best tell the story that you want to tell.

Story sketches

Story sketches convey certain pivotal story moments, prior to boarding out the entire thing from start to finish. Once these key moments are clarified, you can proceed to 'fill in the blanks' of the rest of the story with greater confidence, knowing that your showcase story moments are already solid. Alternately, you can proceed right to the actual storyboarding

Figure 15.20
Story sketches,
Stubborn,
Eustace Ng,
2017.
Developing central
story moments
first can be a good
way to start the
visual storytelling
process.

Rough storyboards

When a student wants specific production feedback on his stop motion film, I always tell him that we'll have a serious meeting once the rough boards are complete. That's because with rough boards in front of us, we'll both be seeing the same version of the film. If there's only a verbal pitch or a written script, there's too many variables floating around. The film he's seeing in his mind won't match the one in mine. But with rough board in front of me, I can really start to evaluate, and eventually help to plan a film. These boards don't have to be pretty, and even basic stick figures are fine. But they do need to be basically clear, and they do need to be *specific*.

What specific angles and set-ups will be used? What will you specifically show, in order to tell the story? Are you consistently using very wide shots? Then you may need to spend a lot of time designing and fabricating sets. As for puppet concerns, that horde of zombies sounds very cool, but your rough boards call for twenty

process, since in the end, the whole story has to work sequentially, not just in portions! Different people like to approach this in different ways.

Figure 15.21
Rough storyboards, *The Champ*, Rosemary Travale, 2014.
These rough boards do an excellent job of indicating the specifics of what the camera will see, but without getting dragged down by details that simply aren't needed yet.

of them! Maybe you can achieve the same thing, story wise, with slightly fewer puppets, which will free you up to address other production issues. These are examples of the kinds of specific concerns that can start to be addressed the instant rough boards are completed.

Figure 15.22
Rough storyboards, *The Arctic Circle*, Kevin Parry, 2010.
Sometimes, rough boards don't need a lot of revising before they move into finals. If it works, it works!

But rough boards don't just clarify production challenges. They also reveal how you specifically plan to connect with your audience emotionally. And that's every bit as important as knowing how many sets and puppets you have to make. What do you show in your story? What do you leave out and allow the audience to imagine, or piece together for itself? How do you develop tense moments within your story? How do you give importance to contrasting quiet parts? What do you emphasize for the audience, so that the audience feels what you want it to feel? The true orchestration of your film should be evident already, in your rough boards, even if it doesn't take on its true flow until you've edited the actual film together.

Camera moves are certainly possible to indicate in your storyboards. They'll just take a bit of planning out, and when you get to the stage of creating your animatic, you'll need to invest some time in creating the movements in Premiere.

One of the most important bits of advice I can offer when it comes to creating rough boards is to always work loose and fast. Nothing is precious at this stage. The time will come to lock things down, but that time isn't now. You may go through half a dozen versions of rough boards for your film, and if you let them be rough now, starting over will be easy, should you need to.

You can dash out a quick template of panels in a sketchbook, find a template online, or develop one yourself in Photoshop. It doesn't matter, yet. You can draw on paper, or digitally, whatever suits you, although digital will make revisions easier, and also allows for easier importing into your animatic (more on that, later in this chapter).

As with your story pitch, it's a good idea to present your rough boards to individuals, and to small groups. You need that audience, and its feedback, to ensure that things are coming through effectively. One person might have entirely new ways of depicting parts of your story, and if those suggestions work, incorporate them. Another person might have a perfect solution to a story issue that you've been struggling with, but that you couldn't solve because you were too invested. Keep your ego out of it, and strive for the clearest, most effective boards that you can create. Then, once you're feeling confident, it's time to move on to finals.

Assuming that you want to work in a standard industry style, you should have your finished character designs, as well as finished designs for sets and props, before moving into the next stage. This way of working is especially helpful if you have a crew contributing work, because having final designs in your final boards ensures that all departments know exactly what is required. Of course, if you're a crew of one, then you can firm up designs as you see fit. Just be aware of what the industry expects.

Final storyboards

As you might expect, final storyboards grow out of your rough boards. They are more carefully crafted, and show even more specifically the details of each of your shots. As for just how detailed final boards are, every filmmaker approaches this in a different way. Some people insist on perfectly accurate character designs, along with designed sets and props. Specific and detailed posing of characters might also

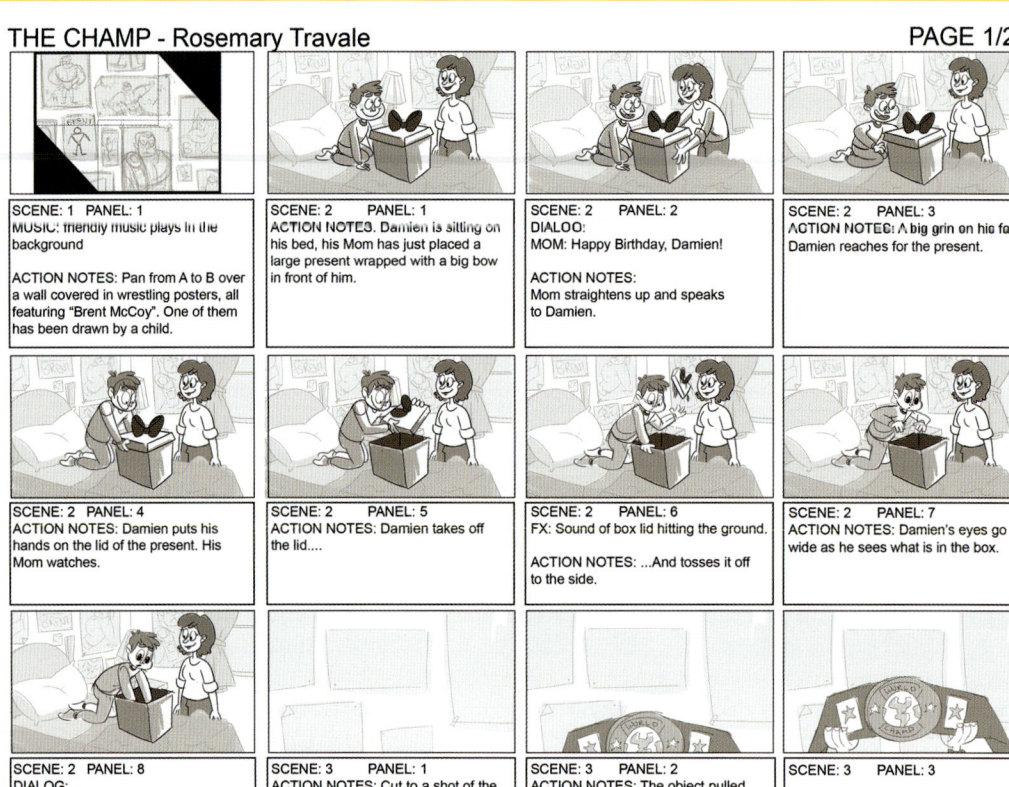

THE CHAMP - Rosemary Travale   PAGE 1/25

SCENE: 1   PANEL: 1
MUSIC: friendly music plays in the background

ACTION NOTES: Pan from A to B over a wall covered in wrestling posters, all featuring "Brent McCoy". One of them has been drawn by a child.

SCENE: 2   PANEL: 1
ACTION NOTES: Damien is sitting on his bed, his Mom has just placed a large present wrapped with a big bow in front of him.

SCENE: 2   PANEL: 2
DIALOG:
MOM: Happy Birthday, Damien!

ACTION NOTES:
Mom straightens up and speaks to Damien.

SCENE: 2   PANEL: 3
ACTION NOTES: A big grin on his face, Damien reaches for the present.

SCENE: 2   PANEL: 4
ACTION NOTES: Damien puts his hands on the lid of the present. His Mom watches.

SCENE: 2   PANEL: 5
ACTION NOTES: Damien takes off the lid....

SCENE: 2   PANEL: 6
FX: Sound of box lid hitting the ground.

ACTION NOTES: ...And tosses it off to the side.

SCENE: 2   PANEL: 7
ACTION NOTES: Damien's eyes go wide as he sees what is in the box.

SCENE: 2   PANEL: 8
DIALOG:
DAMIEN: Oh, wowwwww!

FX: sound of paper rustling as Damien reaches into the box.

SCENE: 3   PANEL: 1
ACTION NOTES: Cut to a shot of the wall above Damien's bed, covered in posters.

SCENE: 3   PANEL: 2
ACTION NOTES: The object pulled from the box rises into view.

SCENE: 3   PANEL: 3

Figure 15.23
Final storyboards, *The Champ*, Rosemary Travale, 2014. Compare these final boards to the rough boards versions, as shown in Figure 15.21. How are the final boards more detailed?

be involved, along with all camera moves and transitions between scenes. Other filmmakers are content with clean and clear panels that are little more than tidied up versions of the rough boards, and that present the characters as they will basically look in terms of their designs. It's up to you, as long as the final boards are tidy, and include the following:

1. Clear numbering of shots, as well as panel numbers
2. Clear depictions of specific characters
3. Clear blocking and staging of characters
4. Clear indications for character movements within the frame
5. Clear transitions between shots (cuts, fade in, fade out, etc.)
6. Clear indication of any dialogue and specific sound effects
7. Clear composition, that ensures all essential action and story is conveyed
8. Clear indication of any specific visual effects requirements, such as green screen or rig removal

As you can see, keeping things clear is pretty darn important! That's because these final boards will eventually go up on your studio wall (more on that in the next chapter), and you want them to be very easy to reference, with all the details that you'll need to create your shots, so that you can quickly refer to them as you set up. These boards also need to be very clear because it's these actual panels that will be directly brought to life, as you create your animatic (see below).

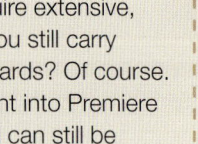

What if your story didn't require extensive, detailed storyboards? Can you still carry onward, using only rough boards? Of course. Rough boards can be brought into Premiere as easily as final boards, and can still be edited together with sound, to create the blueprint for your final film, as you'll see.

SOUND

With the visual component of your story in place, it's now time to think about the other vital aspect of your project, which is the audio. Your story may rely heavily on sound, with narration, lots of dialogue, and heaps of specific sound effects. Alternately, your story may be purely visual, with no dialogue, and only a few sound effects that will emphasize certain moments.

No matter what role sound plays in your film, it's now time to prepare the specific pieces of audio for your film, so that you'll be able to blend these pieces of audio with your visuals, during the creation of your animatic (see below).

Rough voice track vs final voice track

A rough voice track is a temporary recorded version of your dialogue that will serve as a guide throughout production. This guide audio can also be used during animation, depending on the specifics of your film. Assuming that your film has characters speaking lines, one way of working is to do a temporary voice recording now, use that recording during animation, and then have your final voice actor match the animation, in post-production. I've had good results using this method, but it all depends on how talented your voice artist is – not only at performing, but at matching the animation!

Ideally, if your film is dialogue heavy, and if voice performance is essential to your film, you should record your final voice track *now*. Then, when it comes time for animation, you will have the actual, final voice recording to inspire you, and push you, in terms of performance, while you are animating.

Assuming that you have dialogue, and regardless of whether it's rough or final, you'll need to record it. In Chapter 14 we focused on animating with dialogue, so you'll want to refer back to that chapter for specifics on voice recording using Adobe Audition. You'll follow the same process now as you record the voice track for all of your shots.

As you record, be sure to match the naming of your recorded takes to the naming that you used in your storyboards. This will make tracking all the files much easier, further along.

If you're recording final dialogue now, it's essential that you set yourself up carefully, so that you can achieve the highest quality recording possible. This was looked at in some detail, back in Chapter 14. Ideally, this will be done in a formal recording studio, with the help of a recording professional. If that's not possible, do whatever it takes to ensure that you're recording your voice talent in a very clean, clear fashion.

Working with voice actors

Anyone can provide a voice recording for animation. But as with anything in life, some people are simply better at doing this than others. A talented voice artist can bring your written words to life through performance, giving them the shapes, and colours, and dynamic ranges that you imagined while you were writing them.

The right voice (or voices) for your film may belong to a trained actor. After all, they've put in years of hard work to develop these kinds of skills. You can look to acting programs in schools, where you're sure to be able to find folks that would be eager to help. But you might also look to someone who isn't a professional actor, but that just has the right voice for the role, and knows how to use it during recording. Use your ears, and 'listen' around.

Regardless, it will be up to you to direct your voice actor. You'll need to be very clear on what you want, and express that as confidently as you can, so that you can get the best performance from your voice artist. Provide all of the required lines of dialogue to the actor well in advance, and be prepared to answer any questions that your actor may have. At the same time, you'll want to provide room for your voice actor to try his or her own interpretation of things. That's just common courtesy, and it also might result in you getting something wildly exciting that you could never have dreamt of, but turns out to be perfect.

Take care of the actor. Basic things, like providing a bottle of water and a brief break once in a while, go a surprisingly long way. A well-treated actor will reward you with better performances, a better recording, and in the end, better animation. You're both artists, working towards a great performance, and the back and forth required to achieve that can be very rewarding for everyone.

Sound effects

Sound effects are what make your stop motion world sound and *feel* real. They can provide fantastic atmosphere, and when used effectively, sound effects can actually help to tell your story effectively and economically. A character might hear the doorbell ring (a sound effect), walk off screen, and a moment later return with a pizza, freshly delivered. The audience understands what just happened, but it all took place in one simple shot, with no need to fabricate a hallway, doorway, or delivery person!

At this point in the process, there are different ways that you can approach sound effects. As with a film that only has a very small amount of dialogue, you might use temporary sound effects for now. These would be sounds that you find through a sound effects library, through various online sources, or by doing your own recording. Then, in post-production, you could replace these temporary sounds with final recordings.

You're probably best to keep any sound effects that you're actively gathering to a minimum. There's no sense adding to your work at this point, and there will be time in post-production to get serious about sound effects. Focus on essential storytelling sound effects, and ones that are required for animation. For example, if you have a shot of a character using a hammer, then the sound effect for this will be required during animation, so that you can time things effectively. Therefore, that's a sound effect that you'll need to have, now.

Temporary music

As with sound effects, having temporary music at this stage can be helpful. You can use any music, regardless of whether you are cleared to use it in your final film (more on this in the chapter dedicated to post-production). You can use temporary music to convey mood, and to indicate shifts in tempo. It can build tension, or relieve it, and it can even help to emphasize story moments.

Be very careful that you don't fall in love too much with this temporary music. Powerful music, at this stage, tends to be so powerful that it can overwhelm things, and before you know it, you'll be crafting your film to suit the music!

My advice is to only use music at this point if it's absolutely essential to help with storytelling. Otherwise, leave it out for now. I've seen too many projects become overwhelmed by temporary music to recommend otherwise. You'll have time in post-production to get serious about music and ideally, music should be thought of as something that emphasizes and amplifies an *already* strong film, not the other way around.

The exception, of course, is if you are creating a 'music video' type film, that is actually being built *around* a pre-existing piece of music that will be a part of the final film. In this case, your music drives everything as you develop your story and storyboards, and it should continue to do so, as you begin to prepare your animatic.

You now have your essential audio elements, as well as your visual elements (final storyboards). It's time to put them together in a manner that moves you ever closer to the finished film. In other words, it's time to craft your animatic.

THE ANIMATIC

You've got your final boards, and now you've got your audio elements. Like the ingredients for some mysterious dish, you've got everything you need to craft this thing called an animatic. So what is it? What purpose does it serve to your film, and why is it so darn important?

Overview of the animatic

At a basic level, you can think of the animatic as your 'slideshow with audio' version of your film, whose *duration* is the same as your final film. Not only is the overall duration of the animatic the same as your final film, each and every shot within the animatic will be the same duration as the corresponding shot of animation that you're going to create.

This idea of corresponding durations between boards and animatic is a very important one, and merits a closer discussion. Shot 1 in your storyboards may consist of three different panels. Those panels will then be edited together to make Shot 1 in the animatic. This shot, from start to finish, may end up having a duration in your animatic of 3 seconds (a fact you will only know once the entire animatic has been put together). Once you know this, you will then also know that Shot 1, when animated, will also have a duration of 3 seconds. That is the *ultimate* value of the animatic: it determines specifically how much animation you'll be creating, during production.

I've stressed before the connections between filmmaking and music, partly because both film and music progress, and change, over their duration. As you assemble your animatic, using your final boards and essential audio, you'll be creating the overall flow of your film, from beginning to end, right down to the frame. And in very real way, you'll be creating a version of your film that, if it's created effectively, should stand alone as a rough but effective version of your finished film.

You'll achieve this through editing your picture and your sound. As you lay one shot after another, you'll be determining how long those shots are on-screen for, and how they work with your sounds. You'll be *composing* your film in the same way that a musical composer works – by starting at the beginning of the piece, and working your way through to the end. Making your story rise and fall in an effective way, over time, and creating the specific form of your film that will be experienced by your audience, is your ultimate job as a filmmaker. And it starts with the animatic.

One final important consideration. For many years at Sheridan, I worked alongside Kaj Pindal, the devilish Dane who created many remarkable and entertaining cartoons over his long career. Kaj would always emphasize to students, 'Get your story moving!' He was making the point that looking at storyboards only told you that the *boards* were working. But ultimately, you aren't making boards – you're making a film. And films move. Get your animatic underway, and get your film moving on the screen, so that you can see how it *really* functions. And go watch Kaj Pinal's animated films, many of which can be found at the NFB's website!

If you're very new to video editing, you'll have to take some time to get used to Premiere, beyond what is covered here. Like most software, its basic functions are pretty easy to pick up, so you should be able to progress on your animatic pretty quickly, provided your project isn't too complex. For more advanced work, be prepared to invest time in Premiere.

Adobe Premiere part 1: Setting up the animatic project

What you'll be specifically doing in Premiere may be extremely simple, or quite complex. Regardless of the details, you're going to bring your final storyboard panels and sounds into Premiere, align them in a timeline from start to finish, and then edit it all until you have the form of your final film. From start to finish, this task might take you an hour or a week, depending on the film that you're making.

Before starting in, if you drew your final boards on paper, you'll need to digitize them so that you can bring them into Premiere. You'll be able to resize them if needed, once you've imported them. Be sure that your storyboard panels are numbered clearly once they're digitized, and that you keep the numbering consistent as you import into Premiere. If you keep that same numbering consistent into production and post-production, you'll reduce the chances of mis-placing (or altogether losing) vital content.

Depending on what version of Premiere you're using, the basic steps needed to set yourself up may differ somewhat from what follows, since software is always getting updated. Help Menus and online resources are always standing by to help!

STEP BY STEP

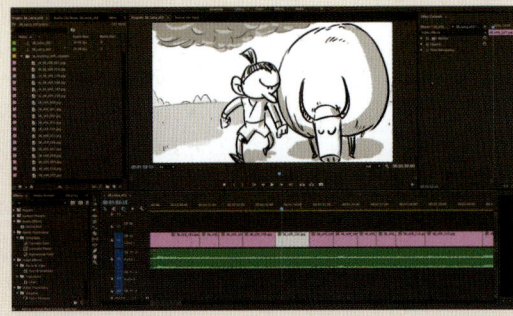

Figure 15.24
Animatic editing workspace, *Stubborn*, Eustace Ng, 2017.
This is the basic workspace in which you'll edit your animatic, once you create your Sequence.

The editing and software skills that you'll develop through working on your animatic will also be put to good use during production and post-production, when you start to assemble your actual film.

1. Launch Premiere, and select New Project. Be sure that you're saving the project to the folder that you created earlier, and be sure to place (and retain) all of your animatic files in that folder.
2. You are now in the Editing Workspace, which is where you'll do most of your editing for the animatic.
3. Before you can do any work on your animatic, you need to create a Sequence. Do this by going to File, then New, and selecting Sequence. As you'll see, there is an array of options. For now, I'd recommend going into the Digital SLR folder, and selecting DSLR 720p24 (see Figure 15.25 for details).

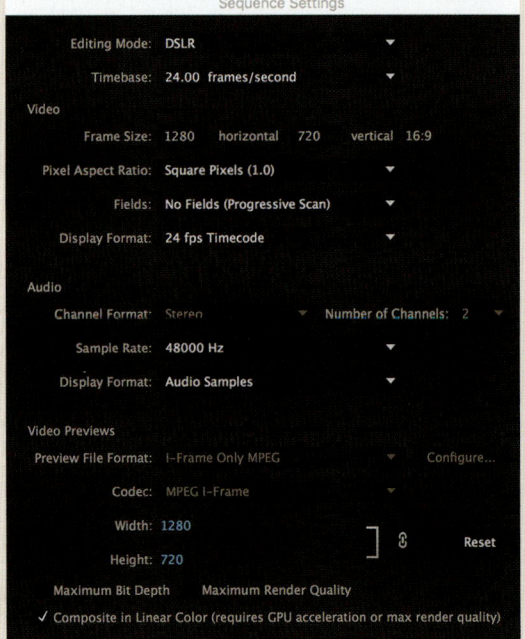

Figure 15.25
DSLR 720p24 sequence settings.
This setting provides you with high definition, correct aspect ratio, and correct frame rate (assuming you are working at 24fps). Other settings can also work, but this is generally a safe choice.

> The Sequence that you set up contains the specific picture, audio, and playback details for your animatic. It's important that you set up your Sequence correctly, so that the duration of the shots you'll be creating (and the duration of your overall animatic) is an accurate guide that you can take onward into production.

4. Now that you've created a Sequence, go to File and select Import. Select your storyboard panels, and bring them into Premiere. You'll see each panel displayed in the Project window.

5. Now import your audio files. They'll appear in the same Project window as your storyboard panels.

6. Drag your first storyboard panel and place it on to the V1 track – this is your main layer for editing your panels. Place your second panel to the right of the first one, and so on. As you place your panels on the track, leave a bit of space between each of them. This will make it easier to grab each panel later on, when you're adjusting its duration.

> Rather than placing all of your panels on the V1 track, you could use a 'checkerboard' style. To do that, place Panel 1 on V1, Panel 2 on V2, and Panel 3 on V1 (the same track as Panel 1). Carry on like this as you lay your panels on the tracks, and you might find it easier to adjust your shot durations later on, simply because each shot has a bit more room around it, on the timeline.

7. If you have audio, you can now bring those files on to the timeline in the same way. You'll place audio on the tracks labeled A (for audio). You'll see various audio tracks (A1, A2, and so on). It's good practice to reserve certain timelines (or tracks) for various sound elements. Typically, you should place dialogue on a specific track, sound effects on their own track (or tracks), and yet another track for music. This will make sound editing much easier, since you'll be able to find various sounds on the timeline quicker, if you know which track to look on.

8. Once you have your panels and audio placed in your timeline, grab the playhead controller (it has a thin vertical line that runs down through all of your tracks), and slide it back to the start of your timeline. The spacebar starts and stops playback, so give it a go. You should see your very roughly assembled animatic, playing out. It won't be timed in a way that's accurate, but finding that correct form is precisely what your task is now. So have fun!

> To move the position of a panel or sound on the timeline, simply grab it and reposition it along the timeline, as needed. Once it's on the timeline, you can change a panel's duration by grabbing its end. Pull it outward to extend its duration, and pull it inward to shorten it.

If you're new to editing motion pictures, it's a very good idea to just play for a while. Get used to the controls in Premiere, and get used to what it's all about. Some time spent playing around in a low-pressure way now is a great way to learn about the software, and about editing.

As with any piece of software, Premiere has a wide array of tools that you can use on your project, but there are a few that you'll go to constantly, as you craft your animatic. Below, I expand on a few that I use a lot when editing.

Essential Premiere tools

Selection Tool

This is the tool that Premiere equips you with from the moment your create a project, and you can think of this as your main editing tool – you'll have it activated more than any of the others.

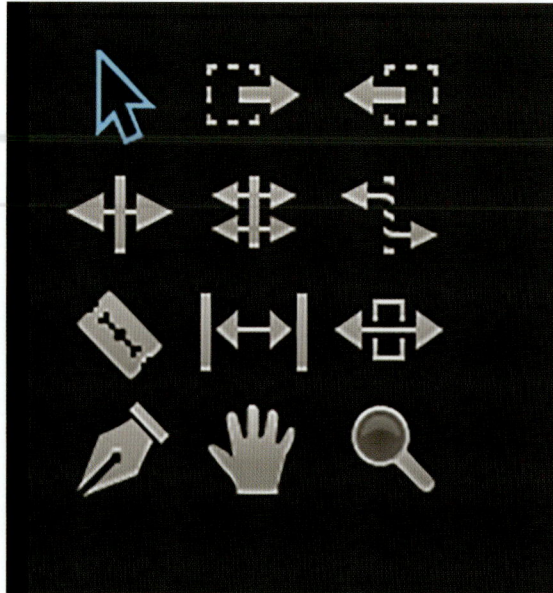

Figure 15.26
Premiere Tools window.
You'll constantly switch between these tools as you work. Hover your pointer over the tool to see its name. The tool highlighted in blue is the Selection Tool.

You can use this tool to grab and move your shots around on your timeline, and also to adjust durations of your storyboard panels.

Track Select Forward Tool

This one takes a bit of getting used to but it's well worth the effort, because it's a fantastic editing tool. It allows you to grab your entire timeline's contents, to the *right* of your selection, and move it as desired. It allows this without changing any of the overall relationships within your edit. This is hugely valuable, since all of those edits may have taken you many hours to create. By using this tool, you can make room around one panel so that you can adjust it, and then move everything back again. With some additional keyboard commands, you can also select the content to the right on *one particular track*, which is also extremely useful.

Razor Tool

This tool allows you to 'cut' a clip (picture or audio) at a certain point. With the clip cut, you can then switch to the Selection Tool and adjust each newly formed clip from its ends, as needed, or move it to wherever it's required. You'll use this tool more often when editing animation rather than when

creating an animatic, but it's still an important one to know about, and to get used to managing.

Beyond the contents of the Tool Box window, there are some other essential tools that you'll find yourself using quite a bit.

The Scale Tool

This tool allows you to change the scale (or size) of a storyboard panel once it's on the timeline. This can be a very useful thing, since as you edit, you may find that you'd like to somewhat change the composition of your shot. This tool lets you do that, and you can then grab the panel and move it around until you're happy. To scale a storyboard panel, click on the storyboard panel, then go to Window, and select Effects Controls. Expand the options for Scale, and you'll be able to adjust the size of that specific panel. This adjusted size will be maintained on your timeline, even to the point of exporting the timeline as a movie file. This process only adjusts the size of the panel on the timeline. If you bring the same panel in again from your Project box, it will be the same size as it was before you adjusted it, so if you need to reuse the resized panel elsewhere, just copy the adjusted panel, and then paste it wherever else it's needed.

Figure 15.27
The Scale Tool within the Effects Control window.
To adjust the image's size you can use the slider, or enter a numeric value. You can also click on the actual image in your edit window, and then grab the edges of the image, and scale it up or down.

The Effects Controller window allows you to manipulate all kinds of things within your picture. For example, you can create movement of panels, in order to simulate camera moves, which can be very handy. Dedicate some time to learning more about what this window can offer.

Video transitions

This set of tools allow you to create certain transitions that will be essential to your animatic. To access these transitions, go to Windows, and select Effects. You'll see a sub-window open up in your Project box. Expand the options for Video Transitions, to see your choices.

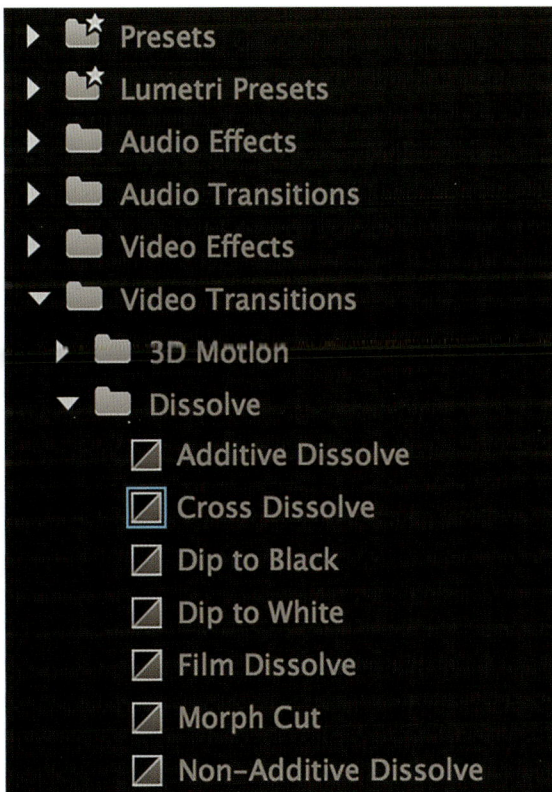

Figure 15.28
Video Transitions window.
In this window you'll find lots of transition effects for your picture tracks. Stick to the classics of film, like dissolves and fades. Unless you're going for a 'cheesy comedy' look, of course.

'Cross Dissolve' is always a safe bet. With it, you can dissolve out of a panel and into black, resulting in a 'fade to black'. Alternately, you can dissolve into a panel from black, creating a 'fade in from black'. To use a transition, simply drag it from its location in the Project box and drop it on to the end of the panel you want to effect. You can then adjust the timing of the effect by grabbing it and sliding it.

THELMA SCHOONMAKER

Most famously known as Martin Scorsese's editor, Schoonmaker has made a stunning career out of mixing pictures and sounds, in order to create some of cinema's more memorable films. Working with live action footage, Schoonmaker takes all of the unassembled work, and gives it shape, to create the final film. She creates the tempo, the flow, and the actual *shape* of the movie. If you carefully study Schoonmaker's editing work, you'll receive a master class in how to build a film, that you can then apply to your own work within animation.

Working with sound in Premiere

In the same way that Premiere allows you to edit your animatic's storyboard panels, it also lets you craft your film's sound. You might just need to move some sound files around on the timeline (using the Selection Tool). Or it might involve actually cutting up your sound files (see the Razor Tool), and patching them back together, again using the Selection Tool. This might be very minor work, as you remove a few microphone clicks here and there. Or it might be a massive undertaking, as you blend parts of various takes of a voice recording session until you arrive at a final performance.

Beyond those tasks, much of your work with sound at this point will involve the 'mixing' of sounds. Mixing refers in part to where your sounds occur on the timeline, but it also refers to overall 'loud vs quiet' considerations. If your voice track, sound effect track, and music track are all very loud, (or very soft) all the way through your film, your audience won't be able to understand what you're trying to communicate. In other words, if you don't give the same attention to sound that you do to audio in your animatic (and later, in your film), no amount of excellent picture editing is going to cover up the sound problems. To ensure that the sounds in your project are flowing in the way that you want, there are a few tools in Premiere that you'll need to master.

Figure 15.29
Audio Track Mixer window.
At the right of the panel, you'll notice the Master slider. This slider overrides all others, and it's generally best to leave this set at '0'.

At this stage, don't invest too much time and energy in doing seriously refined sound mixes. Just worry about basic things like the volume of tracks, and the overall placement of sounds on the timeline. A truly refined sound mix will happen later, during post-production.

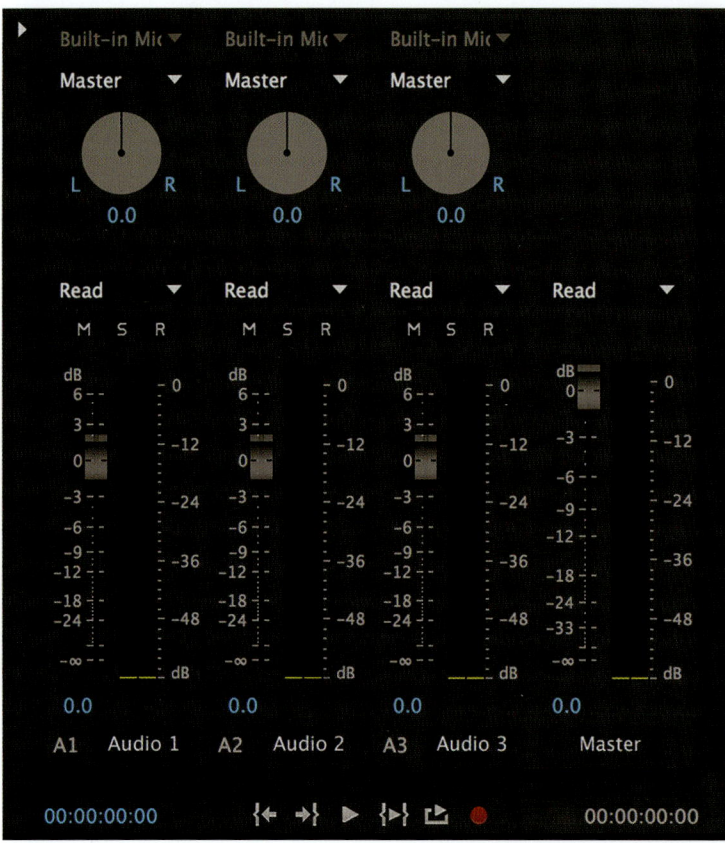

Audio mixing window

This window allows you to control each track's overall volume. To open it, go to Window, and select Audio Track Mixer. As you can see in Figure 15.29, each track of audio has a slider associated with it. Slide it down and the sound becomes quieter. Slide it up, and it gets louder. So if your animatic has the sound of rumbling thunder throughout, you would place the thunder sound effect on a particular audio track, and adjust the track's volume until it reaches a nice 'background' level that doesn't overwhelm the more important sounds that occur (assuming you have other sounds).

You'll also see that each track has a meter. This meter gives you a visual guide to how loud your sound is on that track. If you play your animatic, you'll see any sound on that track represented through the meter, and generally speaking, 'red' is dangerous. It means you've set that track too high, and that you're distorting the sound. Ensure that all of your sounds stay out of the red range, and generally speaking, you should be fine.

Adjusting sound by using this window allows you to adjust audio on an entire track, but what about subtle edits, such as fading sounds in and out? In the example of the thunder sound effect used above, what if there is a moment when you want the thunder to suddenly become much louder, only to then recede? For that, you can use the pen tool.

Pen Tool

The Pen Tool is very useful for subtle audio edits, and you'll find it located in the same box as the Selection Tool. You can use it to place an edit point on an audio file, which you can then grab (using the Selection Tool) and raise up (to go louder) or down (to go quieter, or to fade out completely). To do a fade out, place two edits points side by side. Grab the point on the right, and drag it down. There you go – the sound fades out. To fade *in* a sound, you can place two edit points at the start of a sound, pull them both all the way down, and then raise the second point. You can adjust the duration of these fades by dragging the same points further along the timeline. In this way, you can create endlessly subtle audio edits, as needed.

As any audio engineer will tell you, you need to avoid wearing headphones when editing sound, and definitely don't wear them when finalizing your sound. That's because headphones invariably make your sound louder (and not just louder, but generally different), relative to how the rest of the 'non-headphone wearing' world will hear it. This is important when putting together sound for your animatic, but will be even more important in post-production, when working with your 'real' sound, on your final film. If headphones are needed so that you don't drive others crazy, then make sure you're at least checking your sound regularly without headphones. Your roommates (or cat) will understand.

A final word to the audio-wise, as you think ahead in the filmmaking process: post-production may seem like a long way off, but start looking around now for someone who is an audio specialist, especially if sound is a major component in your film. Quality sound is vital to a film's success, and as dedicated as you may be to animation (and visual things, in general), there are others out there who feel the same way about sound. Wouldn't you like their ears (and their talent) helping you to make your film even better?

It's very important to remember the following: once you're in post-production, and you're editing your actual film, you'll need to come back to your sound again, with renewed dedication. The animatic's sound may be sufficient at that time, and you may be able to use it 'as is' in your final film, but that's rarely the case. At the very least, you'll need to adjust your sound in spots. But you may also need to record (or acquire) final audio recordings, and go through the same editing process as you did with the animatic. It takes time, so allow for it.

Picture editing tips

In the same way that learning how to create quality stop motion takes dedication and time, good editing skills only come with practice. But here are some quick tips that can help you to improve your skills in this area fairly quickly, so that you can craft an effective animatic, and so that you can carry on in the bigger process of making your stop motion film.

Let it be long, at least for now. In time, you'll obviously tighten the duration of all your panels, with some remaining on screen longer than others. But it's hard to know which panels to shorten (in terms of duration) if everything is racing ahead too fast. Let it be overly long. It will feel sluggish, but that's ok for now. Play it all back. Then start shortening the durations of certain panels, until you start to find the visual tempo that works for your story.

Remember that motion picture and music are very similar. Speaking of tempo, don't forget that a piece of music has fast moments, slow moments, intense moments, contemplative moments – and that they all work together to create an overall shape or form. Your animatic (and eventually, your final film) also needs to function in this way. Remember that unless done expertly, 'flat' can cause an audience to wander away, but variations can keep an audience engaged.

Keep playing it back. You'll recall that in the Animation section, I stressed how important it was to always play back your animation, so that you could tell how the overall shot was taking shape. The same practice is essential during editing the animatic. Although the overall form of your animatic is made up of still images (your panels), they only function correctly when played back in relation to all of your other panels in the animatic. Remember, your animatic happens over time, from beginning to end.

Get some fresh eyes on it. You need an audience, to ensure that your animatic is working. For example, you may assume that certain panels are on screen long enough to 'read', but that could be because you've been looking at them for ages, and have gotten too used to them! It's these sorts of things that you need an audience for, to ensure animatic clarity, since you'll simply be too close to the edit to tell.

NORTH BY NORTHWEST, ALFRED HITCHCOCK, 1959

If you think *you're* having a bad day, wait till you see what Cary Grant's character has to deal with in this suspense thriller. It's a great film overall, but in particular, search for the 'crop dusting' sequence, to see some fantastic visual editing. It's man versus airplane, with no dialogue. Watch how each edit helps to tell the story, to explain the action, and to help build tension and excitement. The editing you perform on your film should be just as effective!

Your animatic is complete. Now what?

You now have a specific blueprint for production. More specifically, you have a guide for the actions, acting, blocking, staging, and sound that makes up each shot. You also have the specific duration for each shot, and that's critical, since you need to know that to plan all of your animation.

You can leave your animatic as a Premiere file, and refer to it during production, or you can export the entire project as a movie file. This second option is a bit safer, since it reduces the risk of making accidental changes to the animatic.

Alternately, you can export your animatic shot-by-shot. This can be a good option, since it gives you a specific movie file to reference for each and every shot. A brief search for how to export selected portions of a timeline in Premiere will show you how to do it. Just be sure to name the export the correct shot number, for later reference.

When you're exporting, whether it's your entire animatic or shots, make sure that you don't make any changes to frame rates or playback speed. You want the durations of your export to match the durations in your animatic.

As for audio, your finished animatic also provides you with a precise portion of audio for each shot, that you will take onward into production. You can mark in and out points and export the audio only, or only certain tracks, such as dialogue, and then use that audio in Dragonframe as you animate. See Chapter 13 on Animating Dialogue for more on this.

If you're working with a musician who will be creating a score for your film, you can now provide the musician with a copy of the animatic, which will guide the musician, until you can provide a final edit of the actual film. You'll find more insights into working with a musician in the chapter dedicated to post-production.

Even though your animatic may now be complete, you'll never really abandon it. You'll constantly be updating it during the following stages of filmmaking, and you'll find more on this topic in the following chapter.

A final insight into all of the hard work required to craft an animatic. This whole process of developing an animatic for your film is extremely useful for stop motion, and it's the way that professionals work. But if you'd rather just move into production using only a set of storyboards, and no animatic, it's entirely possible. A very short and simple story may simply not require an animatic. Just remember that if you don't use an animatic, you'll still need to carefully visualize (and time out) each and every one of your shots. Then, be sure to stick to that timing, during animation.

Production planning

Production planning is the stage of making a film that's easy to rush past, if only because it's so exciting to head into the studio and start making stuff. But if you take the time now to specifically think through how you're going to approach all of that fun

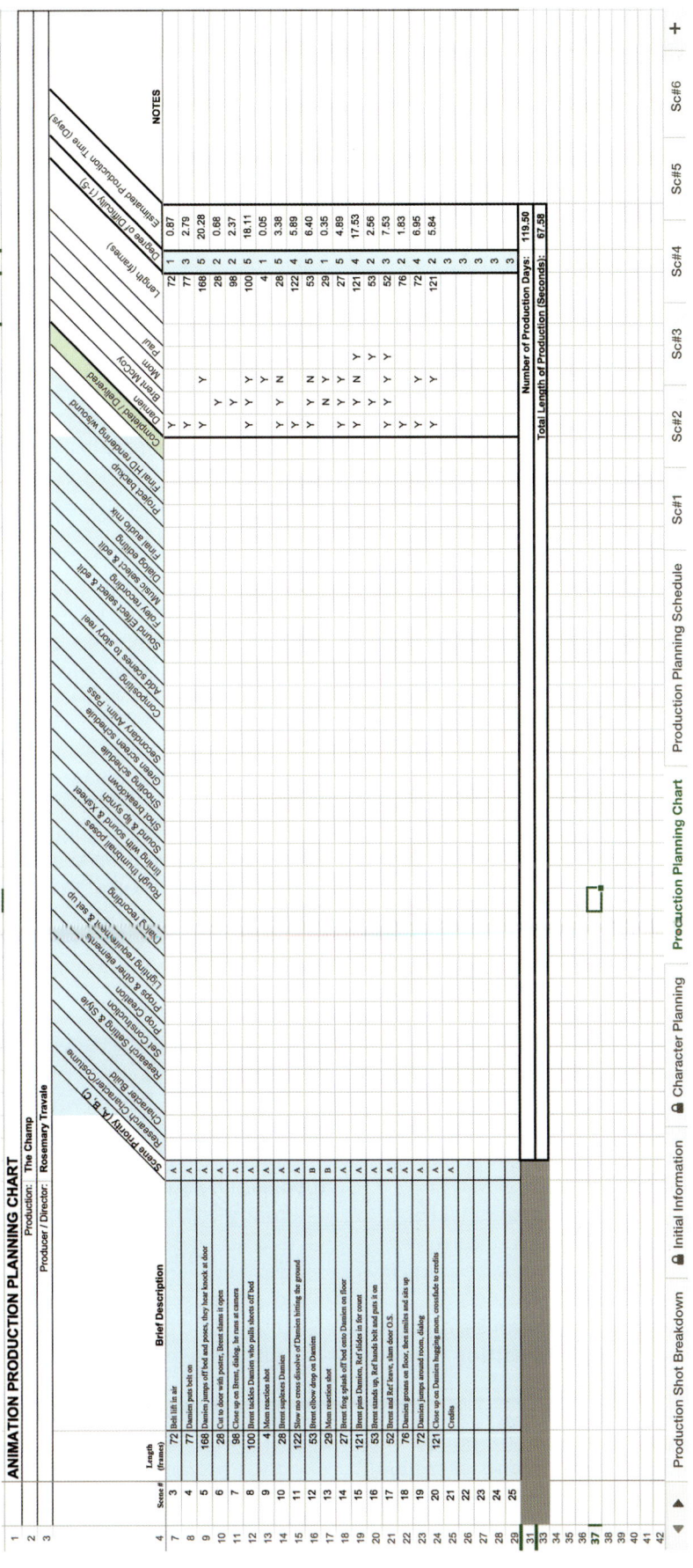

Figure 15.30

Production planning chart, *The Champ*, Rosemary Travale, 2014.

It doesn't take long to figure out the basics of making a spreadsheet, and depending on how complex your project is, it can be a huge help in planning. Use the categories and pages that you see laid out here, to help you organize things.

work, you'll stand a much better change of finishing everything on time. You'll also stand a much better chance of not getting too stressed, when faced with the inevitable challenges that lie ahead.

If your project is modest, and you don't have many time constraints, your plan can be very simple. But if your project is complex, with a range of sets, lighting set-ups, and puppets, you'll need a more detailed plan. And if your project has strict time constraints on top of these challenges, you have all the more reason to be organized, and efficient.

Production schedule

You can't schedule something without a calendar, so dedicate one to your film. Then, ask yourself – what's my delivery date? Yep, just like a baby, your film needs to arrive, all shiny and new, so that the world can adore it. And that doesn't just happen 'whenever'. Even if you have the luxury of a flexible deadline, you need to impose this date, for scheduling purposes. Now you can create what is sometimes referred to as a 'work back plan'. To create this, look at your delivery date, and start moving *backwards*, working your way through all of the stages of making the film (most of which you'll find laid out in this section).

Planning effectively requires asking all sorts of questions: How long do I have access to the space? What about access to the tools, and other equipment? How skilled am I at making the different things required? How quickly can I move through animation? Or, how slowly do I need to go, so that the animation looks fantastic? How

are my post-production skills (if digital effects are going to be required), and how do they stack up against the needs of the project? What about other aspects of life – family, friends, job? Of course, if you're making a project for school, there's also the school's deadlines that have to be considered.

When it comes to animation, you'll need to precisely think through the specifics of all your shots. This will involve reviewing your entire project, shot by shot, and breaking it down, in order to create what we'll call the *shooting order*.

Shooting order

The order in which you'll create your shots has little to do with the actual order of the shots as they appear in your boards and animatic. The reason for this 'out of order' order, as you've probably realized, is efficiency. You don't want to set up the same set a dozen times. Instead, you want to set it up *once*, and shoot all the shots that involve that set. But just how do you go about generating a shooting order? There's no carved-in-stone method, but here's some tips that should help. You'll obviously need to customize, and deviate, from these tips – but they'll get you going in a good direction.

As you'll see from the following tips, creating a production schedule tends to go hand-in-hand with creating a shooting order. You can't have one without the other!

Work from your storyboards. One of the first things you'll need to do once you've moved into production will be to get your storyboards up on the wall (more on that in the next chapter). But why not do it *now*? Seeing your whole project laid out before your eyes will help you to see patterns, and that can be a great help when planning a shooting order.

Group together shots that can be created from the same tripod position. Moving the camera in a major way takes time, and often requires quite a bit of resetting of set pieces, lights, and other studio equipment. Look through your boards, and determine which shots can be created, one after the

other, from one position. Changing the lens angle is fine, as well as other small changes, but by planning this way, it maximizes the day.

If possible, refrain from grouping too many complex shots together. It can be a bit discouraging to go from one intense, back-breaking shot, right into another. If possible, try to place a less-challenging shot after a hard one, not only to keep things rolling nicely (easier shots are quicker to create), but also to keep your spirits up!

'Shoot out' your set. This means you should create all the shots that occur within a given set, before moving on to another. Trust me, you *really* don't want to strike (take down) a set, only to discover that you have to put it back up a few days later, perhaps only to do one more shot!

Group 'special' shots together. By special shots, I'm referring to things like green screen shots, or other kinds of special effects shots (more on those in the next chapter). Any shot that requires an odd or unusual set-up is likely to slow down your overall flow. But if you group them together, at least you can look at your schedule and know that a day of 'weird things' is coming your way. That being said, some people like to mix in oddball shots with normal shots, to keep things interesting. Do what works best for you, but keep this suggestion in mind.

PETE LEVIN, DIRECTOR

Pete Levin is a Los Angeles-based animator, writer, and director, specializing in stop motion animation. For over a decade, Pete has worked for the larger animation studios on productions like *Moral Orel, SuperMansion*, and *Robot Chicken*, as well as independently as an animator and director for television, commercials, and music videos. You can check out his work at www.petelevinfilms.com.

Here's some tips from Pete, when it comes to planning, and shooting.

- It all starts with the animatic. Not only will you know how complex your shot is (number of characters, camera moves, etc.), but you'll know precisely how many seconds/frames you're aiming for it to be and can schedule your animation days accordingly.
- Your production schedule (not to mention your budget) is an ecosystem where everything is interdependent. Choices in puppet fabrication or animatic editing can affect everything all the way down to post-production and VFX.
- Make sure you've allotted time for changeovers between shots – not just setting up new lighting, but also set dressing and securing puppets (especially in crowd scenes).
- If you don't have multiples of a puppet, assume there will be down time with that character, so you can make repairs.
- If you're working on a limited budget or schedule, know going into production which shots you'd like to put more resources into and which shots you can simplify.
- Make sure that the animation monitor is positioned in a place where it will be easy to look at while animating. Animation takes much longer if you're fighting a sore neck or back. Proper footwear and padding to stand on will help with this as well!
- Keep the studio meticulously organized! Finding the right tool for a specific job is important, but you don't want that search to eat up your time!

MARK CABALLERO, SCREEN NOVELTIES

Together with Seamus Walsh and Christopher Finnegan, Mark Caballero runs Screen Novelties, a LA-based animation studio that specializes in stop motion for television and commercials. Their clients include Nickelodeon, Cartoon Network, and Disney, among many others. But basically, they're all about making *very* fun stop motion.

Q. Can you briefly outline the process that Screen Novelties follows for story development, when it's developing its own projects, such as *Krampus Christmas* or *The Witch Doctor*?

A. Sometimes it starts from a story idea, but most often, it grows out of a strong central character, since it's the character that drives the story. And of course, there's doodles. Almost everything starts with doodles. We have our office set up so we can see each other, and see what we're working on, and so if someone has an idea, we just start to draw it up and show it around. Some ideas don't go anywhere, but when something catches on, then we know it has potential. That's a reason to have a formal meeting about it, and see what we can do with it. Then we do whatever it takes to get the idea into some kind of physical form, so that people can start to see it in the same way, literally, that we do. Sometimes an idea isn't something that can be easily expressed through words, or through a written description, sometimes you really do have to *see* it.

Q. **What about when Screen Novelties is developing work for a client?**

A. In this case, a lot of the work comes to us as a script, and we work through that. Like in the case of the *Elf* Christmas special, we went through the script very carefully, in order to work into it our own way of seeing what was on paper. We had to respect the original film, but to do a good job, we really had to approach the whole thing in a way that asked 'How would *we* do this, to make it fun, and to do it in our way, to match our sensibility?' Once we started to approach it that way, it gave us the freedom to really make it our own, and give it a real *reason* to be animated. In the case of *Spongebob*, there's a standard that's already established that you have to live up to, and so you have to rise to that, and make something that's every bit as good, since the audience is going to expect that.

Q. **Great voice acting can provide animators with a lot to work with, when it comes to performance. You've worked with some amazing voice actors, including Tom Kenny and Mark Hamill. Any advice for animation filmmakers who may be working with voice actors, to help them get great animation voice tracks?**

A. As an animator, you *are* an actor. You act, through the puppet. So the more clear you are on what kind of acting is required for the character when you come in to do a voice record, the better, because you can then express that to the actor. And always remember that as amazed as *you* are about their talent, they're every bit as amazed by what *you* do, as an animator, and they want to give you the very best recording possible. Don't be afraid to really give specific and direct notes, because that gives the voice actor something to work from. Mark Hamill is a great example of that, when he was working on *Elf*. He's *such* a talented actor, and he loved checking out the puppet, and really getting into the role, to find something exciting he could give us. He just kept giving us more and more, so we would be sure to have great tracks to work with.

Q. **What's some advice that you'd offer to a stop motion filmmaker who is preparing to step into the production part of the process?**

A. Know your story inside and out. Go to those boards, and know everything awaits you. Be ready to be challenged, and be ready to defend the approach that you want to take. Sometimes, you'll have to fight, and to have a strong vision of what you want to see. You have to find a way to create and then maintain a distinctive approach, and voice. Or at the very least, you need to find a way to hold on to the voice you already *have,* in the face of so much other stuff that's out there.

Know your character really, really well, and if the animation is going to be stylized, you need to really *see* that stylization in your mind, so that you ensure that you get it. In animation, it's really easy for stylization to slip towards realism. It's a natural thing, for that to happen. So you need to really see that style, in order to hold on to it, and achieve it.

16

Production

Now that your story is solid, and your animatic is all ready, it's time to start recording all of those beautiful frames for your film. What will make them beautiful? Your skills and artistic vision, of course, but more specifically, it's the assets that you'll place in front of the camera – the actual stuff. That means your sets and props, and to that end, this chapter will help you to take your designs in this area (that you developed in the previous chapter), and move them onward, into fabrication.

Your film's frames will also be beautiful because of how you've composed and lit them. You'll do this by applying the skills that you developed in the camera and lighting chapters, back in Part 2. But, as you'll see, you'll also be faced with some new challenges in these areas that are particular to filmmaking. This chapter will help you to both recognize and address these challenges.

Finally, your beautiful frames won't be much to look at without quality animation, and to do that you'll make full use of what you learned in Part 3. But just as with lighting and camera, you're going to discover that creating animation for a film has certain distinctions from creating animation for stand-alone shots. This chapter will identify these distinctions, and provide you with specific methods for handling them, as you create your film.

You'll notice that this chapter doesn't examine puppet fabrication for your film. Since all of Part 1 is dedicated to puppet fabrication, you can obviously refer back, as needed. You can also modify those fabrication methods to fit the needs of your film's puppets. Of course, depending on what you've dreamt up for your film, you may need to explore entirely different fabrication methods and materials. Even then, Part 1 should still provide you with solid reference information.

By the end of this chapter, you'll have deeper practical knowledge that you can apply to creating your sets and props. You'll also be equipped with a stronger understanding of the production process that goes into creating a stop motion film. Perhaps most importantly, though, you'll have a better understanding of how to apply the stop motions skills that you've already developed, so that you can create the most effective film possible.

Figure 16.1
Hive set, *Hive*,
Adam Ciolfi,
2016.
A detailed view
of a beautifully
atmospheric stop
motion set.

SETS AND PROPS

The following section will help you to take your designs for sets and props and bring them into the three-dimensional world. As you move through this section, you'll notice that there's no hard distinction made between fabrication for props and fabrication for sets. That's because both tasks call upon the same basic skills, and often use similar materials and tools. That being said, the skills that you developed when making precision small-scale items (as when fabricating Nia in Part 1) will be especially useful when making props, while set-making will typically require 'larger scale' approaches, similar to the ones you used when making the animation deck, back in Part 2.

> If you have a very elaborate set that requires serious wood-working skills (and tools), you may want to bring in extra help. Ideally, your helper would have some set-designing and fabricating skills already. Even if they haven't worked in stop motion, their overall experience and abilities will be extremely useful to your production.

Essential considerations

One of the most exciting things about stop motion is that when it comes to sets and props, it allows artists to create incredibly distinctive and unique worlds. You may have wildly complex designs for a range of giant sets, or you may just need a single wall that you'll place behind your puppet. Regardless of whether you're going big, small, complex, or simple, the following list should help you to think your way through some of the challenges that lay ahead.

Put your storyboards up

This one is so important for all stages of production that you'll see it repeated later in this chapter. Why is it specifically important for sets and props? Getting your boards up on the wall will let you check (and double-check) for every time a prop or a set item occurs within your film. Based on that, you'll know more precisely what's required of that item, before you make it, and before it needs to be involved in animation.

Work to the scale of the puppet

Remember that scale drawing you made of your puppet during its design and fabrication? Be sure to keep using it now. Making a doorway in a set wall? Check the dimensions of the door against your scale puppet drawing. Need to know if a kitchen counter that you're making is the right height? Checking it against your scale puppet drawing will instantly provide you with the answer.

> Floors and ground pieces in stop motion are always a challenge. An uneven style might look great as a design, but it can often become very tricky during animation. Try painted effects, applied directly to the animation deck, or adding texture that is very low relief, so that the ground is still basically flat. This will make it much easier for your puppets to stand and walk!

Know your budget and stick to it

Costs for materials can start to climb very quickly, so you need to be mindful. Plan your spending, and track it! A single trip to the hardware store, if you aren't mindful, can use up all your funds very quickly. And if you are on a very tight budget, try to remember that finding affordable solutions can be a great exercise in creativity.

Think in sections

Assuming that your set has walls of some form, consider fabricating each wall as a separate piece (see more on this below, in the section called 'The basic set wall'). This approach will allow you to connect walls together when needed, and it will also let you *remove* portions so that you can get in for lighting, for camera, and for animation. This also makes moving and storing sets much easier.

Ideally your designs have taken all of this into account but if not, you can still incorporate this approach when building.

Figure 16.2
Projector prop, *The Magic Projector*, Chris Walsh, 2007.
It's great fun to imagine complex props like this one. But they can add serious costs to your production if you have to hire a professional to help you design and fabricate it.

> To make a prop easier for a puppet to hold, consider adding a pin to the prop. Use a pin drill to create a very tiny hole in the prop. Then cut the tip from a sewing pin, and use CA glue to secure the tip in the hole (sharp end out!) You can now carefully pin the prop into the puppet's hand. Just be sure to give your puppet a little hug, afterwards.

Figure 16.3
Picture frame prop, *The Magic Projector*, Chris Walsh, 2007.
In the case of this prop, it needed to be carried around by the puppet for quite a while. Elaborate rigs would be too cumbersome, so ensuring it was light and easy to carry was essential.

Figure 16.4
Texture in stop motion, *Apples*, Neeraja Rajkumar, 2014.
Stop motion is real world stuff, and the real world has textures.
Use this fact to make your film more visually interesting, like in
this student film from National Institute of Design (India).

Embrace texture

Texture is one of stop motion's most basic attributes. Don't fight it. Celebrate it! Sometimes the most amazing imagery in a stop motion film is the result of a textured object being hit with a bit of light from the perfect angle. With this in mind, try thinking of texture in materials as 'free art direction'. Granted, the style of your project may call for completely smoothed out, glossy slickness, and if so, that's fine. But it never hurts to at least consider the roots of the medium as you fabricate items.

Workspace and tools

As you'll see in some of the images that follow, even though we work in miniatures, stop motion sets can get pretty big. And to create something big, you need a big workshop space. But at the other extreme, many beautiful sets for many stop motion films have been made in the good old 'bedroom workshop'. As with all things, you'll need to be creative, as you work with what you have.

Workspace

Depending on the nature of your sets and props, you may need to approach things in the same way as you did with armature-making, back in Part 1. Ideally, you'll want a space with a sturdy table, and a range of tools that are readily accessible (see below).

Some construction noise and mess is inevitable as well, so make sure that your workspace is good with all this. Depending on the materials that you'll be using, ventilation might also be an issue, so having a window that opens to the outside can be important.

Tools

Depending on the details of your project, you may need a range of tools to handle fabrication for your sets and props. Many of these will be the same tools that you used during armature-making, although you'll notice there's a greater focus on tools that are construction-oriented. Fortunately, at least for general set fabrication, there's nothing that's particularly specialized, nor exceptionally expensive. And remember – never buy what you can borrow! Underwear being the exception, of course.

In addition to general hand tools (hammers, screwdrivers, and so on), here's some additional tools that are commonly used for set and prop fabrication:

> The following lists of tools and materials are designed to help you learn more about this part of the process. Use it for reference, but don't feel that you need to buy it all, just because it's listed. Let the needs of your film (and your own resources) dictate that!

- clamps (These are great for securing pieces together while glue is drying. There's a range of styles, but C-clamps are especially useful for larger pieces.)
- utility knife (You want the regular size as well as a small-bladed knife, for precision work.)
- cutting mat
- metal ruler
- spray bottle (Depending on whether it works for your film's look, this is a great and simple tool for 'aging' set pieces. Once a set is finished, you can spray watered-down paint on it, let it dry, and add another layer. The technique takes some practice so try it out on a scrap piece, but when it's done well it can create a lot of visual interest to your world.)
- pin drill (This handy and inexpensive tool lets you drill precise and tiny holes in your set or

props. You'll also need to get the tiny drill bits that go along with it, but considering its low price, it's a tool that's really worth having.)

- helping hands tool (This is a great tool for holding props in place during fabrication. It can also be used during animation, and you'll see an image of it in Chapter 7.)
- cordless drill and drill bits
- hair dryer (A cheap one is extremely useful, for speeding up drying times of paint.)
- screwdriver bits for drill (If you have a lot of larger set pieces to assemble, this is a much faster way to work than inserting screws with a screwdriver.)
- scroll saw (This power saw is an investment, but it can be very useful. Its thin blade allows you to make extremely tight turns as you cut your material, so you can make ornate shapes very easily. If you intend to do any amount of precision cutting for miniatures, this is a very sound purchase.)
- jig saw (This is a general purpose power saw that is very good for most stop motion jobs that you'll encounter. With practice you can use it to cut straight lines, although its main use is for cutting shapes.)
- shop vacuum (A shop vacuum is an industrial strength machine, and will make quick work of just about any mess that you might make.)
- hot glue gun (It may be a common tool, but in fact a hot glue gun is extremely useful when making sets and props. It's very strong glue that dries very quickly making it great for all sorts of set and prop jobs. Consider investing in a better quality one, since you'll use this tool a lot.)

- adhesives (You'll always need lots of glues and tapes. Be sure to refer back to the 'Commonly used materials' section in Chapter 3 for details.)
- safety glasses and safety masks (As with any construction, you need to work safely when fabricating sets and props.)
- assorted general items (This would include paints, brushes, aluminium foil to bulk up the inside of items, spatula, tongue depressors, sandpaper, rags, glues, and tapes.)

> Beyond basic tools, there are many larger power tools that can be very useful, especially for set-making. A table saw for example, is great for accurately cutting larger pieces of wood, and this can greatly reduce your work time. If you have access to such tools and can use them safely, or if you know a skilled person who can use them, then go for it!

Commonly used materials

Every set piece and prop requires its own approach to materials, since it's not only a question of form, but of design. Consider Figure 16.5. In that example, the designs are relatively realistic, with a slight lean towards

Figure 16.5A and 16.5B
Table, lamp, and clock, *The Champ*, Rosemary Travale, 2014.
This desk shows a clever use of balsa wood as a final surface, on top of a basic foam core shape. The clock and lamp base are Sculpey, and the lampshade is simply coloured paper. As for the unfinished back of the desk – this is a great way to save time and resources, as long as you carefully consult your storyboards to ensure that you'll never see the piece from the unfinished angle.

'cartoon'. But what if the design was for a 'caveman' story, and the same objects had to look like they were formed from rock? In that case, the same objects might require very different materials for construction. As you'll find, there's never an easy answer in stop motion for material choices, but honestly – that's part of the fun. Whatever ends up working for a material, works. And what's great about that fact is that sometimes the very cheapest material can provide a perfect look, if that material is utilized effectively.

What follows, then, is a list of common materials used for set and prop construction, along with some insights into how the materials can be put to use. It should help guide you, but always be on the look-out for unusual materials that can provide unique and exciting looks for your project. You won't see yarn in this list, yet a stop motion world whose sets and props are *knitted* could look fantastic!

Board materials

For general set and prop construction, these materials are pretty much essential. They are widely available, highly affordable, easily worked with (since they can be cut with a knife and don't need any saws or power tools). And if they're used mindfully, they can be very strong. They take paint very well, and you can also apply other materials to them, such as plaster (see below). Having an assortment on hand lets you mix and match different thicknesses, depending on what you need to make.

Regular foam core

This board is well-loved by artists all over the world. Essentially, it's lightweight foam with firm board on each side of it, making it very strong and very light. It typically comes in white or black, but you'll also find it in other colours, and you can get sheets of varying sizes. There's really no end to its use in stop motion. It takes paint very well, but it *will* warp if you apply paint to large portions of a sheet, so be careful if you are using it for a set wall, or for a sky.

Double-thick foam core (Gator board)

As you'd expect, this is the thicker, tougher version of regular foam core. It might be a bit harder to track down, but it's extremely useful for making simple set walls (see below). That's because it's far less likely to warp when painted (compared to regular foam core), yet it's still easy to cut with a utility knife.

Cardboard

Yep, the stuff that regular boxes are made with. Look for large boxes from appliance stores. These will provide you with large, clean pieces that are smooth and strong, and can be used for making all kinds of things. Best of all, stores will be more than happy to let you take away all that you can carry, for free.

Illustration board

This board is very thin yet very strong, making it ideal for all kinds of stop motion jobs. Since it's

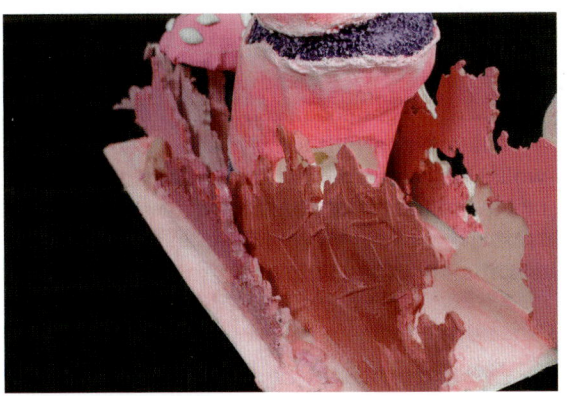
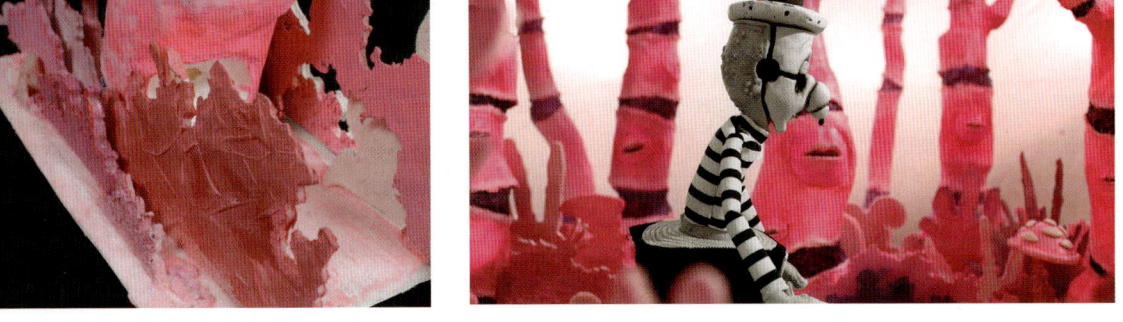

Figure 16.6A and 16.6B
Creative use of foam core, *Never Stop Cycling*, Colin Lepper, 2014.
Foam core is incredibly useful, not only for building objects but also for creating visual layers, as shown in this Sheridan College film. These thin layers can provide a great sense of depth within the frame, without costing a lot in terms of money or labour.

thin, it's often used to add surface-level detail to objects, rather than for actual structures. For example, a house built of foam core could then have window trims and shingles applied that are made from illustration board.

Rigid polystyrene insulation board

That's an impressive name for an impressive material. This is a hard foam board (that's often a very cheery pink colour), that's typically used for insulation purposes. But it also happens to be fantastic stuff for set and prop fabrication. First of all, it's very affordable, very sturdy, and incredibly light. And you can create an endless assortment of things with it. You can carve it, or sand it to an extremely smooth finish. You can glue it on to other things, and it takes paint very well. You can use larger sheets of it to make set walls. There's really no end to its use, and you can see what it looks like in Figure16.8.

It does have a few safety concerns when you're using it. Sanding it creates a lot of fine dust that is toxic, so be sure to wear safety glasses and a safety mask, and be sure to sweep up carefully. Carpentry glue and general white glue are safe to use with this foam, but avoid hot glue, which will simply melt the foam, and will release nasty fumes. But as long as you keep these issues in mind, it's very stable and easy to work with. It comes in different thicknesses, and is typically sold in large sheets. Look for it at most hardware stores.

> Creating skies for stop motion is a challenge unto itself. At a basic level, it's simply a large, thin piece of material, painted appropriately for your world, that's suspended behind your set, either by being taped to the wall or (ideally) being held in place with a grip stand. Bigger is always better when creating skies, since you don't want to run out of it in your wide shots!

Woods

Depending on the complexity and size of your sets, the board materials described above might not offer you enough strength. That's where wood comes in. Many of these woods will require

cutting, either with a hand saw or a power saw of some kind, so you'll need to be prepared for that, in terms of tools and skills.

Masonite (also known as hardboard)

You may recall that this was the sheet material used to construct the animation deck in Part 2. It's very thin, very smooth, quite sturdy, and relatively easy to cut. If you need a sturdier set wall than board materials can provide, then this is a great alternative.

Balsa

This is a great wood for stop motion projects. It's extremely light and easy to work with, as you can readily cut it with a utility knife. You can use it to construct any number of objects, or to add detailing. As you'd expect, wood glue works fantastically well on balsa. This wood is especially useful because it has actual, honest-to-goodness wood grain. In other words, it looks like wood (amazing, I know). If you stain it, or lightly paint it, the grain will come through beautifully. You can find it at art supply stores and craft stores, and it comes in various thicknesses, but the thin sheets are especially useful. Be mindful of cost – if you need a lot, it can quickly get expensive. To keep costs down, consider using it as a final layer on objects, whose basic shape you've made from foam core or cardboard.

Pine

As with masonite, if you built an animation deck, you likely used pine. This is the most common all-purpose wood that's used for most construction. It's strong, light, affordable, and easy to work with. Your set may not require its strength, but for larger projects, it's a must. It's also great for certain props, since it's soft enough to cut easily. For example, if you refer back to the images for the Puppet Smash animation exercise, you'll see that the bat prop I created was made from a piece of pine dowel, and was easily carved by using a utility knife.

Plywood

This wood is similar to masonite, in that it's smooth and comes in sheets, but it's much thicker, and far sturdier. A modest set probably won't require the strength that plywood provides, but it's important to know about it. If you have a large set, you'll need plywood. And because it's thick, you'll definitely need a power saw to cut it.

Sculpting material

Quite a few of these materials will already be familiar to you, since many are used during puppet fabrication. Certain materials listed can be used on their own to create objects, whereas others work best for providing final surfaces on objects.

Mesh wire

Fine-gauge mesh wire is great for creating environments and objects that have irregular shapes, like hills or caves. Once you have your main shape, you'll probably need to add some support material. Once it's sturdy, you can cover the mesh with masking tape, and then apply a finishing material to get your final surface. Watch out for sharp edges – consider wearing work gloves while you work with this material. You can purchase mesh wire at art stores and hardware stores.

Clay

It's not durable, and you have to be careful to not smudge it during animation, but there's no denying that clay can be an awesome material for sets and props. You can use it as a final surface on sets, and its inherent texture when smoothed out looks wonderful.

Regular Sculpey and Super Sculpey

You're probably a pro with these materials already from your puppet making efforts! It's great for creating all kinds of props, and also for creating details for set pieces. When possible, try to 'bulk up' shapes first with aluminium foil, not only so they don't become too heavy, but also to save on the cost of the Sculpey.

Modeling putty

As with Super Sculpey, you're likely familiar with this material by now. It's the two-part compound that provides you with lots of sculpting time, before it hardens on its own. You don't need to bake it since it air-cures, and it can then be sanded, drilled, and painted. You'll find lots of uses for it in the worlds of stop motion set and prop making.

Wood filler

This is a pretty amazing substance. It comes in tubes or tubs, and you can apply it to gaps and spaces in sets and props, in order to create consistent surfaces or to fix mistakes (hey, it happens). Once it's dry, you can sand it flush with your surface, and paint it. You'll see an example of wood filler in Figure 16.8.

> You can use cleaned out yogurt containers for mixing and storing larger quantities of paint, or to hold brush water. The lids provide a great surface for mixing smaller amounts of paint, and you can use the rim as a handy place to rest your brush. Best of all, everything can be rinsed clean and reused. For paint, not yogurt.

Figure 16.7A and 16.7B
Interior cave, *The Shutterbug Man*, Chris Walsh, 2014.
The basic shape for this set was first formed in mesh wire that had simple wooden supports attached. It was then covered in masking tape, then plaster. Sand and pebbles were mixed into the plaster, for additional texture and detail. The final look is appropriately spooky and claustrophobic.

Plaster

Like wood filler, this is a very handy material, that's typically used for filling gaps and holes in the world of construction. Once it's dry, it can be sanded and painted. Beyond filling gaps, it's also quite useful for providing finishes on larger set and prop surfaces. Dried plaster be given detailing through carving, etching, or sanding, before being painted. There's all kinds available at the hardware store. You can get it in powder form (that requires mixing in water), or pre-mixed. Look for the kind that dries quickly.

There are some safety concerns to bear in mind with plaster. Wear a safety mask and eye protection when mixing it (in the case of powdered plaster), and when sanding it, since it creates an extremely fine dust that is not good for your eyes or lungs. It also becomes quite warm as it cures, so don't be surprised when your newly plastered wall starts to give off heat! It cools down rapidly, as it sets.

> Safety with tools and materials is always of utmost importance. Always read material labels carefully. Safety glasses, masks, and work gloves should always be put to good use.

**Figure 16.8
Various fabrication materials.**
On this main piece of polystyrene foam, from left to right: wood filler, plaster with various effects, and an additional piece of polystyrene foam (the blue piece) that has been cut, sanded, painted, and affixed with wood glue.

**Figure 16.10
Airplane, *That One With The Robot*, Erik Blohm-Gagné 2015.**
This item nicely retains the fun stylization of its drawn design (see previous chapter). Its balsa wood core kept it very light for rigging, and its epoxy surface allowed for detailed sculpting and painting.

**Figure 16.11
Exterior house set, *The Arctic Circle*, Kevin Parry, 2010.**
It's amazing what foam core, hot glue, plaster and paint can achieve.

**Figure 16.9
Final set view, *That One With The Robot*, Erik Blohm-Gagné 2015.**
This set features classic indie building materials: cardboard, foam core, and illustration board, all topped with an expert paint job.

Figure 16.12
Exterior street set, *A**hole Robot*, Mad Lab Productions, 2012.
The building front is a combination of polystyrene foam and
illustration board. The window is a sheet of plastic, and had to be
aged quite a bit, so that it wouldn't reflect the animator. The look
of brick on the background wall is a carefully applied paint effect.

Figure 16.13
Various props, *The Shutterbug Man*, Chris Walsh, 2014.
The knife is painted Sculpey. The camera body is illustration board
covered in sandpaper for texture, with a painted masking tape
handle on top. The small lenses on the front of the camera are slices
of hot glue. The book covers are illustration board, whose layers
were then frayed apart with a fine blade, to create the look of pages.

Figure 16.15
City exterior set in progress, *Spider's Anatomy*, Vojtech Kiss,
2014.
Like the spine of a giant creature, this highly architectural set
begins to take form. You'll see how this infrastructure fits into the
final set, later in this chapter.

Figure 16.14
Bedroom set in progress, *I'm Scared*, Pete Levin, 2016. Photo
credit: Colin Crump.
If you have solid carpentry skills, or if you have someone standing
by that can help, a more complex and detailed set like this one
can look stunning. The fine attention to craftsmanship at this
stage will result in a beautiful looking final product.

BLADE RUNNER, RIDLEY SCOTT, 1982

In this sci-fi noir thriller, cultures, languages,
and technologies blend together to form a
world that's as awesome to look at today
as when it was created, over thirty-five
years ago. Many of the stunning sets were
created in miniature, and the more that you
study the designs and fabrication methods
used, the more amazed you'll become at
how convincing and fully realized things
look in the final film. There's no one scene
to highlight in this film, the entire thing is one
remarkable work of visual art.

Useful approaches

Your project's story, budget, design style, and schedule will always prevent things from becoming too streamlined or standardized when it comes to fabricating sets and props. But the following approaches should help, regardless of the specific challenges you face.

Aging is good

Unless your stop motion world needs to look completely pristine, it might benefit greatly from giving it some age. Light switches on walls might have some smudges around them. Lower portions of walls might have flecks, spots, or dusty patches, since they're closer to the dirt that's stirred up when people walk around. Even clean hospital floors have spots that the cleaners missed, and have portions that are worn down more than others. When aging things, work in layers. Add some aging, and see how it looks (ideally in front of the camera, with some lighting). Then add more, if need be. This gradual process also provides a sense of history to your world, since things don't age all at once – they age in increments, over time.

You can quickly age things by creating a very watery dark paint that you then apply with a brush (and then wipe off, leaving a layer of 'age'), or you can apply it with a spray bottle. You can then leave it to dry if you want a spotty look, or wipe it down gently to get a subtle effect. Be sure to test this on a scrap piece first, and if you apply it and it isn't effective, you should be able to wipe it off entirely before it dries. Consider working in layers, drying the paint with a hair dryer to speed things up. You can also 'flick' paint from a brush to create little 'specks', which can break up flat areas nicely.

Patch it, then move on

Mistakes happen. Major problems will need to be taken seriously, but minor gaps, holes, or spaces in pieces can be dealt with. Remember that wood filler is your friend. Use it (or whatever material that's suitable) to fill spaces in, and move on, being sure to give the issue extra attention when it comes time to work on the surface. Once it's a part of your final film, no one in the audience will know, assuming that you patched the problem effectively. Even you will forget there's a mistake in there, eventually!

> Beads of hot glue, once dried, can be very useful – not as glue, but as detailing, since they look like rivets, bolt heads, and buttons. Lay out a row of hot glue beads on a smooth surface, let them cool, then add a coat of paint. Lift them up with a knife, and you can stick them on sets and props, as needed.

Check your progress

Especially as you near completion on a set or prop, try to get it in front of the camera, ideally under lighting that is similar to what will be used in the film. When it comes time for animation, you don't want any nasty surprises in the form of sets or props that look great on their own, but that look all wrong in the context of the actual scene.

Look at things differently

Sometimes the solution for a set or prop challenge exists in the real world, if you know how to see it. A quick example – how do you make a tiny drinking glass? Rather than trying to fabricate one (smooth and clear items are tricky), grab the clear cap off a spray bottle. Done. Once you start seeing set and prop challenges in this way, you'll be amazed at what will start jumping out at you as you wander through dollar stores, thrift shops, and your own junk drawers!

Surfaces are vital

The camera only sees surfaces. This isn't to say that what's underneath doesn't matter but often, what's underneath is just there to provide a basic shape and structure. If you keep this in mind, it can help you to distribute your time, energy, and resources effectively. Get basic shapes created quickly, then spend the majority of your time and effort on the surface layer. A prop that's made of nothing more than cardboard and tape can become something remarkable, once it has an effective skin of plaster, or a masterfully applied coat of paint.

What does the camera see?

Always be thinking about what, *specifically*, will be seen. This will help to prevent you from over-building aspects of sets and props that will never be seen by the camera. Personally, I'll build a *bit* more than what my boards suggest will be seen, but not by much. This allows for some flexibility of camera position and angles during animation.

Thinking about what the camera sees is important for another reason – it can let you play tricks when it comes to sets. Check out the images below for a great example of using 'forced perspective' in stop motion. Want to create vast landscapes when you have limited space? Set up your shot, work out perspective issues in front of the camera, and then see what amazing illusions you can create, right in front of the camera!

The basic set wall

You'll obviously have specific set requirements for your film, but in a lot of cases, a wall of some kind will be involved. The following instructions will provide you with a set wall that can be used on its own as a background, or can be connected to other walls to create a room set. It's quite easy to make and only costs a few dollars, but the basic approach is one that you'll be able expand upon, whatever your needs. Beyond the wall itself, there are windows and doors to think about, not to mention any detailing that the wall may require, such as light switches, window treatments, crown moulding, or baseboards.

But what you'll see below will get you started, and from this basic design you can develop and modify things, as needed.

MATERIALS

double-thick foam core, or rigid polystyrene insulation board (the amount needed will be determined by the size of your set walls. Be sure to use your scale puppet drawing to help determine the wall size.)

TOOLS

hot glue gun (or carpentry glue, if using polystyrene)
cutting mat
utility knife
pencil
ruler

Figure 16.16A and 16.16B
Forced perspective set, *Scrap Metal*, Anthony Straus, 2011.
In this Sheridan College film, a short length of wall, properly designed for forced perspective, creates the perfect illusion of depth, once in place within the shot. Here we see the 'giant' filmmaker checking his work via a live monitor that's just out of frame.

Figure 16.17 The basic set wall.
It's just a flat surface to act as a background – but from this basic set wall, you can create a lot of variations for the specific needs of your film.

STEP BY STEP

1. Determine the width and height of the wall that you want to make. Mark that on to the wall material, and cut it to size. Be sure to make clean and straight cuts, so that your wall will sit neatly on your animation deck.
2. Next, measure and cut a base from the same material. It should run the entire width of the wall. As for how deep to make the base, it should be enough to rest a stack of books or a few bricks on it, in order to keep the wall in place during animation.
3. Carefully glue the wall to the base, so that the wall is flush with the ground, as shown in Figure 16.17. Be sure to use an appropriate glue for the material.
4. Add some triangular support pieces, using scraps of wall material.

That's it! Very simple. If needed, you can use a few small spots of glue to further secure the base to the deck, once it's in place in front of the camera. And if you need to connect the wall to another one, just arrange the walls on the deck, and run a strip or two of masking tape down the seam of the walls, from the back.

This wall can also be used as a simple, generic background piece, which is always handy. You can tack or tape fabric or coloured paper to it, or you can add texture (perhaps with plaster or clay). You can also slap a coat of paint on it, and later repaint it, as needed.

Figure 16.18
The basic set wall, in detail.
You can place this wall directly on to your animation deck, and place some weight on the base to keep it in place.

Figure 16.19
Interior attic set, *The Shutterbug Man*, Chris Walsh, 2014.
This entire set consists of variations on the basic set wall.
You can see the seams for the various pieces, which were all connected with hot glue during animation. During construction, I first carefully framed up the shot, and made as many measurements as I could in front of the camera on to rough pieces of cardboard. Then I transferred those measurements to my proper materials, and only built what the camera would see.

Beyond the basics

What's been introduced so far in this chapter should help you as you approach the challenges of fabricating sets and props, but there's obviously a lot more to be discovered in this particular area, if it excites you. With that in mind, I thought I'd conclude this section with some images of independent projects that go well beyond the basics. By studying these images, you'll be able to pick up further insights into how to approach sets and props. And hopefully, they will also inspire and excite you, as you continue to dream up your own distinctive and amazing stop motion worlds.

Figure 16.20
Hive set, *Hive*, Adam Ciofli, 2016.
This sci-fi/fantasy film provides a stunning example of advanced set design and art direction. No surface has been left unattended, and the sheer intensity of detail, brought to life through heavily coloured lights, is both other-worldly and hallucinatory.

Figure 16.21
City exterior set, *Spider's Anatomy*, Vojtech Kiss, 2014.
The skeletal overhead structure shown in Figure 16.15 is now complete, along with the rest of the set. Realistic aging and lighting, combined with the surreal graffiti, creates a world that is as familiar as any large international city, yet also feels alien and possibly dangerous. A great example of a visually and thematically complex set.

Figure 16.22
Alien space ship, *Dogonauts: Enemy Line*, Justin and Shel Rasch, 2013.
A wonderfully animated film is made even better by the addition of a beautiful designed and constructed alien spaceship.

WINSTON HACKING, ART DIRECTOR FOR STOP MOTION

Winston is an art director for stop motion and for live action film. He's also a collage artist, who creates wonderfully strange worlds, many of which are animated. You can see more of his work at www.winstonhacking.com

Here are some insights from Winston, for when you're designing and building your stop motion sets.

- Whenever possible, make sure that you shoot your sets on a concrete floor. Wood floors will expand and contract and no amount of hot glue will save you from overnight shifts.
- Always block out your scenes before you build – this will prevent you from making things that will never be seen on camera. Get your camera and lenses and build a mock-up of your set. This will tell you exactly what you need to build and how you will maneuver the puppets on the set.
- Make your decks accessible from as many places as possible, and make sure that you have slightly less than a full arm's reach from the furthest point your puppet will be on the set. Make the set floors at a height that is comfortable to animate at – building them too low or too high will result in expensive chiropractic bills.
- Paint your sets with matte paint. You can always add shine – mostly with light, or with different gloss mediums, but taking away shine once it's actually painted into a set is very difficult.
- Build your sets with lighting in mind. Does your indoor set have lots of windows for natural light to pass through? Are there interesting shadows that your set design will generate?
- Set dressing should not be overlooked. It's like creating a painting, using many passes. Put your big elements down first to build your composition – a giant couch, a large painting on a wall or a big, busy carpet that will feature in the shot. Always consider pattern, texture and colour mixing – bringing colours from the wallpaper and working them into the cracks of the floorboards. This technique will really tie everything together.

VISUAL FLOW

Now that you're making a film (and not just creating shots that stand alone), you should stop and imagine a chain. Seriously. Can you see it? That chain is strong, not only because it has strong pieces, but because those pieces are *connected* in a manner that is also very secure. A single animated shot in your film is like a single piece of that chain. It needs to be very strong on its own, that's for sure – but it also needs to connect securely to the shot that came before it, and to the shot that follows. If this connection is strong, you've achieved something that's vital in filmmaking, and that's something called *visual flow*.

We'll define visual flow as the smooth movement of images within a shot, but also (and more importantly) *across edits*. In other words, if one shot in a film transitions into the next shot in a way that is easy to watch, and allows your audience to remain engaged, then we can say that the film has visual flow.

> If your storyboards (and subsequently, your animatic) are solid, visual flow and shot hook-up will already be evident in your film. But remember that it's ultimately how you create your shots on-set, and how they are edited together, that will finally determine the quality of your visual flow.

Shot hook-up is closely connected to this idea of visual flow in filmmaking. Shot hook-up refers to how the end of one shot visually connects (or 'hooks') into the start of the next one. Do they hook-up well? Then the sequence is like that strong chain, with each of its parts securely connected. If the sequence doesn't have strong shot hook-ups, you've got weak connections, and you don't have visual flow. And that means further work is required (either in editing, or possibly in reshooting), in order to achieve flow.

How do you know good visual flow (and good shot hook-up) when you see it? That's the tricky thing. Like good editing, when visual flow and

shot hook-ups are working well, they're nearly invisible! That being said, there *are* specific techniques that you can make use of during stop motion production that will help you to craft something that flows forward, very smoothly.

> You may have a reason for jarring the viewer's eyes, or for making things difficult to follow. If you have a strong reason for this, so be it. But be careful; push the audience away too often, or for too long, and you might not get it back.

Updating the animatic

Updating your animatic is one of the most effective and essential techniques that you can use, in your effort to ensure strong visual flow during production.

This entails importing your completed animated shots into your animatic's Premiere file,

Figure 16.23
Updating the animatic, *The Arctic Circle*, Kevin Parry, 2010. By continually replacing your storyboard panels with your actual animation, you can ensure that your film is taking shape effectively.

and then using those shots to replace the story-board versions of the same shots. In this way, your animatic will eventually evolve *into* your actual animated film, as you continually replace more and more storyboard shots with actual animation.

In a sense, you can think of this updating process as a form of 'early post-production'. That's because post-production is typically the stage when editing occurs (at least in live action filmmaking), but you're doing it now, as much as possible, in order to make sure that your film's coming together effectively.

As you bring in the animated shots to your animatic, you'll see right before your eyes whether visual flow is happening. In fact, you'll be able to judge the effectiveness of every one of the visual flow techniques that we're about to look at, as you update your animatic. Alternately, if you *aren't* updating your animatic, and instead are simply animating shot after shot on its own, you're essentially 'flying blind', since you aren't seeing how those shots are functioning in the *context* of your actual film.

Before you start updating your animatic with your actual shots, be sure to refer to the section called 'Adobe Premiere 2: Working with animation frames' in the next chapter. The process for both importing and working with animation frames in Premiere is a bit different from the one that you used when working with your storyboard panels in the last chapter. It's not complicated, just different – so don't start working with your actual shots in Premiere until you're clear on this process.

Lighting continuity

The process (and art) of lighting during production has a range of its own concerns, of course, but much of what we considered in Chapter 8 can be applied now. One aspect of lighting that's particular to production, however, connects very closely with visual flow – and that's lighting continuity.

If your film has lighting continuity within a given sequence or scene, it has a *consistency* in its lighting as it moves from shot to shot. Let's say your scene begins with a wide shot of a room, and the main source of light is shown

Figure 16.24
Lighting continuity, *Feathers*, Group Film, 2016.
Here are two shots from within the same scene. The main source of light within the scene is sunlight that is coming in through the window. No matter where the camera moves within the scene, the direction and quality of the main light remains continuous.

to be coming from a window on the right-hand side of the screen. You'll want to ensure that all tighter shots within that scene keep the direction, quality, and intensity of the light consistent with what you've established. The camera can move where it wants to, but the lighting should remain unchanged as much as possible.

This consistency helps to create a unified and believable world on-screen, but it *also* helps to reduce visual distraction within your film. In other words, strong lighting continuity helps to increase the overall visual flow of your film.

In your effort to maintain lighting continuity, it can sometimes be useful to plot out your scene in a simple aerial map, marking down the location of the main source of light for the scene. Sketch in your camera positions for each shot as well, and as you light for each shot, refer back to your aerial map, to check for consistency. You'll also want to make use of Dragonframe 4's Media Layers Tool (see below).

You'll often find that you can 'cheat' quite a bit when it comes to lighting, and still maintain overall continuity. A close up shot of a character may require tweaks to the lighting, compared to the wider establishing shot, but as long as you maintain certain important aspects of the lighting – *type, direction*, and *intensity* of the lighting, as well as any major shadows that have been established – you should be fine.

Remember – you want things to flow, from shot to shot, without disruption. If you dramatically change the lighting on your character and background, the audience may not consciously notice the problem, but they'll sense it, and they'll find themselves distracted, even if they don't know why.

> Be sure to make use of Part 2's 'A lighting process for stop motion'. It's useful at any stage, but it can be particularly helpful now, since it's designed to help you light one shot after another as efficiently as possible.

Eye trace

Eye trace refers to the actual movement of the viewer's eyes while watching a film, as each new shot appears. Good eye trace permits for easy watching, as the viewer's attention is directed carefully and purposefully, from shot to shot. If the viewer instead has to shift attention, endlessly, as each new shot appears, then you're dealing with *poor* eye trace – and you've got an exhausted, frustrated, and confused audience.

Good eye trace doesn't mean that nothing moves within your shot! We're dealing with animation, after all, and animation is all about movement. Effective eye trace is simply the way to get over (or through) the edit in a way that doesn't ask the eye to jump excessively. Once you're into that new shot, your animation can move the viewer's eye all that it wants, until the next edit – which will again make use of good eye trace.

In simple sequences of shots that involve little or no movement within the frame (as in the example above), eye trace can be quite simple. But in more complex situations that involve a lot

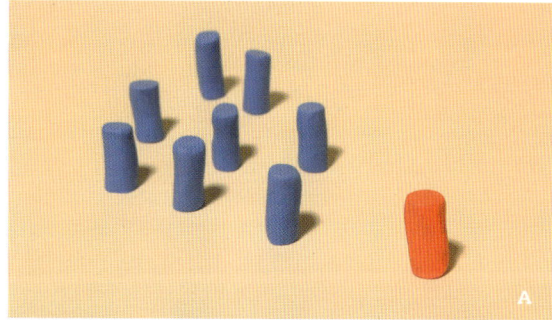

Figure 16.25
Effective eye trace.
As the first shot (A) ends, the location of the main area of interest is maintained as the second shot (B) appears. In this way, the viewer's eye didn't have to move within the frame, which allows for effective visual flow.

of movement, ensuring good eye trace becomes more challenging.

If you want to see excellent eye trace at work, carefully study some sequences from a quality action film. These action sequences typically consist of very fast shots, each of which has information in it that's critical for the audience's understanding of the sequence. With effective use of eye trace (as well as other techniques of visual flow), even the fastest actions and edits come through clearly.

Eye lines

When a character looks at something or someone, either within the shot or off-screen, that act of looking creates what is known as an eyeline. It's a pretty accurate name – just imagine an actual line, perfectly straight, coming out of the character's eyes and directly connecting to what's being looked at, even if it's not on-screen yet.

Eyelines are very strong, and they greatly influence where the *audience* will look. The

Figure 16.26
Eyelines, *The Magic Projector*, Chris Walsh, 2007.
Eyelines help to create connections, across edits. Here, the man is looking down (A). Once the edit occurs, his eyeline connects with that of the boy (B). Eyelines can also cue the audience, so that it knows where its attention is supposed to go. The boy is looking up at the man (B), but as his attention shifts (C), we are ready for the edit, which will reveal to us what the boy is *now* looking at (D).

audience first looks at your character's eyes, and then follows the eyeline to its destination – so if you want your audience to *look* somewhere very specific, your character's eyeline needs to be effectively 'aimed' at that area.

Making good use of strong eyelines can also really help your film to visually flow across edits, as shown in the above images. If you ensure that your eyelines connect between a 'looking' character in one shot, and the thing that is being 'looked at' in the following shot, your audience is much less likely to notice that you've cut from one shot to another. Simply by allowing the eyeline to reach its final destination (which happens when you cut), you're providing visual satisfaction for the viewer – and that helps to ease your film visually, into the next shot.

What if you're animating a character that's wearing a helmet, or that otherwise has its eyes obscured? As long as you animate and pose the overall character in such a way so as to strongly *suggest* that it's looking somewhere specific, you can still establish (and make use of) eyelines.

You can add further strength to eyelines, and achieve greater visual flow as a result, if you match camera angles to eyelines, whenever possible. In the sequence of shots shown above, you'll notice that when we're seeing from the boy's view

(Figure 16.26A), the camera is looking *up* at the man, as if from the approximately height of the boy.

Conversely, when we're seeing from the man's view (Figure 16.26B and C), we're looking *down* at the boy. Again, the result is stronger and more effective visual flow.

Matching on action

Matching on action is a subtle trick of filmmaking that effectively makes an edit invisible. It requires a strong action within the shot to essentially conceal the actual transition from one shot to the next. Because the action is strong, the viewer is too busy noticing the continuing action (across shots) to realize that there's been a cut. The action can be just about anything, as long as it's the main area of interest within the shot.

Matching on action in stop motion relies partially on careful picture editing, but it *primarily* depends upon carefully planned character performance. Careful reference of the action in each shot is critical, so that the shots will hook up seamlessly in editing. It can be a tricky technique to master, but the result of the effort can be truly seamless visual flow.

Matching on action is extremely effective when it's done correctly, but it isn't a technique that you'll be able to use constantly. Lots of edits simply can't be stitched together this way, sometimes because the actions don't match, and other times because there's no strong action to work

with, such as in a series of dialogue shots. But it can be extremely helpful when an action is the central purpose of the connecting shots, as in the example shown below.

Figure 16.27
Matching on action, *The Magic Projector*, Chris Walsh, 2007.
The tighter shot begins with the character sitting (A), but as that shot ends, she begins the action of standing (B), and as we cut to the next shot (C), the action continues, effectively hiding the edit.

Additional tips

When making your way through production on a stop motion film, there's a seemingly endless array of challenges. Some challenges, like finding that puppet eyebrow that just fell on the studio floor, are relatively minor. Others, such as meeting your various production deadlines, are major. Here's a few final things to consider, to help you through the many challenges you'll face.

Put your storyboards up

Sound familiar? This same bit of advice was also offered when looking at sets and props earlier in this chapter, and for very similar reasons. Putting your boards up allows you to see your whole film quickly. It also lets you see relationships and patterns that might help you as you think through camera, lighting, and animation.

Make use of Dragonframe's Media Layers Tool

Essentially, this tool allows you to load reference material (still frames, or movie files) while you're framing up in the Animation or Cinematography Workspace. That seems like a pretty simple thing, but it's incredibly useful for ensuring good visual flow throughout your film. For example, let's say you've just completed animation for Shot 1, and are now framing up for Shot 2, which is a tighter shot on your character. By using the Media Layers Tool, you can load the *final* frame of Shot 1

Figure 16.28
Media Layers Tool.
This tool lets you easily reference frames from other shots. It can help to ensure that your film has excellent visual flow – so be sure to use it!

and, by lowering the loaded frame's opacity, see *both* the frame from Shot 1 *and* the new framing for Shot 2, all in the same window. If you then quickly slide the opacity controller for the loaded frame back and forth, you can effectively 'cut' between your two shots, in order to judge just how well they'll cut together, during editing.

> In earlier versions of Dragonframe, this tool is called the Line-Up Layers Tool. Despite the different name, it functions in exactly the same way.

Keep your action centered

Quite simply, if you can frame up each shot so that the main area of visual interest within the shot is basically centered, you'll be good to go when it comes time to edit your shots together. Of course, you can't always frame up in this way, because every shot has its own individual framing requirements. But if you keep it in mind as you work, and remind yourself that it's a pretty much no-fail way to ensure visual flow (and shot hook-up, and eye trace), odds are good that the concept will find its way into your shots, no matter what, simply because it's so useful. It's all about making things easy to watch, as one shot moves into the next.

Think ahead

A lot of what you do during production is deeply tied to what you *will* do, in post-production. In Part 3, we looked at the slate, which can be recorded at the start of each shot. But you can also shoot an end slate, which offers further information about the shot. This can include things like specific frames that are in need of rig removal, or that need some digital touching up for whatever reason.

You can also be thinking about post-production in the way that you organize and name your files during production. Use the numbering that you used in your storyboards when naming them during production, and carry that naming convention into post-production. This way, you can quickly identify what shot you're handling, and determine where it goes. You'll be glad you did, especially if a shot goes missing in your computer, and you have to track it down!

Minimize the risk

The longer a stop motion shot takes to create, the greater the chance that something might go wrong. Sounds scary, but it's just the way it goes in stop motion. Try to stay focused and 'inside' the shot, both mentally and physically. I'm not saying to skip meals and bathroom breaks, but the more that you can work in a dedicated fashion, without interruption, to get the shot done, the better. The same goes for leaving shots partially done, so that you can complete it the next day. This is fairly common practice on larger productions, but that's partly because those projects have a dedicated lighting and post-production team that can help with corrections, should a light or a set piece shift during the down-time.

> If you need to take an extended break from animating a shot, take your break during a moment when the overall *spacing* in the animation is fairly generous, such as in the middle of a big action. It's easier to carry on animating from a spot like this, compared to a moment when the spacing is very small.

End your day by prepping for the next

As I conclude a work day in the studio, I prefer to finish animating a shot, and then spend the last part of the day preparing for the next day. This preparation might include breaking down dialogue, ensuring that the puppets are ready to go, and arranging whatever props, tools, and gear that might be required in the next shot. Sometimes, I'll also establish a rough frame for the next shot, as well as some rough lighting. All of this preparation work allows me to get into actual animation more quickly the following day, which I find is great for morale (not to mention the production schedule).

Remember the pop-through

You may not need to shoot one for every shot, but a pop-through can help you to resolve all kinds of production challenges. Be sure to refer back to earlier sections, if you need clarification on the various ways that a pop-through can help you during production.

Back it up

You know it's vital, but at the end of a hard day, it's very easy to let it slide. Get in the habit of ending every day with a backup. You will *never* regret the time spent doing it, trust me.

As you work towards completing the production stage of your film, one of the greatest challenges that you may have to overcome is simply *letting go of the shots*. It happens to every artist that aims to create fantastic work: instead of seeing a nice shot in front of you, you only see the rough spots; that bits that *aren't* perfect. Try to remember your bigger objective: to make a finished film, in a given amount of time. It's a hard truth, but you *must* move on, because there is always another shot to animate. And after that, another.

Don't get me wrong – of *course* your shots must look lovely. And I'm the first to admit that any truly rough moments might need to be reshot, or dramatically modified, for the greater good of the film. But you *will* have to find a balance, between wanting the most beautiful, most 'perfect' shot, and arriving at a finished project. A finished film lets you show it to audiences, learn from it, and move on, so that you can make *more* films, each of which will be more amazing. Trying to remember 'the big picture' in this way might help you let go, and carry onward.

Frame by frame, shot by shot, scene by scene – you're building what will become your final film.

More on rigging the puppet

Regardless of how many rig shots you have to handle in your film, it's important to carefully plan each of them in advance of animation. The following considerations will help you during production, but as you'll see, most of them serve the *ultimate* purpose of assisting the process of rig removal, which is the digital process that happens in post-production. You'll find out more about the process of rig removal in the following chapter.

'Clean plate' frames are essential

To digitally remove a rig in post-production, it's extremely important that you capture what's often referred to as a 'clean plate'. This is a frame that you record once your frame is locked, your lighting is complete, and you're ready to start animating. It must be recorded *without* your puppets or other elements that are to be animated (see Figure 16.29A). In post-production, you can then lay the animation frames that require rig removal on top of this clean background plate, and digitally remove the rig. If this all seems a little abstract at the moment, it will make more sense once you've gone through the entire process. Just know that before you animate any rig shot, you really, *really* want to ensure that you've captured a clean plate frame. Without it, effective rig removal will be much harder, if not impossible.

If you also record a clean plate at the end of your shot, you can use it in post-production to fix any shifts that might have occurred with lighting or sets.

Minimize rig shadows

When using a rig, it can be very hard to avoid casting a shadow on to the set. You can see a few such shadows at the right side of the frame, in Figure 16.29B. The fewer rig shadows you have in your frame, the less cleaning up you'll have

Figure 16.29
Rig removal frames, *The Champ*, Rosemary Travale, 2014. To better understand digital rig removal in stop motion, it helps to think in layers. Here, we see the clean plate layer (A), the animation layer (B), and the final rig-free final frame (C), after it's gone through digital post-production. Specific instruction for removing puppet rigs in this layered method is covered in the next chapter.

to do in post-production. Be especially careful of rig shadows falling on elements within the shot that weren't a part of your clean plate, such as puppets or other animated objects.

Keep the rig behind the puppet

This one is very easy to forget when you're busy animating. If the rig stays behind the puppet, you can remove the rig. If the rig moves in *front* of the puppet, how can you remove it, without removing the puppet?! You can see this issue in Figure 16.29B, as the rig comes in front of the Mom puppet's arm. This area of the puppet had to be digitally recreated, during post-production, which is not much fun, even for a few frames. If the problem involved hundreds of frames, you'd be faced with a reshoot.

It's also important to minimize the *points of contact* between the rig and the edge of the puppet, since each point will need to be addressed in post-production. For an example of clean rigging in this way, refer back to Figure 12.24. In that image, the rig is neatly behind Nia, and touches her outline at a single point, making it a fairly easy and quick task to remove it in post-production.

Use tape

If you're shooting on green screen (see below), you can use green tape on the rig so that the rig will blend in a bit to the background. Then, during post-production, you'll have less detailed work to perform. If you're not shooting on green screen, you can still add a coloured tape to the rig, simply to make it stand out more in the frame so that you can spot it during rig removal in post-production. Instead of tape, you can also use coloured shrink tubing. It will serve the same purpose as tape, but will also provide some additional strength to the rig wire.

Figure 16.30
Ossa, Dario Imbrogno, 2016.
Who says you have to remove your rigs in post-production?! In contrast to all of these rig removal concerns, this beautiful film accepts the rig as part of its stop motion world. Rather than distracting the viewer, the rig adds a layer of lyrical self-reflectiveness to the film.

Some final words on animating with rigs during your film. Make sure that you have a good practical understanding of these kinds of shots, both on-set, and in post-production, before attempting a major shot in your film. Consider creating a very brief test shot, then follow the rigging advice here, and the further details on rig removal that you'll find in the following chapter. You can then apply that experience to the shots in your actual film.

Physical special effects animation

Within any film, there's the potential that at least some of the stop motion animation doesn't involve characters. This animation can be broadly referred to as 'effects' animation. In some cases, effects animation is used for emphasizing atmosphere. An example of this might be fireflies, in a shot that's set in a summer field at night. The fireflies aren't *required* for the narrative, but they certainly provide atmosphere. Other times, effects animation is a consequence of something that's occurring in the primary animation. For example, a shot might involve a stop motion firecracker exploding. The firecracker itself might be animated to fall apart into a few pieces, and a sound of a loud bang might be added, but without effects animation in the form a bright flash and a bit of smoke, the final animation isn't going to be very effective.

Often, effects animation is done on-set, at the same time as the shot's main animation. But you can also approach physical effects animation as a task unto itself. You can do this via an 'under the camera' technique, with a green or blue screen in the background, which allows you to crop out the effects in post-production, and then add them digitally to the main shot. This method allows you to spend more time and energy on the effects animation, so that you get it just right. It also lets you adjust the effect on its own, before inserting it into the main animation. You can adjust the effect's timing, its placement within the main animation, and many other characteristics of the effect. Consider this option, as you plan out your physical effects.

Below, you'll find some suggestions for effects materials and methods, but have fun finding new and unusual materials that can be animated in interesting ways, in order to fulfill your specific effects needs. You'll enjoy the creative challenge, and they'll also add a whole other level of visual excitement to your project.

Of course, effects animation doesn't have to be done via stop motion. In post-production, there's a whole range of digital effects that can be created and added into your shots, and we'll look at those options in the next chapter.

Figure 16.31
Water effects, *The Nose*, Neil Burns, 2008.
In stop motion, if it looks right for an effect, you're in business. Here, a thin sheet of black plastic, dragged in increments along the ground, creates the perfect illusion of a flowing river at sunset. Also worth noting are the 'clouds', which are projected on to the wall from out of frame.

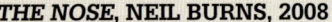

***THE NOSE*, NEIL BURNS, 2008**

This massively ambitious and very funny adaptation of a Nikolai Gogol story is also a superb showcase of practical stop motion effects and in-camera tricks. There's almost nothing that you can't achieve in front of the camera in the world of stop motion, if you have the skills and know-how, and this film sets out to prove it. You'll also find beautifully ornate sets, great animation, and very clever puppet designs. You'll be deeply inspired by this short film, and more than a little amazed.

Water
Small amounts of water

If it's a small volume, water can be very straightforward to create. For example, imagine a shot that involves water flowing from a tap. For this, you could use a thin piece of wire covered in plastic wrap. The wire provides a bit of form to the stream, and the plastic wrap is easily animated, just by shifting or turning it slightly for each frame. Alternately, you could use a strand of hot glue (cooled, obviously), dripped down the wire. Turn that

around, frame by frame, add some flowing water sound effects, and there you go. For teardrops, or rain on a window, you can use glycerine, which can be nicely animated with a toothpick.

Large amounts of water

Big bodies of water can be a lot trickier, since in these cases water moves as a large mass and also in smaller ways, meaning you might be faced with an overwhelming amount of animation, if you try to get really detailed. One approach is to try to stylize things, so that your effect *suggests* water, without having to specifically *behave* like water. For a wide shot of calm water, a large piece of coloured fabric might look great, if it works for your design style. Try working in some gentle folds to give it some detailing. Or perhaps you could use a sheet of blue or green paper with a thin sheet of translucent plastic laid on top, to give a sense of depth and shine. If the water has to be animated, you have a different set of challenges to deal with. You can create a sense of gentle waves or splashes on a plastic surface by animating table salt on top of the plastic. Plastic wrap can look great for quickly flowing water, and even coloured clay, if the look of it works for your project. It all very much depends on what specifically has to happen in your shot, and the visual style you're going for. This is where playing and experimenting comes in, so have fun!

Flashes and fire

These effects, and others like it that involve intense bursts of energy, are lots of fun to do, and you can find all kinds of materials that will look very exciting on screen. If the material is bright, or reflective, you can angle it towards the studio lights to really bring it to life. Since a lot of times these effects are on screen for a very short time (sometimes no more than a frame) selecting just the right shape or pose for the effect is critical. Doing a quick test to determine your shapes or poses in advance can be very helpful.

Remember that in the real world, flashes and fire *emit light*, so beyond the basic effect, consider also aiming a coloured light at the spot that's being effected. The light it provides to the set can help to 'sell' the overall effect. Figure 16.32 makes use of this little trick, with great results. The red light on the wall behind the laser beam is provided not by the beam, but by a light fixture with a red gel, just out of frame.

Flashes

Cartoony flashes, often in a series of increasing and decreasing sizes of replacement pieces, tacked on to a puppet, set piece, or prop, can look great. This works very well for muzzle flashes on guns, or small explosions. You can use them to sell impacts (if your story allows for some cartoony fun), or to suggest 'magic', such as at the end of a wizard's wand. These are super fun to animate, and to watch.

Fire

In certain ways, fire behaves like water. A small amount is fairly easy to manage on-set, while a larger amount can be quite tricky. So be prepared for a challenge if you want to animate a wide shot

of a forest fire! Again, consider finding a stylized way to convey the effect, without having to get lost in hundreds of hours of 'fire' animation. That is, unless you have a burning desire to tackle this kind of challenge. Haven't had a pun for a while, have we? Feels good, doesn't it?

Reflective bits of coloured paper or plastic can look very effective animated through a replacement technique, and if you plan your shapes carefully you can get really appealing 'licks' of flames that always look good. Consider shooting fire separately, and creating a cycle of animation that you can drop in to your main shot in post-production. If you're going to cycle the fire, make sure that you make it a fairly long cycle, with quite a bit of randomness to it, so that you hide the cycled nature of the animation.

> Just as character animation requires you to inhabit the emotional state of the character, good effects animation results from the animator 'getting inside' the effect. Bring it to life for yourself, in your mind, before you animate it. Think about how the effect functions in the real world, and refer to reference material, but remember that ultimately you are creating a *stylized* version of the effect, that needs to match your stop motion world's reality.

Figure 16.32
Laser beam effect, *Scrap Metal*, Anthony Straus, 2011.
Did you know that aluminium foil can be used as a laser beam to defeat giant plant monsters? Another example of how an everyday material, when managed correctly, can be used to achieve very convincing effects.

Figure 16.33
Fog effect, *The Nose*, Neil Burns, 2008.
A beautifully evocative effect, created through the careful planning of physical elements during animation.

Smoke and fog

Smoke

A tried-and-true method for creating smoke (and steam, for that matter) is by animating tiny tufts of cotton, that are placed on the object that's creating the smoke. Plain old cotton balls, pulled apart into smaller pieces, look great, and are so light that they can usually be easily attached with a bit of wax. If the smoke has to be animated along a path, such as smoke that's coming from a moving train's stack, you can try attaching cotton puffs on to thin wire or thread, so that you have a path along which to move the smoke. Cotton is also very handy for creating clouds that have some dimensionality, that can then be lit to convey various moods and weather conditions.

Fog

In a foggy setting, objects that are close to you are still very clear – it's only as they move *away* that they get swallowed up by the whiteness. Because of this, fog is typically only seen in wider shots, meaning it has to cover a large area, and that's always tricky.

Layers of translucent material positioned in front of the camera, such as fine mesh, or certain kinds of paper, as shown in Figure 16.33, can be extremely effective. Look into the world of theatre lighting to find more material choices. You'll have to plan the location of the material to allow access to your set and puppets, and of course do some testing, but if you're going for a mysterious atmosphere, this technique can work wonders.

Camera tricks

Humans have two eyes that face forward, and that allows us to register depth when we look at things. But the camera only has one eye. It doesn't see in depth in the same way that we do, and that means that you can trick it. You can do this by assembling layers in front of it that won't look like they're layers – instead, if they're created and arranged effectively, they'll look like a unified world. Effects that work in this manner always require a fair amount of preparation and patience, but the end result is always worth the effort. Do more research beyond what you see here, and you'll find all kinds of amazing tricks that you can put to use, to make your audience marvel at your movie magic skills.

Figure 16.34
Moving background effect, *The Arctic Circle*, Kevin Parry, 2010. An example of a very clever in-camera trick. The puppet was framed in a medium shot, and animated as if running. At the same time, the tube behind the puppet, serving as the horizon, was rolled away from the camera, frame by frame. The final effect is of a running puppet, and a receding background. The tiny elements in the extreme background remained fixed, adding to the illusion of a vast landscape.

Figure 16.35
Matte painting effect, *The Nose*, Neil Burns, 2008. One of the most intensive camera effects is also one of the most convincing. Here, foreground details are painted on to a transparent layer, with the middle ground consisting of physical sets in front of another painted layer (A). Through the camera (B), it all blends into a seamless effect of incredible depth and realism.

Green screen

Green screen (also known as chroma key) effects shots are all around us, in everything from news and sports programs, to fantasy blockbusters. It's a popular effect in part because it allows filmmakers to greatly expand their worlds in ways that are relatively easy to achieve.

You can shoot all kinds of physical effects on a green screen background, and then lay that effects animation on top of your main animation. You can also animate in front of a green screen when creating your character animation, and then 'drop in' a background later. Want to create a film that has lots of epic, wide backgrounds, but you don't have the physical space (or budget) to fabricate all that? You can create your backgrounds separately, perhaps at a smaller scale, then shoot them as still images that can be inserted during post-production.

When you start thinking in this way, you can also start to imagine backgrounds whose visual style is perhaps different than that of your puppets. You could create drawn or cg backgrounds, that are stills or animated, that can then be 'blended' with your stop motion puppet animation, resulting in a very distinctive hybrid look. You can even use live action footage for backgrounds. To get a sense of what this way of working looks like on set, refer back to Figure 7.2. and in the following chapter, you'll see even more examples of these green screen methods.

Just like rig removal, the more attention that you can give to your green screen work during production, the better your final shot will look. With that in mind, the following tips should help you to arrive at high quality final shots. You'll also find a wealth of online tutorials and references, since this is such a common effects technique.

There's nothing special about green

It's true that a green background can be removed cleanly, but you can use other colours, as well – the most common being blue. What is important is that the colour is vivid, consistent, and without texture. This because the compositing software has an easier time removing one very specific colour, rather than many colours that are nearly the same.

Pick your colours carefully

The background colour that you select has to be a colour that is not present in what you're animating. For example, if your character has a green sweater, you won't be able to use a green background. You'd be surprised how easy it is to forget this rule, and you don't want to realize your error just as you're about to begin animation!

Ensure that your screen lighting is consistent

In the same way that compositing software has an easier time dealing with one specific colour, it also works better when that colour is evenly lit, with no excessively bright or dark areas. Using bounced lighting to light the screen can be one way to approach this, but regardless of how you specifically do it, take your time, and get it right.

Avoid light spill

With your screen lit evenly, you can turn your attention to lighting your characters. As you do this, watch that the light that you are using on your characters doesn't 'spill' on to the screen. More importantly, make sure the screen colour itself doesn't bounce on to your characters, as this can make things quite tricky during post-production. To prevent this, try to keep your characters as far away from your screen as possible. This can be a challenge in a small studio space, but try your best, and you'll find that you have better final results in post-production.

ROBERT MORGAN, FILMMAKER

Robert Morgan is a multi-award winning filmmaker, specializing in stop motion animation. His films – including *The Cat With Hands*, *The Separation*, *Bobby Yeah*, and *Invocation* – have been screened around the world at festivals such as Telluride, Sundance, Rotterdam, and Clermont-Ferrand. They have won over sixty international awards, including a Welsh BAFTA, the Arts Foundation Award for Animation, and a British Academy Award nomination.

Q. Depending on how an artist wants to work, stop motion can be surprisingly spontaneous. On an artistic whim, you can shift your camera or adjust a light. Are you open to that spontaneous way of working on your films? If so, how open?

A. I'm completely open to that spontaneity. In fact, I'd argue that it's an essential requirement of filming stop motion. You have to allow for surprises, and go with them if they work. If you close the door to that then you'll end up with something stiff and lacking in energy. All animation tends to demand a lot of planning and pre-visualization, but I'm pretty insistent that you're killing creativity if you stick too closely to those plans. Of course, if you're working from a commission, it's more difficult to just go off on tangents. But I always try to retain an air of experimentation and possibility when shooting.

Q. Every artist has his or her own process, but can you tell me a bit about the role that storyboards play in your films, specifically while you are in production?

A. It depends on the project. If the film has been commissioned, or has a team involved, then storyboards become a tool for communicating my intentions. But they're usually pretty loose. As mentioned previously, I'm a great believer of spontaneity, so the storyboards are never the bible. If I'm shooting something alone I sometimes don't even use them, unless it's a sequence that really depends on a certain flow of actions, like a fight scene or a chase scene.

During production, I keep it very loose. I usually keep a sketchbook and sketch the storyboards very quickly before a scene to work out the flow, then I'll edit shots together as I go, so that I'm sure I'm getting what I want. And quite often I'll go back and shoot inserts or pick-ups too. So the storyboard is a very loose tool, at least for me.

Q. What are some hazards during production that you've learned to watch out for? Besides kicking the camera!

A. I work with a lot of slimy materials so that stuff tends to get everywhere! Also, I've learned to avoid long wide shots of characters walking in full frame! That's a nightmare that I try to avoid as much as possible. I'd much rather stick a puppet in a coffee mug and slide it around framed from the waist up! I've also learned to be paranoid when getting cheap deals at post-production houses. Make sure they actually care about your film, and treat it with respect. I learned the hard way that's not always the case.

Q. What keeps you going, through all the hard work of production?

A. For me, it's watching back the rushes and cutting scenes together. If I'm capturing some great movement that's giving me that weird, uncanny, hyper-energized motion in the right way, and if the scenes are really working, then it'll keep my own enthusiasm levels up. Enthusiasm is the lifeblood of creativity. Without it, I can't do good work, so seeing the film as it progresses (and liking what I'm seeing) is really important.

Q. Fill in the blank: Stop motion filmmaking is like....

A. Necromancy.

17

Post-production

You've put an incredible amount of effort into your film. It's right there, for all to see, in the lovely shots that you've created, and in the strong visual flow that you've ensured exists from start to finish. Press play on that Premiere file that used to be your animatic, and you should now see the majority of the visuals for your film, working effectively from start to finish. In other words, your film should (basically) be there.

But of course, there is still more work to be done before your film is *truly* complete. You'll want to do a little (or a lot) of polishing, so that your picture edit is just right. And depending on the specifics of your film, you may have a little (or a lot) of digital effects. You'll also need to address the final sound, which is a critical consideration for any successful film. This chapter will help you through all of this, and the great news is that although it's all very important, none of it is as labour intensive as production. That means that you can relax, a least a bit, as you work. You'll even get to sit down while you do it!

By the end of this chapter, you'll finally have what you've worked so hard to achieve through all of these stages of development. Your finished film will be sitting right there in front of you, as a distinctive and unique stop motion film that's finally ready to be shared with the entire world.

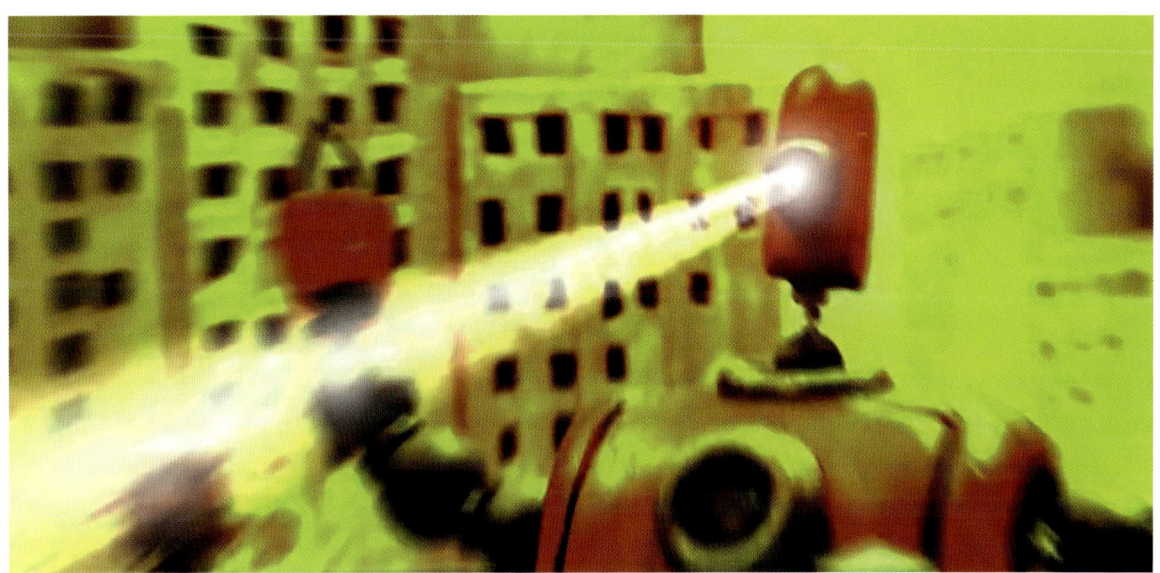

Figure 17.1
Digital effects,
*That One With
The Robot*, Erik
Blohm-Gagné,
2015.
Effective
animation can be
combined in post-
production with
digital effects,
to create a truly
exciting final look
for your film.

PICTURE EDITING

As you put your animatic together, you had to make a lot of big choices. The picture editing that you'll be doing now won't necessarily involve big choices, but it will involve making very important choices, some of them no more than a frame or two in duration. Beyond minor refinements like these, you may decide that your film would benefit from some more serious editing. If that's the case, you'll find some helpful insights below.

> If you haven't already, you really should delete or mute any temporary music that you've been using. It creates a false sense of rhythm and tempo. You don't want something that's not even going to be a part of the final film to influence something as important as your picture edit. The time will come to think about music again for your film, but for now – focus on the picture.

Adobe Premiere 2: Working with animation frames

In the previous chapter, I pointed out that the process for importing and working with animation frames in Premiere is a bit different from working with storyboard panels. It's not a complicated process, but it is important. If you follow it, you'll be ensuring that you're always working with your high-resolution frames, and that those frames are being shown off in their best possible fashion, all the way through the production and post-production pipeline. And when the 'moment of truth' arrives, this way of working with your animation frames will provide you with the best-looking output possible for your final film.

> The following process is for updating your existing animatic Premiere file, although you can certainly follow the same process for working with animation frames, even if you're creating an entirely new project.

STEP BY STEP

1. Establish a specific location on your computer for your folders of animation, and for any other files that you may need to access during editing. Think of this location as fixed, because if you start moving files around, Premiere will need to reconnect with the shots.

2. Go to File, and select Import. Navigate to the X1 folder for the shot that you want to import. As you well know, this folder is where your high-resolution frames are placed by Dragonframe. In the Import window, select the Image Sequence option. This will bring in all of the frames for this shot. Click on the first frame in the X1 folder, then click Import. You'll see your shot in the Project window.

3. Drag the shot over to the timeline, and drop it on its appropriate track. You'll likely receive a notice from Premiere that the clip doesn't match the Sequence's settings. Be sure to keep the existing settings.

4. Adjust the size of your shot to match your editing window, by using the Scale Tool (refer to Chapter 15 on pre-production if you need a refresher on this tool). If you were using a 16:9 mask in Dragonframe, you should be able to match that same framing now in Premiere.

5. Now to adjust the speed of your shot. Since you created your animation at 12 fps, and your Sequence is set for 24 fps, if you don't adjust the shot's speed, it will play back too fast. To do this, select the clip, then go to Clip along the top. Select Speed/Duration. Change your shot's speed from 100% to 50% (see Figure 17.2).

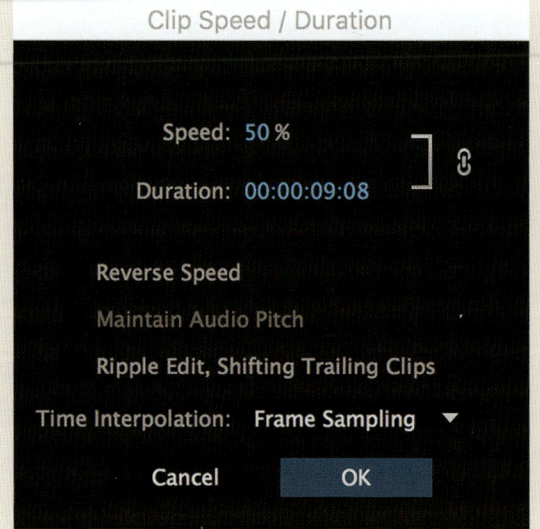

Figure 17.2
Clip Speed/Duration Window.
By adjusting your clip to 50%, your playback speed should now match how it looked in Dragonframe.

6. Play the shot back from its beginning. It should now match the framing you had in Dragonframe, assuming that you were using a 16:9 mask. Its playback speed should also be the same as when you played it back in Dragonframe, assuming that you were animating at 12 fps.

7. Repeat this process for all of your shots as you bring them into Premiere.

You'll likely notice that your shot looks too large in your work window, or too 'zoomed in' for the editing window. That's because the X1 frames are larger than your sequence setting, which isn't a bad thing, since it actually means that your images have exceptional resolution.

You'll notice that we didn't use movie file versions of your shots, but instead we used the actual images themselves. We don't work with movie files because movie exports are often compressed (or otherwise modified) for efficiency, and this potentially compromises image quality.

More picture editing tips

Let's be honest. You tried very hard during production to create each shot perfectly, but sometimes not everything turns out exactly as planned. It's in situations like this that the *real* power of picture editing is revealed. You've no doubt heard the saying 'we'll fix it in post', in reference to production problems. There's some truth in that saying, because for a lot of problems you might face, there are solutions that you can now employ.

The key to finding (and implementing) these solutions requires creativity, and patience. Fortunately, as a stop motion artist, you've got a lot of both traits! Take your time as you work through your editing challenges, and be open to solutions that may completely surprise you.

Beyond fixing problems, you may also discover that editing can provide you with ways to improve your film in ways that deviate from your storyboards, and your animatic. This may require some 'intestinal fortitude' (also known as 'guts') on your part, but you can handle it. Read on.

Be brave

As you edit, you may be faced with some tough decisions. Perhaps portions of shots (or entire shots) that you're very happy with on their own just aren't working that well in the overall film. What should you do? Include it because it's a great shot, even if it diminishes the effect of the overall film? Or remove it, and remove all of that hard work that it took to make a great shot? As you face these hard choices, remember your original objective: to make a great film.

Timing adjustments

Trust me, I know that your intention during production was to create perfect animation that would require no adjustments, ever. That sort of

integrity and dedication was essential during production, to ensure that you were getting the best shots possible. But as you now consider your film, you may be able to 'play' a bit with the timing of certain moments, to make both performances and actions more effective.

To extend a hold, first use the Razor Tool to isolate the frames, then copy and paste the frames. To shorten a hold, you can again use the Razor Tool to isolate the specific frames. Delete the frames, and then pull the shot back together. Keep playing the shot back as you judge things, and remember that you can always undo your modifications, if things aren't improving.

You can also modify the *speed* of your shot, in order to make its timing more effective in the context of your film. The process for doing this is the same as the one that you used for adjusting speed of your imported shots (see above). Just be sure that if you want to modify a specific portion of your shot (rather than the whole shot), that you first isolate the frames you want to affect by using the Razor Tool, before you adjust the speed.

> Remember that Premiere allows you to easily create various versions of your film. Take advantage of this great feature, and create versions that push your film into places you might not have expected.

Visual flow adjustments

The importance of effective visual flow has been emphasized throughout this section. And now that you've nearly done your film, you can consider this stage of picture editing as being a final opportunity to get things flowing as effectively as possible, from beginning to end.

Figure 17.3 Framing adjustments. The original framing is shown in image A, which was created as a medium shot. Image B is the exact same shot, only scaled up in Premiere to create a close-up shot.

Framing adjustments

Adjustments to the framing of your shots can be a great help, especially if some shots simply aren't hooking-up as smoothly as they should. An example could be a shot that you storyboarded, framed, and animated as a medium shot. Yet now, in editing, you've come to realize that this shot would work much better as a slightly closer shot (see Figure 17.3 above). Since your original DSLR frames are of such a high resolution, you can confidently 'blow up' your shot in Premiere by using the Scale Tool, without losing any image quality. Additionally, you can reposition the shot within the editing window, to create new, and more effective, framing. These sorts of adjustments can work wonders, but do use caution as you modify things in this way. Typically, it's just a minor adjustment that's needed, here or there – but it's easy to start changing *every* shot in your film, sometimes dramatically.

Before you know it, you've created more problems then you've solved!

> Adjustments to framing can do more than just help with visual flow. They can also improve story clarity, and they can allow you to emphasize the emotion or the atmosphere of a moment.

Video transitions

Transitions such as fades and dissolves were probably incorporated into your project way back during the storyboard stage, and you'll continue to apply them in the same places now that you're editing your animation. But there's no law stating that in post-production you can't apply a new transition in order to help your film flow more effectively.

As with adjustments to your framing, use discretion as you try out transitions. They can seriously alter the overall 'feel' of your film. They can also be distracting or outright confusing, and if so, discard them. But who knows? Editing is a remarkable process, and sometimes the strangest solution ends up working perfectly!

> If you need a reminder on how to use these specific tools in Premiere, refer back to Chapter 15 that's dedicated to pre-production.

At some point, you're going to stand back from your picture edit and say to yourself 'That's it. It's done'. When that moment arrives, and if you don't have any digital visual effects to do, it will be time to move on to what we'll call 'locked picture', which is examined later in this chapter. However, most stop motion films require a least a bit of digital effects, so let's take a closer look.

Digital visual effects

Digital effects modify or add to our stop motion world, but in contrast to the physical effects that we looked at in the previous chapter, digital effects aren't 'for real'. They're generated by a computer,

Figure 17.4
Chroma, Maxwell Racz, 2013.
In this Sheridan College film, we see a range of digital effects that are very nicely blended with the stop motion world. The butterfly and shadow monster are drawn animation. The trail on the butterfly is yet another effect, and the eyes and mouth on the puppet are also applied digitally, in post-production.

but if they're handled effectively, they often look real, or at the very least, they look carefully integrated into the stop motion world that we're creating.

Sometimes, digital effects are very noticeable, such as a realistic explosion, or tendrils of magical smoke. Hard to miss those effects, since they really show themselves off. But other effects are quite literally invisible. Exposure correction, for example, is all about smoothing out brightness variations in shots, and if it's done well, you'll never know it's been used. And although there are numerous effects applications that can tackle these sorts of challenges, we'll focus our attention on one that's very widely used, and very powerful.

Introduction to Adobe After Effects

If you can visualize an effect, After Effects can help you to achieve it. You can use it for relatively simple tasks such as rig removal (which we'll look at in detail below), as well as for incredibly complex composited shots, that bring together all kinds of wildly imaginative layers into a final amazing shot.

It's important to realize that After Effects is quite a bit trickier to use, when compared to Audition, Premiere, or any other software that we've looked at thus far. If your experience with After Effects is limited, be prepared to invest quite a bit of time in figuring out how to achieve what you're after. For help, you'll find lots of resources online, both through Adobe and through general internet searches.

Since many of the shots that you'll probably want to add effects to have now been edited into your film, you'll need to determine the best workflow for your footage. Ideally, you'd apply effects to the original, high-resolutions frames that you created during animation, in order to maintain the highest image quality possible. If you decide to work this way, make sure that your original frames are backed up, both on your local computer, and on an external drive. Alternately, you can work from a very high resolution movie export (or image sequence export). If you do, be sure that you're exporting at the highest resolution possible.

As with other areas within stop motion that require specialized skills, you may want to bring on someone who is more accomplished to help out with digital effects, at least for any trickier jobs that you may have.

Rig removal using After Effects

If there's *one* specific effects process to cover in After Effects for stop motion filmmakers, it makes sense that it would be this one. Rig removal is such an essential part of our medium, and is required so regularly, that you're very likely to encounter it. And After Effects can help you to do it quite painlessly.

You'll need to be somewhat familiar with After Effects to proceed, but you don't need to be a wizard. Ideally, you should try this out on a very brief test shot, since a few frames of animation with a rig is all you need, along with the shot's clean plate (see the previous chapter's discussion on rigging). Once you've got the hang of how to do this, you can then put the process to work in your actual film.

First, it's important that you visualize what you're about to do. To do rig removal, you're going to lay your frames with a rig on top of the clean plate. Then you'll use what's called a 'mask' to select the area of the rig. This will effectively remove the rig, and *reveal* what lies beneath, which is the clean plate. Then, you'll output all of that as a new series of rig-free images, which you can bring back into Premiere for editing.

Depending on what version of After Effects you're using, the detail that follows may be slightly different for you, since software is always getting updated. Help Menus and online resources are always standing by to help!

STEP BY STEP

1. Launch After Effects, and create a new project.
2. Import your clean plate frame. This is likely the first image in your image sequence.
3. Import your entire image sequence for the shot that requires rig removal. You can include your clean plate in this import.
4. At the bottom of the project window, you'll see several small icons. Locate the one called Create A New Composition. Drag and drop your image sequence frames on to this icon. This will create a new composition that matches the resolution of your frames, which is very important. This will also open a Timeline window for your image sequence. Corresponding with this timeline, you'll see your image sequence listed by name, on the left side of the window (see Figure 17.5).

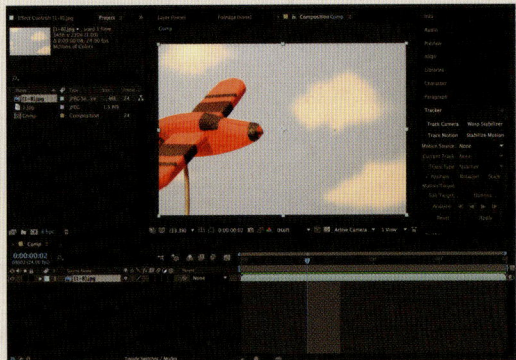

Figure 17.5
Composition for rig removal.
Notice the arrow beside the name of the image sequence. This arrow expands the sequence, to provide you with further options.

In After Effects, you can think of a composition as being the main canvas for your effects shot – in this case, your rig removal work. There are various ways that you can create a new composition, but this method ensures that you'll be working at the resolution of your original frames. If you don't do this, you risk having final frames that are lower resolution than the rest of your film!

5. Drag the clean plate frame into the Timeline window, and drop it below your image sequence. It should now appear in the list on the left below your image sequence. With your footage positioned this way, you're now set up to remove the rig, which will then reveal the clean plate beneath.

6. Grab the playhead in the Timeline window, and slide it to see the frames that require rig removal. If your frames are too big in the Composition window, you can choose 'Fit' in the Magnification option, which is at the bottom of the window.

7. Make sure that your image sequence is selected, and go to the first frame that needs the rig removed. Then go to Window at the top. Select Layer, then Choose Mask, and then New Mask.

8. You'll now see Masks listed, under the image sequence. Expand this, and you'll see Mask 1 listed. Click Inverted (see Figure 17.6). Your first frame for rig removal disappears, but don't worry – it's still there, just hidden. You'll also see new controls at the edge of the window. These controls are for the mask. Grab a corner and drag it down, to reveal your footage. Take some time to play around with the controls, and you'll soon start to understand what rig removal using masks is all about.

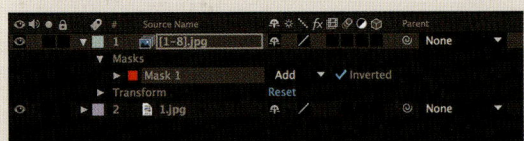

Figure 17.6
Mask settings for rig removal.
Click on the coloured box beside Mask 1, to change the colour of the mask controls. I changed this one to red, so that it was easier to see when doing detailed work.

9. Open the Tools window. Click and hold on the Pen Tool to bring up options, then select Convert Vertex Tool. This allows you to customize the shape of the mask. You can use the 'Command' key (on a Mac) to move an entire control point, and you can then very precisely adjust the mask using the control handles (see Figure 17.7). Remember to zoom in very close for detailed work, and use the Hand Tool to move your image, as needed.

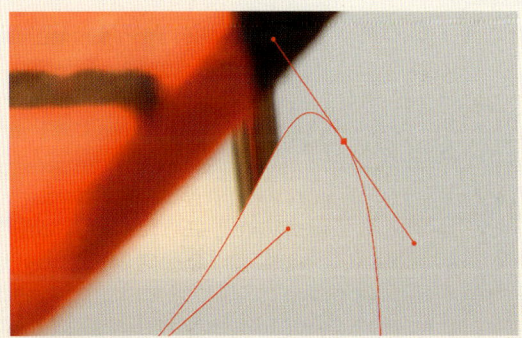

Figure 17.7
Detailed mask adjustment.
The mask control handles take some getting used to, but it's worth the effort, since they allow for extremely detailed positioning.

If you further expand the Mask's options, you'll find a range of controls for ultra-detailed work that allow you to fine-tune the edge of the mask.

10. Once you're satisfied with the mask, expand its options, and click on the stop watch icon beside Mask Path. You'll see a diamond appear on the timeline, which means a key position has been set. This marker indicates that the mask has been confirmed for this particular frame.
11. Move to the next frame, and adjust the mask again, so that the rig is removed. There's no need to 'key' this frame, as After Effects does it automatically. Continue in this way, through all the frames that require rig removal.
12. Before you render out your new rig-free frames, you may need to tell After Effects the specific range of the timeline that you want to export,

otherwise it will continue to render out endless copies of your final frame. If the range isn't set already, there's a slider that you can grab on the timeline to select this range. Set the range for your entire image sequence.

13. Now go to Composition at the top, and select Add To Render Queue. The Render Queue window now replaces the Timeline Window. In the Render Queue window, you'll see a range of options. Click on Render Settings to ensure that the image quality is sufficient. Click on Output Module, and from Format select an image sequence (JPEG, or other). Click on Output To, and select where you want to save the rendered frames, and what you want to call them. It probably makes sense to name them the same as your storyboard shot.
14. On the far side of the Render Queue window, you'll see the Render button. Click this and wait for your new rig-free frames to be created. Take a look at them in detail, to ensure that the rig removal work is clean. If so, you can now import those frames into Premiere as an image sequence, and use them in your film.

A JPEG file loses resolution each time you save it, but that's probably not an issue for you, since you aren't saving more than once. Alternately, you could choose a PNG or TIFF Sequence. These are lossless, but they are also very big frames and depending on how long your shot is, this might be hard for your computer to process.

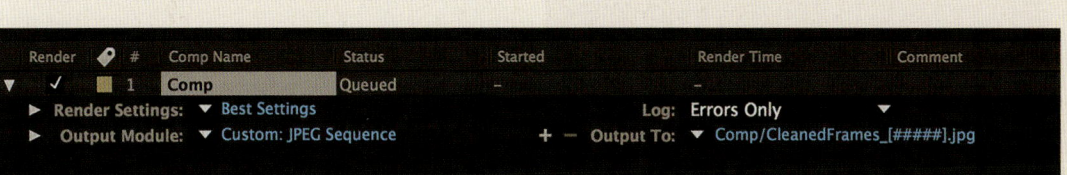

Figure 17.8
Render details.
Try to match your settings to what you see here. Additionally, you can try various settings and do some test renders, in order to determine the specific settings that provide you with the best results.

Various digital effects

It's no exaggeration to say that the creative options within the world of digital effects is limitless. You can always add another layer, or tweak yet another setting, in order to further customize your film. That being said, there are certain core effects that are commonly used in stop motion, and the following section aims to provide you with further insights into those effects.

While some of these effects are simple, others are quite complex, and each requires at least a certain amount of detailed step by step work. This work could involve After Effects, Premiere, or even Photoshop, and in many cases, the same effect could be handled in any of these applications, depending on how you want to approach things. Because of these complexities, you'll find that I've mostly steered away from specific how-to information. Instead, you'll find general tips and advice to help you approach each effect, so that you're working more effectively towards a finished shot. And to inspire your creativity, I've also include images that convey how various stop motion artists have used these effects in their effort to create distinctive and exciting films.

As with other software challenges, you'll find a lot of support for effects tasks through the software's own online support resources, and through more general online searches.

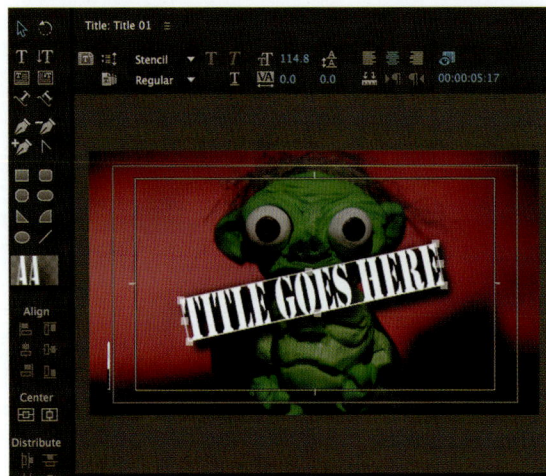

Figure 17.9
Titles in Premiere.
Once you've created the title, just place it on the video layer above your shot, and adjust the title's duration in the same way that you would any timeline file.

Titles

To keep with the physical feel of stop motion, you could create hand-crafted titles and credits, photograph them, and then bring them into Premiere. Or you could create your titles in Photoshop, and again, import them into Premiere. Alternately, it's a pretty simple process if you want to create titles directly in Premiere. Simply go to Title at the top, and select New Title. There's a whole range of options and effects that you can employ. When you're done, you can save the title, and then drag it to the timeline and use it as needed.

To compose a title that will be placed on top of a specific shot, you can position the playhead in Premiere on the shot in question, so that the shot can be seen. Then create a new title, and as you design the title card, you'll be able to see how it will look on the shot.

Exposure correction

This is a very common digital refinement that can be used to generally even out the brightness of your shots so that things flow more smoothly. Alternately, you can adjust the exposure in specific shots to convey a certain feeling or mood. A desert scene, for example, could have its brightness bumped up to create a sun-bleached look, or a cemetery scene could feel more 'night time' by darkening the footage. Adjustments to exposure can result in loss of detail in bright or dark areas, which might not be a problem if that's the look you want, but watch out for this.

Exposure correction can also help to reduce the effects of that constant source of frustration for stop motion artists – light flicker. After Effects has tools and procedures which can allow you to match the exposure between frames, effectively reducing the appearance of flicker. Premiere also allows you to zoom in on specific frames in order to adjust exposure, so if the problem is really noticeable (and you have the time to invest), these kinds of adjustments are worth the effort.

Connected to exposure is contrast, which is also a fairly straightforward adjustment. Reducing contrast can provide your image with a more 'washed out' feel, and if you boost it, you can get a more 'hardened' look. It's worth taking some time to play around with these variables, just to see what you can achieve. You can always hit 'undo', if the tweak doesn't suit you.

Figure 17.10
Colour correction, *Never Stop Cycling*, Colin Lepper, 2014.
In this example of colour correction, After Effects was used
to create a mask area around the character, isolating it from
the intense adjustments that were then performed on the
background's colours. This isolation also allowed any colour in the
character to be drained, without affecting the rest of the frame.

Figure 17.11
Film grain, *The Shutterbug Man*, Chris Walsh, 2014.
Beyond the digital grain that was added here, you'll notice
darkening at the edges of the frame. This slight vignette effect
provides a further analog feel to the digital footage.

Colour correction

As with exposure correction, refinements to the
colour of your film can be done in order to provide
consistency to your entire film, or it can be done
to specific shots or scenes that need a desired
look. Most effects controllers will allow you to
adjust one specific colour, or an entire range,
and the results can be subtle, or startling. Colour
adjustment can have a profound effect on your
film which can be very exciting, but as with any
effect, use some discretion. Remember that your
viewer is going to be taking in a lot of information
already. If a truly wild colour palette is thrown
into the mix, it might result in a worn-out audience. On the other hand, if you're crafting a psychedelic experience that transports the audience
into a different plane of existence, then dial those
colours up. Truly trippy results await you!

Film look

Recording frames in a digital format provides stop
motion artists with all kinds of advantages over
the 'old school' days of recording on physical film.
But for many artists, and for many projects, the
analog warmth of physical media is still desirable. This look is often rooted in something called
grain, and by adding a touch of it to a pristine
digital image, you can provide some 'visual
weight' to your image that it might otherwise
lack. Beyond a bit of grain, you can go *truly* old
school and add scratch, dust, frame jitter, and
vignettes. But do your research so that your effect
has some historical integrity. And presuming that
you'd want to add this effect to your entire film,
use the same caution that you would with any
major effect, and remember that a little goes a

If you're applying a specific effect to a range
of shots within your film, you can first establish the change in one clip, and then apply
the same change to the others. This can save
you a lot of time and effort. A quick online
search will show you how.

> ***GOUTTE D'OR*, CHRISTOPHE PELADAN,
> 2013**
>
> This Danish stop motion short tells the unu-
> sual tale of a dead pirate who meets a flying
> naked woman with an octopus on her head.
> How's that for an original concept? It's a
> great example of how digital effects can be
> used in stop motion to create a final, unified
> look. The entire film takes place in front of a
> wildly stylized sky, on or around a flying ship,
> with characters suspended or floating. Not
> surprisingly, this film has a pretty extensive
> list of digital effects artists in the credits!

long way. Audiences might enjoy a touch of this
effect throughout your film, but slap on too much
and it gets very tiresome, very quickly.

Motion blur

We looked at motion blur briefly in Chapter 9,
mostly in terms of how (and why) it's not naturally evident in stop motion animation. But
when done well, and for the right reasons, some
post-production blur can look great. It's especially

Figure 17.12
Motion blur, *The Arctic Circle*, Kevin Parry, 2010.
As the character is blasted away from the box, the digitally added motion blur really helps to emphasize the speed of the movement. This image also shows off a nice glow and 'blast' effect.

Figure 17.14
Glow effect, *I'm Scared*, Pete Levin, 2016.
All of these spooky bunnies have had glow effects applied to their eyes. Each also has had a rig removed, and several have had their shadows painted in. All of this was done digitally in post-production. Photo credit: Colin Crump.

useful to help convey moments of exceptional speed. The more blur, the faster the action will seem, provided that the spacing in the animation is also doing its part to convey the speed. The trick with adding motion blur is that it requires you to literally blur your animation, and if you have a great looking bit of action, be sure to first consider if you really want to blur it with effects. But since it's typically an effect that's only added for a few frames, you can pretty easily achieve this one in Photoshop. Play around with the effect, ideally on some test animation, to see if you can get it looking right for your film's needs. And if you do eventually use it on your film's frames, as with any digital effects work, make sure that you have copies of your original high-resolution frames, or that you're working in layers so you don't destroy the original image.

Particles and glows

It's hard to imagine a sci-fi or fantasy film being complete without some of these effects. But even

a more realistic film can often benefit from this kind of addition. Imagine a touch of dust floating through a sunbeam, or a background stop light that changes from red to green.

You can download these kinds of effects from an effects company, or use ready-made effects that are provided in After Effects. With further effort, you can craft your own custom layers in After Effects or Photoshop, and apply those. The advantage of custom particles and glows is that they can be integrated more seamlessly into your world, since they can be animated to match the specific needs of your shot.

Since these effects involve light, and light has an effect in a space, whenever possible try to create on-set lighting during production that will work with the digital effect. A glow from within a crystal ball may be a digital addition that's done in post-production, but if on-set the ball was also lit, then the final effect will be more convincing.

Green screen

Animating on green screen can be of particular benefit for filmmakers who have limited space in which to work. If your studio is small, but your imagination is big, green screen might allow you to create huge virtual spaces, while happily working away in your modest room. If you shot physical effects animation on green screen, you can remove the background and then composite the effect quite cleanly on to your animation, allowing you to arrive at a final look that feels quite consistent. Both After Effects and Premiere provide you with very effective tools for removing the green screen, and with some practice (and perhaps some

Figure 17.13
Laser beam effect, *That One With The Robot*, Erik Blohm-Gagné, 2015.
The laser beam consists of several copies of animation layered together digitally, using an assortment of blending modes and blurs. The greenish cast and the image distortion was also done digitally in post-production.

Figure 17.15
Green screen for stop motion, *Bringing Up Bigfoot*, Edward Coughlan, 2013.
In this film from Sheridan College, we see a nice blend of physical and green screen elements. This film also used drawn facial features that were composited on to the puppet during post-production.

Figure 17.16
Stop motion and hand drawn blend, *Doggy See, Doggy Do*, Kathryn Durst, 2012.
This Sheridan College film is a great example of how stop motion can be blended with other methods and approaches, in order to create an on-screen world that is truly unique.

online tutorials), you'll end up with some very nice results, assuming that you set things up effectively during production (see the previous chapter).

Hybrid techniques

Filmmakers can achieve really appealing results by using digital methods to blend in elements that aren't strictly stop motion, but that still have an organic, hand-made feel to them. If done well, the final effect can be really exciting, for both the filmmaker, and for the audience.

The example shown above conveys this idea nicely. During production, the stop motion puppets, with limited facial features, were animated in front of a green screen, along with physically limited sets. Separately, facial features were then animated through drawn animation, and the backgrounds were created using traditional painting and drawing techniques. The facial animation and the scanned backgrounds were then digitally inserted in post-production, creating the final look. It all required careful testing and planning, of course, but the final result is distinctive and appealing. Working in this mixed-media style, with effective use of digital post-production tools, offers endless potential for the filmmaker who wants to utilize a range of techniques and approaches.

CG sets and characters

In keeping with the idea of bringing in drawn elements to the stop motion world, why not computer generate sets and characters? This approach can provide excellent solutions on larger projects, such as feature films, since those projects typically require truly spectacular scenes. But for the independent filmmaker as well, there's no reason – as software becomes more affordable and powerful – that this sort of blending of styles shouldn't be an option. If it works for the world that you see in your head, use whatever tools necessary in order to bring it to life for the audience.

The things that Roy puts up with in this book. What a saint.

**Figure 17.17
CG and
stop motion
characters,** *The
Pirates! Band of
Misfits*, **Aardman
Animation, 2012.**
With so many
characters, this
scene would be
nearly impossible
to manage
entirely in stop
motion. In fact,
only the puppets
on stage are
physical, and the
rest are computer
generated.

SIMON SCHEIBER, ART DIRECTOR FOR STOP MOTION

Simon Scheiber is a self-taught filmmaker, designer, and animator, who works in a range of techniques, including stop motion. Besides working on commissioned projects, he also makes his own films. His short *The Lighthouse* has been shown at more than thirty international film festivals. You'll find out more about his work at www.trimtrab.studio.

Simon has a lot of digital effects skills, and here he shares some insights, on various aspects of effects for stop motion. Some of these tips are quite advanced, and as a result will be more useful to the reader who already has a solid understanding of effects for stop motion.

- In case you record a night scene in front of a green screen you might consider shooting two straight passes to minimize the time you spend in post-production. Shoot one pass with an exposed and one with an unexposed green screen – you can easily automate this task with a DMX controller in Dragonframe. Then use the images with the exposed green screen as a matte pass on the sequence with the unexposed green screen. This way you keep a lot more details and avoid any spilling, unwanted reflection, etc. in your final composition.

- Light fluctuates, which can cause unwanted flickering in your final sequence. In most cases, you can reduce these inconsistencies with de-flicker plugins like Granite Bay's GB Deflicker. These plugins perform an analysis on your composition, and smooth out abrupt changes in luminance.

- If you're using this kind of plugin, place a grey card in the frame, just outside your aspect ratio (this way it will be on every shot, but not on your final composition). Then that grey card can be used as an analysis target for your plugin. In this way, the plugin can compensate for any changes in luminance that occur on the grey card.

- Lighting your chroma key background is all about evenness, consistency, and distance. Choose the right chroma colour for your shot. Chroma green is often used, but it's not necessarily the best colour for your shot. Use your waveform monitor to make sure that your background is evenly lit, and there are no hot spots or shadows. Make sure to avoid as much spilling as possible, by having a clean division of your foreground and background.

THE OUTRAGEOUS BARON MUNCHAUSEN, KAREL ZEMAN, 1962

You'll find very slick, and at times very realistic, digital effects work all around you, but you owe it to yourself to check out this truly remarkable film by yet another Czech master (along with Trnka and Švankmajer). This film in particular shows off some of Zeman's finest effects work. He isn't trying to create realism, but instead to create a truly fantastic world in which live action and animated elements co-exist, to create something utterly unique. Try to bring the same sort of creativity and artistry to your own effects work in stop motion, even if you're working digitally.

Locked picture

Assuming that any digital effects work is now complete, it's time to ask yourself a very important question: are you completely happy with your picture edit? If so, then it's time to lock your picture. As you'd expect, this means you're going to literally lock your picture edit timeline, and refrain from *any* more changes. On your timeline in Premiere, you'll see a lock icon for each track of your film. Go ahead and lock all of your picture tracks. You'll see that they're now greyed out – you can't edit them anymore.

Can't you just unlock them, if you want to mess around again? Of course. But don't. The reason is that every decision that you're going to make in your final *sound* edit depends upon what is happening in your picture edit, right down to the very frame. If you shift anything in your picture *after* you've edited the sound, you'll need to adjust every single one of your sounds to match.

If something absolutely has to change in your picture further along in the process, that's something you'll have to face then. But do everything you can to ensure that doesn't happen. Lock your picture before moving on to final sound.

If that's a tiny adjustment, that's not so bad, but imagine many hours, and possibly days of sound editing work thrown out, because your picture changed. Lock your picture, before moving on to sound.

Sound editing

Even a film with very modest sound elements still needs to sound correct when played in front of an audience. I use the word 'correct' because there's no saying what style your film's sound may have. It may be a loud film or a very quiet film. It may have lots of dialogue or none at all. Music may be a very strong component or be completely absent. But if it sounds *correct*, it sounds as you, the filmmaker, intended it to sound for your audience – and that's vital. Final sound that is unintentionally too loud, or too quiet, or that is otherwise distorted (assuming that the mistake was made by the filmmaker) undermines all of the hard work that's been invested. Poor final sound can, quite simply, ruin a film – there's no other way to put it. But if you follow along with the insights provided in the following sections, you should be able to avoid that fatal problem. Beyond that, you'll pick up a range of insights and workflow tips to help you craft an awesome final sound for your project.

The process of arriving at final sound begins with your temporary sound. For a film that has relatively straightforward audio, many if not all of your temporary sounds might be perfectly fine as final sounds. If this is the case for your film, there's a few relatively simple steps that you need take, and those are as follows.

First, assuming that your dialogue, sound effects, and music are on their own tracks, you'll want to review each element of sound and decide once and for all whether its quality is truly sufficient. If you determine that the quality of your sounds is sufficient, you'll next need to ensure that your sounds are positioned effectively in relation to your images and to your other sounds, that any fades on the sounds are effective, and that the relative loudness of each sound is effective. For some technical insights into this, you can refer back to Chapter 15, when we looked at setting up the animatic.

Adobe Audition is great for recording sounds, but it's also very good at editing and mixing sound. You'll find that it has much better tools than Premiere for sound editing, and since both products are made by Adobe, your files can move back and forth very easily. Alternately, if your sound needs are pretty straightforward, you can work strictly in Premiere.

With this accomplished, you can move on to what we'll call the 'Final Mix', which is the stage of audio work that occurs just before completely finalizing the film. You'll find that section further on in this chapter.

But what if your temporary audio is truly temporary? For a film that is more ambitious in its sound, it may be the case that entirely new audio elements are required. If that's your challenge, then you'll use the temporary sound as a detailed reference point, as you set about the task of securing your final sounds.

That's the focus of the sections that follow, and I'm presuming that you're handling these challenges mostly on your own. Alternately, you could enlist the help of a post-production audio specialist. This can be a very good idea, since as I've already pointed out, a fatal error in your final sound can undermine all of your hard work thus far. If you are working with another artist for this part of your film, you'll find some specific insights below in the section called 'Working with a post-production audio specialist'.

Once you've secured the final sound effects, music, and dialogue, you'll need to repeat the editing process that you did with your temporary sounds, only in more detail, and with more care. This isn't as intimidating as it might seem. For a short film, it shouldn't take too long to recreate your sound edit, especially since you have the temporary version for reference.

Before jumping in to final sound, it's important to realize that by default, Premiere will automatically export your audio in stereo. In general, this is perfectly fine for just about every viewing context. Stereo sound means that your film will sound good in a theatre that has multiple speakers, as well as on a single-speaker device, like a

phone. If you want to create a final sound that has panning stereo, or surround sound (both of which can create highly immersive experiences), you'd be wise to bring on a sound specialist, unless you have very solid skills in this area.

As you edit, it's a very good idea to keep your dialogue track separate from your music and effects tracks. The day may come when you want to replace your dialogue, perhaps with an different language, and this is far easier to accomplish if you only have to replace a *single* track.

Final voice record

You may already have recorded your final dialogue way back in the animatic stage, if you needed to use it to guide you during animation. If that's the case, then you obviously can skip this step. On the other hand, perhaps you used a temporary dialogue recording to guide you during animation, and now the time has come to create your final voice recording.

For this, you might consider recording it in a professional recording studio. This will provide you with extremely clean dialogue recordings, typically with the help of a trained recording engineer who will ensure that the overall quality is excellent.

If you're recording final voice tracks now, your voice actor will face a particular challenge, which is matching the acting performance to the pre-existing animation. This requires a monitor for the actor to view, so that he can practice his lines along with the animation. It sounds tricky, and it is, but a dedicated voice actor (and director) will make it happen.

Final sound effects

It's possible for this section of sound recording to get pretty complex. Does the moving fabric of your character's costume require subtle sounds to be added? What about floorboards creaking, as the character moves through a room? Outside that room's window, is there traffic going by, or are there birds in the trees? Maybe there's both? What kind of traffic? What kind of birds? The more detailed you become with your sound effects, the more 'alive' your world will be for your audience.

Perhaps your world has nothing to hear beyond a ticking clock, marking time in the background of an otherwise silent and lonely scene in which all of the audience's attention will be focused on the performance, or the story. Regardless of whether you're crafting a complex soundscape of effects, or something very stripped down, you have to *obtain* those sounds.

Sound effects libraries

There are remarkably detailed collections of pre-recorded sounds available for filmmakers. Most college-level media programs have quite extensive libraries if you can access them, and if you search online you'll find endless effects that you can purchase for download. You'll also find lots of free downloads, although the quality of these recordings may not be that great, so consider them carefully before using them. Sound effects libraries can do more than provide you with basic sounds. They can offer you a whole other level of creative expression. Take the sound of a whistling kettle, for example. How do you imagine that sound, as you read this? A robust sound effects library might have one similar to that, but it *also* might have half a dozen more to choose from, each with its own particular personality. This can allow you to form a soundscape for your film that's *truly* distinctive.

When considering a pre-recorded sound effect for use, make sure that the sound is isolated, meaning that it doesn't have any other sounds recorded in with it. And unless you're going for comedy or cartoon tropes, try to avoid overused and clichéd sound effects. Instead, search for unique options so that your world sounds as fresh as possible.

Foley

Rather than acquiring pre-recorded sounds, you might decide to go for original sounds, created specifically for your film. This is a process known as 'foley'. It can be a lot of fun to do, since it involves watching your picture edit and creating (and recording) sound effects 'live', as your film plays out. It's most effective for sounds that are made by characters, such as footsteps or fabric movement. Foley sounds will provide you with results that are truly one-of-a-kind, which can really make your film stand out. These 'real' sounds will also cause your animated characters to sound alive, which can be a tremendous boost to your film.

Keep in mind that the process can become pretty elaborate and time-consuming, so ask yourself if you're up for the challenge, before committing. The bigger question won't simply be whether you can create the sound, but can you also effectively record it? Both are essential, of course, if you want the effect to work effectively. If it's feasible, you may want to consider bringing on a specialist to tackle it. You'll find more insights into foley sound later in this chapter.

Figure 17.18
Foley sound recording.
This image shows a foley pit that contains various materials for 'walking' sound effects, such as stone, pebbles, and earth.
Photo credit: Emiliano Paternostro.

Final music/score

If you plan to use music in your final film, will you have the legal right to use it? You'll find more about this topic later in this chapter, but be sure that you're clear on how you want to address it, before getting serious about final music.

If you have music in mind, it might be a single piece, or several, that sit fairly easily in your film's soundscape. A film score, on the other hand, is more of a 'musical companion' for your film's visuals and as such it typically runs throughout, coming to the foreground at times, while receding at other moments, as it blends with the images.

Whatever you're after, a musical element can have a huge influence on the quality of your final film. Music can heighten (or comically undermine) moments of emotion or action. It can foreshadow tonal shifts in the story. Certain characters can even have their own theme music, which can help the audience to feel a deeper connection beyond even what the story and animation can provide. Music can add entertainment in moments that would otherwise run a bit slow, and it can even help you to establish time and place.

You could obtain work that already exists, although allowing another artist to express something original about your film through music can be an extremely exciting collaboration, and one that can certainly allow you to grow as a film-maker. If you plan to work in this way, you'll need to provide the musician with a copy of your film that has locked picture and temporary sound (the musician can remove the sound if needed).

You may also want to provide any 'inspirational' music that might help the musician to understand the mood and style you're looking for.

I've stressed the connection between music and film repeatedly, and at this point the two really converge. Like your visuals, you'll want the score to rise and fall, but also to flow, so watch the film through and try to describe that to the musician. And don't be afraid to talk in *emotions*. How do you want a certain moment to make the audience *feel?*

Once you've gone through the film in this way, it's time to leave the musician alone! You've had your say as the filmmaker – now it's time to let the musical expert sit in the driver's seat, while you wait eagerly to hear the results.

As important as it is to let your musician have creative space, it's also a good idea to establish a date when you'll get to hear a *rough* version of things. This provides you with a chance to provide any (polite) notes, and it helps to lessen the risk that the musician is going off on a path that truly doesn't work for you. At this point, don't be afraid to ask for changes. If the musician is behaving professionally, then requests like this should be accepted happily, and incorporated into the score. It's for *your* film, after all.

But of course, never forget that your musician has invested time and talent into your film, so be respectful and diplomatic as you discuss things. Then, be sure to firm up a date for the delivery of the final music, in a format that allows you to bring it into Premiere.

You might have started a collaboration with your musician way back during the animatic stage. If so, you've likely kept the musician informed and updated with the latest version of your film, right up until locked picture.

Music rights

If you want your film to be seen as widely as possible, then you'll want to ensure that you have the legal rights to use the music that's in your film. Every festival will ask if you do, since a festival doesn't want the legal trouble that can arise from screening something that isn't cleared in this way. Other entities that might want to screen your film for the purposes of earning money (such as broadcasters, distributors, and you, if you plan to sell your film) will also require this, for the same reason.

If you've had original music created for your film, have the musician state, in writing, that you have the right to use that original music. Ideally, the musician will give you permission to use the music in your film across all forms of media, forever. This sounds intense, but it really just means that you are truly clear to use it for your film – online, for festivals, to embed in people's brain chips in the year 2086, you name it – without ever having to ask again. Quite likely, the musician will happily agree and if so, you're done. You probably don't need a fancy contract – just an emailed confirmation should be fine. However, you'll personally need to decide how formal you want to be.

If you want to use *pre-existing* music, you're in for another set of challenges. You'll need to acquire the right from whoever holds it – both for the performance and for the composition itself – and that can get complicated. Personally, I typically avoid this path entirely, since before too long I find that I'm practicing law more than I'm practicing filmmaking!

Alternately, you can enter the world of 'creative commons', and use music that has no legal issues surrounding its use, or that can be legally used, provided that you agree to the terms of the artist. You'll find all kinds of music like this online, and a lot of it is quite good. Many musicians create and post music specifically for this kind of use, so take advantage of it. It can provide you with great results, and it can allow you to avoid any kind of legal hassle.

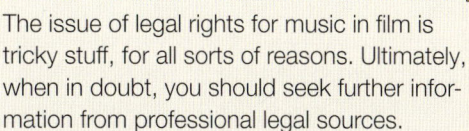

The issue of legal rights for music in film is tricky stuff, for all sorts of reasons. Ultimately, when in doubt, you should seek further information from professional legal sources.

Working with a post-production audio specialist

As you're realizing, post-production audio work can be a rather intense challenge, depending on the needs of your film. As a result, you might have decided that it was a task best left to a specialist. It can be a bit of a relief, if you're able to hand over this task, especially if it allows you to feel secure in the knowledge that your sound is going to be every bit as stellar as your picture.

Figure 17.19 Post-production sound editing, *I'm Scared*, Pete Levin, 2016. A professional sound editing facility can provide your film with amazing audio. Here, the sound editor is using the locked picture as reference. The timecode on the picture allows for more precise referencing, and is easy to apply to your locked picture in Premiere, should your sound person want it. Photo credit: Colin Crump.

Before your sound person can get to work, there's some items that you'll need to provide. We'll take a look at some of them in general, but you'll want to clarify all of this with your audio person, who will be sure to let you know what's specifically required, and who can help you through any technical challenges that you might face at this stage.

Locked picture with 2-pop

The primary item that you'll need to provide is a copy of your film, with locked picture and temporary sound. The sound professional can remove the sound as needed, but at least it will be there as reference. This version that you provide will need to have one simple but very important addition, called a 2-pop. This is a visual reference frame (just one frame), that occurs on your timeline precisely two seconds before the first frame of your film. This provides a visual sync point for all further sound work. It will also provide you with a way to sync up your final sound, when you get it back from your audio person. To add this, you'll obviously need to unlock your picture. Once you've added it, make sure that you lock your picture again.

Separated tracks

Premiere allows you to export each of your film's tracks of audio, in a file format called OMF. These files will contain not just the sounds on each track. They'll also include a wide range of information about the sounds that is required for further editing. Your sound person may eventually replace these sounds with others, but these reference files are still critical. The audio professional will provide you with further details on what (and how) to create these files.

Any additional final sounds

You'll also want to hand over any other pieces of sound (effects, voice, music) that aren't included in the separated tracks. Perhaps you have a few sound effects that you really like, and that would sound great at a certain part of your film, but you just weren't able to get them into the temporary audio. Pass them along, and perhaps they can find their way in.

Your audio person will now need time to work on things. Develop a schedule for this, and sort out stages of development where you'll be able to hear how things are developing. In the end, just as you had to provide specific materials to your audio professional, you can expect certain key elements to be handed *back* to you, so that you can carry on with your final stages of making the film.

The most essential things that you'll receive are called audio stems. These are final audio files, that have all of your sounds as they will occur in your final film. These files can be laid on to your film's timeline and synced with your picture, for exporting as your final film. Your sound person will be able to provide you with further information about all of this, but there are three essential stems that you'll want.

Full mix

This is the most important stem, since it's the one that you'll sync up with your picture. It has everything on it – music, effects, and dialogue. It will also likely be in stereo (which is good), and will be balanced correctly for loudness. In other words, this stem is everything that your final film needs in terms of audio, in one file, that requires no adjustments.

Music and effects

As you'd expect, this stem has your music and sound effects. The nice thing about having these elements together is that the dialogue is not involved. This will allow you the freedom to create alternate versions of your film, as you'll see.

Dialogue

With only dialogue on this stem, you can make a change to it if needed, and you won't have to touch your other sounds. This is important because if you ever want to get your film dubbed into a different language, you'll be able to do that without having to adjust your music and effects (see more on this below, in 'Final output').

Final mix

The final mix is the very last series of steps that you'll perform on your sound, before calling it 'locked'. If you've been working with an audio specialist, this stage is already complete. Just remove any temporary sound files left in your film, and drop the full mix stem on to your Premiere timeline. It should sync up perfectly with your locked picture, and you shouldn't have any other adjustments to make, prior to final steps (see below).

If you've been handling your final sound yourself, the most important thing for you to ensure is that your 'reference level' is set accurately before exporting the final film. Reference level refers to the basic 'loudness' of your film. In a few steps, here's how to tackle this important stage.

1. Don't wear headphones. Ensure that you have the Audio Meters window open. The specific window that you want to monitor is shown in Figure 17.20.

2. Play your entire film through, from beginning to end. As it plays, monitor the window. Most of your film's audio should reside around the −21dB range. Some sounds will be louder (closer to 0dB), and some will be quieter (below −21dB), but overall, your film's sound should reside within this range. You don't want any moment to go beyond 0dB. If it does, your sound will be distorted, and too loud for the audience. This is so important that red warning lights in the window will alert you if this happens, so that you recognize that there's a problem.

3. If your reference level is incorrect, you'll need to go into your sound edit and address the issue. You may need to adjust specific sounds or specific tracks. If you aren't able to resolve things, it's time to get a professional to listen to your project. The expert can help you to isolate and hopefully resolve the issue fairly quickly and painlessly.

4. Once the reference level is correct, give your film one last listen, without headphones, and with your speakers set comfortably. If all sounds well, you can consider your audio locked.

Make sure that you remove any 2-pop references in your film, and make sure that your picture and sound are still synced. Ensure that your Premiere project (and your entire film's contents) are backed up as safely and as thoroughly as possible. Once that's done, take a deep breath, and move on to final steps.

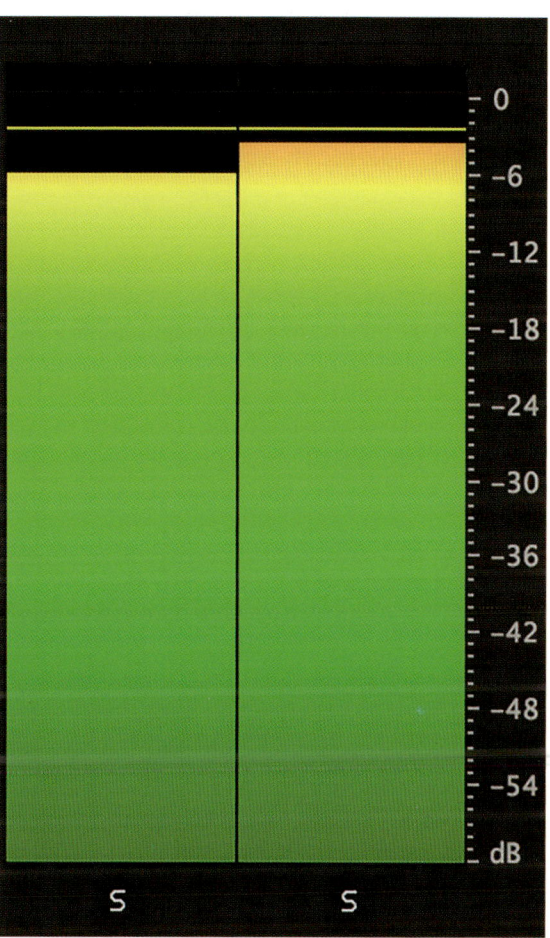

Figure 17.20
Reference level.
This audio meter reading shows the volume of a very loud sound, such as a gunshot, or a very intense musical moment. Notice that it still doesn't quite reach 0dB. If you set your film's reference level this way, your sound will be distortion-free, and just the right level of 'loud'.

EMILIANO PATERNOSTRO, AUDIO SPECIALIST

Emi is a post-production audio professional with many credits to his name, including several feature films as a sound designer. He's also designed and mixed sound for a number of stop motion shorts. He currently works at Sheridan College as a support staff, and instructs in audio production courses.

Here's some tips from Emi, that can help you as you approach the sound for your stop motion film.

- Get help from someone who loves audio. There are a lot of challenges when it comes to making good sound for any motion picture project. Bringing in someone who is passionate about audio will ultimately be more successful than trying to tackle it all yourself.
- Think about the world outside the frame. There's a lot of information presented to the audience on screen through the visuals. The sound in your project is your opportunity to present what the world of the film is like off-screen. Whole worlds can be created through this kind of sound.

- Don't overdo it. The audience can't handle too many elements within a soundtrack at any given time. Too many sounds at once will come across as white noise or static. Don't be afraid to mute or turn down something to allow the other sounds to work.
- Foley and footsteps are vital. This is especially true in stop motion. Since you are working with physical objects, the audience will expect the objects to make a sound when they interact. It's almost impossible to overdo foley.
- Think about what the sound 'could' be. Sometimes the actual object's sound won't provide the most effective film sound. Need the sound of a bone breaking? Try crunching some celery. Want footsteps in the snow? Squeeze a bag of cornstarch. Some of the best sounds created for motion picture have nothing to do with the source, but everything to do with the sound. Think outside the box to achieve what is good, not necessarily what is 'correct'.

FINAL STEPS

You'll be very happy to know that when I call this 'final steps', I really mean final steps! Once you take care of a few minor but important items, that's it.

Technical test screenings

At this point, a spectacular big-budget film that's filled with complex animation, effects, and sound elements shares a common need with a very modest independent project. They both have to have to be screened to ensure that there's no technical issues.

To do this, you'll need to create an exported copy of your film. As you know, export settings in Premiere ultimately determine how your film looks and sounds. What follows are some basic technical settings that should work for just about any screening context. Technical settings of this nature are constantly being modified as standards change, but they should help you to arrive at a final export that looks and sounds as good as possible.

If possible, see and hear your film in a variety of contexts. Test it through the highest-quality projector you can access that's connected to a very good sound system. Test it on the biggest monitor that you can find. Test it on a tablet and on a phone. Test it with headphones, and without. If your test screening results in any nasty surprises, you'll need to unlock your project, and address it. Then export your film again, and try another test screening. Once you're confident that what you're seeing and hearing is what you want to present to the world, then it's time to truly finish things off.

AMANDA STRONG

This stop motion filmmaker draws upon her Indigenous heritage as she creates films that blend traditional stories with modern perspectives. The resulting films are moving poetic fantasies that are courageously honest, and that help to create a stronger voice for a people. Her work is being increasingly recognized around the world, so look for her online, and at festivals.

Adobe Premiere sequence video/audio settings

Timebase: 24.00 fps

Video settings

Frame size: 1280h 720v (1.0000) or
Frame size: 1920h 1080v (1.0000)
Frame rate: 24.00 frames/second
Pixel Aspect Ratio: Square Pixels (1.0)
Fields: No Fields (Progressive Scan)

Audio settings

Sample rate: 48000 samples/second
Stereo

Adobe Encoder Export settings

H.264 encoding
Bitrate VBR 2 pass, Target 25.00mbps
Max 30.00mbps

Final output

One very high quality export of your film, perhaps even the one that you used to do your technical test, might be the only version of your film that you need. This one version should be sufficient for most film festivals, for downloading (if you plan to make it available this way), and for streaming. Additionally, you may want to consider having another version that is slightly smaller in terms of file size, just to make sharing it easier, but with data transfer speeds becoming ever faster, it may not be a concern.

A specialized file format is becoming more of a standard for discerning film festivals, and that's a format called DCP (Digital Cinema Package). This format is specifically designed for theatres that use digital projection. Creating a copy of your film in DCP format isn't something that you can easily do just by choosing certain settings in Premiere. You *can* do it yourself, if you want to get into the associated software that's required, but your best option would be to find a production house that can do it for you. The file will be very large, and not something that you can easily check yourself, so make sure that you use a trusted specialist for this. Most festivals want the DCP copy provided on a drive, such as a usb key, and since you aren't likely to get that key back from a festival, consider getting a few made. This can all start to get expensive, so my advice is to not worry about creating a DCP copy until someone asks you for it because they have committed to screening your film. At that point, you can decide if it's worth the investment.

Are you sitting down? Considering how much standing you had to do during production, you probably are. But if not, take a seat before you read any further. Get nice and comfortable, because I have something to tell you.

You're done. Seriously, you're done. That's it. Finished.

Some brave souls climb mountains. Others dive deep beneath the ocean's surface. You, on the other hand, have just completed an entire film whose world was hand-made. And you did it a single frame at a time. Okay, maybe two frames at a time, but still. Guts. Grit. Gumption. You have them in excess, and the proof is now on the screen. Think about what this accomplishment says about your dedication to your personal artistic vision. Take a moment to consider the following: what you've just crafted didn't exist, but now it does. You've given the world something that's truly one-of-a-kind. That's incredible. Congratulations, and I mean that very sincerely.

Now, call your friends and family. They probably miss you, since you've been so busy on your film. Tell them the good news, and then get ready to celebrate the fact that you, dear stop motion artist, just finished your film. Now, it's time to share it with the world.

ALEXANDER GORELICK, FILMMAKER, STOP MOTION DIRECTOR

Alexander Gorelick is a Toronto-based stop motion and live action director, who has helmed short-format, commercial and television series productions for more than fifteen years. Notable projects include the Gemini-winning series *Life's a Zoo* for Cuppa Coffee Studios, and his own independent feature film, *Luciferous*.

Q. Let's image that a film is completely ani-mated, and that the challenge now is strictly editing picture and sound. No effects work. What are some hazards to watch out for, as a filmmaker moves through this critical stage?

A. Often a filmmaker will discover in the edit that the story needs additional and/or differ-ent shots, not initially boarded. This is to be expected and scheduled for. Otherwise, the filmmaker will have to make a hard choice: either adjust the edit (sometimes significantly) to compensate for the missing story points, or find a way to shoot the required footage.

Q. One of the biggest challenges at any stage of filmmaking is the need to let go, and move on. Post-production is no different, since a filmmaker could endlessly fid-dle around, and the film would never be released to its audience! Any advice on dealing with this?

A. It's a challenge to accept that your edit is complete because filmmaking is so subjective. From day to day, you may see different issues, and want to tackle them. Therefore, schedule a reasonable amount of time to complete the initial edit. Stick to that schedule. Then, show it to a trusted peer who is not close to the project. Make changes based on their notes. Then don't look at it for one week. Repeat the process, if necessary. Make final adjustments. Anything after that will just make it different, not necessarily better.

Q. Like any artist, a filmmaker learns to get better by standing back and reflecting on the finished piece. Looking back over the various films that you've created, can you talk a bit about what they've taught you, about filmmaking?

A. Looking back on my own work, I can say that trusting your instincts during production is the best way to avoid future regrets.

Q. After the dust settles, a devoted filmmaker will soon enough start to imagine her next project. Any advice, as that artist starts out on that new adventure?

A. I think that the next project (which as artists we are often all too eager to move forward into pro-duction) actually takes quite a long time to take shape in the mind and/or subconscious realm. Give it a chance to develop into something more than a fleeting notion. Spend some time with it. Investigate its relevance to you as a human being, and its relevance to your future audiences.

Q. Finally, a personal question – why filmmaking?

A. Filmmaking incorporates writing, painting, sculpting, sound-composing, visual effects, acting, and so on. It is an art-form that can pro-duce content to make people laugh, cry, love, hate, everything in between. And it can cause us to contemplate the nature of humanity.

18

Exhibition and distribution

Now that you've grabbed some much-needed sleep, it's time to think about how to best show off your wonderful film. Many filmmakers quite sensibly like to premiere their film for family, friends, and crew. After that, you'll have all kinds of options for putting your film out there to the wider world. This can be a very simple thing, if you want it to be. You can post it publicly online in minutes, move on in your life, and wait for the world to find it. But since you've invested so much in your project, it's certainly worth considering the range of options that are available to you today when it comes to showing it off.

A newly finished film has a great momentum behind it. That's why media outlets offer a 'New Release' section at the very top of their content list. 'New' attracts audiences. This isn't to say that a strong film won't be strong as time goes on (just look at the dates on many of the films referred to in this book), but at this very moment, your film is automatically attractive to audiences in a very specific way. If you capitalize on this, you won't regret it.

It can feel a bit exploitative – you've worked so hard to create your 'baby', only to now push it out to strangers. But as a professional artist, you'll want to develop not only your artistic skills but also your *promotional* skills. You might be discovered as you humbly toil away in your studio, but why not make it easier for that to happen, by getting your art noticed. Your film will benefit because it's connecting with audiences, and you'll benefit, as the filmmaker.

By the end of this final chapter, you'll have a better understanding of all the different ways that you might share your film, along with some of the pros and cons associated with each. And since making *one* film is never enough, by the end of this chapter you'll also have deeper insights into how you might approach the financial challenges of making your *next* stop motion film.

Figure 18.1
Animation Film
Festivals.
Festivals are a
chance for films
to be appreciated
properly, and for
filmmakers to
connect with each
other as well as
with audiences.

FILM FESTIVALS

Ah, the flashing cameras. The red carpets. The adoring stop motion fans, all begging your puppet for an autograph. A film festival certainly can be an exciting event, but their main importance is that they provide you with an eager and receptive audience. This is becoming an increasingly special thing.

In our digitally connected age, most of the views that your film will receive will be for audiences of one, as people around the world experience it on whatever device is handy (assuming that you make it available this way at some point). Film festivals, by contrast, provide your film with what it *really* wants – a room full of people, all reacting to it simultaneously. And if you find yourself as a member of that festival audience, it can be a seriously exhilarating experience, as your film plays out for everyone.

Beyond the receptive audiences and some occasional spikes of adrenaline, festivals can be good for your overall career, well beyond the specific practice of filmmaking. Imagine a year from now, and your film has been accepted into a few (or more than a few) film festivals. If you include that list of festivals on your resume, anyone looking at it won't just see a list of festival

names. They'll see an artist who takes her work seriously, and in turn is taken seriously by the competitive art world. They'll also see an artist who is talented in a variety of ways, since making a successful film (as you now know) requires a range of skills and talents. All of this great stuff about you will forever be a part of your résumé, if you make some efforts in the coming months to get your film out to festivals.

Film festival essentials

As you think about your film's festival future (try saying that five times fast), there's one very important thing that you need to be aware of before proceeding: the more exclusive a new film is, the more attractive it is to a festival. That's because if a festival knows that the film isn't widely available to the public, then it can leverage that 'exclusive' nature when trying to sell tickets, and when trying to raise its own profile in the highly competitive film festival world. Makes sense, if you're running a festival. But as the filmmaker, this means that if you want to be serious about film festivals, you may need to keep your film away from public eyes, at least for the first six months to a year.

At this point, you might be thinking, 'I just spent ages making this thing, and now I'm supposed to *not* show it?!' I sympathize. And if you're not concerned with film festivals, or with making money from your film (more on that, later in this chapter), then by all means post it publicly, this instant. After all, it's your film, and showing it off to everyone is a very legitimate way to connect with audiences, even if it means bypassing festivals altogether.

If you're unsure about whether to keep your film offline or not, you can't go wrong by doing the following, as soon as you've completed your film: post it on a video sharing site (with Vimeo being a sensible choice), and keep it password-protected. This will allow you to show it to whomever you want to, while also keeping it away from the general public, at least for now. Then, at any point, should you change your mind about the whole festival thing, you can make the film public, and share it as widely as you like.

Finding festivals

The first step towards having your film accepted at festivals is finding festivals that will consider your film! At the time of writing this, a Google search came back with 11,000,000 results on a search for 'film festival', so you're going to need to narrow that down *just* a bit.

Below you'll see a list of recognized animation-only film festivals, to get you started. Each of these festivals takes great care in making its selections, meaning that they show the 'best of the best' for each year. They also attract serious animation fans and professionals, and that is also a good thing for you and your film.

To find more festivals that are worth considering, you can check with local animation societies. They're likely to have a very extensive and reliable list that you can access. Social media groups dedicated to animation are another great source for festival listings, and you can also make use of the databases provided by film festival service sites. You'll find out more about these services later in this chapter.

Your audience is bigger than you realize

Let's imagine that your film revolves around a young girl who lives on a far-away planet. She first discovers and then cares for a delicate space-plant. After much water, sun, and love, the space-plant eventually brings forth beautiful space-flowers, which in turn transform into glittering stars that surround her planet. Poetic, sweet, and very nicely done.

Now let's consider who, outside of stop motion fans, and animation fans in general, might enjoy this film. First of all, it provides a good message to young viewers, which means that a children's film festival might be interested.

Head to the official website for each of these festivals, and from there you'll be able to find relevant details regarding submissions.

- Hiroshima International Animation Festival, Japan
- Seoul International Cartoon Animation Festival, Korea
- Stuttgart Festival of Animated Film, Germany
- Holland Animation Festival, Holland
- StopTrik Festival, Slovenia/Poland
- Fantoche International Animation Festival, Switzerland
- Animafest Zagreb, Croatia
- Annecy International Animation Festival, France

- London International Animation Festival, England
- Festival Stop Motion Montreal, Canada
- Toronto Animation Arts Festival International, Canada
- Ottawa International Animation Festival, Canada
- Chicago International Children's Film Festival, USA
- New York International Children's Film Festival, USA
- Global Animation Syndicate, USA.
- Anima Mundi, Brazil
- Festival Brazil Stop Motion, Brazil
- Melbourne International Animation Festival, Australia

It also has a strong environmental message, which means that a festival that's oriented in this way (there are many) would also like to consider it. The film is set in outer space, which automatically makes it a film of interest to science fiction festivals, and possibly to fantasy festivals. And since your character is a girl, there's no shortage of festivals that want to promote strong female protagonists in films, so there you have yet another range of festivals to consider. What if you're a female filmmaker? Yet again, there are many film festivals that are specifically looking for films from women. Find them, and send them your film.

The point is, beyond animation festivals, there are many, many other kinds of film festivals out there for you to consider. In some cases, a festival may not get many animated submissions, meaning that your film, simply by virtue of its medium, will already stand out to programmers. And standing out in this way is a good thing.

Submission fees

What's to stop someone from sending a short film out to thousands of festivals around the world? Submission fees, that's what. Many festivals charge filmmakers just to consider a film. And if your film doesn't get in, you don't get your money back. This is certainly no fun for the filmmaker, but for the festival, it's a way to generate some much-needed revenue. Theatres and equipment cost money to rent, staff have to be paid, and ticket sales during the festival only go so far. Sponsors may be brought on help cover costs, but no matter what, running a festival is far from cheap.

Of course, knowing this doesn't make it any easier for you, when it comes to dealing with submission fees, and costs can add up quite quickly. One way to save money is to look for 'early bird' rates offered by many festivals, that are quite a bit lower than regular rates. As for the actual cost of submitting, each festival sets its own rate. Most fees are fairly reasonable, while others are ridiculously expensive. My advice is that if a festival's fee makes you gasp for air, avoid it.

The good news is that there are many festivals, including many of the world's leading animation festivals, that have no submission fees, whatsoever. European festivals, for example, very rarely charge submission fees – and there are a *lot* of film festivals in Europe. Many databases and festival guides will allow you to filter your searches, so look for 'no submission fees', and you'll be pleasantly surprised by the options that remain.

You don't have to spend a fortune when submitting your film to festivals. Set a budget that you can live with, formulate a strategy, and spend your money wisely. If you have no money to spend on festivals, don't let that stop you. Keep searching, and you'll find plenty of great festivals that don't charge fees for submissions.

Get organized

Film festivals typically have a 'submission window', which is the specific part of the year during which

Figure 18.2 Film festival tracking sheet. These column headings will help you to keep track of your festival efforts. Consider colour coding any festival that still requires actions on your part, so that you'll quickly spot it each time you return to the sheet.

	A	B	C	D	E	F	G	H	I	J	K	L	M	N
1	FILM FESTIVAL TRACKING SHEET													
2	FESTIVAL NAME	YEAR	LOCATION	DATES	DEADLINE	ENTRY FORM VIA?	SEND TO	ENTERED?	FEE	TRACKING	ACTION REQ	DELIV FORMAT	NOTES	ACCEPTED?
3														
4														
5														
6														
7														
8														

time they accept films for consideration. You'll need to track this date (and any other dates that are important for the festival), in order to keep on top of things. You don't want to miss out on a great festival simply because you missed its submission deadline!

Managing your festival activity is made a lot easier with the help of some kind of tracking sheet like the one shown above. Even if spreadsheets give you the cold sweats, at the very least, make sure that you've got some kind of document that's helping you. Your involvement with a film festival might span many months, from the time that you discover it, to when it opens for submissions, to when you learn that your film was accepted, right through into the actual festival itself. And that's just *one* festival! Imagine having ten, or twenty, all at various stages of progress. But if you're recording all of the details somewhere, you'll be fine.

Toughen up

Your film won't be accepted to every festival that you send it to, and that's no fun. Nobody likes to be rejected. If you film doesn't get in, try not to take it personally. There are many potential reasons that could explain why your film wasn't selected, and none of them have anything to do with your filmmaking skills. Depending on the festival, you may have been vying for acceptance with the very best (and very best-budgeted) film-makers in the world, and that's some serious competition! In many cases, a festival may have liked your film very much, but it may not have been able to fit it in alongside the other strong films.

As you can see, Roy is all about maximizing his audience. If your film isn't effectively put out into the world, it may not get noticed.

Some film festivals have themed programs that you may not have known about, and perhaps your great film just didn't quite suit that theme. There are more fish in the sea, and there's a lot more festivals in the world. Move on to the next one, and don't give the rejections a second thought.

DPK: Digital press kit

A digital press kit (DPK) is a package of information that provides the world with your film's essential details. 'Press' in this case can mean actual press outlets, since there are lots of animation and film outlets online that like to profile new

Figure 18.3
Film poster, *Old Man*, Alicia Eisen, 2016.
An effective movie poster should do its best to sell the actual film. This example shows off the central character, whose unusual designs and textures are big selling points in themselves.

work. But a DPK can also be provided to anyone who wants to know more about your film. This can include festivals, industry contacts, or anyone that might help you to spread the word about your project. It might take a bit of time and effort to create the items, but it's well-invested time, since you can reuse the items again and again to promote your film. Once you have the following items together, keep them all in a handy folder on your computer, so that you can share it quickly.

Don't hesitate to reach out to online outlets (big or small) that you think might be interested in knowing about your film. They constantly need new items to keep visitors engaged, and as a result they may be very happy to post an item about your film. Before reaching out, be sure that you have some public link that you can provide, so that the reader can click and learn more about your film. This could be a link to a trailer, to a social media page that you have for the film, or to the film itself.

Director's photo

Keep it simple and clear. Remember, this image may be included in a festival's program book or website, and someone may need to use it to find you at the festival, so that he can tell you how much he loved your film! If you can't stand the sight of yourself, just tell yourself it's for the greater good of your film, and smile for the camera.

Film stills

Since you have (possibly) thousands of stills from your film's animation, finding a few that look nice shouldn't be hard. These images may be used in press pieces, or by festivals, to help promote your film, so choose carefully. Most filmmakers use images that show off the central character, or the central situation.

Film poster

A simple poster is a great way to promote your film. My advice is to use an image from your film, along with the film's title, your name, and perhaps a contact email. Some filmmakers like to

also include the name of voice actors (if they're higher profile), and some sort of tagline for the film. It's up to you, but when in doubt keep it simple, and you'll be fine. A digital version can go in your DPK, and you can also create some print versions, if required. You can also consider printing some at a smaller size, to act as fun 'postcard' size promo items. Shrink it a bit further, and you have a business card!

Trailer

It might seem odd to make a trailer for a film that might not be much longer then the trailer, but it's a nice way to promote your film, and it gives people something to watch, even if your film isn't publicly available. As you create it, don't give away too much, and remember that the purpose of a trailer is to *entice* the viewer to watch the full film. Make good use of your editing skills, and have fun. As with the poster, when in doubt, keep it very simple. Once it's complete, make sure that you have a copy of the trailer that's high resolution, but that's also easy to upload. You won't want to send your trailer out to everyone, since people don't always want to have to download a video file, but you'll have it if they ask, and you can now post it somewhere, and share the link to that posted version, as a way to promote your film.

Short synopsis

Now that your film is actually done, it shouldn't be too hard to stand back from it and describe it in a sentence or two. A typical DPK synopsis reveals the basic premise or situation, but doesn't reveal the resolution. As you craft it, remember that like the trailer and poster, the synopsis is meant to convince the reader to watch the whole film.

Cast and crew bios

This is a chance to tell the world a bit more about the talented folks that made your film, yourself included. You'll likely want to only list the main cast and crew, and if there's not a lot of professional accomplishments to list, don't worry about it, just do the best that you can. On the other hand, if your crew has worked on great projects that are worth mentioning, then do so! And if your film used voice actors, be sure to list some of their previous credits. It's all a part of getting people to notice, and then watch, *your* film!

Additional information

You may want to list some other, more personal, items that make your film special. This is a chance to push the fact that you hand-made this thing, one frame at a time. You may take it for granted, since you're the one that made it, but take it from me – the process of stop motion increasingly fascinates non-stop motion people, who are astounded by the work involved, and the craft of it all. Make sure that whoever is looking at your DPK knows that your film was made by hand, and is done in stop motion. If you do, then I assure you, they will latch on to this fact, instantly, and will immediately have an 'angle' from which to promote it.

> **IF I WAS GOD ..., CORDELL BARKER, 2014**
>
> This thoughtful and darkly funny short film by the Oscar-nominated Barker uses grade school biology to examine the challenges of growing up. It's packed with all kinds of great stop motion work, and it also serves as a reminder of what the National Film Board of Canada continues to represent in the world of animation. As a government-funded agency, the NFB can support filmmakers through funding productions, but also by handling festival submissions and dealing with distribution challenges.

Once you have the contents of your DPK ready, you'll be able to upload a lot of its content to any festival submission platforms that you may be using (see below), and you'll be able to fire it off to anyone and everyone who wants to know more about your film.

You might also want to set up a shareable and downloadable folder (Dropbox is a trusted service) that contains both your DPK, and possibly even a high-quality copy of your actual film. As time goes on, and as your film gets noticed, you might be approached by someone informally, who would love to show your film at a casual film event. If you have a single link that can provide everything that the person could want, including the film itself, it's a form of 'one-stop shopping' that can make everyone's life just a little bit easier.

Just remember that most festivals have their own formal submission methods, and aren't likely to want to go to your shared folder to grab things. They get so many submissions that if they had to search around for items in this way, they'd never have time to devote to putting on an actual festival!

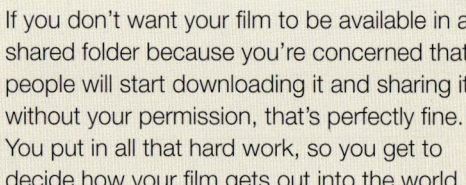

> If you don't want your film to be available in a shared folder because you're concerned that people will start downloading it and sharing it without your permission, that's perfectly fine. You put in all that hard work, so you get to decide how your film gets out into the world.

Festival submission platforms

As you'll discover when you start submitting your film, a festival wants a lot more from you than just the film. Yes, it may want some of your money, but there's also a lot of support information that you'll need to provide, and that's where festival submission platforms come in. These are online services that allow you to find appropriate festivals, submit your film and associated 'stuff', and then track your film's progress with that festival, all in a completely paperless fashion.

It's typically an extremely efficient process, and in recent years, these services have effectively positioned themselves into the film festival pipeline, between filmmakers and festivals. They're so popular now that many festivals will only accept films submitted through one of these services. There are several services out there, and the festival that you're considering will have its own preferred service, but we'll look at one particular platform that continues to distinguish itself.

FilmFreeway

Once you create a free account and basic profile for your film, you'll upload content that's relevant, including items from your DPK. With all of this information stored with the service, you can then search the service's database for festivals. Find one that you want to submit to? A few clicks will provide that festival will everything that it needs to consider your film. You'll then receive updates as the festival processes and considers your film.

If you're submitting your film to a festival that charges for submissions, FilmFreeway will also

Figure 18.4
Festival
submission
platform.
Services like
FilmFreeway
can drastically
simplify the
challenge of
putting together
and managing
film festival
submissions.

handle your credit card transaction. Again, this is a very convenient service, but be careful that you don't go 'submission crazy', and find yourself with credit card debt beyond your wildest dreams! If you keep this in mind, FilmFreeway is very slick, very secure, and very widely used service.

Even if you aren't using it to officially submit to festivals, a festival submission platform can be a great help. They typically have very robust databases that you can sort through, often without even needing to create an account. This allows you to access a very detailed (and current) list of international festivals. From that list, you'll then be able to find the festival's official website, which you can visit directly, in order to find out whether that festival is a good fit for your film.

The festival experience

What can you expect from a film festival, once your film is accepted, beyond the screening of your film? The organizers will likely offer you some form of free pass, or at the very least some free tickets to your own screening. Maybe there's a party that you'll get to attend to celebrate your accomplishment. You can certainly ask, but most festivals aren't in a position to cover your travel or accommodation costs. But they're typically very willing to help you to find a place to stay, or to at least lead you to hotels where they have preferred rates.

Some festivals offer a screening fee to filmmakers, but most do not. And most festivals don't offer cash awards, because they simply don't have the money to do so. Go into a festival being happy that you'll have a receptive audience, and anything that happens beyond that in terms of what the festival offers you will be a bonus.

Figure 18.5
Annecy
International
Animation
Festival, France.
Nestled within
the Alps, on
the shores of its
own sparkling
blue lake, the
animation festival
at Annecy
brings the world
of animation
together each
year, in order to
celebrate the
medium and to do
business.

That being said, a good festival, regardless of their operating budget, is one that thinks about its filmmakers, and wants to help them as best it can. To this end, many festivals will help to connect you with other attending filmmakers and with industry, and will help you to spread the word about your film. You'll know a respectful and professional festival when you experience one, so be sure to return that same respect. Spread the word about that festival, so that other filmmakers know that it's a good one. What goes around, comes around!

Unless you've got the money, it's unlikely that you're going to travel the world, attending every exotic festival in which your film is playing. But if your film *should* get into a festival that means a lot to you, and if it's at all possible, make the trip to

Most film festivals are run by extremely passionate people who work very hard, often on a volunteer basis, to ensure that unique films like yours can be seen by audiences. If not for their efforts, your film might not have any place to be seen outside of the internet, so be sure to show your appreciation to festival staff.

Figure 18.6
Poster with laurels, *The Champ*, Rosemary Travale, 2014.
If your film is accepted into a festival, ask for a copy of the festival's 'laurels'. You can then use them in your effort to promote your film.

attend. The memories that you'll have from attending a festival (any festival) will be vivid, and will only become more valuable as you carry on in life. Think of attending a festival as a chance to let your film pay you back a little bit for all that you've put into it. True, your film isn't going to cover the cost of an airplane ticket, but if it could, I'm sure it would.

If your resources are limited, perhaps you can head to a festival that's closer to home, which can make the trip a lot more affordable. Take a bus, and stay on a friend's couch – do whatever it takes. No matter where in the world the festival is, you'll meet amazing people (both filmmakers and festival-goers), and you'll be proud of yourself, and of what you've made. You'll get to see your film on the big screen, with an audience that can't wait to take it all in, and you'll be inspired to make something else as a result.

If you attend a film festival, will you land a job from it, or win a prize, or secure financing for your next project? Never say never, but most festivals (at least within the short film arena) aren't focused so much on the business, at least not directly. But depending on the festival, you may very well find yourself chatting with industry people, and as a person with a film in the festival, they'll take you seriously. Use the opportunity to make contacts, that you can then keep in touch with as time goes on. Who knows where it all might lead, and that's part of the fun of festivals. They're exciting, and they're hopeful, and they will inspire you, as you move onward.

ERIK GOULET, FESTIVAL DIRECTOR

Erik Goulet is the founder and director of Festival Stop Motion Montreal, which is North America's premiere stop motion animation festival. Dominique Côté is the festival's Programming Director, and between the two of them, they've come up with some very solid advice for you to consider, as you start submitting your film to festivals.

- Don't put an academy leader (the classic 'countdown' seen at the start of films) at the beginning of your film. Most of the time, a festival won't have time to edit this out, and audiences really don't want to see it.
- Keep your final credits to the essentials. There's no need to list your name under every single department – animation, directing, voices, puppet fabrication. This only lengthens the credits, and audiences don't like having to sit through all of that.
- Consider having a separate version of your film that you can post online, or screen privately, in

which you can do whatever you want with the credits.
- Most festivals have a submission form online, but you also will need to send your films and promotion elements (DPK). You should do all of the submitting of material at the same time. It's very hard for a festival to track material that trickles in over several months.
- Read all the of the rules of submission! They have been written for a reason, which is to make things go smoothly for the filmmaker, and for the festival. And if you have question, write to the festival. A good festival will gladly help you out.
- If the festival requires subtitles (check the rules), please do it. It's not much fun to have to do this, but if we love the film, and we want to present it, it would be sad to miss out on screening the film!
- Finally, the golden rule: don't wait to the last minute to send your masterpiece!

ONLINE PRESENCE

As we all know, the internet is essentially a place for cat pictures. But it can also be used for other things, such as representing your film. Back in Chapter 14, we looked at creating an online portfolio to show off your animated work. If you already have something established, that might be the perfect place to post your film now that it's complete, or to at least post updates and information about your film, if it's not publicly available.

Beyond your portfolio, or in addition to it, there's lots of other ways that the internet can be used to support your film. Of course, these methods are ones that we all interact with daily, and as such it's safe to assume that you don't need a lot of 'how to' information. Instead, I'll point out a few best practices that might help you in your efforts to let the world know about your film.

Social media platforms

These notoriously rise and fall in popularity, and you'll no doubt put effort into the ones that appeal to you the most. For all of them though, 'social' is a key concept. No matter what platform you're looking at, it's more beneficial to your film if you're prepared to engage with people. If you post an image of your puppet (as a final creation, or as a work in progress), and someone asks you a question about it, reply to the question. The more people feel connected to your project, the more they're likely to follow it, and support it.

Just how 'behind the scenes' you'll want to be online is an important question that you should ask yourself, if you haven't already. Some filmmakers like to show off every step of the process, and that can be great for building a following. And if you love the art of promotion, and love interacting with people online, social media can be an amazing place not only to share glimpses of your film, but to come up with all kinds of fun and creative ways to bring people closer to your film.

On the other hand, it can also serve to remove some of the 'magic' from your film. When the curtain finally goes up on the finished film, the world might already be tired of it, as a result of your endless (but well-intentioned) updates.

Another question you should ask yourself as you set up social media for your film is how much do you want your film to stand alone as its own thing, and how much do you want it to be an aspect of you. I can speak from personal experience, as a result of making a horror film in stop motion (*The Shutterbug Man*). Horror isn't for everyone, of course, and although I love horror movies, I don't think of myself as a particularly 'horrifying' person in general, so when it came to social media for this film, I set it up on its own, a little bit to the side of my own social media profiles, so that the film could be as creepy and as weird as it wanted to be. It turned out to be good for the film and for its fans, and it also allowed the film to stand (or fall) on its own merits, without 'me' having to get too involved.

How do you see your film, within the realm of social media? Are you comfortable with a series of updates about your own life, *and* the life of your film, weaving together via one profile?

What's best for your film, *and* for you?

Video sharing services

Even if you aren't sharing your film publicly (now, or ever), you may still want to upload it to somewhere and protect it with a password, so that you can share it as needed. And even if your film is private, you may want to use video sharing to publicly post the trailer, or 'making of' footage, or any number of other video clips that might serve to support your film.

With video sharing such a common part of our lives, it might at first seem like a topic not worth examining in more detail, since we all 'get' video sharing. But when you've just completed a film that you've worked really hard on, and that film is now quite possibly a major part of your portfolio, it's good to have some insights into this topic that are coming from a professional perspective.

YouTube

Does YouTube instantly come to mind when you consider the topic of video sharing? If so, you've already been confronted with the biggest advantage that this service has over all others. Just about anyone who has decent access to the internet visits YouTube, making each of them potential audience members for your film. That's staggering, when you image a movie theatre filled with billions of people, watching your film.

YouTube also allows for channel building, and as you continue to create content, a channel can be a very exciting way to get your work seen, and to make some money through advertising revenue (see below).

Speaking of advertising, the role it plays on YouTube can't always be seen as a good thing.

For short films, ads can be more than just annoyances, they can seriously throw off the experience of your film for your audience. And in fact, the entire environment of YouTube, with so many ads vying for the viewer's attention, can sometimes be downright dizzying. It's not an ideal environment when it comes to showing off your great film in the best way possible.

ANT-MAN GOES WRONG!, LEE HARDCASTLE, 2012

In what might be the shortest stop motion film you're likely to find, Hardcastle creates something that's extremely fun to watch. The proof, to some extent, is in the number of views that the film has received on his YouTube channel. As of the writing of this book, Hardcastle is pushing 300,000, for this single film alone. Not bad, for five seconds of animation!

Figure 18.7 Stop motion on YouTube, Richard Svensson. When great content is provided on a channel, viewers don't mind some advertisements tagging along with the excellent videos.

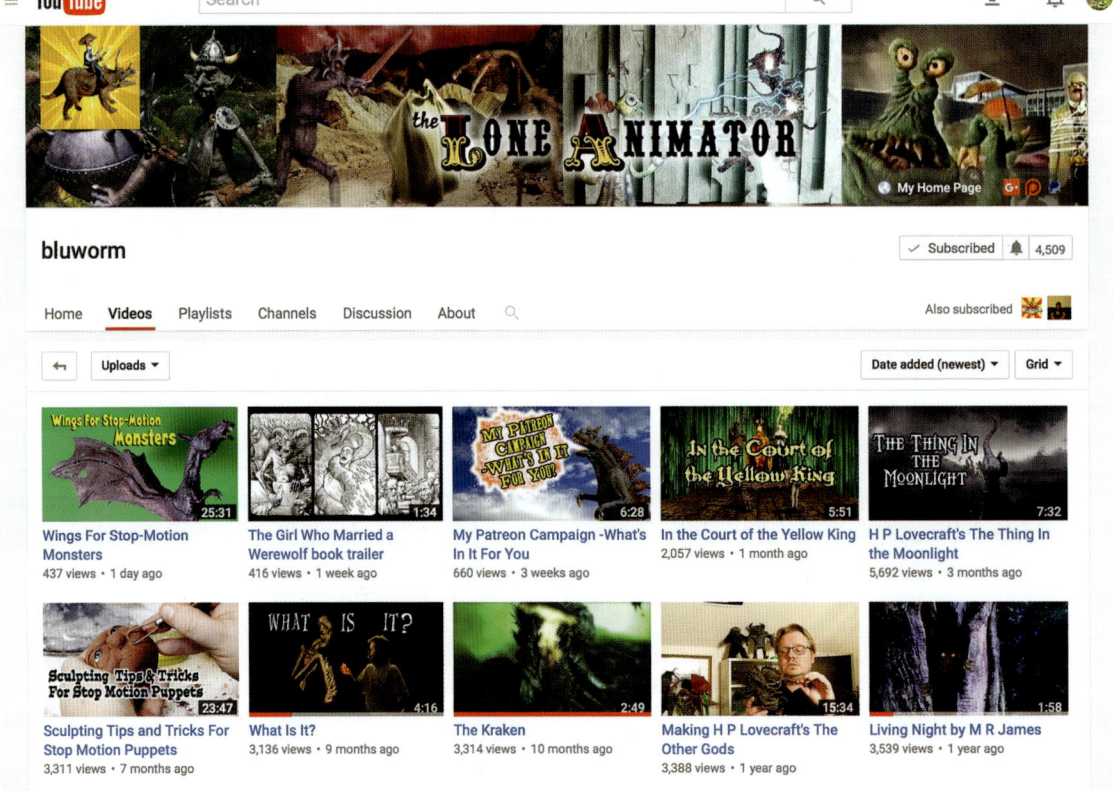

Vimeo

In contrast to the ad-heavy world of YouTube, Vimeo is a tidier forum, by far. No ads, just films. Of course, this can also be a drawback if you're looking to generate ad revenue, but if you want a nice clean viewing experience, Vimeo has YouTube beat. For that reason, if you're going to share your film selectively with professionals or festivals, Vimeo is certainly the preferred place to post. Your film will be given the respect that it deserves, and your audience will be able to focus on what's important – and that's your film.

Does Vimeo attract the same potential viewers as YouTube? Not nearly, so if you're after maximum views, you won't find it through Vimeo. But an effective film *will* earn lots of views on Vimeo, and their curated 'Staff Picks' can seriously boost a film's profile, bringing in remarkable numbers of audience members.

It's important to realize that while Vimeo doesn't push ads in the way that YouTube does, it still can provide filmmakers with monetization options. You can set up your film for paid viewing through Vimeo, and since there's already millions of film-loving visitors moving through their main site, it can make it that much easier to land paying audiences for your film. This, as opposed to setting up your own stand-alone store somewhere else online, where there won't be as many potential customers already browsing the aisles.

> Ultimately, it won't matter which service you use to post your film. If it's a good film, people will find it, watch it, and then spread the word (and the link), so that others can also enjoy it.

Website

Ah, the good ol' website. If you haven't secured a domain already for yourself or for your animation efforts, it's definitely worth considering. A website can provide you with a stable location online that can serve as a portal, leading visitors to anything else that you may have online that's related to your film, such as social media or video sharing sites. As you continue to create animation, and as your online presence expands, you'll be able to grow all of your content in its various (and distinct) social media or video sharing locations, with your *website* providing you with a way to tie it all together in one easy-to-find location.

PINEAPPLE CALAMARI (2014)

Graduation short from the National Film and Television School.

'Stop whatever it is you are doing and give over the next nine minutes of your life to watching Kasia Nalewajka's wonderful stop motion animation Pineapple Calamari, and I promise that you will thank me for it.'
James Marsh, TWITCH

Figure 18.8
Film website, Kasia Nalewajka. A good example of how an artist can showcase her film prominently on her landing page, while also providing separate links to her related art content across the top.

LEE HARDCASTLE, FILMMAKER

The infamous Lee Hardcastle has made a name for himself making extremely intense clay animation, that's primarily viewed via YouTube, where he has a truly astounding number of views racked up. His stuff is shocking, but it's also extremely effective filmmaking. The success he's earned through his own distinctive style has led to client work for companies like Adult Swim, for whom he's created a series of very successful Rick and Morty clips.

Below, Lee offers some tips on creating work and getting it out there, in the age of video sharing and social media.

- Work. Even if you can't work, just work. Shoot commercials, music videos, shorts, make anything and everything. It's very important, just don't stop.
- Know who you're making content for. Remember who your audience is, as a guide to help you make decisions.
- Don't work for free. I offered to work for free more times than I'd like to admit and I was always won over when people said 'You'll get exposure', or 'It'll go on television'. Don't work for things like that. If it's going to take you four days to make, work out what you're happy to be paid for four days, and then add materials on to the fee.
- Social networking is important. Don't be a jerk, look out for your own best interests, and brand yourself. Don't express weird personal opinions or personal dramas. Just keep people up to date and interested, and leave it at that. Spamming is okay but there's a fine line, so keep it in check.
- Know what you want from life and keep in that direction. Personally, I want to be the next Steven Spielberg, so my career decisions have all been made with that in mind. If you don't know where you want to be eventually, then how can you aim towards it?

KIRSTEN LEPORE, FILMMAKER

Kirsten Lepore is an LA-based director and animator, and alumna of CalArts. Her credits include writing and directing an Emmy-winning stop motion episode for Cartoon Network's hit show, *Adventure Time*. Her films have taken top prizes at many festivals, and her client list includes Google, MTV, Facebook, Nickelodeon, Yo Gabba Gabba, Whole Foods, Toyota, and more.

Here's some insights from Kirsten that can help you in your own stop motion filmmaking pursuits.

- Put your work up online! More eyes will see it that way, including diverse, international crowds of potentially millions online, versus maybe thousands of festival-goer types.
- Unless you really hate computers or are super private, an internet presence is very important as a way to establish yourself. Make that web presence cohesive. Don't throw every little test up on Vimeo. Curate your web presence, then make your work as visible as possible.
- Submitting to festivals is also very important. If you get in, and are able to attend, do it! Meeting people in person at festivals is super important. Not only will you make new friends, and maybe have adventures in a new place, but you'll become way more connected to the animation community at large. Although the internet is important, real life human connections are 100 times more valuable. You should also make it a point to attend local animation events and gatherings!

EARNING MONEY FROM YOUR FILM

One way to ensure that your film earns money is to adopt a 'pay to play' policy (you'll find more on this below, when we consider online stores). That means that outside of film festivals, anyone who wants to watch your film will have to pay to do so. Pretty simple concept, and depending on how you look at things, there's a good case for proceeding in this way. By placing a dollar value on your film, you're sending a message to the world that you see your own work as something that's as valuable as any other item in the economy.

You won't find many people that will argue with you on this, but you also may not find a lot of people willing to pay to stream or download your film. After all, in a world where there's so much free content available, why should someone pay to see *your* short film? Beyond the risk that you might not earn much money, another consequence of putting your film behind a paywall is that your film obviously won't be seen by as many people. This fact raises its own set of concerns – don't you want the world to see your hard work? After all, the easier it is to find and watch, the greater the chances are that it (and you) will get noticed. And getting noticed can lead to exciting things, right?

In the same way that you made difficult *artistic* decisions for your film, you're going to have to make difficult distribution and exhibition decisions, now that it's complete. It's not easy finding a path through all of these complexities, but all you can do is consider all of the options as best you can, commit, and then move onward. No matter how you proceed, you'll be learning more about the world of exhibition and distribution in the digital age, and that's increasingly a part of what it means to be a serious filmmaker.

> You can also consider using a paywall for a period of time so that your film can earn some money, before making it public. This might make lot of sense in some ways, but don't forget the people who supported your film with their money! Be sure that you clearly explain your motivations to your supporters, if you move from paid to free.

Distributors

A distributor is someone who will take your film and try to rent it or sell it, in order to make you both money. It's no easy task for a distributor, since short films aren't easy to sell. But if you can find one that wants to take on your film, it might be a good thing, since the distributor may have connections with broadcasters that are willing to pay decent money to show your film.

If you do find yourself considering a partnership of this sort, be sure to carefully go through the terms that they're offering, and seriously consider bringing in a lawyer to advise. Most importantly, make sure that you're clear on what rights are being taken over by the distributor (more on that below), and for how long. Typically, a distribution deal lasts for an agreed upon term, which is often for a number of years, before the film then returns to the filmmaker. If a distributor wants to own your film's rights forever, walk away.

Rights

We looked at this issue in the previous chapter, when looking at final music, but now it's time to think about it from the perspective of your finished film. Assuming that you paid for it yourself, and assuming that any work by others for your film is yours to legally use, then you hold the exclusive rights to your film. That means that you, and only you, get to determine how and where it's shown, and on what platform. So far, so good. But the time may arrive when you'll be asked to give up some of that, so that someone else can show it, for the purpose of trying to make money. In return for this right, you'll receive something, which might be a bit of money outright, or a percentage of the money that your film generates, as time goes on.

If you find yourself having this kind of a conversation, I have two pieces of advice. First, seriously consider having a lawyer look at the offer, and second, determine whether the offer is for 'exclusive' rights, or 'non-exclusive' rights. If the offer is for exclusive rights, that means that the other party wants to be the only one that controls the film, and that can sometimes mean that even *you* can't show it. In this case, you should expect more money, or a bigger share of money that's earned. If on the other hand the rights are 'non-exclusive', that means that that the other party wants the right, but you'll be able to continue to do what you want with your film, including offering the non-exclusive right to others.

As you'd expect, a 'non-exclusive' deal won't provide you with as much money, but it will allow you a lot of freedom to continue using your film, while letting the other party try to earn some money out of your film. Not a bad way to proceed, all things considered. When in doubt, as long as the offer is to gain 'non-exclusive rights', you're probably fine. I'll stress again, though, that you'd really do well to have a lawyer look over things, should you find yourself in this situation.

Online store

Why sign on with a distributor who is going to take a cut of your sales, when you can handle it all yourself, and keep more money? Good question, which is why artist-run online stores have become so popular. With a store, you can sell your film, along with any related items that you think might be of value. The service keeps a portion of your sales, and you keep the rest.

I have very good things to say about Gumroad, which was the service that I used when setting up the store shown here. It was very easy to use, and more importantly, it was very stable and secure. That's critical when people are providing credit card information in order to purchase your film!

As for sales tips, you could consider offering a 'bundled' deal, that might include your film as well as a few other related items. For my bundle, I offered the film, a digital book that expanded the world of the film, and the movie's poster. These items were for sale individually, but were priced slightly more affordably through the bundle. I certainly sold more of the bundle then the other options, because even in the world of independent stop motion films, people love a deal!

When thinking about online stores, it can seem like the perfect plan – make short stop motion films, sell them through your store, and then use the millions that you'll make to buy a tropical island, where you can establish your own state-of-the-art stop motion studio. The reality of your store's sales may be a *little* less exciting than that, but hopefully they'll still be encouraging. I personally made enough from my sales to cover the costs of materials for another short film. Not bad, considering that the film would have generated zero revenue otherwise.

I was happy with these results, but only because I had kept my expectations realistic. If I had already purchased my plane ticket to that tropical island before tallying my sales, I might have been a wee bit disappointed with the way things actually turned out!

Use social media to let people know when (and where) your store will be opening, in advance. Then for every sale, send a follow up email, thanking the person for the support, and ask if you can put the person on a mailing list. They like what you're doing, so keep them informed about your future projects.

Advertising revenue

All of those ads on YouTube have to benefit someone, don't they? They help the advertiser to attract customers, and they help YouTube because the advertisers pay YouTube to post the ads. But they can also benefit filmmakers, at least in terms of generating revenue. If you enable ads for the videos that you post on YouTube, you'll receive some money from YouTube for allowing that to happen. But as with other money-making efforts in the world of short films, you're probably best to keep your expectations modest. You'll receive microscopic fractions of money for your ads. Over time, these tiny drops can fill up the bucket, which will translate into an actual dollar value. And if you gain a strong following, those dollars will increase, since more viewers means more ad revenue coming in.

You'll stand a better chance of earning ad revenue on YouTube if you have more content available beyond your short film, so set up a

CAD$10+

The Shutterbug Man- THE SHUTTERBUNDLE

THE SHUTTERBUNDLE offers all 3 store items (the 1080p Film, the Companion Book, and the Poster), for a DISCOUNTED price. Stock up on all the stop motion horror magic... and save some money at the same time.

Name a fair price: $

I want this!

channel, post your film (with ads enabled), and then keep posting content. One of the challenges that you'll face as an animator is that animation takes *time* (no kidding), and that can mean that you'll struggle to properly 'feed the beast' that is YouTube. It's always hungry for more content, but are *you* able to keep up with that demand, working a frame at a time?

A final bit of honest insight, using my own experiences in the world of making money via YouTube. At the time of writing this, the channel that I maintain for my small business, Mad Lab Productions, has had well over 20,000 views in total. For an average person making some stop motion, it's not bad. So how much money have I earned from my advertising revenue, as a result of those views? Not *quite* enough to buy a nice meal in a fast-food restaurant … but I'm getting close.

The author Kurt Vonnegut said that if you make a work of art to the best of your ability, you'll be rewarded. He wasn't talking about money as a reward, although that might happen. He was talking about the satisfaction of knowing that you made something original. That's an amazing thing, all on its own.

FUNDRAISING

Earning money from an existing film is one challenge, but what about pulling together funds so that you can make your *next* stop motion project? I'd like to say that this is an easier challenge to overcome, but sometimes just getting enough money together for groceries is a battle, let alone getting money together for stop motion films.

Robbing banks can bring in a lot of cash, and quickly, but this probably isn't the most sensible option, for a variety of reasons. Instead, let's take a look at some other methods for raising funds that are a little less dramatic, and a *lot* more legal.

Figure 18.10
The Cat With Hands, Robert Morgan, 2001. Originally slated to show in the early evening, this film found itself moved to a later timeslot, once the commissioning broadcaster saw the final film. This move probably prevented more than a few nightmares for the youth of Britain!

Commissioned films

If you create strong work, and if you do so consistently, then the world begins to take notice. The world in question might be film festival judges or audiences, assorted online communities, or in the case of a commissioned film, a business or a broadcaster (for television or for internet) who has some funds to invest in a project. If you're commissioned to create something,

it can be a pretty great situation, since someone is literally saying 'We like what you do, and how you do it, and we'd like you to do that for us. Here's some money'.

But an opportunity like this doesn't come without certain challenges. If the commission is coming from a business, they may have a particular product that they want you to showcase, and you may suddenly find yourself creating what is essentially a commercial for that product. Before you know it, you're operating in the world of advertising, and that can lead to extremely lucrative projects, each of which you can stamp with your own distinctive style. But this will also mean that you're dealing with clients, and since they're paying, you'll need to address their concerns and do your best to keep them happy. You may find that you're spending more time tending to that, as opposed to creating stop motion.

There's nothing wrong with this per se, and it's a very common way for artists to make money through their art. In fact, many animation studios have built themselves on this method of working. You do the work, you hand it over, and you get paid. But if you have a project in mind that you're very attached to emotionally, or that's really important to you for whatever reason, you should think twice about offering it up to an investor who in the end is going to take it away from you, possibly forever.

If you've got business ambitions to match your artistic ones, don't hold yourself back. Walt Disney got his start in the 1920s by making very modest animations for a small movie theatre client. If it worked for Disney, why can't *you* find clients that would benefit from some online stop motion clips? The approach seemed to work pretty good for Walt.

Art grants

If you're looking for a type of funding that supports your efforts in a very respectful fashion, you can't beat an arts grant. The name says it all – a sum of money that's awarded to you, with no need to pay it back, for the purpose of helping you get your film made. In some cases, such a grant might even help to cover the cost of living, so that you can devote yourself more fully to the project. With an arts grant, the funding body, which may or may not be government-affiliated, will no doubt ask you to thank them in your credits. But that may be about it, in terms of conditions. Of course, you'll also be obligated to actually make the project that you proposed, and to keep to the general process and schedule that was agreed upon.

If this all sounds like a pretty amazing deal to you, you're not alone, and that's the challenge with this form of funding – you won't be the only artist that's eager to capitalize. You may have your work cut out for you, as you try to rise above the other hopefuls, but you shouldn't let that stop you from applying, if you think that your project might be able to secure funding. You can't earn a grant if you don't apply for one! Local arts councils can help guide you, and with some time spent researching online, you'll soon have a better sense of what's available, and whether or not your project might qualify.

If you aren't successful the first (or second, or third) time around, try not to take it personally.

The world of art grants is even more competitive than the world of film festivals! You may be able to reapply the next time that the grant becomes available, or you maybe be able to refine your application without too much effort, and apply elsewhere. An arts grant can be a great way to move your artistic career forward, and to get your next film made, with the support of an agency that *truly* wants to see more art in the world.

Crowdfunding

If you talk to a selection of artists who have met with success through crowdfunding, you'll likely hear recurring observations about the whole process. A good campaign, no matter what platform it runs on, needs to be extremely well organized. It needs to convey updates to backers regularly, and it needs to deliver on perks effectively. It will also, absolutely, take far more time to administer than you ever imagined, back when you were planning it all out. If you want to run a serious campaign to raise funds for your project, give it the same attention that you would your actual film. If you can bring on help to run it, then do so. Don't forget that if you secure the funding that you asked for, you'll soon be up to your eyeballs making that film – yet you'll be obligated to maintain the commitments that you made during the campaign.

There's no shortage of success stories out there (and failures, sadly), so do your research, pay close attention to why they were successful,

Figure 18.11
Birdlime, Evan Derushie, 2016. With great charm, this short film sheds light upon the troubling realities of the exotic bird industry. Its important message (and beautiful look) made it to the screen in part because it was supported by art grants.

and think about how you can follow a similar path to success. One advantage that a stop motion project can have in the world of crowd funding is in the area of rewards. If you plan to use moulding and casting on your film, you might be able to cast some simple but very cool rewards, that a supporter would really cherish. Plastic fridge magnets in the form of your main character? Who wouldn't want one of those?! Just be sure to research the cost of postage, not to mention the cost of silicone and resin, before you commit to mailing them out. You don't want to have to run a *second* crowdfunding campaign, just to pay for the rewards that you owe on the first!

Before you dive into crowdfunding, you'll need to carefully consult the specific platform that you're considering. Here's a quick comparison, of a few major ones, just to get you started. From here, you'll want to carry on with your own online research, before committing.

Kickstarter

As YouTube is for video sharing, Kickstarter is for crowdfunding. It's the platform that typically comes to mind, and that means that a project hosted on this platform is likely to attract more potential supporters, simply because there are more people floating around on it, and looking to it in the press, for new projects to back.

It also adopts the 'all or nothing' approach to funding goals. In other words, if don't achieve your funding goal in the time allowed, that's it. Fail. You don't get any of that money, and your backers do not have their credit cards charged for their contributed amounts. This seriously no-nonsense policy can push supporters to contribute more than they might otherwise, and to support your project more in general, since they know that their invested money *truly* plays a role in whether the project will reach its funding. It also can help you, in terms of realistically planning your project's budget. If you know, with certainty, what your funding amount will be, you can seriously plan for that amount in your budget. Very professional.

The biggest disadvantage about Kickstarter, at least from my perspective *north* of the American border (and perhaps for you, depending on where you are in the world), is that Kickstarter is essentially restricted to U.S.-based projects. This may change in the future, but for now, that's the way the company works. You can get around this

obstacle by having someone in the U.S. sign on as central member of your campaign, but this may not be possible (or desirable).

Indiegogo

Indiegogo is a bit more forgiving, at least when compared to Kickstarter's all or nothing policy for achieving goals. With Indiegogo, you can establish what's known as a 'flexible funding' campaign. This style of campaign will still provide you with your funds raised, even if you don't make your goal. This can obviously be a good thing in some ways, since some funding is better than no funding.

Or is it? If you don't achieve your full funding, how are you going to pay for the balance of your project? Perhaps it means that your project will have be seriously compromised, or left incomplete, and now your investors won't be getting the final film that you promised. Many investors for an independent stop motion film will probably be pretty understanding, but it's not fair to assume that, and you can start to see why risking your money as an investor for this kind of campaign can feel riskier, compared to the 'all or nothing' plan of Kickstarter.

Another major distinction from Kickstarter is that Indiegogo is open to projects worldwide. This makes it a lot more attractive to the wider world of stop motion artists compared to Kickstarter, with its 'U.S. only' policy. It also makes Indiegogo projects attractive to investors who want to see stop motion flourish *internationally*. The more diverse work that's created around the world, from diverse artists with distinct voices, the better it is for the medium.

What you'll raise via crowdfunding isn't 'free money'. It's funding that investors are going to provide, in return for what you say you're going to provide. You don't want to spend the rest of your artistic life running from an online community that's still waiting on rewards (and your film), years after you promised to deliver. And if you're dealing in large sums of money that were invested with you, you might be looking at legal trouble, as well.

Patreon

Patreon is a very interesting model for funding, distinct from crowdfunding. Rather than presenting a specific project for investors to consider, artists can establish themselves on Patreon and then invite support from investors in the form of monthly donations. These investors become, quite literally, patrons of the artist's work. This model can have great advantages for artists, since it can represent a steady (if modest) regular income that can be devoted to ongoing artist efforts.

Because it's more likely to attract supporters who have come to trust an artist's dedication and style, Patreon is particularly attractive to an artist who has accumulated a solid body of work, and who wants to carry on doing just that. It might not be the best method for raising a large sum of money for a specific project, but it might be the perfect solution for ensuring that you have a steady supply of armature wire, foam core, and masking tape.

And if you start to gain wider support, you may find yourself in a position to devote more of your work day to stop motion, since your patrons may be covering some of your actual living costs. Keep making strong work, keep sharing it as widely as you feel is appropriate, and you never know.

> Taxes. There it is, the dreaded 'T' word. If you've got money coming in through fundraising, that's income. And income means that you'll need to contend with income tax. If you've already broken out into a cold sweat as you read this, start the mission to find an accountant who is artist-friendly, to help you understand things better.

Blood, sweat, and saved up money

Remember when you were a kid, and your parents used to tell you that if you wanted that cool new thing, that you'd have to save your chore money until you could buy it for yourself? Little did you know they were helping you to prepare for funding a stop motion film, later in life.

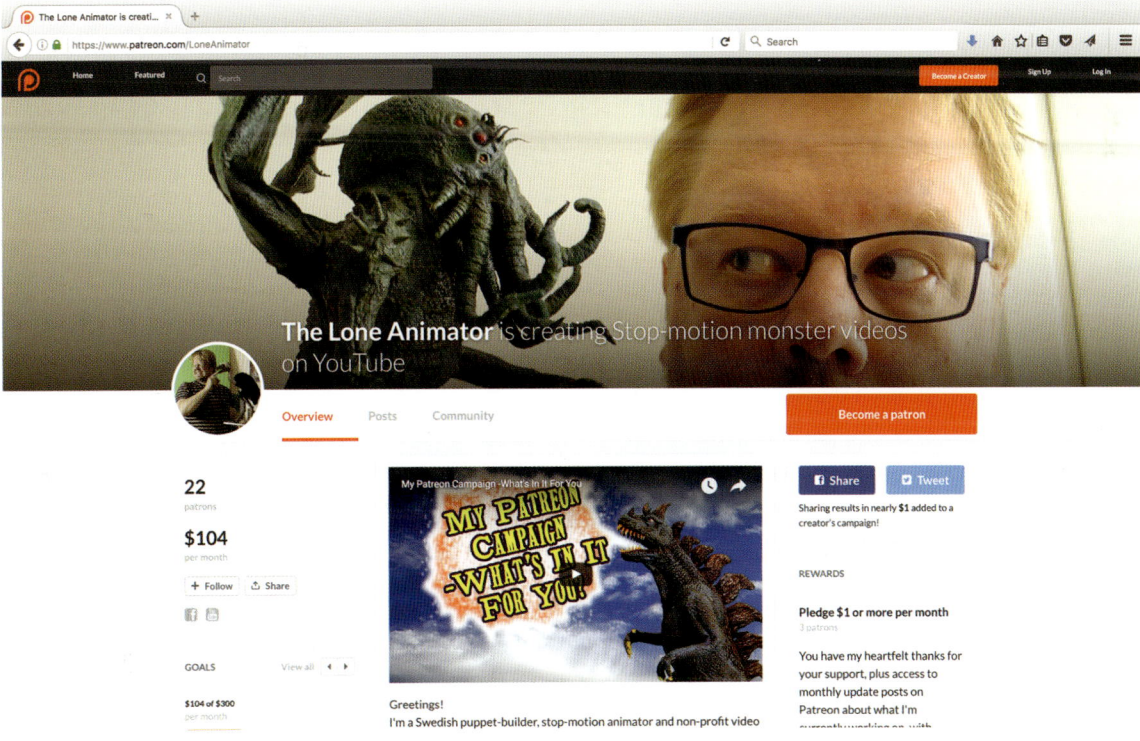

Figure 18.12
Patreon page for stop motion, Richard Svensson. Richard Svensson (aka The Lone Animator) has become known for both his stop motion films, and for his live action tutorials that help to support the medium. He's honest about what he's doing, and he's passionate, and that results in international support via his Patreon page.

Figure 18.13
Bobby Yeah, Robert Morgan, 2011.
Self-funding can be the ultimate way for an artist to establish and maintain supreme creative freedom. It was that kind of freedom that helped produce this film – one of the most wildly unique stop motion worlds that you're ever going to experience.

It's not complicated. Assuming that you have a job, take whatever you can afford to spare from each paycheck, no matter how little, and hold it somewhere as your 'film fund'. If you have to dip into that fund to pay for life's other necessities, then so be it, but go back to adding to that fund as soon as you can. It might take you ages to save enough for whatever your film may require, but you'll get there.

There's nothing radical about this way of thinking. In fact, it's decidedly old school, since there's nothing fast, easy, or internet-based about it. And if you're reaction to this option is to say that real artists shouldn't have to use their own money to make their art, then I'd just point out that a lot of great art has come into the world by using this very method. That's because great art *needs* to be made. It doesn't wait for funding. It forces its way into the world, by any means.

People who find themselves funding their films in this way don't do it because they necessarily choose to, nor because they're independently wealthy. They do it because they *have* to. They're compelled by their films. And what these artists might lack in the way of funding, they more than make up for in sheer passion, dedication, and desire, as they struggle to bring their ideas to the screen in a world that can sometimes make it very hard to get *anything* made, let alone independent stop motion.

PETE LEVIN, DIRECTOR

We first heard from Pete back in Chapter 15, when he offered some insights into production planning. He's back now, this time to share some wisdom about his experiences crowdfunding for a stop motion film. The campaign for his short film *I'm Scared* earned over $80,000 US (more than $15,000 over its original goal).

- Established followers on social media make all of the difference. If you, one of your creative partners, or a friend who wants to help you succeed has a large following on social media outlets, this will help get the word out quickly.
- Get the word out to people you know will support your project before you go live. Once your campaign is released into the world, you'll have a bunch of people who already know about it and are excited on day one.

- Try to tap into a crowd that is fanatical about something (and may have disposable income to invest in that passion). I believe this is why so many projects for gamers do so well on Kickstarter.
- People like physical stuff. It's really tough to sell a film on Kickstarter, but physical objects are a great incentive to help fund a film. Don't have too many different incentives, or things will get too complicated, and expensive.
- Remember to consider the percentage that the crowdfunding website will take, the cost to create any physical products, shipping costs, and how much you may be taxed on this income.
- Make sure it's not just about you, but it's about something bigger and more relatable. Keep detailed spread sheets!!!

Conclusion

As an introduction to plumbing, I'm sure you'll agree that this book has failed pretty miserably. But as a book dedicated to stop motion, I hope that you've found it to be useful, and that overall it's been fun to get through, at least as far as textbooks go.

While writing, I took inspiration from some great guide books that have helped me a lot, as I've learned about making films in general, and about making stop motion in particular. You'll find these books (and others) listed below.

Those books, and others like them, patiently revealed to me how to do magical and mysterious things. They were always there on the shelf, on my desk, or in my backpack, ready to help, no matter how many times I needed to review a process, method, or approach. If I was feeling discouraged, and in need of a reminder of just how amazing all of this stuff really was, they'd do that too, happily. In these ways, a good textbook really is like a good teacher, and I hope that at least in some ways this book can be that for you.

Before we completely wrap things up, I'll ask you to stick with me for just a little bit longer, so that I can tell you about one particular stage in my own stop motion journey. I think that it might prove useful for you, as you carry on.

Throughout much of my life, I had been a big fan of stop motion. As I learned more about live action film production, I found myself moving closer and closer to stop motion, but I still never imagined that I could actually make something in the medium. It was too mysterious, and too complex, or at least that was how it seemed. When the time came to actually try my hand at it, I was very excited, but also very intimidated. I had a very good teacher (Alex Gorelick, who provided some great tips back in Chapter 17) but was I going to be able to face the challenge? I had a lot to overcome, after all. My formal training had been in live action, so I didn't even know much about animation, let alone stop motion!

In the introduction to this book, the motto 'Animate, Eat, Sleep, Repeat' was presented light-heartedly, but that really *was* the life that I was living, when I set out to learn. I dove in, hard. The world didn't see much of me at that stage of things. I was much too busy putting myself through my own intensive stop motion boot camp. In the end, this intensive approach led to good things for me professionally. I soon had my first job as a stop motion animator on a television series, and from there I carried onward.

This process that I had put myself through was formative for me as a person, as well as a stop motion artist. I had learned how to animate a puppet (well enough, at least, to get me started), but I had also learned to believe in myself, and in my ability to overcome obstacles. That's a lesson that I've carried with me ever since, and it's one that I try to impart to my students who are starting out, not only as stop motion artists, but as young adults.

Stop motion is hard. That's not a flaw that needs to be fixed, it's something to be celebrated. The medium is amazing because of that fact, not despite it. It's a proving ground, in which you can chart your own personal development, even as you create incredible art.

A lot of my early stop motion work was done with the help of someone that you've seen a lot of in this book, and that's Roy the puppet. As you may recall, Roy isn't just an illustrated character, he was the first stop motion puppet that I ever worked with. Roy (the actual, physical puppet) is still with me today. In fact, he sat on my window ledge throughout the entire writing of this book, offering me endless encouragement, and reminding me to approach my writing with the same enthusiasm and dedication that I had used when I was animating him, many years ago.

And since a big part of being a good stop motion animator is taking a step back so that the *puppet* can take the lead, it seems only fitting that the last word of this book should go to Roy.

Figure 18.14
The real Roy.
Roy says, 'Thank you for loving stop motion. It wouldn't exist without you!'.

Further reading

Books about puppets

Blumenthal, Eileen. *Puppetry: A World History*. Abrams. 2005.

Gross, Kenneth. *Puppet: An Essay On Uncanny Life*. University of Chicago Press. 2011.

Leach, Robert. *The Punch and Judy Show: History, Tradition and Meaning*. University of Georgia Press. 1985.

Nelson, Victoria. *The Secret Life of Puppets*. Harvard University Press. 2001.

Books about stop motion

Brierton, Tom. *Stop-Motion Armature Machining: A Construction Manual*. Mcfarland & Co Inc Pub. 2002.

Harryhausen, Ray & Dalton, Tony. *Ray Harryhausen: An Animated Life*. Aurum Press Ltd. 2003.

Harryhausen, Ray & Dalton, Tony. *A Century of Stop-Motion Animation: From Melies to Aardman*. Watson-Guptill Publications. 2008.

Lord, Peter. *Creating 3-D Animation*. Abrams. 1998.

Priebe, Ken. *The Art of Stop-Motion Animation*. Course Technology PTR. 2006.

Priebe, Ken. *The Advanced Art of Stop-Motion Animation*. Course Technology PTR. 2010.

Purves, Barry. *Stop Motion: Passion, Process, and Performance*. Focal Press. 2008.

Purves, Barry. *Stop-motion Animation: Frame by Frame Film-making with Puppets and Models*. Bloomsbury. 2014.

Shaw, Susannah. *Stop Motion: Craft Skills For Model Animation*. Focal Press. 2004.

Books about animation and performance

Ed Hooks' books *Acting For Animators*. Routledge. 2011.

Acting in Animation. Heinemann Educational. 2005.

Respect for Acting by Uta Hagen. 2nd edition. Jossey Bass. 2008.

Audition by Michael Shurtleff. Walker and Co. 1978.

Acting Skills for Life by Ron Cameron. 3rd edition. Dundurn. 1999.

Miyazaki, Hayao. *Starting Point*. VIZ Media. 1996.

Thomas, Frank & Johnston, Ollie. *The Illusion of Life*. Walt Disney Productions. 1981 (reprinted many times).

Books about story development

Achtenberg, Mark. *Get Your Hero Up A Tree*. Runamok Books. 2018.

Buchbinder, Amnon. *The Way of The Screenwriter*. House of Anansi Press. 2005.

Field, Syd. *Screenplay: The Foundations of Screenwriting*. Dell Publishing. 1979.

Glebas, Francis. *Directing the Story: Professional Storytelling and Storyboarding Techniques for Live Action and Animation*. Focal Press. 2008.

MacDonald, Brian. *Invisible Ink: A Practical Guide to Building Stories that Resonate*. Libertary Company. 2010.

McKee, Robert. *Story: Style, Structure, Substance, and the Principles of Screenwriting*. It Books. 1997.

Paez, Sergio & Jew, Anson. *Professional Storyboarding: Rules of Thumb*. Focal Press. 2012.

Yorke, John. *Into the Woods: A Five-Act Journey Into Story*. Overlook Books. 2015.

Books about film and filmmaking

Bordwell, David & Thompson, Kristin. *Film Art: An Introduction*. McGraw-Hill Education. 10th edition, 2012.

Hames, Peter (editor). *Dark Alchemy: The Cinema of Jan Svankmajer*. Wallflower Press. 2008.

Katz, Stephen. *Film Directing: Shot by Shot: Visualizing from Concept to Screen*. Michael Wiese Productions. 2011.

Mackendrick, Alexander. *On Film-making: An Introduction to the Craft of the Director*. Faber & Faber. 2005.

Murch, Walter. *In The Blink of An Eye*. Silman-James Press. 2005.

Zettl, Herbert. *Sight, Sound, Motion: Applied Media Aesthetics*. Wadsworth Publishing. 7th edition, 2013.

Books about drawing and sculpting

Bridgman, George. *Constructive Anatomy*. Dover Publications. 1973.

Bruckner, Tim, Oat, Zach & Procopio, Ruben. *Pop Sculpture: How To Create Action Figures and Collectible Statues*. Watson-Guptill Publications. 2010.

Faraut, Philippe & Faraut, Charisse. *Portrait Sculpting: Anatomy and Expressions in Clay*. PCF Studios Inc. 2004.

Norling, Ernest. *Perspective Made Easy*. Dover Publications. 1999.

Simon, Howard. *Techniques of Drawing*. Dover Publications. 1972.

Stanchfield, Walter. *Drawn to Life: 20 Golden Years of Disney Master Classes: Volume 1: The Walt Stanchfield Lectures*. Focal Press. 2009.

Woodcock, Vincent. *How To Draw and Paint Crazy Cartoon Characters*. Barron's Publishing. 2007.

Index